San Diego

THE INSIDERS' GUIDE® TO

San Diego

by
Jacquelyn Landis
and
Eva Shaw

The Insiders' Guide®
An imprint of Falcon® Publishing Inc.
A Landmark Communications company
P.O. Box 1718
Helena, MT 59624
(800) 582-2665
www.insiders.com

Sales and Marketing: Falcon Publishing, Inc.
P.O. Box 1718
Helena, MT 59624
(800) 582-2665
www.falcon.com

•

FIRST EDITION
1st printing

•

•

Printed in the United States
of America

•

Cover photos, clockwise from top left: child at Carlsbad by CeCe Canton; surfer at sunset by Bob Yarbrough, San Diego Convention and Visitors Bureau; Mission de Acala by James Blank, San Diego Convention and Visitors Bureau; spine photo by San Diego Convention and Visitors Bureau.

•

Publications from *The Insiders' Guide*® series are available at special discounts for bulk purchases for sales promotions, premiums or fundraisings. Special editions, including personalized covers, can be created in large quantities for special needs.
For more information, please contact Falcon Publishing.

ISBN 1-57380-077-5

Preface

Welcome to San Diego, a.k.a. America's finest cities.

Haven't seen the word "cities" showing up in the glossy advertisements? That's because they're only talking about the city of San Diego. As Insiders know, San Diego is more than one location or destination.

We're inviting you to create a relationship with all of the enticing locales that form greater San Diego. It's filled to the brim with America's best places to visit and live. To be more exact, the region stretches from Orange County to our international border with Mexico. On one side, you'll find the Pacific and on the other the mountains, and the glorious desert beyond.

Think of San Diego as a welcoming hug; it's that comfortable here. Like many first-time visitors, you might even be a bit surprised by the diversity. Our region may challenge every preconceived idea you have about California. This isn't Los Angeles or Orange County with that rush-around attitude and never-ending sprawl.

Life here in San Diego is a bit slower — "cherished" — some say. We seem to take recreational time more seriously than other areas do. But don't mistake the gentler pace for commonness. We have boatloads of cultural activities to satisfy even the most discriminating tastes. And our easygoing spirit doesn't keep us from being ambitious. San Diego strives for — and achieves — worldwide recognition. It's a mix that works.

In San Diego you'll find cutting-edge biotech and telecommunications firms right beside industry leaders in sporting goods and agriculture. To make it more engaging, staffers of these businesses are rubbing elbows with internationally known artists, actors, writers and craftspeople. Together they're creating one of the country's most eclectic lifestyles and cultures. And consider that all this is almost always happening under a cloudless sky in a perfect climate.

On any given day, you'll have a smorgasbord of possibilities only San Diego can offer. At daybreak start on a beach walk with a stop at a surfer hangout for the best breakfast burritos in town. Your biggest problem? Which beach and which outdoor restaurant. Want to have lunch featuring succulent burgers (veggie or traditional) at a cowboy eatery, where country music brings out the best of the sunshine and sage? Again, you'll have to make a choice. How about topping that off with a mountaintop dinner under the stars? Maybe you'd rather do it on a boat touring the bay. It's all here and more.

We can offer a choice of weather, too. For those folks who actually like to shovel snow, San Diego's boundaries encompass towns that experience the four seasons. That's right. Every winter our mountain communities get that fluffy, white stuff. If you prefer wearing cotton January through December, that's practically a given (career allowing, of course). Clothing here is typically San Diego casual, except for occasions when grown-up clothes are required.

One of the sweetest parts of being in San Diego is that you never run out of choices for shopping, culture, watersports, kidstuff and old-fashioned fun. To whet your taste for the region, think of Balboa Park, our zoo, the Wild Animal Park, and the miles of hiking, biking, and walking trails. If you're thinking of relocating, consider the choices of universities and schools, healthcare (we think it's the best in the nation), and retirement living. One of these may cinch your decision to make San Diego home.

San Diego is the second largest city in California, and yet tourism is still a basic of our economy. There's no "high season" because this is a year-round resort. Are you aware

Photo: James Blank/San Diego Convention and Visitors Bureau

The biggest problem with a San Diego beach walk is choosing which beach to walk on.

that San Diego combines 101 official neighborhoods, 18 incorporated cities and habitats
for every taste? We're talking hometowns with
diverse and on-the-go community spirits,
towns that are cosmopolitan yet cozy. San
Diegans know their neighbors and are darn
proud of it.

Unlike other regions of the country, here
in San Diego you'll never feel like an outsider.
Although the number of those born in San
Diego is growing, most of us selected San
Diego as the place to live, go to school and to
raise a family because we like it here. Sometimes our tie to San Diego starts with a day
visit or a long holiday and then becomes a
reason for returning again and again. That's
how the San Diego connection becomes
fused; it's like joining a big, adopted family.

Whether you're visiting, relocating or re-
kindling your ties with San Diego, it's nearly
guaranteed that in less than twenty-four hours
you'll feel at home. Want a preview? Just flip
through these pages or select your favorite
chapters to get an overview and then details
of San Diego, the region and the city.

So, you're coming to San Diego and have
time to explore. The Daytrips chapter gives
you great getaways including ever sunny Palm
Springs and Temecula's lush Wine Country.
What if you want to just relax? The Spas and
Resorts chapter can direct you to a place
where you can tune up your body and mind.
And if you're bringing along your sweetie, the
Bed and Breakfast Inns chapter can help you
find the perfect romantic getaway.

Whether you want to go south of the border or play golf, we've included chapters to
give you those choices and focus on your desires and needs. We've tried to cross-refer-
ence information to make the book user-
friendly. However, you know your needs best
so be sure to browse the index for specifics.

We hope you'll stop in on-line with a visit
to our Insiders' Guides web site at
www.insiders.com. While there you'll find a
page for comments and suggestions. Please
use it. Or do it the customary way: Write us or
the editors with your own Insider's tips, comments, or questions at Insiders' Guides, P. O.
Box 1718, Helena, Montana 59624. Your in-
sights and pointers will make the next edition
more valuable, and besides, we love hearing
from friends. In our book anyone who enjoys
San Diego is a friend.

Welcome to San Diego. It's a great place
to visit and it's the best place to call home.

About the Authors

Jacquelyn Landis

A native San Diegan, Jacquelyn Landis has never seriously considered settling anywhere else. Her San Diego roots run deep: Jackie's ancestors arrived in San Diego in the early 1900s and quickly established themselves in the business community. Landis Street, which stretches east from North Park all the way through City Heights, was christened in honor of her great-grandfather, a physician, and her grandfather and great-uncle, who owned a drug store and soda fountain in Mission Hills.

An alumna of the University of San Diego, Jackie credits her demanding philosophy professors for pounding home the fundamentals of writing, while at the same time encouraging her love for the craft. Formerly the managing editor for Emery-Dalton Books, Jackie is now a freelance writer who ghostwrites health and psychology self-help books and celebrity autobiographies. But when the opportunity arises to write about her hometown, she has yet to be able to resist. Her work has appeared in *San Diego Magazine*, San Diego pictorial books and a variety of San Diego business and community newspapers. She also is an editorial consultant, offering advice and guidance to other writers.

Jackie currently lives in Linda Vista, overlooking bustling Mission Valley. Wanderlust strikes occasionally, and it has taken her to the four corners of the world. But San Diego always beckons. Jackie knows she's spoiled. When you can go to the beach in January, drive a short hour to play in the snow in the Laguna Mountains and keep going over the mountains to the warmth of the Borrego Desert, why live anywhere else?

Eva Shaw

As far as Eva Shaw is concerned, there's no other area on the planet that compares to San Diego. It has been her hometown for almost 30 years, chosen for the climate, diversity and spectacular array of outdoor activities.

Eva teaches creative writing with the University of California Extension Programs and at conferences throughout the United States. She holds a doctorate in eschatology from Westbrook University. She is the award-winning author of more than 40 books, including the best-selling *The Successful Writer's Guide to Publishing Magazine Articles, Writing the Nonfiction Book, and For the Love of Children*, as well as *What to Do When a Loved One Dies*. She's currently working on books about safety for women and gardening as therapy, and she "dabbles" in writing fiction.

Her writing has appeared in the *San Diego Union Tribune*, *San Diego Business Journal* and scores of national publications. Eva is a ghostwriter, lecturer, public speaker and advocate for family and women's issues. She was recently honored with North San Diego County's Woman of Merit Award. A nationally recognized television guest on *Leeza*, A&E Network, MSNBC and *Maury Povich*, Eva has enlightened audiences with her expert knowledge on topics ranging from grief management to wellness.

Eva lives in Carlsbad, a pearl on the string of coastal communities in San Diego County. When not writing, teaching, speaking and volunteering at the Florence Crittenton Center and other charities, Eva tends her flower garden (at last count there were nearly 100 rose bushes); plays fetch with Zippy, a Welsh terrier; and hikes San Diego County and the world with her husband, Joe, and their son, Matt.

Acknowledgments

Eva Shaw and Jacquelyn Landis

When we began this book in early January 1998 we were colleagues. We quickly became friends and are now the closest of friends. An added pleasure and dimension to our friendship happened when we discovered that our funny bones were in the same spots. Without each other's support, warmth and mutual admiration, this collaborative project would never have gone so smoothly, perhaps never have been possible.

"Thank you, Jackie. You're the best."

"Thank you, Eva. You're the best."

"No, you're the best."

"No, you're the best."

"You're the best."

"You're the best."

Ad infinitum...

Table of Contents

Directory of Maps

San Diego County

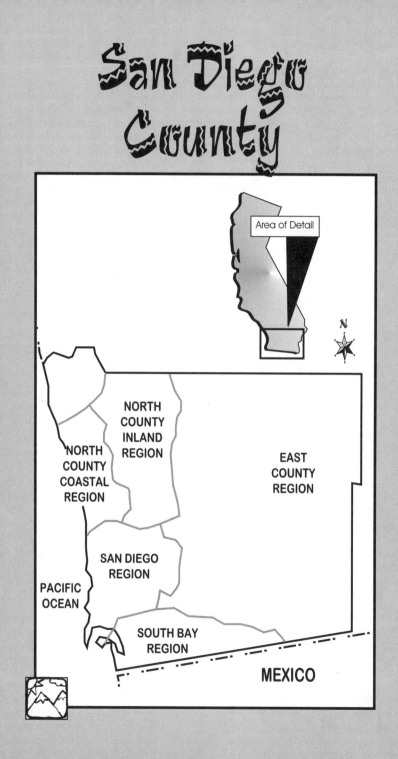

Area of Detail

N

NORTH COUNTY INLAND REGION

EAST COUNTY REGION

NORTH COUNTY COASTAL REGION

SAN DIEGO REGION

PACIFIC OCEAN

SOUTH BAY REGION

MEXICO

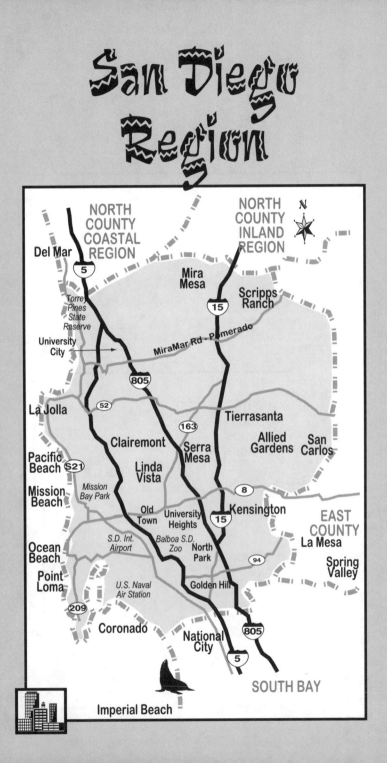

Downtown San Diego

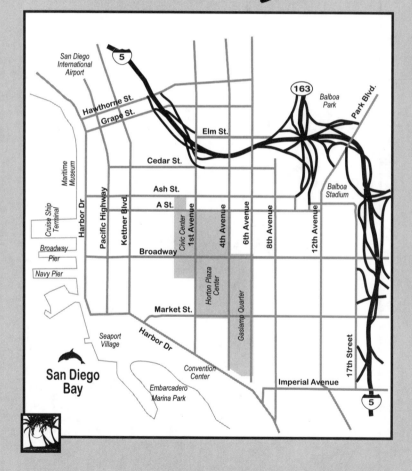

San Diego International Airport

Hawthorne St.
Grape St.
Elm St.
Cedar St.
Ash St.
A St.
Broadway
Market St.

Maritime Museum
Cruise Ship Terminal
Broadway Pier
Navy Pier

Harbor Dr
Pacific Highway
Kettner Blvd
Civic Center
1st Avenue
4th Avenue
6th Avenue
8th Avenue
12th Avenue
17th Street

Horton Plaza Center
Gaslamp Quarter

Balboa Park
Park Blvd.
Balboa Stadium

163

5

Seaport Village
Harbor Dr
Convention Center
Embarcadero Marina Park
Imperial Avenue

San Diego Bay

North County Coastal Region

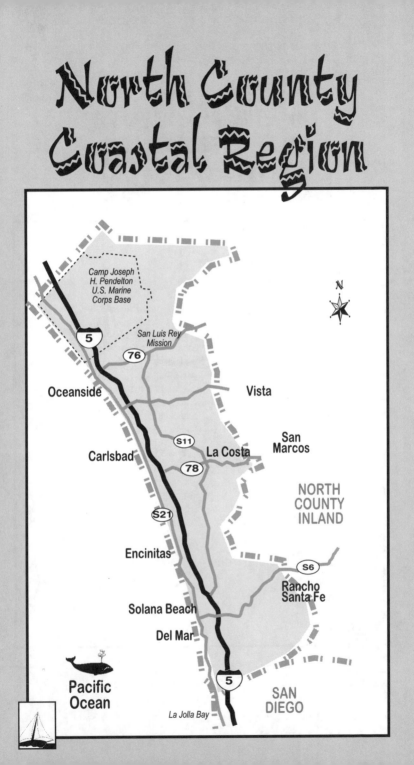

North County Inland Region

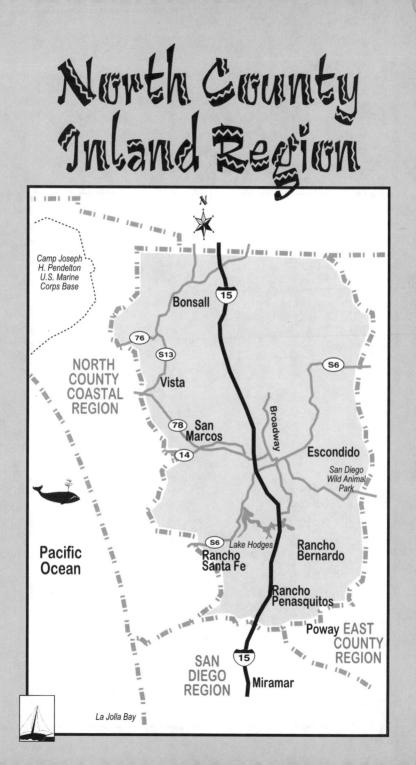

East County Region

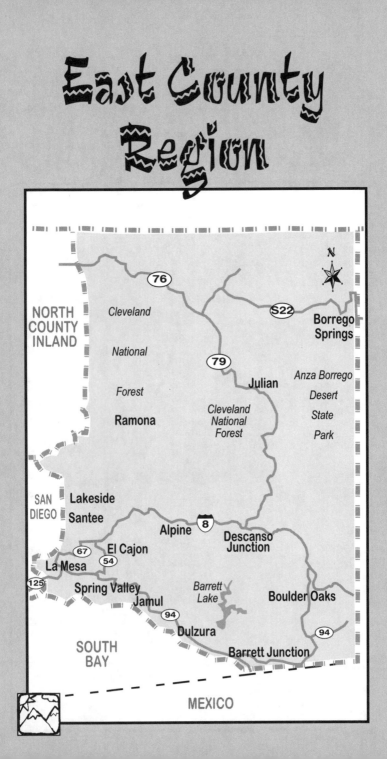

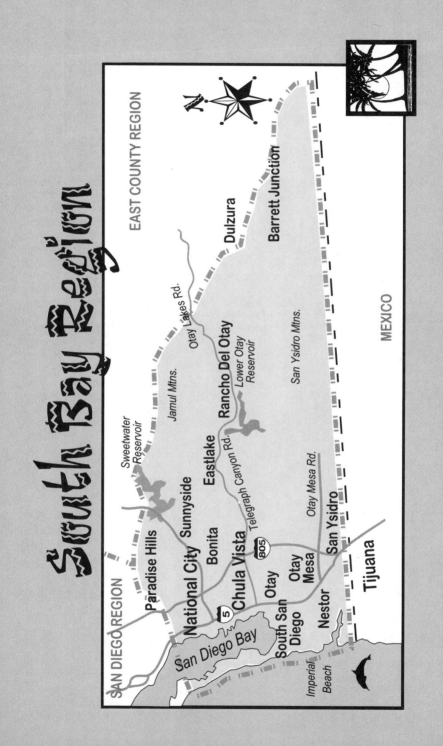

Most visitors and residents think of San Diego in regions.

How to Use This Book

Most visitors and residents think of San Diego in regions. We fondly refer to them as North County Coastal (not a "real" county, rather a local nickname), North County Inland, East County and South Bay.

The actual city of San Diego includes those spectacular buildings and the gorgeous harbor you may have seen if you arrived at the San Diego International Airport, locally known as Lindbergh Field. For our purposes this **San Diego** area (the downtown) includes the Gaslamp Quarter, Uptown and Hillcrest, San Diego's beaches, Coronado, La Jolla, the Golden Triangle and the inland communities such as Allied Gardens and the Midway District. Some Insiders will bristle at the divisions. It's tough to slice a perfect pie. Our goal with the format was to make it easy for newcomers and tourists to get around.

To make it less complicated to locate what you want and need in San Diego County, we've broken the region into the four, smaller areas noted above. These are the labels Insiders use, too, so you'll see and hear these areas referred to in the newspaper, on television and in conversations.

Just for now, think of the regions making a circle around our county. Out of the city proper we move north, up the coast using Interstate 5, to **North County Coastal**. This area includes the beach communities that touch or are close to the Pacific Ocean. Included in the area are the cities of Rancho Santa Fe, Del Mar, Solana Beach, Cardiff and Encinitas (with its neighborhood region called Leucadia), La Costa, Carlsbad and Oceanside.

Inside the coastal area and to the east of the ocean is the region we called **North County Inland**. It includes the communities of Vista, San Marcos, Escondido, Fallbrook, Valley Center, Bonsall, Rancho Bernardo, Rancho Penasquitos and Poway.

The next region is **East County**. For our purposes it includes the cities of La Mesa, Lemon Grove, Spring Valley, El Cajon, Santee, Bonita and Lakeside. East County, for our book, also embraces the mountain towns of Alpine, Pine Valley, Ramona, and Julian out to the desert area of Borrego Springs. In the desert, we're lucky enough to have the communities of Boulevard, Campo and Dulzura along with others.

Completing the circle is the **South Bay** area. It includes Chula Vista, National City, Imperial Beach and San Ysidro. Since much of our region is bicultural, you'll find information and recommendations on activities, shopping, accommodations, nightlife, etc. for Mexico in our chapter titled South of the Border.

When organizing the book we elected to do so, for the most part, by the natural regions. It made sense. Like most decisions, there were exceptions and that's where "for the most part" strolled into the picture. Sometimes, such as in the chapter on Higher Education, we've listed colleges and universities by category and then alphabetically. Watersports and our Media chapter are also organized by categories.

Even if your family has been in California since the Gold Rush days, you'll enjoy reading the History chapter to get the full scope of San Diego. It will give you a feel for San Diego's terrain, our traditions and

our colorful and somewhat checkered past. In the Area Overview we'll bring you up-to-date on our industries, cultural activities, distinct population, role in the international marketplace and our close bonds with Mexico.

Annual events are listed with month-by-month notations. So if you're visiting San Diego County in August, you may want to find out about the Roar and Snore Camp Over at the Wild Animal Park in Escondido, the Weed Show in Julian and the Toshiba Tennis Classic in La Costa. These events are just examples of the many possibilities we've listed.

You'll notice by looking at the Table of Contents that we've devoted separate chapters to Golf, Spas and Resorts, Retirement, and Balboa Park. These are "big ticket items" in our county and make us unique. In Balboa Park alone, you can find museums, activities, and concerts along with the world-famous San Diego Zoo and its treasure trove of botanical exhibits. As long-time residents of San Diego we know that you can't just devote one afternoon to our Balboa Park; it deserves repeat visits.

Determined to make the book really usable, we've cross-referenced places and events. We've tried to keep repetition to a minimum but have allowed some duplication of entries to save you the trouble of flipping back

and forth. For example, a great picnic area might be mentioned in the Parks chapter and in the Kidstuff chapter. Each entry will probably be slightly different depending on its placement. For example, the entry in Kidstuff might include the fact that this is the site of Easter egg and candy hunts for youngsters. Check the index if you want to read everything on a particular site.

The book's regional divisions and cross referenced entries should make it easy for you to find the closest bed and breakfast inn, Asian grocery store, Cinco de Mayo fiesta or water park. However, keep in mind that Insiders never blink at traveling across the county for dinner, to visit a theater or to attend a festival or event. For instance, when snowflakes sprinkle Mount Laguna on U.S. Interstate 8, San Diegans often take off to let the kids (of all ages) play in the snow. For those of us living on the coast (our slang for the beach communities) it's a fun drive that's well worth the time. Since we feel that all of San Diego is our backyard, distance isn't an obstacle. Don't make it yours.

Our roads and highways are clearly marked and referred to locally by number. As an example you'll hear people say, "Take 5 to 78 and then 15." Translated that means to go north on Interstate 5 to U.S. Highway 78, which begins in Carlsbad and takes travelers to the North County Inland area. After about twenty miles, U.S. Highway 78 easily merges with Interstate 15 and the signs are large and noticeable.

When navigating the county by car, we recommend buying a map. Most bookstores have them. Maps are also available at the Transit Store, 102 Broadway. The Transit Store is on the northeast corner of First Avenue and Broadway and the phone numbers are (619) 234-1060 and (619) 233-3004. They're open Monday through Friday 8:30 AM to 5:30 PM, Saturday and Sunday noon to 4 PM.

Parking isn't a big problem in the county. However, if you're attending a well-publicized event, parade or a Chargers football game you could be in for short hike. Remember, sneakers are acceptable here; comfortable clothes are the fashion choice for most San Diegans.

Throughout the book distances and times are given from the downtown area of San Diego, travelling on multi-lane freeways and highways, unless noted otherwise. Allow about 20 minutes to get from the hotels downtown to Del Mar. Rush hours and the occasional rainstorm always play a role in the time it takes to get anywhere. So if you're meeting friends after work at a microbrew pub in Solana Beach (North County Coastal) and it's stormy, give yourself extra time. Yes, there are traffic jams even in Paradise.

A few words on our area codes. It's doesn't take a rocket scientist to notice that the region is booming. (Although we have plenty of rocket scientists in the area who will discuss this at length.) With a recent influx of high-tech firms and high-tech folks, we finally stretched the limits of our area codes. Pacific Bell added some and then even more. As we go to press, we have three area codes for the county, so next to each telephone listing you'll find the area code along with the phone number. In June

2000, a fourth will be added. Therefore if this book is more than a year or two old, double-check the area code before making a call.

Now for addresses. We provide street addresses, where available, to help you find your way around. Reading the Getting There/Getting Around chapter will help you further, by identifying some of San Diego's major districts. Once you know those, you can take a shuttle from the airport to the Gaslamp Quarter, for example, by asking for it by name. No numbered address needed, unless you want to go to a specific building in the area.

Throughout the chapters, we've included Insiders' Tips. These are recommendations you won't find in tour books and are guaranteed to make your visit or move here more enjoyable or memorable. The Close-ups will help let you meet the people and places that make the area exceptional. For instance, we've even included a once-secret guacamole recipe that recently received a first-place ribbon at a local avocado festival. Folks in San Diego County eat a lot of avocados. In fact, more avocados are eaten here than anywhere else in the country. Check out the festival and recipe in the Annual Events chapter.

We hope you'll make this book your own. We wrote it for you. You might want to keep it in your desk for daydreaming or trip-planning purposes. You could put it in your briefcase to study during your morning commute or your flight into Lindbergh Field. Or add it to the glove box of your car when you're maneuvering around San Diego.

Use highlighting pens, sticky notes and corner folds on the pages to plan an itinerary, a weekend, a holiday adventure or your future. You've already started to feel comfortable here because, at this very moment, all of San Diego is at your fingertips.

San Diego still preserves its low-key and slow-paced image right alongside its more polished one.

Area Overview

Word has it that San Diego, now ranked the sixth-largest city in the United States, will probably drop to seventh once the results of Census 2000 are in. It appears that its neighbor to the east, Phoenix, will pass it by and take over the sixth slot. Guess what? That doesn't bother San Diegans a bit. It's not a sign that things have taken a turn for the worse in San Diego. In fact, just the opposite is true. The economy is strong, jobs are plentiful, crime is down and the weather is still balmy. All it means is that Phoenix is growing faster than San Diego. Good for them.

San Diegans have always appreciated quality over quantity, and while all reports indicate continued population growth, city leaders prefer to be ready for it. Predictions are that the next 20 years will bring more than a million newcomers to San Diego, and those already here are taking steps to ensure that the same quality of life they now enjoy will be preserved for generations to come.

So if San Diego slips to the seventh-largest spot, it's hardly a tragedy. In spite of the city's burgeoning reputation as a major player in international business, in spite of the fact that it continues to grow on a dozen different levels, it still relentlessly preserves its low-key and slow-paced image right alongside its more polished one.

Regions

Describing San Diego geographically can sometimes be a challenge. It's a city, but within that city are over 100 separate, identifiable neighborhoods. It's also a county. And within San Diego County are 18 incorporated cities (including the city of San Diego) and many more unincorporated towns and communities. The county stretches south from the Orange County line all the way to the U.S.-Mexico border. Its western boundary is the Pacific Ocean, and its eastern reaches include the Laguna Mountains and the Anza-Borrego Desert.

When locals try to describe where they live, they usually tack a few qualifiers onto the end of their description. Someone living in the tiny northern town of Jesmond Dene, for example, would say "I live in Jesmond Dene, a little town in San Diego, in the North County." Or even if their hometown is within the city limits, it occasionally needs a bit more information to pinpoint its location. "I come from Nestor. It's in San Diego, in the South Bay." Even though residents of every locale within the boundaries of the county feel enormous pride for their neighborhood, sometimes it's just simpler to say we all live in San Diego. And that's what most Insiders do.

To make things easier for you to understand, we've separated the county into five regions: San Diego proper, North County Coastal, North County Inland, East County and the South Bay. The lines separating the regions are indistinct, and some locals may disagree about which region, in fact, contains their neighborhood. But each region has different characteristics that give it a definable flavor all its own. As you travel around the county, you'll soon discover that San Diego is indeed a complex place. And we have little doubt that you'll like what you find.

www.insiders.com

See this and many other **Insiders' Guide®** destinations online.

Visit us today!

San Diego

It would be easy to say that the city of San Diego is where all the action is. That may have been true at one time, but not anymore. Everything that makes San Diego a great place to visit and an even greater place to live can also be found in one or more of the other regions. But San Diego is still the heart of the county, the metropolitan center, and where the largest concentration of people live. From the lazy, sun-soaked beaches to the no-nonsense high-tech companies in Sorrento Valley; from the nightlife of the Gaslamp Quarter to the bedroom communities nestled inland, San Diego has it all.

The rhythm of life is a little faster in San Diego than in other regions of the county. A good number of the major businesses are within the city limits. If you fly into Lindbergh Field, San Diego's International Airport, you'll notice that you're almost downtown already. Of course, you probably figured that out while your plane was making its hair-raising descent through the maze of high-rises.

Within San Diego are three separate business areas: Downtown, Mission Valley and the Golden Triangle. Although downtown will always have the highest concentration of banks and law firms, and Mission Valley has more than its share of real estate companies, the Golden Triangle is where the newcomers and the upstarts are congregating. Located east and north of La Jolla, the area is home to most of San Diego's high-tech, biotech and telecommunications firms.

The neighborhoods within the city limits are defined by several factors: the people who live there, the types of houses and in many cases, what's nearby. For example, communities like Mission Valley, the Golden Triangle and the College area, which are close to universities, naturally tend to have lots of twenty-something inhabitants. La Jolla, on the other hand, is inhabited by an upscale population with the financial resources to afford the multimillion-dollar ocean-view homes. For a detailed description of where San Diegans call home and who lives where, be sure to check out our Neighborhoods and Real Estate chapter.

Both urban and suburban neighborhoods are plentiful in San Diego, and there's never a shortage of entertainment and recreation to be found. But true San Diegans realize that a large part of San Diego's appeal is contributed by the surrounding regions and the bounty they offer.

North County Coastal

Stretching north from Del Mar to Oceanside, San Diego's North County Coastal region has some of the area's prettiest beaches, the most offbeat clubs, one of the largest assortments of antique shops and its

---

INSIDERS' TIP

Carlsbad, in North County Coastal, was named after Karlsbad, Bohemia, because the mineral water found in the city was similar to that in the German town. The spelling was changed to give it a more Americanized look.

own collection of emerging high-tech and manufacturing businesses. In short, North County Coastal has just about everything San Diego has — even it's own airport. You can catch regular commuter flights to Los Angeles from Palomar Airport in Carlsbad.

Also in Carlsbad, behind the rainbow of flower fields visible from Interstate 5, is an explosion of new office complexes. Numerous businesses new to San Diego have chosen to make Carlsbad their home, and this new business community has provided an economic shot in the arm to North County Coastal as well as to the rest of the county.

Houses in beach communities such as Del Mar, Solana Beach and Encinitas command some of the most spectacular views in California, while just a few miles in from the coast, interspersed among thousands of eucalyptus trees, is the village of Rancho Santa Fe. Here you will find sprawling estates, a gentrified country atmosphere and some of the most expensive real estate in the United States.

A few hours spent driving around North County Coastal will explain why this region has grown so quickly in recent years. It's just like San Diego — only different. It's different in that it's a little farther away from what most people know as San Diego, and it maybe has more of a vacation atmosphere. But those differences give it its own special charm.

North County Inland

Continuing the circle of San Diego County, we come to North County Inland. Home to the cities of Vista, San Marcos, Escondido and Poway, North County Inland also has smaller communities with such charming names as Harmony Grove and the Elfin Forest. These are not misnomers, either. Trees, chaparral, horses and hiking trails are abundant, and life

has a decidedly more rural flavor, with lots of trees, hills and canyons.

As more and more people gravitate to San Diego, many have found their way to North County Inland, where housing tends to be more affordable and the traditional neighborhood is more common than it is in San Diego proper. Even though many residents commute to San Diego for work, they don't seem to mind. They prefer the more relaxed atmosphere of the northern region over the hustle and bustle of San Diego.

An emerging trend in North County Inland is to live, work and play within the confines of the region. Many have moved or started their businesses close to home, avoiding the commute altogether, and taking advantage of the quality of life to be found in the northern reaches of the county.

The communities are a good mix of folks who have been around for a couple of generations and young families just starting out. Families are drawn to North County Inland for another reason too: top-notch schools. Poway High School, for instance, has one of the highest percentages of graduates in the county who go on to college.

East County

Largest in terms of physical area, East County includes the suburban communities just east of the San Diego city limits, the Laguna Mountains, the Cuyamaca Mountains, Palomar Mountain and the desert city of Borrego Springs. East County is where you'll find the hottest temperatures during the summer months and the coldest in wintertime.

East County is even more rural than North County Inland. East County residents share their neighborhoods with farm animals and country western bars. And if you're looking for the ultimate cowboy hat or the perfect pair of boots, you're in the right place.

INSIDERS' TIP

The name of the East County town of Jamul literally translates to "slimy water." It's a Digueño Indian word that fortunately also translates to "antelope spring."

But don't let the casually rugged appearance of some of the inhabitants fool you. Hidden treasures of a most sophisticated nature abound in the region. The East County Performing Arts organization in El Cajon stages a variety of wonderfully entertaining productions every year. The annual Oktoberfest in La Mesa draws folks from all over the county. And the Palomar Observatory, in the Palomar Mountains, is a magnet for international astronomers as well as the simply curious. Borrego Springs, located in the desert east of San Diego's mountains, is home to one of the finest resorts in the county, La Casa del Zorro (see our Spas and Resorts chapter for a detailed description).

East County has more than its share of pleasures to be sampled. And give the residents credit for having figured out how to enjoy the best of both worlds. They have the serenity of the quiet life, but the lights of the big city are only a short drive away.

South Bay

At the southernmost end of the county, the South Bay has beautiful beaches and great neighborhoods. By now you've noticed that's not unique within the county. But South Bay does have something that no other region can claim: an international border. Only 20 minutes from downtown San Diego, the U.S-Mexico border is the gateway to Baja California and a whole different set of experiences, many of which you'll find described in our South of the Border chapter.

Even locals are surprised to learn that within the entire county, South Bay's Chula Vista has a population second only to the city of San Diego. Chula Vista is also home to Rohr Industries, an aircraft manufacturer and one of the county's largest employers.

As the county's population slowly spreads to outlying regions, the South Bay has not been ignored. As in North County Inland, many young neighborhoods, such as EastLake and Otay Ranch, are springing up to complement the older ones, like National City, Imperial Beach and San Ysidro, and home prices are among the most affordable in the county.

An Olympic Training Center opened recently in the South Bay. So did an enormous water park and the Coors Amphitheater, a 20,000-seat venue for concerts. As with San Diego's other regions, the South Bay is constantly looking to the future and finding ways to make its little corner of paradise even better.

Government

Describing the structure of government is almost as confusing as describing the geography of San Diego, but if you remember the cities and the regions within the county, then you'll have a pretty good idea of the various governments, which tend to follow those same separations. The city of San Diego has a mayor and an eight-member city council, which represents eight different areas within the city limits. The 17 other incorporated cities within the county also have mayors and city councils.

Representing the entire county is a board of supervisors, composed of five elected members who represent areas that generally correspond to the regional divisions we use here. So even those hardy souls who live in the most remote speck on the county map still have an elected official representing their interests. Those who live in any of the incorporated cities are lucky enough to have two.

Demographics

To give you an idea of the geographic reach of San Diego, it lies in the southwest corner of California, 120 miles south of the city of Los Angeles. The city of San Diego encompasses an area of 320 square miles; add in the other four regions, and the area of the entire county jumps to 4,255 square miles. The population of the city is about 1.2 million, while the county's numbers climb to 2.8 million.

Like most other major cities in the United States, San Diego's minority population has increased significantly in recent years, especially because of its proximity to the U.S.-Mexico border. Estimates are that the His-

Photo: San Diego Convention and Visitors Bureau

San Diego Bay offers a combination of harbor, urban and coastal lifestyles.

panic population will increase to 30 percent within the next 15 years, and the Asian population will jump to 11 percent.

In addition to being the sixth-largest city in the country (at least for the time being), San Diego is the second-largest city in California, behind Los Angeles. Living in the shadow of that megalopolis to the north has been both a blessing and a curse. National newspapers and magazines tend to overlook San Diego in favor of Los Angeles. When something newsworthy happens in La Jolla or Rancho Santa Fe, it will often be referred to by the national press as "a community south of Los Angeles."

Even though locals bristle at that kind of liberal manipulation of county lines, there's a certain quiet satisfaction in believing that their city still has an aura of secrecy about it. It's not that we mind sharing it with visitors,

we just prefer to keep it as quiet as possible. No one wants to spoil a good thing.

Industry and Jobs

Ask an Insider what the top industry is in San Diego and the likely response will be, with hardly a pause, "Tourism." Well, sometimes even Insiders can be wrong. Although tourism has been and will continue to be a driving force in the San Diego economy, it's not number one. It's not even number two. San Diego's industries rank as follows: manufacturing, the military, tourism, construction and agriculture.

From the early days, manufacturing has been a leader in supporting the local economy. The types of goods produced have shifted in the past decade, however.

INSIDERS' TIP

In 1985 the Cabrillo National Monument was the most-visited national monument in the United States, attracting 1,720,000 visitors. The next year it lost its number-one status to the Statue of Liberty, but each year since it's still been the second or third most visited monument in the country.

Mayor Susan Golding

When Susan Golding was elected mayor in 1992, she had big plans for San Diego. In addition to some top priorities such as public safety, economic development, education and neighborhood revitalization, she was thinking even bigger. So big, in fact, that most locals scoffed when she revealed her plan to try to snare the 1996 Republican Convention. No thanks, said many. They had been down that road before. San Diego was the chosen site for the 1972 convention, but at the last minute the Republicans packed their bags and went to Miami instead. It still smarted.

But Susan Golding is not a woman to let a few naysayers rain on her parade. She put together a team that included then California Governor Pete Wilson and former President Ronald Reagan and just about every business owner in San Diego. She pleaded, cajoled, twisted arms and finally convinced city leaders that San Diego could indeed be a contender.

When the city officially threw its hat in the ring and ended up as one of the three finalists for the convention, along with San Antonio and New Orleans, Mayor Golding went into overdrive. No problem was too big to overcome and she took personal responsibility for glitch control. When some site-selection committee members complained that the convention center was too small, Mayor Golding staged a mock convention to prove how smoothly it would go.

When the committee was poised to decide and made its final trip to San Diego, its lucky members were treated to a show they will never forget. Wining and dining were the least of their entertainment. They were treated to behind-the-scenes tours of the zoo and the Wild Animal Park, trips to the Del Mar Racetrack, helicopter rides, shopping and golf. By the time they left town, there was little doubt which city would emerge as the hands-down winner.

The Republican Convention was an unqualified success. That only inspired Mayor Golding to reach higher. San Diego hosted the 1998 Super Bowl at Qualcomm Stadium, it's second time staging the football extravaganza, and it looks as though the city will have a place in the regular rotation for future Super Bowls. Looking even further into the future, Mayor Golding has already spearheaded successful ballot proposals to expand the convention center (maybe for another political convention?), and build a new baseball-only ballpark for the San Diego Padres. A new showcase central library is at the top of her priority list too.

Lest you get the impression she's interested only in high-profile projects, think again. Mayor Golding understands that from a safe city, all else follows. As a result of her efforts, the city has more police officers, a new community-policing structure and tough curfew policies for minors. Crime is down 35 percent in San Diego as compared to 1992.

Mayor Susan Golding

The mayor also understands that the best form of crime prevention is a job. By cutting business taxes and easing permit restrictions, she has given local businesses the freedom and flexibility to succeed, and San Diego's economy has never been better. San Diego currently has one of the lowest unemployment rates of any major city in California, thanks in no small part to the mayor's programs.

Mayor Golding embraces the idea that San Diego is a city of neighborhoods. She has fought to decentralize municipal government and give control back to the neighborhoods. Community police storefronts have helped bolster relations between the public and the police and has led to increased neighborhood pride.

It's no surprise that Susan Golding was overwhelmingly reelected in 1996 with 78 percent of the vote. She has put San Diego on everyone's map and has even christened it with a new nickname: The First Great City of the Twenty-first Century. And even though she'll be long out of office by the time 2018 rolls around, rumor has it that she now has her sights on that year's Olympic Games. No surprise, really. She has a habit of going for the gold.

The aerospace industry used to be the giant in town, now there are any number of manufacturing companies fighting to be on top. For example, San Diego has become the golf-equipment manufacturing capital of the world, employing about 11,000 people locally.

Biotechnology firms account for 22,000 jobs, and more than 500 software firms keep 13,000 people working. Qualcomm, the homegrown telecommunications company, employs more than 8,000 all by itself. But the leader in the employment race for the foreseeable future is the electronics business, which employs more than 35,000 San Diegans. The greatest opportunities are in engineering, and the shortage is severe. Many companies have launched international searches and are stuffing employment packages with perks to try to lure engineers to San Diego.

The ties between San Diego and its good neighbor to the south continue to strengthen. A joint international marketing program with Baja California helps attract investment in research and in manufacturing, and a vigorous trade between the two countries helps bolster the emerging maquiladora industry. Maquiladoras are companies with offices and manufacturing facilities on both sides of the border, a venture that has been quite successful for the two countries.

The military remains a strong contributor to the economy, pumping nearly $10 billion annually into the local coffers. Tourism, even though it ranks third, will never be under-appreciated, as 14 million visitors yearly add another $4.4 billion to the pot. And more than 124,000 San Diegans work in fields directly related to the tourist industry, including lodging, food service, attractions and transportation.

Construction is recovering from its slump of the early to mid-1990s, and builders are frantically trying to construct the 400,000 housing units needed for those expected million new residents coming. And finally, agriculture holds steady in the fifth slot. We have a theory about that. It must be all the avocado groves that boost the agriculture business. After all, most San Diegans consider guacamole a separate food group.

INSIDERS' TIP

To report a crime in progress, or for any life-threatening situation, dial 911 immediately. If you are the victim of a crime that happened while you were away, or to give information concerning a crime or any suspicious activity, call the police at (619) 531-2000.

Cost of Living

There's a price to be paid for living in a paradise where the weather's great, jobs are plentiful and attitudes are casual. A true dollars-and-cents price. The cost of living in San Diego is undeniably higher than in many other cities, and the main reason is real estate. Real estate has traditionally been the barometer of the local economy, rising and falling with the fortune of the rest of the city. However, even at its lowest, real estate is rarely a bargain in California's southernmost cul-de-sac. Housing prices fluctuate, of course, but the median resale price of a single-family house in the county is about $210,000 and climbing.

Gasoline prices seem to be higher than in other places, too. And since San Diegans tenaciously cling to their autos as the preferred mode of transportation, they pay for it.

But the good news is that bargains are always to be found. Inexpensive dining, off-price shopping and discount entertainment opportunities are common. With judicious planning, a visit or even a permanent move to San Diego doesn't have to break the bank.

Weather

San Diego is famous for many things: the zoo, Sea World, Balboa Park, Dr. Seuss and Scripps Institution of Oceanography, to name a few. But ask anyone what comes to mind when they think of San Diego, and more likely than not they'll say the weather. Let's face it. The average daytime temperature is 70 degrees, and most days are sunny. Humidity is usually low, even during the summer, and winter temperatures rarely dip below 40 degrees at night. It doesn't get much more pleasant than that.

Of course, if you travel to the far ends of

the county you can find some extremes. Desert temperatures in Borrego Springs soar over 100 degrees for most of the summer, and the mountains get cold enough to keep snow on the ground for at least a few days during the winter. But aside from a few heat waves during the summer and cold snaps during the winter, it's generally comfortable around town most of the time.

Visitors from the Midwest are astonished to find that a winter wardrobe is nonexistent in San Diego. Most locals' idea of a winter wardrobe is their summer wardrobe — with a sweater. And no matter how cold it gets during the winter months, some stalwart souls refuse to give up their shorts.

Rainfall averages less than 10 inches per year, except in the El Niño years, when anything can happen. The only other weather oddity is the occasional condition known as a Santa Ana. During a Santa Ana, hot and dry winds blow in from the desert, the temperature climbs into the high eighties or low nineties and the humidity plunges to 10 percent or less. Most common during the late fall or early winter months, these winds usually last only a few days, and are more a subject for water-cooler conversation than a cause of major discomfort.

Earthquakes

Anyone who has endured an earthquake of any magnitude will confirm that they are nothing to be scoffed at. They are every bit as frightening as a tornado or a hurricane and can cause devastating damage. The good news is that the big ones are few and far between. Even though earthquakes are almost a daily occurrence in and around Southern California, most are too small to be noticed. The wise traveler or resident is prepared for any eventuality, though, and will have evacuation routes planned in advance, just as you would in case of fire.

Photo: Dale Frost/Port of San Diego

A downtown San Diego skyline is the backdrop to a group of sailing enthusiasts.

The White Pages of the local telephone book have comprehensive instructions and suggestions for earthquake safety. Knowing what to do ahead of time will lessen the scare factor of the occasional shaker.

Crime and Personal Safety

We want your time in San Diego to be safe. Although crime is down according to police and sheriff's department statistics, this still is a big city, and it still has crime and safety issues like every other large city. It's always wise to keep in mind the same basic safety precautions you would take in your hometown or in any other major metropolitan city.

Whether sightseeing, dining or shopping, it's a good idea to travel in groups. There's safety in numbers, and you will lessen the opportunity to be singled out as a target. Also, try to have a good idea of your current surroundings and where you're headed. The more confident you appear, the less vulnerable you are to unscrupulous strangers.

Finally, like every other major city in the world, San Diego has a homeless population concentrated in its urban areas. Most homeless people are harmless, but some are chronic criminals and drug or alcohol abusers who are eager to take advantage of the unsuspecting. We suggest you treat transients with respectful caution, and avoid contributing to panhandlers.

Now, you have an idea of what San Diego is all about, hop in your car, head for the trolley and explore. You'll like what you find. And don't forget to bring your *Insiders' Guide*.

San Diego's Lindbergh Field sits right smack in the middle of the city, so when you land, you're already here. You don't have to spend an hour or more finding your way into the city.

Getting Here, Getting Around

San Diego is a destination city. In fact, it is often referred to as the cul-de-sac of the Southwest, a distinction that rankles most locals, but ultimately they grudgingly agree. Few people come through San Diego on their way to someplace else, as they do with major hubs like Los Angeles, Chicago or Dallas. Of course, Lindbergh Field is called San Diego International Airport, but unless you're headed to Mexico, leaving the country usually involves a stop in Los Angeles first. Once you're here, well, there's really no reason to go anyplace else aside from an occasional daytrip. As you'll soon discover, that's not such a bad thing. The city has more than enough attractions and entertainment to amuse even the most hard to please. And if you're really determined to go someplace else when you leave San Diego, we'll get you there...eventually.

Another distinction San Diego has is the location of its primary airport, Lindbergh Field. It sits right smack in the middle of the city, not on the outskirts of town like most major airports. That means when you land, you're already here. You don't have to spend an hour or more finding your way into the city. Oh, and just a word about the landing. Because the airport is right next to downtown, your pilot will have to navigate some high-rises during final approach. But don't let that worry you — they've been doing it for years and they're used to it. Just wave to the office workers on the top floors as you fly by.

We've designed this chapter to help you find your way to San Diego and how to get around once you're here. We've included all the traditional modes of transportation as well as a few that may surprise and delight you, such as water taxis and ferries. Just be sure to always have a map with you, and you'll find your way around with ease. If you do get lost, half the fun of traveling is finding your way home.

We're delighted that you've chosen San Diego as your home base. So we'll let you in on a little secret. Los Angeles is only two hours north by car, train or bus. Imagine Disneyland, Knott's Berry Farm, Universal Studios, Rodeo Drive and Hollywood, and you may decide to take a daytrip to visit our neighbor to the north. We won't hold it against you. We'll be here to welcome you back at the end of the day.

Getting Here

By Air

San Diego International Airport/ Lindbergh Field
3707 N. Harbor Dr., San Diego
• (619) 231-2100

Named for aviation pioneer Charles A. Lindbergh, whose famed *Spirit of St. Louis* was built in San Diego, San Diego International Airport carries his name as tribute to his epic solo flight across the Atlantic Ocean. Lindbergh Field opened in 1934, and although the airport has changed substantially over the years, it remains at its original location — sandwiched between Pacific Highway and Harbor Drive.

Nearly 14 million passengers travel through the airport annually on more than 500 daily flights. Terminal 1 has been in existence since 1967, with quite a bit of remodeling in the ensuing years, and Terminal 2 opened in 1979. The Commuter Terminal was added in 1996 and handles 25,000 passengers daily, and a major expansion and renovation of Terminal 2 was completed in 1998.

For the past 30 years, even while in the midst of remodeling, talk about the airport has mostly been, where should we move it? The drawbacks to having an airport in the middle of the city are many: The land the airport occupies is precious. Nearby residents constantly complain about airplane noise, and many consider the steep descent to pose a hazard with every landing. But 30 years of talk have produced nothing — not even a consensus of opinion on whether it should be moved, much less where it should go. Chances are it'll stay right where it is. For convenience and proximity to downtown, it can't be beat.

Arrivals

Terminal 1 and Terminal 2

Once you have deplaned, signs will direct you to the baggage-claim area as well as to ground transportation. If you've arrived at one of the far gates, it can be a bit of a hike, especially in Terminal 2, so muster up your extra energy and concentrate on the delights that await you. You'll have to take the escalator or elevator down to the baggage area, but once you're there, lighted signs will indicate which carousel will deliver your bags. Should your bags not arrive (this almost never happens in San Diego, but then, we believe hardly anything bad ever happens here), lost-baggage offices are conveniently located in the claim area, and friendly agents will do their best to reunite you with your luggage.

Located within the baggage-claim area are rental car and hotel information boards with telephones that will connect you directly to your preferred agency or hotel for pick-up, information and reservations. As you leave the baggage area, you can proceed directly to the outside curb if you are taking the Metropolitan Transit Service bus called the Airport Flyer. The bus stop is curbside as you exit either terminal, and the 10-minute Airport Flyer service will transport you to or from downtown, Amtrak, the Coaster, the Trolley and other bus routes for a $2 fare.

Otherwise, after you claim your luggage, take the elevator or escalator back upstairs to cross the pedestrian bridge to the transportation plaza. There you will find taxis, shuttles and rental car transport.

Commuter Terminal

If you're arriving by commuter flight from the Los Angeles, Fresno, Santa Barbara or San Francisco areas, you'll probably land at the Commuter Terminal. Smaller but just as efficient, the Commuter Terminal has much the same system as Terminals 1 and 2. The only difference is that ground transportation is available curbside as soon as you leave the baggage area; you needn't cross a pedestrian bridge. In addition to taxis, shuttles and the Airport Flyer, a complimentary red airport shuttle bus transports passengers between the Commuter Terminal and Terminals 1 and 2.

Rental Car Agencies

Alamo	(619) 297-0311
Avis	(619) 231-7171
Budget	(619) 297-3360
Dollar	(619) 234-3388
Enterprise Rent-a-Car	(800) 736-8222
Hertz	(619) 231-7000
National	(619) 231-7100
Thrifty Car Rental	(800) 367-2277

Departures

The most convenient way to reach the airport is to have a friend drive you, or take a cab, bus or shuttle. Access to Lindbergh Field is from Interstate 5, either south or

Photo: Dale Frost/Port of San Diego

The San Diego Airport is graced with sculpture and a colorful flag display.

north. If you're traveling south, take the Sassafras Street exit, and follow the airport signs to Laurel Street, where you will turn right. Laurel Street feeds into North Harbor Drive, which takes you directly to the airport. From I-5 north, take the Hawthorn Street exit to North Harbor Drive and turn right. Signs will direct drivers to specific airlines at the three terminals.

Ticketing is downstairs at both the Commuter Terminal and Terminal 1, and upstairs *and* downstairs in Terminal 2, depending on your airline. A variety of shuttle services are available to transport you to the airport, as well as taxis and park-and-ride facilities. If you drive your own car and wish to leave it in airport parking while you're away, the rates are as follows:

0-1/2 hour	$.50
1/2 - 1 hour	$1
1-6 hours	$1 per hour
6-7 hours	$8
7-8 hours	$10
8-24 hours	$12
Per day after 1st day	$18

(includes any part of the following day)

Private Airport Shuttles

Rates vary widely from company to company. Some charge a per-person rate, others a per-carload rate. Still others charge by the mile. Van or sedan service is available, depending on the company.

5 Star Shuttle	(800) 543-9222
Airport King	(619) 521-1199
Airport Shuttle	(619) 234-4403

INSIDERS' TIP

If you're picking up or dropping off passengers at San Diego International Airport, keep in mind that both arrivals and departures share curb space in front of the terminals. Traffic is always heavy, and airport security is vigilant. Don't leave your car unattended or linger longer than necessary.

Cloud 9 Shuttle	(800) 974-8885
Coronado Livery	(619) 435-6310
Prime Ride Shuttle	(800) 789-5254
San Diego Xpress	(619) 220-8454
Supreme Shuttle	(800) 565-7021
Torrey Pines Transfer	(858) 587-1184

Many travelers take advantage of the numerous park-and-ride facilities located near the airport. You can park your car in their secured lot, and they will shuttle you to and from the airport for a fee that is substantially less than the airport's parking fee. Fees range from $6 to $11 per day, depending on their proximity to the airport. Here are a few park-and-ride companies:

Aladdin Parking Garage
(619) 696-7275
Ladki Airport Parking
(619) 294-6858
Laurel Travel Center
(619) 233-4841
Park and Ride Co.
(619) 295-1503
San Diego Airport Parking
(619) 574-1177

Regional Airports

The following airports located around the county are mostly private or small airports serving small planes and corporate aircraft. The exception is Palomar Airport in Carlsbad, which, in addition to its private aircraft facilities, has daily commercial flights to Los Angeles.

Landing information and fees should be obtained in advance from each airport. As the fees and availability change frequently, we recommend you contact the desired airport well in advance of your arrival to make arrangements for landing.

Brown Field Municipal Airport
1424 Continental St., San Ysidro
• (619) 424-0455

Owned and operated by the city of San Diego, Brown Field is located just north of the U.S.-Mexico border and has two runways, 8,000 and 3,000 feet long. The airport has two fuelers and three FBOs (Fixed Base Operators) for full-service maintenance. Amenities include a restaurant and bar, and rental car arrangements can be made at the airport.

Gillespie Field
1640 N. Johnson Ave., El Cajon
• (619) 449-0611

Located in East County, Gillespie Field has two runways, 5,300 and 2,800 feet respectively. Fuel services are available at the airport, but it has no maintenance facilities. Inside the small terminal is a comfortable lounge with soft-drink and coffee vending machines. Rental cars are not located on-site, but Enterprise Rent-a-Car has an arrangement with Gillespie Field to pick up travelers and transport them to the agency, usually within 30 minutes. Advance arrangements with most rental agencies can also be made to have a car waiting on arrival.

Montgomery Field
3750 John Montgomery Dr., San Diego
• (858) 573-1440

City-owned Montgomery Field has one 4,600-foot runway. Located in the Kearney Mesa business district of San Diego, the airport has full fueling services as well as three FBOs for aircraft maintenance. Car rentals are available, and the Casa Machado restaurant and bar is situated overlooking the runway.

Oceanside Municipal Airport
480 Airport Rd., Oceanside
• (760) 966-2940

Oceanside Airport has one runway, 3,061 feet in length. Full-service fueling is available, as well as an FBO that services both planes and helicopters. Inside the terminal is a small lounge complete with snack and coffee machines. Rental cars are available from the airport.

McClellan-Palomar Airport
2198 Palomar Airport Rd., Carlsbad
• (760) 431-1328

Fifteen daily flights to and from Los Angeles International Airport are available from McClellan-Palomar on American Eagle and United Express Airlines. Most of the traffic at Palomar, however, is private aircraft. The

Photo: Dale Frost/Port of San Diego

Passengers arrive at the San Diego Airport.

single runway is 4,600 feet for landing and 5,000 feet for take-off. Three FBOs provide full-service maintenance and fueling. A restaurant is located on-site, and rental cars are available too.

By Train

Amtrak

Reservations (800) USA RAIL (872-7245)
Oceanside Station
• 235 S. Tremont St. • (760) 722-4622
Solana Beach Station
• 105 Cedros Ave. • (858) 259-2697
San Diego's Santa Fe Depot
• 1050 Kettner Blvd. • (619) 239-9021

Traveling by train is probably one of the more pleasant ways to reach San Diego, and train routes feed from every part of the country. Scenic rides down the coast of California are popular; so are the over-land routes through the deserts east of San Diego. Amtrak makes three stops in San Diego County: Oceanside, Solana Beach and the Santa Fe Depot in downtown San Diego.

Taxi stands are prominent at all three stops, and bus service is available from all three too. The San Diego Trolley, which serves much of San Diego, also has a station at the Santa Fe Depot.

Should you be leaving San Diego by train, checked baggage service is available at all stations. If you're packing a bicycle for that spur-of-the-moment ride, some trains are equipped with coach cars that have a bicycle storage area. Bikes can be carried on with no advance reservation, but it's advisable to check in advance to make sure your train has the special car.

Reservations may be made in advance through any travel agent, at Amtrak stations or by calling the 24-hour toll-free num-

---

INSIDERS' TIP

Sometimes a special event deserves a special touch. Ask your hotel concierge or receptionist to help you arrange for private limousine service to drive you in style to the wine country or a restaurant or even for a day of sightseeing. Enjoy a bit of luxury.

Photo: Thom Vollenweider

The Greyhound Bus Line takes many visitors on day excursions to nearby Tijuana.

ber listed above. Tickets can also be purchased the day of travel at Amtrak stations. Amtrak accepts cash and all major credit cards. If you're 62 or older, a personal check will be accepted. Animals are not permitted on trains unless they are certified guide or service animals accompanying passengers with disabilities, and Amtrak requires that you carry the necessary documentation.

By Bus

Greyhound Bus
• (800) 231-2222, Fare and Schedule
Information

If you're on a tight budget, Greyhound Bus may be the perfect solution. In an effort to attract more customers, it seems that Greyhound always has some kind of special, such as two-for-one fares. If you're traveling with children Greyhound offers half-price fares for kids 11 years of age and younger. Babies younger than 2 travel for free.

Greyhound has several stations throughout San Diego County, which we've listed below. Go Greyhound, and leave the driving to them!

San Diego:
120 W. Broadway • (619) 239-3266
El Cajon:
250 S. Marshall • (619) 444-2591
San Ysidro:
799 E. San Ysidro Blvd. • (619) 428-1194
Oceanside:
205 S. Tremont St. • (760) 722-1587
Escondido:
700 W. Valley Pkwy • (760) 745-6522
Vista:
130 Eucalyptus • (760) 631-7715

By Car

To reach San Diego from Washington, Oregon or Northern California, take I-5 and keep your car pointed south; it'll lead you all the way into the city. If you're not in a hurry and would like a more scenic drive,

Calif. Highway 101, which begins in Eureka, California, is a nice alternative. It'll keep you close to the coast as you drive through such picturesque towns as Big Sur, Monterey and San Luis Obispo. From points east, hook up with Interstate 15 in Nevada or Utah, or Interstate 8 in Arizona. Both freeways end up in San Diego. I-15 takes you through Las Vegas and the high desert in eastern California, and I-8 is a pretty drive through the Laguna Mountains that separate San Diego and the Imperial Valley.

Getting Around

Now that you're here, let us show you how easy it is to move around the county. You have many options: auto, bus, taxi, trolley, train and a few unusual modes, too. Take a map and your *Insiders' Guide* and go exploring.

By Car

Roadways

California is known for its excellent freeway system, and San Diego has one of the best systems in the state. Aside from normal morning and afternoon congestion during commute hours, San Diego has managed to avoid the dreaded gridlock that Los Angeles is notorious for. With a combination of interstate, state and county highways, navigating the county should be a snap. If you're in the exploring mood and happen to see one of San Diego's trademark blue and yellow signs with a big white seagull on it, follow it. That's the sign for a scenic drive, and there are many throughout the county, especially along the coastline. They will lead you on a drive that will show you some of the most beautiful sights in San Diego.

All interstate and state highways have emergency call boxes spaced every quarter mile or so. These provide direct connections to emergency services, such as police, ambulance, fire and towing.

U.S. Interstate Highways

Interstate 8

I-8 begins at the western edge of San Diego, at Sunset Cliffs Boulevard., and travels east through Mission Valley, East County, across the mountains and into Arizona. It's the main east/west artery in the city. Every north/south interstate, state and county route intersects with I-8.

It has a tendency to bunch up in the Mission Valley area during rush hours, the westbound lanes in the morning and the eastbound lanes in the afternoon. But unless an accident results in a major clog, rush hour traffic is relatively easy to endure.

Interstate 5

I-5 begins at the U.S.-Mexico border and ends at the U.S.-Canada border. It meanders north along the coastal region of San Diego, offering some spectacular ocean views before veering inland once it passes the county line.

Its rush-hour bottlenecks are in North County Coastal: during morning hours they happen in southbound lanes; the ones leading north back up in the afternoon.

Interstate 15

The second major north/south freeway is I-15. Its southern leg emerges from I-5 in National City, and it travels north through inland San Diego and North County, eventually leaving the county in Riverside. One portion of I-15 remains unfinished, between Landis Street and El Cajon Boulevard in central San Diego. This short, one-mile stretch must be traveled on surface streets and is almost always heavily congested any time of day. Construction is underway to complete this section of I-15, but the date

Photo: San Diego Convention and Visitors Bureau

Passengers using the San Diego Airport find exciting surroundings as they move through the airport's terminals.

of completion is uncertain. Many drivers bypass the missing link by taking Interstate 805 north to California Highway 163, which reconnects with I-15 in the Miramar area.

Rush-hour slowdowns are in North County Inland, southbound in the morning and northbound in the afternoon. However, I-15 has the distinction of having the only HOV lane (High-Occupancy Vehicle) on county freeways. Its HOV lane is an eight-mile stretch that bypasses much of the traffic back up. The direction of the lanes is switched from south to north to accommodate morning and afternoon heavy traffic.

Interstate 805

I-805 provides a much-needed north/south inland sweep between I-5 and I-15. It emerges from I-5 in San Ysidro, just north of the U.S.-Mexico border, and makes its way north through central San Diego, reconnecting with I-5 in Sorrento Valley at the infamous "merge." Traffic at the merge is always heavy as North County residents make their way home during the afternoon commute.

California State Highways

All state highways have the familiar green sign with white numbers that designate them as California highways, but in truth, some are little more than surface streets or roadway extensions of highways that may or may not be completed one day. Here we will mention only those that qualify as true highways. If you're looking at a map and see the California State Highway designation, and it hasn't been described here, keep in mind that it may well be a winding, two-lane road through the mountains or a busy commercial street that you'd just as soon avoid.

INSIDERS' TIP

Killing time while waiting for a flight? Check out your favorite website at one of Lindbergh Field's Internet kiosks.

California Highway 54

We'll start in the South Bay with Calif. 54. This is a fairly new and very short freeway that travels east/west and connects I-5 and I-805 and has been helpful in relieving a lot of traffic on South Bay surface streets.

California Highway 94

Moving north, you come to Calif. 94, another east/west freeway that travels east from I-5 and eventually connects with Calif. 125 in the East County. Also called the Martin Luther King Jr. Freeway, it is heavily traveled during commute hours, west in the morning and east in the afternoon. If you bypass Calif. 125 and stay on Calif. 94, it turns into a surface road that becomes a scenic back route through the foothills of East County, near the Mexican border.

California Highway 163

Calif.163, also known as the Cabrillo Freeway, has historic status in San Diego. It is a north/south freeway whose southern end is in downtown. As it travels north, it winds through Balboa Park, and is about as scenic a freeway as you'll ever see, surrounded by lush greenery and soaring trees. If you drive it during rush hour, south in the morning and north in the afternoon, you'll have ample opportunity to enjoy its beauty. It continues north through Mission Valley and ultimately connects with I-15 near the Miramar Marine Corps Air Station.

California Highway 125

Now we're moving into the East County, where you'll find Calif. 125. It is a north/south connector between I-8 and Calif. 94. It's a short freeway, but provides a much-appreciated link between the two freeways.

California Highway 67

Calif. 67, another north/south freeway, is even shorter than Calif. 125, but it eases congestion for commuters traveling to and from Lakeside and Santee in the East County. If you're looking for an adventure, keep driving north on Calif. 67 to Ramona, a slowed-down, laid-back community on the way to the mountain town of Julian. It's a journey back in time.

California Highway 52

Calif. 52 has been called San Diego's godsend. It is an east/west freeway that intersects four other major north/south freeways: I-5, I-805, Calif. 163 and I-15, and eventually comes to an end in Santee, in the East County. It doesn't seem to suffer the same rush-hour traffic as San Diego's other freeways, and it has provided a much-loved link between the coastline and East County.

California Highway 56

Located just south of Del Mar, Calif. 56 will one day be a sorely needed east/west link between North County Coastal and North County Inland. Right now, it is only a

Photo: Dale Frost/Port of San Diego

A plane arriving at the busy San Diego airport pulls up to the terminal.

mile or two long, beginning at I-5 and moving east for just a few exits.

California Highway 78

This is the existing major east/west artery connecting North County Coastal with North County Inland. Calif. 78 begins in Oceanside and travels east through Vista and San Marcos, before turning into a surface street in Escondido and continuing to Ramona. It too is heavily congested during rush hour — in both directions, both morning and afternoon.

San Diego County Routes

Identified by a white hexagonal sign with a black "S" followed by a number, county routes are exclusively surface streets and roads. Some are major business streets, others are scenic drives that meander through the back country. If you're looking to get somewhere fast, don't mistake a county route for a shortcut. The county route designation is mostly an indication of who is responsible for maintenance — in this case, the county rather than the city in which they are located.

Taxi Service

San Diego has about as many taxi companies as it has animals in the zoo. Fees vary from taxi to taxi, but all are clearly posted on the outside of the cab. If you're catching a taxi from the airport, they will be queued up in the transportation plaza outside the terminals. It's customary to take the next taxi in line, and there will often be a facilitator present to offer assistance.

Taxis usually gather around major hotels and are available on demand. If none are immediately available, your hotel doorman or receptionist will be happy to call one for you. Generally speaking, taxis aren't hailed from the street; they don't spend a lot of time cruising for fares. If you're leaving a club or restaurant, ask the host or hostess to call a taxi for you.

Be wary if a taxi driver doesn't engage the meter as soon as you depart. This is strictly against the law, and you should bring it to the driver's attention.

Here are a few taxi companies:

Airport Cab	**(619) 280-5555**
American Cab	**(619) 234-1111**
Diamond Cab	**(619) 474-1544**
North County Cab	
	(San Diego) **(619) 260-1003**
	(North County) **(760) 480-9833**
Orange Cab	**(619) 291-4444**
San Diego Cab	**(619) 226-8294**
Yellow Cab	**(619) 234-6161**

Public Transporation

Metropolitan Transit System

• **(619) 233-3004**

The Metropolitan Transit System (MTS) includes the bus system and the San Diego Trolley. Dating back to 1886 the MTS began when the first streetcar made its way up Fifth Avenue from the downtown waterfront. San Diego was the second city in the nation to replace the horse with electric streetcars, but by 1945 all the streetcars had been replaced by buses.

The bus system covers 635 miles on 29 fixed routes and serves the cities of San Diego, El Cajon and La Mesa in the East County, and National City and Chula Vista in the South Bay, and some of the unincorporated areas too. The system also connects with other regional systems. Also included in the system is Direct Access to Regional Transit (DART). Residents of Paradise Hills, Mira Mesa, Rancho Bernardo, Scripps Ranch and the mid-city areas can call ahead to DART at (619) 293-3278 for transport to the nearest bus stop.

All buses are equipped to carry bicycles on racks mounted on the back of the bus. Most bus route fares are $1.75 one-way, and exact change is required. Deposit your fare into the box by the driver when you board an MTS bus. Children five years and younger ride free with any paying passenger, and discounts are available for seniors. Day Tripper passes provide unlimited access to all MTS buses, the Trolley and the San Diego-Coronado Ferry. They are available for one day ($5), two days ($8), three days ($10) or four days

Photo: San Diego Convention and Visitors Bureau

The Coaster runs through a downtown San Diego intersection.

($12). Passes can be purchased at the Transit Store at 102 Broadway, San Diego.

Transfers are free, just ask the driver for one when you board. When you board the next bus, hand the driver your transfer. Transfers are good for two hours. Printed bus routes and schedules are available in many hotels and at the Transit Store.

North County Transit District
Route Information:
(NorthCounty Coastal)• (760) 722-6283
(North County Inland) • (760) 743-6283

The North County Transit District (NCTD) serves all of North County, both coastal and inland. Connections to San Diego MTS buses are plentiful and easy, and many routes connect to Greyhound, the Coaster and Amtrak at the Oceanside and Solana Beach Transit Centers.

Basic fares are $1.50 for adults and free for children ages 5 and younger traveling with any fare-paying passenger. Seniors and the disabled (with NCTD photo ID card) pay $.75. Transfers are free.

Coaster
• (800) 262-7837 or (760) 722-6283

The Coaster operates regional rail service between Oceanside and San Diego. The blue, green and white express train mainly serves commuters, but it's a good way to travel between San Diego and North County Coastal. Moving north from the Santa Fe Depot in downtown San Diego, it stops in Old Town, Sorrento Valley, Solana Beach, Encinitas, Carlsbad Poinsettia, Carlsbad Village and Oceanside.

Numerous roundtrips are scheduled during weekdays, and a modified schedule is offered on Saturdays. Extra trains are added during special events such as

INSIDERS' TIP

Traffic reports will often refer to a back-up at the "merge" or the "S-curve." The merge refers to the area just north of La Jolla where I-5 and I-805 join to become one freeway going north; the S-curve is the portion of I-5 that runs through downtown, snaking back and forth like an S.

Ferry passengers disembark at the San Diego ferry landing.

Photo: Dale Frost/Port of San Diego

the annual Street Scene in downtown San Diego or the annual Holiday Bowl at Qualcomm Stadium.

Tickets are purchased from vending machines on the station platform before boarding the train, and the machines accept cash (dispensing a maximum of $10 in change), VISA and MasterCard. Fares range from $3 one way to $3.75, depending on the distance you travel. All tickets must be validated before boarding the train by validating machines that are also located on the station platform.

Passengers must present a validated ticket to the conductor, ticket inspector or police upon request. Coaster tickets provide a free transfer to all connecting San Diego MTS buses, Trolley and NCTD buses within two hours from the time validated. Your Coaster ticket also provides a free transfer to the Airport Flyer, which departs for Lindbergh Field from the Santa Fe Depot in San Diego.

San Diego Trolley
• (619) 233-3004

A light rail system with bright red cars, the San Diego Trolley serves San Diego,

East County and the South Bay. Riding the Trolley is so much fun that it's arguable whether it's a form of transportation or a pleasure excursion. But because it's so efficient and connects to so many other forms of transportation around town, we'll consider it transportation for the time being.

Connections to the Trolley from Amtrak and the Coaster are available at the San Diego Santa Fe Depot, and an additional connection from the Coaster is available at Old Town.

The Trolley has two lines, the Blue Line and the Orange Line. The Blue Line is an S-shaped line that serves San Diego from the Rancho Mission stop (east of Qualcomm Stadium and near San Diego Mission de Alcalá), west through Mission Valley and Old Town, and south through downtown to the U.S.-Mexico border. The Orange Line makes a loop through downtown San Diego serving Centre City as well as Seaport Village, the Convention Center and the Gaslamp Quarter, then continues to the East County, serving El Cajon and Santee.

Trolley tickets are purchased at vending machines located on the station platform and are priced according to the distance to be traveled. One-way fares range from $1 to $2.25, with senior and disabled-rider discounts available. Passengers with bicycles are charged 50 cents extra. Day Tripper passes give visitors one- to four-day unlimited access to the Trolley, MTS buses and the San Diego-Coronado Ferry for the same prices as listed under the MTS section. Passes can be purchased at Trolley stations or at the Transit Store at 102 Broadway, San Diego. If you're using a prepaid pass, you must validate it before boarding the Trolley. Special validating machines are located on every Trolley platform near the ticket-vending machines.

Trolley tickets serve as transfers to MTS buses, with connections at most stations. Keep your tickets with you while on the Trolley. They won't be collected as you board, but Trolley officers periodically check to make sure all passengers have tickets.

San Diego-Coronado Bay Bridge

This graceful blue bridge soars across San Diego Bay and links downtown San Diego with the peaceful island enclave of Coronado. The views of both the San Diego skyline and Coronado are breathtaking from the top of the bridge. The bridge is quite high and narrow, and the trip across can be a little hair-raising. So if you're the driver, let your passengers describe the view to you.

It is the only toll bridge in San Diego County, and the fare crossing from San Diego to Coronado is $1. If you're traveling in the reverse direction, from the island back to downtown, the fare is free. Car-poolers are exempt from the $1 fare too. Just bear to the right as you come to the end of the bridge and sail right through the carpool lane.

San Diego-Coronado Ferry
• (619) 234-4111

If you prefer a waterborne approach to Coronado, try taking the ferry across San Diego Bay. Ferrying passengers and bicycles only (no autos), it departs from the San Diego Harbor Excursion Dock at 1050 North Harbor Drive, San Diego, and docks at the Ferry Landing Marketplace on Coronado. It leaves San Diego every hour on the hour from 9 AM to 9 PM Sunday

through Thursday, and until 10 PM Friday and Saturday. It leaves Coronado every hour on the half hour beginning at 9:30 AM to 9:30 PM Sunday through Thursday, and until 10:30 PM Friday and Saturday. The fare is $2 per person, one way.   If you're bringing your bike, the fare is $2.50.

San Diego Water Taxi
• (619) 235-8294

San Diego Water Taxi offers on-call boat transportation service along San Diego Bay for a $5 per person fare. Operating between the hours of 10 AM and 10 PM, you can take in skyline scenery on your way to waterfront hotels, restaurants and shopping centers. San Diego Water Taxi offers service to all points in San Diego Bay including Shelter and Harbor Islands, Coronado, Downtown, Chula Vista and the South Bay.

Crossing the Border

No visit to San Diego would be complete without a trip across the border to Mexico. All the details of a visit to Tijuana and beyond are covered in our South of the Border chapter, but we'll give you a general idea of how best to approach it here.

If all you're planning is a shopping and dining expedition to Tijuana, the best way to get there is via the San Diego Trolley. The Trolley ends right at the border, and you can walk across. Should you be driving, you can park in one of several lots on the U.S. side of the border and, again, walk across. Once you've passed through the border checkpoints, you can hail a Tijuana taxi to take you to the main shopping area or the restaurant of your choice.

For the more adventurous, it's perfectly safe to drive south of the border. Just remember that the streets are not laid out quite as efficiently as they are north of the border, and it's easy to get lost. Also, be sure to purchase Mexican insurance from one of the many storefront insurance shops before you drive into Tijuana. If you were to have an accident, your Mexican insurance policy will make life much easier while dealing with the local authorities.

What finally started San Diego on the path to becoming a city was the same commodity that fuels its economy today: real estate.

History

Historians pay scant attention to Juan Rodríguez Cabrillo. After all, he was just one of many Spanish explorers who set out in the wake of Christopher Columbus to chart new territory for Spain. When Cabrillo sailed with his two ships into San Diego Bay on September 28, 1542, he wasn't eager to spend much time exploring. Profit and glory lured him northward. Cabrillo's quest was to discover a northwest passage linking the Pacific and Atlantic Oceans. Still, he couldn't help admiring the natural attributes of the bay he had happened upon: Its south-facing opening between the Point Loma peninsula and Coronado made a U-turn and traveled southward between the mainland to the east and a narrow stretch of land to the west that merged several miles south. Cabrillo took note that San Diego Bay was uniquely situated with natural defenses against unwanted intruders.

The First San Diegans

Cabrillo's arrival on the eve of the feast day of St. Michael the Archangel inspired him to name his discovery San Miguel. Thus christened, the territory and its inhabitants said farewell to Cabrillo and his fellow explorers, who were never to be seen again. Yes, there already were settlers before Cabrillo arrived. We give Cabrillo credit for being the first European to set foot on San Diego soil, but he certainly did not "discover" it. As far back as 9000 B.C., Indians now known as the San Dieguito were settling in San Diego. They were descendants of Asians who had traversed the bridge of land that connected Asia and North America in prehistoric times, and of others who had traveled westward across North America, crossing the Sierra Nevada Mountains and moving down the coastal plains.

The Kumeyaay Indians joined the San Dieguito around 1000 B.C., and they shared the beauty of San Diego undisturbed until Cabrillo's arrival more than six centuries later. Although they greeted Cabrillo guardedly, they had nothing to fear. Spain and the rest of the world ignored the new possession for six decades. Their loss. What attracted the San Dieguito and the Kumeyaay and ultimately kept them here was the weather. It was similar to the Mediterranean's but even better. The area escaped the cold weather patterns that besieged the north and also managed to avoid the tropical humidity that enveloped the regions to the south. Mild winters and long summers were the norm. Through the centuries since Cabrillo stopped here, most who have visited San Diego have all agreed that it has the most enviable climate on Earth.

In 1602 another of Spain's explorers, Sebastián Vizcaíno, sailed into San Miguel during a voyage to inspect his country's holdings claimed by those who came before him. Fortunately for the resident Indians, Vizcaíno had no more interest in settling the territory than did Cabrillo. His only contribution was to rename the city San Diego, in honor of his flagship's Franciscan patron saint, Saint Didacus of Alcalá. Like Cabrillo, Vizcaíno quickly left to sail northward, and the Indians once again were left in peace.

Reluctant Colonization

By the mid-1700s Spain's reluctance to colonize its holdings in Mexico's Baja California and the rest of California was overcome by the encroachment of Russian fur traders. Moving down the coast of the Pacific Northwest and into California, they threatened to claim Spain's territories for themselves. Spain may not have had much interest in colonization before, but the possibility of losing something they believed was rightfully theirs was motivation enough. Still, there was the problem of the local Indians. Charles III, king of Spain, figured the best way to establish authority among the Indians was to enlist them.

So, along with Don Gaspar de Portolá, the Catalonian captain in charge of the military forces, King Charles sent Father Junipero Serra, a Franciscan priest who would establish a string of missions throughout California and attempt to convert the Indians to Christianity. De Portolá and Serra began their quest in Loreto, Baja California, and finally arrived in San Diego in 1769. Although de Portolá quickly pressed on, Father Serra remained behind and dedicated the first of 21 missions in California on July 16, 1769. Located atop Presidio Hill, Mission San Diego de Alcalá overlooked the bay and the Pacific Ocean beyond.

Father Serra soon learned that the best way to convert the local Indians to Christianity was to virtually conscript them into service for the mission, and in the process they were renamed Digueño, after his new mission. History has treated Father Serra kindly, rightly crediting him for the establishment of the mission system that prospered well into the 19th century, and for generating a strong foothold of Christianity in California. But his detractors are critical of his mistreatment of the Indians who served him. History books have universally glossed over the fact that Father Serra's preferred method of conversion was physical rather than spiritual. Many Indians lost their lives at the hands of the Spanish newcomers when they resisted their authority.

Mission San Diego de Alcalá remained on Presidio Hill for only five years before it was moved to its current location in Mission Valley, on the banks of the San Diego River. Conflict between the Indians and the soldiers, as well as the need for a better water supply, prompted the move.

Nevertheless, the mission system was a success, Spain laid claim to California, and peace reigned until 1821, when Mexico declared its independence from Spain.

Soon after, the mission system, with its profitable trade industry, would die. San Diego and its Mission San Diego de Alcalá were now under the authority of Mexico and would remain so until the end of the war between the United States and Mexico. Seeing the strategic value of San Diego's natural harbor, the United States was quick to wrest control of it from Mexico and met little resistance. By the time the war ended in 1847 and San Diego, along with the rest of California, officially became part of the United States three years later, the population was about 350, mostly settled in at the foot of Presidio Hill, in an area now known as Old Town.

The Beginnings of a City

Released from the control of Mexico, San Diego seemed perfectly poised to begin growing. It didn't happen as quickly as you might think. By the end of the Civil War, the population of Old Town had dwindled by half, mainly because everyone was flocking to Northern California to join the gold rush. What finally started San Diego on the path to becoming a city was the same commodity that fuels its economy today: real estate.

Visitors coming to San Diego for the first time are sure to notice a certain similarity between the names of some prominent structures: Horton Plaza, the Horton Grand Hotel, Horton Street, Horton House, Horton's Tavern. Alonzo Erastus Horton was the city's official founding father, and he was among the first to recognize the value of real estate in San Diego. Unlike others before him, he wasted little time in capitalizing on it.

Horton was living in San Francisco when he attended a lecture on the ports of California. The discussion about the prospects of San Diego caught his interest, and within three days he was on a steamer to San Diego with dreams of building a great city. He pulled into San Diego Harbor on April 15, 1867, disembarking at what is now the foot of Market Street. Horton's first stop was Old Town, the original settlement

Photo: CeCe Canton

San Diego Mission de Alcalá stands as a reminder of the tremendous influence the mission had in the beginning of this city.

nestled beneath the burned-out ruins of the old Presidio. Scarcely disguising his contempt for what he saw, he declared his intention to relocate the heart of the city to the area near the wharf. "I have been nearly all over the United States," Horton said, "and that is the prettiest place for a city I ever saw."

Horton's first land purchase was enviable even by nineteenth-century standards: 960 acres for $265, or about 27½ cents per acre. Within three years New Town had far outpaced Old Town with a population that had swelled to 2,301. The economy of the young city was precarious, however, because it was tied so closely to land speculation. From 1867 forward San Diego's economy would fluctuate between boom and bust as the price of real estate rose and fell.

In Search of a Railroad

Adding to the uncertain land market was speculation about the arrival of a railroad. Three barriers kept stalling the prospects: the two natural barriers of the mountains to the east and the ocean to the west, and the political barrier of the Mexican border to the south. Commerce-hungry San Diegans would not give up their dream, though, and whenever rumors spread that the railroad was finally coming, land prices would soar. Then when the bubble burst with the news that there would be no railroad, the real estate market would plummet, followed by the population, and the city's economy wold be left in shambles. In 1872 the news was that San Diego would become the western terminus for the Texas

& Pacific. What followed was wild speculation. Residents and outsiders alike scraped together whatever money they could get their hands on to buy property and build, build, build. The population soared to 5,000. But when railroad plans fell through, the economy collapsed and the population dropped to less than 1,500.

Alonzo Horton took a financial bath during the bust of the 1870s and was never again the same driving force in San Diego. His contribution to the city is well remembered, however, as is evidenced by the many visible tributes to him.

The railroad did finally make its way to San Diego in the mid-1880s. The Santa Fe-Atlantic & Pacific Railroad built its West Coast terminus in National City, just south of San Diego. The line went north and then east, through Barstow in central California. Once again the economy boomed, and the population grew to 35,000. New Town boasted 71 saloons, playing host to such notable visitors as Wyatt Earp, who lived in San Diego for a time and operated a handful of gambling casinos in town. Prostitutes were abundant, occupying 120 bawdy houses, and nearly outnumbering the more traditional business people. Hotels, restaurants, rooming houses, opium dens and dance halls were bursting at the seams.

But true to the shape of San Diego's short history, bust was right around the corner. The Santa Fe-Atlantic & Pacific Railroad never became much more than a spur line. Most of the real rail traffic went north to Los Angeles, already a commercial rival. By 1889 San Diego had crashed again. The wharves and warehouses were empty, and half the city's population had disappeared because of a lack of industry to support it. Those who had their fortunes tied up in real estate suffered greatly as the bottom dropped out of the land market. Once again, San Diego would have to reinvent itself.

Spreckels to the Rescue

Whenever San Diego seemed to be suffering the most, whenever its fortunes looked especially bleak, a savior was inevitably waiting in the wings. As was the case with Alonzo Horton, John D. Spreckels was captivated by the temperate climate of this city by the bay. Heir to the Spreckels sugar fortune, he liberally poured his family money into his adopted city and for the next 20 years laid claim to much of its assets. He owned the streetcar system, most of Coronado and North Island, the historic Hotel Del Coronado (a million-dollar property even then), two of the three newspapers (one of which still exists today, *The San Diego Union-Tribune*, whose history is detailed in our Media chapter), the water company, the ferry system and numerous commercial businesses.

Spreckels's most prized holding was undoubtedly the Hotel Del Coronado. A favorite getaway for hordes of the rich, famous and notorious, it was also home to Tent City. In the summer of 1900 Spreckels erected a sea of tents on the beach just southeast of the hotel, where families could spend the summer in a casual but elegant fashion, literally living in a luxurious tent on the sand. Along with the square tents, Tent City featured a dance pavilion, shops, restaurants, regular entertainment, an indoor swimming pool and a floating casino. The resort was so popular it remained open every summer until 1938.

Ignoring that stunningly clear introduction to a tourist industry, city leaders held fast to the notion that the fortunes of San Diego were inextricably linked to the railroad. That coveted rail line, the San Diego & Arizona Railroad stretching east through the mountains, finally became a reality in 1919. And it was Spreckels who guaranteed the financing.

An Exposition and a War

If early city leaders had one fault, it was their failure to instantly recognize the value of San Diego's natural attributes: its climate and its deep-water harbor. No railroad and no piece of land would chart the course of the city's future in the way those two features did.

To celebrate the opening of the Panama Canal, San Diego hosted an exposition in 1915 to 1916, which lured thousands of tourists. They marveled at the beauty and mild weather. And when they went home, they told their friends about this newfound paradise. They came back — in droves. Then, when Congress declared war on Germany in 1917, San Diego was remembered because of its strategic importance during the Spanish-American War. The army set up Camp Kearny, the navy took over North Island on Coronado and the marines established their recruit depot just to the north and across the bay from the naval base. The military was here, and it never left. In that brief span, between 1915 and 1917, San Diego's future as both a tourist mecca and a military town was entrenched.

The Panama-California Exposition drew thousands of visitors from all over the country. Located in what is now the heart of the city — Balboa Park — the exposition gave birth to much of the park itself. By the early 1920s Balboa Park had become the site for the now world-famous San Diego Zoo. (Be sure to read all about the history of the Zoo in our Balboa Park chapter.) Founded by Dr. Harry Wegeforth with animals left over from the exposition, it was funded in large part by Ellen Browning Scripps, who also was a major benefactress of Scripps Institution of Oceanography in La Jolla. In 1937, with the aid of funds advanced by the Works Progress Administration, actors Pat O'Brien and Bing Crosby co-founded the Del Mar Racetrack, a lure for locals and for bored Hollywood denizens. With attractions such as the racetrack, Balboa Park, the long-established Hotel Del Coronado resort, pristine beaches and the gambling houses across the border in Tijuana, San Diego soon became impossible to resist. The Los Angeles film colony discovered the beauty and energy of its neighbor to the south, and quickly made San Diego a regular daytrip. Tourists from

INSIDERS' TIP

If you're interested in learning more about the beginnings of San Diego, the California Room at the San Diego Central Library, 820 E Street, (619) 236-5800, has a comprehensive collection of excellent books on both San Diego and California.

other parts of the country found myriad reasons to stay for the summer.

San Diego's leaders finally conceded that maybe there was life beyond the railroad. Real-estate speculation proved to be a hard habit to break, though. It remains the sport of choice for many San Diegans even today.

The Aerospace Industry and Another War

In 1927, in an old building that once housed a fish cannery, a small aircraft company was working frantically to finish constructing a special airplane. Ryan Airlines, co-owned by aviation pioneers Claude Ryan and B. F. Mahoney, began regular flights between San Diego and Los Angeles in 1925 and had a sideline division for aircraft construction. What they were constructing then, a plane Ryan built in just 60 days, was the *Spirit of St. Louis.* Soon after, Charles Lindbergh made his historic flight from New York to Paris and planted the seeds for San Diego's budding aircraft industry.

Following closely behind Ryan and Mahoney was Major Reuben H. Fleet, who moved his Consolidated Aircraft Corporation from New York to San Diego. With mergers, his company eventually would become Convair, then General Dynamics, a giant in the U.S. defense industry and one of the largest employers in San Diego. Fred Rohr, a metal smith who had worked on the *Spirit of Saint Louis*, formed his own aircraft company, which is still located just south of the city limits in Chula Vista. Rohr Industries also would become one of San Diego's largest employers, and now has

branches and subsidiaries all over the country.

World War II was rapidly approaching, and the aircraft industry thrived, fed by defense contracts. Already a dominant presence in San Diego, the military increased dramatically as war loomed on the horizon. The army set up two new camps, Camp Callan near La Jolla and Camp Elliott on Kearny Mesa. Not to be outdone, the navy purchased Camp Pendleton for a marine base. Camp Pendleton is a massive area of land that stretches north from Oceanside all the way to the Orange County line, and today is the only undeveloped coastal land between San Diego and Los Angeles. The navy also installed its 11th Naval District Headquarters here, as well as the Naval Training Center and the Miramar Naval Air Station.

Consolidated Aircraft fared well during the war. More than 2,000 PBY Catalinas, a twin-engine flying boat, were manufactured by Consolidated and used extensively by American and British air troops. They proved their value time after time. A Royal Air Force Catalina tracked the *Bismarck* for nine days and nights until the British sank the German sub. A U.S. Navy Catalina spotted a Japanese submarine lurking at the entrance to Pearl Harbor.

At the war's end, many active-duty military personnel stationed in town wisely decided to stay. The population boomed to over 330,000, and San Diego enjoyed a post-war prosperity throughout the 1950s.

A New Direction

Peacetime had its price, and those who paid were in the aircraft and aerospace business. The industry suffered a severe

Photo: Dale Frost/Port of San Diego

The Star of India rests in San Diego harbor.

decline that threatened the economy of the entire city. Experts around the country were predicting that San Diego was about to bust once again. But seasoned locals scoffed. They knew the history of their town, and that history was a long tale of booming and busting. This time, they knew, it was simply a matter of looking in a different direction to lay the groundwork for the future economic health of the city.

Dr. Jonas Salk, developer of the polio vaccine that bears his name, opened the Salk Institute for Biological Studies in 1963. Scenically located in La Jolla, it has become a world-renowned research facility specializing in molecular and cellular biology and neuroscience. Around the same time, the University of California at San Diego opened its 1000-acre campus, also in La Jolla. The origins of the university lie with Scripps Institution of Oceanography, which had long been a member of the University of California's statewide system. Saturated with scientists, the institution needed larger facilities not only to enhance its own capabilities but to also attract the best research scientists in the world.

The military was firmly in place, even in peacetime, and tourists kept coming in greater numbers every year. Real estate values were ebbing and flowing just as they always had. And now with the establishment of a world-class research facility and a science and engineering-based university, the groundwork was firmly in place for San Diego's new course. It was almost as if the city could anticipate the explosion of high-tech and biotech that was about to

INSIDERS' TIP

Benjamin Harrison was the first U.S. president to visit San Diego, in 1891. He was treated to a reception at the Hotel del Coronado and a rally at Horton Plaza.

rise to the top of the world's research and manufacturing industries. When that explosion came, San Diego was ready.

High-Tech, Biotech and Brain Power

The 1980s and 1990s have seen an influx of high-tech and biotech companies that was beyond the wildest dreams of those who had pinned their hopes on these industries. Pharmaceutical companies, biotech researchers, electronics and telecommunications companies make up the bulk of the newcomers, and more are coming. One telecommunications titan, Qualcomm Inc., has made its intentions perfectly clear. It started here, and it's here to stay. Founded by Dr. Irwin Jacobs, a former professor at UCSD, Qualcomm is bent on integrating into the community.

When expansion of San Diego's stadium hit a roadblock because of lawsuits filed by opponents, it looked like the Chargers and the Padres would have to seek another venue — perhaps in another city. At issue was the $18 million needed to finish the expansion. Enter Qualcomm. The $18 million deficit disappeared, the stadium expansion was completed, and now Qualcomm gets national exposure every time a game is televised. Why? Because the savvy execs at Qualcomm gently suggested that an appropriate thank-you for their generosity would be to rename the stadium "Qualcomm Stadium." The city was only too happy to comply.

San Diego is prospering as the millennium approaches. Tourism, the military, manufacturing and, of course, real estate development, are all contributing to a healthy economy and a population that continues to grow: 2.8 million countywide by last count. Surprisingly, agriculture is a major contributor to San Diego's financial health, too. Avocado groves and fields of strawberries, lettuce and tomatoes are a familiar sight in the northern reaches of the county.

The icing on the cake of San Diego's prosperity is its growing enclave of higher learning. Known by locals as the "alphabet soup," UCSD (University of California, San Diego), SDSU (San Diego State University), USD (University of San Diego) and CSUSM (California State University, San Marcos) head the list of prestigious institutes. Gaining in stature is Point Loma Nazarene University, a high-quality liberal arts college situated on the bluffs of Sunset Cliffs, overlooking the ocean. Added to this collection of four-year universities is an impressive array of community colleges. The result is a stunning production of brain power. (See our Higher Education chapter for more details.)

The majority of graduates stay in San Diego once they finish school. No surprise there. It's a hard place to leave. A cool 30 percent of San Diego's populace hold college degrees, and no other region in the United States has more Ph.D.s per capita. We're proud of our eggheads. They are a generation of movers and shakers who are well-poised to lead us into the twenty-first century.

The Flavor of San Diego

The image many easterners have of San Diego is blond surfer boys and even blonder girls in bikinis languishing under palm trees on the beach. Granted, most

---

INSIDERS' TIP

Two Academy Award-winning actors were born in La Jolla: Gregory Peck and Cliff Robertson. Peck graduated from San Diego High School, Robertson from La Jolla High.

inhabitants take advantage of the beach as often as they can, but they do have jobs. Plus, palm trees don't grow well in sand.

San Diego is a city that constantly contradicts its small-town image. It was host to the 1996 Republican Convention and also to a presidential debate that same year. Two Super Bowls have been contested here, with the promise of more to come. San Diego is home to a first-rate opera company, dozens of theaters and hundreds of art galleries.

The city has a large and diverse ethnic population that is well reflected in its many neighborhoods. Its proximity to the Mexican border has naturally resulted in a well-established and growing Hispanic community, and most locals find it to their advantage to have more than a passing knowledge of Spanish. Cultural events and festivals regularly celebrate the heritage of a multitude of ethnic groups.

Although San Diego is proud of the bold steps it has taken to embrace the future, it still clings tenaciously to its roots. Its Spanish and Mexican heritage runs deep. The pace is a little slower than in most big cities, and San Diegans are more easily identified as laid-back than hard-driven. Most believe they have found the best of all worlds. The industries of the future are already here. Educational opportunities abound. And then there's that weather.

Cabrillo could see it. So could Vizcaíno, de Portolá and Father Serra. Alonzo Horton and John Spreckels figured it out, too. Paradise lies here sandwiched between the mountains and the ocean in a place called San Diego.

San Diego has hundreds of accommodations from which to choose, everything from a bare-bones motel on the sand to a luxurious, fully appointed hotel designed to cater to your every whim.

Hotels and Motels

It didn't take San Diego's founding fathers too long to figure out that their city by the bay had the potential to become an irresistible destination for visitors. Along with the first buildings in downtown San Diego — the general stores, saloons and rooming houses — came places for guests to hang their hats. And as increasing numbers of tourists targeted San Diego for their vacations, hotels began to spring up to accommodate them.

Today there are hundreds of places from which to choose, everything from a bare-bones motel on the sand to a luxurious, fully appointed hotel designed to cater to your every whim. If your idea of a room is only a place to hang your clothes and grab a few hours sleep, you'll find it here. But if you plan to spend a lot of time in your room or enjoy the touches of luxury that only top hotels can offer, you'll find that too. You need only decide what best fits your style and budget.

Even though San Diego is a year-round destination for visitors, it does have a high season during the summer months. Summer is when you're least likely to find your first choice in accommodations unless you plan ahead. The good news is that there are so many hotels and motels spread throughout the county that you can almost always find an available room, even on short notice. Even during Super Bowl week in 1998, when hotels were sold out a year in advance, rumor had it that rooms were still to be found here and there. So if you're the spontaneous type who likes to pack a bag on Friday night and see what you can find once you arrive, chances are a nice room will be waiting for you somewhere in the county.

Your choice of accommodation really depends on your individual plans. If you're visiting friends or relatives, it makes sense to book a room close to their neighborhood. If hiking and nature walks are high on your itinerary, you might look at facilities in the East County or North County Inland to be near the foothills and local mountains. If sun and sand are your first priority, you would naturally want to investigate beachside hotels and motels.

If you plan to do it all — sightseeing, shopping, dining, the beach and nightlife — you really can stay just about anywhere in the county. If you're without a car, though, we recommend that you check out some of the more centrally located facilities in North County Coastal, downtown San Diego or Mission Valley, so you can take advantage of the Coaster and the San Diego Trolley for transportation.

Whatever your idea of the perfect holiday may be, we'll give you a good cross-section of available accommodations. We'll describe each facility and give you an idea of what makes it unique and desirable. We'll also list special amenities such as workout rooms or business centers. If the hotel has a great restaurant, we'll be sure to mention it.

In San Diego hotel and motel ownership frequently changes — sometimes overnight — especially among the chains. So don't be surprised if you call one of our listings and the facility has a different name. If this happens, be sure to ask if the accommodation has undergone any significant changes with the new ownership. Remember too that the quality of chain hotels can vary from city to city. What might be an outstanding hotel in your city might be a little less desirable someplace else. So read our descriptions carefully, and we promise to steer you in the right direction.

We've divided this chapter into our usual regional designations: San Diego, North County Coastal, North County Inland, East County and South Bay. For your convenience, San Diego has been further divided into the areas most visitors target in their search for a hotel or motel. Bed and breakfast inns and vacation rentals are covered in separate chapters; campgrounds and RV parks are noted in our Recreation chapter.

Reservations

It's always a good idea to make your reservations as far in advance as possible, especially if you have your heart set on a specific facility or part of the county. If you're planning a beach vacation and decide to take your chances when you get here, you might find yourself spending much of your time commuting to the beach from a hotel in an outlying area. Beach accommodations typically fill up quickly, far in advance of summer months.

When you make your reservation, most facilities will require a major credit card to hold your room for you. Should you decide to cancel, policies vary from hotel to hotel, so be sure to inquire when you make the reservation. Most require a specified lead time for cancellation to avoid a charge to your credit card. Unless we designate otherwise, all listings accept major credit cards.

Be sure to ask about check-in and check-out times too. Most check-in times are around 3 PM, and checkout is usually around 12 PM. If those times don't fit with your schedule, ask about early check-in or late checkout. Many facilities are happy to adjust to your plans for no extra charge or offer to store your luggage, but some will charge extra fees if you're too early or hang around too long after checkout time.

Also keep in mind that all the hotels and motels we list here offer smoking and non-smoking rooms. If this is important to you, be sure to specify your preference when making your reservation. If you can't bear the thought of leaving your pet at home while you're vacationing, you may be in luck. Many hotels and motels these days are putting out the welcome

mat for furry guests. We've noted those facilities that do accommodate pets along with any restrictions or special policies. In accordance with federal law, all hotels have accommodations for the disabled. Just be sure to specify your needs to the reservations clerk.

Price Code

Prices are based on a one night's stay for two people during summer months. Keep in mind that room rates can be somewhat lower during winter months. San Diego's 10.5 percent hotel tax is not included in these rates.

$	$50 to $100
$$	$101 to $150
$$$	$151 to $200
$$$$	$201 and higher

San Diego

Beaches and Mission Bay

Best Western Blue Sea Lodge
$$-$$$ • 707 Pacific Beach Dr.,
San Diego, CA
• (858) 488-4700, (800) 780-7234

At the Blue Sea Lodge you can choose from 100 luxury oceanfront rooms or standard rooms with private balconies or patios. Some rooms feature sunken tubs and skylights too. Start your morning with coffee on the patio by the oceanfront pool and spa, which has direct access to the beach. Then spend the rest of the day sightseeing, swimming or strolling along the beach boardwalk.

No restaurants are on-site, but dozens are within four or five blocks. If eating in is more your style, ask about suites with kitchens. A few are available.

Catamaran Hotel
$$-$$$ • 3999 Mission Blvd., San Diego
• (858) 488-1081

Long a fixture in the beach area, the Catamaran's 315 rooms offer unparalleled access to both the beach and the bay. All rooms and suites are graciously appointed and have all the amenities you would expect from a first-rate hotel. Most rooms have a refrigerator, and all have their own balcony or lanai.

Your hosts will be happy to arrange watersports for you: sailboating, pedal boating, sailboarding and lessons. Two authentic sternwheeler boats cruise Mission Bay nightly from the Catamaran, offering cocktails and dancing. The Cannibal Bar on the premises is a San Diego favorite for its live music and dancing. For a quieter atmosphere, try Moray's for cocktails and piano music. The Atoll Restaurant serves breakfast, lunch and dinner daily, including an award-winning Sunday brunch.

Dana Inn
$$ • 1710 W. Mission Bay Dr., San Diego • (619) 222-6440

Guests choose from either bayfront, poolside or garden view rooms at the casual Dana Inn in the heart of Mission Bay Park. The best of Mission Bay and the surrounding beaches await visitors at the Dana Inn, recipient of San Diego's "Finest Service Award." Only a 10-minute walk from Sea World, the inn has 200 rooms, a bayview pool and spa, tennis courts, shuffleboard and Ping-Pong — plenty to entertain the whole family.

All rooms have refrigerators. Room service is offered, or you can enjoy family dining at the Red Hen Country Kitchen restaurant on the premises.

San Diego Hilton Beach & Tennis Resort
$$$$ • 1775 E. Mission Bay Dr., San Diego • (619) 276-4010, (800) 445-8667

Completely renovated in 1996, the San Diego Hilton is an oasis of palm trees and sand with a mirage-come-true in the form of beautiful Mission Bay right alongside the hotel. The Mediterranean-style resort has 357 rooms. Standard guest rooms have courtyard and garden views; suites have expansive bay views.

Activities galore await you at the San Diego Hilton. Take a walk down to the bay, which is just steps away, or play tennis on the lighted courts. Maybe you'd like to swim in the hotel's

huge pool or try the spa — both have a bay view. If you're in the mood for something different, take a cruise around Mission Bay on the Hilton Queen, an old-fashioned paddlewheel boat. Dine at either the casual Cafe Picante, serving breakfast lunch and dinner, or the more upscale Cavatappi, which serves Italian cuisine nightly.

San Diego Paradise Point Resort
$$$-$$$$ • 1404 W. Vacation Rd., San Diego • (858) 274-4630, (800) 344-2626

For the best combination of luxury and a beach vacation, the Paradise Point Resort is a great choice. The 462 lanai guest rooms have a variety of layouts, and all have patios and a spectacular garden, lagoon or bay view. Studio and one-bedroom suites are also available.

The resort is perfect for quiet strolls where you'll find surprises at every turn: lagoons with water lilies, fountains, waterfalls, bridges and botanical treasures. For more active pursuits, try one of six pools (one has a swim-up bar), or swim and sunbathe on the mile of sandy beach surrounding the resort. Tennis, sailing, volleyball and bicycling are there for the taking, and an 18-hole putting course will help you refine your stroke. Paradise Point also has a fully equipped fitness center.

The Dockside Restaurant serves dinner nightly, and be sure to stop in at the Barefoot Bar, a legendary hangout for Insiders. Also on the premises is the Village Cafe, which is open for breakfast, lunch and dinner daily. Small pets are welcome at Paradise Point for a one-time $20 fee. Guests must sign a damage waiver.

Seacoast Suites
$ • 4760 Mission Blvd., San Diego • (858) 483-6780, (800) 554-6555

The 50 rooms and suites at Seacoast offer few frills, but for proximity to the beach, it can't be beat. It's located one block away from the beach boardwalk and Pacific Beach, one of San Diego's most popular beaches.

Rooms and suites all come equipped with king-size beds; suites have microwave kitchenettes. The rooms are comfortable, clean and air-conditioned. The facility itself is in the heart of the beach-area business district and has dozens of restaurants and shops within a five-block radius.

Coronado

Best Western Coronado
$$ • 275 Orange Ave., Coronado • (619) 437-1666

One of the best values in Coronado, the Best Western's 63 rooms and suites offer comfort and convenience to all of Coronado's attractions. The Old Ferry Landing, with its shops and restaurants, is a short two-block walk away, and the downtown village of Coronado is about 10 blocks in the other direction.

All the rooms and suites are decorated in a contemporary style, and they all have a view of the quiet courtyard in the middle of the hotel. Government and military travelers especially appreciate the Best Western Coronado because it's close to North Island Naval Air Station. Also available for guests are on-site laundry facilities and a complimentary continental breakfast.

Crown City Inn
$-$$ • 520 Orange Ave., Coronado • (619) 435-6750, (800) 422-1173

One of the nicest features of Coronado is that it's a small island, jam-packed with things to do. And the Crown City Inn is right in the middle of it all. Walk five blocks in one direction and you'll find beautiful, white-sand beaches. Five blocks in the other direction brings you to San Diego Bay and the Old Ferry Landing.

The inn itself has 33 newly redecorated rooms, including a few one-bedroom suites. If you're not in the mood for a day at the beach, relax by the pool in the courtyard, or catch up on your laundry at the on-site facilities. The inn's Cafe Bistro, open for breakfast, lunch and dinner, is known for its excellent French/American cuisine. You're welcome to bring the family pet for an additional $8 per night.

Hotel del Coronado
$$$$ • 1500 Orange Ave., Coronado • (619) 522-8000, (800) 468-3533

Don't let The Del's 692 rooms lead you to believe you'll get lost in a maze of structures and people. Despite its size, The Del has created a comfy, cozy and luxurious atmosphere that will make you feel like its most treasured guest. All the rooms in the main building have been painstakingly restored and are one of a kind in their decor. Rooms in the Ocean Tower combine the grandeur of the past with the conveniences of the present. No matter where you choose to stay, you'll be overwhelmed by the surrounding beauty of the Pacific Ocean, the San Diego skyline and the beautifully landscaped grounds of the hotel.

Guests need not stray far from the hotel to enjoy all the elements of a true Southern California vacation. Within the hotel are eight restaurants and lounges, and many more are just a few blocks' stroll away. You can enjoy tennis on The Del's oceanside courts or golf at the nearby Coronado Golf Course. The Del has its own boathouse from which all sorts of water activities can be enjoyed: sailing, fishing and whale watching, to name a few. Round out your day with a few laps in one of the heated pools and a therapeutic massage in The Del's spa. And of course, the hotel has its own shopping arcade, which is sure to provide you with the perfect memento of your stay. Look for the Close-up on the Hotel Del

Coronado in this chapter for the history of this fascinating landmark.

Loews Coronado Bay Resort
$$$$ • 4000 Coronado Bay Rd., Coronado • (619) 424-4000

If you're ready to splurge and indulge yourself in the ultimate luxury hotel, Loews is the place for you. Located on a private peninsula a few miles south of Coronado, its 440 guest rooms and suites all have spectacular views of San Diego Bay, the Pacific Ocean, Loews' private marina or one of the sparkling pools. This is a true destination resort (check our entry in Resorts and Spas), so get ready to be pampered.

Everything you'd expect in a resort is here: a full health club, three pools and five tennis courts. In addition, Loews has a fully equipped Business Center for those who are combining work with pleasure. On the grounds of the hotel is the divine Azzura Point Restaurant (see our Restaurants chapter for all the scrumptious details), noted for its elegant cuisine and atmosphere. For more casual dining, guests can take advantage of RRR's Cafe and Gourmet Market for breakfast lunch and dinner as well as take-out deli. If you simply can't drag yourself away from the pool, the Astra Pool Pavilion has an outdoor bar and grill. And guests can relax after a long day in the Cays Lounge, which offers evening entertainment and large screen televisions. Loew's welcomes small pets at no additional charge.

Downtown/Gaslamp Quarter

Embassy Suites Hotel
$$$ • 601 Pacific Hwy., San Diego • (619) 239-2400, (800) 362-2779

Downtown's Embassy Suites is in an ideal location: slightly removed from the hustle and bustle of downtown, yet close enough to walk to many of its attractions and restaurants. On one side of the hotel, the view is of San Diego's sparkling harbor. The other side offers a view of the stately skyscrapers that populate the heart of downtown. Each of the 337 suites has a living area (complete with refrigerator, microwave and wet bar), and a separate bedroom and bath. An indoor pool area with a sauna and whirlpool is a nice place to relax after a long day sightseeing.

Seaport Village, with its shops and restaurants, is only one block away from the hotel (see our Shopping and Attractions chapters for the lowdown on Seaport Village), and the Convention Center is a short three blocks away. Plus, all the shopping, dining and nightlife of downtown and the Gaslamp Quarter are within less than a mile.

Children younger than 18 stay for free with their parents.

Holiday Inn on the Bay
$$ • 1355 N. Harbor Dr., San Diego • (619) 232-3861, (800) 877-8920

This is one of the best locations in San Diego County. The 600-room twin high-rise towers of the Holiday Inn lie at the foot of downtown on the embarcadero, close to everything there is to see and do. Rooms have a view of either San Diego Bay or the city lights and lots of special amenities: voice mail, data ports and workspaces, to name a few.

Workouts are a breeze in the poolside exercise facility, and a waterfront jogging trail is right across the street. The Elephant & Castle is an English-style pub and restaurant that's open for breakfast, lunch and dinner and comes equipped with pool tables and dartboards. You can dine in style at Ruth's Chris Steakhouse, or grab a sandwich at Hazlewood's Deli. All of Downtown's attractions are a few blocks away, and harbor cruises, the Maritime Museum, the Star of India and the San Diego-Coronado Ferry are right across the street from the hotel. You may bring your pet along, but you must pay a $100 deposit, $75 of which is refundable.

Horton Grand Hotel
$$-$$$ • 311 Island Ave., San Diego • (619) 544-1886, (800) 542-1886

In 1986 the Horton Grand was built, brick by brick, from two original Victorian hotels in the heart of San Diego's Gaslamp Quarter. Today you can enjoy the elegance of the turn-of-the-century era in this painstakingly recreated hotel. No two rooms are alike, and all are furnished with Victorian draped queen-size beds, antiques and gas-burning fireplaces.

The Ida Bailey Restaurant is located on the premises, serving breakfast, lunch and dinner as well as a sumptuous Sunday brunch. High Tea is served on Thursdays, Fridays and Saturdays, and live entertainment is offered in the Palace Bar on those same evenings. Horse-drawn carriages depart from the Horton Grand's doorstep to take guests on a romantic tour of the Gaslamp Quarter. Shopping, restaurants and nightlife are all within two or three blocks. Pets that weigh less than 14 pounds are accepted here for a $25 nonrefundable fee.

Super 8 Motel Bayview
$ • 1835 Columbia St., San Diego • (619) 544-0164, (800) 537-9902

Though it's a little off the beaten path, this motel is easy on the wallet. It's located near the Little Italy neighborhood of San Diego (which has a ton of great restaurants), and the nightlife of downtown is a five-minute drive away.

The motel's 136 rooms are clean, contemporary and comfortable. It has a pool and a spa, and offers a complimentary continental breakfast every morning. Ask for a bay-view room, and your hosts will bend over backward to accommodate you.

U.S. Grant Hotel
$$$ • 326 Broadway, San Diego • (619) 232-3121, (800) 237-5029

The U.S. Grant has been a San Diego landmark and gathering place since 1910. As you might expect, you'll see lots of polished wood and antiques here. The 280 large and beautifully furnished guest rooms and suites offer the ultimate in classic comfort and elegance. The Grant Grill has been part of the downtown dining scene for years, and the Grant Lounge is a favorite hangout for Insiders who enjoy live jazz and billiards. The Sidewalk Cafe serves bistro-style lunches and dinners daily. Across the street from the Grant is Horton Plaza shopping center (see our Shopping chapter) and the famous Gaslamp Quarter. Small pets are welcome

at the Grant, and they get a free ride with no additional charges.

Westgate Hotel
$$$-$$$$ • 1055 Second Ave., San Diego • (619) 238-1818

Whether you're traveling for business or pleasure, the Westgate provides an unforgettable experience in luxury. Each of the 223 guest rooms is unique in its design and offers a variety of amenities, including two-line phones and data ports. A complimentary private car is provided to take you to business or social appointments, the airport, Sea World and the San Diego Zoo.

The Westgate is located in the heart of Downtown, across from the Horton Plaza shopping center and the historic Gaslamp Quarter. Afternoon tea is served in the Grand Foyer, and candlelight dining can be enjoyed at the hotel's Fontainebleau Restaurant. For more lively entertainment, try the Plaza Bar.

La Jolla/Golden Triangle

Colonial Inn
$$$ • 910 Prospect St., La Jolla • (858) 454-2181, (800) 826-1278

The perfect blend of European ambiance and traditions of hospitality can be found at the Colonial Inn. Its 64 luxury rooms and 11 elegant suites are exquisitely decorated to create a romantically posh environment. No matter where you are in the hotel you'll have an incomparable view, either of the coastline or the beautiful village of La Jolla.

A pool is on the premises, and the hotel offers privileges at a nearby health club for its guests. Putnam's restaurant is on-site, serving lunch and dinner daily. But the inn is virtually steps away from La Jolla's numerous fine restaurants, shops and galleries, so be sure to go exploring.

Embassy Suites Hotel
$$$-$$$$ • 4550 La Jolla Village Dr., San Diego • (858) 453-0400, (800) 362-2779

Like its sister hotel in downtown San Diego, the Embassy Suites in the Golden Triangle offers 335 full suites consisting of living room, bedroom and bath. This is a popular hotel among business travelers, but many visitors enjoy it as well because of its proximity to La Jolla and to University Towne Center, one of San Diego's nicest shopping malls. (Check our Shopping chapter for all the details on UTC.) The mall is right across the street from the hotel and has an abundance of stores, restaurants and a multiplex theater.

The Coast Cafe restaurant on the premises is open for breakfast, lunch and dinner, and many top-notch restaurants are within a few blocks. For visitors who plan to do a lot of sightseeing, this is a centrally located spot that's hard to beat. La Jolla is a five-minute drive away, downtown San Diego is 15 minutes south, and North County Coastal's hot spots are 15 minutes north. Children younger than 18 stay for free with their parents.

Hyatt Regency La Jolla
$$-$$$ • 3777 La Jolla Village Dr., San Diego (858) 552-1234

Located in the heart of the Golden Triangle, just east of La Jolla, the Hyatt Regency offers all the amenities travelers have come to expect from fine hotels. Eleven acres of lush gardens surround this 400-room hotel, and the architecture and décor reflect the style of ancient Rome. The hotel's Aventine Sporting Club is a 32,000-square-foot health spa that's sure to challenge even the most fitness-oriented. And, of course, tennis and a swimming pool are part of the package, too.

Choose from five restaurants featuring a diversity of cuisines, or sample one of the many other restaurants that are within a five-minute drive. University Towne Center, one of San Diego's finest shopping malls (as detailed in our Shopping chapter), is three blocks away. Small pets (meaning weighing less than 25 lbs.) are allowed for a $100 refundable deposit.

La Jolla Beach Travelodge
$-$$ • 6750 La Jolla Blvd., La Jolla
• (858) 454-0716, (800) 578-7878
La Jolla Cove Travelodge
$-$$ • 1141 Silverado St., La Jolla
• (858) 454-0791, (800) 578-7878

Both of La Jolla's Travelodges offer the best value for those determined to stay in La Jolla and stick to a budget too. They both have little in the way of extra amenities, but are clean, spacious and comfortable.

The La Jolla Beach Travelodge has 44 rooms and is located outside the village, but just a block or two from the ocean. It's perfect for those who want to spend most their time on the sand.

The La Jolla Cove Travelodge has 30 rooms and is in the middle of the village. If shopping, dining and art galleries are more to your taste, this is the spot for you. All of those and more are within a few blocks.

La Valencia
$$$$ • 1132 Prospect St., La Jolla
• (858) 454-0771, (800) 451-0772

A landmark in La Jolla, La Valencia is the essence of Old World elegance and luxury. Overlooking La Jolla Cove, its 100 guest rooms and suites are custom decorated with a European flavor, and rooms have either a garden or a sweeping ocean view. Even though you're just a whisper away from the ocean, the hotel has a swimming pool and whirlpool spa as well as a fitness room.

The Mediterranean Room/Tropical Patio serves breakfast, lunch and dinner daily. For a more intimate dining experience, try the Sky Room Restaurant on the tenth floor, which has 12 tables overlooking the cove. Also, be sure to stop by the Whaling Bar & Grill for lunch, dinner or cocktails with friends. Nestled right in the heart of the Village of La Jolla, La Valencia is the perfect place to create memories to last a lifetime. Small dogs are allowed in a few of the bungalow rooms.

Sea Lodge
$$-$$$ • 8110 Camino del Oro, La Jolla
• (858) 459-8271, (800) 237-5211

Step onto the balcony of your room at the Sea Lodge, and you can almost touch the waves. It has become one of California's favorite oceanfront retreats, with its 128 luxury rooms set amid fountains, courtyards, fresh flowers and ocean breezes. The architecture is reminiscent of old Mexico, and Mexican antiques are everywhere you turn on the grounds of the hotel.

The Sea Lodge offers an array of

amenities: fitness center, tennis, pool and spa, sauna and volleyball on the beach. The oceanfront Shores restaurant offers breakfast, lunch and dinner daily.

Mission Valley

Doubletree
$$ • 7450 Hazard Center Dr., San Diego • (619) 688-4088

Located in the heart of Mission Valley's shopping district, the Doubletree has the added bonus of being right across the street from a San Diego Trolley station, which will take visitors to all points of interest in San Diego. The hotel's 300 guest rooms and suites all have mini-bars and PC data ports for those who don't like to be disconnected.

Swim in the indoor/outdoor pool, or get a good workout in the fitness center. Casual all-day dining is available at the Fountain Cafe, and you can dance the night away at Club Max, the red-hot nightclub on the premises. Enjoy the freshly baked chocolate chip cookie

Hotel del Coronado

Rarely does a mere hotel achieve legendary status, but the Hotel del Coronado has accomplished just that. Built more than 100 years ago in the seaside village of Coronado, The Del has maintained a tradition of lavish service in a fairy-tale setting surrounded by mystery and wonder. The grounds sprawl over 26 acres of

lush beachfront property, and the hotel itself is an architectural marvel. Some compare it to a confection as elaborate and pristine as a wedding cake. Frank L. Baum, who wrote *The Wizard of Oz*, based his design of Emerald City on the hotel's turreted architecture. Everywhere you turn is a nook, a cranny, a gazebo or an alcove that makes you feel you're uncovering a secret that no one has ever found before.

Two Midwestern builders dreamed up The Del. Back in the 1880s, before Coronado was developed, Elisha Babcock and H. L. Story could see promise in the barren landscape. They spared no money or effort, importing lumber and laborers from San Francisco to help construct their vision. A mahogany bar was built in Philadelphia and delivered fully assembled to Coronado by ship, traveling all the way around South America. Babcock and Story spent a cool $1 million to realize their dream — an amount unheard of in those days — $600,000 for construction and $400,000 for furnishings.

The Del quickly became world famous, and even though it now is more than a century old, it has never sacrificed its old-world charm and elegance.

The hotel has attracted its share of legendary guests. Fourteen U.S. presidents

Photo: Hotel del Coronado

For more than a hundred years, the historic Hotel del Coronado has been a San Diego landmark and a favorite destination for visitors.

have stayed at The Del, starting with Benjamin Harrison in 1891. Over the years Franklin Roosevelt, John Kennedy, Ronald Reagan and Bill Clinton have all been guests. In 1970 The Del was the site for the first state dinner to ever be held outside the White House, honoring President Richard Nixon and Mexican President Gustavo Díaz Ordaz. The elaborate dinner was held in the Crown Room and was attended by more than 1,000 guests.

But more than just politicians have added their luster to the hotel. Charles Lindbergh was honored at The Del after his historic 1927 flight across the Atlantic Ocean. And in 1920 England's Prince of Wales (who later became King Edward VIII) was an honored guest, and it has long been rumored that the Del was where he met Wallis Simpson, the woman he abdicated the throne to marry.

Hollywood was quick to discover The Del too, and frequently used the hotel grounds and interior for filming movies. Most famous, of course, is the romantic comedy *Some Like It Hot*, filmed in 1958 and starring Marilyn Monroe, Jack Lemmon and Tony Curtis. Naturally, in 1995, when the Marilyn Monroe postage stamp was released, the only logical place for the unveiling was The Del. More recently, the Del has served as backdrop for movies such as *The Stunt Man*, starring Peter O'Toole, and *Mr. Wrong*, with Ellen DeGeneres. And there has never been a shortage of fine entertainers, either. During the summers of 1949 and 1950, the flamboyant pianist Liberace entertained in the Circus Room.

For those who have an affinity for the supernatural, The Del does indeed have a resident ghost. Although hotel management would like that particular legend to die, it refuses to fade away. In fact, it's a poorly kept secret that the 1972 television series *Ghost Story* was filmed at The Del. Hotel officials insist the site was chosen for its Victorian atmosphere, but we know better. So if you'd like to add a little adventure to your holiday, ask the receptionist for the haunted room when you make your reservation. Stories of ghost sightings are all just part of the allure.

Today the Hotel del Coronado is as modern as the discriminating traveler demands, but it has never sacrificed its original design and beauty. Thanks to ongoing renovations, the hotel retains the polish of its youth. A recent five-year makeover totaled $50 million, and all guest rooms, public spaces and meeting rooms were refurbished, including the oceanfront ballroom and the Prince of Wales Grill. The hotel has been designated by Congress as a National Historic Landmark and is dedicated to protecting its architectural integrity. This is no small task when you consider that every modern service and comfort must continually be provided for guests in order to keep them coming back.

Over the years, even though ownership of The Del has changed hands several times, the owners have never missed a step. The hotel is as beautiful as it was the day it first opened to the public in 1888, and it will continue to be a source of great pride in San Diego for generations to come.

---

that awaits you on arrival. Pets are allowed only in the smoking rooms, but there is no additional charge.

Hanalei Hotel
$-$$ • 2270 Hotel Circle N., San Diego • (619) 297-1101, (800) 882-0858

Here's an Insiders' secret: the Hanalei Hotel is one of the best bargains in San Diego County. It's a full-service luxury hotel

for a price that fits most budgets. Surrounded by Southern California's signature palm trees and tropical plants, the Hanalei feels like an exotic resort, right in the heart of the city.

The hotel's 416 rooms and suites have been recently refurbished, and the swimming pool, whirlpool and fitness center are there to please the most discriminating traveler. Islands Restaurant serves authentic Polynesian cuisine for dinner and Sunday brunch, and the Peacock Cafe is open daily for lunch and dinner. The Ploynesian Pu Pu Bar offers live entertainment four nights a week. A $25 deposit will secure accommodations for your small pet.

Handlery Hotel & Resort
$$ • 950 Hotel Circle N., San Diego
• (619) 298-0511, (800) 843-4343

Each of the 217 contemporary rooms at the Handlery provide spacious comfort and a traditional San Diego atmosphere. Guests will enjoy a workout in the fully equipped Health and Fitness Club. Practice your swing on the hotel's own driving range, or indulge in a game of tennis on one of eight lighted courts. Three swimming pools (including a five-lane lap pool) are waiting to cool you off, and you can reward yourself with a relaxing massage to top off your busy day.

Mission Valley and Fashion Valley Shopping Centers (check out our Shopping chapter for details) are nearby, as are movie theaters and tons of restaurants. Or if you prefer to stay close to home, dine at Postcards American Bistro, which serves breakfast, lunch and dinner daily.

Marriott Mission Valley
$$ • 8757 Rio San Diego Dr., San Diego
• (619) 692-3800, (800) 842-5329

Mission Valley can't be beat for its easy access to all of San Diego's attractions, and the Marriott Mission Valley is perfectly situated to take advantage of the best the city has to offer. The 17-story, 350-room hotel has a swimming pool, championship tennis court with night lighting, a health club with a whirlpool and sauna and a specially designed jogging trail.

Two blocks away are the new Rio Vista Shopping area and Mission Valley Shopping Center, and Qualcomm Stadium is just minutes away by car or trolley. The Gratzi Grill serves breakfast, lunch and dinner, or grab a snack in Chats Sports Bar or at the Splash Pool Bar. Pets are welcome, but guests must pay a $200 deposit, $150 of which is refundable.

Quality Resort
$ • 875 Hotel Circle S., San Diego
• (619) 298-8282, (800) 362-7871

This beautifully landscaped 20-acre retreat has an ideal location, casual elegance, generous amenities and attentive service. The 202 rooms are family friendly, with lots of room to spread out and relax. Kids will be pleased by the swimming pool and in-room Nintendo, while adults will enjoy the cocktail lounge with pool tables, the whirlpool spa and the 27,000-square-foot athletic and racquet club.

A 24-hour restaurant is located on-site, and room service is available too. For even more convenience, there's a liquor store and small market. The resort provides complimentary transportation to shopping, trolley stations and Old Town.

Town & Country Hotel
$-$$ • 500 Hotel Circle N., San Diego
• (619) 291-7131

Spread over 40 acres of landscaped grounds, the Town & Country is a San Diego landmark. Amidst hundreds of palm trees are two guest-room towers and a sprawl of ranch-style garden bungalows. All together, the Town & Country has 1,000 rooms. It also has an on-site convention center, which makes it a favorite place for small conventions and gatherings of all kinds.

Kick off your shoes and jump into one of four swimming pools, or choose from five restaurants, which offer everything from fine cuisine to casual fare. Also available are barber and beauty services.

INSIDERS' TIP

Whenever making reservations or inquiring about a room, ask about professional, AARP, AAA and student discounts. Sometimes you can get a significant discount. At other times you may receive just a few dollars off the price.

Old Town

Best Western Hacienda Hotel
$-$$ • 4041 Harney St., San Diego
• (619) 298-4707, (800) 528-1234

Terraced on a hillside overlooking Old Town State Park is the all-suite Hacienda Hotel. Decorated with handcrafted Santa Fe furnishings, each of the 150 guest suites opens onto a courtyard or a balcony, inviting in those fresh Southern California breezes.

Suites have either one or two queen beds and come equipped with microwave ovens and refrigerators. You can take an afternoon dip here in the pool or at the spa — or if you've had a long day, how about a relaxing water massage?

When hunger strikes, you need venture no farther than the grounds of the hotel to Acapulco, a casual Mexican restaurant that serves breakfast, lunch and dinner daily. A spectacular brunch is offered on Sundays, complete with a roving mariachi band to treat you to the ultimate Old Town experience.

Old Town Travelodge
$ • 2380 Moore St., San Diego
• (619) 291-9100, (800) 578-7878

Most travelers are familiar with Travelodge's basic clean and comfortable motels. Old Town's version fits the mold well, and even has the requisite swimming pool. What gives this facility an edge is its location — right smack in the middle of one of the most desired vacation areas in San Diego.

Rooms with either one or two queen beds are available, and all are nicely decorated in an Old California style. Modem jacks are installed in all rooms, and Internet access is available too. Another plus is the on-site guest laundry facilities. Guests can also enjoy a complimentary continental breakfast.

Ramada Limited
$$ • 3900 Old Town Ave., San Diego
• (619) 299-7400, (800) 451-9846

Located in the heart of historic Old Town, the Ramada Limited combines old California charm with European flair. The inn's 125 guest rooms and six suites are designed to resemble comfortable bed and breakfast accommodations, updated with modern appointments. If you're in the mood for a late-night snack and just don't feel like trekking outside your room, we've got you covered. Each room comes complete with a microwave oven and refrigerator you can stock with goodies.

When you're ready to unwind, there's no better place than the central courtyard with its pool, spa and sundeck. After a day of sightseeing or basking in the sunshine, you can take a five or 10-minute stroll to more than 30 restaurants, which offer everything from casual Mexican fare to fine seafood or ethnic cuisine.

Point Loma/Harbor and Shelter Islands

Best Western Island Palms Hotel
$$-$$$ • 2051 Shelter Island Dr.,
San Diego • (619) 222-0561,
(800) 345-9995

A common sentiment among visitors is, why come to San Diego if you don't stay on the water? The Island Palms is surrounded by the blue waters of San Diego Bay and offers a resort-like atmosphere for guests who want to get away from it all and still be close to San Diego's attractions.

The 97-room hotel has a bayside swimming pool and spa, and all rooms and suites have spectacular bay views. If you plan to settle in for a while, take advantage of the oversized suites with full kitchens. The hotel's Doc Masters waterfront restaurant is a San Diego fixture for dining and unwinding with friends in the lounge.

Humphrey's Half Moon Inn
$$$-$$$$ • 2303 Shelter Island Dr.,
San Diego • (619) 224-3411

A tropical paradise on the bay is the best way to describe the Half Moon Inn on San Diego's Shelter Island. Its 182 rooms and suites are nestled among lush gardens, palm trees, ponds and waterfalls. Award-winning Humphrey's Restaurant is on-site and in charge of room service, so if you're in the mood to dine in, it won't get much better than this.

Guests who visit from June through October are in for a special treat. Humphrey's Concerts by the Bay series (see our Nightlife chapter) takes place right on the grounds of the hotel. Enjoy the evening breezes by the pool or from your balcony while you enjoy music from jazz and pop entertainers such as Ray Charles, Kenny G, Ringo Starr and more. Kids will enjoy the pool and the continuous Ping-Pong games.

Travelodge Harbor Island
$$ • 1960 Harbor Island, San Diego
• (619) 291-6700, (800) 578-7878

Most folks are familiar with the comfortable but few-frills reputation of Travelodges across America. This one, however, is head and shoulders above the rest and qualifies as a full-fledged hotel. Located on beautiful Harbor Island (right across from the airport), the 207 rooms overlook San Diego Bay and the lively marina. All rooms have a view, either of the city or the bay, and all have balconies or patios.

The Waterfront Cafe offers a fabulous breakfast buffet every day and is open for lunch and dinner, too. Harbor Island is home to several other fine restaurants, too.

Vagabond Inn Point Loma
$ • 1325 Scott St., San Diego • (619) 224-3371, (800) 800-522-1555

This is strictly a bare-bones accommodation, but for convenience to Point Loma's fishing docks, it's a gem. Directly across the street are deep-sea fishing boats waiting to take guests on half-day or daylong ocean fishing trips. And for those to whom fishing is secondary, shopping and many restaurants are within a few blocks.

The 40 guest rooms are clean and comfortable, and the motel is within a 10- or 15-minute drive to most of San Diego's attrac-

tions. Pets are welcome for an additional $10 per night.

North County Coastal

Best Western Marty's Valley Inn
$ • 3240 Mission Ave., Oceanside
• (760) 757-7700, (800) 747-3529

Located about 20 minutes east of the heart of Oceanside, the hotel has been an accommodation mainstay since the seventies. There are 111 guest rooms (including accessible rooms for the disabled), which are furnished in the modest, practical style of any Best Western. The hotel has a conference center and a casino card room. There's a pool at the hotel, and dining and shopping are nearby.

Best Western Stratford Inn Del Mar
$$ • 710 Camino del Mar, Del Mar
• (858) 755-1501

One of the best bargains in Del Mar, this hotel is within walking distance of village eateries, boutiques and bookstores, and nifty pubs where you can find some live music. There are 93 rooms, and for days when you'd rather not deal with beach sand, there's a pool.

If you're staying for a week, ask about discounts. The hotel has some rooms with kitchenettes but these are reserved early during both the summer and winter seasons. Book ahead if you want a place to cook.

Carlsbad Inn Beach Resort
$$$ • 3075 Carlsbad Blvd., Carlsbad
• (760) 434-7020

This popular hotel is a block from the ocean and only steps away from Fidel's, one the best and most affordable Mexican restaurants in the county (for more on Fidel's see our Restaurants chapter). If you have

INSIDERS' TIP

When making reservations, ask about special packages that may include admission to attractions (like the San Diego Zoo or Sea World) that you'd planned to visit anyway. You might save some money.

your heart set on a Carlsbad hotel, make reservations ahead of time. The hotel is popular, especially with families, because of the casual atmosphere. While it's pricey, keep in mind that you're right across a small street from huge, sandy beaches, and within walking distance to the shops and stores and restaurants in Carlsbad, and about five blocks from the Coaster station. When you get here you do not need to move the car for the entire vacation. You'll find 60 rooms, some with adjoining rooms and some mini-suites.

There's all you'd expect here, from a pool to rooms with tiny kitchens. Alas, there's no room service, but there are cafes by the dozen in downtown Carlsbad and upscale places for dinner too. If you're car-less or like to hike along the famous Carlsbad beach, this is a perfect choice.

Days Inn
$ • 133 Encinitas Blvd., Encinitas • (760) 944-0260

Recently renovated, the Days Inn is clean and convenient. It fits well into most travel budgets too. Located off I-5 at Encinitas Boulevard, the hotel has a Denny's on the property. Directly across the street, you'll find fast food, but a short drive will take you to Encinitas, Del Mar or Carlsbad for more upscale eating. The hotel doesn't have a pool, but it's just a quick jog to Encinitas's Moonlight State Beach where there's sand and sunshine nearly year-round.

Del Mar Hilton
$$-$$$ • 15575 Jimmy Durante Blvd., Del Mar • (858) 792-5200

Stay at this Hilton and you can walk to the Del Mar Fairgrounds, including the on- and offsite horse race track. It's a popular hotel so if you're determined to stay here during the racing or fair season, make plans well ahead. There are 254 rooms and some suites. There are meeting rooms and a lounge that invites you to linger. There's a spacious pool and restaurant on-site.

Doubletree Hotel Del Mar
$$-$$$ • 11915 El Camino Real, Del Mar • (858) 481-5900, (800) 222-8733

Just east of the ocean communities of Solana Beach and Del Mar, the Doubletree Hotel Del Mar offers 220 luxuriously appointed rooms, oversized and warmly decorated. There are four suites. Rooms come with everything from coffee makers to two-line phones with modem hookups. Accessible and nonsmoking rooms are available.

Along with that fresh-baked chocolate chip cookie you'll find every night right in your room, you'll be able to relax even if you're visiting on business. Breakfast, lunch and dinner are served in the hotel's restaurant and on the patio. There is an exercise room and outdoor pool. Families love the children's playroom and separate wading pool. Within minutes, guests can be splashing in the Pacific or swinging a golf club at one of the many courses in the area. The hotel is near the Del Mar Fairgrounds and racetrack, too.

Four Seasons Aviara
$$$-$$$$ • 7100 Four Seasons Pt., Carlsbad • (760) 603-6800

With 331 rooms, many oversized and all with wonderful views, this is a destination location for anyone who loves luxury. See the Spas and Resorts chapter for details on the resort, including those famous "Four Seasons" beds you may have heard about on the *Rosie O'Donnell* and *Oprah* shows.

There a championship golf course, two pools (one that's strictly for kids), poolside lounging and afternoon tea. Dining in the hotel's restaurants is a delight. There's one "fine" restaurant — Vivace — and another extra nice California Bistro (which is also 4 star). California Bistro is more casual and open for breakfast, lunch and dinner (see our Restaurants chapter); Vivace is open only for dinner.

This is where Insiders come, whether it's for a quiet chat and iced coffee at poolside or a more elaborate event like a romantic second honeymoon. If Four Seasons Aviara sounds good, you'll want to read more about it in our Spas and Resorts chapter.

Pets are welcome here at the Four Seasons Aviara, as long as they weigh less than 15 pounds. Guests with pets are required to pay a $100 nonrefundable fee.

Holiday Inn Carlsbad-by-the-Sea
$$ • 850 Palomar Airport Rd., Carlsbad
• (760) 438-7880

Close to the highway, close to LEGOLAND California (see our chapter on Kidstuff), close to the Carlsbad Flower Fields (see our Annual Events chapter), close to the Carlsbad Company Stores (see our Shopping chapter) and close to the technology centers of the North County, this recently renovated hotel is an obvious choice for many travelers. You can't miss it: A 50-foot Dutch-style working windmill sits atop the buildings. There are 144 rooms.

The hotel is about an hour's drive from downtown San Diego and offers a pool and on-site dining. Remember, directly across the street from the hotel is the not-to-be-missed Belle Fleur (see Restaurants) and the quicker eateries in the Carlsbad Company Stores mall. You'll find your favorite fast-food places right in the neighborhood, too.

Inns of America
$ • 751 Raintree Dr., Carlsbad
• (760) 931-1185

This Carlsbad chain hotel offers few frills, but it's convenient, well maintained and inviting. There is a pool, and the beach is about a five-minute drive west. If you're a budget-minded traveler, this is your hotel. There's no extra charge for those glorious sunsets you can see from some of the rooms. There's a restaurant on-site and good eating choices within minutes in the village area of Carlsbad and in various shopping centers near the hotel. And if you're traveling with your pets, you'll definitely want to stay here as they're a "pets welcome" policy. There's a $10 pet charge, which is due on check in.

L'Auberge Del Mar
$$$$ • 1540 Camino Del Mar, Del Mar
• (858) 259-1515, (800) 553-1336

Many people think of L'Auberge as a spa (see our chapter on Spas and Resorts) and they're right. It has wonderful possibilities if you're looking for relaxation; it also has beauty and rejuvenation programs. Yet it's also a convenient and enjoyable hotel located in the seaside village of Del Mar. Be sure to read more about the lovely beaches in Del Mar in our Beaches and Watersports chapter.

There are 120 deluxe rooms and elegant suites; there's a sports pavilion and pool. Along with the breathtaking views of the Pacific, you'll be treated to nearby golf, tennis, horseracing and, of course, the village's delightful restaurants, sidewalk cafes, boutiques and bookstores, all within walking distance. (See the entries in our Shopping chapter.)

La Costa Resort and Spa
$$$$ • 2100 Costa Del Mar Rd., Carlsbad
• (760) 438-9111

Since the seventies, La Costa Resort and Spa has been known for quality; it continues to be a benchmark for luxury in the hotel industry. The goal for the resort is to maintain privacy while providing every comfort for guests. As a guest yourself, you'll meet visitors from around the globe and those who live in Carlsbad. Insiders know this is a great getaway. The facility offers a range of spa choices (see our chapter on Spas and Resorts) and a hotel's "menu" of incomparable opportunities for recreation and relaxation. Ask about special package offers when making reservations and be sure to treat yourself to a spa experience.

La Costa has two championship golf courses, 21 tennis courts, the La Costa Racquet Club, five swimming pools, a full conference center, five restaurants, two lounges, walking paths and of course, the world-class spa. It also happens to be the home of the Toshiba Tennis Classic (see our Spectator Sports chapter) where top-ranked women tennis pros compete each summer.

Motel 6
$ • 750 Raintree Dr., Carlsbad
• (760) 431-0745
$ • 1006 Carlsbad Village Dr., Carlsbad
• (760) 434-7135
$ • 6117 Paseo Del Norte, Carlsbad
• (760) 438-1242

Like other Motel 6's throughout the country, this trio of North County Coastal bud-

Sometimes San Diego hotel guests arrive by boat.

get hotels is clean and functional. Kids stay free. Ask about AAA and AARP discounts. Pets are welcome at Motel 6's, with no extra charge or special room designation.

If you're going to spend hours outdoors, visiting the local attractions or doing business in the area, then it's tough to go wrong with the basics provided by Motel 6.

Oceanside Marina Inn
$-$$ • 2008 Harbor Dr. N., Oceanside • (760) 722-1561

Small (only 57 rooms) and convenient to the marina, this is the hotel of choice for those who motor or sail in for a vacation. There are some rooms with tiny kitchens, many with wonderful views, and in case you don't love walking on the golden Oceanside sand (on one of the best sandy beaches in the area), or playing in the Pacific waves, the hotel has a pool. If you're looking for a romantic getaway, ask about the rooms with fireplaces and balconies.

There isn't a restaurant on-site, but dining is close by, and if you're so inclined, you can rent a sail boat or book a fishing trip just steps from your hotel.

Olympic Resort Hotel & Spa
$$ • 6111 El Camino Real, Carlsbad • (760) 438-8330

Located within minutes of Carlsbad's Palomar Airport, this hotel includes 80 oversized rooms, a well-equipped fitness center, two heated pools and five lighted tennis courts.

There's a restaurant on-site and banquet facilities, yet most people don't visit for these reasons. It's the golf right at the hotel that draws in travelers. Yes, a driving range and putting greens are straight out back — barely 50 feet from the hotel. The championship golf courses at La Costa and

---

Mission Valley's hotels are the tops in luxury and the best of bargains. The facilities are centrally located, close to restaurants, shopping and theaters and offer great amenities.

Four Seasons Aviara are within a five-minute drive.

Radisson Inn Encinitas
$$ • 85 Encinitas Blvd., Encinitas
• (760) 942-7455, (800) 333-3333

Do you need sea breezes? How about great sunsets? How about highway convenience? Then this North County Coastal Radisson is the right choice. It has 94 rooms, some with kitchenettes. There's a restaurant on-site and dining within a five-minute drive. Of course, it has the prerequisite pool and lounging features and is especially popular with seminar groups and corporations that use the hotel for retreats and meetings. If you're traveling with your pet and want to stay here, there's a $50 nonrefundable charge and the pet must stay in a portable kennel that you'll need to bring.

Rancho Valencia Resort
$$$ • 5921 Valencia Cir., Rancho Santa Fe
• (858) 756-1123

About 30 minutes from downtown San Diego, Rancho Valencia is elegant and a top choice for spa and resort fans (see our chapter on Spas and Resorts). You'll find upscale touches throughout the restored adobe brick home that was built in the 1940s.

The lovely accommodations are limited to 43 luxurious casita suites spread around the lush grounds. There is a garden pool and beauty spa, 18 tennis courts, golf privileges and fine dining. Within minutes, you'll find elegant dining; you can walk to many of the restaurants. There are also great hiking and biking trails right out the hotel's door. Be warned, you may become addicted to the ambiance of Rancho Santa Fe; it's that lovely.

North County Inland

Best Western Escondido
$-$$ • 1700 Seven Oaks Rd., Escondido
• (760) 740-1700, CA (800) 752-1700,
USA (800) 528-1234

With 100 rooms and a location that's near the highway and the heart of Escondido, Best Western Escondido is the choice for people on the go. It's about 10 minutes to championship shopping at North County Faire (see Shopping), 15 minutes from championship golf courses (see Golf), and 20 minutes to the Wild Animal Park (see Attractions).

Good news for families: There's no extra charge when children stay with an adult guest. There isn't a restaurant on-site, but many Escondido restaurants are nearby. Ask about the discounted golf packages for your family golfers.

Comfort Inn
$ • 1290 W. Valley Pkwy., Escondido
• (760) 489-1010, (800) 228-5150

Whether you're just passing through or stopping to sample some of North County Inland's fun attractions, the Comfort Inn is a budget-right choice. The 95-room facility has a pool and the amenities that you'd expect at any Comfort Inn throughout the country.

Doubletree Carmel Highland Resort
$$$ • 14455 Penasquitos Dr., San Diego
• (619) 672-9100, (800) 222-8733

Situated just off Interstate 15 in the Carmel Mountain area and about 23 miles north of downtown San Diego, this hotel/resort offers 173 sleeping rooms, suites, two bi-level and four two-room parlor suites. The rooms are oversized and inviting.

If you need a quiet hideaway, you'll enjoy the hotel. But it's not just for sleeping. The Wild Animal Park, Sea World, and the Zoo are freeway close, and on-site you'll find an 18-hole golf course (par 72), five lighted wind-sheltered tennis courts, a state-of-the-art, 5,500-square-foot health and fitness center and heated outdoor pools. There are also whirlpool spas, steam rooms, and therapeutic massage opportunities.

Doubletree Club Hotel
$$$ • 11611 Bernardo Plaza Ct., San Diego • (858) 485-8250, (800) 222-8733

Right in the heart of Rancho Bernardo, the Doubletree Club Hotel is popular with those coming to San Diego for business and pleasure. The facility has 209 sleeping rooms and there are free chocolate chip cookies nightly. Amenities include a complimentary full, hot breakfast and complimentary cocktails each evening. Your room includes a spacious desk, two telephones with voice mail, data ports, in-room coffee, movies, irons and ironing boards and blow dryers. There is a heated pool, workout room, and jogging track. This is also a favored facility for conferences, retreats, seminars and meetings, since computer hookups and telephone service are available. There's a restaurant on-site.

With a lakeside setting overlooking Webb Park, you'll be close to business but feel a world away. The hotel is about 25 minutes from downtown San Diego.

Holiday Inn Express
$$ • 1250 W. Valley Pkwy., Escondido • (760) 741-7117

Newly refurbished and awaiting travelers, the Holiday Inn Express has 86 rooms, many with mini-kitchens, and offers two-room suites to give that extra elbow room often necessary when traveling. Rooms include microwave ovens and refrigerators. There's a free continental breakfast. There's a fitness room, heated pool and spa. Golf packages can be arranged.

Quails Inn Hotel at Lake San Marcos Resort
$$ • 1025 La Bonita Dr., Lake San Marcos • (760) 744-0120, (800) 447-6556

Quails Inn Hotel is conveniently located off California Highway 78 in San Marcos, yet once you're settled in one of the 140 oversized rooms, you'll feel a million miles away from anything as routine as traffic and work. Situated on the shores of Lake San Marcos, Quails Inn Hotel offers a variety of accommodation options, from standard rooms to spacious lakeside accommodations. One- and two-room suites and cottages are available, some overlooking the lake. Room amenities include coffee makers and hair dryers. The hotel is very popular with those who have retired and provides activities and social mixers for guests who love to mingle.

The hotel is pet friendly too, but there's a $10 per day extra charge when your pet stays with you. However, for seniors, they're now offering a 10 percent discount on room rates, so this may easily make up the extra cost.

Guests here have access to the 18-hole championship Lake San Marcos Country Club, known for its 6515-yard, par 72 course. Its third hole is rated one of the toughest in San Diego County. There's also a challenging executive course for those who are perfecting their game. The facility includes a fitness room, canoes, walking and hiking trails, and three restaurants. It's minutes from San Marcos' "restaurant row" where the dining possibilities range from seafood to Mexican favorites (see our Restaurant chapter for more about the choices you'll find).

Pala Mesa Resort
$$$ • 2001 Old Hwy. 395, Fallbrook • (760) 728-5881, (800) 722-4700

About an hour's drive north of San Diego and just off I-15, you'll find one of the area's nicest resorts, where you can leave your hectic city life behind. Pala Mesa Resort has 131 oversized guests rooms and suites clustered in a two-story California ranch-style building that's nearly touching the golf course. Rooms come with well-stocked refrigerators, data ports and large work desks.

This is the home to the Golf Digest School (for golf) and features an impeccable golf course designed in a classic style that challenges players at every turn. There are four lighted tennis courts, a workout room, dining at the hotel's restaurant and relaxing at the lounge. Be sure to read more about the golf facilities at this resort in our Golf chapter.

Pine Tree Lodge
$ • 425 W. Mission Ave., Escondido • (760) 745-7613

This is a no-frills lodge that's in the hub of Escondido. Declaring that "seniors are welcome," this modest lodge appeals to older travelers and to regulars who travel I-15. For them, and maybe for you, it's the hotel of choice, since it's clean and affordable. Some rooms have fully stocked kitchenettes. There are restaurants, discount stores and supermarkets nearby. Your furry friends are welcome at Pine Tree

Lodge too, although if anything is destroyed it must be paid for, and there's a one-time pet-in-the-room fee, depending on the size and type of pet. For instance, the fee for a Golden Retriever to share your room is $40.

Radisson Suite Hotel
$$ • 11520 W. Bernardo Ct., San Diego
• (858) 451-6600, (800) 333-3333

With 174 suites offering amenities not usually found in hotels, this work and pleasure hotel, close to Rancho Bernardo's technology hub, is gaining in popularity.

Year after year the hotel receives the Radisson President's Award for quality. In addition to the complementary full American buffet breakfast, there are complimentary evening cocktails at poolside in the cabana cafe.

For business travelers and for meetings, there's 800-number access, data ports, computer and printer options, and spacious work areas in each room. On the fun side, there's an exercise room, heated pool and spa, nearby golf, tennis, and walking and hiking trails.

The hotel is about 20 minutes from the Wild Animal Park and a half-hour from the mountain hamlet of Julian.

Rodeway Inn
$ • 250 W. El Norte Pkwy., Escondido
• (760) 746-0441

In the center of Escondido, the Rodeway Inn provides all the comforts you'd expect in a service-oriented hotel. Families with kids and seniors who travel take note: Rodeway offers senior discounts and kids younger than 18 stay free. Kitchenettes are available and restaurants are in walking distance.

Super 8 Motel
$ • 528 W. Washington Ave., Escondido
• (760) 747-3711

Whether you're on a travel budget or just like the convenience of Super 8 motels, this Escondido location is a good choice. The hotel is near the Wild Animal Park, close to the corporate centers of Rancho Bernardo, and blocks from the freeways. This Super 8 is a 48-room hotel that offers AAA and senior discounts. Of course, there's no restaurant on-site, but there is a complimentary continental breakfast and guest laundry facility. You'll find all your favorite fast-food restaurants within walking distance; more upscale dining is just minutes by car.

Travelodge
$ • 16929 W. Bernardo Dr., San Diego
• (858) 487-0445

This is a thrifty, popular choice for those who are in Rancho Bernardo for business and pleasure (kids stay free with a paying adult). The hotel is freeway convenient. This hotel offers free continental breakfast (there's a restaurant close by) and free cable and HBO in all rooms.

Welk Resort Center
$-$$$ • 8860 Lawrence Welk Dr., Escondido
• (760) 749-3000, (800) 932-9355

Welcome to this golfer heaven. Many people select this hotel as a destination spot for that reason alone. Companies and corporations use it for retreats and seminars and families love it for the outdoor attractions, including the golf, swimming, biking and walking opportunities.

Pets are welcome here, but you need to know that you and Fluffy will be staying in a "smoking" room. There's a $50 fee, with $25 refundable to you if your stay is "accident" free.

Located in North County Inland, about 45 minutes from downtown San Diego off I-15 and 10 minutes from the city of Escondido, the resort is situated on 600 beautiful acres. There are 132 rooms and suites, many right on the greens. There's a pool, spa and beauty facilities, and a workout room too.

East County

Best Western Continental Inn
$ • 650 N. Mollison, El Cajon • (619) 442-0601

This AAA, triple-diamond rated hotel makes you feel comfortable. Recently modernized, this Best Western is a good choice for families who want to stay near the San Diego freeway or who are coming to visit San Diego State University. Golfing buffs

Photo: Thom Vollenweider

Hotel del Coronado guests enjoy the warm weather as they browse the hotel shops and grounds.

choose it since it's close to the East County and San Diego courses. Some suites have spas; some have kitchenettes. There is a honeymoon suite, and there are meeting rooms, too.

Best Western Santee Lodge
$ • 10726 Woodside Ave., Santee • (619) 449-2626

As with other Best Westerns, this hotel offers good, basic hotel service. There are 46 rooms, a small pool, and you can find restaurants, including the mandatory fast-food kind, nearby. If you're coming to the East County on business, take note: This Best Western has data ports in some of the rooms.

Comfort Inn-La Mesa
$ • 8000 Parkway Dr., La Mesa • (619) 696-7747

Whether you're just passing through or stopping to sample some of East County's attractions, you'll find the Comfort Inn always clean and hospitable. There's a small pool, and pets are welcome (with a refundable deposit). There are 127 rooms and lower rates are available for weekly stays.

Days Inn La Mesa Suites
$ • 7475 El Cajon Blvd., La Mesa • (619) 697-9005

This clean, comfortable and affordable place is the right fit for travelers who enjoy a suite, rather than a single room. Some suites have mini-kitchens. It's conveniently situated off Interstate 8 and close to San Diego State University. There are restaurants nearby.

Holiday Inn Express-La Mesa
$ • 9550 Murray Dr., La Mesa • (619) 466-0200

With 78 spacious standard rooms and two-room suites, the Holiday Inn Express provides a lot for your money. There's no extra charge for children who stay with adults. The location is convenient to down-town La Mesa, the "Q" (Qualcomm Stadium) and San Diego State University.

The hotel has a pool and a whirlpool and offers a free complimentary breakfast. Ask about the weekly and monthly discounts for those who are staying in East County more than a few days.

Julian Lodge
$-$$ • 2720 C St., Julian • (760) 765-1420, (800) 542-1420

In the heart of this quaint, somewhat touristy village loaded with antique shops and tempting cafes, the Julian Lodge is a wonderful getaway place. If you're planning to visit during any of the holidays, especially the December ones when there may be snow in Julian, make reservations well ahead, since the Lodge has only 23 rooms. There's dining and shopping all around the hotel and biking and hiking trails just minutes from the hotel's front door. Ask about packages for Valentine's Day (it's truly romantic) and Apple Days.

La Casa Del Zorro Desert Resort
$$ • 3845 Yaqui Pass Rd., Borrego Springs • (760) 767-5323, (800) 824-1884

This is one of the jewels of East County. La Casa Del Zorro is a four-star, four-diamond desert resort. Some of the casitas have private swimming pools and some have baby grand pianos. (Be sure to read about this resort in our Spas and Resorts chapter and about the location in our Parks and Recreation chapter.)

Located in the Anza-Borrego Desert State Park, it offers numerous outdoor possibilities from hiking to sunbathing. The hotel is about two hours from San Diego and features 77 two-and three-bedroom casitas; most include fireplaces and individual patios. Pets are welcome here with some restrictions: There's a $100 refundable cleaning fee and an extra $50 per day, per pet, fee. There are only two casitas that are

---

INSIDERS' TIP

Are you going to visit the area during one of the major holidays? Plan ahead and make your reservations early, especially if you have your heart set on staying right at the beach.

designated for pets and their people, and they are available for smokers and non-smokers.

You can dine in the hotel's restaurant and get a desert sunset for the asking — check out the stargazing — that's free too. You can sip iced tea or soda (or a more grown-up choice) in the lounge.

The hotel is popular throughout the dry, warm winter months and especially in the spring when the desert bursts with flowers. If you're planning a March or April visit, make reservations ahead of time.

Motel 6
$ • 550 Montrose Ct., El Cajon
• **(619) 588-6100**
$ • 7621 Alvarado Rd., La Mesa
• **(619) 464-7151**

Like other Motel 6's throughout the country, the East County motels are clean and functional. Kids, accompanying an adult, stay free. There are various discounts available, including ones for AARP members.

If you're going to spend your time here visiting the local attractions or doing business, then it's tough to go wrong with the basics, and Motel 6 has them down pat. As with other Motel 6 hotels, your pet is welcome in these two facilities.

Palm Canyon Resort
$-$$ • 221 Palm Canyon Dr., Borrego Springs
• **(760) 767 5341**

Spacious grounds with oodles of hiking, biking, walking and sunset watching possibilities, this is a perfect choice for a getaway. The 14-acre complex is situated next to Anza-Borrego State Park, so if you're planning to come to the desert to see Mother Nature's spring flower show, make plans early. All hotels fill up quickly between November and May. Note that there's a three-day notice required on all canceled reservations.

Pine Hills Lodge
$-$$ • 2960 La Posada Way., Julian
• **(760) 765-1100**

An intimate, 18-room hotel that's rustic and attractive, it's popular with those who want to escape from hectic San Diego living and breathe in that pine-filled mountain air. This hotel isn't for every traveler. If you need — yes need — a TV in your room, find another place to stay, since the Pine Hills Lodge doesn't have them. It also manages to be very popular without air conditioning. What you do get is a great location, wonderful friendly service and a restaurant on-site. Be sure to have some of that world-renowned Julian apple pie.

Travelodge El Cajon
$ • 471 Magnolia, El Cajon
• **(619) 447-3999**

This is a thrifty, popular choice of hotel for those who visit the East County. The hotel has 47 rooms and allows pets in some of the rooms. There's a small pool and free cable and HBO in all rooms. There's a free complimentary continental breakfast and there's dining nearby.

South Bay

Holiday Inn Express
$ • 4450 Otay Valley Rd., Chula Vista
• **(619) 422-2600**

For freeway convenience, sparkling clean rooms and proximity to one of South Bay's premier attractions, Whitewater Canyon, the Holiday Inn Express can't be beat. Furnished in Spanish-southwestern style, the 118 spacious and beautiful rooms make you feel like you're in a bed and breakfast inn. A complimentary continental breakfast only reinforces that notion. The inn is located just west of Interstate 805.

Beaches are a 15-minute drive from the inn, but what might impress the kids even more is the fact that Whitewater Canyon Waterpark, with its wave pools and water slides, is just a five-minute drive away. We describe it in detail in our Attractions chapter.

La Quinta Inn
$ • 150 Bonita Rd., Chula Vista
• **(619) 691-1211, (800) 687-6667**

The La Quinta Inn in Chula Vista maintains the high standard that the inn has set nationwide. You can choose from 142

Photo: James Blank/San Diego Convention and Visitors Bureau.

A nighttime view of the San Diego skyline can be seen beyond this busy marina.

rooms with either a king-size bed or two doubles. Renovated in 1994, the spacious rooms, furnished in contemporary style, offer spacious comfort as well as closeness to all of South Bay's attractions.

When you pry open those sleepy eyes, La Quinta's First Light breakfast is ready for you in the lobby: cereals, fresh fruit, pastries, bagels, juice and coffee. Or if a Grand Slam is more your style, take a short walk next door to Denny's. Then it's back to the inn for a dip in the refreshing pool. Small pets are welcome here.

Radisson Suites
$ • 700 National City Blvd., National City
• (619) 336-1100

For the business traveler or the visitors who simply like to spread out, the Radisson Suites is an exceptional bargain. Located just east of

I-5, each of the hotel's 168 suites has either a city or a bay view. Modern and comfortable, all suites are equipped with computer modems, and all have Internet access.

Laundry facilities are available for guests, as is a complimentary continental breakfast. Or if you're in the mood to lounge around your suite, choose from a full room service menu. The Radisson's central location makes access to beaches and to Mexico just an easy drive. If your favorite family pet does not reach your knees, it's welcome here for a $25 refundable deposit.

Ramada Inn South Bay
$ • 91 Bonita Rd., Chula Vista
• (619) 425-9999

If you're visiting family or friends in either Chula Vista or Bonita, you can't go wrong with the Ramada Inn. Located right

INSIDERS' TIP

Are you planning to work during your stay? Ask about computer hookups, data ports, large desks, modems, fax machines and rooms with multiple telephone lines when making reservations.

on the border between the two communities, it's only a few minutes' drive to everything — shopping, golf and the beach.

Its 97 rooms are comfortable and clean, and a bonus is the casual Love's Restaurant on the premises. It's open for breakfast, lunch and dinner. Laundry facilities are available on-site, and a whirlpool spa awaits your aching bones at the end of a long day.

Seacoast Inn
$-$$ • 800 Seacoast Dr., Imperial Beach
• (619) 424-5183, (800) 732-2627

Affordable accommodations right on the sand are hard to find in San Diego County, but the Seacoast Inn is just the ticket. The motel's 38 rooms on two floors either have a beach view or look out over the inviting pool and courtyard. If you have a large group or are planning a private function, ask about the third floor Penthouse Suite. Rooms have either a king-size bed or two doubles, or you might try one of the suites that comes with a fully equipped kitchen and a private beach deck.

The Imperial Beach Pier is just steps away for romantic moonlight strolls or to satisfy fishing enthusiasts. And after a day spent exploring San Diego or lazing on the beach, fresh coffee is always waiting for you in the lobby. This is the perfect place to stay if you're planning to attend the Imperial Beach Sand Castle Contest (described in our Annual Events chapter), so make your reservations early.

Travelodge
$ • 394 Broadway, Chula Vista
• (619) 420-6600, (800) 578-7878

Like Travelodges across the country, this one will feel familiar. Its 80 rooms have few bells and whistles, but are dependably clean and comfortable. And if Mexico is high on your agenda, you're in the right place. The international border is less than a 10-minute drive from the motel.

This Travelodge is relatively new, built in 1990, and if you are a business person, you'll be happy to know there are computer modems in each room. A complimentary continental breakfast is offered every morning, and although there is no restaurant on-site, many fine restaurants are within a few blocks.

Bed and breakfast inns in the San Diego region have a flavor that's strictly Southern California.

Bed and Breakfast Inns

Bed and breakfast inns in the San Diego region have a flavor that's strictly Southern California. Each of the bed and breakfast inns has an easygoing ambiance that makes you long to check in and dread saying good-bye. These inns are special, warm, restful and inviting. They've been chosen because we'd enjoy revisiting them or would recommend them to our closest friends.

These are not the bare-bones accommodations found in some parts of Europe. You know the places: one bath down the hall, "take a number please," and a pint-sized sleeping room where if you sneeze your next door neighbor might respond, "Bless you."

All of the rooms at the bed and breakfast inns described in the chapter have private baths, unless otherwise noted. Most have enticing, easy-to-get-to locations, which also happen to be some of our favorites places in San Diego County.

For instance the Victoria Rock Bed and Breakfast Inn, in the East County mountain community of Alpine, receives a few inches of snow each winter. It's an especially sweet spot for a winter-weekend getaway, more so if you plan to drive the extra 20 minutes to walk, frolic or hike in the snow.

The Leucadian Inn by the Sea, in North County Coastal, is so close to the Pacific that you're surrounded with ocean breezes — just the right prescription for even the most ragged spirit. The town that Insiders call Leucadia is actually part of the city of Encinitas. Everything you could want for a relaxing weekend is there and all within walking distance. The town will remind you of a fifties beach and delight you with its many tiny hangouts where you can munch inexpensive fish tacos and its swank restaurants that also offer four-course dinners.

As you look over our listings, keep in mind that it's wise to call and double-check rates and availability of rooms. All of the bed and breakfast inns encourage reservations. If you want to book for a holiday, say Christmas or Valentine's Day, we recommend you do so months ahead so you won't be disappointed. Unless otherwise noted, the inns we've included all accept MasterCard, Visa or cash, but do not accept indoor smoking or pets. Assume too, that children are discouraged, unless we tell you otherwise.

Some of the bed and breakfast inns featured here serve a continental breakfast, with plump muffins and fresh juice, along with coffees and teas. It's simple but enough. Others have a full European-style (sometimes called gourmet) breakfast. These are the breakfast feasts of which fantasies are made, that spoil you to the bone while you're enjoying every minute of munching. Some of the inns have in-room eating options too — nice if you'd prefer to have a romantic breakfast on the balcony or in your room. Our entries will tell you what to expect.

In all of the bed and breakfast inns we've featured there is a comfortable sitting room, parlor or library. You may find overstuffed chairs loaded with pillows, lots of reading material, perhaps a puzzle in progress or a stack of board games, maybe a player piano, a decanter of sherry and some crackers and maybe — but not always — a television. (Some inns only have a television in the main part of the house, but not in individual bedrooms; some don't have televisions at all.)

Even when the bed and breakfast inn's parlor is deliciously old-fashioned, it's not unusual to find the rooms decorated in anything from African safari themes to South Seas motifs. Most are typically furnished with antiques and fresh flowers, lovely furnishings and plump comforters. The morning paper will probably be placed by your door as might a rose or decanter of coffee. Some of the inns have lovingly-placed extras in each of the rooms such as bowls of local fruit or plates of homemade cookies to nourish your inner child and that adult you often have to be.

If you haven't tried a bed and breakfast inn and need a few days off or want to stay somewhere unique when you're visiting San Diego, these entries will help you design the perfect getaway.

Price Code

Our prices indicate a one-night double occupancy at high-season rates.

Less than $65	$
$66 to $95	$$
$96 to 140	$$$
$141 to $200	$$$$
More than $20	$$$$$

San Diego

Balboa Park Inn
$$$ - $$$$ • 3402 Park Blvd., San Diego • (619) 298-0823

Does Paris in the '30s appeal to you? What does The Noveau Ritz conjure in your imagination? These are the names of just two of the Balboa Park Inn's 25 uniquely decorated luxury rooms. Host Edward Wilcox welcomes you to the complex of four Spanish colonial buildings that contain a novel assortment of themed rooms and suites. Paris in the '30s has a romantic wood-burning fireplace and a dreamy canopy bed. The Noveau Ritz is decorated in black, gold and burgundy art deco, with lots of mirrors, a separate kitchen and a private door to the sun terrace.

Nestled in a quiet residential neighborhood on the north edge of Balboa Park, the inn is a short walk away from the San Diego Zoo, museums, shops, restaurants and the Old Globe Theater. And it's just a few minutes' drive from downtown and the Gaslamp Quarter. Fresh fruit, juice, warm croissants, cinnamon buns and muffins are standard breakfast fare served either in your room or suite, on the sun terrace or in the peaceful courtyard.

This is one of the rare bed and breakfast inns that allows smoking in some of its rooms and also welcomes children. In fact, kids younger than 12 stay free when sharing accommodations with their parents.

Banker's Hill Bed & Breakfast
$$$ • 3315 Second Ave., San Diego • (619) 260-0673

Built in 1912, Banker's Hill is a historic Craftsman home with a fully restored Victorian interior, including all-new baths. Craftsman homes are common in San Diego, and they feature wide porches and interiors with lots of built-in shelves and cabinets. Each of the seven guest rooms is true to its original design, yet features contemporary decor. Both gay and straight Insiders have discovered that here they can step back in time while surrounded by modern luxuries and amenities. Located adjacent to the neighborhood of Hillcrest, guests need only take a short walk to find shops, restaurants, gyms and gay and lesbian clubs.

In addition to a continental breakfast, perks include a newly built pool and hot tub, billiard table, suntan bed, workout room and on-site laundry facilities. If you're searching for even more fun, Balboa Park, with the San Diego Zoo, museums, tennis courts and golf course is only four blocks away.

The Bed & Breakfast Inn at La Jolla
$$$$$ • 7753 Draper Ave., La Jolla • (858) 456-2066

Here is a rare opportunity to stay in an architectural gem that is also a registered San Diego Historical Site. Designed by noted architect Irving Gill, the house was built in 1913 and is one of Gill's finest examples of Cubist-style architecture. The lush, original gardens were planned by renowned horticulturist Kate Session, who was also responsible for founding Balboa Park.

Get ready to be pampered. Fireplaces and ocean views are available in many of the nine guest rooms in the main house and six in the annex. Fresh fruit, flowers, a glass of sherry and a terry robe await you upon check-in, and wine and cheese are served as an aperitif every evening. A gourmet breakfast is yours to enjoy in the dining room, on the patio or sun deck or in your room.

Each room is decorated differently, from the nautically themed Pacific View Room to the Oriental-style Windansea Room, with its rattan furniture. If a splurge is in order, try the Irving Gill Penthouse, a spacious suite at the tip of the house with an incomparable view of the Pacific Ocean.

Coronado Victorian House
$$$$$ • 1000 8th St., Coronado
• (619) 435-2200

Have you ever dreamed of reenacting Romeo and Juliet? It's a fantasy you can indulge while staying in the Romeo and Juliet Room at the Coronado Victorian House. With its brass bed that rises four feet above the ground, stained-glass doors leading to the Juliet balcony and Jacuzzi bath with double showerheads, this room is the ultimate romantic dream.

Owner Bonni Marie Kinosian has transformed her home, which is a registered San Diego Historical Landmark, into a posh bed and breakfast inn that re-creates a variety of innovative settings in its seven rooms. One feature that's a favorite among guests is the 40-foot dance studio in the house, where Bonni Marie leads stretch and exercise classes and teaches dance classes ranging from two-step to ballroom.

Breakfast is a gourmet delight, including homemade yogurt, beautiful fruit platters, fresh-squeezed juice, scones, muffins, and omelets or other sumptuous breakfast entrees. In the afternoon, tasty treats such as homemade meatballs are offered for hors d'oeuvres.

Located on the peaceful island of Coronado, Victorian House is within walking distance from pristine beaches, shops, restaurants and theaters. Children are welcome at the Coronado Victorian House.

Elsbree House
$$$ • 5054 Narragansett Ave., San Diego
• (619) 226-4133

If you're craving a vacation at the beach but still want the homey atmosphere of a bed and breakfast inn, Elsbree House is the solution. This recently constructed Cape Cod house is just a short half block from the Ocean Beach Pier and public beach, and only two blocks from the O.B. business district, with its restaurants and antique shops.

Innkeepers Katie and Phil Elsbree have created a modern escape to paradise. The six rooms are decorated in country English-Victorian style. Each has a private entrance and a balcony or patio all to itself, where you can relax with a book or write your own great American novel. In the morning, enjoy a self-serve continental breakfast of homemade bread and muffins, cereal, fruit and yogurt in the dining room. At sunset, stroll along Sunset Cliffs for a panoramic view of the Pacific Ocean.

Ask the Elsbrees, and they'll reveal the secret of Elsbree House: It's the best place to kiss in Southern California.

Heritage Park Bed & Breakfast Inn
$$$ - $$$$ • 2470 Heritage Park Row,
San Diego • (619) 299-6832

If you happened to catch a recent issue of *Country Inns Magazine*, you may already know that Heritage Park Inn is San Diego's highest-rated bed and breakfast inn. Step across the threshold and you'll

INSIDERS' TIP

Julian, snuggled in the mountains above San Diego, has more than 20 bed and breakfast inns and has a Bed and Breakfast Guild. To get up-to-the-minute information about rates and availability, call the guild at (760) 765-1555.

understand why. This magnificent 1889 Queen Anne mansion has twelve antique-filled guest rooms, featuring feather beds, clawfoot tubs, whirlpools and robes so fluffy you'll loathe to take them off.

Heritage Park is the centerpiece of a collection of Victorian mansions located on a hill above historic Old Town, one of San Diego's favorite visitors' destinations. Peace and quiet are the norm, and yet the bustle of shops, restaurants and the theater are just steps away. It's a great place for a family vacation because of its proximity to Old Town, and children are welcome here. Since 1992 owners Nancy and Charles Helsper have delighted their guests with a full candlelight breakfast, as well as afternoon tea on the veranda. Should you opt for an evening in, classic films are shown nightly in the sitting room.

www.insiders.com

See this and many other **Insiders' Guide®** destinations online.

Visit us today!

Recently completed is the Drawing Room, a professionally designed and decorated room that is a romantic fantasy come true, complete with soft colors, lighting and fabrics and a whirlpool for two. It's so romantic it practically whispers in your ear.

Keating House
$$ • 2331 Second Ave., San Diego
• (619) 239-8585, (800) 995-8644

Immerse yourself in nineteenth century Victorian luxury. Keating House, a beautifully restored Victorian home (and a San Diego Historical Site, sits proudly in a residential neighborhood full of elegant homes. Owner Larry Vlassoff has tastefully recreated the splendor of the Victorian era in each of the six rooms in the main house and two in the guest cottage. If you're a fan of English-style bed and breakfast inns, you'll be undaunted by the rooms in the

main house, which share a bath. If you prefer more privacy, the guest cottage rooms have private baths.

A full gourmet breakfast is served every morning in the dining room, and a cozy parlor offers the perfect setting for conversation or the opportunity to curl up in front of the fireplace with a favorite book. Lush tropical grounds surround the house, and several seating areas in the garden and on the front porch allow visitors to drink in the sweet aroma of roses and jasmine and the vibrant colors of bougainvillea, orchids and jacaranda.

Close to downtown, Hillcrest and Balboa Park, Keating House is ideally located for the visitor seeking quiet rejuvenation combined with lots of activities.

San Diego Yacht & Breakfast
$$$$ • Marina Cortez, Harbor Island, San Diego
• (619) 297-9484, (800) 922-4836

Many bed and breakfast inns are located near the water, but few can say they're on the water. Picture drifting off to the land of nod while being gently rocked by the tide, and waking up to the glorious sun, water and blue sky and a full gourmet breakfast. Choose from a luxury yacht, sailboat or a floating dockside villa, with space for two to six guests.

Each guest receives a voucher for a full breakfast at one of the nearby hotels, along with discount coupons for dinner. Or, should the mood strike you, your hosts will arrange to have dinner delivered for a romantic evening on the fantail of your boat. Spacious staterooms have private baths, and all boats have a fully stocked galley, TVs, VCRs and telephones. Bring the kids along because there are plenty of activities to

INSIDERS' TIP
If you will be arriving late in the day and don't know the area, check the Restaurants chapter for places to eat near your bed and breakfast inn. Ask the bed and breakfast innkeeper for recommendations too.

Photo: CeCe Canton

Heritage Park, with its beautiful Victorian houses, is the location of one of San Diego's finest bed and breakfasts.

keep everyone occupied. If you crave water activities, kayaks, Waveriders, fishing and whale-watching cruises can be arranged.

North County Coastal

The Cardiff-by-the-Sea Lodge
$$ - $$$ • 142 Chesterfield Ave., Cardiff • (760) 944-6474

You may have read about this bed and breakfast inn in *Sunset* magazine, seen it as a prize on *Wheel of Fortune* or heard Insiders talking about it. Overlooking the Pacific in the beach town of Cardiff, this sparkling clean and luxurious inn offers lush gardens and an open-pit fire ring that is high on the rooftop. Imagine roasting marshmallows as you watch the sun shimmering in the west. Yummy, to say the least. These attributes are tough to top.

Owned by Jeannette and James Statser, long-time Insiders themselves, the inn's interior is graced with original art and handcrafted touches. The Southwest Room, for instance, looks like it's straight out of New Mexico with hues of tan, pale pink and the palest of blues. The crowning glory is the Sweetheart Room and it's Jim's favorite too. Here you'll find hearts everywhere, from the ceiling to the heart-shaped tub for two. Breakfast is simple and good and all homemade — Jim's the chef — with muffins, fruit, coffees and teas.

All rooms are equipped with queen beds, custom furnishings, oversized baths and showers. There are 17 rooms and a roof garden that's becoming popular for weddings and receptions. Rates here go up during holiday weekends, and you can also expect to pay more for luxury suites or a spectacular view.

INSIDERS' TIP

Do you need accommodations for a wheelchair? Ask about accessibility when you call.

Leucadia Inn by the Sea
**$$ • 960 N. Highway 101, Leucadia
section of Encinitas • (760) 942-1668**

Do whimsical birds, flower leis, a palm tree right in your room give you a hint that this inn is a bit on the unique side? If so you're right and the new-to-the-inn community Leucadia Inn by the Sea is making waves. All the rooms have a theme from the Tropical (the one mentioned above and the most requested) to the New Orleans suite.

Owned by Mary and Ray Trimmins, who are also innkeepers for the Butterfield in Julian, this seaside inn is within walking distance of the Coaster station and a block from the beach. The breakfast package includes a $6 certificate at your choice of local eateries. If that's not enough the Timmins can offer you more than just a room. How about a romantic rendezvous for dinner at your favorite restaurant, a dozen long-stemmed roses, chilled cider and breakfast for two in the morning? Hot air balloon rides, limo service, bi-plane trips and surfing lessons can also be arranged.

Pelican Cove Bed and Breakfast Inn
**$$ - $$$ • 320 Walnut Ave., Carlsbad
• (760) 434-5995**

Only 200 yards from the Pacific, the Inn is strolling distance from the antique shops and fine eateries in the village area of Carlsbad. (If you love to antique shop, be sure to read our Shopping chapter for tips on things to do in Carlsbad.) That would make it nice. But what makes this inn special is the TLC poured on by owners Kris and Nancy Nayudu and the soft luxury and romance of the rooms.

There are only eight of them in this small inn, but each one comes with a fireplace, television, and European (make that fat and fluffy) bedding that surrounds you like a huge hug. Some rooms have spa tubs. The Balboa, with twin beds, is done in lavender florals and green stripes. The Del Mar, an Insiders' favorite, is done in tones of white; staying in this room feels rather like walking in the foam from ocean waves. As a matter of fact the carpet color is called sea foam green. Unlike other bed and breakfast inns, Pelican Cove isn't a foo-foo antique-strewn establishment. The decor is inviting and uncluttered.

The grounds are studded with flower gardens and trees. There's a sun porch and garden for lounging. The innkeepers make beach chairs, towels and picnic baskets available for those who can break away from the inn for a day on the beach.

The inn "draws the nicest people," says innkeeper Nancy. "Sometimes they bring us presents." While gifts are not required, compliments are always forthcoming when breakfast is served. "We have a different, hot entree that's included in the full breakfast everyday." On the day one Insider visited the inn, the savory menu included a blended ham and asparagus egg dish, plump blueberry-studded and crunchy nut muffins, scrumptious fruits and coffee that rivaled that of the best coffeehouse in town.

If that isn't enough, the inn is wheelchair friendly. Be aware that rooms cost more over holiday weekends, so be sure to ask when you call for reservations. There's courtesy pickup at the Amtrak station and Palomar airport. If you're arriving by Coaster, a pickup might be arranged. Ask when you call for reservations. FYI: the Coaster station is about 2 miles north of the inn.

North County Inland

Fallbrook Country Inn
**$$ • 1425 S. Mission Rd., Fallbrook
• (760) 728-1114**

Popular as a getaway, the Fallbrook

INSIDERS' TIP

Most bed and breakfast inns have a more restrictive cancellation policy than other accommodations. When making reservations ask about the cancellation policy. Sometimes there may be a charge for canceled reservations.

Photo: Bob Yarbrough/San Diego Convention and Visitors Bureau

Many popular bed and breakfast inns are a short distance from a relaxing stroll on the beach.

Country Inn has a romantic side since it specializes in wedding accommodations. In addition to the graciously appointed bridal suite, the inn offers 27 country-style rooms for family and friends. The garden, a riot of cascading annuals makes a perfect setting for the ceremony.

Pam Lushanko, innkeeper at Fallbrook Country Inn, likes to tell guests, "Let me show you that Fallbrook and the Fallbrook Country Inn offer the stuff dreams are made of. This is the perfect place to begin a happily-ever-after life." Pam has been in the inn-keeping business just a few years and has loved every second of it. She shares the daily chores with husband Larry and her parents, Barbara and Tom Crail.

All rooms have king or queen-size beds, cable and color television, spacious baths and patios. Sixteen of the rooms have kitchenettes, but you needn't cook since there

are fine restaurants and cafes within walking distance.

The inn offers mid-week discounts as well as weekly and monthly rates that are seductive to Canadian visitors (getting away from THAT winter) and Arizonans (cooling off in Fallbrook during THAT summer). Maybe they'll appeal to you too.

What's for breakfast at this bed and breakfast inn? Pam entices you with muffins, hot rolls, juices and fruits (remember this is citrus and avocado country) and coffees and teas. "Homemade jams and jellies are made right here in Fallbrook," Pam explains. You can spend your days lounging pool side, visiting the antique stores that are aplenty in Fallbrook, or checking out the art galleries and handcrafted jewelry stores that dot the main street of Fallbrook. Special golf packages and wedding party packages are available.

INSIDERS' TIP

A large number of bed and breakfast inns have websites where you can pull up information as well as photos of the rooms. When calling on the phone for information, be sure to ask about the website address.

East County

Brookside Farm Bed & Breakfast Inn

$$$ • 1373 Marron Valley Rd., Dulzura
• (619) 468-3043

Tucked away in East County about 2 miles from the tiny community of Dulzura is an inn whose reputation has spread around the country. The inn is actually about 30 miles from downtown San Diego but in environment and flavor it's as different from its big-city neighbor as night from day. We're talking a farm, with animals, farm-style breakfasts, and country hospitality, coupled with gourmet treats and all combined in a place you're sure to remember.

"We have regulars, snow birds, who come from Wisconsin each winter just to be with us," say Sally Guishard, who along with husband Edd are creators of this oasis. Edd's in charge of the mouth-watering food. He's a veteran of the restaurant business, having been a chef at some of the areas leading eateries. The fresh herb and vegetable garden, the orchard, the berry patch and the vineyard supply produce for the table, jams and jellies, and toppings for the waffles that are part of the breakfast fare that Edd talks about with pride. Sally is in charge of the baked goodies: breads, rolls, cakes and pies as good as you think Mama should have baked. Meals are served in the main dining room at 9 AM.

Each of the ten rooms has a distinct personality — from the Victorian pinks of Jennie's Room to the cool blues of A Room with a View. One Insider who treks to East County every spring says her favorite room is the Mexican-flavored La Casita, with its private patio, Monet-inspired sun porch and the view of the gardens.

All rooms have queen-size beds; several have fireplaces or wood-burning stoves; some include private balconies and patios. Sally's crafts and original artwork grace the inn

and there are decorative splashes everywhere. No, you won't find in-room phones or television at Brookside Farms, but you will find homey nooks, friendly farm animals, and an honest-to-goodness gurgling brook that is nearly guaranteed to soothe away city woes.

We'd be remiss if we didn't mention the "gourmet weekends." On these days Edd provides cooking courses. Friday night you'll begin with a course called "meals in a minute"; Saturday morning and afternoon the focus is on gourmet dining. The cost of $220 to $270 includes two nights' accommodation and the classes.

Butterfield Bed & Breakfast

$$$ • 2284 Sunset Dr., Julian
• (760) 765-2179, (800) 397-4262

Beneath majestic pine and oak trees on a serene hillside that's just footsteps from the historic town of Julian, is the comfortable, inviting Butterfield Bed & Breakfast.

Breakfast is a grand affair with country gourmet served in the Garden Gazebo in the summer and by the crackling hearth when winter sets in. Mary and Ray Trimmins, the innkeepers at Butterfield, can do something special if that tickles your fancy and can offer a romantic dinner and horse-drawn carriage ride. Reservations for this extra must-do activity are required.

There are five rooms at the inn and each features a fireplace and a television. One Insider will not stay at the Butterfield unless she can sleep in the Rosebud Cottage. It's decorated in country decor with a potbelly stove, sitting area, knotty pine ceilings and a world away from reality.

Rockin' A Bed and Breakfast

$$$ • 1531 Orchard Ln., Julian
• (760) 765-2820

Just a "piece up the road" from the historical town of Julian the Rockin' A Bed and Breakfast offers four country-style accommodations. Each room has a unique personality. You might choose the duck room with a queen-size bed and private jetted tub for two. The horse room, deer room and bird rooms have private baths and fireplaces.

To make a stay extra restful all rooms feature European-style feather-filled body pillows covered with cuddly comforters. In the parlor and den there's a wood-burning stove and the rooms open to a spacious wood deck.

Breakfast is a production, real country-style cooking. "You'd have to stay quite a few days for the possibility of a repeated menu," says Gil. He explains that guests love the country biscuits and gravy, the specialty pancakes and all the meat and fruit plates.

Wandering around the grounds is part of the Rockin' A experience. There's a ¾-acre pond, magnificent oak grove and an orchard, where you can eat the fruit (in season) straight from the trees. After that strenuous morning you could relax on the deck with Julian apple pie and a cup of hot or cold cider.

The Rockin' A is walking distance (about 10 minutes at a moderate pace) to Julian's quaint restaurants and shops. "Down the road a piece" and about a 15-minute drive is Santa Ysabel mission as well as Dudley's Bakery. After dinner at one of Julian's cafes, you can return to the Rockin' A, sit outdoors and count shooting stars. Now that's relaxing.

Victoria Rock Bed and Breakfast Inn
$$ • 2952 Victoria Dr., Alpine
• (619) 659-5967

This bed and breakfast inn is small (just four rooms) and Insiders believe that's what makes it inviting — along with the fact that it's in the mountains and off the beaten path. The Victoria Rock Bed and Breakfast Inn, owned by Darrel and Helga Daliber, is not to be missed if you love staying in intimate inns.

The inn has recently seen major renovations and the rooms are lovely, bright and fresh. One Insider says his favorite has to be the South Seas room with a strong nautical theme. The room has a full bath as well as an Enchanted Grotto Shower. That's Victoria Rock talk for an 8-foot waterfall/shower.

Another Insider says her favorite place to stay at this inn is the Antique room. It features an oversized four-poster bed, delightful Victorian furnishings and a turn-of-the-century ambiance.

Breakfast is hearty and scrumptious. On the day one Insider stayed at the inn, breakfast was the specialty of the house, southwest style eggs Benedict. "This recipe was once a secret but that's not so now since so many guests have asked for my recipe," says Darrel. Open year-round, smart guests book well ahead for holidays and longer-than-weekend stays.

These are not places to leave your belongings while you go out sightseeing; they're destinations in themselves. They're places where time slows, relaxation begins, tensions melt, and you leave your worries behind.

Spas and Resorts

Go ahead, say the names: La Costa, Cal-a-Vie, the Golden Door. It's impossible to do so without a sigh. These resorts are known here and throughout the world as part of what draws travelers to our region.

Whether you're living here or visiting, the spas and resorts of the San Diego region are diverse, exciting, and available. The spas are easy to get to and many are just a short drive from downtown San Diego.

Here in San Diego, some hotels are called resorts and some resorts have fitness and beauty spas on the grounds. In this chapter we've only included those spas and resorts that have special health, beauty, recreation or relaxation programs and whose main thrust is to nurture the mind and body. These are not places to leave your belongings while you go out sightseeing; they're destinations in themselves. They're places where time slows, relaxation begins, tensions melt, and you leave your worries behind.

And they are the cream of the crop. Here are the places we'd like to revisit or would suggest to a best friend. In fact, here are some of the most prestigious spas and resorts in the world. So if you're looking to relax, rethink fitness goals, revitalize your spirit and play some sports, read on. The spas and resorts in this chapter will give you plenty of opportunities.

The first thing you may notice is that they're all different. Some, like the Golden Door, cater to women (although they do have a few weeks a year when men are invited). Others have incomparable spa and beauty facilities, but do not offer separate healthful or calorie-conscious meals.

Some of the spas and resorts included in this chapter have day-spa packages where you can have all the fitness classes and pampering you want and then go back home or to your hotel at day's end.

We've tried to include this information.

We've also tried to give you an idea about current prices. You may note that we have not used the usual dollar-sign price keys with these entries. This is because some spas charge by the week, others by the day; some include spa services in their prices and some do not; and because many offer a multitude of "packages," each different and difficult to compare. Nevertheless we've included the charges for typical, popular packages or lodging options, so you can decide which ones are likely to fall within your budget. For even more detailed information, you may want to call the spas to get their brochures and to be put on their mailing lists for upcoming spa-related events. (You might even receive a discount coupon that could make your spa visit even more delicious.)

Be aware that sometimes spas offer two-for-one specials and group discounts (in case everyone in your office or investment club wants to come too). A few of the spas have seasonal packages and there are discounts available. However, here in San Diego it's resort time 365 days a year so don't expect to save a lot by visiting in an off season.

Cal-a-Vie
2249 Somerset Rd., Vista
• (760) 945-2055

Cal-a-Vie, nestled away in North County Inland, is a sweet refuge from the stresses and strains of modern living. With only 24 guests, and a staff that outnumbers guests, the privacy and pampering are beyond compare. The four-star cuisine is an adaptation of classical gourmet foods, minus the fats. The emphasis is on flavor and the exquisite art of presentation.

The fitness course, tailored for each guest, is invigorating. You'll find classes from aerobics and body shaping to pool activities and stretching. There's a long morning and afternoon hike within the 125-acre landscaped compound. Even the most indulgent guests feel spoiled by soothing European therapies such as massage, body scrubbing and aromatherapy. A favorite is the seaweed wrap said to promote detoxification and replenish nutrients in the skin.

You'd think all this would be enough, but that's not so. The main objective of Cal-a-Vie is to re-educate guests about the fundamentals of a healthier life style. Evening lectures cover topics such as fitness, nutrition, safe and sane weight loss, and stress management. There's also a class on cooking low-fat, highly delicious food.

Cal-a-Vie has women-only and co-ed sessions. All sessions begin on Sunday afternoon and end the following Sunday morning. There's complimentary transportation from Lindbergh Field.

The spa offers package plans. The European Plan includes meals, accommodations, all therapeutic treatments and fitness classes for about $4,500 a week. The California Plan includes meals, accommodations, all fitness classes and six body treatments for just less than $4,000.

Four Seasons Resort Aviara
7100 Four Seasons Point, Carlsbad
• (760) 603-6800

About 40 minutes from downtown San Diego, just off Interstate 5 at the La Costa Boulevard exit, that spa and resort feeling hits. You feel it the minute you pull into the winding drive and make it up the incline to the white Spanish colonial-style building atop the hill. If you love Four Seasons quality, you'll be gaga over this newly built diamond.

The resort features 331 generously sized guests rooms and suites with prices ranging from $305 for a moderate room to $4,000 for the Presidential Suite with three bedrooms and a view that will knock your socks off. Each upper-story room opens onto a private balcony; ground-level rooms have private, landscaped terraces. All feature the famous Four Seasons bed that movie stars and many regular folks say is the best in the universe.

www.insiders.com
See this and many other
Insiders' Guide®
destinations online.
Visit us today!

The grounds are lush, and the adjacent golf course, designed by Arnold Palmer, was recently featured in *Golf Digest* and *Golf* magazine. (See the chapter on Golf for the scoop on this side of Aviara.) There is a promising rose garden (remember it's a new facility so the landscape isn't fully established) where plenty of couples have already said "I do."

The spa and fitness center are open to registered guests only, so Insiders sometimes register for a night to get that luxurious pampering. In one of the spa's seven treatment rooms you can enjoy a massage, scrub or wrap. One Insider says be sure to try the chamomile body scrub (60 minutes cost $90) for a gentle loofa experience. Another prefers the Moor Mud Wrap that costs $70 for 60 minutes.

The hair salon is operated by the internationally known stylist Jose Eber. If you'd like to have Mr. Eber coif your hair, make plans ahead of time.

INSIDERS' TIP

Spa Finders, a national network of spas and resorts, can help you find the right one for your needs. You can reach them at (800) 255-7727.

The fitness center is beyond high-tech — tiny televisions are attached to some of the treadmills so you won't lose track of CNN while you're racking up the miles.

When fitness and pampering are complete, you can take a dip in the pool, then have a healthful and beautiful lunch poolside or in one of the private cabanas, and then lounge away the afternoon in the library. "A glass of sherry?" the food server may suggest.

This really is a family place too, with a special Kids for All Seasons program offered during weekends, summer months, traditional school breaks and holidays. There are supervised outdoor activities like nature hikes and water fun in the separate kids' pool, and indoor play inside a playroom that features a teepee for storytelling-time. The cost for guests is $30 for a full day; the concierge can also arrange babysitting. Staff members are CPR certified.

Golden Door
777 Deer Springs Rd., San Marcos
• (760) 744-5777, (800) 424-0777

Town & Country magazine pretty well sums up this spa: "The Golden Door is everything everyone has always said it is — and much, much more." Most San Diegans forget about this world-renowned health and beauty spa, and since it's tucked away in North County Inland off a country road surrounded by a high fence, that's logical.

The Golden Door has been rated as America's number-one spa by numerous spa guides and travel books. If you need some extra TLC and can afford the exclusive pampering, then pick up the phone and reserve your spot now at about $5,000 a week, slightly less in the winter months.

Packing for a stay at the Golden Door is simple because the spa provides everything. It suggests you bring personal basics (like toothbrush, aerobic and hiking shoes, swimsuit and undergarments); the rest will be waiting for you.

Nestled in 350 acres, including orchards and gardens, the Golden Door provides plenty of room for hiking and other outdoor activities. The formal landscaping here was designed by the famed Takendo Arii. Among the resort's features are three guest lounges, a dining room, indoor and outdoor exercise studios, the new Dragon Tree Gym, swimming pools, tennis courts and plenty of graduated walking trails. Activities are

Photo: Thom Vollenweider

There's lots of room for relaxing around this pool at the La Costa Health Spa.

geared to individual guests' requests according to their level of fitness, which is evaluated along with their range of motion, as staff create one-on-one fitness plans. There's also a customized take-home training program.

The Beauty Court is where you'll find steam rooms, saunas, showers, Swiss hoses, a fan-shaped therapy pool, and sequestered rooms for body scrubs and lulling herbal wraps. There are fitness classes too, taught by well-qualified instructors. These are small classes, (only 39 guests attend the spa each week, and staff outnumber guests four to one) so everyone receives plenty of attention. The clientele include movers and shakers from around the planet and those you see on the big and little screen. In other words, The Golden Door is an exclusive hangout.

For most of the year this is a women-only spa, although there are couples' and mens' weeks. The menu is gourmet and healthful, providing an innovative cuisine that's low in sugar, sodium and cholesterol yet rich in fiber and good taste. Evening programs might range from cooking demonstrations to lectures.

La Casa Del Zorro Desert Resort
3845 Yaqui Pass Rd., Borrego Springs
• (760) 767-5323, (800) 824-1884

As a relaxation spa, this resort is one of the best; however, you must remember it is in the desert. It does get hot. Fall, winter and spring may be the optimal times to visit. Nonetheless, some Insiders prefer the summer when they relish that dry, hot air and have lots of elbow room at the popular resort.

About an hour and a half and 90 miles northeast of San Diego in East County, La Casa Del Zorro offers you unique surroundings: It's smack dab in the 600,000 acres of Anza-Borrego State Park. Positioned on 42 acres of natural landscape, lush gardens and waterscapes, La Casa Del Zorro has

77 luxurious and spacious accommodations ranging from rooms and suites to casitas with one to four bedrooms. All rooms come with first-class amenities from coffee makers and plush bathrobes to a morning newspaper and service bars.

Here in the desert, it's quiet. It can be really quiet at night. That's why this is some Insiders' favorite spot on earth. During the day, guests like to hike or bike the miles of specially designed trails. Afterwards they can watch sunsets the color of rainbow sherbet. At night, in this isolated spot, they can gaze at a sky overflowing with stars. Take along a simple astronomy guide and you'll enjoy your stay even more.

You won't find any specific fitness or beauty regimen here; rather you can choose your own healthy activities. There are six championship night-lit tennis courts and guided desert walking and bicycling tours. If you're a golfer you'll find a couple of courses within quick driving distance, but there's also a nine-hole putting green right on the grounds. The resort also offers shuffleboard, a life-size chess set, and a complete high-tech fitness center

The resort's spa side is staffed with specialists who offer hair and nail services along with facials (a full facial is $65). You can include a Swedish, shiatzu or sports massage in your resort package for $85 an hour. Services are a la carte. A casita (a 4-bedroom suite with pool) costs about $775 a night. A standard room is $115.

When you're tired of staring at those stars, there's nightlife at Casa Del Zorro. At the Fox Den there are special events featuring jazz, blues, swing and classic musical performances.

La Costa Resort and Spa
Costa Del Mar Rd., Carlsbad
• (760) 438-9111

Thirty miles north of San Diego, minutes from I-5, is the 450-acre luxury resort of La Costa. Along with the two 18-hole champion-

Afternoon Tea (and More) at Aviara

Have you dreamed of quietly elegant afternoons sipping tea and sampling delicate morsels that taste even better than they look?

If the grandeur of afternoon tea is your idea of good living, then the Four Seasons Resort Aviara should be included on your dance card whether you're a registered guest or a visitor. While you might find afternoon tea provided at some teashop in San Diego, Aviara does it with Four Seasons style. We're talking top drawer.

At Aviara, tea comes with a plethora of finger sandwiches, Sultana scones with rose petal jelly (that's to die for), lemon curd and Devonshire cream, delicate pastries and petit fours. As for the tea, there are plenty of choices, including herbal and fruit infusions and the standards such as Darjeeling, English Breakfast, Wild Sweet Orange and Zen.

While you're waiting in the lounge of the Carlsbad resort, allow your mind to contemplate the origins of tea time, an addictive custom. The first afternoon tea was ordered by Anna, seventh Duchess of Bedford, in 1840. Apparently, Anna was tired (or grew hungry) during the long, dull space between meals. One afternoon about four,

— continued on next page

Photo: Four Seasons Resorts Aviara

Whether you're lingering next to the fountain or lying by the pool, the Four Seasons Resort Aviara is a treat to the senses. Days can be as busy or idle as you like. There's golf, tennis, nature trails, hiking possibilities, beauty and pampering treatments, a well-stocked fitness center and private cabanas. Everything you need or want is minutes away from your room.

during her weary, low-energy time, she regally asked something like, "Bring me some tea, bread, butter and cakes." This refreshing, light meal lifted Anna's spirits and blood-sugar level. Her idea spread like honey on a hot scone. Friends, family, royals and commoners decided it was the "in" thing and the practice became as English as Buckingham Palace. In 1865, the Aerated Bread Company opened London's first teashop for the public.

Just a note for trivia lovers: Afternoon tea is a grand affair with delicate cakes and sandwiches. High tea is the American equivalent to supper, a sturdier meal, and may have been most popular originally, with those who lived in the north of England.

Now return to Carlsbad and the Four Seasons Resort Aviara. Afternoon tea is served daily in the hotel's Lobby Lounge, from 2:30 PM until 4 PM, and it is deliciously accompanied by a pianist or harpist who sets the mood. You can lean back in one of the richly decorated sofas or overstuffed chairs, you can admire the tables decorated in crisp linens and you can breathe in the fresh rose petals sprinkled around the tables. The view is the focal point, with floor-to-ceiling windows that frame views of the Pacific and the resort's luxurious Palm Courtyard.

Afternoon tea is $16; with the addition of a glass of sparkling wine, port or sherry the cost is $21. Insiders recommend making reservations for afternoon tea, especially during the holidays. The number is (760) 603-6800.

ship golf courses, a 21-court racquet club, the award-winning restaurants and lounges, you have the Spa.

Covering more than 75,000 square feet, the La Costa Spa is the largest spa in North America. There are separate locker and spa facilities for men and women, and co-ed work-out rooms providing the finest in weight and cardiovascular equipment. Supervised exercise classes challenge even the most fit.

Knowing the reputation of La Costa Resort and Spa, it's easy to put your health and beauty in the hands of these professionals. With the menu of services, most a la carte, even the most persnickety can find a health and beauty favorite.

Let's start with food: By arrangement you can have a personal consultation for health management, which includes an analysis of your present nutritional habits. You'll get handouts and printouts. Costs for nutritional services range from $70 to $130. If you're serious about turning over a new nutritional leaf, sign up for the super-market and healthy-eating seminar.

In the Lifestyle Program, which costs $135 per one-hour session, you'll learn about healthful eating behaviors and ways to reduce stress. You'll also receive a lifestyle evaluation. The fitness programs include yoga, water aerobics and aerobics combined with toning and resistance training. For $55 per 30-minute session, you can have a body-composition analysis and a personal consultation with an exercise physiologist. You can have the services of a personal trainer for a cost of $50 for 50 minutes.

If beauty and relaxation top your list, you'll be interested in the facials, which start at $50 for 30 minutes. Massages (reflexology to shiatzu) are $95 for 60 minutes. An Insiders' favorite is the La Costa Glow ($150 for 90 minutes), which is touted as a ten-

4.9 Million People Can't Be Wrong:
The Legacy of Lawrence Welk Continues

Over 35 years ago, Lawrence Welk purchased a small parcel of land just north of San Diego, California. There, he founded a haven for virtues, family values, and endless relaxation. Today the **Welk Resort Center** still keeps those ideals. Nestled on 600 acres of rugged hills and valleys, two beautiful golf courses, a live Broadway-style theatre, and deluxe accommodations await you. And it's only minutes from some of San Diego's famous attractions, including the all-new LegoLand, California.

sion-relieving, hydrating treatment but is considered by some to be just simple, indulgent pleasure.

Ask about the special four-day Renewal (about $1,500) and the seven-night Lifestyle package, which is about $3,000.

L'Auberge Resort and Spa
1540 Camino Del Mar, Del Mar
• (858) 259-1515

Have a yen to be treated like you personally owned the entire state of California? Then take a closer look at L'Auberge Resort and Spa, in North County Coastal. Located in the heart of Del Mar, one of Southern California's most picturesque coastal villages, the boutique resort (as it calls itself) offers 120 luxury guest rooms and suites. Rooms are well appointed and inviting. Prices range from $169 to $950 for the rooms.

As a guest, you may use the Sports Pavilion featuring the latest in exercise and fitness equipment. You can have a fitness instructor develop and supervise a personal workout plan – or just have the teacher accompany you on a sunrise or sunset walk along the sand, or a vigorous trail hike in Torrey Pines State Park. Additionally, there's golf and tennis nearby. Afterwards, you can choose from a tantalizing menu of massage, skin and body treatments; and hair, nail and facial treatments. Insiders recommend the exclusive hydrotherapy and body purification programs.

You'd expect fine dining and will get it at Pacific Terrace, the dining room at L'Auberge and at the resort's Durante's Pub (ask the food server about the nightly special appetizers).

Loew's Coronado Bay
4000 Coronado Bay Rd., Coronado
• (619) 424-4416

About 20 minutes south of downtown San Diego, Loew's Coronado Bay Resort has an exquisite location, which is fitting for this exclusive resort snuggled on a private peninsula in San Diego Bay.

All rooms include custom furnishings, fully stocked mini bar, two telephones, king-size bathrooms with oversized tubs and luxury from top to bottom. That gives you the statistics; now let's get to important stuff — like cooking classes lead by the resort's top chef ($30 per class), Kung Fu lessons ($15 per person), free nature hikes, tennis clinics ($20 per person) and yoga ($15 per person). And that's just a sampling. Guests also have access to bikes and in-line skates, boats, golf, tennis, the health club (private men's and women's steam rooms). Do you want to charter a yacht? Just talk to the concierge. Be sure to take the resort's herb-garden tour; it's free and the beds of flowers and pungent herbs are sure to please and impress you.

The Commodore Kids Club has a supervised program providing entertainment for kids ages four to twelve. Activities include arts and crafts, Ping Pong, board games and movies. The cost is $40 per child; evening care is $25 per child. As an extra service to you and your children, the management will gladly "kidproof" your room to help keep yours safe and happy during your visit.

The accommodations range from $285 for a standard bay-view room to $1500 for the presidential and hospitality suite.

Rancho La Puerta
Tecate, Baja California, Mexico
• (760) 744-4222, (800) 443-7565

Nestled in 300 acres of scenic countryside, just 3 miles south of the border, Rancho La Puerta is in a world of its own. More than 150 guests a week visit this valley where hiking trails cross the habitats of the spa's eco-sanctuary.

Unlike some other health and beauty spas, Rancho La Puerta is co-ed. Yet from its beginning over 50 years ago, it was recognized that men and women require distinct fit-

INSIDERS' TIP

Some spas are fancy and people dress up for dinner. Others are more casual. When making reservations, ask about the type of clothing you'll need to bring.

Photo: San Diego Convention and Visitors Bureau

This Anza-Borrego desert plant in bloom is just a sample of the beauty
in the surrounding desert.

ness regimens, therapy and workouts, so there are separate exercise centers, and beauty treatment facilities. Be sure to sample the Kneipp herbal wrap (it will relax even the most Type A overachiever). The Ranch, as Insiders call it, provides multiple facilities for saunas, steams and nude sun bathing, whirlpool and hot tubs. It also boasts one of the highest ratios of staff per guests of any spa. Ponder that for a moment and you may want to get to a phone to make reservations now.

The feeling throughout the Ranch is one of relaxation and comfort. There are over 60 fitness classes and conditioning programs. There's plenty of pampering. And if you needed any more reasons to consider the Ranch think about this: Rancho La Puerta is the birthplace of spa cuisine, with most of the fresh produce served here

coming straight from the Ranch's organic gardens. It's honest food, offered at the peak of flavor. The Ranch and The Golden Door (see above) are currently owned by the same company, and while the Ranch is in the wilds, comparatively speaking, this is not a country cousin. Everything is first-rate and appealing.

Accommodations at the Ranch consist of individual Spanish-colonial inspired cottages, most with private patios and fireplaces. The secure grounds are landscaped with lovely gardens. The facility includes six lighted tennis courts, six aerobics gyms, a weight-training gym with advanced equipment, three pools, five whirl-jet therapy pools and three saunas and steam rooms. There are beauty and skin care opportunities similar to those found at the Golden Door (see above). If you go, be

INSIDERS' TIP

Are you aware that the massage you have at a spa or resort has more than feel-good benefits? Massage therapy is now being used in treating conditions like carpal tunnel syndrome and for reducing the pain of arthritis.

Photo: Dale Frost/Port of San Diego

Night offers a unique vista of the fabulous San Diego skyline.

sure to include the Better Breathing class and the African Dance Workout in your schedule.

The question about drinking water was on the mind of one Insider during a visit to the Ranch. Although the tap water is chlorinated and fine for baths and showers, it's not recommended for drinking. For that and for tooth brushing, there's a filter faucet in the kitchen or bath of each ranchero or hacienda. Bottled mineral water is always available too.

The second question most people ask is: How do I get there? If you're coming in from San Diego's Lindbergh Field, a regularly scheduled spa bus can take you to the Ranch. Guests are asked to arrive on Saturday for the seven-day program; the Ranch is about an hour's drive from the airport. During the drive, chipper staff members offer mineral water, snacks and information on what to expect and what one can expect to accomplish.

Spa packages are for seven days; prices range from $1,500 to $2,300 and are all-inclusive except for Mexican tax and modest charges for special treatments. Ask about special discounted packages, such as the Summer Savings program, and the just-for-couples week for those who want to share new life-enhancing habits.

Rancho Valencia Resort
5921 Valencia Cir., Rancho Santa Fe
• (858) 756-1123

About 30 minutes and seemingly 3 million light years away from the city of San Diego, Rancho Valencia is elegant and secluded. In North County Coastal, it is a neighbor to the elite Rancho Santa Fe community and fits in just fine, thank you very much. The restored adobe brick home was built in the 1940s and the hacienda has hosted countless notables such as Bill Blass, Bill Gates, Merv Griffin, Jack Kemp and Eva Gabor.

INSIDERS' TIP

Most spas have a non-smoking policy. If you smoke, ask about the restrictions when making reservations.

Guest accommodations are limited to 43 luxurious casita suites spread around the lush grounds. There is a garden pool and spa, 18 tennis courts, golf privileges and fine dining. The staff here must be trained in mental telepathy. They seem to know what you need or want even before a request is spoken. Now that's service.

This isn't strictly a fitness and beauty resort; like Rancho La Puerta in Baja California, it is also a respite for the senses. The spa and fitness program are not afterthoughts, but rather well-planned offerings. The spa experience includes accommodations, breakfast, an assortment of massages (try the warm-oil massage or the deep-tissue massage), services such as the body wrap or Ayurvedic aromatherapy facial, which features a blend of herbs and essential oils for cleansing and exfoliating the skin. Prices include complimentary use of tennis courts and the fitness center. The two-night package ranges from $1,400 to $1,700 per couple.

A la carte fitness possibilities include a personal bicycle tour lead by a fitness instructor for $75 per session and a two-hour hiking tour through Torrey Pines State Park for $25.

Other packages include the two-night "Yours & Mine," which makes a popular Valentine or anniversary getaway. This package includes spa pampering (massages and facials like those described above), together with two rounds of 18-hole golf, cart included, for $1,500 per couple. The two-night golf package (yes, with two rounds at the course and some golf lessons) plus the pampering, is also $1,500.

An Insiders' favorite is the one-night Romantic Getaway that pours on the champagne. You and your lover will be treated to a private breakfast, one-hour Swedish massage for each of you and a candlelight dinner served fireside in your own suite or the signature restaurant. That package costs only $725 per couple.

You'll find fine dining at the resort and steps away in the city of Rancho Santa Fe.

The staff can arrange for hot-air balloon trips, horseback riding, beach walks, polo lessons or a day trip to Disneyland.

Welk Resort Center
8860 Lawrence Welk Dr., Escondido
• **(760) 749-3225 (800) 932-9355**

Remember the famous band leader? Lawrence Welk loved the area of Escondido where he "discovered" a secluded valley. Once you see the area, you'll understand why he wanted to build a resort here. The air is dry and clear, the breezes are gentle, and why, yes, it's a perfect place to play Welk's favorite sport: golf. While Welk is gone, his memory and love of comfortable, wholesome living continues in the surroundings of the resort. Today those who remember Welk's bubbling television show enjoy the resort, and even those too young to remember, or have missed the reruns on television, come here to unwind and to play.

Let's get to the specifics: There are three 18-hole courses for players of all levels. The Oaks Par 3 course is ideal to work on your short game, and the famous Fountains Executive Course is designed by renowned golf course architect David Rainville. With plenty of sand traps, water hazards and challenges, the Meadows Lake Championship course is the ultimate experience.

Located in North County Inland, about 45 minutes from downtown San Diego off Interstate 15, 10 minutes from the city of Escondido, the resort is situated on 600 beautiful acres. Room prices range from $80 to $120 a night depending on location, and the resort offers shopping, a relaxing, fitness center, spas, a beauty salon, pool and dining possibilities. Insiders agree that the fun of the Welk Resort (above and beyond the golf, in the opinion of some Insiders) is the award-winning live theater where Broadway musicals are performed in casual settings. For further information on the Welk resort, see our entries in the Golf, Arts, and Restaurants chapters.

Vacation rentals are plentiful and offer a cost-effective way to spend some time in San Diego, especially if you're bringing the whole family along.

Vacation Rentals

We're about to let you in on a secret — the secret to becoming a real San Diegan, even if only temporarily. Whether your stay in San Diego is short, long or indefinite, one of the best ways to enjoy and assimilate the true San Diego experience is by living it in a vacation rental. Within minutes of unpacking your bags, you'll find yourself doing the same things the natives do. The only difference is, you don't have to go to work.

Vacation rentals are plentiful and offer a cost-effective way to spend some time in San Diego, especially if you're bringing the whole family along. From a quaint 1940s cottage to a modern, fully appointed condominium to a grandiose house in La Jolla, if you can imagine it, you'll find it.

The vast majority of vacation rentals hug the beach, mainly because that's where most people want to be. Picture waking up to the sound of the ocean waves gently breaking on the shore and having that first cup of coffee on a deck or patio just steps away from the sand. Or perhaps you're more inclined to be inland a few miles, in the wooded enclave of Rancho Santa Fe or on the fairway of a world-class golf course.

From Oceanside in North County Coastal to Imperial Beach in the South Bay, you can choose from an array of amenities and price ranges. The primary appeal to staying in a fully furnished house, condo or cottage, aside from the lower cost, is that you can fend for yourself, not having to rely upon hotels and restaurants for your needs. It's a much more casual existence. Plus, many people love being absorbed by the local culture, mingling with neighborhood residents, browsing nearby shops, even making the obligatory trip to the local laundromat.

So pack your bags lightly (remember, we're very informal here), bring along your sunscreen and become a bona fide San Diegan. Imagine lazy days on the beach, a glass of champagne while watching the sunset, a leisurely dinner and an evening stroll along the water. Then you'll understand why so many people have discovered that a vacation rental is the ideal way to go.

Rental Agents and Independent Owners

Even though most vacation rentals are independently owned, the majority are managed by property management companies. Although you can find beautiful properties that are for rent directly by their owners, unless you have a reliable word-of-mouth referral or good photos that show the interior and exterior, we strongly recommend that you use an established agency. Properties managed by rental agents are uniformly well maintained, the renting agents are completely familiar with the units they are renting and you will have few surprises. Agents will be more likely to have brochures too, so you can get an idea of what you're renting ahead of time.

One of the benefits of vacation rentals in San Diego is that many of the properties are occupied by their owners at least part of the year. As a result, most are beautifully upgraded and maintained.

Some vacation rental companies advertise their properties only on the Internet, but

Bayfront vacation rentals sometimes include amenities like these catamaran sailboats waiting on the beach.

the ads come complete with pictures and detailed descriptions of the house or condo. This is especially true for rentals in the inland and southern regions of San Diego. A browse around the Internet might be time well spent, particularly if you're looking for something other than beach property. Just search on "San Diego Vacation Rentals," and you'll be overwhelmed by the number and variety of rentals.

Short-term and Long-term Stays

Although shorter stays are usually available during the winter season, most rentals require a minimum of a one-week stay during the summer. Some of the higher-end properties in La Jolla and Rancho Santa Fe, for example, might require a one-month commitment during the tourist season. Long-term stays, usually considered to be for the whole summer, are also an option. If you plan to stay longer than that, you may as well rent privately if for no other reason than to avoid local hotel taxes, which must be collected on vacation rentals.

Rates and Reservations

Not surprisingly, rates fluctuate greatly between the summer and winter seasons. The summer season generally runs from June

INSIDERS' TIP

Even though June signals the beginning of the summer season, it often is a gray, overcast month. The marine layer that locals wryly refer to as "June Gloom" settles in along the coast, and oftentimes the sun makes only an occasional appearance during the entire month. Keep it in mind if you're planning a beach vacation.

through September; winter is considered to be October through May. Summertime rates are naturally significantly higher than winter rates, ranging from $600 per week to $3500, while winter rates drop by about $300 to $500 per week. So if you'd like to join the ranks of "snowbirds" who flee the harsh winters of the Midwest and the East for a respite in temperate San Diego, you'll probably find some good values.

Keep in mind, too, that quoted rates do not include the required 10.5 percent hotel tax, and you will also be required to pay an advance reservation fee and security deposit. Most properties require a 30-day or 60-day cancellation notice to refund the full amount of your deposit. Some will withhold a portion of your reservation fee regardless of how early you cancel.

We highly recommend that you make your reservations well in advance of your visit. Some properties are booked for the summer by January, so the earlier you can make plans, the better.

Kids and Pets

Nearly all rentals welcome children. In fact, most encourage Mom and Dad to bring the kids. San Diego has much to offer the whole family. Most will have a limit on how many people can occupy a property, but they are designed to accommodate as many as possible. Property managers are happy to work with you to make sure your entire group is comfortably accommodated.

For the most part, pets are not allowed. If you're set on bringing Fluffy or Fido along, you might have more luck renting from individual homeowners, most of whom list their properties in the classifieds section of *The San Diego Union-Tribune* or on the Internet. If you play detective and search thoroughly enough,

you should be able to find a place willing to host your four-legged family member.

Parking

If there were a way to sugarcoat this issue, we would. But the truth is, parking at the beach is always...well, we'll say, a challenge. Nowhere is that more true than in Mission Beach during the summer. If you're driving into town and considering a Mission Beach rental, a garage or reserved parking space may be one of the amenities you'll wish to place near the top of your list. Even if you're lucky enough to find an overnight parking place on the street, should you decide to go for a drive the next morning, by 10 AM you will not find another place to park when you return. You'll be forced to park in a lot miles away and shuttle back and forth.

Just in case you're tempted to squeeze your car into a likely spot in one of the alleys, be forewarned. If one of your wheels even kisses the red line that screams "no parking," your car will be towed. And parking enforcement is a constant, vigilant presence in Mission Beach during the summer months. You'll have to pay not only the towing charges but also a painful parking fine. The good news is that even though parking is difficult at best, the payoff is worth it. Most people take it in stride and simply plan ahead. Plus, the other beach areas aren't quite as bad. You might end up having to hike a little, but you should always be able to find something.

Rental Agencies

T. L. Pace Real Estate
5713 La Jolla Blvd., La Jolla
• (858) 454-1123
If you're looking for the ultimate luxury va-

Photo: Dale Frost/Port of San Diego

Visitors who choose bayfront vacation rentals reap the benefit of a colorful view when the sailboats are afloat.

cation, T. L. Pace Real Estate offers magnificent individual homes for rent in La Jolla, the tony beachfront village that has some of the country's most valuable real estate. You're not likely to find any bargains here, but if you're willing to part with upward of $10,000, you'll get a month in a La Jolla house that is the stuff dreams are made of.

Penny Property Management
4444 Mission Blvd., San Diego
• (858) 272-3900, (800) 748-6704

Since 1965 Penny Property Management has been helping vacationers find the perfect beach rental. Specializing in Mission and Pacific Beaches, Penny also has a few hard-to-find rentals in Ocean Beach and La Jolla. All of Penny's booking agents are familiar with each property they rent and can help you find

exactly what's right for you, from a no-frills unit to a luxury penthouse in the sky. Penny can also help with babysitting needs.

Realcor Property, Inc.
731 S. Hwy 101, Ste. 1P, Solana Beach •
(858) 793-3600

Realcor specializes in vacation condos and houses from La Jolla north to Oceanside, and occasionally offers a property in Rancho Santa Fe or a condo in the Aviara Four Seasons Resort. Included in Realcor's territory are Del Mar, Solana Beach, La Costa and Carlsbad, areas that are highly sought after for their proximity to the Del Mar Racetrack and North County Coastal golf courses. Most of Realcor's properties are high end, but all are exquisitely maintained and appointed to provide a memorable San Diego experience.

INSIDERS' TIP

Most locals claim to have seen it, but only a lucky few really have. We're talking about the "green flash," a brilliant green light that appears for a split second right at sunset. Watch for it in the western sky over the ocean at the precise moment the sun dips below the horizon.

San Diego Vacation Rentals
2613 Mission Blvd., San Diego
• **(619) 296-1000**

Like its cohorts, San Diego Vacation Rentals specializes in beach rentals, focusing on Mission Beach, Ocean Beach and La Jolla.

Whether you're looking for a large, luxury house located right on the beach or bayfront sand, or a secluded cottage tucked away on one of Mission Beach's courts, San Diego Vacation Rentals can help you find a dreamy vacation home.

**San Diego has more
than 2,500 restaurants.**

Restaurants

After you spend the day swimming, surfing and sailing, or rock climbing in the backcountry, or sailing above the earth in a hot-air balloon, what is it that everyone wants to do? Why, eat, of course! Whether you're grabbing take-out from a fast-food place or dining in luxury at an exquisite restaurant, eating is truly one of the great pleasures of life. And we aim to help you find the best eats in the county, no matter what you're in the mood for. Tough assignment, we know, but someone had to do it.

We've canvassed the county from one end to the other to find the very best San Diego has to offer. Our biggest problem was deciding what to include. After all, San Diego has more than 2,500 restaurants, and try as we might, we just couldn't sample them all. But years of dining out and an all-out recent assault on local establishments have made us confident that we can steer you toward exactly what you have in mind.

You'll probably notice that we've included a lot of Mexican restaurants, and for good reason. Being so close to the U.S.-Mexico border has resulted in an abundance of them, from tiny, hole-in-the-wall fast-food places to elegant establishments featuring upscale Mexican food. Everyone loves the typical tacos, quesadillas and enchiladas, but we've also included some of the newer restaurants that are introducing locals to authentic Mexican fare from deep within the various regions of Mexico.

As always, remember that San Diego is a casual place. Very few restaurants have any kind of a dress code. The key phrase seems to be "casual but elegant." However, a few of the top-notch (meaning expensive) restaurants do insist that gentlemen wear jackets and that both ladies and gentlemen refrain from wearing shorts or jeans. If such a requirement exists, we'll be sure to mention it. It's not a bad idea to call ahead if you have any doubt, though.

Most restaurants accept reservations except for the ultra-casual places, and we recommend that you make them, especially on weekends. Most also accept all major credit cards; the exceptions are noted. The exceptions are usually small fast-food places that just aren't equipped for credit cards but are certainly worth experiencing. If a restaurant is especially family-friendly, we've mentioned it, but you're likely to see children dining right along with Mom and Dad just about everywhere.

California has tough smoking laws. Smoking is prohibited in all restaurants and bars, unless you're seated in an outdoor patio or terrace. Luckily for smokers, the summer months afford numerous opportunities for outdoor dining.

As usual, we've divided the chapter by geographic region, with one slight deviation. Restaurants in the city of San Diego have been further broken down into groupings by neighborhoods for your convenience. Each restaurant has also been identified by its cuisine.

So go exploring and try something new. We know you'll be pleased by what you'll find.

Price Code

Our price code includes the average price of dinner for two, excluding cocktails, wine, appetizers, desserts, tax and tip.

$	Less than $15
$$	$16 to $30
$$$	$31 to $40
$$$$	$41 and higher

San Diego

Coronado

Azzura Point
Loews Coronado Bay Resort
$$$$ • Continental
• 4000 Coronado Bay Rd., Coronado
• (619) 424-4000

When you initially peer at the menu prices, you might gulp a little, but the first bite could easily induce you to take a second mortgage on your house so you can return night after night. Chicken isn't just chicken here, it's *poussin*, and it's delicately bathed in flavors of citrus and rosemary and served with creamy polenta, swirled with even creamier mascarpone cheese. The beef tenderloin is prepared the way it was always intended: crisply seared and rosy inside, fork-tender and melt-in-your mouth heaven. Served with sautéed portobello mushrooms and a polenta fritter, it'll linger in your dreams for a long while.

Desserts are unusual — and unusually good. Our favorite is the chocolate volcano cake, which cradles molten mocha lava. If you want just a sampling of the chef's magic, the adjacent Azzura Point Bar serves tapas-style hors d'oeuvres. You'll see folks trying to appear as though they're used to cuisine this fine, but usually by the time they're halfway through the appetizer, the jig is up. Prepare to swoon. Dinner is served nightly except Monday.

Chez Loma
$$$$ • French/Continental
• 1132 Loma Ave., Coronado
• (619) 435-0661

The finely restored house Chez Loma calls home is a Coronado historical monument, and its award-winning cuisine has received nationwide distinction. The restaurant is broken up into several intimate dining areas that almost make you think you're dining at home, that is, if you have a resident chef who can prepare updated French and Continental classics.

Menus change with the seasons, but some standouts are the horseradish-encrusted Atlantic salmon with smoked tomato vinaigrette. Duck, lamb, seafood and pasta dishes are also treated to the chef's special touch. The complementary focaccia bread with seasoned olive oil is out of this world. A carefully selected wine list complements the menu, and the bar offers premium selections. Chez Loma serves dinner nightly and a fine Sunday brunch.

Mexican Village
$ • Mexican
• 120 Orange Ave., Coronado
• (619) 435-1822

Since the mid-1940s, Coronado's Mexican Village has been serving both Mexican and American dishes in its historical landmark building. Colorful murals adorn the walls, and lively music keeps diners peppy. You'll see lots of families dining here as the restaurant has special menus for children and for seniors, too.

The restaurant is noted for its romaine salad, and the Mexican pizza is a menu standout. Chimichangas, deep-fried burritos with a variety of fillings, are a favorite item, too. Mexican Village serves lunch and dinner daily, and is open for breakfast on Sundays.

Prince of Wales Grill
$$$-$$$$ • Continental
• Hotel del Coronado, 1500 Orange Ave.,
Coronado • (619) 522-8496

Recently remodeled, the Prince of Wales Grill, is an airy and elegant oceanfront restaurant specializing in grilled prime meats, seafood and other fresh seasonal selections. Floor-to-ceiling windows afford a spectacular view of the ocean, and the lengthy menu offers fare equally pleasing. Broiled salmon and swordfish dishes are the most popular, but the lamb chops with Anasazi beans is an unusual but successful pairing. For an appetizer, try the grilled prawns served with a plum salsa, two flavors that blend beautifully.

If you're a dessert lover, save room for the luscious banana macaroon bread pudding. The wine list has few bargains, but the selections are quite good. This is one of the few restaurants in San Diego that actually has a dress code. No jeans or shorts are permitted, and jackets are recommended. Dinner is served nightly.

Rhinoceros Cafe
$-$$ • American
• 1166 Orange Ave., Coronado
• (619) 435-2121

American bistro-style cooking is featured here in this cozy cafe. Choose from steaks, poultry, fresh fish and shellfish dishes as well as a selection of delicious pasta entrees. Thick and juicy chops are a popular choice among meat lovers, as is the Southwestern meat loaf sandwich. Lighter eaters lean toward the pasta dishes or the herb-sauced poached salmon. A good selection of beer and wine is offered.

The atmosphere is casual, and all menu items are available for take-out if you're in need of a night in. Dinner is served nightly, lunch from Monday through Saturday. Breakfast is served on Saturday and Sunday.

Downtown/Gaslamp Quarter

Athens Market
$$ • Greek
• 109 W. F St., San Diego
• (619) 234-1955

Located in the historic and beautifully restored Senator Building, the Athens Market is a haven for the relaxed dining crowd.

Proprietor Mary Pappas offers a comprehensive Greek menu with large portions and high quality. All the traditional favorites are covered, including moussaka and spanakopita, but if you like lamb, don't miss the roasted lamb served here. It's especially nice.

San Diego Chargers owner Alex Spanos is a regular at Athens Market, as are members of the downtown legal community. There's a full bar that keeps things lively. Dinner is served nightly, and the restaurant is open for lunch Monday through Friday.

Bayou Bar & Grill
$$ • Creole/Cajun
• 329 Market St., San Diego
• (619) 696-8747

Walls adorned with memorabilia of Mardi Gras, and music evoking the New Orleans Jazz Festival create a festive atmosphere at the Bayou Bar & Grill. Its Creole/Cajun cuisine has become a favorite of Insiders who keep coming back for such specialties as Mardi Gras pasta, crawfish etoufee and soft shell crab.

All entrees get the Cajun treatment: Pork chops, duck and chicken are all standouts in their mildly spicy sauces. Entrees are accompanied by a salad of greens, pecans and mandarin oranges tossed with a poppy-seed dressing.

Open for lunch and dinner daily, the Bayou also has a Sunday champagne brunch in addition to its regular menu. The restaurant is located in the Gaslamp Quarter within walking distance of the convention center, Horton Plaza and Seaport Village. It has a full bar as well as a selection of New Orleans food specialties for sale.

Bella Luna
$$ • Italian
• 748 Fifth Ave., San Diego
• (619) 239-3222

For a long while, you couldn't throw a cannoli without hitting an Italian restaurant in the Gaslamp Quarter. Many have come and gone, but the ones that remain are those that have gotten it right from the beginning. Bella Luna continues to offer the excellent regional food of Capri in its small but chic establishment. The name translates to "Beautiful Moon," and moon-themed artwork covers the walls.

The menu is light and imaginative including lots of fresh seafood and pasta, as well as a tasty breaded veal chop covered with a blend of arugula and fresh tomato. Daily risotto dishes are Insiders' favorites, but if it's available, try the shrimp salad or the tender crepe stuffed with salmon. One specialty always available is the grilled half chicken. Dinner is served nightly.

Blue Point Coastal Cuisine
$$$ • Seafood
• 565 Fifth Ave., San Diego
• (619) 233-6623

You'll feel like you're walking into a San Francisco supper club when you enter Blue Point. With its large wooden booths and dining tables off to one side and a massive bar dominating the other, the mood is elegant and upbeat. In fact, you'll probably be inspired to order one of the dozens of specialty martinis to complement appetizers, which can be ordered at the bar.

Our favorite entree is the Hawaiian ahi, served with wild mushrooms and ginger butter. But you can't go wrong with any of the seafood items here, like crab cakes or catfish, all of which are served with lots of organic vegetables. Dinner is served nightly.

Cafe Sevilla
$$ • Spanish
• 555 Fourth Ave., San Diego
• (619) 233-5979

The only way to truly appreciate Cafe Sevilla is to go at least twice, because the first time you visit, it's almost mandatory to have the paella Valenciana. This traditional Spanish dish is loaded with clams, mussels, calamari, shrimp, chorizo and roasted chicken, all cooked in an aromatic saffron rice. When you return, you can enjoy one of the other fine entrees, such as New York steak with Riojo sauce or roasted chicken in garlic sauce.

Should you wish to sit at the bar and make a meal of tapas, which are Spanish appetizers, try a sampling of croquettes of shrimp, mushrooms sautéed in a garlic wine sauce or fried calamari. If you'd really like to make a night of it, make reservations for the Flamenco dinner show that's winning citywide raves. See our Nightlife chapter for more happenings at Cafe Sevilla. Dinner is served nightly.

Croce's
$$$ • International
• 802 Fifth Ave., San Diego
• (619) 233-4355

Croce's nearly defies description, as it is much more than a restaurant. It's actually two restaurants, a jazz club, a sidewalk dining spot and a concert venue. And they all flow into one another with an electric mix of great food, divine music and fun-loving folks. For dining, Croce's is truly an experience; to find out more about it as an entertainment spot, check our Nightlife chapter. Owner Ingrid Croce, widow of legendary singer Jim Croce, opened the first arm of her restaurant when the Gaslamp Quarter was in the early stages of its revitalization. Over the years it has spread out into adjacent buildings. The chef keeps diners coming back for such treats as a breaded Alaskan halibut with prawns, served with a spicy Indonesian sauce. The menu changes with the seasons, but there's always a good selection of pastas and fresh fish as well as inspirations like the grilled lamb salad. Croce's is open for dinner nightly and offers late-night dining, too.

Dobson's
$$$ • Contemporary American
• 956 Broadway Cir., San Diego
• (619) 231-6771

For power lunches and after-theater

Photo: Dale Frost/Port of San Diego

A Seaport Village restaurant at sunset will offer picturesque dining.

dinners, Dobson's is a great choice. This is THE spot in San Diego to see and be seen, either at the saloon-style bar downstairs, or the upstairs loft dining room. The hands-down Insiders' favorite menu item is the signature mussel bisque with a puff-pastry crust, a delicacy owner Paul Dobson introduced at the St. James Bar and Grill when he opened that restaurant, too (see our entry under La Jolla/Beaches).

You'll also find lots of seafood specialties on the seasonal menu, as well as meats and poultry that mingle French tradition with modern California style. Many go to Dobson's just to hang out at the bar, which is next to a huge front window, affording a view of the constant parade of downtown movers and shakers. Dobson's is open for lunch Monday through Friday and for dinner Monday through Saturday.

The Field
$ • Irish
• 544 Fifth Ave., San Diego
• (619) 232-9840

The food at this eatery/pub is down-home Irish, corned beef and cabbage being the main menu item. But it's corned beef and cabbage unlike any you've ever had before in the United States, we'll wager. Thick slabs of corned beef that look like prime rib are accompanied by tender, sautéed cabbage that has none of that stink-up-the-kitchen aroma we're all familiar with. We know that boiled potatoes don't sound too sexy, but give them a try. Combined with the other flavors on your plate, they're a winner.

The interior of the restaurant is furnished with tables, farm tools and equipment all imported, piece by piece, from Ireland. If you

---

INSIDERS' TIP

If you find that evening is approaching and you don't have a dinner reservation, go early. Most restaurants start serving as early as 5 PM, but the dinner crowd doesn't start arriving until about 7 PM. Chances are you'll be able to get a table.

have even a smidgen of Irish in you (as we all do on St. Patrick's Day), you'll feel right at home here. The menu also includes fish and chips and some outstanding breakfast selections. Lunch and dinner are served daily, and brunch is served on Saturdays and Sundays.

La Provence
$$ • French
- **708 Fourth Ave., San Diego**
- **(619) 544-0661**

If you appreciate fine ambiance, La Provence has it in spades. The dining room is full of fascinating decorations that create the quintessential Country French mood. The food is bistro style, with some creative dishes that have elevated this casual restaurant into the stratosphere as far as most local reviewers are concerned. Starters include a terrific spinach salad with shrimp wrapped in basil and prosciutto. Bouillabaisse is equally satisfying, and the onion soup is worth coming back for.

La Provence serves wine and beer only. It's open for dinner nightly, lunch Monday through Friday and brunch on Saturday and Sunday.

Las Cuatro Milpas
$ • Mexican
- **1857 Logan Ave., San Diego**
- **No phone**

A Barrio Logan mainstay since 1933, Las Cuatro Milpas is a storefront eatery offering authentic Mexican specialties such as chorizo bowls, a spicy Mexican sausage combined with beans and rice. The dangerously fiery salsa concocted on the premises is a mandatory addition to every dish, and the warm tortillas are unlike anything you'll ever find in a supermarket. Over the years the restaurant has expanded its seating into adjacent buildings, which provide plenty of room for family-style eating. But don't be surprised if you find yourself dining on savory pork or chicken tacos in your car or while perched on the curb, be-

cause lines often snake out the door and down the street during lunch time.

The specialty of the week is served on Saturdays only, when Las Cuatro Milpas opens at 6 AM to dish up steaming bowls of menudo, a legendary hangover cure. The restaurant is open for breakfast and lunch every day except Sunday. Take-out is available as well as bulk purchases of most menu items. Be sure to bring cash; no credit cards are accepted.

Hillcrest/Uptown

Cafe on Park
$ • American
- **3831 Park Blvd., San Diego**
- **(619) 293-7275**

An American-style bistro, this small and cozy eatery offers hearty breakfasts, lunches and upscale fare for dinner. Even during the week the cafe is busy from the moment it opens until closing. Breakfast seems to be the standout of the day. You can choose from all the standards — eggs, pancakes, cereals — but they're all prepared with a twist. Eggs are called "scrambles" and are combined with a variety of ingredients, including peppers, onions, chilies, beef and more.

Most diners are regulars, and most have their favorite dishes, except for one Insider who says his favorite menu item is whatever's in front of him at the time. Imaginative sandwiches, salads and pasta items distinguish the lunch menu, and dinner includes such specialties as crab fritters with Thai mustard sauce and butternut squash risotto. Cafe on Park is open for breakfast, lunch and dinner Tuesday through Saturday.

Chilango's Mexico City Grill
$ • Mexican
- **142 University Ave., San Diego**
- **(619) 294-8646**

Mexican fast-food places are never in

short supply around town, but few of them feature regional cuisine like Chilango's. Dishes such as pork adobada, lean pork with a rich, sun-dried red chile sauce, is served over thick corn masa patties and topped with pinto beans, guacamole, and crumbled Enchilado cheese. Or try a burrote, a giant flour tortilla burrito stuffed with pollo asado pibil, chicken marinated in tangy-sweet orange juice, achiote and spices.

Dining-in facilities are limited to a few tables inside and out, and you'll probably see far more orders to go than to eat in. But if you can dispense with candles and linen, the food makes up for the lack of ambiance. Chilango's also serves breakfast tortas, tacos and burrotes along with a selection of sweet Mexican pastries. The restaurant is open for breakfast, lunch and dinner daily and does not accept credit cards.

Corvette Diner

$ • American
• 3946 Fifth Ave., San Diego
• (619) 542-1001

Music from the '50s, eclectic decor (including a vintage Corvette) and simple diner fare have made this restaurant a family favorite. Burgers, sandwiches, fries and milkshakes are the mainstays here, and all are first rate. Kids love the Corvette Diner because it's loud and there's lots to look at while awaiting their meal.

Waiters and waitresses are relentlessly cheerful and efficient, and the music eventually creeps into your brain. Your toe will be tapping before you know it. The restaurant is open for lunch and dinner daily.

Extraordinary Desserts

$ • Desserts
• 2929 Fifth Ave., San Diego
• (619) 294-7001

Who hasn't fantasized about skipping dinner and going straight to dessert? This is the place to indulge the fantasy. Owner Karen Krasne, whose sweet creations have been featured in *Bon Appetit*, has carved a niche for those who want to throw caution to the wind and relax with a dessert that's as beautiful as it is tasty. Picture a tender, flaky napoleon, filled with whipped cream and fresh berries, dusted with powdered sugar and topped with edible flowers.

Or if chocolate is your only idea of dessert, you'll have plenty to choose from. Dense chocolate tortes, huge brownies and cookies and luscious chocolate cakes are yours for the choosing. Tart and sweet lemon tortes awaken the sense buds, and several kinds of buttery shortbread rekindle memories of Grandma's kitchen. Extraordinary Desserts also serves a large selection of coffees and teas, the ideal accompaniment to your sweet delicacy. The restaurant is open to satisfy your sweet tooth for breakfast, lunch or dinner every day, including Sunday when a continental breakfast is the highlight of the day.

Kemo Sabe

$$$ • Southwestern/Asian
• 3958 Fifth Ave., San Diego
• (619) 220-6802

As pleasing to the eye as it is to the taste buds, Kemo Sabe grabs your attention as soon as you walk through the door with its unusual collection of sculpture and other art pieces. Even the entrees are works of art — you'll hear lots of oohs and aahs as dishes are placed before diners. And what dishes they are. The perennial favorite is Skirts on Fire, a skirt steak grilled and seasoned with spices that will ignite your senses (and your mouth — but pleasantly).

For appetizers, try the mixed satay, skewers of grilled chicken, shrimp and steak seasoned with Thai spices and served with a peanut dipping sauce. To complement your dinner, Kemo Sabe's bartender

---

INSIDERS' TIP

Watch for restaurant specials and coupons in Thursday's *San Diego Union-Tribune*. Oftentimes, you'll find two-for-one or early-bird specials that can save you a bunch.

has created a large selection of custom martinis. The Insiders' favorite is the Blue Glacier, a concoction of Bombay Sapphire gin, Skyy vodka and blue curaçao, with an orange twist. It goes down quite nicely. Lunch is served Monday through Friday, and dinner is served nightly.

Laurel
$$$ • Southern French
• 505 Laurel St., San Diego
• (619) 239-2222

Laurel is a recent addition to San Diego's restaurant scene that was immediately embraced by a crowd that keeps coming back for such treats as duck confit on garlicky mashed potatoes. Another entree the chef has trouble keeping in the kitchen is the Provençal chicken roasted in a clay pot. Appetizers are unusual — and unusually good — like the Roquefort tart baked on a savory walnut crust.

Service is perfect. The night we visited Laurel, the waiter brought a small sample of wine for us to try that was other than what we ordered simply because he thought we might like it better. He was right, and we were impressed. Desserts are heavenly, especially the warm fruit tarts with caramel ice cream. If you're in the mood for lighter fare but still want the Laurel experience, you can sip and nibble at the spacious bar. Laurel serves dinner nightly.

Mission Hills Cafe
$$ • Continental
• 808 W. Washington St., San Diego
• (619) 296-8010

Unassuming from the outside, the interior of this casual bistro is graciously appointed with nice linens, beautiful floral arrangements, excellent service and a varied menu that's sure to please everyone in your party. The restaurant is actually quite large, occupying two rooms that are usually filled, even on weeknights.

The pear Cambozola salad is a delectable lunch entree or an even better way to begin dinner. Baby greens topped with imported Cambozola cheese, a creamy cheese with a tangy, Roquefort-like flavor, are paired with garden-fresh sliced pears

and strawberries. Dinner selections include pastas, poultry, seafood and various meats, including an oven-roasted lamb shank with a house-made tomato garlic sauce. The satiny garlic mashed potatoes served alongside are worth ordering on their own. An excellent wine list offers wine by the bottle or the glass. The cafe is open for breakfast lunch and dinner every day but Monday

MIXX
$$ • Global
• 3671 Fifth Ave., San Diego
• (619) 299-6499

"Cuisine with no ethnic boundaries" is the motto at MIXX, and the eclectic offering of entrees gives testament to that philosophy. Upon entering, diners are ushered past a cozy bar area, through the cocktail lounge, which features nightly entertainment, and up a short flight of stairs to the dining room that overlooks the action below.

Standouts on the menu are the salmon in a spring roll wrapping, served with a Dijon and ginger sauce, and the pan roasted trout with its creamy horseradish sauce. Also popular are a selection of pastas and the wild boar meat loaf. Salads, including a tasty combination of greens, apples, walnuts and Gorgonzola cheese, can be ordered for half price if accompanied by an entree.

MIXX is open for dinner nightly.

Montana's American Grill
$$ • American
• 1421 University Ave., San Diego
• (619) 297-0722

Insiders who make it a habit to dine again and again at Montana's do so for one reason. They know their favorite dish will be consistently perfect every time they order it. Owner Francisco "Pancho" Marty has created an ambiance that is a magnet for locals and visitors, and the chef has created a menu that features an innovative combination of flavors.

Many entrees have Southwestern accents, such as the grilled Anaheim chiles with three cheeses and smoked tomato salsa appetizer. For those who like to splurge on meat dishes when they dine out, the mixed grill features three cuts that change daily and always get Montana's signature grilling. A cozy, clublike atmosphere envelops you as soon as you walk through the door, and the bar, with its intriguing, artsy light fixtures, is always alive with conversation. Hang around for the divine desserts made on the premises, especially the smooth-as-silk sourdough bread pudding with berries. Montana's is open for lunch and dinner Monday through Friday and for dinner on Saturday and Sunday.

Saffron Noodles and Saté/Saffron Thai Grilled Chicken
$ • Thai
- **3737 India St., San Diego**
- **(619) 574-7737**

These side-by-side eateries have the same ownership and serve Thai favorites for takeout or to eat in. Saffron Noodles and Saté offers mouthwatering combinations of chicken, beef and pork saté served with jasmine rice, cucumber salad and peanut dipping sauce. There's also a large selection of noodle dishes served in traditional Thai style, flavorful and spicy. Next door at Saffron Thai Grilled Chicken, tender, Thai-style roasted chicken is served with your choice of five sauces and a terrific Vietnamese coleslaw topped with chopped peanuts. There's no seating on this side, but all menu items can be ordered from either restaurant if you're eating in.

Saffron was listed in *USA Today* as one of the ten best places in the country for take-out. Insiders have discovered the place, and it's not uncommon for lines to be a bit long. But it's worth the wait for these savory Thai delicacies. Saffron serves lunch and dinner daily.

La Jolla/Beaches

Bird Rock Cafe
$-$$ • California/International
- **5656 La Jolla Blvd., La Jolla • (858) 554-4090**

Step into this cozy, cottage-like restaurant and prepare yourself for a delightful meal. Depending on your appetite, you can order from among small, medium and large plates, and even the large plates are reasonably

priced. Free-range chicken is a standout, as is the ever-changing risotto and the crab cakes.

The food is unpretentious, but the quality is excellent. Beer and wine are served. The Bird Rock Cafe is open for dinner nightly.

Brockton Villa
$ • Continental
- **1235 Coast Blvd., La Jolla**
- **(858) 454-7393**

Although the food is equally good at lunch and dinner, breakfast is what draws the big crowds to this quaint, century-old beach cottage overlooking La Jolla Cove and the Pacific Ocean. Wander in around breakfast time, put your name on the list, then help yourself to a cup of coffee and a newspaper and lounge around the deck with the rest of the crowd waiting to be seated.

Once you're seated either inside or on the outside terrace, choose from some amazing breakfast dishes, like steamers, Greek-style eggs scrambled with feta cheese, or banana pancakes dotted with big banana chunks. Orange French toast is a keeper, too. The lunch menu features shrimp and chicken salads, and at dinner, don't miss the California seafood stew. Breakfast and lunch are served daily; dinner is served Tuesday through Sunday.

George's Cafe & Ocean Terrace
$-$$ • Contemporary California
- **1250 Prospect St., La Jolla**
- **(858) 454-4244**

This is al fresco dining at its best, on a rooftop terrace with an unimpeded view of La Jolla Cove, and memorable California cuisine to boot. Lots of pastas are offered, like the fettucine with rock shrimp in garlic Parmesan sauce. Seafood offerings include a pan-seared king salmon that's served with couscous. Or try the deep-fried prawns accompanied by sweet potato cakes.

The lunchtime menu has great sandwiches and salads, but the star is the quesadilla with spicy-hot Jamaican chicken. The Ocean Terrace is open daily for lunch and dinner, and has late-night dining on Fridays and Saturdays.

Marine Room
$$$$ • French
• 2000 Spindrift Dr., La Jolla
• (858) 459-7222

Venerable is the most appropriate word to describe the Marine Room. It has withstood the test of time, reinventing itself a number of times over the years to appeal to new generations of diners. In addition to fine French cuisine, the restaurant is noted for its ocean view. And it's not an ordinary ocean view, we might add. It's right on the water, and during storms, waves often crash against the triple-thick glass windows facing the ocean, putting on a show of Mother Nature's ferocity.

But back to the food. Sample a juicy veal chop baked with an airy Parmesan soufflé, or rack of lamb in an exquisite mustard-pistachio crust. Or you might try a starter of greens tossed with pecans and Asian pears, rounded out with bits of goat cheese. The Marine Room is open for lunch Monday through Saturday and brunch on Sunday. Dinner is served nightly.

St. James Bar & Restaurant
$$-$$$ • Californian
• 4370 La Jolla Village Dr., La Jolla
• (858) 453-6650

Tucked away on the ground floor of a high-rise office building, it's an unlikely place for a restaurant, but patrons have found it to their liking. The elegant interior includes a massive wooden bar that has become a casual after-work meeting place. If, after happy hour, you're hungry but don't feel like moving too far, you can dine in the bar from the same menu offered in the main dining room.

From opening day, the standout on the menu has been the superb mussel bisque with puff pastry. Burrowing your way through the flaky pastry is a treat in itself, but the creamy, savory bisque that awaits below its golden crown is the real treasure. Other menu item fare just as well, like the Maryland crab cakes with corn mango chutney, or the Pacific salmon teriyaki served with spinach and oriental rice. Meat dishes, including a rack of lamb or a veal chop with a Chardonnay and sorrel sauce, are equally tempting.

An extensive wine list complements the full bar. Lunch is served Monday through Friday, and the restaurant is open for dinner Monday through Saturday.

Sante
$$$-$$$$ • Italian
• 7811 Herschel Ave., La Jolla
• (858) 454-1315

Sante offers several options for diners: See and be seen in the gracious dining room, or enjoy an intimate tête-à-tête in one of two sidewalk patios or at one of the few tables tucked away in the bar. Wherever you choose to dine, rest assured the chef is determined to make you happy. The fare is classic northern Italian, ranging from antipasti, flavorful soups, bitter salads and beautifully composed pastas to game, veal and fresh seafood.

One characteristic that distinguishes Sante is that the chef will happily compose a dish on the spot to suit your taste just in case it doesn't appear on the menu. The night we dined at Sante, we were the fortunate beneficiaries of a spur-of-the-moment, divinely inspired risotto with shellfish. The bar is a comfortable and happy spot for before or after-dinner drinks. Sante is open for lunch Monday through Friday, and for dinner nightly.

Saska's
$$ • American
• 3768 Mission Blvd., San Diego
• (858) 488-7311

Let's say you've pushed the day into nighttime, it's midnight and you haven't eaten yet. Where do you go to get dinner other than a "Grand Slam" at Denny's? Since the mid-1950s Saska's has been the solution for late-night diners looking for a steak, a lobster tail or even a good plate of pasta. Saska's stays open until 2 AM during the week and until 3 AM Fridays and Saturdays, adding first-rate breakfast items to the menu at 11 PM.

Even if you tend to dine at more conventional hours, it's worth a trip to Mission Beach to experience this legendary restaurant. The food is consistently good, especially the teriyaki steak and chicken, and there's usually a member of the Saska family behind the bar or roaming about to make you feel at home. Saska's serves lunch and dinner daily and brunch on Saturdays and Sundays.

Thee Bungalow
$$-$$$ • Continental
• 4996 W. Point Loma Blvd., San Diego
• (619) 224-2884

Make a point of visiting this longtime resident of Ocean Beach. Owner-chef Ed Moore caters to his customers, who are extremely loyal, changing the menu and prices constantly to adapt to their tastes and moods. One dish that is almost always available is the roast duck, and for good reason. It's superb, as are the fresh fish dishes, innovative soups and veal creations.

You can dine in the dining room, formal in construction but relaxed in mood, or in the outdoor patio. Watch for value-priced midweek and early-bird dinners. Thee Bungalow is always trying something different and fun, like the recent recreation of the last meal on the Titanic. Dinner is served nightly.

Mission Valley/Inland

Adams Avenue Grill
$$ • Global • 2201 Adams Ave., San Diego
• (619) 298-8440

Whatever your favorite meal is, you're likely to find it on the menu here. Everything from Thai to Italian to American to Southwest is represented. The mystery is how they all come out so well. The angel hair pasta with roma tomatoes, garlic, basil and balsamic vinegar is finished with a splash of burgundy that gives this traditional dish a nice twist. Equally pleasing is the Thai salad, a mixture of snow peas, Napa cabbage and mixed greens tossed with roasted peanuts and a spicy peanut dressing.

Although offered as an appetizer, the Southwest black bean soup served with shrimp and jalapeño quesadilla makes a full lunch.

Desserts include a chocoholic's delight, a six-layer fudge cake that's more than a pound per slice. Plan on a trip to the gym if you finish the whole thing. Lunch and dinner are served Tuesday through Sunday.

Canyon Cafe
$-$$ • Southwestern
• 1640 Camino del Rio No., San Diego
• (619) 296-2600

Tucked away at the eastern end of Mission Valley Center (we've covered this shopping mecca in our Shopping chapter) is this outstanding restaurant that specializes in regional Southwestern cuisine that is so good that the place is usually packed. Fortunately, it's quite large, with two indoor dining rooms and a big outdoor terrace, so there's rarely a wait.

One Insider keeps coming back for the portobello mushroom sandwich that's served with melted cheese and a tangy sauce. We lean toward the chicken and goat cheese quesadilla, a combination of flavors that keeps us smiling. Appetizers are out of the ordinary, including a tortilla soup with a spicy tomato base, crisp tortillas and melted cheese. Even if you forego dessert, you'll still be given a sweet farewell: a tiny roll of white chocolate studded with pecans. Canyon Cafe is open for lunch and dinner daily.

Kensington Grill
$$ • American
• 4055 Adams Ave., San Diego
• (619) 281-4014

The owners bill their restaurant as "New American cuisine," and while we might be hard pressed to define it, we don't care. Whatever it is, it's great. This is a neighborhood restaurant with a large and lively bar on one side and a smallish dining room on the other. A few tables line the sidewalk for outdoor dining.

We strongly suggest you start your meal with a delectable mango and brie

INSIDERS' TIP

Many restaurants can package full meals for take-out service. Call ahead and pick up your order on the way to the beach or an outdoor concert.

quesadilla. It sounds unusual, but it's sinfully good. Then move on to such dishes as grilled salmon or a remarkably good gumbo brimming with shellfish. You can even get a burger here if you're searching for comfort food. Dinner is served nightly.

Prego
$$ • Italian
- **1370 Frazee Rd., San Diego**
- **(619) 294-4700**

As you approach Prego through the sunlit courtyard, you'll get the feeling that you're walking into a large Italian villa. Once inside, the sights and sounds of regional Italian cuisine being prepared in the open kitchen will get your mouth watering. Begin with the fresh garlic-rosemary bread baked in Prego's wood-fired oven, then graze through such tasty antipasti as the grilled radicchio, endive, eggplant and portobello mushrooms accompanied by prosciutto-wrapped goat cheese.

Chicken, seafood, pork chops and steak all get the Prego treatment, and be sure to ask about the risotto of the day, a creamy arborio rice dish that changes according to the chef's whim. Lunch is served Monday through Friday, and dinner is served nightly.

Seau's: The Restaurant
$$ • Californian
- **1640 Camino del Rio No., San Diego**
- **(619) 291-7328**

San Diego's own Junior Seau, star defensive back for the San Diego Chargers, opened this restaurant to immediate acclaim. Junior's aim was to have an all-out sports bar that was all things to all people. He's darn well done it, too. Food is not secondary here. It ranges from pizzas, salads and pastas to sandwiches and grilled fresh fish. And most menu items are quite good, especially the Greek salad, a toss of greens, feta cheese, Greek olives and tomatoes dressed with a tangy herb vinaigrette.

Of course, baseball, basketball, football and every other sport on earth is continuously broadcast from TVs placed everywhere. There's a full bar, and cigar aficionados have their very own lounge for an after-dinner stogie. Ventilators keep the room from filling with smoke. Located in Mission Valley Center, Seau's is open for lunch and dinner daily.

Trophy's Sports Grill
$ • Californian
- **7510 Hazard Center Dr., San Diego**
- **(619) 296-9600**
- **4282 Esplanade Ct., San Diego**
- **(858) 450-1400**
- **5500 Grossmont Ctr. Dr., La Mesa**
- **(619) 698-2900**

We can't mention one sports bar/restaurant without giving equal space to the other standout in town. Trophy's predates Seau's, and it has held its own against the young upstart by sticking to its tried-and-true formula. The range of menu items is predictable — pizzas, pastas, burgers and sandwiches — but you'll find some unusual variations here that are quite good, like the pizza with artichoke hearts and bacon.

Trophy's is a kid-friendly place, providing a place mat and crayons at each table setting. This tends to bring out the kid in most adults, too. Wide screen TVs are in the bar, and smaller ones are sprinkled throughout the rest of the restaurant. Trophy's is open for lunch and dinner daily.

Old Town/Point Loma

Great Wall Cafe
$-$$ • Chinese
- **2543 Congress St., San Diego**
- **(619) 291-9478**

Mexican food has long been the dominant force in Old Town, but that's starting to change. One of the most welcome deviations is the Great Wall Cafe, where you can enjoy good-quality Chinese meals on a wide, outdoor terrace that surrounds a rather small indoor dining room. We usually opt for outdoors to sample such treats as minced chicken in lettuce leaves and Szechuan dumplings that are on the spicy side.

If you like a taste of everything, try Buddha's Jump Over the Wall, a hot pot full of meat, seafood and vegetables. Or if you really want to go all out, we can heartily recommend the Peking Duck. Lunch and dinner are served daily.

Photo: San Diego Convention and Visitors Bureau

Many San Diego restaurants feature fresh lobster, like the ones in this fisherman's catch.

Old Town Mexican Cafe
$ • Mexican
• 2489 San Diego Ave., San Diego
• (619) 297-4330

No trip to San Diego is complete without stopping for lunch or dinner at "Old Town Mex," as Insiders call it. You'll be hard pressed to tell the locals from the tourists here, because everyone is too intent on the lively conversation and the steaming plates of Mexican food. There's usually a wait, so a good place to hang out (if the bar is full) is on the front sidewalk, where you can watch fresh tortillas being made by hand.

You'll find the usual combination plates of enchiladas, tacos and burritos, but the dish that keeps everyone coming back is the carnitas. You'll understand why when a plate of roasted, shredded and seasoned pork is placed before you with its accompanying hot tortillas, avocado, onions, tomatoes and cilantro. Warm chips and salsa

are served with every meal. Breakfast, lunch and dinner are served daily.

El Agave
$$-$$$ • Nouveau Mexican
• 2304 San Diego Ave., San Diego
• (619) 220-0692

We wandered into this place looking for the Italian restaurant that formerly occupied the premises, took one look at the more than 200 varieties of tequila lining the bar, and decided to stay. It was a good decision. Sipping tequila is an art form here. Once you make your choice, it's served in a miniature carafe and is accompanied by a small glass of sangrita, a cool mixture of tomato juice and lime intended to cool the fire of the tequila.

Moving on to the menu produces even nicer surprises. This is food with a Mexican influence, but there are none of the combo plates with rice and beans typically found

---

INSIDERS' TIP

Although it's been a few years since San Diego rationed water (because of the severe drought conditions), you may still have to order water with your meals.

in Mexican restaurants. A good way to sample a variety of appetizers is to order the sampler, which includes tiny quesadillas, tacos and tamales, all with unusual but delicious regional Mexican fillings. The watercress salad is also a star. Peppery watercress is quickly wilted in bacon drippings and served with warm tortillas in which to wrap it. Entrees include a variety of seafood, and chicken with several variations of molé sauces. If you've never tasted mole, we strongly recommend it. It is a complex sauce that combines dozens of flavors and ranges from mild to fiery. Lunch and dinner are served every day but Tuesday.

Pizza Nova
$$ • Californian
• 5120 N. Harbor Dr., San Diego
• (619) 226-0268
• 3955 Fifth Ave., San Diego
• (619) 296-6682
• 8650 Genesee Ave., La Jolla
• (858) 458-9525
• 5500 Grossmont Center Dr., La Mesa
• (619) 589-7222

When the first Pizza Nova opened on the harbor in Point Loma, it didn't take Insiders long to figure out that it served a multitude of purposes. It's a great restaurant for casual dining, for dates, for the whole family, for a quick bite or for a leisurely meal. Other locations began opening around town, and they all have become fixtures in their respective neighborhoods.

Pizzas are innovative, like the ever-popular Thai Chicken — ginger-marinated chicken breast, green onions, bean sprouts, carrot slivers, cilantro and roasted peanuts. The chopped salad almost overflows with generous chunks of salami, fontina cheese, turkey breast and tomatoes. And the sinfully good fettucine with prawns and prosciutto in a garlic cream sauce spiced with crushed red peppers and topped with Parmesan has been a menu mainstay for years.

Pizza Nova is open for lunch and dinner daily. All menu items are available for take-out, and delivery is available to most locations.

Point Loma Seafood
$ • Seafood
• 2805 Emerson St., San Diego
• (619) 223-1109

Enter Point Loma Seafood, make your way to the counter and prepare to be dazzled by the display of fresh seafood for sale by the pound. Then remind yourself that the same seafood you see before you is the main ingredient in wonderful sandwiches, salads, soups and platters of fried fish served with coleslaw and french fries. Sushi and ceviche appetizers fly out the door every day, as do the shrimp and crab Louie cocktails.

Favorite sandwiches are the imaginative crab cake sandwich and the squid sandwich on sourdough bread. Several outdoor tables are situated harborside, but they become extremely crowded around lunchtime. So if you have a picnic in mind, this is a great place to stop. Don't miss the large selection of smoked fish. Combine it with some fresh sourdough bread, and you'll have a tasty snack. Lunch and dinner are available daily, but closing hours are early — around 7 PM.

North County Coastal

Al's Cafe
$ • American
• 795 Carlsbad Village Dr., Carlsbad
• (760) 729-5448

Here's an old-fashioned, downtown cafe where you can enjoy breakfast and lunch inside or beneath an umbrella at one of the tables set out on a quiet side street. There are specials served every day. The all-you-can-eat fish and chips (for about $6) is a bargain. It's about seven blocks east of the

Carlsbad shopping district of antique stores (mentioned in our Shopping chapter) and in the heart of downtown Carlsbad.

Angelo's Burgers
$ • American
• **621 N. Coast Hwy., Oceanside**
• **(760) 757-5161**
• **1050 S. Coast Hwy., Oceanside**
• **(760) 757-4064**
• **2035 S. Coast Hwy., Oceanside**
• **(760) 967-9911**
• **608 S. Coast Hwy., Oceanside**
• **(760) 943-9115**

Angelo's has been a favorite beach restaurant hangout for Insiders since the mid-1970s and continues to serve up great big burgers and mountains of fries for under $4. The quality and price are hard to beat. This is a no-frills burger joint (that starts the day with large breakfast burritos and other morning specials). You order at the counter and spread your food on plastic tables. You can dine in or outside.

The gyros sandwiches are excellent and under $3. Hungry for a giant hot pastrami sandwich? Angelo's is your place. Try the homemade onion rings and zucchini strips, deep fried but cooked in cholesterol-free corn oil. Sure, you can't eat this way all the time, but hey, once in a while is fun, and doubly so if you're on vacation, it's the middle of the week or you need good fast food. All locations are open daily for breakfast, lunch and dinner.

Bellefleur Winery & Restaurant
$$$ • California, Southwestern and Mediterranean
• **5610 Paseo Del Norte, Carlsbad**
• **(760) 603-1919**

This restaurant is a find and it's convenient too, right off Interstate 5 and Palomar Airport Road, in Carlsbad. It's a half-block walk north of the Carlsbad Company Stores shopping center (see our Shopping chapter). The food is ultra-fresh tasting and seasoned in a way that might make your tastebuds ask: "Where has Bellefleur been all our lives!"

Service is fabulous. Lunch prices are very modest, but bring your credit card for dinner if you plan to include an appetizer, drinks, dessert and a cordial or sherry to end your experience.

At a recent lunch we had the fresh salmon burger with watercress, lemon pepper aioli and quinoa salad, all for about $9, and the presentation of the ample portions was done with a master's hand. Dinner choices, also luscious and stunning, range from certified Angus beef to sea bass with Maui Onion Risotto. The wine is excellent and priced at $5 for a glass of the Bellefleur Winery brands (which we highly recommend). Bellefleur Winery, for your information, is located in Fallbrook, and has won numerous awards and recognition. This Carlsbad restaurant is open daily, except Monday, for lunch and dinner.

Budapest Express
$$ • Hungarian cuisine
• **315 S. Hwy. 101, Solana Beach**
• **(858) 259-4465**

Take a culinary expedition to Hungary without leaving North County Coastal at this Insiders' favorite ethnic eatery. The decor tries to be European, but that's tough since the restaurant is just blocks from the ocean and the fragrance of the breeze is sweetly North County.

Food is rich, savory and plentiful here and Insiders say that the choices are hard to make since everything is great. We liked the Budapest Platter. It has stuffed cabbage, red cabbage, breaded mushrooms, Wiener schnitzel, gypsy steak and Hungarian sausage. Yes, it's for two. Unless you're big eaters, you'll have some to take home. Budapest Express is open for lunch and dinner and reservations are recommend.

Bully's
$$ • American
• **1404 Camino Del Mar, Del Mar**
• **(858) 755-1660**

Want a place you can count on every time for good food? Bully's is your answer. This prime rib and steakhouse has been a tradition in North County Coastal since the early 1970s and deserves many repeat visits. They have great steaks, fresh seafood, ribs, succulent chicken, plump sandwiches and a children's menu too.

We always consider ordering other salads and then our hearts (and taste buds) are won over with the classic Caesar salads, either plain or loaded with shrimp or chicken.

Bully's is popular in the summer months, but you can sit outdoors or in the pub and sip and wait. Bully's is open for breakfast, lunch and dinner daily as is its "sister" Bully's at 5755 La Jolla Blvd., in La Jolla.

California Bistro
$$ • California Cuisine
- **Four Seasons Resorts Aviara**
- **7100 Four Seasons Pt., Carlsbad**
- **(760) 603-6800, (800) 332-3442**

The California Bistro is open for breakfast starting early in the day and, as you might expect from a top-rated hotel, everything is fresh and created to please. (See our chapters on Spas and Resorts and Golf for more about the Four Seasons Resorts Aviara.)

Breakfast might start with smoked salmon with chive scrambled eggs on brioche toast (for about $11.00) or you could go lighter with pink papaya and a huge muffin. We highly recommend the honey sunflower toast and the chocolate rolls. There's a wonderful buffet available during breakfast and lunch.

If you're visiting the California Bistro for lunch, you cannot go wrong with the "Bistro Dishes." They range from Spicy Ginger Shrimp with shiitake, snow peas, bean sprouts and egg noodles (about $14) to Mom's Meatloaf, served with green beans, buttermilk-smashed potatoes with gravy and button mushrooms (at about $13). Once you make it past the scrumptious starters, dinner could be Cavatappi Pasta with banana peppers, grilled cilantro chicken with mild chipotle chili sauce ($13.50), oven-baked sea bass with a root vegetable vinaigrette, or Braised Lamb Shank Redemption, served with French lentils and sautéed summer squash (about $15) will also tempt you.

On Friday nights there's a seafood buffet that defies description because the choices are enormous. At $26 for adults, it's a bargain. On Sundays there is an extravagant Sunday brunch. It's $28 for adults and $14 for children younger than 12. The restaurant's menu is marked with choices that are lower in calories, cholesterol, sodium and fat so if you're visiting and enjoying the spa program, you can eat healthy foods. The California Bistro is open daily for breakfast, lunch and dinner.

Chin's Szechwan Restaurant
$$ • Szechwan
- **2959 Madison Ave., Carlsbad**
- **(760) 434-7117**
- **1506 Encinitas Blvd., Encinitas**
- **(760) 753-3903**
- **4140 Oceanside Blvd., Oceanside**
- **(760) 631-4808**

While Chin's has a lot of locations, it's a San Diego exclusive and some of the best Szechwan we've had. Actually we were torn about including our favorite Chinese eatery because, by golly, it's already really popular.

The decor is what you'd expect from nearly any Chinese restaurant, but the food is better. Vegetable dishes are hot, crispy and good. Service is excellent and strangely enough, each time we've been there, seating is possible the moment we walk in the door. Maybe it's just our Insiders' good fortune or because we've come in before the dinner crowd. Chin's has the prerequisite "family" style dinners and early-bird specials, too. Service is excellent. It's open daily for lunch and dinner. You can get take-out if you're headed to the beach or an outdoor concert.

Coyote Bar & Grill
$$ • American
- **300 Carlsbad Village Dr., Carlsbad**
- **(760) 729-4695**

This hot spot in downtown Carlsbad is mentioned in our Nightlife chapter, but it's more than a place to meet and mingle. Insiders come here for American food with a Southwestern flavor. At lunch, there's the working crowd from nearby offices and the Palomar Airport industrial area. At dinner, it's families and then couples. The couples often stay for the live entertainment and party atmosphere. Food is grilled over a wood fire. Salads are fresh and lively. You can eat inside or, as we recommend, on the patio. Open for lunch and dinner daily.

East of...

$ • Global Cuisine
- **3870 Valley Centre Dr., San Diego**
- **(858) 259-3278**

In the Del Mar Heights area of North County Coastal, this cafe's menu has been inspired by the travels of its owners Mark Spanjian and Craig Wiese. Years ago they took a 40-foot sailboat and traveled the ocean. Today, they have one of the hottest cafes in the area where you can sample recipes they gathered during their travels. East of... features rolled sandwiches, elaborate salads and sizzling meat combinations such as the shawarma (a tightly rolled, hand-held sandwich filled with the marinated meat of your choice and roasted vegetables). Take our advice and try it. Sit inside in the simple cafe or on the patio. The cafe is open for lunch and dinner.

Fish House Vera Cruz

$$ • Seafood
- **417 Carlsbad Village Dr., Carlsbad**
- **(760) 434-6777**

Just three blocks from the beach and three blocks south of the Coaster station and Carlsbad's antique stores (see our Shopping chapter), Fish House Vera Cruz is one of the best seafood restaurants on the planet. Fish is grilled to perfection over mesquite wood and is always succulent and fresh. They have a standard menu and catch-of-the-day choices, too. If you're from out of the area, the thought of eating grilled shark might be a bit much. Get over it if you want some really great fish and a great price, because shark has been a mainstay on San Diego's menu for years. The Sopa de Pescado (a spicy soup loaded with bite-sized pieces of delicate fish, tomatoes, carrots and potatoes) is served with lemon, and is so luscious that the kitchen sometimes runs out. No wonder Fish House Vera Cruz is popular.

If you're determined to eat here, come at an off time, such as mid afternoon or just before the lunchtime crowd to avoid a long wait. They don't accept reservations. Unfortunately this "find" isn't much of a secret to Insiders and folks come from Orange County, Riverside County and throughout our county to eat here. Like its "sister" at 1020 San Marcos Blvd., San Marcos, (760) 744-8000, the restaurant is open daily for lunch and dinner.

Fidel's

$$ • Mexican
- **3003 Carlsbad Blvd., Carlsbad**
- **(760) 729-0903**
- **607 Valley Ave., Solana Beach**
- **(858) 755-5292**

If you've ever fantasized about the perfect Mexican food — hot, fresh, and abundant—Fidel's is your ticket to taste-bud heaven. It happens to be our Insiders' favorite. And we're tough to please when it comes to Mexican food.

The restaurants have been in business since the 1940s and both locations are popular. On a Saturday or Sunday, especially during the summer, you probably will wish that they took reservations; but they don't, so have a seltzer or glass of wine on the patio and be patient. You'll be rewarded.

Here's a tip: Come before the dinner crowd. As a matter of fact, come for happy hour when the drinks are more reasonable and the appetizers plentiful. Lunch prices are affordable and in the $5 to $8 range; dinner is a bit more pricey, but still easy on the wallet. Ask for the salsa fresca with any meal. It's an explosive combo of onion, chili, cilantro and tomato and made on the spot just to thrill your taste buds.

Try the tender, piquant carne asada or the Tostada Suprema, which is a massive plate of shredded chicken (or beef) loaded down with guacamole, olives, tomatoes, beans and lettuce. The Carlsbad location is about one block from the ocean, two blocks from the Carlsbad shopping dis-

---

INSIDERS' TIP

Saving calories so you can indulge in dessert? Have the food server bring your salad with dressing on the side or substitute lemon as a low-calorie choice.

trict, and four blocks from the Coaster station. (See our Shopping chapter for more on this location.) The Solana Beach Fidel's is about 2 miles north of the Del Mar Fairgrounds (See our Attractions chapter). Both locations are open for lunch and dinner and have happy hour and early-bird specials.

Greek Corner Cafe
$$ • Greek
• 2939 Carlsbad Blvd., Carlsbad
• (760) 603-9672
• 1845 Marron Rd., Carlsbad • (760) 434-5557

If you love Greek food and think you've had the best on the planet, you might want to give that a second thought once you've tried the Greek Corner Cafe. Everything we've had there is beyond delicious — it makes you want to sing out in happiness, and possibly never want to leave. Seriously, the meals, such as the gyros plate for two, are bargains. Most meals are priced in the $10 to $19 range. They have low-fat and vegetarian dishes too. You can dine inside or on the patio. You can't rush this experience because you'll want to savor every bite. Open for lunch and dinner, you may love the Greek Corner Cafe as much as we do and wonder if it's wise to tell another Insider about this find.

Greek Village
$$ • Greek
• 6030 Paseo Del Norte, Carlsbad
• (760) 603-9672

This is the place if you want Greek food and want to hear the oud while you're dining. At the Greek Village, off Palomar Airport Drive and I-5, the combination sizzles, as does the food. (The restaurant is just two blocks south of the Carlsbad Company Stores, mentioned in our Shopping chapter.) Specialties of the house and favorites of Insiders are the souvlaki, moussaka and fettucini ala Greka. You can't go wrong with the gyros platter for only $9.95.

The Greek Village starts serving up food at 10 AM daily with breakfast choices that include loukaniko and gyros to mundane stuff like a big farm-style breakfast of eggs, bacon, and toast. Lunch is a smaller version of dinner and hot and cold sandwiches. You can

dine inside or on the patio. Senior discounts are available. Call about the free Greek dancing lessons and evening musical performances. The Greek Village is open daily for breakfast, lunch and dinner.

Jake's Del Mar
$$ • Seafood
• 1660 Coast Blvd., Del Mar
• (858) 755-2002

Here's a classic, waterfront restaurant and a sure thing if you're hungry for seafood and atmosphere. The view, right on the ocean, is impossible to beat. Take a hint, and call for a reservation or be disappointed with a long wait. It's a good party place and draws in a fun-loving Friday night crowd. But after you've partied, stay for the Asian seafood cocktail followed by the tortilla-crusted halibut with avocado/mango salsa. Open for lunch and dinner daily and on Sunday for brunch.

Mille Fleurs Restaurant
$$$$ • French
• 6009 Paseo Delicias, Rancho Santa Fe
• (858) 756-3085

Here's the benchmark for all French restaurants in the county. Mille Fleurs, in the upscale area of Rancho Santa Fe, attracts national attention and constantly wins culinary awards. It's also the place where notables, celebrities and the wealthy gather when they want superb service and great food. People become hooked on Mille Fleurs and often try to think up special occasions so they can come here to celebrate.

The cuisine is fine dining at its best and the extraordinary wine list (with prices to match) makes perfect sense. Open daily for dinner only. By the way, for this dining experience you'll want to change out of the T-shirt and shorts and slip into a blazer and slacks.

Pacific Breeze Cafe
$$ • California Eclectic
• 1555 Camino Del Mar, Del Mar
• (858) 509-9147

It's quaint. It has great food. It's popular and it's in downtown Del Mar. You'll want to eat tacos, salads, baked goods, soups and light entrees on the patio while you sip some home brew. An Insiders' favorite at Pacific Breeze Cafe are the barbecued fish tacos, followed by a margarita. Open for breakfast and dinner, the Pacific Breeze is conveniently located in the Del Mar Plaza (see our Shopping chapter).

Pizza Port
$$ • Pizza
• 571 Carlsbad Village Dr., Carlsbad
• (760) 720-7007
• 135 N. Hwy. 101, Solana Beach
• (858) 481-7332

Here's where you'll find praiseworthy pizza that's a cut above the most chi-chi pizza's you've had. Better yet, they brew on-site and provide just the right micro-brewed beer to go with your choice.

Decor is of the wooden picnic-table variety with big screen televisions flashing sports, and the music is sometimes loud and the conversation even louder. We've seen people hang around outside waiting for tables.

Yes, the Pizza Port restaurants are popular. We've talked about Pizza Port in our Nightlife chapter so if you want the scoop on what happens at night, read that entry. Pizza specials and microbrew choices vary and sometimes they sponsor beer-tasting contests in which the public can participate. The Pizza Port pizzerias are open daily for lunch and dinner.

Prontos' Gourmet Market
$ • Italian
• 2812 Roosevelt St., Carlsbad
• (760) 434-2644

Here's an eating jewel that's tucked away in the heart of the village of Carlsbad, near the antique shopping district (see our chapter on Shopping). Once you stop here, you may not want to tell any friends for fear it will become crowded.

Sandwiches are stuffed with meats and vegetables, prices are easy on the wallet, and everything is fresh and tasty. You get choices of breads and side dishes with each sandwich and there are salads too. Most folks take out and get back to work, but there's a shady patio where you can dine outdoors.

Prontos' is open for breakfast and lunch every day except Sunday and stays open late enough in the afternoon so you can stop and pick up a prepared meal, like the lasagna, or a sandwich for supper on the way home from work.

St. Germain's Cafe
$ • European Sidewalk Cafe
• 1010 S. Coast Hwy. 101, Encinitas
• (760) 753-5411

It's impossible to pinpoint a "type" for this quaint cafe set in Encinitas; locals just go there because the food is always wonderful. Here eggs Benedict are served all day long and at a reasonable $4.95. You can also get Eggs Acapulco (topped with zesty Spanish sauce) and a dozen other breakfast varieties. All food is served with fresh fruit or their yummy cafe potatoes. Belgian waffles, sandwiches and soups are always good choices, too. Open for breakfast and lunch each day.

Sandbar Cafe
$$ • American
• 3878 Carlsbad Blvd., Carlsbad
• (760) 729-8561

Here's a beach hangout that has dancing and entertainment in the evenings and good food all the time. Be sure to check our Nightlife chapter for more on this club and others where you can dance to live music and have dinner too. The Sandbar's menu has an extensive seafood array featuring shrimp, calamari, fish tacos, shark burgers and oysters, along with burgers, sandwiches and salads.

The location is spectacular. It's straight across the street from the ocean and you do not have to pay extra for the sunsets. They come with the territory. If you want to dance and party at the club side of the cafe, there's a $3 cover charge. The Sandbar is open for lunch and dinner every day.

Stratford Court Cafe
$$ • American
• 1307 Stratford Ct., Del Mar
• (858) 792-7433

Stratford Court Cafe is nestled in old Del Mar and serves up home-baked favorites, over-stuffed sandwiches, crispy salads and something they call the Wake Up

Call. It's a double espresso, Ghirardelli chocolate and fresh, nonfat vanilla yogurt that always gets high marks from choco-holics. We love the Garden Wrap, available at lunch. It's a rolled sandwich filled to the brim with sun-dried tomatoes, cucumber, red onion, sprouts, low-fat cream cheese and Parmesan peppercorn. Still unde-cided? How about the Blast? It's bacon, lettuce, fresh apple butter, and smoked turkey on a rolled sandwich.

The Stratford Court Cafe has dining inside and on the sidewalk and it's open for break-fast and until the mid-afternoon for lunch. Try to head here during the times when working folks are working and you won't have to wait long for a table.

Sydney's Australian Grille
$$ • American/Australian
• Doubletree Hotel in Del Mar
11915 El Camino Real, San Diego
• (858) 481-5900

Forget airfare to the Land Down Under. Here at Syndey's Australian Grille you can have some prawns from the barbie or emu skewers (marinated then broiled emu filets served with apricot chutney). The signature dish is spiced salmon with grapefruit mint sauce. An Insid-ers' favorite is the Tasmanian tournedos (twin petite fillet of beef covered in a wild mush-room glaze). If your tastes are more ordinary than emu, try the Outback salmon salad or the Bondi Beach fish and chips. Open for lunch and dinner, the Grille has a children's menu and happy-hour specials.

That Pizza Place
$ • Pizza and more
• 2622 El Camino Real, Carlsbad
• (760) 434-3171
• 1810 Oceanside Blvd., Oceanside
• (760) 757-6212

That Pizza Place restaurants are neighbor-hood pizza eateries (that serve salads and subs too) and have live entertainment on some eve-nings. Call the numbers above for more infor-mation on groups and times. They've been in North County Coastal since 1979 and are proud of the local connection. The places are the gathering holes for commu-nity sports teams; they flock in after games.

As you might expect the atmosphere is super-casual and no one will notice if your baseball shirt has grass stains on it or your soccer uniform is caked with mud. Why you might even get a round of applause.

The house special pizza is pepperoni, ham, salami, mushrooms, olives, bell peppers and sausage — you have to ask for ancho-vies. It's always served up hot and fresh. We think the best things to eat at That Pizza Place are the Roll'N The Dough sandwiches. They're like a pizza burrito. For about $3 you can even get the Kitchen Sink, a com-bination that has about everything on it. If that's not enough, there are special lunch deals, like a small pizza, large soft drink and a trip to the always-fresh salad bar for about $4.50. You can dine in (with picnic-table elegance) or take it out. For a de-scription of That Pizza Place at night, check out our Nightlife chapter. The restaurants are open for lunch and dinner daily.

Trattoria Postano
$$ • Italian
• 2171 San Elijo Ave., • Cardiff
• (760) 632-0111

Welcoming and relaxing is the atmosphere of this cafe just a few blocks from the ocean in Cardiff and Cardiff State Beach (see our Beaches and Watersports chapter). There's an excellent salad selection; a tangy citrus sauce graces the warm Maine lobster salad priced at less than $13. You'll find seafood, a slew of pasta choices and vegetarian specialties, too. The decor is California/Italian, crisp and clean with great service. Lunch and dinner are served daily.

Vivace
$$$ • International/California cuisine
• Four Seasons Resorts Aviara
• 7100 Four Seasons Pt., Carlsbad
• (760) 603-6800, (800) 332-3442

The decor of this popular restaurant is so inviting (some tables have fat easy chairs and sofas rather than straight backed, restaurant-style chairs), you might try to stay forever. When the food arrives you'll be dazzled. Oh, such a display — it's art that makes you want to savor every bite. It's one of those eating experiences where you can linger over your food, loving the antipasto and appetizers, adoring the soups, diving into the main courses and cherishing every bite of the dessert. As you make reservations on a beautiful summer evening, ask for a table overlooking the balcony, the lagoon and the Pacific beyond.

To say that Vivace is a respectable restaurant is like saying a Jaguar is a nice car — this is great stuff. Once you've treated yourself to dinner at Vivace, you may be too spoiled for other restaurants. If you're a seafood lover, try the charred mint-marinated swordfish in basil-infused oil (about $22) or the seafood cioppino (a blend of lobster, shrimp, scallops, clams, mussels and white fish for about $27). It's impossible to go wrong with the oregano-crusted rack of lamb with capponata (about $26) or the wood-grilled veal chop with baby artichokes, pearl onions, stewed cannellini beans in a rosemary veal reduction (about $28).

Vegetarian Insiders say you have to try the oven-baked vegetables with wild mushrooms, scented with fresh herbs and garlic olive oil (about $15). All desserts are $6.50. If you have room, try the Warm Bitter Sweet Chocolate Melt over cranberry ice cream. Vivace is open daily for dinner only.

To read more of what to do at this resort, please read our chapters on Golf and Spas and Resorts.

North County Inland

The Barbeque Pit
$ • American
• 727 Center Dr., #119, San Marcos
• (760) 432-0177

Since 1947, the Barbeque Pit has been serving up tender, succulent choices of carved-to-order beef, ham and rib dinners that bring customers back again and again. Try the chicken, or if you're a hot-sausage fan, you can't go wrong with their spicy choice.

On Friday's the specialty is shredded pork, not just on a sandwich, but piled high on a toasted bun. Side dishes include macaroni and potato salads, coleslaw and French fries. The Barbeque Pit has good grub, the decor is without pretension and it is open for lunch and dinner.

Centre City Cafe
$ • American
• 2680 Escondido Blvd., Escondido
• (760) 489-6011

"Homestyle" is the best word to describe the food choices at this cafe, which is in the heart of Escondido. Prices are on the moderate side and the selection is vast. The menu leans toward Southwestern-style cuisine. For dessert, try the hot fudge brownie smothered in ice cream — it's easily enough for three people. There are early-bird specials, too. Centre City Cafe is open for breakfast, lunch and dinner.

Chieu-Anh
$$ • Vietnamese
• 16769 Bernardo Center Dr., Rancho Bernardo • (858) 485-1231

Chieu-Anh has to be included in a culinary tour of North County Inland because the foods are fresh and combinations unique even for this cuisine. It's tucked into a shopping mall and you might walk past without hardly giving it a second thought, except for the fragrances emanating from the eatery. We love the specialty of feather-light Vietnamese crepe filled with grilled chicken and shrimp. There's a tangy and sour soup with tamarind flavor that's excellent, and the shrimp on sugar cane is a smoky, savory delight. The restaurant is open Tuesday through Friday for lunch and Tuesday through Saturday for dinner.

Chin's Szechwan Restaurant
$$ • Szechuan
• 631 S. Rancho Santa Fe Rd., San Marcos • (760) 591-9648

While Chin's has a lot of locations — there are three in North County Coastal — it's a San Diego exclusive. If you have the hots for Szechuan, you'll be in spice heaven here, and they can make every dish on the cool side, too. This is one of our very favorite dining experiences and all in California casual without any pretension.

The decor is what you'd expect from

nearly any Chinese restaurant. Vegetable dishes are hot, crispy and good. Service is excellent and we've had good luck with seating — perhaps because we've come before the standard dinner hour. Chin's has family-style dinners and early-bird specials, too. It's open daily for lunch and dinner. You can get take-out if you're headed to an outdoor concert or home after a long day.

Debbi Ann's Kitchen and Pie Shoppe

$ • American
• 868 E. Vista Way, Vista
• (760) 757-1549

Entering this cozy restaurant is like walking into the perfect kitchen. The decor, frilly and flowery, is easy on the eye, and the prices are easy on the wallet. Every day there's a lengthy list of specials displayed as you walk in and on chalkboards around the dining room. This is the ultimate in American foods.

On a recent visit, the specials of the day were broasted chicken (very tender), Swiss steak, baked ham, and lasagna, all priced under $6. The meals came with soup or salad and dessert. They offer senior discounts after 11 AM in the morning.

For breakfast there's an impressive variety of omelets as well as sausage gravy and fried potatoes, fried chicken livers and eggs and even a breakfast steak. We told you this was comfortable American cuisine. If you're there at lunch and huge sandwiches are your soft spot, consider the Hopeless, for about $5.50. It's grilled kielbasa sausage, onions and cheese on rye with sauerkraut. Debbi Ann's has salads, if you're thinking that a Hopeless might be hopelessly too much. The restaurant is open daily for breakfast, lunch and dinner.

DiCrescenzo's

$ • Italian
• 11627 Duenda Rd., Rancho Bernardo
• (858) 487-2776

One day when we took a friend from the East here, she questioned our sanity. You see, this is an order-at-the-counter and eat-outdoors place, and it's so popular with the working crowd from the high-tech compa-

nies in Rancho Bernard, you may have to stand in a long line and then get your lunch in a bag. Trust us, it's worth it.

Insiders keep a menu in their desks and call ahead so they can pay and pick up their choices without the wait. Prices are nearly as good as the food. The baked ziti with French bread is just $3.75. The subs, featuring Genoa salami, ham capicolla, mortadella, provolone cheese and all the other veggie fixings are under $5, unless you're picking up one for the whole office that serves 20 people. That sandwich is only $39.95. The menu includes low-fat items, too.

DiCrescenzo's is open for lunch and dinner and what it lacks in atmosphere, it more than makes up for in flavor.

Fish House Vera Cruz

$$ • Seafood
• 1020 San Marcos Blvd., San Marcos
• (760) 744-8000

Okay, we've heard it: The only good seafood is served along the coast. Not so. And you'll know it once you've visited Fish House Vera Cruz. Each time we eat here, we're reminded of that fact. The seafood, from lobster to calamari, is grilled over mesquite wood and is always succulent and fresh. If you're from out of the area, the thought of eating grilled shark might be a bit much. But if you try it you'll learn why shark has been a mainstay on San Diego's menu for years. Fish House Vera Cruz is popular so if you're determined to eat here and if you can arrange it, visit at an off time, such as 4 PM or just before the lunchtime crowd leaves their offices. Unfortunately this "find" isn't much of a secret to Insiders. Like it's "sister" at 417 Carlsbad Village Dr., Carlsbad • (760) 434-6777, it's open daily for lunch and dinner.

Gumbo Pot

$$ • Cajun and Creole
• 11655 Duenda Rd., Rancho Bernardo
• (858) 673-3850

The Gumbo Pot bills itself as a "country Creole bistro, with a relaxed inviting atmosphere." We saw what that meant when we walked in for our first visit: Water and soft drinks are served from canning jars,

Bayside restaurants offer scenic views and fascinating atmosphere.

Zydeco and New Orleans jazz play in the background, and the walls are decorated with posters celebrating the culture and heritage of Louisiana.

If Creole cuisine is new to you, you'll probably like the Gumbo Ya-Ya (with chicken, sausage, okra and tomatoes served with rice) and you'll be stuffed for about $7. There's a savory seafood gumbo with oysters, shrimp and white fish that's cooked in a thick roux-flavored sauce, and the jambalaya (for about $9) is a casserole of chicken, sausage and shrimp simmered with spices. Watch out: We think we're addicted to the jambalaya.

Can you fit dessert? If so, try the sweet potato pie (for about $3), and you may not need to eat for a week. The Gumbo Pot is popular so you may have a wait, but it's worth it. It's closed Monday, but open for lunch and dinner the rest of the week.

Hot Wok Cafe
$ • Mandarin and Szechuan
• **1252 E. Mission Rd., San Marcos**
• **(760) 735-9988**

Whether you decide to dine inside or take home the treats, the Hot Wok is popu-

lar and gives you plenty of choices and plenty of food.

A special noodle soup for just $4.95 easily serves two. The honey spice shrimp and Szechuan-style egg foo young are two of the popular choices, but as Insiders know, it's nearly impossible to make a bad choice with this much good food. The place is busy and tends to be noisy, so if you're looking for a romantic Chinese place, put out the chop sticks on your own dining room table and order carryout as many do. It's open daily for lunch and dinner.

La Paloma Restaurante
$$ • Mexican
• **116 Escondido Ave., Vista**
• **(760) 92084**

When Insiders get into discussions on the best Mexican food in the area (and this is serious business — opinions and chili peppers have a lot in common), La Paloma always wins praise. Okay, we admit: We love Mexican food.

Located out of the usual restaurant area, La Paloma serves up fresh, savory, and spicy favorites. Although it's a struggle to name the best choices, we love the shrimp and lobster meat fajitas (at about $15), and for about $13, the camarones con pollo cilantro (tender shrimp and sliced chicken breast sauteed in sauce and spices and topped with cheese, avocado and cilantro).

All meals are served with rice, beans and tortillas. You can be cautious with tacos and tostadas and burritos (all priced in the $7 range) or reckless with bistec vaquero, a large steak char-broiled and topped with mushrooms, garlic and onions or the Pancho Villa ribs smothered in a zesty barbecue sauce. There are half-price happy hour specials Monday through Friday and early-bird dinners Sunday through Thursday. La Paloma is open daily for lunch and dinner and you can dine indoors or on the patio. Choose the patio if you love everything that's great about San Diego.

Lake Wohlford Cafe
$ • American
• 25484 Lake Wohlford Rd., Escondido
• (760) 749-2755

You could call the decor at the Lake Wohlford Cafe "funky" and not be too far from the mark. The cafe is casual and makes you feel like it's okay to have fun. At this cafe, no one will even notice if you've dripped catsup or eaten the fries with your fingers—why you're suppose to, right?

Burgers and fries and lots of American food are on the menu. Call about their special all-you-can-eat catfish dinners. See our Nightlife chapter to find out about Jack Johnson's *Live! The Hank Williams Sr. Tribute Show,* which features 1950s music and happens the last Friday of every month. The cafe is open daily for breakfast, lunch and dinner.

Mama Cella's Italian Kitchen
$$ • Italian
• 16707 Bernardo Center Dr., Rancho Bernardo
• (619) 613-7770

Do you crave a meatball sandwich? How about a grinder? Or a sandwich that's loaded beyond dripping with eggplant

Parmigiana on a bun? Stop in at this no-frills, but great-food Italian restaurant. It's a hot spot with the work-day folks from Rancho Bernardo; the staff is quick and efficient. The pizza selection, according to Insiders, is tops, especially the Toscana (about $16), which includes pesto, mushrooms, cheese and chicken. Mama Cella's is open for lunch and dinner.

Nami Seafood Buffet Restaurant
$$ • Japanese, Seafood
• 240 E. Via Rancho Pkwy., Escondido
• (760) 738-7522

Have you ever seen a 160-foot Japanese seafood buffet? This is not a "fish story," because when you visit Nami, you'll see it and more. The buffet is huge and the food is top drawer. And it's an all-you-can-eat affair. They have the seafood buffet every day and also feature 40 variations of sushi. If you don't eat seafood but still want to go with friends, you can order teriyaki beef and chicken, great vegetable creations and a fruit bar. The buffet will tempt you with 20 different kinds of desserts, too.

The Nami is open daily for lunch and dinner. FYI: The restaurant closes during the middle of the afternoon to set up for dinner. Senior discounts for those more than 65 years old could make this a sure bet for the older seafood-loving eater.

Passage of India
$$ • Indian
• 13185 Black Mountain Rd., Rancho Penasquitos • (858) 484-9688

Here's a place to have authentic Indian food, and a welcome addition to all of the Italian, fast food and seafood places in the southern portion of North County Inland. Your palate will be tempted with an array of curries, tandoori oven specialties, vegetarian items and entrees of chicken, seafood, beef and lamb.

If you like buffets, this one is a bargain with its assortment of ethnic fare. The buffet, as we recently told a friend from Milwaukee, is a good way to try some dishes that are unfamiliar. Most likely, you'll be head over heels in love with this place after just one bite. The lunch buffet is about $6 and at dinner it's a reasonable $8.99. Passage of India is open for lunch and dinner daily.

San Marcos Brewery & Grill
$$ • American
• 1020 San Marcos Blvd., San Marcos
• (760) 471-0050

See our Nightlife chapter for details on this popular brewpub. Lots of people start with beer and appetizers — perhaps onion ring flowers or potato skins smothered in chives, bacon and sour cream — and then go on to dinner. The fine brews that are on tap combine well with the good grill grub of burgers, chicken or steak. The San Marcos Brewery & Grill is open for lunch and dinner daily.

Sirino's Restaurant
$$ • Italian
• 113 W. Grand Ave., Escondido
• (760) 745-3835

The dining room is unassuming — some say uninspired — but any thought of the dulls will end in a flash when you breathe in the fragrances coming from the kitchen, and ultimately to your plate. Here's a fine Italian restaurant in downtown Escondido that's worth the drive from other parts of the county.

We recommend the pastry Florentine. It's an overstuffed turnover bursting with spinach, Stilton cheese and veggie goodies. The night we visited, the baked penne with crayfish was a treat and the ravioli stuffed with veal was superb. While these Insiders had to pass on dessert, other diners in our party didn't. They said the choices were worth the calories. Open for lunch Tuesday through Friday and dinner Tuesday through Saturday.

Thai Express
$ • Thai
• 11975 Carmel Mountain Rd., Ste. 606, San Diego • (858) 485-5459

In the Carmel Ranch Mountain Town Center of San Diego, this small restaurant serves up quick, wonderful and inexpen-

sive Thai foods. Many Insiders stop on their way home from the office or during lunch for a filling and price-wise meal. For about $6 you can get a classic chicken satay or skewered marinated chicken both served with a creamy, pungent peanut sauce and a tart cucumber dip. The vegetarian spring rolls are only about $5 and the salad selection is worth the trip here. Try the elegant yum woosen; it's minced chicken and shrimp tossed with onions, cilantro and clear noodles with a spicy lime dressing. It's under $8. There are noodle dishes, tasty soup and entrees that can be a la carte or with rice and soup. Get your food as hot or as mild as you choose, but choose to frequent this tiny eatery. It's open daily for lunch and dinner.

Welk Resort Center Restaurant
$$ • American
• 8860 Lawrence Welk Dr., Escondido
• (760) 749-3000, ext. 2129

If you've browsed through the book, you've already read our Golf, Spas and Restaurants chapters and know that the Welk Resort Center is host to an eclectic collection of things that are fun. Here's another reason to go to North County Inland— good food at a good price.

The restaurant's quality surprised us on some recent visits. Hospitality was warm, food hot and well presented and there's a lavish carved-meat buffet and salad bar that could knock your socks off (it's available during the dinner theater performances). On the menu you'll find seafood, Angus prime roast beef and chicken along with international favorites. The restaurant is open daily for breakfast, lunch and dinner.

Wildwood German American Restaurant
$$ • German-American
• 1415 S. Mission Rd., Fallbrook
• (760) 731-0007

Hungry for bratwurst sausages, dumplings that nearly float into your mouth, and apple strudel nestled in a cloud of whipped cream? If your mouth is watering at these visions, head straight for the Wildwood German American Restaurant. Specialties of German food include breaded pork loin fried crisp and tender in the Wiener schnitzel style, and sauerbraten that is savory and nearly melts on your fork.

The dining room has high ceilings and is decorated with cozy bric-a-brac and candles on the tables. Entrees include crusty wheat bread (hot from the oven), soup or salad. Ask for the house horseradish dressing if you want to zip up those greens. The restaurant is open daily, except Tuesday, and for dinner only.

East County

Barona Casino
$ • American
• 1000 Wildcat Canyon Rd., Lakeside
• (619) 443-2300, (888) 722-7662

You've read about this casino in our Attractions and Nightlife chapters and here it is again. The casino has a Vegas-style buffet, called the International Buffet. The food themes change often, but what doesn't change is the variety and excellence of the menu. Recently it was a Western Round-Up BBQ Buffet, featuring steak, chicken, ribs, burgers and hot dogs, corn on the cob, bacon baked beans and corn bread.

On Mondays it's a South of the Border Buffet, that includes spicy choices from tacos to tamales. The buffet is open for lunch and dinner. Another restaurant, the Side Court gives you 24-hours a day eating and snacking possibilities. Remember that one must be 18 or older to be present in the casino, even for dinner, after 8 PM.

Dudley's Bakery and Cafe
$ • American
• Calif. Hwy. 78 and 79, • Santa Ysabel
• (760) 765-0488

The bakery and cafe are East County treasures. To visitors, Santa Ysabel might seem to be smack dab out in nowhere yet Insiders drive from all over southern California for a loaf of Dudley's bread and if they're patient, they wait for a table in the cafe.

You'll want to read about the bakery in our Shopping chapter if you're planning a trip

to this part of the county. The food is good enough to warrant the wait you may have on some weekends; it's also a fun stop to or from a Julian outing. Open daily for breakfast, lunch and dinner.

Giacopelli's New York Deli
$ • American
• 2512 Jamacha Rd., El Cajon
• (619) 670-4320

Insiders come here for the hero sandwiches and the mountain-high piles of cold cuts stuffed into a crispy Italian roll. Some say it's the only place in East County where you can get a decent New York-style hot dog (which comes from a cart inside the store). Even if you're not from the Big Apple, you'll like the slowly simmered sauces that include marinara, creamy vodka and tomato for pasta or a meatball sandwich. Giacopelli's New York Deli is open for breakfast, lunch and dinner. Call ahead if you want to order and pick up a sandwich.

Julian Grille
$ • American
• 2224 Main St., Julian • (760) 765-0173

Go for the pie — apple pie, that is, and the pie that's put Julian on the map. And be sure to save room after the large servings of American-style choices served at the Grille. This is where the Julian Insiders and visitors eat, and during Apple Days and when the art and photo shows are held, it can be busy. See our Bed and Breakfast Inns chapter for accommodations in the area. Service is good at the Grille and the food worth the wait.

The Julian Grille is a nice tradition for every trip to the mountain community and it's open for breakfast, lunch and dinner every day.

La Mesa Ocean Grill
$$ • Seafood
• 5465 Lake Murray Blvd., La Mesa
• (619) 463-1548

Here's the place if you've been craving lobster in a big way. They're big, sweet and straight from New England. The whole Maine lobster includes deviled clam, clam fritters, corn on the cob, red potatoes and corn bread for about $17. The Big Kahuna Fried Fishermen's Plate (about $20) will stuff you with Arctic cod, shrimp, scallops, calamari, crab cake, deviled clam, clam fritters, French fries, coleslaw and corn bread. You may just want to order one dinner and split it between two. Ask about the daily specials. La Mesa Ocean Grill, a find in East County, is open daily for lunch and dinner.

Lader's Italian Gourmet
$$ • Italian
• 5654 Lake Murray Blvd., La Mesa
• (619) 463-9919

Lader's is family run and friendly. The food shouts: Italian. Portions are large. The emphasis is on fresh ingredients and you can taste the difference in the vegetables and pasta sauces. With your first bite, you'll know that the ingredients didn't come from a can. There's a casual, family atmosphere, with checkered tablecloths. Lader's is closed on Mondays and open for lunch and dinner the rest of the week.

Mario's de La Mesa
$ • Mexican
• 8425 La Mesa Blvd., La Mesa
• (619) 461-9390

"This is down home cooking," say some Insiders after sampling the food at this lesser-known, but wonderful nonetheless, Mexican restaurant. The food arrives in generous helpings, the menu is extensive, and the service is better than home. You can be sure to get smiles with every order here. There's a Don Gallo sauce that is a creamy covering for some of the seafood dishes. It's innovative and down right tasty too. There's a "build your own" taco bar and all the standards you've come to expect from Mexican restaurants. It's open daily for breakfast, lunch and dinner. On Sunday, it opens for brunch and then heads straight to dinner.

Pinnacle Peak Steak House
$$ • American
• 7927 Mission Gorge Rd., Santee
• (619) 448-8882

Let's say you're in East County, maybe visiting Summers Past Farms or the casinos (see our Attractions chapter). It hits you. You're hungry for a steak, and not just any steak will do. You want a cowboy-size portion with beans and bread and barbecue sauce that's rich and red. The answer to your need to feed is the Pinnacle Peak, a cowboy eatery where the staff, if necessary, will forcibly take your tie and suit jacket. All the beef (and chicken) choices are grilled to perfection over an open mesquite fire.

If you and a sweetie are lookin' for candles and romantic mushy mood music and a place where the ostentatious nouveau victuals are no bigger than your thumb, do not, we repeat, do not come to Pinnacle Peak. This is the steak house where the slogan is "beef is our business" and they mean business. Once you see the size of the steaks and burgers, you'll agree that they don't mess around with huge appetites.

The restaurant is a fun experience, a great place for families and a favorite among residents from all over the county. Pinnacle Peak is open for lunch and dinner every day.

Romano's Dodge House
$$ • Italian
• 2718 B St., Julian • (760) 765-1003

This restaurant is just a block off Main Street in downtown Julian. It is an Insiders' favorite, too. There's a classic, Julian-style rustic decor and a fine selection of Italian specialties. Ask about the daily specials and check out the pizza variations. Credit cards are not accepted here, but it is open for lunch and dinner daily.

Singing Hills Country Club Dining Room
$$ • American
• 3007 Dehesa Rd., El Cajon
• (619) 442-3425

This dinner-only dining room, with great steak, seafood and chicken choices, always gets a thumbs-up. When we visit with friends and family for the Sunday brunch, our loved ones are blown away. There are so many choices of mouth-watering dishes that selections might be almost impossible.

Photo: San Diego Convention and Visitors Bureau

Sunset on the coast surrounds diners with the colors of the San Diego evening.

Why, you may have to sip champagne while you map out an eating strategy.

The dress is casual, decor is of the Southwest style, and there's a view of the lush, green golf course. The dining room is open daily; brunch is served only on Sundays. Reservations are recommended. You may want to read more about Singing Hills Country Club in our Golf chapter and reserve a tee time before sampling this restaurant.

Village Garden Restaurant & Bakery
$ • American
• 8384 La Mesa Blvd., La Mesa
• (619) 462-9100

Homestyle cooking with a flair is what you'll find at the Village Garden Restaurant & Bakery. Go for the food and stay for the dessert. One of the days we ate here, we sampled Idaho pan-fried trout with hushpuppies (the daily special). Everything was crispy, hot and tasty. Then we did the nearly impossible: saved room for dessert and managed to eat every morsel of the strawberry pie. We didn't know pie could be that good. You can dine inside or on the patio. The eatery is open for breakfast and lunch Monday through Wednesday, and Thursday through Sunday it's open for breakfast, lunch and dinner.

Viejas Casino & Turf Club
$-$$ • Buffet and Food Court
• 5000 Willows Rd., Alpine
• (619) 445-5400

For everything you can expect at this ultra-popular casino, be sure to read our entries in the Nightlife and Attractions chapters. You can also expect casual dining and fine dining, in very easygoing surroundings. Check out the grand buffet (much like those you may have seen in Las Vegas or Atlantic City). There's also the new China Camp Express for Asian foods and other 24-hour restaurants to make your gaming experience complete. Restaurants are open daily for breakfast, lunch and dinner.

South Bay

Anthony's Fish Grotto
$-$$ • Seafood
• 215 Bay Blvd., Chula Vista
• (619) 425-4200
• 1360 N. Harbor Dr., San Diego
• (619) 232-5103
• 9530 Murray Dr., La Mesa
• (619) 463-0368
• 11666 Avena Pl., San Diego
• (858) 451-2070

San Diego's Ghio family has established a long tradition of good, reasonably priced seafood at their grotto restaurants. When you enter the grottos, you'll feel you've been transported to an underwater cave, complete with sea animals, coral and shells. The exception to this decor is the Harbor Drive restaurant, which is open to the bay to take advantage of the view.

Seafood salads are the gems of the lunch-time menu, especially the seafood combo — chunks of lobster, shrimp, crab and avocado served over fresh greens and topped with Anthony's signature dressing. For more hearty appetites, choose from a variety of fish from both the lunch and dinner menus, including, sole, sea bass, halibut and swordfish that are grilled, sautéed or broiled according to your desire. Anthony's is open for lunch Monday through Saturday, and for dinner nightly.

Bob's by the Bay
$$ • American
• 570 Marina Parkway, Chula Vista
• (619) 476-0400

Bob's is probably the most popular restaurant in the South Bay, and for good reason. The food is consistently well prepared, and the menu features entrees that are perennial favorites. For instance, the grilled shrimp, two skewers of shrimp seasoned with citrus and butter, then grilled, is paired with fresh seasonal vegetables and basmati rice — just right for a dinner that's filling but on the light side. Grilled chicken alfredo is another crowd-pleaser — marinated, boneless chicken grilled and served over fettucine with a basil and parmesan cream sauce.

This is a busy hangout for the after-work crowd, too, and a good place to meet friends for a drink before dinner. Bob's is located close to the water in the Chula Vista Marina and is open for dinner nightly and for lunch Monday through Friday. On Saturdays lunch is served at the outdoor Bayside Grill, and on Sundays a lavish brunch buffet is served.

The Butcher Shop
$$ • American
• 556 Broadway, Chula Vista
• (619) 420-9440
• 5255 Kearny Villa Rd., San Diego
• (858) 565-2272

As its name implies, The Butcher Shop specializes in beef: prime rib, top sirloin and just about any other cut that strikes your fancy. Picture a darkened dining room with paneled walls and red fabric booths, and you'll probably guess this restaurant is a holdover from the days of three-martini lunches in a smoke-filled room. Although the interior design hasn't changed much, the ambiance is a lot more refined.

The restaurant also caters to lighter eaters by offering chicken and fish dishes, but then spoils all your good intentions by serving them with irresistible, giant twice-baked potatoes and piping hot garlic bread. Dinner is served nightly, and lunch is served Monday through Saturday. On Sundays The Butcher Shop opens in the early afternoon for a late lunch or early dinner.

D'lish
$-$$ • Pizzas, Pastas, Salads
• 386 E. H St., Ste. 211, Chula Vista
• (619) 585-1371
• 2260 Otay Lakes Rd., Chula Vista
• (619) 216-3900
• 7514 Girard Ave., La Jolla
• (858) 459-8118

Whether take-out is on the agenda or you're dining in, D'Lish serves up gourmet salads, pizzas and pastas with a different but delicious twist. The Caesar salad, for example

is made with roasted red peppers and kalamata olives, a tasty combination of flavors. Another menu favorite is the chicken sun-dried calzone, made with chicken, sun-dried tomatoes, marinara sauce and sour cream. Or, try the shrimp-scallop angel hair pasta served with red onions, bell peppers and zucchini.

The atmosphere is casual but elegant, with both table and booth seating. A fire pit keeps diners toasty warm on chilly winter nights. The menu may vary slightly at the different locations, and everything on the menu is available for take-out. Lunch and dinner are served daily.

House of Munich
$$ • German
• 230 Third Ave., Chula Vista
• (619) 426-0343

If you're a schnitzel fan, the House of Munich is just what the doctor ordered. Try Wiener Schnitzel, Jager Schnitzel or Holstein Schnitzel. Or if you prefer to jump off the schnitzel bandwagon, sample one of the other authentic German entrees, like sauerbraten or hunter stew. Traditional treats such as potato pancakes and cabbage rolls are quite good, too.

The restaurant is in a building that resembles a chalet, and some nights you'll find traditional accordion music being played (see our Nightlife chapter for more details). German beers are always on tap, so get ready for a total German experience. The House of Munich is open for lunch Tuesday through Friday, and for dinner Tuesday through Sunday.

The Old Bonita Store
$$ • Mexican
• 4014 Bonita Rd., Bonita
• (619) 479-3537

It's ironic that the closer you get to the U.S.-Mexico border, the scarcer the fine Mexican restaurants become. But if you're searching for a restaurant with strong influences of Baja California and Mexico in the South Bay, look no farther than the Old Bonita Store. All the standard Mexican fare is served here, such as combination plates and a la carte tacos, burritos and enchiladas, but the real treat is the bucket of Baja-style lobster for two.

The bucket includes slipper lobster tails, shrimp, grilled chicken and carne asada, plus Ceasar salad, rice, beans and tortillas. The atmosphere is party-like and casual. Everyone has fun at the Old Bonita Store. It's open for lunch and dinner daily.

Sunday Brunch in San Diego

If you're like most Insiders, you wake up on Sunday morning with one thought: where shall we go for brunch? San Diego is a big brunch town, and chances are good that your favorite restaurant will have its own version of the weekend ritual. Most include complementary champagne, and the serving style leans heavily toward buffet. The following list will give you an idea of where some of the best buffet brunches in town are, but don't hesitate to do some exploring. We haven't found a bad one yet. Our price code is the same one we've used throughout this chapter and indicates the cost of brunch for two, excluding cocktails (although most brunches include complementary champagne), tax and tip. Most brunches start at 9 AM or 10 AM and wrap up by 2 PM or 3PM.

$$	Bali Hai • 2230 Shelter Island Dr., San Diego • (619) 222-1182
$$$	Del Mar Hilton • 15575 Jimmy Durante Blvd., Del Mar • (858) 792-5200
$$$$	Hotel del Coronado • 1500 Orange Ave., Coronado • (619) 435-6611
$$$	Humphrey's • 2241 Shelter Island Dr., San Diego • (619) 224-3577
$$$$	Hyatt Regency • One Market Pl., San Diego • (619) 687-6066
$$	Bob's by the Bay • 570 Marina Pkwy, Chula Vista • (619) 476-0400
$$$$	Loew's Coronado Bay • 4000 Coronado Bay Rd., Coronado • (619) 424-4000
$$	Quails Inn • 1035 La Bonita, San Marcos • (760) 744-2445
$$$$	Rancho Bernardo Inn • 17550 Bernardo Dr., San Diego • (858) 675-8550
$$$	Reuben's • 880 E. Harbor Island Dr., San Diego • (619) 291-5030
$$$$	Hilton Torrey Pines • 10950 N. Torrey Pines Rd., La Jolla • (858) 558-1500
$$	Singing Hills Resort • 3007 Dehesa Rd., El Cajon • (619) 442-3425
$$	Tomatoes • 4346 Bonita Rd., Bonita • (619) 479-8494

While the city isn't known for the kind of trendy, chic and wild nightlife you might find in Hollywood or Manhattan, San Diego's after-hours personality is alive and well.

Nightlife

After a hard day playing outdoors, who wants to have more fun? Most of us in San Diego. While the city isn't known for the kind of trendy, chic and wild nightlife you might find in Hollywood or Manhattan, San Diego's after-hours personality is alive and well.

Here you can choose from a smorgasbord of nighttime pleasures. In this chapter we'll give you the rundown on hangouts, clubs, bars and brewpubs, independent coffeehouses and places that are worth checking out. We've actually decided to include that category — worth checking out — since some nighttime entertainment just doesn't fit into a formula (like concerts in the park). As a note, we didn't list every Starbucks in the county. Just follow your nose to find them or check the listing in the phone book for the closest place for coffee.

We'll steer you clear (by not mentioning them) of those places with questionable reputations and head you toward the ones that can make your trip even better. If there's a cover charge or a specific dress code for a nightspot, we've added that information, but keep in mind, things change.

Since San Diego's population looks young, don't be shocked if you're carded. Club owners and barkeeps have the right to ask anyone for ID at any time. Even if you're in the over-30 crowd, you'll need to carry identification. We have been carded well past college age and said "Thanks very much!" As we go to press there's no smoking in public establishments. Some bars get around the law, but in most, smokers are welcome only outdoors. On the other end of the scale, the Bitter End, a cigar and martini bar in the Gaslamp Quarter, encourages plenty of puffing amid the upscale surroundings.

While the regions other than San Diego proper excite the crowd that's looking for nightlife, many people also drive into the city to visit the Gaslamp Quarter and the clubs and hotels in La Jolla and downtown. If you're visiting or making San Diego your home, you'll want to browse through the entire section, knowing that to find the right nightlife for you, you may need to drive for a half-hour to find it. That's a small price to pay for a great time.

When we formulated our list, made phone calls and took field trips (it was a tough job but someone had to do it for you), one thing was clear: Clubs, pubs, coffeehouses and the rest change. One spot might be hot with rock music and then a month later change ownership. The next time you visit you might find a jazz band or a poetry reading or a passle of square dancers. So though we've tried to make our listings as current and accurate as possible, you still might want to make some calls to check on the types of music or entertainment you'll find.

With all the directions and advice out of the way, it's time to introduce our entries and give you the lay of nightlife land. Have fun — it's abundant in San Diego and waiting for you right now.

Nightclubs

San Diego

Barefoot Bar and Grill
San Diego Paradise Point Resort
1404 W. Vacation Rd., San Diego
• (858) 274-4630

You can get here by boat, tie up, climb ashore and start dancing. The Barefoot is legendary in San Diego because of the unusual way some people arrive. Don't worry if you're boatless though; more conventional methods will get you here too. The sound is different every night, from reggae to pop to classic rock to blues. Even though the bar is on the grounds of a resort hotel, you'll find lots of locals of all ages here. There's a $3 cover charge on Friday, Saturday and Sunday.

Bitter End
770 Fifth Ave., San Diego
• (619) 338-9300

This is a classy joint at the corner of Fifth and F streets habituated by denizens of the Gaslamp Quarter. Nominally classified as a martini and cigar bar, it will actually serve you any concoction your heart desires. The crowd tends to be of the Baby Boomer ilk during the week, but gets a bit younger on weekends, when a DJ spins dance music. After 8:30 PM on Fridays and Saturdays, a cover charge of $7 will get you through the door.

www.insiders.com

See this and many other
Insiders' Guide®
destinations online.

Visit us today!

Blind Melons
710 Garnet Ave., San Diego
• (858) 483-7844

This is not a place to dress up. Throw on a pair of jeans and come dance to the sound of the blues from nationally known artists. The cover charge varies according to the notoriety of the band, but it ranges from $3 to $7. This is the epitome of a beach bar, so expect the crowd to have a free-and-easy attitude.

Cafe Sevilla
555 Fourth Ave., San Diego
• (619) 233-5979

Nibble on Spanish tapas or enjoy a full meal at this trendy restaurant/club in the Gaslamp Quarter. Different shows are presented during the week: samba, flamenco, Spanish rock, salsa and merengue. On weekends it becomes a Latin-Euro dance club. During the week the cover charge is $5. On Fridays and Saturdays it's $8. Like most places in the Gaslamp, the age of the crowd is varied, ranging from those barely old enough to

get through the door to the gray-haired set looking for some lively good times.

'Canes Bar and Grill
3105 Ocean Front Walk, San Diego
• (858) 488-1780

This is a lively spot located in Belmont Park in Mission Beach. On a normal night, the crowd is usually made up of 20-somethings, but special concerts will draw a mixed-age group. Some concerts are open to revelers as young as 18. In addition to concerts, 'Canes has music festivals, local bands and lots of special activities. The rooftop deck overlooking the ocean offers a nice respite from the activity below. Admission varies according to the event; call for prices.

Cannibal Bar
Catamaran Resort Hotel
3999 Mission Blvd., San Diego
• (858) 488-1081

The Cannibal Bar has had some staying power. Trendy hangouts tend to come and go, but this one has been around a while. Live entertainment and dancing are featured Wednesday through Sunday, and the sounds are eclectic: reggae, blues, zydeco, alternative rock, acid jazz and good old-fashioned rock and roll. Occasional special concerts are presented, too, for which tickets must be purchased ahead of time. Cover charges fluctuate, ranging from nothing to $10. During the summer months, bands will play from 3 PM to 7 PM Fridays and Saturdays on the beach next to the hotel.

Coronado Island Marriott
2000 Second St., Coronado
• (619) 435-3000

If you're looking for a night of jazz, try the

INSIDERS' TIP

There's a no-smoking law for bars, pubs and restaurants in San Diego. Some locations may even ask you not to smoke on the street in front of a club.

La Provence Bar inside this posh resort. Top-notch jazz artists play on Fridays and Saturdays in a decidedly upscale atmosphere. This is where you go when you want to dress up a little, sip a glass of champagne and feel the romance in the air.

Croce's Restaurant & Jazz Bar
802 Fifth Ave., San Diego
• **(619) 233-4355**

Croce's has become an institution in San Diego for its fine dining and outstanding entertainment. Owned by Ingrid Croce, widow of singer Jim Croce, the bar features international jazz talents and an occasional appearance by A. J. Croce, son of the legendary crooner, who has made his own mark on the music scene. Upstairs is the Top Hat Bar & Grille, which showcases blues and rock. The whole scene is noisy and exuberant and more fun than you could think up on your own. The cover charge is $3 during the week, $6 on Fridays, $7 on Saturdays, and it will get you into both the Jazz Bar and the Top Hat. If there's a special event, the cover might be slightly higher.

Dick's Last Resort
345 Fourth Ave., San Diego
• **(619) 231-9100**

Granted, this is a chain outfit with a reputation for being slightly uncouth at times. But take it from us, there's some great music going on here. Talented local bands play every night, and folks of all ages dance, have a beer, throw wadded up napkins at each other by way of introduction and just generally let their hair down. Give it a try; you'll find all types of music, from rock to pop to salsa to soul.

In Cahoots
5373 Mission Center Rd., San Diego
• **(619) 291-8635**

Polish up those boots and get ready for some line dancing and two-stepping. Dancing to DJ-spun country music is what's happening here, and this is a great place for singles of all ages to meet and mix in a friendly, non-threatening atmosphere.

Drink prices are inexpensive, but the main draw is the dancing. The cover charge is $5 on Wednesdays for the special mid-week party, $2 on Thursdays, and $3 on Fridays, Saturdays and Sundays.

Kensington Club
4079 Adams Ave., San Diego
• **(619) 284-2848**

What used to be just a neighborhood bar has gained some panache and has been discovered by folks outside the surrounding area of Kensington. Live entertainment is now being featured on Fridays and Saturdays, and the format varies. If you're really concerned about what you hear, call ahead of time. Or if you feel adventurous, just show up and enjoy whatever's on the agenda. It may be pop, it may be rock, it may be rockabilly. The cover charge varies from nothing to $5.

Patrick's II
428 F St., San Diego
• **(619) 233-3077**

When you've got a hankerin' for the blues, look no further than Patrick's II. A mainstay in the Gaslamp Quarter for years, this is a small club that is usually packed with people of all ages soaking up the blues. Quarters are close, but the crowd is friendly and the music can't be beat. During the week there's no cover charge; on Fridays and Saturdays it's either $3 or $4.

Winston's Beach Club
1921 Bacon St., San Diego
• **(619) 222-6822**

This beach-casual club in Ocean Beach features standout bands ranging from reggae and ska to alternative, blues, funk, soul and acid jazz. The crowd is mixed; you'll see all ages here having fun no matter what type of music is playing. The cover charge is $5.

INSIDERS' TIP

While the legal drinking age is 21, you'll have to be 18 to get into the door of any club that serves alcohol.

North County Coastal

Belly Up Tavern
143 S. Cedros Ave., Solana Beach
• **(858) 481-9022**

A classic in the county, the Belly Up Tavern has been bringing top performers and newcomer groups to the music scene since the 1970s and continues to do so. Ticket prices vary. Music varieties stretch from salsa and ska to bluesy rock and Big Band. Call the club's line, noted above, for information, buying tickets over the phone and subscribing to the Belly Up's newsletter of events.

North County Inland

Club Tropics
740 Nordahl Rd., San Marcos
• **(760) 737-9402**

A hip club with a $1 cover charge, Club Tropics attracts a college-age crowd and working folks too. You'll be bombarded with music from the 70s, 80s and 90s, from hip-hop to reggae all the way to disco. According to one of the bartenders, this is the place for the "hot college babes." So you won't be disappointed, *hot* and *babes* are both in the eye of the beholder and the bartender. (Be aware that a "Hot College Babe" is also an alcoholic drink, so perhaps that's what the bartender meant.) Call for ticket information on special events. Friday and Saturday nights feature local pop radio personalities who spin the music.

Leo's Little Bit O' Country
680 W. San Marcos Blvd., San Marcos
• **(760) 744-4120**

Country music bounces off the walls at Leo's and is well blended with good fun and laughter. Insiders who love country say that

the best moments are on Tuesdays during the West Coast Swing dance lessons, and on Thursday through Saturday when country-western dance lessons are given for free.

East County

Dirk's Nightclub
7662 Broadway St., Lemon Grove
• **(619) 469-6344**

Dirk's fun party atmosphere is a big draw for the 30 to 50 age group — you know the people — the ones who remember Buffalo Springfield, Fleetwood Mac and Sting. And college students who like this vintage music come here too. Dirk's is popular, and the best part is that the music is classic rock with live groups on the weekends. Call to find out about upcoming special events, such as the 50's theme parties and other theme events. Everyone in the East County, from city mayors to college students, gives this club a thumbs-up. There's never a cover charge to get you in the door.

Ox Bow Inn
9816 Campo Rd., Spring Valley
• **(619) 469-9616**

The age group attracted to this country-western nightclub is across the board and loud and fun and out for a great time. The live music performances on Friday, Saturday and Sunday evenings start at about 8:30 PM. The food's worth saving your appetite for with burgers high on most Insiders' lists. Call for more information about upcoming performers.

Pine Valley House
28841 Old Hwy. 80, Pine Valley
• **(619) 473-8708**

Love country music? Need some two-step tips? Head east to Pine Valley and enjoy live entertainment every Saturday night when this

---

INSIDERS' TIP

The churches and synagogues in our community are involved in nightlife too, often providing the venues for performances and sports tournaments. If you're looking for singles fun and are new in town, check out our Worship chapter to give you a start on making connections and new friends.

country-style club rocks. Here's where the 50-plus mob gathers for a good old time. This is the denim and boots crowd, but you won't be turned away if you're not wearing appropriate cowboy attire. On some holiday weekends there are no scheduled performances, so if that's important to you, call ahead to see what's being offered.

South Bay

The Butcher Shop
556 Broadway, Chula Vista
• (619) 420-9440

The Butcher Shop is legendary all around San Diego County for it's top-quality dining. But if you feel like hanging around after dinner, this Chula Vista restaurant offers live contemporary music Saturday through Wednesday from 8 PM to midnight.

Di-mond Jim's Nightclub
773 Third Ave., Chula Vista
• (619) 585-7323

Dance to live classic rock music every night in this South Bay hotspot. The crowd at Dimond Jim's tends to be of all ages. Dress is casual, and there's no cover charge. A few billiard tables enhance the scene for those looking for a break from the dance floor.

Bars and Brewpubs

San Diego

Coronado Brewing Co.
710 Orange Ave., Coronado
• (619) 437-4452

Right in the heart of scenic Coronado is this lively brewpub, which has five varieties of beer on tap. You can lift a pint or two and have a bite to eat for lunch or dinner. The menu includes casual fare: hamburgers, salads, pizzas and pasta. Live entertainment pops up occasionally on Saturday nights, but it's a sporadic thing, so call ahead if you need live music to accompany your brew.

Hang Ten Brewing Co.
310 Fifth Ave., San Diego
• (619) 437-4452

Open daily from 4 PM, Hang Ten is the newest entry in San Diego's brewpub scene. In addition to 10 beers on tap, you can dine on innovative cuisine that combines California and Asian influences. For those who'd prefer a cocktail, Hang Ten also has a full bar. There's no live entertainment here, but folks enjoy the classic rock that broadcasts continuously.

Hyatt Regency
1 Market Pl., San Diego • (619) 232-1234

As you step off the elevator and wander into the bar on the 40th floor of the Hyatt Regency Hotel, you might wonder what makes it worth a visit. You'll quit wondering as soon as you look out the window. This is the best place in San Diego to have a cocktail with a view of the harbor on one side and a view of city lights on the other. The interior of the bar is dimly lit so as not to distract from the glorious sights outside. It's comfortable, romantic and breathtaking.

Karl Strauss Brewery & Grill
1044 Wall St., La Jolla
• (858) 551-2739
1157 Columbia St., San Diego
• (619) 234-2739
9675 Scranton Rd., San Diego
• (858) 587-2739

One of the first brewpubs to open in San Diego, Karl Strauss's has maintained its qual-

Nightlife in the heart of The Gaslamp Quarter is a bar hopper's paradise.

ity and reputation through the years. From its first location in downtown San Diego, it now has expanded to three locations, all of which have 12 fine brews on tap. There's also a wide menu of casual dining selections, including sandwiches, salads, pastas and pizzas. This is a great place for late-night dining. The kitchen stays open until 10 PM during the week and until midnight on weekends.

The Lamplighter
817 W. Washington St., San Diego
• **(619) 298-3624**

There's a pool table, a full bar and a neighborhood crowd that couldn't be friendlier at the Lamplighter. Bartenders are exuberant in their attention to customers; some are a show in themselves. But if you want to put on your own show, Karaoke starts at 9 PM Tuesdays through Saturdays.

McP's Irish Pub and Grill
1107 Orange Ave., Coronado
• **(619) 435-5280**

There's never a cover charge at McP's, and you get a lot for the price of a beer and a burger here. Every night has a different band playing blues, rock and Irish music, too. This is favorite hangout of Coronado locals and visitors alike.

Milligan's Bar and Grill
5786 La Jolla Blvd., La Jolla
• **(858) 459-7311**

Wednesdays through Saturdays you'll find live music in Milligan's spacious bar. The music is heavy on jazz and blues, but occasionally there will be a performer who ventures into different territory, such as acoustic guitar. Milligan's is known for its wide selection of martinis.

The Pennant
2893 Mission Blvd., San Diego
• **(858) 488-1671**
The Beachcomber
2901 Mission Blvd., San Diego (phone unlisted)

Although these two bars are separate establishments, it's nearly impossible to visit one without going next door to the other. They both are typical beach bars: shorts-and-sandals casual. The difference between the two is that The Beachcomber has live music, wall-to-wall people (some dancing, some just chatting), and The Pennant is a little quieter. It's a place you can go to catch your breath, watch a game on TV and carry on a conversation. The Pennant also has an upstairs deck that's a godsend on hot summer afternoons and evenings. The crowd at both places is mixed, from college students to grizzled beach rats to tourists, so everyone fits right in.

Red Fox Room
2223 El Cajon Blvd., San Diego
•(619) 297-1313

There was a time when the Red Fox Room was one of the most elegant lounges in town. Its grandeur may have faded a bit, but its popularity has continued over the years. Today it's a piano bar where you can sing along while cozied up with your sweetie in its hallmark red vinyl booths and be assured that your cocktail will be served with panache. The crowd is older during early hours, but as the evening wanes, the age group gets decidedly younger.

San Diego Brewing Co.
10450 Friars Rd., San Diego
• (619) 284-2739

If you're serious about your beer drinking, this is the place to go. Fifty brews on tap will keep you sampling indefinitely. Talk with the knowledgeable staff about the different varieties, and be sure to try one new to you. Pace yourself with an extraordinary burger or bowl of chili, then sit back and enjoy the sporting events that are broadcast on two big-screen and 12 regular TVs.

Trophy's Sports Grill
7510 Hazard Center Dr., San Diego
• (619) 296-9600
4282 Esplanade Ct., San Diego
• (858) 450-1400
5500 Grossmont Ctr. Dr., La Mesa
• (619) 698-2900

This homegrown sports bar/restaurant has flourished in all three of its locations, and for good reason. The restaurant itself is good: eats are cheap and quality is high. Plus, you can usually see at least one of the TVs from anywhere in the restaurant. The bar has big-

screen TVs along with normal-sized ones, and if there's a game in progress anywhere in the country, it's likely to be on. The lobby of the restaurant is filled with huge collections of sports memorabilia. This is a fun place for families and singles.

Whaling Bar
La Valencia Hotel, 1132 Prospect St.,
La Jolla • (858) 454-0771

Once an elite hangout for Hollywood types in town for the thoroughbred races at Del Mar, today the Whaling Bar has matured into an elegant gathering place for La Jolla locals and visitors. Entertainment is a piano bar, which naturally encourages the singer in us all to join in, and most folks do. The bar has recently undergone a mammoth renovation and is now up to date while retaining its old-world style.

North County Coastal

Bar Leucadia,
1542 U.S. Hwy. 101, Encinitas (Leucadia)
• (760) 753-2094

Here's a neighborhood hangout and bar that has live music on Sundays (4 to 8 PM) and Karaoke on Wednesdays (9 PM to 1 AM). But that's not the reason why people congregate here.

Bar Leucadia has the same quality as television's *Cheers*: It's a comfortable place to be, mingle, laugh and have a good time. You can also play darts and shuffleboard and there are pool tables, too. Insiders say it's thumbs up for this neighborhood pub.

Coyote Bar & Grill
300 Carlsbad Village Dr., Carlsbad
• (760) 729-4695

The age and musical tastes of the crowds

INSIDERS' TIP

Looking for clubs, performances, and other fun stuff? Check the *"Night and Day"* section in *The San Diego Union Tribune* or pick up a copy of *The Reader,* the weekly tabloid of film, music, theater and cool stuff that's available free of charge at bookstores, libraries, and music outlets.

who frequent the Coyote change quicker than Dennis Rodman's hair color. Music and people spill out the door, off the patio and into the parking lot, especially when the weather is perfect — and that happens year-round in San Diego. We've heard that right now it's the baby boomers who are coming for the rock classics. A while back, it was elbowroom only with the college-age crowd.

So call and find out who's playing if that's important for your good time. For all we know, by the time the book is in your hands there might be string quartets playing at the Coyote. Seriously, the Coyote is a popular hangout with loud music, lots of laughter, and live entertainment on weekend evenings.

Pizza Port
135 N. Hwy. 101, Solana Beach
• (858) 481-7332

Yes, you'll get pizza, but you'll also get some great microbrewed beers with it. The

Sweet Baby — Here's the Cheathams

Jeannie and Jimmy Cheatham and their Sweet Baby Blues Band play in the Kansas City blues style. Asked for a definition, Jimmy says, "It's unrestrained, exuberant, soulful, rollicking, growling, howling, roaring, wicked, virtuous and wild." Jeannie adds, "It's truthful too."

Whether you're sitting in a club or concert hall or have their CD plugged into your car's player, don't be surprised if you find yourself singing along — even if you haven't heard the song before. You'll also be nodding in agreement to the lyrics. Their music speaks loud and clear about love, friendship, worry and joy, and in a way that seems downright personal. It'll make you feel good — so much so you might get addicted.

Jeannie and Jimmy have been producing this feel-good music so long and so well

that they're considered legends, both by fans who circle the globe and by fellow musicians. Jeannie, with her seductive, powerful voice, and Jimmy, who is a trombone genius, are the cornerstone of their band. Partners in music and marriage, they spark wherever they play, giving seamless performances to standing-room-only crowds. One of those huge crowds will happen in Escondido on December 31, 1999. That will be the couple's third performance at Escondido's "First Night," and they are sure to be among the most popular performers of the evening.

Jeannie Cheatham's music started in her soul at nearly the same instant she was born. She can remember when she didn't play the piano (she began at five), yet knows life truly began when she did. Although most fans don't know it, she didn't consider herself a vocalist at first. Her singing has evolved in the last decade and now fans won't do without it.

Jeannie began performing and defining her style in the church choir in her hometown of Akron, Ohio. Since those days she's performed with scores of greats, including Sippie Wallace, Big Mama Thornton, Cab Calloway, T-Bone Walker, Diana Washington and Jimmy Witherspoon. Additionally, Jeannie was featured in *Three Generations of the Blues*, a public-television special featuring Jeannie, Sippie Wallace, and Big Mama Thornton. The film won rave reviews from jazz fans and African-American critics throughout the country. Currently Jeannie is helping the Smithsonian with its project of recording interviews with the great women of jazz.

Photo: Meredith French

La Jolla residents and internationally known blues and jazz performers, Jimmy and Jeanne Cheatham sing the praises of San Diego at blues and jazz clubs and concerts throughout the area and around the world.

— continued on next page

Before moving to San Diego in 1978 and selecting the Golden Triangle as a home base, Jeannie and Jimmy did their share of gigs in clubs and concert halls. For a time, they taught at the University of Wisconsin. It was the easygoing environment and climate that pulled the Cheathams to San Diego. Jimmy was soon recruited by UCSD to teach music and Black musical history. "I retired in 1993 with Professor Emeritus status," he says chuckling; Jeannie adds the punch line: "Sure he retired, for about fifteen minutes before the regents realized they couldn't do without him." Jimmy brought such energy to the program, that they hired him back. He can still be found in the classroom he loves.

Jimmy has played base trombone with Duke Ellington, Lionel Hampton, Thad Jones, Ornette Coleman and was musical director for Chico Hamilton. Jimmy arranges all the music for the band and with Jeannie co-writes some of the songs that have secured their place on the charts and in jazz history.

Each musical success has produced another and they just seem to be getting better. If you can't find their CDs it's because their music doesn't stay in stores very long. *Meet Me with Your Black Drawers On*, *Back to the Neighborhood*, *Love in the Afternoon* and *Homeward Bound* have topped the blues and jazz charts. The band has performed for packed houses at the Long Beach Blues Festival and the Long Beach Jazz Festival, San Francisco Blues Festival, Playboy Jazz Festival, Monterey Jazz Festival, Chicago Jazz Festival, and scores of others. Jimmy and Jeannie recently made front-page news during a tour in Japan.

As Jeannie says, "Music is alive in our souls and it comes out in the songs and melodies." Crowds respond to that, and also to their obvious enjoyment of one another, which comes out in the teasing and good-natured fun that audiences enjoy so much.

As we go to press, there's rumor of a book deal for Jeannie's memoirs. Meanwhile, Jimmy and Jeannie are polishing up the band's newest songs for an album that will feature Jeannie's golden voice and magic fingers at the piano and Jimmy's arrangements and his magnificent horn playing. While they won't share the details yet, it's sure to roar and rattle, seduce and soothe you.

---

music makes this place feel like party time, even though it's not live.

The microbrew choices vary and the pub also has a large selection of imported beers if you prefer something more continental with that garlic and feta pizza. Call for upcoming events such as the microbrew brewing contests.

Sandbar Cafe
3878 Carlsbad Blvd., Carlsbad
• (760) 729-8561

An ultra-popular beach club and hangout where the age bracket of the patrons runs from late 20s to the older-than-50 crowd. There's a $3 cover charge and on the week-

ends, especially in the summer, the place can be packed. There's a big dance floor, and the music varies: country on Tuesdays, rock and roll on the weekends, blues on Monday and reggae on Thursdays.

Tournament of Champions Lounge
La Costa Resort & Spa
2100 Costa Del Mar Rd., Carlsbad
• (760) 438-9111

A lounge and gathering spot for visitors and guests of the famous resort (please see our Spas & Resorts chapter for more details), this is normally a quieter nightspot for the 40-and-older crowd. There's live music and the variety changes often.

Downtown San Diego lights up the night with skyscraper light shows.

North County Inland

Beaver Creek Saloon
1320 E. Valley Pkwy., Escondido
• (760) 746-7408

If you love country music and want to be with people who know how to have Western-type fun, then this could be your spot of choice. The Saloon, decorated in (what else?) Western style, has live entertainment Tuesdays and Thursday through Sunday nights and boasts one of the largest dance floors in the county. Need another reason to visit Beaver Creek Saloon? How about free dance lessons every night?

San Marcos Brewery & Grill
1808 W. San Marcos Blvd., San Marcos
• (760) 471-0050

The number of microbrews on tap daily changes, and some Insiders say when the honey-wheat ale is available, get a pitcher because one glass won't be enough. The food is okay, the service is quick and friendly, but Insider's come for the brew.

This microbrewery draws the after-work crowd, students from nearby Cal State San Marcos and Palomar College, and families too. It's busy on Friday and weekends and even in winter it's fun to sit outdoors around the open-air fire pit.

East County

Blarney Stone Pub Too
7059 El Cajon Blvd., La Mesa
• (619) 463-2263

A traditional Irish pub where the Guinness is dark and the traditional Celtic music is loud and makes you want to dance or at least tap your toes. Call for a schedule of performers; band auditions are Wednesdays.

South Bay

Cafe Lamaze
1441 Highland Ave., National City
• (619) 474-3222

Piano bars seem to be making a resurgence, and Cafe Lamaze is no exception. Sip champagne or your favorite cocktail while listening to the smooth sounds of a variety of pianists, all with their own specialties. But they all like requests, and they'll all encourage you to sing along.

House of Munich
230 Third Ave., Chula Vista
• **(619) 426-5172**

Come on, admit it. You like accordion music — we all do! But how often do you have the opportunity to hear it played seriously and at its best? Here's your chance. Enter into the House of Munich with its German ambiance and accordion music played Friday through Sunday. It's a different experience and one well worth trying.

J.J.'s New Sports Bar
2638 Main St. (inside Marisol Nightclub), Chula Vista
• **(619) 429-8045**

Watch your favorite sport every night of the week at J.J.'s, or you can take a break on Tuesdays and try a little Karaoke. The crowd is friendly here and all ages are welcome. Only one thing is required: You have to root for the home team.

Coffeehouses

San Diego

Java Joe's
4994 Newport Ave., San Diego
• **(619) 523-0356**

Head to Ocean Beach and this way-cool coffeehouse for live music every night but Tuesday. Monday is open-mike night, which always produces some interesting and sometimes surprising entertainment.

Lestat's Coffeehouse
3343 Adams Ave., San Diego
• **(619) 282-0437**

Nightly entertainment is featured here: jazz, acoustic, folk and even some music from the middle ages every once in a while. Monday is open-mike night for aspiring performers looking for an audience.

The Living Room
5900 El Cajon Blvd., San Diego
• **(619) 286-8434**
1417 University Ave., San Diego
• **(619) 295-7911**

The name says it all. When you walk into the Living Room, you'll feel like you're in your own home. Relax on a comfortable sofa, enjoy a light bite to eat and an outstanding selection of coffees while you listen to a rotating group of comedians and musical performers. Spanish guitar and acoustic are the most common, but check to see what's up before you go. The El Cajon Boulevard site is popular with college students as it's close to San Diego State University. The University Avenue location draws a more eclectic crowd.

Red's Espresso Gallery
1017 Rosecrans St., San Diego
• **(619) 523-5540**

If you're looking for something a little different, try this coffeehouse in Point Loma. There's plenty of music, blues and jazz predominantly, but you can also get in on poetry readings, a chess club and an Art Bell (the late-night radio talk-show host) discussion group.

Twiggs Tea and Coffee Company
4590 Park Blvd., San Diego
• **(619) 296-0616**

Something is going on at Twiggs nearly every evening. Most performances are acoustic/folk music, but occasionally a jazz or pop

INSIDERS' TIP

The Indian gaming casinos are excellent nightspots for fun seekers. At the casinos you'll discover dancing and live music, but you may not be able to find a beer. Only Viejas serves alcohol.

Photo: James Blank/San Diego Convention and Visitors Bureau

Nestled at the foot of San Diego's skyline along the embarcadero, Seaport Village offers fine shopping, dining, entertainment and sightseeing.

artist will make an appearance too. This is a spacious coffeehouse with lots of room to spread out and get comfortable.

North County Coastal

Esmeralda Books & Coffee
1555 Camino Del Mar, Del Mar
• (858) 755-2707

An independent bookstore that sells great coffee, Esmeralda's ambiance encourages you to linger, sip and buy a smashing selection of books. On the weekends, along with books, there's live entertainment and highbrow events like poetry readings. (Be sure to read more about Esmeralda in our Shopping chapter.)

The store is a popular Insiders' hangout for bibliophiles, local authors, poets and others who stop in for a browse and conversation. The store is in the Del Mar Plaza. It's open seven days a

week and stays open until 11 PM on Friday and Saturday nights.

La Costa Coffee Roasting
6965 El Camino Real, Carlsbad
• (760) 438-8160

A family-style hangout where people come to mingle, have coffee and relax, especially after taking in a movie at the multiplex theater or visiting the branch of the Carlsbad City library right in the same shopping center. There's live entertainment — perhaps a guitarist, cellist, or bluegrass banjo player — on weekend evenings. If you're looking for a coffee-related gift to take back home, there are walls of designer, silly, and fun coffee mugs.

Roasting Plant Coffee Co. and Cafe
3870 Valley Center Dr., Del Mar
• (858) 793-6777

Insiders come here for the live music on Thursday and Friday evenings — which might be anything from jazz to southern-style music to classical to rock. You'll see all age groups here enjoying the good, strong coffee — and snacks too.

North County Inland

Grounds-Zero
212 E. Grand Ave., Escondido
• (760) 480-5777

Great, comfortable atmosphere and great coffee is only better with the blues jam sessions on Monday nights. Call the Grounds-Zero for other events — many are spontaneous and some are scheduled.

Java Central
11738 Carmel Mountain Rd., Carmel Mountain Ranch • (858) 674-0804

It's impossible to tell what music or performer will appear at Java Central, a relaxed place to meet friends and enjoy the nightly live entertainment. What you know you'll get is a superb cup of coffee — as exotic or as normal as you choose. We like the friendly staff and cozy feeling of the place; others must too since it can be busy.

Metaphor Cafe
258 E. Second Ave., Escondido
• (760) 489-8890

Here's a place for coffee, perhaps a snack and comfortable surroundings in which you can enjoy the poetry readings, the jazz jams and a comedian or two. The Metaphor Cafe alternates between quiet and crowded.

Mikey's Coffeehouse
12222 Poway Rd., Poway
• (858) 486-7924

The coffeehouse is popular with the early evening crowd that needs a place to meet and mingle after a movie, long work day or just to get out and about. The live entertain-ment might include a jazz group, a singer, a guitarist or a blues band. Call for a week's worth of possibilities.

East County

Coffee Merchant
5500 Grossmont Center Dr., La Mesa
• (619) 460-7393

Whether you want decaf or the real thing, this is a great little coffeehouse for grabbing a quick cup or hanging out with friends (or a good book). There's a complete espresso and dessert bar and live music every Friday evening, played by a jazz group, perhaps, or a guitarist singing Latino melodies.

Original Cajon Coffee Company
330 N. Magnolia Ave., El Cajon
• (619) 588-6376

You can drink your java inside or out on the patio. The Original Cajon Coffee Company has specialty coffee and a good, plain old cup of brew. It's a nice place to meet friends whether you're on the way to a SDSU game, out shopping or on the hunt for the perfect antique.

Worth Checking Out

San Diego

4th & B
345 B St., San Diego • (619) 231-4343

This is a relatively new indoor concert and dance venue that has already made its mark on San Diego. Current performers as well as legends from the past appear regularly at 4th & B, like Sister Hazel, Sonia Dada, the Squirrel Nut Zippers, Stephen Stills and Eddie Money. When no concert is scheduled, you can always enjoy dancing to live music. Tick-

INSIDERS' TIP

The bar or club in your hotel or any of the hotels in our Hotel Chapter may have a big screen that's tuned to a big game or movie and an opportunity for conversation.

ets are available at the box office from 10 AM to 5 PM or by calling Ticketmaster at (619) 220-8497. You must be 21 or older for admission.

The Comedy Store
916 Pearl St., La Jolla • (858) 454-9176

What started in Los Angeles has made its way south to La Jolla. First-rate comedians entertain, and sometimes a big name will roll in. Check out the Dreamgirls Revue held weekly, featuring comedy and celebrity lookalikes. If you're an aspiring comic yourself, check for open-mike night when you can try your act on a captive audience. Open Tuesday through Sunday, there's a two-drink minimum and an $8 cover charge on Tuesday, Wednesday and Thursday, $10 on Friday and Saturday and $5 on Sunday.

Humphrey's Concerts by the Bay
2241 Shelter Island Dr., San Diego • (619) 523-1010

Every summer Humphrey's stages this unique outdoor concert series that features top-name performers such as David Sanborn, Boz Scaggs, the Doobie Brothers and Harry Belafonte. If you have access to a small boat, you can motor up to the concert site and listen to the music from the water. For those who prefer to see what they're hearing, tickets are available in advance by calling Ticketmaster at (619) 220-8497 or can be purchased at Humphrey's box office. Food, beverages and cocktails are all sold on-site.

SOMA Live
5305 Metro St., San Diego • (619) 239-7662

This is a rock concert venue that caters to the teenage and early twenties set. Top-name acts inspire moshing and crowd surfing amongst this very young crowd. Recent bands have included Misdirection, User Friendly, N.I.V. and Good Riddance. We can't claim to recog-

nize these groups, but our young Insider sources assure us they're hot. The concerts are well supervised, and you'll see lots of parents coming to pick up their kids at the end of the evening. Call for concert and ticket information.

North County Coastal

Concerts Under the Oaks
Quail Botanical Gardens, 230 Quail Gardens Dr., Encinitas • (760) 436-3036

A series of concerts that range from jazz favorites like The American Song Book and Kendra Eskau and Friends to a bluegrass band. This is an early night out (the concerts begin at 6 PM). Call for a list of upcoming Sunday evening concerts. Ticket prices are $15 for a single concert and light dinner to $40 for the summer series.

Carmel Valley Summer Serenades
3520 Long Run Dr., Solana Beach • (858) 481-1339

These are free concerts under the summer stars with views of great sunsets, too. The locations vary; they're currently in the Del Mar and Solana Beach area. Call for a line up of concerts and locations.

TGIF
Carlsbad Arts Office
1200 Carlsbad Village Dr., Carlsbad • (760) 434-2904

Sponsored by the Carlsbad Arts Office, the TGIF Jazz in the Parks concerts bring live performances in from around the country and the county. The free summer concerts are popular with Insiders and visitors. The concerts, held at different parks in the city of Carlsbad, start at 6 PM and end around 8 PM. Past performers have included Earl Thomas and the Blues Ambassadors, Billy Thompson and Yavaz performing Latin jazz. Most Insiders pack picnics or stop for sandwiches on route. Be sure to bring lawn chairs or blankets.

That Pizza Place
2622 El Camino Real, Carlsbad
• (760) 434-3171

Call for a schedule as the nightly jazz and rock groups change. We recently went to hear a banjo group; they were a blue grass, knee-slapping dynamite group. We came away congratulating ourselves for finding such great music where most people wouldn't expect it.

That Pizza Place usually has a loud and fun crowd: families, singles, and couples eating pizza (some say the best on the planet), drinking beer and dancing too.

This is a good place to shake off the workday frustrations on the dance floor and meet friends, too. (For more details on what Insiders choose to eat here, check out our Restaurants chapter. Here's a clue: Try the "kitchen sink.")

North County Inland

Lake Wohlford Cafe
25484 Lake Wohlford Rd., Escondido
• (760) 749-2755

Leave your fancy duds in the closet when you head for this fun, funky, country-style cafe and pub. This isn't a chi-chi microbrew pub or oh-so-cool coffeehouse, but here you'll get burgers that are big and extra crunchy fries. Depending on who's at the cafe, the noise and fun level change.

On the last Friday of every month, check out Jack Johnson's 1950s vintage music review called *Live! The Hank Williams Sr. Tribute Show*. It's fun and there's no cover charge. Remember if you're a burger lover, bring along your appetite.

East County

Back to the 50s Car Show
La Mesa Blvd., from Date St. to Grant St., La Mesa • (619) 465-1571

This isn't the club scene or a hot hip-hop nightspot, but those in East County know that a visit to the Car Show means a good time will be had by all. Every Thursday starting at about 6 PM, you'll be treated to live music performances and DJs spinning CDs, great looking cars (how do they keep them that clean?), and food vendors. Call for information about parking your own hot rod among these beauties.

Barona Casino
1000 Wildcat Canyon Rd., Lakeside
• (619) 443-2300, (888) 722-7662

The Barona Casino provides all the gaming fun you can handle (see our chapter on Attractions for more about the gambling side). As for nightlife, you'll have no trouble finding music, dancing, and other pleasures. The Casino features more than 12 hours of non-stop live music on the casino floor, seven days a week. The acts change often, and we've enjoyed performances by talented local bands that specialize in country music (yes, you'll find room to dance) to great jazz groups. If you get hungry, there's a Vegas-style buffet and Side Attractions food court, too. You might even get to mingle with television, film and music superstars who frequent this casino.

Viejas Casino & Turf Club
5000 Willows Rd., Alpine
• (619) 445-5400

As this ultra-popular Viejas Indian Casino says, "We've got more fun," and when you go for entertainment, you won't be disappointed. Of the three main casinos, this is the only one

---

INSIDERS' TIP

A bar hopper's paradise is found in The Gaslamp Quarter. A huge concentration of unique and exciting clubs and bars are within a few blocks of one another, most of them easy walking distance. See how many you can sample in one evening, it will be a challenge. Then be sure to take a taxi home.

that can sell alcohol. Call for the latest lineup and performance times.

Be sure to look at the entry under Attractions for more on this night and day spot and the other casinos. Although not complete as we go to press, a new shopping outlet with upscale and discount stores is going up on the Casino & Turf Club property. A highlight is the NightFire!, an interactive fountain, fire and laser light display.

Sycuan Casino
5469 Dehesa Rd., El Cajon
• (619) 445-6002

The Sycuan Casino, in East County's El Cajon, gives you gaming fun and live entertainment. In case you haven't caught on, the casinos (Barona, Sycuan and Viejas) are popular places to nightlife hop in the East County. In addition to gaming, Sycuan has featured internationally as well as locally famous entertainment — names such as Phyllis Diller, America, BJ Thomas, The Turtles, Mark Lindsay and the Shirelles. Be sure to call for upcoming events and performances.

South Bay

Coors Amphitheatre
2050 Otay Valley Rd., Chula Vista
• (619) 671-3500

This brand-new concert amphitheatre adds a much-needed performance venue to the South Bay and to San Diego County. The amphitheatre seats 20,000, and in its inaugural season showcased such acts as Elton John, Santana, the Spice Girls, Chicago and the B-52s.

Concerts and events will be expanded in years to come. Tickets can be purchased at Ticketmaster at (619) 220-8497.

The area's malls, shops, stores and districts are huge and eclectic.

Shopping

If shopping is your hobby, passion, indulgence or sport of choice, San Diego will satisfy you. The area's malls, shops, stores and districts are huge and eclectic. We think San Diego has about the best shopping on the planet. The choices might even be a bit overwhelming.

So in this chapter, we've included need-to-know shopping information and then presented the best in shopping experiences. As shoppers at heart, we've put a lot of enthusiasm behind the lists we give you in this chapter. The places we've included are the ones we tell our friends not to miss.

Like the malls. Some, like the Fashion Valley Mall in Mission Valley, could easily become an addiction. Like the shopping districts — including Adams Avenue, with its blend of coffee pubs, new and used bookstores and antique emporiums. Here you can read about the district in San Marcos (in North County Inland), that has more than 50 furniture stores. You'll find information on the Carlsbad Company Stores too, where you can find specialty stores from Donna Karan to Ralph Lauren. Although it might be different in your city, here in San Diego County the shopping centers are often a blend of specialty stores like these, national chains such as Sears, and discount stores too, like Marshalls Department Store. Of course, that information is here too.

We've included our favorite stores specializing in resale and consignment clothing, and then added swap meets (and a few flea markets). Half the fun of shopping in these specialty places is that you never quite know what you'll find, and if you'll need it, until you see it.

We've also given you a taste of the antique stores in the area. Our list is far from a telephone-book tabulation, though. Use it as a basic introduction only. If you're really hooked on antiquing, we recommend that you visit some of the stores and get a newsletter (we'll tell you about that too), which should lead you to even more stores to try. And while you're off on your hunt you might want to scan the listings for other possibilities. If you've traveled the hour and a half to East County's Julian Shopping District, for example, you may find some surprises to take home along with your antiques. This quaint mountain town is heaped to heaven with little shops that sell country accessories, collectibles and crafts — not to mention fudge, ice cream and apple cider.

We're both book lovers. Therefore, we've given you a good sampling of what's available in this area and we've mentioned unusual stores because we're especially fond of them. Keep in mind, though, that the phone book's Yellow Pages can be helpful too, because we couldn't include every possibility.

After organizing all our favorite stores into tidy categories, we discovered something was lacking, so we created a new section. It's called "Unique and Intriguing". Here you will find stores that may tickle your fancy with unusual or hard-to-find offerings, like those little cookies you nibbled in Vienna, the right color chaps for your western-wear outfit or perhaps a fragrant bouquet of dried herbs. If reading about them appeals to you, they're probably worth the visit, even if they're a ways from the place you're staying.

We've organized this chapter by shopping category; within each of those you'll find the usual regional divisions. So if you're a used book buyer, hooked on swap meets or thrill to consignment store buying, then you'll want to look for those categories, see what each of San Diego's regions has to offer, and perhaps hop in your car for one of those long shopping trips Insiders are known to take. (If you have to make that long drive to Julian, you can replenish your shopping energy with a slice of the city's famous apple pie.)

Perhaps, though, all the stores you want to see will be within a few blocks of your hotel doorstep. In either case, with your *Insiders' Guide* in hand, you're ready. Put on your shopping shoes (best make them comfortable), grab your sense of adventure, and head to the stores. You won't be disappointed

Malls

San Diego

Clairemont Town Square Shopping Center
4186 Clairemont Mesa Blvd., San Diego
• **(619) 276-6462**

Recently renovated, Clairemont Town Square is anchored by **Burlington Coat Factory**, **Circuit City** and **Michael's**, a giant arts and crafts store. The center has lots of little shops too, like the charming **Dear To My Heart Doll Boutique**. Several fast-food places are sprinkled throughout the mall, and **Acapulco Mexican Restaurant** is nearby, as is the **Outback Steakhouse**, for a sit-down meal and a chance to rest your feet. Also located in the center is the newly built **Pacific Theatres Town Square**, with 14 screens and all stadium-style seating.

Fashion Valley
7007 Friars Rd., San Diego
• **(619) 688-9113**

This is San Diego's largest shopping mall, and it has just undergone a $120 million expansion and renovation. The big department stores are **Neiman Marcus**, **Nordstrom**, **Macy's**, **Saks Fifth Avenue**, **Robinsons-May** and **JC Penney**. And just about every other

Fresh and Fabulous Farmers' Markets

Picture succulent produce, aromatic herbs and field-fresh flowers. Now put that vision smack dab in the center of a convenient neighborhood parking lot and you'll get a peek at what our area's farmers' markets have to offer. Insiders adore the outdoor markets and many plan shopping and meals around the produce that they buy there.

At all the farmers' markets mentioned you'll find vegetables at peak perfection, oodles of flowers from the exotic (protea anyone?) to the familiar (flawless roses, perky daisies and more), and exquisite fruits, many cut and offered for sampling. Each stall holds something different: one may have herbs, plants and organic eggs; another pies and breads. Some of the markets listed have specialties too, like tamales, or roasted-on-the-spot peanuts. As you visit them you'll find that each one has a flavor of its own; part of the fun of shopping the markets is discovering what each place and even each stall has that makes it unique.

Many shoppers arrive just as the market opens; others go when it's convenient. Most of the farmers' markets are open for about three hours and are always held outdoors. Although winter rainstorms have been known to put a damper on some farmers' markets, it usually takes a good soaking storm to shut one down. So don't go if it's pouring.

Remember that the produce found at the farmers' markets is seasonal. If you're visiting in December and looking for vine-ripened strawberries, you may be out of luck. Check that same market between March and June and you'll dazzled by the choices.

Prices and quality vary from vendor to vendor at the markets, so it's best to have a shopping game plan. As we discussed the advice we might give to you, we found that our own methods were the same: We always walk the entire market before buying, making mental notes of where to select the best chocolate-brown macadamia nuts, rich green Fuerte avocados and pickling cucumbers. Most vendors have enough change for customers, yet we always make sure there are dollar bills in our pockets so that shopping is quick and easy.

We've listed the markets by days of the week rather than regions. So if your dinner party is on Thursday and you really need field-perfect squash, mouth-watering melons and magnificent mushrooms, just find a market that's open that morning, and you'll know which direction to head.

SUNDAY	**San Diego**: at "The Boulevard" at Marborough Street (3 blocks east of 40th Street), 10 AM to 2 PM; **Hillcrest**: at the Department of Motor Vehicles parking lot at 3960 Normal Street, 9 AM until noon.
TUESDAY	**Coronado**: at the Old Ferry Landing, corner of Third Street and B Avenue, 2:30 PM to 6 PM; **Escondido**: at Grand Avenue and Broadway Street, 3 PM to 7 PM; **Chula Vista**: between Third Avenue and E and F Streets, 3:30 PM until 6 PM.
WEDNESDAY	**Escondido**: across from the North County Fair Shopping Mall, 3660 Sunset Drive, 9 AM until noon; **Ocean Beach**: at the 4900 block of Newport Avenue, 4 PM to 8 PM; **Carlsbad**: on Roosevelt Street between Grand Avenue and Carlsbad Village Drive, 2 PM until 5 PM.
THURSDAY	**Oceanside** (downtown): Coast Highway and Pier View, 9 AM to 12:30 PM; **Mission Valley**: at Hazard Center, Friars Road at Calif. 163, 3 PM to 6:30 PM; **Chula Vista**: at Third Avenue and E Street, 3 PM to 6 PM.
FRIDAY	**Rancho Bernardo**: at the Bernardo Winery, 13330 Paseo del Verano Norte, 9 AM to noon; **La Mesa**: at 8500 Allison Street (east of Spring Street), 3 PM to 6 PM; **Fallbrook**: at Village Square at Main Street, 9 AM to 1 PM.
SATURDAY	**Pacific Beach**: at Promenade Mall, Mission Boulevard, Reed Avenue and Pacific Beach Drive, 8 AM to noon; **Vista**: at the corner of Eucalyptus Street and Escondido Avenue (Vista City Hall parking lot), 8 AM to 11 AM; **Poway**: in Old Poway Park, corner of Midland Road and Temple Street, 8 AM to 11 AM; **Del Mar**: in the City Hall parking lot at the corner of El Camino del Mar and 10th Street, 1 PM to 4 PM.

specialty store you can think of is there, too. Fashion Valley has more than 200 of them, including **Tiffany & Co.**, **Talbots**, **Gap**, **Banana Republic**, **Crate & Barrel**, **See's Candies**, and many, more. **Restoration Hardware** is one of our favorites. It's a hardware store that's enticing to both men and women for its one-of-a-kind reproduction treasures.

Nearly two dozen restaurants, bistros and eateries offer everything from a leisurely meal with wine and cocktails to a quick snack while on the run to the next store. If you're looking for something truly unusual, check out the kiosks located throughout the mall. They offer unique gifts and mementos that are hard to find elsewhere. If a movie is on your agenda, you can't go wrong with the brand-new **AMC Theater** right in the middle of the mall. Eighteen screens and stadium-style seating provide the ultimate movie-going experience.

Horton Plaza
Fourth Ave. and
Broadway, San Diego
• (619) 238-1596

Known for its highly acclaimed architecture and eye-catching color scheme, Horton Plaza is home to more than 140 shops, anchored by **Nordstrom**, **Macy's** and **Mervyn's**. San Diego's version of **Planet Hollywood** is in the shopping center, as is **FAO Schwarz**, the **Warner Brothers Store**, the **Disney Store**, **Victoria's Secret**, **Ann Taylor** and **Abercrombie & Fitch**.

Some of our favorite restaurants are inside the mall too, such as the **California Cafe** and the **Panda Inn** for great Chinese food. Or if you're looking for something different, the international food court can't be beat for quick and tasty treats. For entertainment, check out the 14-screen theater or take in a play at the **Lyceum Theatre**, located one level below ground floor in the mall.

Mission Valley Center
1640 Camino del Rio N., San Diego
• (619) 296-6375

Just a hop, skip and a jump away from Fashion Valley is Mission Valley Center. This is a mall that was in decline until it reinvented itself with the addition of a 20-screen AMC movie theater and a bunch of new stores. It now is one of the most popular malls in the county, especially among teenagers. Besides **Macy's Home & Furniture**, **Montgomery Ward**, and **Robinsons-May** there are more than 100 specialty shops and restaurants.

Nordstrom Rack, **Loehmann's** and **Bed, Bath & Beyond** are the big draw for adults; teens like to shop at **Express**, **Lerner New York** and **Charlotte Russe**, and can always be found in **Starworks Arena**, an interactive

entertainment center that features virtual reality games and simulations. **Ruby's Diner**, **Canyon Cafe** and **Seau's The Restaurant** (check out the latter two in our Restaurants chapter) are the main dining spots in the mall, but don't miss the food court that has everything from soft pretzels to fish tacos.

University Towne Center
4545 La Jolla Village
Dr., San Diego
• (858) 546-8858

Having just spent $12 million to create a more parklike setting, UTC has become a place where shoppers are encouraged to slow down and linger. Tranquil touches including grass and fountains are found throughout the mall. You'll find more than 155 stores too, including **Nordstrom**, **Macy's**, **Robinsons-May**, **Sears** and specialty stores like **bebe**, **Crate & Barrel**, **charles david** and **Ann Taylor**.

Choose from Chinese, Japanese, Mexican or California bistro cuisine offered by four full-service restaurants. Or sample from the variety of treats available in the huge open-air food pavilion. A movie theater and an ice rink (see our Recreation chapter for more information on the ice rink) are guaranteed to entertain both kids and adults.

North County Coastal

Plaza Camino Real
2525 El Camino Real, Carlsbad
• (760) 729-7927

For some people this mall is the hub for all shopping in North County Coastal. Plaza Camino Real is an enclosed regional mall that boasts over 140 specialty stores including those where you'll find upscale women's clothing, shoes, toys and kitchen gadgets. The anchor stores are **Sears**, **Robinsons-May**, **JCPenney** and **Macy's**.

There are more than 21 food specialty shops where you can select everything from pizza to pretzels and a few **Mrs. Fields** cookies to ward off the shopping hungries. There are places to sit and people watch, good book stores, clothing stores, accessory boutiques and a western wear outlet. The mall was originally designed and built in the late 1960s and in 1997 underwent a beautification program, which has drawn more upscale stores and shoppers.

Del Mar Plaza
1400 Maiden Ln., Del Mar
• **(858) 792-1555**

Found on the corner of Camino Del Mar and 15th Street, the many shops of the Del Mar Plaza open onto a courtyard.

This mall offers an eclectic array of shopping choices. Here you'll find stores like **Sole Comfort** (featuring specialty shoes including Birkenstock), **Moonbeams** (with heavenly clothing for children) and **Chicos** (an exclusive line of all-cotton clothes for women). You'll also find the **Good Nature Market** (natural foods and natural health care), **Modera** (a gallery of modern artifacts by design), **Esmeralda** (the bookstore you may have read about in our Nightlife chapter) and an all-American hamburger and malt shop. If you shop here in the evening, you get an added bonus: Wait on the balcony facing west and get a $1 million view of the sun setting over the Pacific.

North County Inland

North County Fair Mall
272 E. Via Rancho Pkwy., Escondido
• **(760) 489-2332**

North County Inland's largest enclosed mall is anchored by **Nordstrom**, **Macy's**, **Robinsons-May**, **Sears** and **JCPenney**. You'll find 160 specialty shops including **Godiva** chocolates, **Crabtree & Evelyn**, **Mrs. Fields Cookies**, **No Fear**, **Lane Bryant**, **Singers! Karaoke Store**, **Eddie Bauer**, **Natural Wonders** and **San Diego Padres Clubhouse**.

There are 15 restaurants that are open for lunch and dinner, along with a nifty food court that offers everything from pizza to Indian foods. Throughout the mall there are plenty of places to sit and people watch — a favorite pastime for those who come along with a true shopper. Parking on weekends can be tricky but there always seems to be enough. Be sure to check out **Calido Chili Traders**, (760) 489-

5740, for some of the neatest and strangest foods that are definitely hot stuff.

East County

Grossmont Center
5500 Grossmont Center Dr., La Mesa
• **(619) 466-5306**

Recently renovated and highly spiffy, the Grossmont Center has attracted shoppers from East County and the mountain communities since it was founded in 1965. Currently there are over 100 stores. Anchor stores include **Macy's**, **Montgomery Wards**, **SuperSports USA by Oshmans** and **Target**. You'll find specialty stores that are unique, including **Chic Wide Shoes**, **Shavers and Small Appliances**, **Cutler's Cupboard** (a knife store) as well as **Kids R Us**, **Barnes & Noble**, and a **Cost Plus World Market**.

South Bay

Chula Vista Center
555 Broadway, Chula Vista
• **(619) 422-7500**

Located right in the heart of Chula Vista, this mall is home to **Macy's**, **Mervyn's**, **Sears** and **JC Penney** as anchors, and more than 100 specialty stores. Browse among the vitamins and natural food items at **Pleasant House of Natural Foods**, or shop for men's and women's clothing at **Raya's for Him & Her**.

A **CinemaStar Luxury 10 Theater** is in the mall, and so are lots of fast-food places where you can grab a snack.

Plaza Bonita Shopping Center
3030 Plaza Bonita Rd., National City
• **(619) 267-2850**

South Bay's only enclosed, climate-controlled shopping center, Plaza Bonita is anchored by **JC Penney**, **Montgomery Ward**, **Mervyn's** and **Robinsons-May**. More than 130 specialty shops, like **Miller's Outpost**, **Foot Locker** and **Kinney Shoes** will keep you shopping for hours.

When you need a break, stop in at **Applebee's Restaurant** or one of the many restaurants in the food court. There's also a six-screen **Mann Theater** in the center.

Discount and Outlet Shopping

San Diego

Burlington Coat Factory
3962 Clairemont Mesa Blvd., San Diego
• **(858) 272-1893**

Located in the Clairemont Town Square Shopping Center, you'll find much more than just coats (although there's no shortage of those).

Burlington is the second largest off-price clothing store in the country, offering fashions for the whole family. Most styles are in season, but in some cases sizes and selection are limited. Additionally, Burlington has shoes, accessories, linens and baby furniture.

Designer Labels for Less
4240 Kearny Mesa Rd., San Diego
• **(858) 874-3823**

Career clothing and dressy casual wear are the specialties at this Insiders' favorite. Both prices and quality are consistently good, and if you're looking for upscale lingerie, look no further. Designer Labels for Less has a vast collection of beautiful, lacy sweet nothings for a fraction of the original cost. Some children's and men's clothing is available too.

La Jolla Village Square
8657 Villa La Jolla Dr., La Jolla
• **(858) 455-7550**

This almost qualifies as a mall, but it's really a discount shopping center, and a pretty spiffy one, at that. It's a popular shopping destination because of its **Starbucks Coffee**, offbeat fast-food eateries and 12-screen theater.

Mixed in with the leisurely crowd, however, are the power shoppers looking for bargains at **Marshalls**, **Cost Plus**, **Linens 'n Things**, **Famous Footwear**, **Ross Stores** and **Crown Books Superstore**.

A gigantic **Ralph's Grocery Store** is on the premises as is **Trader Joe's** for international wines and delicacies.

Loehmann's
1640 Camino del Rio N., San Diego
• **(619) 296-7776**

San Diego's version of this national discount store is located in the east wing of Mission Valley Center (see our entry under Malls). Famous for its discount women's designer clothes, it's also a great place to find bargains on sportswear, shoes and lingerie. Loehmann's has a good children's department too, and has just recently added a menswear section. Don't forget to check out the back room, where top-of-the-line designer formal wear and more casual duds can be had for deep discounts. Wear your best underwear — fitting rooms are communal.

Mission Valley Center West
1100 Camino del Rio N., San Diego
• **(619) 296-6375**

Mission Valley Center's little sister, located just to the west of the main shopping center, has **Old Navy** and **Marshalls**, two discount giants. You'll also find a **Borders Books & Music** and **Just for Feet** athletic shoes. When you're ready to hit the links, stop in at **Golfsmith** for all your golfing equipment and supplies. A giant **Gateway** computer store should fulfill all your techno-wishes.

Nordstrom Rack
1640 Camino del Rio N., San Diego
• **(619) 296-0143**

This is where all those beautiful but pricey clothes from Nordstrom end up. You can get great deals on ladies', men's and children's

---

INSIDERS' TIP

Many specialty stores also sell books. If you're looking for a book on climbing opportunities, a sporting goods specialty store such as Adventure 16 or REI might have a better selection than a bookstore.

clothing as well as shoes, accessories, lingerie and some home decor items. Don't expect the same selection or level of service you'd find at Nordstrom's regular department stores, but the values make it a worthwhile visit. The Rack is located in the east wing of Mission Valley Shopping Center (see our entry under Malls).

Park Valley Center
1550 Camino de la Reina, San Diego
• (no phone)

Do you love the clothes at Saks Fifth Avenue but hate spending the big bucks? Then head for **Off 5th** in this new shopping center. It's a beautiful store that is orderly, clean and inviting, just like the original Saks, but with price tags that are much kinder to your wallet. The shopping center is located just north of and across the street from the giant Mission Valley Center, and also has a **Crown Books Superstore**, **Aaron Brothers Art & Framing**, **Zainy Brainy** for the kids and a **Mikasa** store for china and crystal. Some of the stores are full price, but there are several discount shops and boutiques too.

Shoe Pavilion
4240 Kearny Mesa Rd., San Diego
• (858) 492-9833
3337 Rosecrans St., San Diego
• (619) 222-6787

In these warehouse-style stores you'll find quality brand-name men's and women's shoes for about half the retail price.

The shoes are displayed on counters with boxes piled up underneath, and it's strictly self-serve. But friendly salespeople are always glad to answer questions or help you find something special.

North County Coastal

Carlsbad Company Stores
Palomar Airport Rd. and Paseo del Norte, Carlsbad • (760) 804-9000

Carlsbad Company Stores is a new potpourri of specialty stores from **Ralph Lauren**, **Donna Karan** and **Royal Dalton** outlets to **Rockport**, **Tommy Hilfiger**, The **Gap**, and

Hush Puppies. North County shoppers who love those exceptional brand names love coming here.

As we go to press, there are more stores just moving in; when this mall is completed you'll be able to enjoy about 75 fine clothing and accessory stores. The mall is in a great location, too, especially for tourists: Both LEGOLAND (see our Kidstuff chapter) and the Carlsbad Flower Fields (see our Annual Events chapter) are the same area.

Should you start fading while you're picking the perfect little black dress or searching out some super-cool sneaks, you'll find chain shops like Starbuck's, a fast Asian food restaurant, an old-fashion malt shop with enormous burgers and a real California smoothie (juice) bar. Or if you'd like to pop outside, you can find fine dining without even moving your car. Just a short block north is Bellefleur (see our Restaurant chapter), which features fresh and flavorful California-style cuisine and excellent local wines.

On weekends the stores are busy and during the holidays the Christmas decorations are magnificent. Last year there was a 50-foot decorated tree. There's lots of parking and the mall is wheelchair accessible.

Marshalls Department Store
685 San Rodolfo Dr., Solana Beach
• (858) 755-0791

While there are other Marshalls Department Stores in San Diego, many Insiders consider this North County Coastal store to be the best. We're talking primo prices and larger selections, from shorts and T-shirts to business suits.

This store is bigger than the others, for one thing. It stocks higher quality merchandise at the excellent discount prices one expects from Marshalls. Close by are other specialty stores that move in and out of the strip mall. Currently, you'll find an accessories shop, a lingerie store, an office supply store, and a bagel and coffee cafe.

UFO
1120 N. Melrose Dr., Vista
• (760) 941-2345

No, you will not find E.T. at this store, but rather great bargains from the Upholstery Fab-

Horton Plaza shoppers enjoy the sun and the whimsical sculptures.

ric Outlet. If you're in the market for fabric or for the accessories it takes to recover or design anything, this is the store. At UFO you'll be tempted by first-class merchandise. Although the sales happen rarely, the clearance table always holds a few finds.

North County Inland

Kids Warehouse
1617 Capalina Rd., San Marcos
• **(760) 471-5442**

If you're looking for a priced-right bit of baby's room equipment, then Kids Warehouse will help you find it. They have enough cribs, beds and accessories to make a mom or dad's head spin.

The staff are experts at helping find the right furnishing for your needs.

San Diego North County Factory Outlet Center
1050 Los Vallecitos Blvd., San Marcos
• **(760) 471-1500**

At this center's 27 outlets you can expect

to pay from 25 to 75 percent less than at department stores. Among the shops are **Maidenform**, **Dress Barn**, a book discounter and a top shop.

You'll also find stores for party goods, books, linens, frames and luggage.

East County

GTM Discount General Store
8967 Carlton Hills Blvd., Santee
• **(619) 449-4953**
7551 Broadway Ave., Lemon Grove
• **(619) 460-2990**

This is a discounter with a true no-frills ambiance. These stores specialize in merchandise that's discounted because it's slightly damaged (yet very usable) or because the original store isn't carrying the item any more. Oftentimes you have to look five times before you can figure out why the item is in the store. The products come from suppliers such as Costco and 130 other vendors. We've found bargains on everything from beauty aids to pet food. Plan on a stop at GTM if you love a deal that feels like a real bargain.

South Bay

JC Penney Furniture Outlet Store
741 Broadway, Chula Vista
• **(619) 422-4486**

Furniture bargains here border on the un-believable. Sofas, recliners, dining-room fur-niture, bedroom pieces, all have been slashed (the prices, that is, not the furniture). Most have been marked down already or are canceled special orders or discontinued items. Regard-less of their origin, you'll save 40 to 60 percent on all items in the store.

San Diego Factory Outlet Center
4498 Camino de la Plaza, San Ysidro
• **(619) 690-2999**

Head for the U.S.-Mexico border, but take the last exit before you leave the country (don't worry — plenty of signs will alert you to the fact that the last-chance exit is approaching). What you'll find is San Diego's first factory outlet center and still one of the best. Nearly 40 outlet stores offer outstanding bargains for grown-ups and kids alike. Women will appre-ciate the outlet stores for **Calvin Klein**, **Maidenform**, **Nine West** and **Georgiou**, while men will be looking for bargains at **Docker's**, **Van Heusen**, **Van's** and the **Nike Factory Store**. Kids' bargains are found at the **Toy Liquidators Outlet**, **Carter's Childrenswear** and **Oshkosh B'Gosh**. Plenty of discount housewares are available too, as are leather goods, vitamins, fragrances and cosmetics.

Shoe Pavilion
304 E. H St., Chula Vista
• **(619) 691-7621**

Like its sister stores in San Diego and North County Coastal, Shoe Pavilion offers no-frills shopping, but excellent quality, selection and price in brand-name and designer shoes for

men and women. Don't miss the clearance racks, where prices are often as much as 75 percent below retail.

UFO-Upholstery Fabric Outlet
1918 Roosevelt Ave., National City
• **(619) 477-9341**

Even if you have no plans to reupholster any of your furniture, a visit to UFO will change that kind of thinking in a hurry. What seems to be miles and miles of racks of fabric will in-spire your creative spirit, and you're sure to find something you can't live without or the perfect fabric to recover Aunt Matilda's an-tique chaise. UFO, along with its sister store in North County Inland, is an Insiders' secret not to be missed.

Shopping Districts

San Diego

Adams Ave.
Between 30th and 40th Streets

Informally known as San Diego's Antique Row, this stretch of Adams Avenue is filled with antique stores, art galleries, used-book shops, collectibles and home furnishings. This is a browser's paradise. As you leisurely stroll from shop to shop, you can take a break at one of the many pubs, coffeehouses or res-taurants that are mixed in with the stores.

Be sure to stop in at **Eclectic Treasures** at 3027 Adams Avenue for a one-of-a-kind an-tique or collectible to add to your collection. And don't miss the **Prince and the Pauper** at 3201 Adams Avenue for collectible children's books. **TaTa Lane** (3328 Adams Avenue) for vintage clothing is an Insiders' favorite, as is **Rosie O'Grady's** pub, a longtime fixture at 3402 Adams Avenue.

INSIDERS' TIP

Most San Diego stores open at 10 AM and close anywhere between 6 PM and 9 PM. On Saturday and Sunday evenings they may close earlier. In popular visitor areas such as in Pacific Beach or the Gaslamp District, hours are sometimes longer.

Bazaar Del Mundo
Juan St., in Old Town State Historic Park, San Diego • (619) 296-3161

Sometimes shopping is more than just shopping — it's an experience. And Bazaar Del Mundo offers an unparalleled experience for the whole family. Enjoy the international sights, sounds, fragrances and flavors of the Bazaar as you discover treasures from around the world in the 16 shops and four restaurants. The **Guatemala Shop** offers hand-woven textiles, ethnic clothing and folk art. At **Earth, Wind & Sea** you can find unusual plants, fountains, chimes and garden accessories.

Entertainment is usually on hand, too, in the form of lively mariachis and Hispanic dancers swirling in their colorful costumes. When hunger strikes, sample the Mexican cuisine at **Casa de Pico.** (Don't forget to try one of their giant margaritas.) Or if Italian food appeals to you, **Lino's** offers pasta, pizza, sandwiches and salads.

Ferry Landing Marketplace
1201 First St., Coronado • (619) 435-8895

Not really a mall, not really a neighborhood shopping district, the Ferry Landing Marketplace is nevertheless a fun-filled shopping area. This is the perfect spot for souvenir shopping at places like **Captain Coronado's Trading Company** or the **Coronado Ferry Company**. Fine art can be found at the **Southwestern Indian Den** or the **Art for Wildlife Galleries**, and don't miss the **Coronado Psychic**, a new-age gift shop.

Grab a snack from one of the fun eateries in the Marketplace, or dine in style at **Peohe's Restaurant** overlooking San Diego Bay and the city skyline.

Gaslamp Quarter
Fourth and Fifth Aves. Between Broadway and K St., San Diego

Interspersed among the nightclubs and restaurants in the Gaslamp are dozens of unique shops, ranging from the well-know **Z Gallerie** at 611 Fifth Avenue to the **Cuban Cigar Factory** at 551 Fifth Avenue. Part of the appeal of shopping in the Gaslamp is that the stores are open late on weekends. So after dinner in one of the dozens of restaurants in the Quarter, you can browse leisurely through the shops.

You'll find vintage clothing stores and boutiques that specialize in offbeat fashions. For collectors, art galleries and rare print stores are abundant. And if you're having trouble deciding what to buy, you might consult one of the resident psychics or palm readers who have set up shop in the Gaslamp.

Hillcrest
Fifth Ave. between Robinson and Washington Sts.

A funky and cool collection of shops and eateries line Fifth Avenue in Hillcrest. You'll find vintage clothing at **Buffalo Exchange** at 3862 Fifth Avenue, and across the street at 3823 Fifth Avenue is the **Blue Door Literary Bookstore**, legendary for its offbeat collection of books. Don't forget to pop in at **Bad Habits**, at 3850 Fifth Avenue. Even if you're not a smoker, you'll admire the huge variety of cigars, pipes and accessories on display.

Farther up the street is **Village Hillcrest**, a small shopping center that has a **Body & Bath Boutique**, the **Candy Depot** and several other specialty stores and restaurants. The **Hillcrest Cinema** is inside the Village, where first-run art films are shown.

La Jolla
Prospect St. and Girard Ave.

La Jolla is famous for its upscale shopping district, and it's hard to argue that there's a better location. Sunshine, the ocean and streets teeming with happy shoppers combine to make this an out-of-the-ordinary shopping excursion. Here you'll find ultra-trendy boutiques, world-famous clothing designers' stores, art galleries and just enough offbeat stores to keep things interesting.

One of our favorites is the **Silver Store**, at 7909 Girard Avenue. Silver treasures from dining utensils to tea services to jewelry all can be found here, usually at a discount. You'll find lots of restaurants along both Prospect and Girard, including San Diego's **Hard Rock Cafe**, plenty of casual bistros and lots of full-service restaurants.

Ocean Beach
Newport Ave., between Sunset Cliffs Blvd. and the beach

Downtown OB is overflowing with antique stores, art galleries, card and gift shops, jewelry stores and places to scout out active wear (you are at the beach, after all). Newport Avenue is the heart of Ocean Beach, and in addition to the regular shopping opportunities, a special festival or fair is usually happening on weekends during summer months, complete with craft booths for even more shopping.

Seaport Village
West Harbor Dr. at Kettner Blvd. (next to the Hyatt Regency San Diego)
• (619) 235-4014

We included Seaport Village in our Attractions chapter simply because there's so much to do here: dining, seaside entertainment, a carousel for the kids. But we just had to include it in Shopping too, because some of San Diego's most interesting stores are here.

Where else can you find a store like the **Captain's Cove**, which specializes in nautical treasures? Or discover your family coat of arms at **European Heritage**. The **Gingham Goose** is a country store, and **Scandinavian Specialties** imports treasures from Sweden, Norway and Denmark. Fifty-two unique stores make up Seaport Village, and for the dedicated shopper, it's a place not to be missed.

North County Coastal

Cedros Avenue Stores and Design Centers
Cedros Avenue • Solana Beach

Here you'll find wonderful shops from **Adventure 16** (the outdoor gear and camping specialty store) at 143 S. Cedros Avenue to a host of high-end and lower-scale antique stores. Be sure to stop at **Peck & Peck Antiques** at 241 S. Cedros Avenue for that perfect item for your home or office or the folks back home. In the same district you'll find cafes and pubs including **Belly Up** (which is mentioned in the Nightlife chapter).

There are more than 50 storeowners who support one another in the shopping and design center for the North County Coastal area. Parking is mostly on the street, but there are lots places on side streets. FYI: The district is about three blocks south of the Coaster train stop in Solana Beach. Check the Coaster schedule to make sure you can get to and from the district at convenient times.

State Street Stores
Between Oak St. and Beech St. on both sides of State St., Carlsbad

If you're looking for an antique, an addition to your baseball-card collection, are just nuts about rare books or need a good cup of coffee, you'll find it all in this shopping area. Within the four-block plus shopping district, you'll be treated to about 40 antique stores, boutiques and small shops.

Be sure to browse through **DeWitts Antiques and Collectibles** for jewelry and glassware (there are over 50 dealers combined in this store at 2946 State Street and there's a licensed appraiser on-site). Don't miss **Postal's Antique & Collectibles**, 2825 State Street for inkwells, pottery, bookends and furniture. At **Vintage Antiques**, 505 Oak Avenue, you'll find rugs, books and paintings along with the usual antique fare.

Mixed among the shops and cafes are boutiques like **Kobos**, at the corner of Carlsbad Village Drive and State Street (2998 State Street). This shop features trendy and sensible beach clothes and California casual sportswear. If you're headed up to North County from downtown San Diego, check the

Coaster train schedule to make your trek more enjoyable. The station is right in the middle of this shopping district.

North County Inland

San Marcos Shopping District
Los Vallecitos Blvd., San Marcos

In this district, furniture is the name of the game. The stretch of these stores is found along 2 miles of Los Vallecitos Boulevard in San Marcos. (You can find it between the Sycamore Drive and Rancho Santa Fe Road exits on Calif. Highway 78.)

Stores here sell everything from bedding to bar stools at excellent prices. Sears has a large furniture store called **Homelife**, at 860 Los Vallecitos Blvd. (760-471-1710). As we go to press, there's a new antiques mall being constructed along the same street right next to an **Ethan Allen** showroom. If you're shopping for bargains, watch for the sidewalk sales, which are held on most major holiday weekends, and advertised in the newspapers.

Carmel Mountain Shopping area
San Diego

If you're traveling on Interstate 15 through the Rancho Bernardo, Carmel Mountain area, there's a shopping district that will fit your basic needs. Take the Carmel Mountain exit and go east. Here's where you find a **Marshalls** Department Store, **Staples**, **Target**, **Michael's** (the craft store), **Borders Books and Music**, and a fine selection of chain and fast-food restaurants, including **In 'N Out Hamburgers**.

East County

Julian Main St. Shopping District
Julian

Julian's antique stores are mostly located around Main Street in the downtown area, which is about five easy blocks long. That said, if you don't look out the car windows while driving into town you'll miss other stores along Calif. Hwy. 78 as it winds up to this mountain village.

Be sure to visit some of the antique stores

on Julian's cozy side streets too, such as **Applewood & Co.**, 2840 Washington Street, (760) 765-1185, and **Julian Farms Antiques**, 2818 Washington Street, (760) 765-0250. When you get to town, stop at the Julian Town Hall (on Main and Washington Streets) and pick up an antique newsletter giving brief descriptions of shops and any specialties. You can also ask about the best places for the famous Julian apple pie and cider, but you may just have to do the sampling yourself. (The truth is, all the pies and cider we've tasted — and we've tried to be fair — are luscious. Be sure to buy enough to take back with you.)

La Mesa Blvd. Shopping District
La Mesa

Sometime in the 1980s store owners along La Mesa Boulevard looked around and decided it was time to spiff things up. And so they did. This shopping district now includes coffee pubs, tidy cafes, inviting boutiques and antique shops — nearly 20 at last count — all within the downtown area of La Mesa.

Two favorite Insider antique stores are the **Antique Radio Store**, 8376 La Mesa Boulevard, (619) 668-5653, for radio buffs, and **Granny's Antiques**, 8360 La Mesa Boulevard, (619) 562-3387, where you never quite know what treasure you'll discover.

South Bay

Chula Vista
Third Avenue, between E and G Streets, Chula Vista

Once a declining business district, Third Avenue has been revitalized and is now the hub of downtown shopping in Chula Vista. Restaurants, an old-fashioned movie theater, a performing arts theater and, most important, lots of shops now line the busy street.

Stop in at **Riviera Bakery** at 315½ Third Avenue for a sweet treat, or if your wedding day is approaching, feast your eyes on the bridal confections at **Bridal World**, 250 Third Avenue. As you amble up and down the pedestrian-friendly street, you'll find card shops, antique stores, a specialty food market and a few boutiques, too.

Resale and Consignment

San Diego

All Baby Needs
10615 Tierrasanta Blvd., San Diego
• (858) 292-8226

Savvy Insiders know this is where to go to stock up on infant clothing and furniture. Everyone knows how quickly babies outgrow their clothing, so the merchandise here is hardly worn, as good as new and priced right. Resale baby furniture and accessories are great bargains here, too.

Big City Woman
4185 Adams Ave., San Diego
• (619) 521-0121

This store is a much-appreciated rarity — it specializes in resale fashions for women size 16 and up. Most resale and consignment shops have a marginal selection in the plus sizes, but at Big City Woman, you'll find a wide array of in-season fashions. The store is open Tuesday through Saturday.

Designer Resale Boutique
690 University Ave., San Diego
• (619) 692-3343

A consignment boutique, it offers better-quality women's clothing and accessories. You'll find some designer labels and a good selection of seasonal and current styles. The clothing is "gently worn" and ranges in size from 2 to 22. Shop every day except Sundays.

Dress to Impress
4242 Camino del Rio N., San Diego
• (619) 528-9797

If you're looking for a special dress to wear for a formal occasion, Dress to Impress may be your answer. You'll find a large selection of women's formal wear in all sizes both for sale and for rent. Better-quality sportswear, dresses and suits are also available. The store is open every day but Sunday.

Encore
7655 Girard Ave., La Jolla
• (858) 454-7540

Occupying what was once an upscale department store, Encore specializes in way-up-scale women's resale designer clothing. All the big labels are here. You might not find the bargain basement prices that you would at other resale and consignment shops, but the selection and quality are fabulous.

Mr. C's Clothiers
4242 Camino del Rio N., San Diego
• (619) 528-8738

Right next door to Dress to Impress is the place for men's resale and consignment clothing. From casual to dressy, quality and price combine to make this store a real find for male bargain hunters. Mr. C's is open every day except Sunday.

Reruns
1015 C Ave., Coronado • (619) 435-5444

Specializing in resale clothing from newborns to teens, this is the spot to take the kids. And just so Mom and Dad don't feel left out, right next door at 1017 C Avenue is **Coronado Classics**, which has adult resale gems. Both stores are open every day but Sunday.

Wear It Again Sam
3922 Park Blvd., San Diego
• (619) 299-0185

This store is worth a visit just to see the latest finds. Specializing in vintage clothing from the 1900s through the 1960s, there's always something unusual to be found. Men's

---

INSIDERS' TIP

Here in San Diego, shopping attire is California casual. Nice sneakers, sandals, shorts and shirts are suitable for malls and stores. In the shops in La Jolla, Del Mar and Rancho Santa Fe, you may feel more comfortable with a slightly upscale version of this very same dress code.

and women's clothing, shoes and accessories that you haven't seen in years are sure to capture your imagination.

North County Coastal

Always Fabulous
1217 Camino del Mar, Del Mar
• (858) 481-8866

From accessories to jewelry, from clothing to shoes, you can select top-of-the-line styles (yes, that have been placed here on consignment) for a fraction of the original cost. As with all resale and consignment shops, the merchandise changes often. Are you after something special or a period piece of clothing? See if a staff member might give you a call when items like you're looking for come in.

Coastal Consignment
860 First St., Encinitas • (760) 943-1199

High quality and comfortable prices: This could be Coastal Consignment's slogan as it surely says what the store is all about. There's furniture and collectibles, antiques and used furniture. Ask about the free lecture series. Insiders know the lectures are great places to learn about buying antiques, restoration and collecting future collectibles.

Double-Take
144 E Vista Way, Vista • (760) 758-4840

Looking for a snappy sixties outfit, a dress first worn in the 1920s, or just something really cool? Visit the resale shop and have fun trying on the fashions. This is a great place for accessories and that perfect bit of rhinestone jewelry. The store also features designer brand-name clothing from Liz Claiborne to Carole Little. The store is closed on Sundays.

Earth Angels
1919 Apple St., Oceanside
• (760) 757-1120

A children's resale boutique, here you'll find top brand names like Gap, Gymboree, Guess and more. Call ahead if you're looking for a specific size as merchandise changes often. The store also carries a range of children's furniture, from cribs to lighting accessories.

Hand Me Ups
12750 Carmel Country Rd., Del Mar
• (858) 794-7311

Here you'll find upscale clothing for kids including brands like Gap, Quicksilver, Gymboree and Oshkosh with new and resale sizes ranging from 0 to 12. You'll also find toys, furniture, equipment and maternity wear.

Two Sisters Consignment Home Furnishing
616 Stevens Ave., Solana Beach
• (858) 755-4558

If you love to browse through collectibles and those nearly antique pieces of furniture you may remember from Mom's or Grandmother's home, this store is a find. Most of the pieces are well within a family's budget.

There's a large supply of home furnishing in nearly perfect condition, and the best part is that consignments arrive daily. While you're in the neighborhood, check out the Cedros Avenue stores and design center.

North County Inland

Deborah's
1624 E Valley Pkwy., Escondido
• (760) 743-8980

This is a huge, one-stop resale store for items for the entire family. In business since 1974, Deborah's has jewelry, shoes, accessories, furniture, household items, toys, and gift items. The store sells only items in very good and nearly perfect condition and has a large supply of department store brands.

The store is open from 9 AM to 7 PM during the week. Saturday the store closes at 6 PM and on Sunday the hours are 11 AM to 5 PM.

East County

Conceptions
10438 Mission Gorge Rd., Santee
• (619) 596-2229

Conceptions offers baby clothing,

Horton Plaza, an exciting multi-level shopping area in downtown San Diego, is a must-see for those who really love to shop.

children's clothing, clothes for the expectant mom as well as accessories. They purchase gently used clothing and equipment and are always looking for special treasures for baby and mom.

Lil' Folks
375 Broadway Ave., El Cajon
• (619) 447-0991

Here you'll find new and used quality children's clothing, furniture and toys. Sizes range from preemies up to 6X. The store is open seven days a week and brand names include Guess, Oshkosh, Gymboree, Gap and Carters.

Picket Fences and Twice is Nice Resale Stores
7435 Broadway St., Lemon Grove
• (619) 462-7238, (619) 460-3353

A children's and women's resale store combined, these stores are two good reasons to visit Lemon Grove. The stores have baby and children's clothing and will buy, sell and trade women's clothing. You may need to make an appointment if you're interested in selling.

Picket Fences and Twice is Nice Resales are fun shops. If you're looking for something special — such as a baptismal gown or a tux for a two-year old— call ahead, as unique items move quickly.

South Bay

Disabled American Veterans Thrift Store
881 Broadway, Chula Vista
• (619) 232-0141

If you're a dedicated bargain-hunter, get ready to dive into the largest of the Disabled Vets' stores. You may have to plow through a lot of stuff before you come upon what you're seeking, but that's half the fun. And there's a ton of quality mixed in with the stuff that might

be best classified as "junque." Clothing for the whole family, accessories and home furnishings are just some of the treasures you'll find. Be sure to check out the collection of silk ties. It's a great way to add to your collection for a fraction of retail price.

Value Village
2756 Main St., Chula Vista
• (619) 232-6251

If thrift-store shopping is your hobby, then this is another one worth a look. Thousands of resale items, all slashed to a minute fraction of their original price, await your keen eye. Like all thrift stores, you'll have to work to separate the wheat from the chaff, but many a great value is to be found. You'll find an abundance of clothing and household items.

Bookstores

San Diego

B Dalton Bookseller
Horton Plaza, 407 Horton Plaza,
San Diego • (619) 615-5373
Mission Valley Center, 1640 Camino
del Rio N., San Diego • (619) 291-1315
University Towne Center, 4505 La Jolla
Village Dr., San Diego • (858) 453-8755

B Dalton has been around a long time. Even though it doesn't compete with the superstores in terms of volume of titles, it's a consistently good bookstore with up-to-date stock and friendly salespeople. Plus it has the added benefit of being inside a mall, so it's easy to stop in while you're shopping for other things, too.

Barnes & Noble Booksellers
7610 Hazard Center Dr., San Diego
• (619) 220-0175

With more than 150,000 titles, Barnes & Noble is one of the giants in town. The Hazard

Center location is roomy and spread out, and there's a coffee house next door where you can spend a few quiet moments with your new book. Part of the special appeal of Barnes & Noble is the huge children's department.

Bay Books & Cafe
1029 Orange Ave., Coronado
• **(619) 435-0070**

Coronado's Bay Books has one of the largest selections of national and international newspapers and magazines to go along with its extensive collection of new books. Best sellers, fiction, mysteries, travel, children's books, cookbooks and gardening books highlight the collection. You'll have plenty of opportunity to peruse your selection in the reading room or at the espresso bar.

Bookstar
3150 Rosecrans Pl., San Diego
• **(619) 225-0465**
8650 Genesee Ave., San Diego
• **(858) 457-4561**

Owned by mammoth Barnes & Noble, Bookstar is a smaller version of the giant superstores. Don't think for a moment you won't find a huge selection of titles; these stores are just a little smaller and have a cozier atmosphere. The Rosecrans Place store, for example, is in an old movie theater, and as you move through the store toward where the screen used to be, the floor gently slopes, just the way it did when theater seats occupied the floor instead of bookshelves.

The sales staff at Bookstar is great for helping you locate a title in their computerized inventory. And if what you want isn't in stock, they'll be happy to order it for you.

Borders Books, Music & Cafe
1072 Camino del Rio N., San Diego
• **(619) 295-2201**

This mammoth 25,000-square-foot bookstore is located in the Mission Valley Center West shopping mall, and like its counterparts across the country, it is a combination bookstore, music store and cafe.

In addition to carrying more than 200,000 book titles, music selections and videos, the store features the Borders' Cafe Espresso, where customers are encouraged to sip a cup of coffee while they read their latest purchase.

Something special always seems to be going on at Borders, whether it's a book signing, a live music performance or a childrens' event. The comfortable interior induces shoppers to hang around and enjoy all the acitivity.

Controversial Bookstore
3021 University Ave., San Diego
• **(619) 296-1560**

Since 1964 this bookstore has been selling just about everything except mainstream books. Spirituality, religion, metaphysics and wellness are among the popular subjects here. Also offered are new-age music and videos, crystals, jewelry, tarot cards and other gifts.

Crown Books
4711 Clairemont Dr., San Diego
• **(858) 483-3891**
1776 Garnet Ave., San Diego
• **(858) 272-5909**
1640 Camino de la Reina, San Diego
• **(619) 296-5578**
3309 Rosecrans St., San Diego
• **(619) 224-2713**
8657 Villa La Jolla Dr., La Jolla
• **(858) 450-0577**

Crown Books guarantees the lowest prices on their huge selection of titles. Deep discounts make Crown the best bookstore in town for bargain hunters. Plus, they also have the added convenience of having the most locations around the county. The La Jolla store occasionally has interesting authors come in for signings.

Family Christian Store
3231 Sports Arena Blvd., San Diego
• **(619) 224-2863**

Serving the Christian community, this store has a wide selection of religious books, CDs, tapes and gift items. It's also a treasure trove of church and Sunday school supplies. If there's something you need that is not in stock, the staff is great for handling quick mail orders.

Gaslamp Books, Prints, Antiques & Museum
413 Market St., San Diego
• **(619) 237-1492**

For that one-of-a-kind find, this is the place. You'll be amazed by some of the old magazines, prints and books you can find here. Complementing all the reading material is a nice collection of antiques. And be sure not to miss the **Wyatt Earp Museum** on the premises. It's a little-known tidbit of history that Wyatt Earp was a saloon owner in the early days of San Diego. This is the kind of place that's discovered by accident — that's how we found it; it's a treasure, and we're happy to share it with you.

John Cole's Book Shop
780 Prospect St., La Jolla
• **(858) 454-4766**

As you enter the front door of this vine-covered cottage, you'll be transported back to a time when book buying was a quiet, leisurely pursuit. Long a mainstay in La Jolla, John Cole's specializes in art books, architecture, travel, cookbooks, fiction, children's books and books on Baja California. Don't miss **Zach's Music Corner** inside the store, where you'll find CDs and harmonicas.

Upstart Crow Bookstore & Coffee House
Seaport Village, 835 W. Harbor Dr., San Diego • **(619) 232-4855**

Long before coffeehouses became popular, and eons before anyone thought to combine a coffeehouse with a bookstore, Upstart Crow was doing it, and doing it well. Located right in the middle of the chaotic (but fun) Seaport Village, it's an oasis of calm. You can enjoy a steaming cup of coffee or tea while you're surrounded by stacks and stacks of books, all begging for a reader. Although small, the store has a good cross-section of titles, plenty to keep you occupied.

Wahrenbrock's Book House
726 Broadway, San Diego
• **(619) 232-0132**

No one knows exactly how many books are in Wahrenbrock's — not even the owners. But look around you and you'll surely guess that there must be at least a million. Most of the books are used, but Wahrenbrock's does have some new ones scattered about its three floors. Loosely organized by subject matter, the books offer a browser's paradise. And if you're looking for something specific, ask a staff member.

Even with all those titles and no real system to catalogue them, the staff usually knows exactly what they have and where it can be found. If you have a rare book, this is a great place to get an appraisal.

Warwick's
7812 Girard Ave., La Jolla
• **(858) 454-0347**

If a celebrity author comes to San Diego for a book signing, Warwick's is where he or she will likely end up. In recent years this venerable bookstore has hosted Norman Schwarzkopf, Margaret Thatcher, Maya Angelou, Doris Kearns Goodwin and Newt Gingrich, to name just a few. Large for an independent, Warwick's carries 40,000 titles along with books on cassette, large print books, maps and globes. One half of the store is dedicated to gifts and stationery, so chances are you'll find a nice memento in addition to a new book. You're sure to see just as many Insiders shopping here as visitors.

The White Rabbit
7755 Girard Ave., La Jolla
• **(858) 454-3518**

Just as Warwick's is a legendary bookstore in La Jolla, White Rabbit holds its own for its inventory of children's books. With more than 30,000 titles, this is the place to go for that hard-to-find kids' book you've been looking for. The staff is expert in all things literary (kidwise, that is) and will graciously assist you with phone and mail orders. Kids love the weekly story time, too.

North County Coastal

Barnes & Noble
11744 Carmel Mountain Rd., San Diego
• **(858) 674-1055**
12835 El Camino Real, Encinitas
• **(760) 481-4039**

Barnes & Noble's two fine chain bookstores are justly proud of their commitment to customer service. If you need a book, they'll help you find it, and if it's not in the store they'll special order it for you. Since the stores are open all week, they're convenient to visit too. Both have large children's departments, and sometimes have story times or special kids events. In these locations there are more than 150,000 titles close to your book-loving fingertips.

Bookstar
2500 Vista Way, Oceanside
• (760) 721-0706

Bookstar, a sister in the Barnes & Noble bookstore family, is a popular spot for book lovers who like in-store readings, and book discussion groups. Kids come for the children's "PJ" story time (with milk and cookies).

There are special events too, ranging from musical performances to Martha Stewart-style craft demonstrations. Pick up a store newsletter for up-to-the-minute information.

Book Works
2670 Via de la Valle, Del Mar
• (858) 755-3735

The Book Works has been helping book lovers satisfy their reading needs since the late 1970s. Located at the Flower Hill Center, it offers new and best-selling books, as well as some used ones. It also offers magazines (both foreign and domestic), unusual cards and stationery, English garden statuary and vintage decorative accessories.

You can also get a cup of coffee or tea next door at an Insiders' cafe paradise, the Pannikin Cafe.

B. Dalton Bookseller
2525 El Camino Real, Carlsbad
• (760) 729-5988

Found in the Plaza Camino Real Shopping Mall, this smallish bookstore is high on customer service. You'll find a friendly staff and a well-rounded selection of books and magazines. If you need a good read and you're in the mall, this is the store for you.

Chronicles
677 San Rodolfo St., Solana Beach
• (858) 350-0485

A Christian bookstore and cafe, you can browse through an excellent selection of bibles, Christian calendars, and faith-oriented materials and then enjoy the gallery and cafe. They also sell music, cards and gifts.

Circle of Friends Bookstore
704 N. Hwy. 101, Encinitas
• (760) 633-4254

Located in a place Insiders still think of as Leucadia, the Circle of Friends Bookstore is actually in the city of Encinitas. This metaphysical bookstore makes you feel welcome the moment you walk through the door. If intriguing topics are your cup of tea, you'll find just what you want here, in books on yoga, healing, Sufism, Buddhism, Taoism, Zen, channeling, sex, meditation, tarot, relationships, witchcraft, shamanism and more. This store is a great resource if you're looking for unique and handcrafted jewelry, gifts, cards, or incense. The staff loves to provide information on metaphysical topics so don't be shy about questions.

Coronet News Stand
111 S. Coast Hwy., Oceanside
• (760) 722-3233

This is the place for all your magazine needs; it sells well over 5,000 periodicals, the largest selection in Southern California. This is the place to look if you need an out-of-town or foreign magazine or newspaper.   So if you're looking for the latest issue of *Le Monde*, the French magazine *Match*, or the German newspaper *Der Spiegel* or something more obscure, this is the place.

If it's Sunday and you must read an edition of the *Detroit Free Press* or the *Boston Globe* or the *Chicago Tribune*, call the Coronet before dashing up the coast. The store is open from 8 AM until midnight seven days a week.

Crown Books, Superstore
1092 N. El Camino Real, Encinitas
• (760) 944-8151
2180 Vista Wy., Oceanside
• (760) 721-6216

If you love Crown Books this super store must be on your shopping tour. As with other Crowns in the national chain, this one is big, and the staff is helpful. Crown routinely discounts books on the best seller list and can special order your favorite titles (if you can't find them among the many choices). As with other Crowns, the stores have a helpful you-do-it computerized system to help you locate books.

Esmeralda Books & Coffee
1555 Camino Del Mar, Del Mar
• (858) 755-2707

Besides best-selling books, this independent bookstore offers unique selections, especially in the areas of fiction, travel, art, design, poetry, travel, and cooking. It also sells children's books. Esmeralda also offers free gift wrapping, shipping options, and special orders. Located upstairs in the Del Mar Plaza (see our listing under Malls), it's a great place to come for a cup of coffee, browsing, and, if you like literature, free readings by local and nationally known authors.

The store closes at 9 PM on weekdays, but on the weekends you can shop late: Friday and Saturday nights it's open until 11 PM. Be sure to read more about Esmeralda in our Nightlife chapter.

Family Christian Book Stores
2229 El Camino Real, Oceanside
• (760) 722-5323

A spacious addition to the chain of Family Christian Book Stores, this Oceanside branch includes religious-oriented books with a strong Christian slant. You'll also find music, videos and gifts as well as cards. They have a children's book and parenting section and they also carry Sunday school supplies.

Heaven on Earth
768 First St., Encinitas• (760) 753-2345

A metaphysical and spiritual bookstore, Heaven on Earth offers books on well-known topics like astrology and lesser-known ones like Celtic crop circles and sacred altars. It also has a wonderful selection of music, cards, jewelry, incense, crystals and spiritual art.

Paperback Book Exchange
578 Carlsbad Village Dr., Carlsbad
• (760) 729-4100

If you love to read and are looking for bargains, you must stop in at the Paperback Book Exchange. This store is just one half block east of the antique, cafe and coffeehouse shopping district of downtown Carlsbad and about two blocks south of the Coaster station.

Most of the books have been pre-read (i.e., they're used), and the prices are right. If you're hooked on an author of paperback fiction, call the store to see which titles are in stock, since inventory turns over quickly.

Phoenix Phyre Bookstore
282 N. El Camino Real, Encinitas
• (760) 436-7740

This metaphysical bookstore has been in North County Coastal since the mid-1970s. Here you'll find candles, oils, and jewelry along with a fine collection of books on topics ranging from traditional metaphysics and spirituality to recovery material and videos.

If you simply must know your future or have questions about a specific forecasting technique, you're in luck: There are daily psychic readings and monthly psychic fairs that host guest metaphysical experts. If you're looking for a spiritual piece of artwork (including ones in glass, wood or pottery), you'll especially enjoy the gallery. Call for a subscription to their newsletter, which lists upcoming events and readings.

Waldenbooks
2525 El Camino Real, Carlsbad
• (760) 729-1286

Right inside the west end of the newly renovated Plaza Camino Real, Waldenbooks carries the top-selling hardbounds and softbound books. The store also has an extensive selection of art, oversized, and technical books. Check out their computer books and ask about upcoming book signings. They have an especially well-rounded selection of romance titles. The staff works hard to accommodate customers' special requests.

INSIDERS' TIP

If you've purchased a bulky item at one of the malls, ask if you can leave the purchase with their customer service department until you finish shopping. Life will be easier if you don't have to carry extra bags.

North County Inland

Barnes & Noble
1066 W. Valley Pkwy., Escondido
• (760) 738-7168
11744 Carmel Mountain Rd., San Diego
• (858) 674-1055

Part of the fine chain of bookstores found throughout the country, these stores, with their atmosphere of calm, are especially inviting on a hectic weekend. While some bookstores have noisy, boisterous events, here you'll find people who've come to quietly browse, and the staff is happy to have them.

In no time at all, shoppers can be directed to a special book or have it special-ordered. As at other Barnes & Nobles, there's a sizeable selection of children's books and a place for kids and parents to sit and preview the books.

Borders Books and Music
11160 Rancho Carmel Dr., San Diego
• (858) 618-1814

While the address says the store is officially in San Diego, it's really in the Carmel Mountain/Rancho Bernardo/Poway region of the county. To find the store, take the Carmel Mountain Drive exit from Interstate 15 and go east. The store is immense, as you'd expect a Borders to be. It's a busy place with lots going on. If you're the type who loves a cozy, peaceful (read that quiet) bookstore, you won't find your bibliophile heaven here. It can get noisy, busy and crowded on weekends. The children's area is in the back of the store; this is where the many storytimes are held and where parents can sit and read to their little ones. Pick up a newsletter of current events including poetry readings and author book signings.

There's a cafe on-site for a cup of tea or coffee and a sweet treat, and no one looks twice if you take the snack to a comfortable reading area.

Cassidy's Books
742 S. Rancho Santa Fe Rd., San Marcos
• (760) 727-8640

For book lovers, this is a page-turning paradise. You'll find one of the largest selections of new and used books in the county right at Cassidy's. They carry hard-to-find editions and collector's copies; if they don't have the title you want, they'll start a search and then order it for you.

Heritage Books
1785 S. Escondido Blvd., Escondido
• (760) 746-6601

In the center of Escondido, this independent bookstore provides book lovers with first editions, rare books, collectable books, and signed editions. Heritage both buys and sells, and has a large children's section too. Their slogan is, "We'll search the universe for your books," and although space travel doesn't really come within their realm of service, the staff does give it their best shot.

Crown Books, Superstore
632 N. Escondido Blvd., Escondido
• (760) 480-0111
16775 Bernardo Center Dr., San Diego
• (858) 487-3698

These North County Inland Crown Books stores are everything you'd expect in a super store, plus you get a staff at each location who cares about your book-buying tastes and needs. You'll find special events, signings, readings and overstuffed chairs so you can sit and preview books before writing that check. Call for an event calendar.

Village Books
130 N. Main Ave., Fallbrook
• (760) 728-1680

In the downtown area of Fallbrook, this cozy store stocks best-selling books and some inviting selections. Unlike some impersonal mall superstores, Village Books has a staff that loves their customers and makes sure everyone is happily reading. If you're visiting this area, stop in for a good book and ask about upcoming events and readings. While the store is off the beaten track, it attracts celebrity authors and local writers too. Depending on the event, the store can become jammed with book buyers and readers.

Waldenbooks
200 E. Via Rancho Pkwy., Escondido
• (760) 746-4859

Located at the North County Fair Shopping Mall, this Waldenbooks is especially inviting when you've been on a shopping spree. There's a calm atmosphere in the store and the staff is very willing to allow you to browse. They'll special order books too if they don't have them in their large stock.

Ask about upcoming events, including signings by local and national authors.

East County

Barnes & Noble
5500 Grossmont Center Dr., La Mesa
• **(619) 667-2870**

Located in the newly renovated Grossmont Center, this Barnes & Noble, like others in the chain, has a real commitment to customer service.

All Barnes & Noble stores are open seven days a week, have large children's departments, and put more than 150,000 titles close to your book-loving finger tips. Pick up a newsletter to find out about their children's story hour, book discussion groups and author book signings.

Bookstar
8501 Fletcher Pkwy., La Mesa
• **(619) 466-1688**

Bookstar, a sister in the Barnes & Noble bookstore family, is a popular literary spot for book lovers because of its in-store readings and book discussion groups. Children come for the "PJ" story time. Other special events range from musical performances to crafts demonstrations. And when people aren't hanging around for the special events you'll often find them chatting at a table or reading quietly in the overstuffed chairs. This is the place to find that just right book for entertainment and information. The store is open seven days a week.

Family Christian Book Stores
8227 La Mesa Blvd., La Mesa
• **(619) 462-9550**

This is East County's religious bookstore. Family Christian sells the latest Christian best sellers as well as hard-to-find Christian materials and book titles. The store has a Spanish-language section, a children's section and a section on parenting. It also sells tapes, videos and gifts.

Lemon Grove Book Store
7904 Broadway Ave., Lemon Grove
• **(619) 463-2503**

Primarily a used-book store, the staff enjoys long-term reading relationships with customers. Part of Lemon Grove since the late 1970s, the store draws neighborhood regulars who come here to chat about their favorite books. The staff can help you locate out-of-print editions and special order books too. So if you're looking for a hard-to-find title, see if they can track it down for you.

Miner's Bible Book Store
733 Main St., Ste. A, Ramona
• **(760) 788-9141**

This store is filled to the brim with new and used bibles, and special ones, too. You'll find home-study courses, videos, CD's, tapes, gifts and lots of Sunday school materials. The store provides rentals and sales on some items and there are also cards and gifts for the Christian book buyer.

Romance World
929 E. Main St., El Cajon
• **(619) 588-5494**

If you adore romantic fiction, head to Romance World for oodles of books from authors ranging from Debbie Macomber to Barbara Cartland. Even if you have to make the drive from another part of the county, if you

---

INSIDERS' TIP

Don't forget to check out the bookstores at San Diego's local universities. Not only do they carry a good selection of books, they also have clothing and other items with the school's name and logo.

Photo: Horton Plaza

A good look at Horton Plaza can take time, so plan for an afternoon or day of shopping.

love this genre, you have to visit this store. Here you'll find romance books from the top to the bottom of the shelves. You might get to see one of your favorite authors too, as the store attracts big-name romance authors for signings, readings and special events. Call for an events schedule or to find out what's going on in the store. The staff will special order hard-to-find books.

Yellow Book Road
8315 La Mesa Blvd., La Mesa
• (619) 463-4900

A children's and teacher's resource bookstore, people come from throughout the county to find materials and wonderful books. If the staff doesn't stock what you're looking for, they will get it. There's a newsletter and calendar of events, and they draw in famous children's authors for signings.

South Bay

B Dalton Bookseller
Plaza Bonita Shopping Center, 3030
Plaza Bonita Rd., National City
• (619) 267-1294

For the largest selection of titles, this is South Bay's best bet. You're likely to find exactly what you're looking for in this pleasant, well-organized store. Like all B Daltons, this store is open daily and has friendly and helpful sales people.

Bayfront Bookstore
1000 Gunpowder Point Way, Chula Vista
• (619) 422-2481

Part of the Chula Vista Nature Center, this bookstore specializes in books on birds, animals and ecology. Enhance your apprecia-

---

INSIDERS' TIP

Farmers' Markets are fun outings for the whole family. If you discover an unusual fruit or vegetable, just ask the farmer for cooking or eating recommendations.

tion of nature by browsing amongst the naturalist books, supplies and gifts. While you're there, indulge yourself in a tour of the Nature Center (we tell you all about it in our Attractions chapter).

Crystal Light & Power Co.
286 Third Ave., Chula Vista
• **(619) 422-4443**

Enter the realm of the metaphysical as you look for the perfect book to nurture your soul. In addition to the collection of new age books, Crystal Light & Power Co. has crystals, tapes and CDs and gift items.

Family Christian Store
639 Broadway, Chula Vista
• **(619) 425-4223**

Like the other stores in this chain, Family Christian Store serves the Christian community with a wide selection of religious books, CDs, tapes and gift items. For church, Sunday school supplies and special orders, this is a great source.

Gracie's Book Nook
1722 Sweetwater Rd., National City
• **(619) 474-4464**

For the best in bedtime reading material, Gracie's is the place. The "gently read" selection of titles includes mystery, romance, general fiction, true crime and science fiction. It's always a pleasure to search the shelves for the latest gem to hit Gracie's, and you can't beat the prices. If you're like most Insider bibliophiles, you know what a treat it is to find a great used bookstore, and Gracie's is tops in South Bay.

Antiques

San Diego

Adams Avenue Antique Row
Adams Ave., between Texas St. and 40th St., San Diego

You could make a day of browsing through the nearly two dozen antique shops that stretch along Adams Avenue. **Leapfrog Collectibles** at 2604 Adams Avenue specializes in lamps

and chandeliers as well as pottery, art glass and paintings. Or stop in at **Resurrected Furniture** at 3504 Adams Avenue if you're looking for the perfect piece to complete a room. The **Antique Seller** at 2938 Adams Avenue is overflowing with collectibles certain to wiggle their way into your heart.

Coronado Antiques & Consignments
1126 Orange Ave., Coronado
• **(619) 435-7797**

Located in the heart of the shopping district in beautiful Coronado, this store is heaven for the antique shopper. You'll find lots of sterling silver, estate jewelry and fine porcelains. Coronado Antiques also specializes in American and European furniture, painting and bronzes. And don't think you won't find those precious decorative arts that charm the soul — they're overflowing with them. The store is closed on Sundays.

D.D. Allen Antiques
7728 Fay Ave., La Jolla • **(858) 454-8708**

Shopping in La Jolla always results in something special, and nowhere is that more true than at D.D. Allen Antiques. You'll marvel at the antique linens and quilts, or the baskets and beadwork. If figurines are on your list, D.D. Allen has tons of them, along with antique furniture, oil paintings, silver, bronze, crystal and glass. D.D. Allen is usually closed on Sundays.

House of Heirlooms
801 University Ave., San Diego
• **(619) 298-0502**

This upscale shop is an Insiders' favorite for its comprehensive selection of quality antiques. Among the treasures you'll find here are antique English and American furniture, silver, china, cut glass, brass and oodles of decorative accessories.

Mission Gallery Antiques
320 W. Washington St., San Diego
• **(619) 692-3566**

If you're a serious antique collector, you've come to the right place. The Mission Gallery has museum-quality furnishings from the seventeenth, eighteenth and nineteenth centuries.

You're sure to appreciate the fine American and European oil paintings, silver, porcelain, Persian rugs and estate jewelry.

Ocean Beach Antique Row
4800 block of Newport Ave., San Diego

Dozens of antique stores line Newport Avenue, some in malls or centers, some standing alone. The **Newport Avenue Antique Center** at 4864 Newport Avenue, for instance, has more than 18,000 square feet of antiques and collectibles. Whether you're looking for old prints, silver, toys or dolls, you'll find it all and more here. Just across the street at 4847 Newport Avenue is the **O.B. Collectors Mall** with a similar collection of antiques. Or check out the small but charming **Alive Again Antiques** at 4861 Newport Avenue. You're sure to find that special treasure.

Olde Cracker Factory Antiques
448 W. Market St., San Diego
• (619) 233-1669

Three floors of antique and specialty shops await your inspection in this restored warehouse. You're most likely to find collectibles here more often than serious pieces. But as antique shoppers know, the unexpected treasure can pop up any time, any place. The Olde Cracker Factory has been known to produce many a find. Plus, it's a delightful place to browse. Shops are open every day but Monday.

Papyrus Antique & Unusual Shop
116 W. Washington St., San Diego
• (619) 298-9291

If you're searching for the trendy but unusual, this is the place for you. Papyrus has a variety of Art Deco, Moderne, Hawaiiana and early California nostalgia pieces. You'll also find some interesting jewelry pieces, lighting fixtures and furnishings. The store is closed on Tuesdays.

North County Coastal

Antique Warehouse
212 S. Cedros Ave., Solana Beach
• (858) 755-5156

Under one warehouse roof (perfect when you want to shop for antiques and it's wintry outdoors), this mall has more than 100 shops, and new merchandise arrives daily. Use this store if you're on a Cedros Avenue antique hunt as a good starting point for your journey.

There's great variety here: shops that specialize in bottles, brass and Depression glass and vintage clothing, western gear and pewter. There's always coffee and refreshments for the weary shopper. Parking and all shops are on ground level. Ask for the warehouse's newsletter which lists upcoming antique events.

DeWitts Antiques & Collectibles
2946 State St., Carlsbad
• (760) 720-1175

One of the many antique stores lining State Street in Carlsbad, DeWitts is an excellent point of departure for those who love the quest for collectibles, true antiques, period furniture, glassware, toys and Americana. Among the 50 dealers here you might find Hummels, silver, records, linens and furniture.

Be sure to stop at the other State Street antique stores (between Beach and Oak streets), which specialize in everything from Americana to restored lighting fixtures. DeWitts is within four blocks of the Coaster train station.

Estate Sale Warehouse
1719 S. Coast Hwy., Oceanside
• (760) 433-6549

This store is more on the collectible end of antiques than others, but if you're looking for good quality, used furniture — perhaps doing a room in sixties retro — than head to Oceanside. You'll find unusual period pieces and truly great prices.

McNally Company Antiques
6033-L Paseo Delicias, Rancho Santa Fe
• (858) 756-1922

McNally's is the place if you're looking for 18th and 19th century furnishings or just love to browse through classic furniture. Here you'll find estate pieces, *objets d'art* and investment collectibles. They also carry quality items in silver. The store isn't open on Sunday; the days of the week the hours are 10-ish to 5-ish. Really, that's what the sign says on the door.

Vinge Antiques
505 Oak Ave., Carlsbad • (760) 729-7081

Just slightly south of the other antique stores in the shopping district, you'll cross Carlsbad Village Drive to find Vinge. It's worth the two block walk to discover their china (lovely tea pots were everywhere during our last visit), Depression glass and glassware that some of us used in the 1960s and 1970s (which is selling for collectible prices now), and paintings too.

North County Inland

Antique Village
983 Grand Ave., San Marcos
• (760) 744-8718

Antique Village has more than 65 stores, and that makes for excellent shopping. You'll find everything from unique collectible garden accessories to glassware collectibles here. And if you love oak and vintage furniture, there's sure to be a piece to tempt you.

This store has the largest selection of antiques in North County Inland. If you're looking for something distinctive and adore the country look, head in this direction.

Ivy House Antiques & Consignments
3137 S. Mission Rd., Fallbrook
• (760) 728-7038

This antiques store specializes in estate sale collectibles so you never quite know what you'll find. During past visits we've seen and been tempted by paintings, fine vintage linen and quilts, Native American items, and Oriental accessories. They also stock furniture and consignment items.

Hidden Valley Antique Emporium
333 E. Grand Ave., Escondido
• (760) 737-0333

Imagine more than 10,000 square feet of antique shopping. It's here at Hidden Valley Antique Emporium. Currently there are more than 60 shops under one roof, and they have layaway. They're open until 7 PM on Tuesday evening (other days the hours are from 10 AM until 5:30 PM). Parking can be found along nearby side streets.

This Old House
30158 Mission Rd., Bonsall
• (760) 631-2888

Antiques, dolls, glassware and oak and Victorian furniture are the stars of this 7,000-square-foot antique mall. There are more than 50 dealers and that number is growing. Many of the stores specialize in toys and western items. For those antique shoppers always looking for a clock to add to a collection, this is the place to start (At our last visit they had an overload of collectible time machines).

East County

Alpine Heavenly Hill Antiques
2327 Alpine Blvd., Alpine
• (619) 445-9255

This store is paradise for those who love antique oak, wicker and handmade giftware. There's an excellent selection (at least when these Insiders where last visiting) of vintage linens and children's items.

Blessings Galore!
8290 La Mesa Blvd., La Mesa
• (619) 463-8941

This is a store filled with heirlooms that you can add to your own pleasurable living. The store has primitives, antiques, florals, Victorian accessories and bits of Americana. Blessings Galore! carries many one-of-a-kind collectibles and the staff is helpful whether you're picking out a nostalgic gift for yourself or someone dear.

J K Corral Antiques & Specialty Store
2526 Alpine Blvd., Alpine
• (619) 445-0315

If you're searching out Western gear, Western collectibles and other Western furnishing this is the store for you. Insiders rave about the accessories. Perhaps you'll find a Hopalong Cassidy mug or a Roy Rogers lunch box. Perhaps you'll find a more authentic collectible from the real Wild West.

Ramona Antique Mall
872 Main St., Ramona • (760) 789-7816

Quality antiques, furniture and vintage toys,

this store also specializes in books and jewelry. Call ahead if you're looking for quilts. During a recent visit the store had a large selection.

Unique Stuff
2253 Alpine Blvd., Alpine
• (619) 445-3508

Whether you're headed to Alpine for a bed-and-breakfast-inn vacation or just coming up for a drive or to play in the snow, Unique Stuff offers an antique-lovers rest stop. Unique Stuff has antiques and collectibles, glassware and jewelry. They also specialize in vintage linens. As a sideline, the store carries crafts and supplies including those for tole painting.

South Bay

Bush Antiques
460 Third Ave., Chula Vista • (619) 426-2181

A little bit of everything is what you'll find at Bush Antiques. Glassware, linens, books, magazines, kitchenware and some silver are the headliners. Look a little deeper though, and you're likely to discover some fantastic furniture pieces as well as tons of collectibles. The store is closed Sundays and Mondays.

Gibson & Gibson Antique Lighting
180 Mace St., Chula Vista • (619) 422-2447

Antique Lighting is the specialty at Gibson & Gibson, both originals and reproductions. Does your home need an antique lamp to set off your favorite room? This is the place to find it. Open daily except Sunday, the staff suggests making an appointment ahead of time so they can best help you find the perfect piece.

Third Avenue Antiques
269 Third Ave., Chula Vista
• (619) 476-7222

Is Depression glass high on your list of collectibles? You'll find it in abundance here, along with ceramics, figurines and furniture. If you're looking for antique costume jewelry, you're sure to find the perfect piece from the large collection at Third Avenue Antiques.

Swap Meets and Flea Markets

San Diego

Kobey's Swap Meet
3500 Sports Arena Blvd., San Diego
(at the Sports Arena) • (619) 226-0650

Opened in 1980, Kobey's has become San Diego's largest open-air swap meet. Both new and used merchandise as well as many a hidden treasure can be found at Kobey's, and you don't need a fortune to come home with lots of goodies. Clothing, jewelry, collectibles, electronics, fresh flowers, baked goods and produce are just some of the items to be found. Live entertainment is usually on hand, and food and beverage is available on the premises.

Kobey's Swap Meet is open every Thursday, Friday, Saturday and Sunday from 7 AM until 3 PM. Admission is 50 cents on Thursdays and Fridays; $1 on Saturdays and Sundays. Children younger than 12 are admitted free.

If you pick up a copy of *This Week In San Diego*, available in most hotel and motel lobbies, it usually has a two-for-one admission coupon to Kobey's.

North County Coastal

Cedros Avenue Jumble Flea Market
On a lot south of Cedros Trading Company, 307 S. Cedros Ave., Solana Beach • (858) 755-0444

If you're addicted to flea markets, this "jumble" sale is a must. It happens every Sunday from 10 AM to 5 PM and there's no admission fee. You'll find delightful hand-painted fabrics and clothing, designer purses, crafts and antiques. It's all housed under brightly colored tents that suggest a Southern European flea market. There's food and entertainment, and while parking can be tricky, there are plenty of side streets where you can leave your car and walk the few blocks to the market.

Oceanside Drive-In Swap Meet
3480 Mission Ave., Oceanside
• **(760) 757-5286**

The swap meet is held 6 AM to 3 PM each Friday through Sunday, and on holiday Mondays, at this Oceanside location. Treasures to trash are found here and only you can determine what each item or category this merchandise fits into.

There's new and used merchandise, and bargaining is encouraged by many of the regular vendors. This swap meet is said to be one of the biggest in Southern California. Most Insiders agree that it's definitely one of the largest in North County. Admission is 50 cents on Saturday and 75 cents on Sunday. During June there's a "monster garage sale-a-thon" that brings even more sellers and buyers to the location. If you want to participate or go there to buy, call for more information.

Seaside Bazaar
One block south of Encinitas Blvd. on First St., Encinitas

Every weekend for the past 20-plus years, vendors and shoppers have been coming together at this vacant lot to sell, buy and marvel at the merchandise: crafts and antiques, treasures and collectibles along with flowers, plants, home decorator items and clothing. *Sunset* magazine wrote it up recently as one of the "secret finds along the coast." A secret no more, this North County Coastal sale still offers opportunities to find a bargain if not an outright prize. Hours are flexible; vendors start to set up in the morning and in the summer you may still find vendors and shoppers out in the early evening. There is no admission fee.

North County Inland

Escondido Drive-In Swap Meet
635 W. Mission Ave., Escondido
• **(760) 745-3100**

The swap meet is held year-round, Wednesday through Sunday, from 7 AM until 4 PM. There are food booths, a farmers' market, and lots of treasures in new and used merchandise. Admission is 50 cents on Wednesday and Saturday, 35 cents on Thursday, and 75 cents on Sunday.

East County

Spring Valley Swap Meet
6377 Quarry Rd., Spring Valley
• **(619) 463-1194**

If beauty is in the eye of the beholder, then you may find some beautiful items for sale at this East County swap meet. When you do go, you can never predict what will be there. And isn't that half the fun?

Generally speaking, there's new and used merchandise, antiques, collectibles, farmers' market produce, foods and stuff that you probably just have to take home. The admission is 50 cents for adults and the vendors are open from 7 AM to 3 PM on Saturday and Sunday throughout out the year.

South Bay

Kobey's MarketPlace
Coors Amphitheatre
2050 Otay Valley Rd., Chula Vista
• **(619) 523-2700**

Kobey's Swap Meet is legendary in San Diego, and now it has moved into the South Bay and set up shop in the parking lot of the Coors Amphitheatre. Although smaller than the San Diego version, the South Bay swap meet is much the same as its big brother in terms of the merchandise for sale. You'll find both new and garage-sale type items being sold by private vendors, including jewelry, craft items, sportswear, baked goods and much more.

For now, Kobey's MarketPlace is open on Saturdays and Sundays only, from 7 AM until 3 PM. Admission is $1 for adults and free for children younger than 12. Parking is free.

National City Swap Meet
3200 D Ave., National City (at the Harbor Drive-in Theater) • **(619) 477-2203**

Every Saturday and Sunday 50 cents will get you into this swap meet that's primarily of the garage-sale variety. Household items and collectibles are abundant, but you will find some new items, too. Show up early; things usually start rolling by about 7 AM, and you don't want to miss any great bargains. Half a dozen snack bars and food vendors are scattered throughout the swap meet. Be sure to wear a hat and bring your sunscreen.

Unique and Intriguing

San Diego

The Black
5017 Newport Ave., San Diego
• (619) 222-5498

Back in the 1960s and early 1970s, this was the best-known "head shop" in town. In addition to the requisite incense and psychedelic art pieces, you could find some accessories of dubious legality. Those days are long behind us though, and today The Black specializes in more mainstream items. It hasn't lost its hippie flair, however, and you'll marvel at some of the gift items that you probably didn't know still existed. The Black also has a fine selection of cigars, pipes and pipe tobacco.

Hillcrest Ace Hardware
1007 University Ave., San Diego
• (619) 291-5988

Looking for some nuts and bolts? You'll find them here, along with thousands of things you'd never expect to see in a hardware store. Time after time we hear locals say they stopped into Hillcrest Hardware and had a hard time leaving. There's just so much to look at. Along with traditional hardware items, check out the plants, gift items, antique hardware pieces and all those other little things you never thought you needed until you saw them here.

Museum Shops of Balboa Park
Balboa Park, San Diego

Every single museum in Balboa Park has a large gift shop offering distinctive gifts from around the world. You could plan an entire day around nothing but shopping in Balboa Park, especially if you're looking for something a little different.

Books, textiles, jewelry and ceramics are available at the Mingei International Museum. At the Museum of Photographic Arts you'll find photo kits, cars, posters and frames. Or how about some sports-related gift items from the San Diego Hall of Champions? See our chapter on Balboa Park for a complete listing of museums and their locations.

99 Ranch Market
7330 Clairemont Mesa Blvd., San Diego
• (858) 565-1199

Have you ever wandered into those mysterious, small Asian markets that are stuffed with unusual food items you've never seen before? Imagine that small market expanded to supermarket size, and you'll have an idea of what 99 Ranch is like. It's huge — make no mistake — and if you're seeking an obscure Asian food or ingredient, you'll find it here. Don't miss the fresh fish display. Dozens of varieties of freshly caught fish will get your mouth watering.

Sew & So
7333 Clairemont Mesa Blvd., San Diego
• (858) 573-1853

Buttons and bows don't even begin to describe the array of special items at Sew & So. Literally thousands of buttons in every size, shape and color are available, as are hundreds of ribbons and unusual trims. If you're crafting a bridal headpiece, choose from a variety of forms and decorative accessories to create a memorable confection. Or if you're building your own costume, you'll find plenty of fabrics and trims to gussie up your most elaborate creation.

Walter Andersen Nursery
3642 Enterprise St., San Diego
• (619) 224-8271

When you step into Walter Andersen's you'll find the usual assortment of trees, shrubs, bedding plants, bulbs and garden tools. What makes this nursery different is the staff. If you need advice, an opinion or just

INSIDERS' TIP

Good prices are in the eye of the beholder. You may want to shop around for the best deals.

some conversation about what's growing in your garden, the certified nursery professionals are only too happy to oblige. You'll learn more here in an hour than you would in a month of horticultural study. In other words, these folks know their stuff, and they're glad to share it. Just in case you're looking for something exotic, Walter Andersen has that too, along with many native plants and trees.

The White House
7927 Girard Ave., La Jolla
• **(858) 459-2565**

Here's an interesting twist — women's clothing and accessories all in shades of white. Just walking through this classy store makes you feel like you're shopping for the perfect outfit for an afternoon sipping Bellini cocktails on a terrace overlooking Italy's Lake Como. From casual to dressy, the prices are affordable, and the clothes are adorable. The White House has a store in the Del Mar Plaza shopping center, too (see our entry under North County Coastal).

Whole Foods
711 University Ave., San Diego
• **(619) 294-2800**
8825 Villa La Jolla Dr., La Jolla
• **(858) 642-6700**

Farmers' Markets are ideal for picking up organic produce and other goodies, but they're usually open only one day a week. When the urge strikes for freshly picked strawberries or whole grain breads, Whole Foods is open every day. You won't find a larger array of organically grown produce, whole grains, fresh fish, poultry and meats, and herbs and vitamins. Inside the store is Mrs. Gooch's Cafe, where you can enjoy everything from a cup of coffee to a full meal.

North County Coastal

Anderson's La Costa Nursery
400 La Costa Ave., Encinitas
• **(760) 753-3153**

Possibly the best nursery and garden specialty store ever conceived, Anderson's La Costa Nursery is far from a secret, although

their "secret garden" is not to be missed. This is the place to wander and dream of what your garden can be and then to select perfect plants (that will thrive after they're home).

In addition to plants, trees and specialty items (such as bromeliads and proteas and huge potted palms) you'll find an enticing collection of wind chimes, bird feeders, statuary and garden art. The herbs and perennials are worth the drive from all points in the county and in the winter months, you can get David Austin and Old English roses here that are hard to find at other nurseries. Call ahead if you're searching for something special; their knowledgeable staff can answer your plant care questions.

Begonia Gardens
695 Normandy Rd., Encinitas
• **(760) 436-2194**

Twice a year (April 1 to September 15, November 1 to December 22), the gardens are open for retail sales. Here you'll find perfect tuberous begonias of all varieties, from tiny hanging plants to monster-size specimens in colors only Nature can make. At Christmas the nursery has a fine collection of field-fresh poinsettias.

Some Insiders bring their out-of-town plant-loving friends to the nursery; it's beautiful, unique and makes for a wonderful outing.

British Food Centre-South
1378 S. Solana Hills Dr., Solana Beach
• **(858) 755-6161**

If you love anything from the British Isles or you're missing home, then head to British Food Centre-South. You'll find all the right teas and teacakes. What's more, you'll find teacups, tea caddies, tea cozies and tea spoons (the kind you place loose tea in to steep right in your cup).

In the same shopping area as Marshalls Department store (see the entry in this section under Discount Shopping), this is a fun place for a quick Brit fix.

Carlsbad Danish Bakery
2805 Roosevelt St., Carlsbad
• **(760) 729-6186**

If you're visiting the antique shopping district in Carlsbad, you may want to take a short walk (one block east and one block north) to 2805 Roosevelt Street, where you'll find this hidden secret of sweet temptation. The Carlsbad Danish Bakery can offer you a perfect muffin or sweet treat (try the oatmeal cookies and the bran muffins — they're to die for) and a hot cup of coffee or tea.

Their wedding and special-occasion cakes are known as the best throughout North County Coastal. They are beautiful and taste even better. Take home a loaf of their multi-grain bread, too.

This is a popular Insiders' hangout — often packed—so you may have the chance to browse through the offerings before it's your turn at the counter. You can eat here too, inside, or in the fresh air; try coffee and cake at an umbrella-covered table. The bakery choices run out after about 3 PM and the bakers don't make the same treats every day, so it's best to come early. The bakery is closed on Sundays.

Hadleys Fruit Orchards
6115 Paseo del Norte, Carlsbad
• (760) 438-1260

A mainstay of southern California since 1931, Hadleys tempts shoppers with dried fruits and nuts from around the world. There's also a fine selection of fresh fruits and produce, and traveler's snacks too. Some believe Hadleys has the best selection on the West Coast. Maybe that's why those tour buses that visit the best places in Southern California always stop here. When they do, travelers often try one of their strange-sounding specialties — sweet, creamy date shakes. If you buy a gift here, Hadleys can arrange to ship it.

Hadleys Fruit Orchards is near LEGOLAND, the Carlsbad Company Stores, Carlsbad State Beach, and the Carlsbad Flower Fields, so check the index if you're in the neighborhood and want to find more to do and see.

Mary's Tack & Feed
3675 Via De La Valle, Del Mar
• (858) 755-2015

This is a horse-lover's and pet-lover's shopping heaven and the best place along the coast if you need a bale of hay or a new set of spurs. Frequented by the upscale residents of Rancho Santa Fe and Fairbanks Ranch, the store is a fun browse and the staff is friendly and knowledgeable on pet-oriented topics.

If you're shopping in Del Mar and have had enough of the designer shops and coffee pubs along the coast highway, head inland about 2 miles for some real-life shopping. Adjacent to Mary's you'll find shops and stands that sell plants, fresh vegetables, strawberries in season, flowers and country-style collectibles.

North CountyInland

G & B Orchids
2426 Cherimoya Dr., Vista
• (760) 727-2611

If you're hooked on orchids, you'll have to include this place on any plant-seeking expedition. Here you'll find cymbidiums, oncidiums, phalaenopsis, cattleyas, and dendrobiums by the score. All plants are of premium quality and the helpful staff will tell you what each plant requires to keep it happy. They'll also give you plenty of instruction on how to get started in the exotic world of orchids.

S. B. Nickerson Nursery
1761 E. Mission Rd., Fallbrook
• (760) 728-8379

S. B. Nickerson's has been compared to plant lovers' heaven. It's worth a field trip here if you adore plants and all that goes with them. You'll find more than 30 acres of them plus a gift shop. Trust us. If you love to garden you will find something you must have. Be sure to

---

INSIDERS' TIP

Sally Gary's *San Diego's Deals & Steals*, found at bookstores around the area, is a must-have for all serious shoppers. The guide offers savvy tips on where to find everything at bargain prices. It's a good reference guide for antique shoppers, too.

visit the model gardens to get landscaping ideas. The store also sells custom plant baskets, fountains and indoor plants. This is one of the best gardening stores in North County Inland.

East County

Branding Iron
629 Main St., Ramona • (760) 789-5050
An old-fashioned Western apparel and tack store, the Branding Iron has everything from silver bits and spurs to horse blankets and felt cowboy hats. You'll also be tempted with jeans, western clothing, boots, moccasins and western collectibles and if you happen to need some hay or oats for Trigger, you're in the right place too. This is a real Western-wear store and shopping is just part of the experience as you tour the aisles.

Dudley's Bakery
Calif. Hwy. 78 and 79, Santa Ysabel
• (760) 765-0488
This bakery is a treasure, and while visitors might see it as being smack dab out in nowhere, they have to admit it's busy. In fact, people drive from all over southern California for a loaf of Dudley's bread. And if you're just going to Julian, it's an absolute "must stop."

The bread is so good you'll want take some home, but which loaf? There are 17 different types of bread to tempt you. Dudley's also has a cafe, which is especially busy during holidays and on weekends. But that's OK. While you wait you can snack on the bread you've bought.

Siempre Bella
8341 La Mesa Blvd., La Mesa
• (619) 698-9008
If you're searching for a romantic dress and all the Victorian accessories you could dream of owning, the Siempre Bella is not to be missed. There is a full range of women's sizes including those for full figures. You'll find original and antique wedding gowns, hats, shoes, bustles and special-occasion dresses. The store has a variety of laces, velvet creations, designer originals and children's clothing too.

Summer Past Farms
15602 Old Hwy. 80, Flinn Springs
• (619) 390-1523
This is possibly one of the most thrilling experiences for any gardener, plant lover, craft maker and nature person within the entire county. Some say it's like plant heaven here on earth.

People come from around the world to visit Summer Past Farms, yet many locals don't even know it exists. Here you'll find a delightful gift shop crowded with books to inspire any gardener, designer or herbal crafter. Plenty of dried herbs are on display and for sale, and the flowers you'll see in arrangements (both dried and fresh) come straight from the farm's fields. Start with the herb nursery and then make a stop at the espresso bar. You can visit the herbal soap shop and factory, a children's garden, a vegetable garden, a cutting garden and fragrance garden. The store holds craft demos and classes. If you're hooked on crafts, you'll want to call ahead for a brochure (or send a self-addressed, stamped envelope to the address above, including the zip code (92021) and then find out what will be offered during your visit.

We recently attended a free seminar on how to grow, enjoy, cook with and soothe the body with lavender. These delightful seminars happen throughout the year. Call for their schedule.

The farm is closed on Monday and Tuesday. There is no admission charge, but be warned, one visit and you'll be hooked.

INSIDERS' TIP

Have you ever fallen in love with an item in an antique store? Consider making your buying decision right then. If you come back later the item may have been snapped up by the very next shopper.

South Bay

General Bead
317 National City Blvd., National City
- **(619) 336-0100**

Whether you're looking for a few beads to decorate your favorite jacket, or you need hundreds of beads for that special craft project, you won't be disappointed at General Bead. Choose from among 18,000 items spread out over 3,000 square feet. Beads of all sizes, shapes and colors will dazzle you and inspire your creative nature.

Music Trader
481 Broadway, Chula Vista
- **(619) 585-3472**

Do you have old CDs or cassettes that you no longer listen to? Then trade them in at the Music Trader. You can sell or trade your oldies for something that appeals to you more, or just browse through the latest offerings for something new and unusual. The store specializes in R&B, rap and oldies. Videos, video games and laser discs are also bought and sold.

My Bridal Gown
1050 Highland Ave., National City
- **(619) 474-4025**

You'll be overwhelmed by the more than 1,000 designer bridal gowns that this store stocks. Expert bridal consultants will help you select the perfect gown in sizes 4 to 44 for a storybook wedding. If there's something special you have in mind, My Bridal Gown will order direct from the manufacturer at a substantial savings. Your attendants will be delighted by the large selection of bridesmaids' dresses and accessories.

National City Mile of Cars
National City Blvd., between 24th and 30th Sts., National City

If you're in the market for a new car but are undecided about exactly what you want, drive to National City, park and start walking. Car dealers line National City Boulevard. Every make and model you could possibly think of is here, so you can test drive all your favorites, without having to visit dealers all over town.

We're justly proud of the famous San Diego Zoo and its "sister," the Wild Animal Park, a 2,300-acre park that's home to 1,600 mammals, butterflies and bromeliads.

The historic San Diego Museum of Art, located in the heart of Balboa Park, provides a rich and diverse cultural experience for more than 500,000 annual visitors. The museum's nationally renowned permanent collection includes European, American, Asian and contemporary art, most notably Spanish and Italian old masters, South Asian paintings, 19th- and 20th-century American paintings and sculptures, and works by contemporary California artists. In addition, the museum regularly features major exhibitions of art from around the world, as well as an extensive year-round schedule of supporting cultural programs and educational opportunities.

EXHIBITION SCHEDULE
(PARTIAL)

El Alma del Pueblo: Spanish Folk Art and its Transformation in the Americas
August 28, 1999 - October 31, 1999

Star Wars: The Magic of Myth
September 25, 1999 - January 2, 2000

Pacific Arcadia: Images of California 1600-1915
October 30, 1999 - January 9, 2000

Picturing Paradise: San Diego in the Eye of the Artist, 1875-1940
October 30, 1999 - January 9, 2000

Land of the Winged Horsemen: Art in Poland, 1572-1764
December 18, 1999 - February 27, 2000

Eastman Johnson: Painting America
February 26, 2000 - May 21, 2000

SAN DIEGO MUSEUM OF ART
1450 El Prado, Balboa Park • (619) 232-7931
www.sdmart.com

San Diego. From a couple of angles.

Our spacious two-room suites are ideal when traveling with your family. The living room sofa-sleeper provides that extra space. Conveniences include wet bar, refrigerator, microwave, coffeemaker, two telephones and two TVs. Enjoy a complimentary, full cooked-

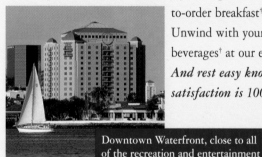

to-order breakfast[†] each morning. Unwind with your favorite beverages[†] at our evening reception. *And rest easy knowing your satisfaction is 100% guaranteed.*

Downtown Waterfront, close to all of the recreation and entertainment activities including the San Diego Zoo, Gaslamp Quarter Restaurants, Seaport Village and Horton Plaza Shopping.

**Embassy Suites®
San Diego Bay –
Downtown**
601 Pacific Highway
San Diego 92101-5914
619-239-2400 • Fax 619-239-1520

Just minutes from La Jolla's shopping and beautiful beaches, golf at the famous Torrey Pines, Del Mar Fairgrounds, University of California, San Diego, Sea World, the San Diego Zoo and Wild Animal Park.

**Embassy Suites®
San Diego – La Jolla**
4550 La Jolla Village Drive
San Diego 92122-0436
619-453-0400 • Fax 619-453-4226

EMBASSY SUITES®

www.embassy-suites.com
1-800-EMBASSY

What a difference a stay makes.℠

Attractions

Besides the glorious climate, why do so many people visit and settle in San Diego? Attractions. We have them by the boatload and they're as varied as the county itself.

Sure, we have the places to go and the things to see that you've read about in glossy publications and books. We're justly proud of the famous San Diego Zoo and its "sister," the Wild Animal Park, a 2,300-acre park that's home to 1,600 mammals, butterflies and bromeliads. We love to talk about the history of Old Town, the array of creatures at Sea World, and the San Diego Hall of Champions with its collection featuring more than 40 sports and a mountain of memorabilia.

As Insiders, we smile when pointing out that attractions in San Diego can mean more than viewing dinosaur bones, marveling at Native American artifact collections, touring working wineries or even screaming on a roller coaster. These are fun, but there's more.

For instance, there are the museums that are as far from the run-of-the-mill variety as you can get. Take the Surf Musuem in Oceanside where you can learn the history of surfing (it began in 1907), or the Antique Gas and Steam Engine Museum in Vista, where you can see working exhibits of gas, steam and horse-powered engines. If you're interested in little-known historical sites, it's thumbs up for the San Pasqual Battlefield State Historical Park where the bloodiest battle in the Mexican-American war occurred. Want to visit some lovely gardens? You can't beat the tranquil beauty of the Quail Botanical Gardens. (It's tucked away in Encinitas and even some Insiders don't know its there.)

Now blend this kettle of interesting places with the excitement of casinos, high-energy fun at water parks and the thrill of rollercoastering at Belmont Park in Pacific Beach. Focus on that and then include the smidgen of education you'll snatch at a visit to the observatory at Palomar Mountain and you've taken just a sip of the attractions that are all within an hour's drive of downtown San Diego.

While often described as "for the tourist," you're likely to meet more Insiders at these places than those visiting from other areas. San Diegans like to enjoy our hometown attractions again and again. And we do.

The problem, as Insiders see it, is that there are so many things to do here that you just can't visit for a day or two. You must live here to make sure you do every one justice.

In this hefty chapter we've included our favorite attractions, including the quirky ones, the notable ones and the ones we always share when best friends come to town. Prices and hours are as current as we can make them. You may want to call ahead, however, in case prices or hours have recently changed.

As you browse through this chapter, keep in mind that these activities and not-to-be-missed places may also be described in other chapters. For instance, there is so much to see and do at Balboa Park that you'll find an entire chapter devoted to this jewel of San Diego. Other entries may reappear in Kidstuff or Parks or Nightlife So to get the most of our chunk of paradise, you'll want to refer to the index to get all the details on your favorites. Like most of our other chapters, this one is organized by geographic region and then by alphabetical listings within each region.

With all that said, it's time for fun. So grab your camera, pack a lunch or some snacks for the road, and let's hit it. There's plenty to do in San Diego and just so many hours in a day.

San Diego

Balboa Park Visitors Center
1549 El Prado, San Diego
• **(619) 239-0512**

Balboa Park is truly the heart of San Diego, both geographically and emotionally. You could spend a whole day in the park and barely scratch the surface of all there is to do. Rather than try to cram Balboa Park into a few short paragraphs, we've devoted an entire chapter to an in-depth description of all it has to offer. But just to give you a taste of what you'll find, we'll start with, of course, the world-famous San Diego Zoo. That's a day's expedition all by itself. Another day could easily be spent going through its museums — the Aerospace Museum, the Natural History Museum, the Automotive Museum and the Model Railroad Museum, just to name a few. The Miniature Railroad and the historic Merry-Go-Round are favorites with the kids, and both adults and youngsters flock to the Ruben H. Fleet Space Theater and Science Center for IMAX films and hands-on exhibits. If you plan to spend the day at Balboa Park, turn to its chapter and we'll give you the whole lowdown, including some tips on scheduling your time.

www.insiders.com
See this and many other
Insiders' Guide®
destinations online.
Visit us today!

Belmont Amusement Park
3146 Mission Blvd., San Diego
• **(619) 491-2988**

Home of the Giant Dipper, one of two remaining antique wooden roller coasters in California, Belmont Park is full of rides, restaurants and attractions for the whole family. In the tradition of Coney Island in New York, Belmont Park sits alongside the beach, and the ocean view from the top of the Giant Dipper is spectacular.

Besides the roller coaster, you can enjoy Bumper Cars, a Tilt-a-Whirl, the Liberty Carousel, the Sea Serpent ride, a Crazy Submarine and Baja Buggies. If those seem too much for the young ones, they'll surely enjoy Pirates Cove, a soft-play facility with over 7,000 square feet of tunnels, slides and a ball pool. Adults and kids will enjoy the Prime Time arcade

game center and Cyber Station, which has a collection of the latest electronic games. For the adventurous, the "Trampoline Thing" awaits, a giant trampoline where you can do spins, flips and jumps, all with the guidance of an able-bodied and vigilant assistant.

For those who prefer tamer pursuits, try San Diego Sand Art, where you can create beautiful sand crafts. Or go for a swim in the indoor plunge, a nice alternative to the salty ocean. Built in 1925, it's Southern California's largest indoor swimming pool. When you get hungry, a large food court has numerous fast-food establishments, or enjoy one of the fine oceanfront restaurants within the park.

Belmont Park's hours are Sunday through Thursday, 11 AM to 8 PM, and 11 AM to 10 PM on Friday and Saturday. Admission to the park is free; rides and attractions are priced separately. For good, old-fashioned family fun, try combining a day at the beach with a visit to Belmont Park.

Cabrillo National Monument and Tidepools
1800 Cabrillo Memorial Dr., San Diego
• **(619) 557-5450**

High above San Diego Harbor, at the tip of the Point Loma peninsula, is the Cabrillo National Monument. The monument commemorates the 1542 landing of Juan Rodríguez Cabrillo in what is now San Diego and acknowledges that he was the first European to set foot on the west coast. After stopping at the Visitor Center, which has information about the park, exhibits and films, make a beeline to the Old Point Loma Lighthouse for a trip back in time. Your tour of the lighthouse, built in 1854, will remind you of the days of sailing ships and oil lamps. Back when it was a work-

---

INSIDERS' TIP

At local attractions, food can be pricey, especially for families. Consider packing a picnic or stopping at one of the less expensive restaurants listed in the Restaurants chapter.

Photo: San Diego Wild Animal Park

Giraffe feeding at San Diego's Wild Animal Park is a popular attraction for all ages.

ing lighthouse, its light could be seen 39 miles out to sea.

Once you've taken in the panoramic views of the harbor from the lighthouse, stroll along the 2-mile bayside trail that descends 300 feet through the cliffs and is surrounded by native sage scrub, prickly pear cactus and yucca. It passes remnants of the defense system used to protect the harbor during both World Wars. Finally, take a short drive down to the tidepools, and discover the marine plants and animals that have adapted to survive in the harsh conditions of pounding surf and shifting tides that leave them exposed to the sun for a part of every day. Check out the shore crabs, bat stars, dead man's fingers, sea hares and many other fascinating sea creatures.

The park is open every day from 9 AM to 5:15 PM. Admission is $5 per vehicle and $2 per bicyclist, jogger, walker or city-bus passenger. Keep in mind that the rocks around the tidepools are slippery, and the barnacles can be sharp. Be sure to wear sturdy, non-slip shoes. And remember, collecting marine animals, shells or rocks is prohibited by federal law.

Corporate Helicopters of San Diego
3753 John J. Montgomery Dr., San Diego • (858) 505-5650, (800) 345-6737

For a thrilling, bird's-eye view of San Diego, take the tour that adventurous souls swear by: a sky tour over the best of San Diego. Soar past the San Diego skyline in a quiet, jet-powered helicopter. See Old Town and the San Diego-Coronado Bay Bridge as you fly across San Diego Bay. View the beauty of Sunset Cliffs, Mission Bay and La Jolla. Thirty minutes later you're safely back on the ground with a never-to-be-forgotten memory. The 30-minute San Diego tour is $120 per person. Other tours are available too, including a North County tour and one that goes south to the U.S.-Mexico border. Or if you have something

special in mind, a customized aerial adventure can be arranged.

Family Fun Center
6999 Clairemont Mesa Blvd., San Diego • (858) 560-4211

Like its sister Fun Centers in Escondido, Vista and El Cajon, San Diego's version of the Family Fun Center has enough going on to entertain and occupy kids (and Mom and Dad too) for a full day or evening. In addition to the attractions offered by the other centers — miniature golf courses, batting cages, bumper boats, go-carts, and huge arcades — San Diego's also has a laser-runner venue and a Country Fair Fun Zone with amusement park rides. (See the North County Inland section for more information on other Family Fun Centers.)

Operating hours vary, depending on weather and the time of year, so be sure to call before you go. Generally the Fun Center opens at 11 AM Monday through Friday and 9 AM Saturday and Sunday. Closing hours are midnight Sunday through Thursday and 1 AM Friday and Saturday. The various attractions are priced separately, but an all-day pass can be purchased after 4 PM on Friday and at any time on Saturday and Sunday. The cost is $18.50 for those 57 inches and taller and $14.50 for those shorter.

Gaslamp Quarter
Between Fourth and Sixth Aves., below Broadway, San Diego • (619) 233-4691

No matter what you're seeking — dining, entertainment, history or shopping — you'll find it in the Gaslamp Quarter. Covering an area of more than 16 blocks, the Quarter was named for the gas lamps that lit the evening sky in the late nineteenth century.

By day, stroll through the district and go back in time to the days when lawman Wyatt Earp operated three gambling houses and the

---

INSIDERS' TIP

Visit the Downtown Information Center for maps, literature, videos and free downtown-area trolley and walking tours. The Information Center is located at 225 Broadway, Suite #160, between Second and Third Avenues.

Photo: San Diego Convention and Visitors Bureau

A visit to the Carlsbad flower fields will brighten anyone's day.

area was a thriving red-light district. Drink in the beautifully restored Victorian houses, including the William Heath Davis House, the Gaslamp's oldest surviving structure. Browse among the antique shops, art galleries, boutiques and specialty shops.

By night, join the crowds who fill the streets as the gas lamps begin to glow. Take in a lively happy hour or enjoy fine dining at one of more than 60 restaurants serving a variety of cuisines: Italian, French, Spanish, Greek, Asian, and even Californian. After dinner, have a cup of coffee or tea at one of the many coffeehouses that dot the area.

Then the fun begins. Choose from Dixieland jazz, hip hop, country or Spanish flamenco in the clubs and cabarets that have made the Gaslamp one of Southern California's finest entertainment centers. If you're looking for nightlife in San Diego, you won't be disappointed by the Gaslamp Quarter.

Harbor Tours

Hornblower Cruises & Events, 1066 N. Harbor Dr., San Diego • (619) 686-8715
San Diego Harbor Excursion, 1050 N. Harbor Dr., San Diego • (619) 234-4111

See San Diego the way Cabrillo first viewed it — from the water. Both Hornblower Cruises and San Diego Harbor Excursion offer one- and two-hour narrated tours of San Diego's beautiful and diverse natural harbor. Among the many sights you'll see are the U.S. Navy fleet, the *Star of India* sailing ship, the Cabrillo National Monument, the San Diego-Coronado Bay Bridge and the historic Hotel del Coronado. Enjoy the sights and the sea air from pleasant sun decks or comfortable inside seating. Snacks and beverages are available on board.

Prices for the one-hour tour are $12 for adults, $10 for seniors and military, and $6 for children 4 to 12. Two-hour tour prices are $17 for adults, $15 for seniors and military, and

INSIDERS' TIP

If you're planning a visit to the tidepools, check the tide tables before you go. Low tide is the optimum time for an up-close look at the vast array of marine creatures.

$8.50 for children 4 to 12. Dinner cruises are available too, if you'd like to take in the stunning nighttime skyline. Cruise schedules vary depending on the season, so be sure to call ahead for departure times. And even though it may be a warm day, the air can get a little chilly on the water, so it's a good idea to bring along a light jacket or sweater.

Mission San Diego de Alcalá
10818 San Diego Mission Rd., San Diego
• (619) 281-8449

In 1769, when Father Junipero Serra established the first of 21 missions at what is now Presidio Park, little did he know that a few years later the mission would be moved. Strife with the local Indians and the need for a better water supply prompted the move to the present location in Mission Valley, where today it is a favorite visitor attraction as well as an active parish church.

Completely restored in 1931, the mission is truly San Diego's most famous historical landmark. The on-site museum displays artifacts unearthed during archeological digs over the past several years. It also provides visitors a detailed history of Father Serra's work as well as a chronicle of the early days of San Diego. The serene gardens surrounding the property are a favorite spot for relaxation and contemplation, as is the beautiful chapel. The mission is open daily from 9 AM to 5 PM. Admission is $2 for adults, $1 for seniors and students, and 50 cents for children younger than 12. Cassette players are provided for self-guided tours.

Old Town State Historic Park Visitor Center
4002 Wallace St., San Diego
• (619) 220-5422

No visit to San Diego is complete without a day spent where California began. Even Insiders frequently feel the need to rediscover their roots in historic Old Town, where there's always a fiesta in progress. It was here that Father Junipero Serra established his first mission in 1769, and it was here that the fledgling city took hold.

The park includes a main plaza, where Kit Carson was among those who raised the first American flag in 1846. Surrounding the plaza are historic buildings, including the Mason Street School (San Diego's first schoolhouse), exhibit museums and living history demonstrations. Also around the plaza are meticulously restored historic houses such as La Casa de Bandini, La Casa de Estudillo and La Casa de Pedroarena.

On the streets leading to the plaza are surprises galore: a professional theater, artisans, galleries and shops with traditional Mexican wares. When the aroma of restaurant delicacies proves irresistible, choose from one of 37 fine restaurants that offer the best in Mexican and international cuisine. Be sure to try a traditional Margarita; Old Town's are the biggest in the world. Enjoy live mariachi bands and traditional dancers everywhere you turn. And if you're looking for even more excitement, don't miss the Whaley House, an officially designated haunted house.

Free historic walking tours are offered daily at 2 PM from the Visitor's Information Center at 4002 Wallace Street, just across from the western edge of Old Town Plaza. The tour includes many of the museums and historic buildings, including the Seeley stables, the Blacksmith Shop, the Dentist Shop and more. Or if you prefer a self-guided walking tour, pick up a free copy of the *Olde San Diego Gazette*, an entertaining souvenir guide of San Diego that will steer you through the park with ease. It's available nearly everywhere in Old Town.

Be sure to observe the local artisans as they practice their crafts. Watch glassblowers create artistic treasures from 2,000-degree molten glass, or observe diamond cutters as they delicately shape their brilliant stones.

INSIDERS' TIP

At the Zoo and the Wild Animal Park, you can rent lockers. The lockers are wonderful for a picnic lunch, film, and the extra items families need. You can also rent strollers and wheelchairs.

A group of children are entertained by a local juggler at Seaport Village.

Woodcutters, potters and weavers are abundant too. While you're out walking, don't miss touring Heritage Park Village, a collection of beautifully restored Victorian homes that were moved to their current site in Old Town in the early 1970s.

Finally, if you're searching for the perfect gift to take home, don't miss the Bazaar del Mundo, 17 international shops in a beautiful garden setting surrounded by Mexican-style buildings. Plan to spend the better part of the day in Old Town in order to fully enjoy the food, fun and history of old San Diego. The park is open every day except Thanksgiving and Christmas, from 10 AM to 4:30 PM. Admission is free.

San Diego Maritime Museum
1306 N. Harbor Dr., San Diego
• (619) 234-9153

Immerse yourself in San Diego's exciting maritime history by touring a collection of three historic ships docked along the picturesque embarcadero. The 1863 *Star of India* is the oldest actively sailed square-rigged ship in the world. Aboard the ship you can learn about her colorful history of collisions, mutiny, dismasting and entrapments. Next is the 1898 ferryboat *Berkeley*, which was relocated from San Francisco and features daily demonstrations of its triple-expansion steam engine. During its time in San Francisco, the *Berkeley* was used to evacuate survivors of the 1906 earthquake and ensuing fires. Last but not least is the 1904 *Medea*, one of three surviving great steam yachts. It saw service in both World Wars, under three navies and six national flags.

All three ships have exhibits chronicling their respective histories, demonstrations of nautical skills, maritime art and interactive activities for children. Hours are 9 AM to 8 PM daily. Admission is $5 for adults, $4 for juniors 13 to 17 and $2 for children 6 to 12. Children younger than 6 are admitted free.

Sea World
Sea World Dr., 1 mile west of I-5,
San Diego • (619) 226-3901

More than just a marine-life entertainment park, Sea World is committed to the health and preservation of all marine species. A prime example is the yearlong effort to rescue and rehabilitate J.J., an abandoned California gray whale calf. Near death when she arrived at Sea World, she was nurtured back to health and released into the ocean to join her fellow whales on their annual northward migration. Similar rescue-and-rehabilitation efforts are frequently on display for visitors to witness and learn from.

But don't think for a moment that you'll be lacking in visceral thrills at the 150-acre park. At the Wild Arctic attraction you can journey to the frozen North on a 400-mph jet helicopter expedition. When you land you'll find yourself eye-to-eye with polar bears, beluga whales, walruses and harbor seals. Or visit the Manatee Rescue attraction, or the interactive dolphin habitat. How about a trip to Rocky Point Preserve, home to bottlenose dolphins and Alaskan sea otters? And don't forget the favorite thrill of all: seeing Shamu, the Killer Whale, perform. Afterward, visit "Shamu Backstage," an interactive killer whale experience.

Sea World features five shows and more than 20 exhibits for the whole family. The park is open daily at 10 AM during fall, winter and spring, and at 9 AM from mid-June through Labor Day. Closing time varies depending on the time of year. Admission, which includes all shows and attractions, is $34.95 for adults and $26.95 for children 3 to 11. Children 2 and younger are admitted free.

Seaport Village
849 W. Harbor Dr., San Diego
• (619) 235-4014

Nestled at the foot of San Diego's skyline along the embarcadero, Seaport Village is one of San Diego's premier sites for dining, shopping, entertainment and sightseeing. Four bayside restaurants provide breathtaking views of San Diego Bay as well as outstanding continental cuisine. Or if you're in the mood for something a little more casual, sample an international treat at one of more than a dozen eateries situated throughout the village—everything from Chicago hot dogs to an authentic Italian cappuccino.

If shopping is the order of the day, you'll find many a precious treasure at Seaport Village. Handcrafted gifts, original art, souvenirs, toys and fashions are among the unique items awaiting your scrutiny. The kids are sure to head for the restored 1890s Looff carousel, and they will delight at the ongoing parade of mimes, clowns and street performers. Then stroll along the boardwalk for an up-close view of the embarcadero, or hop aboard a horse-drawn carriage for a romantic and scenic tour of the area.

Shops are open from 10 AM to 9 PM from September through May, and until 10 PM during summer months. Admission to the village is free.

Sightseeing
Gray Line Tours San Diego
1775 Hancock St., Ste. 130, San Diego
• (619) 491-0011

A comfortable coach can sometimes be the very best way to take in the highlights of San Diego. Gray Line offers a variety of tours, all narrated by experienced driver-guides. Among the most popular is the San Diego City Tour, which will show you Downtown, the Gaslamp Quarter, Point Loma, Balboa Park, the beach areas and more. Affordably priced at $25 for adults and $11 for children 3 to 11, tours depart from major area hotels. Also available are Seaport Village/Harbor Cruise tours, south of the border tours, the San Diego Zoo and Sea World, San Diego Wild Animal Park and tours to attractions outside the county such as Disneyland and Universal Studios. All fares include admission to attractions. Reservations must be made in advance.

Old Town Trolley Tours
2115 Kurtz St., San Diego
• (619) 298-8687

Hop aboard an open-air trolley on wheels, and take a leisurely approach to sightseeing. Start your two-hour tour at any of nine locations in Old Town, the Embarcadero, Seaport Village, Downtown, Coronado or Balboa Park. Stay on as long as you like, or get off at any of the stops to shop, sightsee or dine. When you're ready, climb back aboard the next trolley and resume your tour, which is fully narrated with colorful anecdotes, humorous stories and historical facts. Call Old Town Trolley Tours for a complete list of their stops, or check to see if your hotel has a map. Tour prices are $20 for adults and $8 for children 4 to 12.

Photo: Bob Yarbrough/San Diego Convention and Visitors Bureau

Colorful species of fish swim in their underwater world at the Birch Aquarium at Scripps.

Stephen Birch Aquarium-Museum at Scripps Institution of Oceanography
2300 Expedition Way, La Jolla
• (858) 534-3474

Have you ever been eye to eye with a fish bigger than you? Here's your chance to get up close and personal with more than 3,000 native fish from the cold waters of the Pacific Northwest to the balmy seas of Mexico and the South Pacific. The largest oceanographic museum in the country, the Stephen Birch Aquarium-Museum gets you as close to ocean life as possible without getting wet. The aquarium-museum is part of world-renowned Scripps Institution of Oceanography and is dedicated to educating the public about marine science.

Kids especially enjoy the recreated tidepool on a plaza overlooking the coastline and the interactive oceanographic museum with its hands-on exhibits of seawater recycling, global warming and earthquakes. Also part of the aquarium-museum is a specialty bookshop featuring a wide selection of educational gifts, books and souvenirs. Hours are 9 AM to 5 PM daily, except Thanksgiving Day and Christmas Day when the museum is closed. Admission for adults is $6.50. Seniors 60 and older are $5.50, students (with I.D.) and juniors 13 to 17 are $4.50, and children 3 to 12 are $3.50. Children younger than 3 and members of the military (in uniform) are free.

Whale Watching
H&M Landing, 2803 Emerson St., San Diego • (619) 222-1144
Hornblower Cruises & Events, 1066 N. Harbor Dr., San Diego • (619) 686-8715
Islandia Sportfishing, 1551 W. Mission Bay Dr., San Diego • (619) 222-1164
San Diego Harbor Excursion, 1050 N. Harbor Dr., San Diego • (619) 234-4111
Seaforth Sportfishing, 1717 Quivira Rd., San Diego • (619) 224-3383.

Every year, visitors and locals have the opportunity to experience the excitement of seeing one of the largest creatures on earth, the California gray whale. Between December and March more than 25,000 of these magnificent creatures pass San Diego as they leave their feeding grounds in the Bering Sea for their calving grounds in the lagoons of Baja California, five thousand miles to the south.

Theirs is the longest migration of any mammal on earth.

Most whale-watching cruises are two to three hours long, and all vessels have comfortable indoor and outdoor seating. Expert commentary by experienced captains and naturalists accompany each tour. Food and beverages are available on most tours, but amenities and prices vary from company to company. Be sure to phone ahead for information and reservations.

North County Coastal

California Surf Museum
308 N. Pacific St. at Third St., Oceanside • (760) 721-6876

"Don't wait for the tide to come in, come over to the California Surf Museum," is the slogan of this slightly offbeat and wonderfully fun museum. Located at the top of the Oceanside pier, this attraction is a must for surfers and want-to-be surfers, too. The goal of the museum is to preserve surf lore and legends of California and the Pacific Rim. There's a gift shop with surf stuff you just might have to buy.

You'll find colorful displays, photos that chronicle surf history and learn trivia — did you know surfing began in 1907? The displays change every six months. Through photos, clothing and memorabilia, you'll find out about surfboards, surfers, surfing records, surf clothing and possibly more than you thought possible about boards. For instance you'll see redwood and mahogany "planks" from the 1930s, hollow wood boards, and boards constructed from balsa, foam and fiberglass.

The museum is open Monday, Thursday and Friday, noon to 4 PM, and on weekends 10 AM to 4 PM. During the summer months, the museum is also open on Tuesday and Wednesday, from noon to 4 PM. Admission is free; donations are suggested.

Carlsbad Flower Fields
Palomar Airport Rd. and Paseo Del Norte, Carlsbad • (760) 431-0352

This annual event is greatly anticipated by half the population of San Diego and the surrounding areas. The six-week flower show between March and mid-May is breathtaking. You'll see acres of ranunculas in brilliant whites, yellows, oranges, pinks and reds. There are also rows of mixed colors. Plan to stay at least an hour. Parking is free, but there's a small entrance fee. Admission in 1999 was $2.50, with discounts for children and seniors.

The flowers you'll see are produced for their bulbs and tubers so you won't be able to actually walk in the beds. However, you can buy bouquets, tubers, and flower-field boutique items at the gift shop on the grounds.

Carlsbad Children's Museum
300 Carlsbad Village Dr., Ste. 103, Carlsbad • (760) 720-0737

This kids' museum features hand-on exhibits for children ages 2 through 12. Kids explore a fishing boat, create crafts, laugh at themselves in the magic mirror, and experiment on computers. Favorites are the Castle Play area and the Kids Market where children can learn the workings of a supermarket, including how groceries are moved along on a conveyor belt. Hours are limited during the school year; summer hours are 10 AM to 5 PM daily There's a $3.50 admission fee; children younger than 2 get in free of charge. See the Kidstuff chapter for more details.

Heritage Park Village and Museum
220 Peyri Rd., Oceanside • (760) 433-8297

This attraction is situated on land that's now part of the San Luis Rey Mission and it celebrates the beginning of the city of Oceanside, one of the oldest incorporated cities in San Diego County. Walking down the main thoroughfare of Heritage Park Village is like walking down Main Street in the American West. Kids especially enjoy it. A small-fry Insider recently said, "It's just like a movie set."

You'll stroll by the first general store, the Portola Inn, a blacksmith shop and livery stable. Along the way you'll also pass by Oceanside's original city jail, Libby School (the first public school) and the newspaper office. And you'll also see Mrs. Nellie Johansen's house, built in 1886 and moved to Heritage Park in 1976 through the efforts of the Friends of Heritage Park Village and Museum. Guided tours are available by arrangement, and the

Photo: Bob Yarbrough\San Diego Convention and Visitors Bureau

Costumed dancers perform for visitors to the Old Town section of San Diego.

entire area can be reserved for special events. An Insider was recently married in the serene garden area of the park. The grounds are open 9 AM to 4:30 PM; the buildings are open for visitation Sundays only, from noon to 4:30 PM. Call for special tour information. Admission to the park is free.

LEGOLAND California
One LEGOLAND Dr., Carlsbad
• **(760) 918-5346**

Home of the only educational amusement park devoted to those ever-popular LEGO BRICKS, this is a not-to-miss experience for kids and parents. Here you won't find that thrill-a-minute excitement of Magic Mountain and Disneyland; the excitement here is a different kind and every bit as good.

Open since March of 1999, the park is about 40 minutes north of San Diego in Carlsbad, on a 128-acre hill overlooking the ocean. (Take the Cannon Road exit off Interstate 5.)

LEGOLAND is a mix of education, adventure and fun designed for kids 12 and younger and their parents. It took over 30 million LEGO blocks to build the models and displays here; 20 million alone were used in Miniland. Be sure to kneel down and get close to them — many displays have "hidden" design elements that will make you and your kids laugh out loud.

LEGOLAND has six theme areas, each leading easily into the next. **Village Green** includes an opportunity to drive your own Jeep on an African safari; you'll see life-sized LEGO giraffes, zebras, lions and other wildlife. A boat ride takes you through storybook adventures (be sure to look for Little Red Riding Hood carrying something you'd never expect to see in Red's hands). In **Fun Town**, kids drive real electric cars and earn their official LEGOLAND

INSIDERS' TIP

An ideal place for shoreside whale watching is the observation deck located on the grounds of the Cabrillo National Monument. High-powered viewers are available to help you catch sight of the migrating gray whales.

Old Town architecture brings the flavor of south of the border to San Diego.

driver's license at a Driving School. There are also kid-size LEGO helicopters (yes, kids pilot them) and Skipper School where you can captain real boats.

At **The Ridge**, you can enjoy the Sky Cycle, where you pull yourself up to the top of a tower for an overhead view of the park, and then free-fall down to the ground. (No. There are no jerky scary crashes; they're all controlled, easy landings.) At **Castle Hill**, there's a fun Dragon roller coaster, a royal joust, and a chance for kids to enjoy a treasure hunt before moving over to the Hideaway to climb balance beams, walls and curvy slides.

In **Imagination Zone**, families are invited to play with LEGO toys (little ones can start with the larger-sized DUPLO blocks). Older kids can test out LEGO's latest innovations in this area. This is where they can build and program cutting-edge computerized LEGO blocks into robots. The last area (and the favorite of these Insiders) is **Miniland** where you'll see reproductions of American landmarks. You can get up close and personal by walking around Miniland or by taking the Coast Cruise grand tour.

There are more than 25 specialty shops and carts, and open air restaurants where you can get everything from a quick snack or salad to a sit-down dinner of ribs and chicken. The park prides itself on fresh, wholesome foods that will enhance the experience.

The park is open every day of the year. Single-day admission (on-site, no pre-visit booking available) is $32 for adults, and $25 for children ages three through 16. Senior admission (for those older than 60) is $25. Parking is $3 for cars, $8 for campers. If you plan to visit the park and want to stay close by, we recommend you make hotel reservations in advance. And take our advice: Wear comfortable shoes, use sunscreen and bring a hat. Also, take your time; remember, you can come back.

(For more details, be sure to read about LEGOLAND in the Kidstuff chapter.)

Mission San Luis Rey de Francia
4050 Mission Ave. and Rancho del Oro Dr., Oceanside • (760) 757-3651

Of the 21 California missions, this is probably the least known and one of the prettiest, especially as renovation efforts continue. It was founded in 1798 as the 18th in the string of missions that dot the state.

Strolling through the grounds, church, garden and museum you'll be treated to early artwork, historical artifacts and Native American historical displays. Be sure to visit California's first pepper tree and the *lavanderia,* or laundry area, used by the Native Americans and early mission settlers. You can also visit Mission San Luis Rey cemetery, which dates back to 1798 and is still being used by members of all faiths.

Worship services are held at the mission; the holiday masses often draw families of all denominations. Admission to the museum is free; hours are Monday through Saturday, 10 AM until 4:30 PM and Sunday 11:30 AM until 4:30 PM. The gift and bookstore is open daily, 9 AM until 4:30 PM.

Oceanside Harbor
Harbor Dr., Oceanside

This is the quintessential California pleasure harbor. Here you'll see beautiful boats, restaurants dotting the waterfront and sailors, strollers, in-line skaters and artists all capturing their own vision of fun.

The harbor is used by more than 900 pleasure crafts and sport-fishing boats. Unlike other ports, all boats are visible from the two-lane road that hugs the harbor. You'll find fine restaurants to simple fish-and-chips hangouts and shops that sell everything from shell wind chimes to upscale clothing.

Insiders visit the harbor for a leisurely walk and to admire the sunset. Families and working folks picnic on the grass and share lunch with the ever-present, ever-hungry flock of seagulls. There's no admission fee.

Oceanside Pier
West end of Mission Ave., Oceanside

The pier is a popular fishing, meeting and whale-watching spot for Insiders and visitors too. At its current length of 1,942 feet it is one of the longest wooden recreation piers on the West Coast.

A license is required to fish from the beach; no license is required to fish from the pier. There's a bait shop on the pier. If you don't catch any, you might stop at Ruby's, a fifties-style restaurant that's drawing interest from around the county. This outing is easy on the wallet, as there's no admission fee.

Quail Botanical Gardens
230 Quail Gardens Dr., Encinitas
• **(760) 436-3036**

In the midst of developments and tucked away on a quiet country road, Quail Botanical Gardens is a favorite nature retreat for Insiders. Ask five people about their favorite parts of the garden and you'll receive five different answers. There's a tropical area, desert display, seasonal "English" plantings with walls of cascading annuals, and an orchard with tree specimens, including guava, macadamia nut, and loquat. You'll see cork oak, the bird garden that attracts birds and butterflies, and a large display of those local plants used by Native Americans for food and medicine.

There are guided tours by arrangement and self-guided tours available with the user-friendly brochures found at the trailhead. There's also a bookstore/gift shop and a small attached nursery, which sells plant starters. The plant sales, scheduled throughout the year, are a hit in the community. Recently, Quail Gardens has become a popular place for garden weddings, so your visit might just include a bit of romance.

The Garden is open daily from 9 AM to 5 PM; the shop is open from 10 AM to 4 PM. The $2 entrance fee is on the honor system; you'll find donation boxes at the edge of the parking lot.

North County Inland

Antique Gas and Steam Engine Museum
2040 N. Santa Fe Ave., Vista
• **(760) 941-1791**

Located about an hour's drive from downtown San Diego, this is California's only museum devoted to early engines and turn-of-the-century farm equipment.

If you want to see what early farm life was like, this is the place. Located on more than 40 acres, most in cultivation, the museum collects and displays historical gas-, steam- and horse-powered equipment. Period displays include a blacksmith shop, country kitchen and parlor, a steam-operated sawmill and a small, gas-powered train.

There's a threshing bee and antique en-

Photo: San Diego Wild Animal Park

The cheetah poses as visitors watch at the "Heart of Africa" in the San Diego Wild Animal Park.

gine show held twice a year. Admission to the museum is free; if you come for one of the events, the charge is $6. The museum is open 10 AM until 4 PM daily.

Bates Nut Farm
15954 Woods Valley Rd., Valley Center
• (760) 749-3333

At Bates Nut Farm, you'll find nuts. That's a given, but you'll also find an 8-acre park and farm zoo and special events.

Insiders enjoy the shaded park for family picnics — especially popular for Mother's Day and the 4th of July. Kids of all ages adore the pumpkin patch, which is open from September until Halloween. At the patch you can walk out into the field to pick the perfect pumpkin — or two or three or four. Pumpkin picking is a wonderful family sport and a tradition among Insider families. While the prices might be slightly higher than you'd find at the grocery store, the quality is supreme. Later in the year Bates is the place for Christmas trees, too.

The grounds also include a nostalgic country gourmet food store and a "Farmer's Daughter" gift shop. Cultural events and arts and crafts fairs are held throughout the year. Admission is free.

Blue Sky Ecological Reserve
14644 Lake Poway Rd., Poway
• (858) 679-5469

A wilderness area that's managed jointly by the Department of Fish and Game and the City of Poway, Blue Sky Ecological Reserve is located on Espola Road, about a half mile north of Lake Poway Road.

The reserve offers hiking, guided mountain and wildlife walks, campfire programs and even an Owl Prowl. (See the Parks chapter for more details on these special events.) Call for reservations for programs and a list of upcom-

INSIDERS' TIP

Some attractions, such as wilderness areas, allow Fido (on a leash and accompanied with poop bags). Others do not allow dogs. Before leaving for an attraction with your canine companion, call the appropriate information number to make sure you'll receive a warm welcome.

ing events, many well suited for school-age children. Admission is free and donations are welcome.

Be sure to bring along your own water when visiting the reserve since there are no drinking-water facilities.

Deer Park Winery and Auto Museum
29013 Champagne Blvd., Escondido
• (760) 749-1666

Don't let the name mislead you. This is a fun outing and a great place for a picnic. And if you're a car lover, definitely add this attraction to your social calendar.

Deer Park Winery and Auto Museum can be found at the Lawrence Welk Resort, which is 45 minutes north of downtown San Diego on I-15. At the winery and museum, you'll be surrounded with 15 acres of vineyard, orchards, grape arbors, gazebos and shady oaks inviting you to linger. But don't linger too long, since you'll want to visit one of the country's largest collections of vintage convertibles and Americana. Just what is Americana? According to an Insider, a doll collector, who pleaded that we not forget her favorite attraction, that means Barbie dolls (hundreds). You'll also see neon car-dealership signs, old-time radios and vintage wine-making equipment.

Admission to the winetasting room and a free sampling of the award-winning wines is free. Admission to the museum is $6 for adults, and $4 for seniors; children ages 12 and younger get in free.

Escondido Historical Society's Heritage Walk and Grape Day Park
321 N. Broadway, Escondido
• (760) 743-8207

Besides nature, you can enjoy a bit of history in this downtown park, which is lovely, shady, and the home of some of Escondido's historic buildings. On a typical Sunday you'll find lots of Insider families here.

The Escondido Historical Society maintains the buildings, which you can visit. So come see the city's first library, a barn with a windmill, a Victorian house, the 1888 Santa Fe Railroad depot, a railroad car and the model train. You can also visit a working blacksmith shop.

There is no entry fee and buildings are open Thursday through Sunday from 1 PM to 4 PM.

Family Fun Center
830 Dan Way, Escondido
• (760) 741-1326
1525 W. Vista Way, Vista
• (760) 945-9474
6999 Clairemont Mesa Blvd., San Diego
• (858) 560-4212
1155 Graves Ave., El Cajon
• (619) 593-1155

Take your choice of locations; all Family Fun Centers are just what they say — great family fun. And while they charge separately for activities during the week, weekends are priced right. On Saturday and Sunday general admission is $17.50, and those who stand less than 57 inches get in for $13.50.

Call for times since the various venues keep different hours. Generally, they're open from about 11 AM until 10 PM, while the Kids Country Fair attraction closes earlier.

So what can you do at Family Fun Center? How about playing on miniature golf courses, or riding the bumper boats or trying your luck in the batting cages? You'll also find go-carts, huge arcades, the Kids Country Fair, a giant maze and at the Vista center a place for laser tag. For kids the Vista center also includes Kidopolis, a soft play area that really tickles small-fry imaginations.

Orfila Vineyards
13455 San Pasqual Rd., Escondido
• (760) 738-6500

Looking for an outing that's tasty and free? Try a visit to this working vineyard. Located near the Wild Animal Park, this is an award-winning winery by any standards. You'll see hillsides planted with Chardonnay, Merlot, Syrah, Sangiovese and Viognier grapes, and listen to savvy staff as they graciously answer any questions on wine buying and drinking, whether they come from experts or novices. Admission is free. The vineyard is open 10 AM to 6 PM daily; there are self-guided tours throughout the day. At 2 PM, you can enjoy a guided tour of the facility.

While some come just to sample and buy wine, others bring picnic lunches or purchase gourmet snacks from the tasting room and then enjoy their newly purchased wine right on-site. But whether you enjoy the wine here or at home (or both!), the visit here makes for a perfect day.

Palomar Observatory
Highway of Stars (off Calif. Hwy. 76), Palomar Mountain • (760) 742-2119

When you wish upon a star and desire to learn more about the heavens above, you might want to visit this observatory owned and operated by the California Institute of Technology. It's a working observatory so there's no peering through the huge 200-inch Hale telescope or taking a nighttime star tour. What you do get — all for free — is to participate in a self-guided tour, see the educational video and visit the gallery dome to see the telescope.

The facility is open daily (except Christmas Eve and Christmas) from 9 AM until 4 PM. The gift shop, jammed with star- and galaxy-related stuff is open weekends only, from September to June. There are nice hiking trails and here on the top of the mountain there are great views in all directions. You'll want to pack a picnic since there's no restaurant in the area. Be aware that in the winter, Palomar Mountain may get snow, so if you're planning a trip in December or January, you may be required to have chains for your car.

San Diego Wild Animal Park
15500 San Pasqual Valley Rd., Escondido • (760) 747-8702

With more than 2,100 acres this may be the largest, most authentic animal park outside of Africa and worthy of more than one or 10 visits. It's a favorite hangout of Insiders who buy a yearly pass and spend many days visiting the animals, the flora and the shows. One Insider hikes the trails every Sunday to keep fit, and yes, she does visit the animals. The gorilla enclosure is her favorite, especially, she says, "When there are toddler gorillas."

Right along with the entrance fee you get the 50-minute monorail ride. Be sure to bring a light sweater if you're visiting in the early morning or in winter; it can be cool and breezy on the monorail. It's worth every goosebump though for the photo and viewing opportunities.

The park is noted for its educational programs, African village, and the higher-than-average birth rate for endangered species. Even those who shy away from typical zoos often give the Wild Animal Park a thumbs up. The zoo's staff works hard to make sure all the critters are happy, and that equates to wonderful visits by the human species.

Winter hours are 9 AM to 4 PM; summer hours are extended until 9 PM on weekends and 6 PM weekday nights. Admission for adults is $18.95, for seniors $17.50, and for ages 3 to 11 $11.95; children 2 and younger get in free. Parking is $3. Ask about the combination ticket for the Wild Animal Park and the Zoo.

San Pasqual Battlefield
State Historic Park and Museum, 15808 San Pasqual Valley Rd., Escondido • (760) 489-0076

Just down the road from the San Diego Wild Animal Park and a millions miles away in focus is the San Pasqual Battlefield. It's a historic park that celebrates those who participated in the 1846 San Pasqual Battle, called the bloodiest battle of the Mexican-American War. There's a visitor center and a hiking trail and the prerequisite stone marker that describes the historical significance of the area. At the center you'll find an exhibit and video films. In December there's a reenactment ceremony commemorating the battle.

The center is open Friday through Sunday, 10 AM until 5 PM. Admission is free. There

---

INSIDERS' TIP

The Flower Fields in Carlsbad draw BIG crowds, including organized groups, tour buses filled with visitors, and lots of people from Southern California. To avoid the crushing traffic, visit before noon on a weekday during the blooming season, from March to mid-May.

are picnic tables and volunteers on staff to answer questions.

The Wave Waterpark
161 Recreation Dr., Vista
• **(760) 940-9283**

It's a strange feeling to put on a swimsuit or grab your beach towel for a day in the waves and then head away from the ocean, but Insiders do it all the time. The Wave Waterpark is a hot place to cool down on any San Diego day from May through September.

This $3.8 million state-of-the-art aquatic park is municipally operated and geared to families. Its attractions include the Flow Rider, four water slides, a Crazy River, a competition pool and a children's water playground. In addition, swimming lessons and aquatic programs are offered throughout the year. Admission for those older than 7 is $8.95, for seniors it's $6.95, and for those ages 3 to 6 it's $6.95. Children younger than 2 are welcomed without a fee.

East County

Barona Casino
1000 Wildcat Canyon Rd., Lakeside
• **(619) 443-2300, (888) 722-7662**

As the slogan says and the casino's song will have you singing, "It's the magic of Barona." Grown-up fun is the bill of fare at this Barona Indian gambling center. You can try your luck at over 1,000 video and video poker machines, Joker's Wild "21" poker and satellite wagering. There's high-stakes bingo, too.

There's also great entertainment: Internationally known singers and musicians perform at Barona. If you need another reason to visit, how about the Las Vegas- style buffet and food court? Barona's is air-conditioned and open 24-hours a day. Admission is free.

Computer Museum of America
7380 Parkway Dr., La Mesa
• **(619) 465-8226**

Depending on your age, the Computer Museum of America can be a trip down memory chip lane or a first look at the beginnings of cyber technology. Located on the campus of Coleman college, one of the county's technical schools, the museum strives to preserve the major milestones in computer development. (Much original equipment has been lost since "antique" computers were once melted down and recycled for their solid gold components.)

Three not-to-be-missed pieces are the Royal Precision LGP-30, a rare computer, representing the end of the vacuum-tube era (it originally sold for $50,000); the Commodore PET 2000-8, one of the first competitors to the Apple II, boasting an all-in-one-combination monitor, CPU and keyboard; and the Altair 8800, adding a chapter to the Bill Gates epic.

With changing exhibits, special interactive events, and over 100 pieces of history on display, the Computer Museum of America has fun stuff.

Call for hours and admission fees. The museum's volunteer staff can provide educational programs and other special programs for your group.

Heritage of the Americas Museum
2952 Jamacha Rd., El Cajon
• **(619) 670-5194**

Set on the campus of Cuyamaca College, this museum attracts some folks who just come for the view. It's located atop a hill that overlooks the entire El Cajon valley area and that's quite a sight on a perfect San Diego day.

The museum is known for its cultural and educational displays, which reflect the natural and human history of the Americas. Don't expect this to be the Smithsonian, but rather a carefully selected collection of minerals and meteorites, fossils, seashells, tribal tools, effigies, baskets, jewelry and artifacts. There's a small art gallery too. The museum is open Tuesday through Friday from 10 AM until 4 PM, Saturdays from 1 PM to 5 PM. Admission is $3 for adults; students with ID card pay $1, and kids younger than 13 are free.

Sycuan Casino
5469 Dehesa Rd., El Cajon
• **(619) 445-6002**

The Sycuan Casino, in East County's El Cajon, isn't just another place for adult fun: It has some unusual gambling games. These include Sycuan Aces, Pai Gow, Caribbean Stud and Video Pull Table Machines. You'll also find satellite wagering, and a 24-hour card room. High-stakes bingo is the biggest draw, right along with the buffet and the restaurants. Call for a schedule of live entertainment. Admission is free of charge, but you must be 21 to gamble in California, even on Indian reservations.

Viejas Casino & Turf Club
5000 Willows Rd., Alpine
• **(619) 445-5400**

As this ultra-popular casino says, "We've got more fun." They really work at the fun portion, too, and include high-stakes poker, video tournaments, satellite wagering and Indian blackjack. There's a popular non-smoking area in the casino, too. Located on the Viejas Indian Reservation, the club is open 24 hours a day and there's no admission fee.

As we go to press, Viejas continues in mega-renovation mode, which will bring this popular stop into the next decade of entertainment and adult fun. Currently on the premises are four restaurants ranging from the snack-attack style to the exclusive sit-down variety. There's also full cocktail service throughout the casino.

For those who enjoy gambling and the high-energy of casinos, this is an attraction to add to your itinerary.

South Bay

ARCO U.S. Olympic Training Center
1750 Wueste Rd., Chula Vista
• **(619) 482-6222**

One of only three official Olympic Training Centers in the country, the ARCO Center is where Olympic hopefuls train for international competition. Unlike its sister facilities in Lake Placid and Colorado Springs, the ARCO Center is the only year-round warm-weather venue

for track and field, kayaking, field hockey, cycling, soccer, archery and rowing.

Officials at the Training Center like to say that visitors get the "red, white and blue carpet treatment" when they come for a tour. From the Olympic Path, guests can view the entire 150-acre campus, including the athletes' dormitories, training fields and tracks. The Chula Vista site has the largest permanent archery range in North America, four soccer fields, an all-weather hockey field, a 15,000 square-foot boathouse and four tennis courts. In addition to those stellar facilities, the Center provides a 400-meter track, six acres for field events and a cycling course.

Free tours are offered daily from 9 AM to 4 PM Monday through Saturday, and from 12 noon to 4 PM Sunday. Tours depart every hour on the hour in the morning, and every hour on the half-hour in the afternoon. Be sure to stop in the Spirit Store, where you'll find a wide variety of Olympic merchandise and memorabilia. Although tours are free, donations are gratefully accepted to further the Olympic dream for the Training Center's athletes.

Chula Vista Nature Center
1000 Gunpowder Point Dr., Chula Vista
• **(619) 422-2473**

Did you know that burrowing owls imitate the sound of a rattlesnake to fool potential predators? Hear it for yourself at the Chula Vista Nature Center. Located in the Sweetwater Marsh National Wildlife Refuge, it's one of the few remaining habitats of its kind on the Pacific coast. A haven for more than 215 species of birds, some endangered, the Nature Center's observation tower provides the perfect venue for watching the birds go about their daily routine.

In addition to birds, a variety of seemingly fierce creatures native to San Diego Bay can be found—and petted. Bat rays and leopard sharks are among the intimidating but harmless water babies awaiting the attention of the curious.

INSIDERS' TIP

Weather in San Diego can be changeable. Those Pacific breezes aren't always balmy. Insiders layer clothing and keep a sweatshirt in the car, just in case it turns cool.

If a bird, bug and nature walk appeals to you, check with the Nature Center for its schedule. Many such tours and walks are provided to the public.

Hours are 10 AM to 5 PM Tuesday through Sunday. During June, July and August, the Nature Center is open on Mondays too. It's closed on major holidays. Admission is $3.50 for adults, $2.50 for seniors 65 and older and $1 for juniors 6 to 17. Children younger than 6 are admitted free.

To reach the Nature Center, from I-5, take the E Street exit in Chula Vista, and go west to the parking lot.

Free shuttles from the parking lot to the facility run about every 25 minutes.

Whitewater Canyon Waterpark
2052 Otay Valley Rd., Chula Vista
• **(619) 661-7373**

Waves and slides and lots of cool, cool water promise to keep you smiling on a hot summer day. Whitewater Canyon has 16 water slides, including body slides and single and double tube slides that take you on a wild plunge into the water below.

While your heart stops pounding from the thrilling descent, let the waves in the 24,000 square foot pool gently splash over you. Or romp with the kids in the four-story interactive family play structure as buckets of water up-end unexpectedly and hidden water guns squirt without warning. For toddlers, Whitewater Canyon has a smaller play structure with gentle water play.

When you're ready to dry off, join a volleyball game on one of the sand volleyball courts. Or grab a snack at one of three different snack bars or several specialty booths featuring pizza, hamburgers, hot dogs and ice cream.

The waterpark is open from 10 AM to 6 PM on weekends only from early May until mid-June, when it opens daily until Labor Day. Admission is $21.99 for those 48 inches and taller, and $15.99 for those shorter than 48 inches.

LEGOLAND, the country's only educational amusement park devoted to those ever-popular LEGO bricks, is wholesome fun for kids or kids at heart.

Kidstuff

It's not hard to find things for kids to do in San Diego. Most of what makes San Diego special — the Zoo, Sea World, Wild Animal Park, the beaches — appeals to kids just as much as it does to adults. Even though kids can have as much fun doing all the things that grown-ups enjoy, there are times when they need something a little different, something that's designed just for them. And that's what we'll help you discover in this chapter.

We've found the special little treats just for kids and given you the lowdown on them all. For instance, no child can resist the Children's Museums (one in San Diego, one in Carlsbad), where they can get their hands on interactive displays geared specifically for the younger set. Or maybe the kids would enjoy hearing the San Diego Youth Master Chorale, or seeing a performance by the San Diego Junior Theatre or the Escondido Theater for Families.

Lots of one-time events are staged especially for kids, too, and although we can't ever predict what's coming, we'll tell you where to look to find Frisbee demonstrations, yo-yo clinics and kids' craft sessions. Most bookstores have story times for kids; we've clued you in on the ongoing ones. Libraries are a good place to check out, too. Most have reading programs for kids ranging in age from toddlers to teens.

A great resource for kidstuff is in the "Calendar" section of *The San Diego Reader*, a weekly tabloid that comes out on Thursdays and can be picked up free at bookstores, libraries, convenience stores and hundreds of other locations throughout the county. It lists a ton of special events just for kids.

Don't forget that what's particularly appealing to kids can often be fun for adults, too. We've covered all the big draws in our Attrac-

tions chapter, but we've done some cross-referencing here so you won't forget the things to do that are extra special for the kids.

If an adult's presence is required at a children's event or attraction, we've made note of it. If your child needs to bring along anything extra, we've mentioned that too. Keep in mind, though, that it's always a good idea to phone ahead and get all the particulars. It's nice to touch base with the folks who organize these events; you'll have peace of mind and the kids will know what's in store ahead of time.

San Diego

Barnes & Noble Bookstore
7610 Hazard Center Dr., San Diego • (619) 298-4306

Kids' story time is every Saturday at 11 AM. Special guests like Ms. Frizzle make regular appearances with stories, fun and lots of surprises. Barnes & Noble also has occasional story times for children with special needs. Often the morning program will be repeated in the afternoon for hearing-impaired kids. Sometimes snacks are provided, but if they aren't, try to send something with your child that won't make much of a mess. It's a good idea to send along a favorite toy with younger children (not the squeaky kind, though). There's no cost for admission, but you should call for reservations.

Baseball Academy
San Diego State University
College Ave., north of Montezuma Rd., San Diego • (619) 594-4186

Do you have a budding Tony Gwynn who'd like a few pointers on baseball techniques? At the Baseball Academy kids younger than 13 can get one-on-one, personalized coaching sessions from experienced baseball trainers. In addition to the training, participants receive a video analysis of their performance. The cost is $30 per half-hour, and kids can take several sessions or just one.

Bookstar
3150 Rosecrans Pl., San Diego
• (619) 225-0465

Kids love Monday Night Storytime at Bookstar. Every Monday from 7 PM to 8 PM, a different story is read. Sometimes the subject is animals; sometimes it's the ocean and its many wonders. The topic is different every week, and kids are encouraged to bring related items for show-and-tell. Snacks are usually provided during Storytime.

Once a month, Nanny Brit makes an appearance. Sometimes she brings a surprise guest, sometimes is just Nanny herself. Always there are stories, songs and laughter. Nanny Brit comes on either the second or third Saturday of every month. All events are free, but call Bookstar ahead of time to find out exact times and dates and what's on the agenda.

www.insiders.com

See this and many other
Insiders' Guide®
destinations online.

Visit us today!

Camp Sea World
500 Sea World Dr., San Diego
• (619) 226-3903

For preschoolers through high school seniors, Camp Sea World has one of the coolest summer-camp programs around. It's an adventure filled with animals, games, crafts and learning, and it all adds up to a whole bunch of fun. Camps for preschoolers are designed for children ages 3 and 4 (with parent involvement), and the level of activities and learning experiences accelerate for older kids.

Camp Sea World runs from 8:30 AM until 12 noon, and there's an extended camp that lets kids stay in the park to enjoy an afternoon of games, shows and animal attractions. Extended camp ends at 5 PM. Or, have the kids pack a sleeping bag for a nighttime Sea World adventure. Campers explore the night world of marine animals and spend the night in the Wild Arctic attraction. Sleepovers include games, videos, dinner, breakfast and a T-shirt. The sleepover program is available to children in grades 2 through 5.

Prices vary depending upon which camp is selected, but generally run from $15 for a single-day camp to $70 for a sleepover.

Children's Museum
200 W. Island Ave., San Diego
• (619) 233-5437

Housed in what once was an old electrical warehouse, the sparkling new Children's Museum has interactive arts and activities designed to enlighten and entertain young minds. Both permanent and traveling exhibits inspire children to learn by encouraging a hands-on experience. The Dino Car has been a favorite for some time. It's half auto, half dinosaur, created entirely by kids. There's a supervised play area within the museum where kids can work with clay and paint, and rotating educational programs keep things interesting.

The Children's Museum appeals most to kids ages 2 to 12. It's open from 10 AM to 4:30 PM Tuesday through Saturday, and from 11 AM to 4:30 PM on Sundays. Admission is $4. Kids younger than 2 are admitted free.

Children's Pool
Coast Blvd., south of Jenner St., La Jolla

City engineers gave Mother Nature a helping hand when they built a sea wall to partially enclose a natural inlet. The result is Children's Pool, a protected cove with gentle waves (actually, they're more like a vigorous ripple) and lots of sand. In recent years, sea lions have discovered Children's Pool and have taken up residence on the sand, giving kids a close-up look at these amazing sea creatures.

On any sunny day you'll see lots of chil-

Photo: Dale Frost/Port of San Diego

With mom helping, this baby is getting a first-time view through the telescope.

dren with their families building sand castles and watching the humorous sea lions, who provide an entertaining and educational show of their own. The downside is that the water is no longer accessible because of the sea lions, but the show they put on is worth a trip to Children's Pool.

Chuck E Cheese's
9840 Hibert St., San Diego
• (858) 578-5860
3146 Sports Arena Blvd., San Diego
• (619) 523-4385

Put on your best game face, Mom and Dad, and prepare for an assault on the senses. Kids absolutely love Chuck E Cheese's for its noise, shows, constant activity, games, rides, prizes and pizza. The motto is, "It's a magical place where a kid can be a kid." Although it may be a bit much for adults looking for a peaceful meal, the smile on the kids' faces makes it all worthwhile. Large

groups are welcome (call in advance), and birthday parties and other gatherings can be arranged ahead of time. Admission is free, and the restaurant is open for lunch and dinner every day but Monday.

Family Fun Center
6999 Clairemont Mesa Blvd., San Diego • (858) 560-4211

We covered the Family Fun Centers located throughout the county in our Attractions chapter. But they're worthy of a mention here, too, simply because kids go wild over the variety of activities they can dive into, such as batting cages, miniature golf, arcade games, go-karts, laser tag and amusement park rides.

Operating hours vary, depending on weather and the time of year, so be sure to call before you go. Generally the Fun Center opens at 11 AM Monday through Friday and 9 AM Saturday and Sunday. Closing

INSIDERS' TIP

A day spent in the backcountry parks can be tons of fun. Just make sure you check with park rangers or officials to get a heads-up on any hazards such as poison oak, rattlesnakes, bobcats or ticks.

Photo: Dale Frost/Port of San Diego

The look on this carousel rider's face tells the story...it's fun.

hours are midnight Sunday through Thursday and 1 AM Friday and Saturday. The various attractions, priced separately, range from about $2 for an individual ride in the Fun Zone to $5.75 for miniature golf. An all-day pass, though, can be purchased after 4 PM on Friday and at any time on Saturday and Sunday. The cost is $18.50 for those 57 inches and taller and $14.50 for those shorter.

La Jolla YMCA Day Camps
8355 Cliffridge Ave., La Jolla
• (858) 453-3483

La Jolla's YMCA has created a series of special-interest day camps that run for one-week periods during the summer. For kids who want to learn water skiing, an intense, five-hours-per-day instruction camp is held at the Mission Bay Aquatics Center. Or if your junior Bill Gates wants to learn more about computers, a week spent at the Futurekids Computer

Learning Center is sure to sharpen up those skills.

Dozens of other camps are available too, including cooking, mountaineering, ice-skating, arts and crafts and many more. Most camps are geared for kids from 7 to 13 years old, and prices vary, ranging from $95 to $405 for a one-week session. YMCA members get a discount on camp fees.

Marie Hitchcock Puppet Theater
2130 Pan American Rd. W., Balboa Park,
San Diego • (619) 685-5045

Named for San Diego's original Puppet Lady, who charmed local kids for decades with her amusing puppet acts, the Marie Hitchcock Puppet Theater is now home to the San Diego Guild of Puppetry. It's a group of professional and amateur puppeteers who perform year-round at the theater, staging both marionette and hand-puppet performances. Occasionally the

Guild will stage a ventriloquist act, too. The theater also hosts traveling shows that produce a variety of events.

It's a small theater — only 230 seats — so it's a good idea to get there a little early to get the best seats. No refreshments are sold during performances, and food isn't allowed in the theater. Shows usually run about 30 to 45 minutes. Tickets are available at the theater on the day of the performance; no advance reservations are required. Show times are 10 AM and 11:30 AM Wednesday, Thursday and Friday; 11 AM, 1 PM and 2:30 PM on Saturdays and Sundays. Admission for adults is $2; children 3 to 17 are charged $1.50. Children 2 and younger are admitted free.

Mission Valley YMCA Day Camps
5505 Friars Rd., San Diego
• **(619) 298-3576**

For kids who think the X Games are the hottest thing going, here's their chance to get some firsthand experience with extreme sports. Campers ages 12 to 15 can participate in X-treme Teen skating. Campers of all ages can join one of a variety of other camps, including cheerleading/dance, marine life, woodworking, wake boarding and laser tag.

The cost of the camps vary depending on the chosen activity, but they range from $95 to $405.

Nighttime Zoo and Wild Animal Park Adventures
Balboa Park and Escondido
• **(619) 234-3153**

Held at the Zoo and Wild Animal Park, the park adventures happen in the evenings when the animals are most active (they choose to snooze during the afternoon's heat). During the summer the facilities stay open late for special educational and kids' programs, and continuing shows. The trams run and humans can wander the grounds until 10 PM throughout the summer. Stroller and wheelchair rentals are

available. Pack a picnic dinner to eat at any of the wonderful sites. There are lockers you can rent where you can store extra gear and supper. It may be cool in the evenings. Admission ranges from $15 to about $20; discounted admission is available for children, seniors and active military. Be sure to read more about the Zoo in our chapter on Balboa Park.

San Diego Junior Theatre Casa del Prado Theatre
1800 El Prado, Balboa Park, San Diego
• **(619) 239-1311**

Since 1948 the San Diego Junior Theatre has provided classes in acting, voice, dance and other specialties like accents, dialects and stage makeup for kids ages 6 to 16. One or two-week class sessions are offered during the summer, and one-class-per-week sessions that last 10 weeks are available the rest of the year.

Students who have taken or are currently enrolled in Junior Theatre classes are eligible to audition or be part of the stage crew for the five productions given every year in the Casa del Prado Theatre. Recent productions have included such hits as *Joseph and His Amazing Technicolor Dreamcoat*.

Even if the kids aren't interested in classes, the productions themselves are always crowd-pleasers, enjoyed by children and adults alike. Ticket prices range from $5 to $7 for children younger than 14, and from $7 to $9 for adults. Class prices vary widely depending on the type of class and the age of your child, but they range from about $100 to $200. Call the theatre for current production information, class schedules and prices.

San Diego Youth Master Chorale
c/o Keiller Middle School, 7270 Lisbon St., San Diego • **(619) 685-7701**

Youthful voices charm listeners with their versions of songs from some of today's most popular children-oriented musicals, such as *The Secret Garden*. Broadway tunes take on a whole different flavor for youngsters when they hear them performed by kids their own age.

The Youth Master Chorale performs in various locations around San Diego, and performances are usually free. Call for the current schedule.

Summer Sports Camps
University of San Diego
5998 Alcalá Park, San Diego
• (619) 260-4593

The University of San Diego offers one and two-week sessions and day and resident programs for campers ages 6 to 17. Camps are focused on improving skills in baseball, basketball, softball, swimming, soccer, volleyball, tennis, crew and water sports. Those who would like to try a little bit of everything can enroll in the All-sport camp. Campers can either stay in dormitories on the beautiful USD campus, or go home at the end of the day.

The USD Sports Camp program is dedicated to providing a unique athletic experience that is tailored to the individual needs of each camper. Emphasis is on personalized instruction and increased performance. Plus, the university organizes an abundance of free-time recreation opportunities and activities. Costs range from $195 to $495.

Zany Brainy
1520 Camino de la Reina, San Diego
• (619) 291-9500

More than just a toy store, Zany Brainy is event central for kids. Special programs and demonstrations are going on all the time, like performances by children's recording artist Eileen Barnett, who sings Broadway show tunes for kids. Or kids can learn how

to do tricks with yo-yos, or master the art of Frisbee throwing. All special events are free, and most are scheduled on weekends. Call the store for the latest lineup and times.

North County Coastal

Carlsbad Children's Museum
399 Carlsbad Village Dr., Ste. 103,
Carlsbad • (760) 720-0737

Busy small hands are welcome at the museum. It's just for kids. Located near the beach and Carlsbad's State Street shopping district (see our Shopping chapter), it delights children ages 2 through 12 with interactive exhibits that change often.

Here kids can create crafts and experiment on computers at various activity centers. The Fishing Boat sparks imaginative play, and so does the Castle Play where kids can dress up and act out medieval fantasies. At the Kids Market children can learn the workings of a supermarket, including a conveyor belt that works.

Did you know that in "real" grocery stores — just like at the Kids Market — the conveyor belt is moved along by a switch on the floor? Accompanying the kids to this museum might be a good educational experience for you too.

During the traditional school year, call ahead, since times are limited. In the summer the museum is open between 10 AM and 5 PM. There's a $3.50 admission fee.

Carlsbad City Library
1200 Carlsbad Village Dr., Carlsbad
• (760) 434-2870

This feels like the most-visited library in the state and it's a great place for kids. Along with a huge collection of books, videos, and tapes, there are reading programs, story hours, and free and fun activi-

At the Heart of Africa in San Diego's Wild Animal Park, wondrous sights like this thrill kids of all ages.

ties from magic workshops to cultural activities. There are lots of arts and crafts programs designed to please even the most particular child. Kids can also find homework help and computer mentoring in this safe environment. Stop in for a program and newsletter that details the free activities.

The library sponsors programs such as "Totally Teen Reading X-treme," teen murder mystery nights and the incredibly popular (for the last 25 years!) summer reading program.

The ribbon cutting for the second full-service city library at 1775 Dove Lane, (760) 434-2865 in the La Costa section of Carlsbad was in August of 1999. With city and taxpayer approval, the library on Carlsbad Village Drive might soon be renovated too, so if you're reading this in late 2000, call for updates.

If you're going to that library on Carlsbad Village Drive for some summer fun, do like the Insiders. Park off Elmwood Street, just east of the library, in the unpaved parking lot. You'll always find room there.

Remember that many of the libraries in the county can fill you in on kids' programs offered at other libraries, so if you're interested be sure to ask.

Chuck E Cheese's
2481 Vista Way, Oceanside • (760) 439-1444

If you and the kids need a shot of intense family fun, steer the car to Chuck E Cheese's. It's a restaurant like no other because here kids really are encouraged to be kids. Sure you'll get pizza and soda and then the family can wrap it up with plenty of activity and excitement.

No one has to be quiet or use proper manners here — the noise and enthusiasm level is always on full blast. Call ahead if you're bringing a big group or planning an event.

San Diego County Fair
Del Mar Fairgrounds, 2200 Jimmy Durante Blvd., Del Mar • (858) 792-4252.

Even though we've mentioned this huge fair in the Annual Events chapter and you can read the details there, please don't think of it just as an adult attraction. It's truly kid-style fun.

Pre-fair tickets and family passes can make the fair more affordable. In past years, we've saved about $20. During the three-week event, one day is specially designated for kids — and they get in free.

When you're at the fair, pick up a free listing of events for the day. Some favorites with kids, in addition to the food and the midway rides, are the collection contests, the animals, the horse shows, and the special events like sheep shearing and herding demonstrations.

There are free shuttles available from various locations in the county. Admission is $8.

Remember lots of things happen year-round at the Fair Grounds — including plenty of kids' events. Do like Insiders and call the 24-hour event hotline at (858) 793-5555 to get the scoop for what's happening right now.

J.W. Tumbles
292-A El Camino Real, Encinitas • (760) 942-7411

An activity center and gym strictly for kids, J.W. Tumbles offers kid-style fitness and exercise programs and classes. The staff here, too, can help you create great birthday parties.

Kids Night Out is popular with kids and parents, so reservations are recommended.. On Fridays from 5:30 PM to 9:30 PM, parents can drop off children from ages 3 to 10 for supervised activities (from coloring to games) and fun themed parties. The food that's available runs along the pizza

This young lady has found a field full of flowers bright enough to match her smile.

and soda line. The cost is $20 per child for the four hours.

LEGOLAND California
One LEGOLAND Dr., Carlsbad
• (760) 438-5346

If you're a kid or a kid at heart, you have to visit LEGOLAND California, in North County Coastal. It's the country's only educational amusement park devoted to those ever-popular LEGO bricks. The park is wholesome fun for the family; LEGO makes kids and their parents comfortable and provides gentle entertainment the moment you walk through the gates. There are no scary breath-snatching rides and nothing that will make even the youngest have bad dreams.

The park officially opened in March 1999 and expects about 2 million visitors in its first year of operation. We recommend going, if you can, at a less busy time, such as midweek during the traditional school year. You'll probably wish you could spend two or more days at the park, but remember, it'll be here for a long time, so don't rush so much that you and the kids can't

hang out and enjoy the magic. The 128-acre park includes The Beginning where you'll want to start your LEGOLAND adventures. This is where you will enjoy the market place and LEGO shops. Then you can move to the Village Green for a boat ride down Fairy Tale Brook (a place that reminds us of our favorite tales). In Village Green, you'll also be treated to Safari Trek, a venture into the wilds of Africa to see giraffes, zebras, lions and more, all made from LEGO bricks. There's the Waterworks, an interactive water play area where kids do play with water; there's also DUPLO for younger guests, a puppet theater, magic theater and snack shop.

You can then move on to the Ridge, LEGO maze and Sky Cycle where you cycle your way around in a zany people-powered car. The way it's planned this self-propelled ride will take you up Kid Power Tower. At the top — guess what? — you can experience the exhilarating "free-fall" to the bottom. (Parents: This is all very safe and won't scare even the youngest child). Too cool? You bet.

There's more child-oriented pleasure with Fun Town (with a LEGO driving school, LEGO boats and LEGO helicopters), Castle Hill (for medieval scenes and encounters), Miniland (the heart and soul of LEGOLAND California and by far the favorite place for adults) and the popular Imagination Zone. The Imagination Zone emphasizes the learning center and exploration with LEGO bricks.

The best part (and we checked twice) is that you can visit without kids and have a great time. The park is open year-round, rain or shine. Non-summer hours are from 10 AM to 5 or 6 PM and summer hours are from 9 AM to 8 PM. In addition to the rides and family fun, there are family restaurants throughout the park that serve only the freshest, healthiest foods. Adult admission is $32; seniors and children ages 3 through 16 enter for $25, and children younger than three get to visit (with an adult) free of charge. Parking is $6 for cars, $8 for RVs, and bicycles park free of charge.

Best photo ops for the park? From the Garden Restaurant near Castle Hill, on the promenade heading into the Imagination Zone and anywhere in Miniland.

Insider tips for this park are simple: 1) Wear a hat or sunscreen or both, 2) wear your most comfortable shoes since you'll be doing a lot of walking, and 3) rent a storage locker for extra jackets, the LEGO purchases you'll have to make, and (if you have one) the diaper bag.

Silver Bay Kennel Club Dog Show
Del Mar Fairgrounds, 2260 Jimmy Durante Blvd., Del Mar • (858) 558-0507

Grown-ups (along with dog breeders and handlers) go to the show to see the competition. Kids love it to see how working dogs work, the pampered pooches compete and the demonstrations. All animal-loving kids, future vets, and children with incredible curiosity (and what kid doesn't have that) talk about this premier

dog event for years. Kids can get up close to elite canines (with permission from the handlers please) before and after competition times.

There is no admission fee for this event that happens each February. If your kids love dogs, keep a watch at pet-food centers and in the newspaper for other dog shows around the county. Show dates change each year, so watch the paper or call the fairground's info line.

(Be sure to check out our Annual Events chapter for other free, kid-oriented things to do from rodeos to toys shows that happen at the fair ground year-round.)

YMCA
200 Saxony Rd., Encinitas
• (760) 942-9622
1965 Peacock Blvd., Oceanside
• (760) 758-0808

The Y has been an important part of kidstuff throughout the county for years. Their varied programs are well-supervised, age-specific and lots of fun. Choose to have the kids experience horseback riding, surfing, skating, crafts, gymnastics or a dozen other fun camps and workshops. There's a popular skateboard park at the Encinitas Y and a climbing wall at the Y in Oceanside. There are also classes and sporting teams for parents and teens as well as family campouts. Call for prices, locations, and a current schedule; Y members receive a discount on events and trips.

North County Inland

Bates Nut Farm
15954 Woods Valley Rd., Valley Center
• (760) 749-3333

At Bates Nut Farm, kids can be kids as they discover and touch farm animals. There are wonderful places to let the smaller set run as you put out a picnic lunch. In the fall, plan a trip here to pick a pumpkin. Bates fields will be blanketed with bright orange, plump pumpkins. You might want to bring along a wagon as you go out to find your own. (You'll be disappointed if you don't bring your camera; the snap shots are sure to make the aunts, uncles and grandparents smile.)

At Christmas, you can select the perfect tree at Bates Nut Farm, and while you're there, you might want to take a horse-drawn hayride too. For many families that's become a holiday tradition.

(Mom and Dad will enjoy the craft shows that are scheduled during the fall and December holidays. Parents will also like the gourmet foods found at the Bates general; after all this fun you'll need some healthy snacks.)

See Attractions for a full idea of what's in store for kids and grown ups at Bates Nut Farm.

Blue Sky Ecological Reserve
Espola Rd., north of Lake Poway Rd., Poway • (619) 679-5469

If you have curious kids who love everything that has to do with the outdoors then you'll want to take a trip to Blue Sky Ecological Reserve. Be sure to read the entry in the Parks chapter.

The reserve's 700 acres of wilderness are located about 20 minutes from I-15. For those who haven't had a chance to see what San Diego County might look like without freeways, houses and cars, it's an eye opener. Please remind the kids; it might be a new concept for them.

At the reserve you might spot a coyote, deer, fox, or snake. It's recommended that you always stay on the paths. There are birds in abundance. Bring drinking water since this is a wilderness area. There are special kids' tours and guided tours and an information kiosk with a display of plants and animals that are native to the area. Call for details and to receive a free newsletter.

California Center for the Arts
340 N. Escondido Blvd., Escondido
• (800) 988-4253

Families will find lots to do at this cultural center right off I-15 in downtown Escondido. You'll find Education at the Center, which features art and acting classes and other related programs for both kids and adults. Call for a current program of activities and pricing information.

On Sundays throughout the year you and the kids will be treated to Theater for Families. Kids get to meet the artists before and after the show. The shows are just an hour long, accommodating a kid's attention span and need to get up and move. Kids can also do hands-on art projects, participate in the after-show entertainment, and buy snack foods like popcorn, ice cream and soda.

Programs and plays here are by top performers who specialize in children's productions. Insiders and visitors have been recently treated to *Treasure Island*, brought here by the Omaha Theater Company for Young People, *The Jungle Book*, from Theatreworks USA, and *Island of the Skog* from the Dallas Children's Theater on Tour. Ticket prices are about $10, call for reservations and seating.

Chuck E Cheese's
624 W. Mission Ave., Escondido
• (760) 741-5505

There's fun aplenty at this kids-oriented restaurant that has foods and activities for kids. This restaurant probably the one most requested by the seven and younger set, and plenty of teens go there, too. If you and the kids need a shot of intense fun, steer the car to Chuck E Cheese's.

INSIDERS' TIP

Halloween can be scary for pets (especially those who have recently moved into any San Diego neighborhood). Always bring your pets inside on Halloween. And if you want trick-or-treaters, just keep your home's porch light on. Turn it off, and the kids are signaled to go elsewhere.

Family Fun Center
830 Dan Way, Escondido
- **(760) 741-1326**
1525 W. Vista Way, Vista
- **(760) 945-9474**

Take your choice of locations and then turn to our Attractions chapter to read about all the fun your kids can have here. On Saturday and Sunday general admission is $17.50; prices during the week are slightly less. For people who stand less than 57 inches, the price is $13.50.

At each Family Fun Center, you'll find activities from miniature golf to bumper boats to a giant maze. At the Vista center there's a place for laser tag. The Vista center also includes Kidopolis, a soft play area that really stimulates small-fry imaginations.

Palomar College Programs and Workshops for Kids
Palomar College Community Services, 1140 W. Mission Rd., San Marcos
- **(760) 744-1150 ext. 2702**

Palomar College's Community Service office offers great summer fun for kids with a number of programs ranging from ice-skating lessons to magic workshops. There are golf lessons, figure skating, and camps, too. Call for a catalogue if you're out of the area. Price for workshops range from $39 for the magic class to $195 for a five-day (half-day) camp.

Roar and Snore Camp Over
San Diego Wild Animal Park, 15500 San Pasqual Valley Rd., Escondido
- **(760) 738-5049**

While you'll meet other adults who go on this once-in-a-lifetime camp, there are plenty of families. For kids and parents who love animals, it's a memory in the making. See our chapters on Attractions and Annual Events for more details. Be sure to read our chapter on

Balboa Park, too, that tells all about our world-famous San Diego Zoo.

Costs range from about $90 for adults to about $60 for kids 8 and older. There are hikes, instructional programs, campfires. Campers have all meals outdoors. Kids and parents need to bring sleeping bags and a sense of fun. The camp happens on Friday, Saturday and Sunday summer evenings only; call for reservations and a recommended equipment list.

The Wave Waterpark
161 Recreation Dr., Vista
- **(760) 940-9283**

This is a wet and wild adventure for kids and parents. Be sure to read all about it in the Attractions chapter, then come sample the fun at this $3.8-million state-of-the-art, municipally operated family aquatic park. It's open from May through September. If you're interest in swimming lessons for the kids, it's wise to reserve a space ahead of time.

The attractions include the Flow Rider, four water slides, a Crazy River, a competition pool and a children's water playground. Admission for those older than 7 is $8.95, for seniors it's $6.95, and for kids ages 3 to 6 it's $6.95; children younger than 2 are admitted free.

YMCA
1050 N. Broadway St., Escondido
- **(760) 745-7490**

You can depend on the Y for quality year-round fun. There are summer day camps, overnight campouts, classes, crafts, and good wholesome fun when you participate in the Y programs. For youngsters in the 10 and older group there are youth events, and the Y has after-school programs too.

When you call for details and a current schedule, ask about family camping experiences, such as those at Lake Sequoia.

INSIDERS' TIP

Many communities and local churches have Easter egg hunts where kids search for candy eggs and have lots of fun — most of the time for free. Look for the lineup of these events in your local community newspaper or call the local parks and recreation department.

Photo: CeCe Canton

Two smiling girls find something to pose with....the ranunculus flowers in Carlsbad.

Call for prices, information and a current schedule of events. Y members receive a discount on the programs.

East County

Cuyamaca Rancho State Park
Calif. Hwy. 79 between Hwy. 78 and I-8, eastern San Diego County
• (760) 765-0755

If you're a camping family and love to explore, this state park should be on your must-do list. You and the kids will be treated to wilderness areas, a museum with Native American artifacts and more than 120 miles of walking and equestrian trails. Some of the trails are easy walks, perfect for smaller children; others are more challenging.

The wilderness area covers more than 25,000 acres in East County, including heavenly wildflower meadows, Green Valley Falls and the ruins of a gold mine, the Stonewall mine. There are two developed campgrounds with 166 units, group campsites and cabins. There is even an equestrian campsite. You'll want to look at the Parks chapter for a full overview of this natural adventureland and of other parks throughout the county that

have special kids programs. Most programs are seasonal and change themes often.

Chuck E Cheese's
5500 Grossmont Center Dr., La Mesa
• (619) 698-4351

Okay, so it's loud inside. Okay, kids run around a lot. And that's more than okay if you and the kids need to laugh, get wild and have some fun. Kids need time out of their stress-filled days too, and Chuck E. Cheese is often the right prescription. This La Mesa restaurant is a carbon copy of others — same pizza, soda and fun. This is a popular place for pint-sized sports teams.

As with other Chuck E Cheese's, kids run wild and parents know from the noise alone that their children are having fun. If you're new in the community, this is a great place to meet other families.

Family Fun Center
1155 Graves Ave., El Cajon
• (619) 593-1155

In our Attractions chapter, you'll find all the details about this great activity center. On Saturday and Sunday general admission is $17.50; those who stand less than 57 inches get in for $13.50.

Photo: San Diego Sports Fishing

The waters off San Diego produce many big fish—and big smiles.

Here you'll find old- and new-fashioned fun: miniature golf courses, batting cages and bumper boats, as well as go-carts, an arcade with the latest video games, the Kids Country Fair and a giant maze.

Mother Goose Parade
W. Main and Chambers Sts., El Cajon
• **(619) 444-8712**

The parade is usually held the last weekend in November and really gets the family in the mood for holiday fun. The parade begins at 12:30 PM on W. Main and Chambers streets and continues east on Main to Second Street then north on Second to Madison. This is an old-fashioned children's affair with lots of local turnout. You'll see floats, clowns, bands, equestrians, civic leaders and representatives of charitable organizations.

There's no admission fee. Be sure to bring lawn chairs or blankets for sidewalk sitting. Bring your own lunch or buy food from vendors, then try some of the peanuts or candy for sale. You'll be able to buy banners and toys here too.

YMCA
8881 Dallas St., La Mesa
• **(619) 464-1323**
7733 Palm Ave., Lemon Grove
• **(619) 667-2955**
8669 Magnolia Ave., Santee
• **(619) 449-9622**

The Y is more than just a great place to workout — it's a kidstuff favorite with important learning programs, child care resources, summer classes and camps that are run on age-specific levels. The Y could

---

INSIDERS' TIP

If you're looking for something low-key that won't cost an arm and a leg, grab a couple of blankets, pack a quick lunch and head for the nearest neighborhood or community park. Most maps of the county clearly show where they are, or call Parks and Recreation at (858) 694-3030 or (619) 685-1350 for the location of the nearest park. Mom and Dad can relax while the kids romp in the playground, bike, skate or toss a ball around.

be your best resource if you're looking for family fun throughout the county. Call a location that's close for programs and outings, costs and information. Y members receive a discount on camps and programs.

South Bay

Border View YMCA Day Camp
3085 Beyer Blvd., Suite A-103, San Diego • (619) 428-1168

Like most YMCA camps, this is a traditional day camp that offers 10 one-week sessions during the summer months. It's designed for children ages 5 to 12 and includes arts, crafts, sports, swimming and field trips to other locations and attractions around the county that have maximum "kid appeal." The weekly cost ranges from $65 to $120.

Chuck E Cheese's
1143 Highland Ave., National City • (619) 474-6667

This is a carbon copy of the other Chuck E Cheese's kids' restaurants in the county. You'll notice that they've popped up in every one of our regions, and for good reason: kids absolutely love them. For more information, see our entry under San Diego.

Discovery Zone
510 Broadway, Chula Vista • (619) 427-1291

This is another place that's likely to rattle the senses of adults, but has just the right level of noise and activity for kids. Discovery Zone is a safe and soft supervised play area where kids can climb, jump, crawl, slide and swing. A plastic ball pool is a favorite of the really young ones, and a separate play area is toned down a lot for toddlers.

A large arcade is one of the favorite hangouts in Discovery Zone; here kids can play electronic games and win tickets to be accumulated and traded in for prizes. Plenty of refreshments can be purchased at snack bars, from pizza to ice cream. Hours are from 10 AM to 8 PM Monday through Thursday, 10 AM to 9 PM on Friday and 11 AM to 7 PM on Sunday. Admission is $5.99 for kids ages 3 to 12. Children 1 or 2 years old are charged $3.99. Adults and babies younger than 1 enter free.

Fun-4-All
950 Industrial Blvd., Chula Vista • (619) 427-1840

This is a smaller version of the Family Fun Centers around San Diego County, but kids still find plenty to do here. Miniature golf is a favorite, as are the batting cages and the bumper boats. Kids will find enough attractions here to keep them busy for a couple of hours.

Fun-4-All is open Monday through Thursday from 11 AM to 10 PM; Fridays, 11 AM to midnight; Saturdays, 9 AM to midnight and Sundays, 9 AM to 10 PM.

Miniature golf is $5 for adults and $4 for children younger than 12. Bumper Boat rides are $3.50 for adults and $1.75 for those shorter than 44 inches. A dollar will get you 20 pitches in the batting cage, and a free bat and helmet to use, but an ID card is required.

Whitewater Canyon Waterpark
2052 Otay Valley Rd., Chula Vista • (619) 661-7373

Something about waterparks is irresistible to kids, so when you toss out the idea of a day at Whitewater Canyon, the suggestion is sure to be met with cheers and shouts of approval. Even if adults don't like to admit it, they get a kick out of waterparks, too. It must be that combination of warm sunshine, cool water and knowing your kids are having an excellent time.

We've covered Whitewater Canyon in detail in our Attractions chapter, so we'll just give you the basics here.

You'll find body slides, tube slides, a giant wave pool, a four-story interactive family play structure and a scaled-down structure for younger children.

Plenty of refreshments are available from a variety of snack bars and specialty food booths. The waterpark is open from 10 AM to 6 PM on weekends only from early May until mid-June, when it opens daily until Labor Day. Admission is $21.99 for those 48 inches and taller, and $15.99 for those shorter than 48 inches.

The park is not something you can absorb in a day; like a rich dessert, it's better savored at a leisurely pace to fully enjoy its lavishness.

Balboa Park

San Diego is famous for its natural attributes — the sparkling beaches, the curving harbor, the imposing ocean bluffs, the blooming desert. It's also noted for its manmade landmarks, such as the Hotel del Coronado, the San Diego-Coronado Bay Bridge and Sea World. But San Diego also has a spot that is the best combination of natural and manmade: Balboa Park.

Most San Diegans believe that Balboa Park was born along with the Panama-California Exposition, held in 1915 and 1916 to celebrate the opening of the Panama Canal. But the seeds of the park were actually planted — literally — in 1892. Kate Sessions, a noted horticulturist, leased 30 acres of Balboa Park from the city to use as a nursery. In exchange, she agreed to plant 100 trees a year in the park for the next 10 years. It was Sessions who set the standard for the landscaping in the park, which today has vast displays of exotic and drought-resistant plants and trees.

The manmade attributes of the park came later. Many Spanish-style buildings were constructed for the Panama-California Exposition. More were added for the California Pacific International Exposition in 1935. After both expositions, the buildings evolved into homes for museums and exhibits, and most of them remain today, carefully reconstructed, restored and refurbished. At the conclusion of the first exposition, Dr. Harry Wegeforth, a local physician, gathered together a few animals to start a small zoo, which today has grown into the world-famous San Diego Zoo. From those beginnings grew Balboa Park as we know it today, the jewel in the crown of San Diego's attractions.

The park is not something you can absorb in a day; like a rich dessert, it's better savored at a leisurely pace to fully enjoy its lavishness. The zoo alone can take up the better part of a day, and to see and appreciate the rest of the park can easily consume another day. As you read this chapter, you will probably pick and choose from the things to see and do, but we recommend that you try not to stick too closely to a strict agenda. It's inevitable that you'll get distracted by something. Besides, that's half the fun.

In this chapter we'll describe the zoo, museums, gardens and other attractions so you can get an overview and see what appeals to you. The park is spread out over 1,400 acres, and even though that sounds enormous, most everything is within an easy walk of any place you park. (Parking in all lots, by the way, is free.) Should you get tired of walking, though, just hop on the free Balboa Park Tram that runs continuously from 9:30 AM to 5:30 PM daily. Tram stops are located throughout the park as well as in outlying parking areas.

Loads of places to picnic are scattered throughout the park, and it's a great way to take a midday break from all the activity. One prime spot is the grassy area surrounding the Moreton Bay Fig Tree, which was planted in 1915. Located immediately behind the Natural History Museum, this magnificent tree has been a favorite of generations of children who have climbed over its gnarled roots and swung from its lofty branches. If lunching al fresco isn't your style, there's no lack of spots that provide food and beverage, from hot dog stands to the Lil' Miss Muffins Cafe in the Casa de Balboa to the peaceful Sculpture Garden Cafe next door to the San Diego Museum of Art.

The park is loaded with art museums and a noteworthy theater, too, which is covered in greater detail in our Arts chapter, but we'll mention them, just so you'll know they're here and you won't miss anything. We'll also include some references to attractions with particular appeal to kids, which we'll spell out in our Kidstuff chapter.

Balboa Park is located in the heart of the city, just north of downtown San Diego. It's accessible by auto or by Metropolitan Transit bus. From Interstate 5 north or south, take the Pershing Drive exit, and follow the signs to Balboa Park. Once you're there, a good place to start is the Visitors Center, located in the House of Hospitality building at 1549 El Prado, (619) 239-0512. Friendly receptionists can answer questions, give you maps and steer you in the right direction if you get turned around.

Many of the attractions — the gardens in particular — don't have an actual street address, so we'll describe their locations to make them easy for you to find. Signage pointing the way to just about everything is excellent in the park, but still it's a good idea to carry a map showing exact locations of the various plazas and buildings. Most hotels have Balboa Park maps, and as noted above, they are also available at the Visitors Center. So carve out a day or two from your schedule, gather up the family and don't forget your *Insiders' Guide*. Art, science, culture, history, animals, bugs and botany all await.

Aerospace Museum
2001 Pan American Plaza
• (619) 234-8291

Have you ever wondered what it was like that day at Kitty Hawk when the Wright Brothers made the first powered flight? You can relive that thrilling day in history at the San Diego Aerospace Museum, along with other landmark events and innovations in the history of aerospace. See the Spad, the Nieuport and the Albatros from World War I, and the Spitfires, Zeros and Hellcats from World War II.

The Aerospace Museum's collection has aviation memorabilia and more than 65 foreign and domestic aircraft, including present-day spacecraft. Don't forget to visit the International Aerospace Hall of Fame, which honors aero-engineers, pilots and aviation industrialists.

The museum is open daily (except Thanks-

giving and Christmas) from 10 AM to 4:30 PM. From Memorial Day through Labor Day, hours are 10 AM to 5:30 PM. Admission is $6 for adults, $5 for seniors 65 and older, $2 for children 6 to 17, and free for children younger than 6. Active-duty military members are admitted free too, and admission is free for everyone on the fourth Tuesday of the month.

Alcazar Garden/Palm Canyon
Located adjacent to the House of Charm

Patterned after the gardens of Alcazar Castle in Seville, Spain, Balboa Park's version is distinguished by its ornate fountains and colorful Moorish tiles. It's a beautifully symmetrical garden, with individual areas bordered by boxwood hedges and planted with more than 7,000 annual flowers for a year-round vibrant display.

Just across the road and behind Alcazar Garden is Palm Canyon, a tropical oasis of more than 2-acres graced by 450 palm trees representing 70 species. Most prominent in the canyon are Mexican fan palms that date back to the early 1900s.

Both Alcazar Garden and Palm Canyon are open daily, and there is no admission fee.

Automotive Museum
2080 Pan American Plaza
• (619) 231-2886

The automobile holds such fascination for Americans that it has become integrated into our culture, our way of life and our technological advances. The San Diego Automotive Museum has gathered an impressive collection of the objects of our fascination to take you back in time or to help you imagine autos of the future. Along with automotive memorabilia, see exotic road cars, the historic Model-A, gas-guzzling muscle cars and luxurious Rolls Royces.

The on-site restoration facility gives visitors a glimpse of restoration techniques, and the research library, which is open to the pub-

---

INSIDERS' TIP

If museum browsing is high on your list of priorities, try to schedule your visit some other day than Monday. Many of the museums are closed Mondays, year-round.

This little girl, like most small visitors, likes the horses used by the mounted police who patrol the 1,400 acres of Balboa Park.

The Casa de Balboa and the House of Hospitality are beautiful and unique examples of Balboa Park's historical architecture.

lic, contains rare publications, photos and vintage films. Museum hours are 10 AM to 4:30 PM daily, and 10 AM to 5:30 PM during summer months. Admission is $6 for adults, $5 for active-duty military and seniors, $2 for children 6 to 15 and free for children younger than 6. Or visit the museum on the fourth Tuesday of each month, when admission is free.

Botanical Building and Lily Pond
North side of El Prado, between Timken Art Museum and Casa del Prado
• no phone

Walking down El Prado, the main pedestrian mall in the park, you can't miss the reflecting lily pond. What you'll notice first are the creamy white lilies and lotus flowers floating on the surface of the 193-foot by 43-foot pond. Then you might spot a turtle or two sunning themselves on the lily pads, or bright orange koi swimming amongst the lilies. It's hard to imagine that the pond was used as a therapy pool during World War II for injured sailors sent over from nearby Balboa Naval Hospital.

A little less striking from the outside, but glorious on the inside, is the Botanical Building that sits behind the pond. At 250 feet long by 75 feet wide and 60 feet tall, it was the largest wood lath structure in the world when it was built in 1915. Inside you'll find more than 2,100 specimens of tropical plants and trees, along with changing seasonal flowers. Orchids, lilies, plants and flowers you never dreamed existed all await your admiration as you meander along the shaded paths.

INSIDERS' TIP

Ranger tours are scheduled for 12 PM on Wednesdays and 11 AM on Sundays. Experienced rangers give you historical insight into the Prado, along with the history of the two expositions held in the park. Meet in front of the Visitors Center.

Tours

Explore the exotic horticulture, the architectural beauty and the historical wonders of Balboa Park by taking one of several free tours. Meet in front of the Botanical Building at 10 AM on Saturdays, except those falling within the holiday break from Thanksgiving through mid-January. No reservations are necessary, but tours will be canceled if it's raining or the group is fewer than four people. All walking tours are easy paced and last about one hour. For more information, call the Park and Recreation Department at (619) 235-1121.

History Walk — First Saturday
This tour blends a little bit of everything: history, architecture and horticultural delights. You'll meander up and down the two-block El Prado area while your tour guide describes the history and architecture of the various buildings. You'll also get background information on some of the many botanical specimens for which the park is noted.

Palm Walk — Second Saturday
Delve into the world of palm trees. Learn about their structure, growth and landscape value as your guided tour takes you into Palm Canyon, where a huge collection of palm specimens awaits your inspection.

Tree Walk — Third Saturday
Famed horticulturist Kate Sessions made sure Balboa Park had a vast array of exotic trees. Your guide will introduce you to many of these rare beauties. You'll see some in the Botanical Building and many others that have been planted over the years, all within a few blocks walk.

Desert Walk — Fourth Saturday
Kate Sessions was also devoted to cultivating drought-resistant plants. After all, San Diego is a desert. See the wide variety of American, African and Baja California desert plants as you tour the Desert Garden across from the Natural History Museum.

Tour del Dia — Fifth Saturday
Explore the Palisades area, where the California Pacific International Exposition was held in 1935, and learn about its historical and horticultural roots. Like the other tours, this is a short walk that's equivalent to a few blocks.

The Botanical Building is open daily except Thursday, from 10 AM to 4 PM. Admission is free.

Carousel and Miniature Railroad
Park Blvd. and Zoo Pl., behind the Spanish Village Art Center • no phone

Built in 1910 and imported from New York, the "merry-go-round" has been a park fixture since 1912, with its menagerie of animals hand carved by European craftsmen. It's one of the few remaining carousels in the world where you can still go for the brass ring and win a free ride.

From mid-June through Labor Day the carousel operates from 11 AM to 5:30 PM every day. The rest of the year it opens on Saturdays, Sundays, holidays and during school vacations from 11 AM to 5:30 PM. Tickets are $1.25; children younger than a year old ride free. Adults should plan to accompany smaller children.

Next door to the carousel is the miniature railroad. The 1/5-scale locomotive takes a three-minute, 2½ mile ride around 4 acres of Balboa Park. It's a replica of the General Motors F3 diesel, which pulls the Santa Fe's Super Chief. More than 5 million passengers,

Sunday in Balboa Park will find jugglers and musicians entertaining park visitors.

Photo: San Diego Convention and Visitors Bureau

young and old, have enjoyed the ride through the years. Adding to the atmosphere is the conductor in a railroad cap and overalls who not only shouts "All aboard" but also serves as engineer for every ride.

The Miniature Railroad runs on Saturdays, Sundays and school holidays from 11 AM to 4:30 PM. Admission for "children 1 to 99" is $1.25; children younger than a year old ride for free. Kids younger than 5 must ride with an adult.

Centro Cultural de la Raza
2125 Park Blvd. • (619) 235-6135

Located just south of the Pepper Grove picnic area, the Centro Cultural de la Raza is an internationally recognized art space that hosts exhibitions and performances showcasing Latino/Chicano artists. The building itself is a work of art. Stroll around the perimeter of the circular building and you'll see that the exterior is one long mural depicting themes from Mayan, Native American and Chicano culture.

For more information about the Centro Cultural de la Raza, please see the entry in our Arts chapter. There you'll find greater detail on its exhibits, community outreach programs and special performances. The Centro is open Wednesday through Sunday, 12 PM to 5 PM. Admission is free.

Hall of Champions
2131 Pan American Plaza
• (619) 234-2544

Uniforms, trophies, photographs and other memorabilia from San Diego's sports stars adorn the walls of the Hall of Champions museum. The jerseys of baseball legend Ted Williams are here: the ones he wore when he belted his first homers for the Padres' Pacific Coast League team, and ones he donned in his more famous days with the Boston Red Sox. You'll also find items representing boxing great Archie Moore, tennis star Maureen Connolly, Bill Walton of basketball fame, the Chargers' Dan Fouts and many others. Local talents from Over-the-Line (see our Spectator Sports chapter for the lowdown on this homegrown sport), golf, the Holiday Bowl, swimming and horse racing are all honored too.

The Hall of Champions is open daily from 10 AM to 4:30 PM. Admission is $3 for adults, $2 for seniors 55 and older and active-duty military, and $1 for children 6 to 17. Children younger than 6 are admitted free.

House of Pacific Relations, International Cottages
Pan American Rd. W. • (619) 234-0739

Founded in 1935, the House of Pacific Relations is an organization dedicated to fostering cooperation and understanding among its international groups. More than two dozen countries are represented in the organization, and most of them have their own cottages in Balboa Park. The cottages are furnished and staffed by members of the respective groups and present exhibits that showcase their history, culture and traditions.

Cottages are open on Sundays from 12 PM to 5 PM, at which time group members, dressed in traditional costumes, are present to welcome visitors and answer questions. Adjacent to the International Cottages is the Hall of Nations, which also has international exhibits. Groups that do not have cottages rotate their exhibits in the Hall of Nations.

On Sundays from March through October, special Lawn Programs are held on the outdoor stage in the cottage area at 2 PM. Members perform ethnic songs and dances and serve food native to their country. Programs last one hour. Admission is free to all House of Pacific Relations events (except films); donations are gratefully accepted. On the fourth Tuesday of each month, Children Around the World Films are shown. Admission is free.

Inez Grant Parker Memorial Rose Garden/Desert Garden
Located across Park Blvd., opposite the Natural History Museum

Stopping to smell the roses has never been sweeter. This stunning, award-winning garden shows off more than 2,200 rose bushes in 178 varieties. Peak bloom time is during April and May, but most of the roses bloom clear through December. If you're in the mood for romance, the Rose Garden is the most popular wedding spot in Balboa Park.

With the heady fragrance of roses still lingering, walk a few yards north and visit the 2½ acre Desert Garden. Kate Sessions, the horticulturist who was largely responsible for turning Balboa Park into a botanical wonder, was fascinated by drought resistant plants. The Desert Garden displays many of the speci-

Photo: Balboa Park Administration

Children have been enjoying this carousel since 1912.

mens Sessions introduced to the park, as well as succulents and other drought-resistant varieties from around the world.

The Rose Garden and the Desert Garden are open daily, and admission is free.

Japanese Friendship Garden
Located between the House of Hospitality and the Spreckels Organ Pavilion • (619) 232-2721

Peaceful and serene describe the atmosphere once you pass through the massive wooden gates at the entrance to the Japanese Friendship Garden. Funded by a grant from the San Diego Art and Culture Commission, the garden was built as a tribute to San Diego's sister city of Yokohama. The garden demonstrates the sister cities' shared values of beauty in nature, respect in friendship and hopes for the future.

Exhibits within the garden change monthly, displaying Japanese art, folk crafts and Japanese culture. The Friendship Garden is open Tuesday, Friday, Saturday and Sunday from 10 AM to 4 PM. Admission is $2 for adults; $1 for seniors 65 and older, disabled persons, military, students and children 7 to 17. Children 6 and younger are admitted free. The garden is open free of charge on the third Tuesday of every month.

Marie Hitchcock Puppet Theatre
Pan American Plaza • (619) 685-5045

Named for San Diego's original "puppet lady," the Marie Hitchcock Puppet Theatre has been charming local kids and their moms and dads for decades. The San Diego Guild of Puppetry, a group of professional and amateur puppeteers, performs year-round with marionettes, hand puppets and ventriloquists. For more information, see our entry in the "Kidstuff" chapter.

Show times are 10 AM and 11:30 AM Wednesday, Thursday and Friday; 11 AM, 1 PM and 2:30 PM on Saturdays and Sundays. Admission for adults is $2, and for children 3 to 17 is $1.50. Admission is free for children 2 and younger.

Mingei International Museum
1439 El Prado, House of Charm • (619) 239-0003

Many cultures are adopting the word "Mingei" to mean "art of the people." The San Diego Mingei International Museum is dedicated to furthering the understanding of art of all cultures of the world. The goal is to open a window to a broad view of the creative potential of all people. The Mingei Museum displays indigenous arts and crafts of unsurpassed beauty. Frequently changing exhibitions present essential art forms, such as ceramics, textiles, baskets, pottery, toys, furniture and other objects of daily use. Numerous videos are also available for viewing at the museum, including *American Expressions of Liberty: Art of the People, by the People, for the People*.

The museum is open Tuesday through Sunday from 10 AM to 4 PM. Admission is $5 for adults, and $2 for students and children 6 to 17. Admission is free for children younger than 6. Admission is free for everyone on the third Tuesday of each month.

Model Railroad Museum
1649 El Prado, Casa de Balboa, Lower Level • (619) 696-0199

Check out the largest operating model-railroad exhibit in America. More than 24,000 square feet of model train exhibits await your delighted observation. It's a toss-up which attraction kids love more: the train exhibits or the interactive Toy Train Gallery, where they (and you too) can play engineer.

INSIDERS' TIP

If you plan to spend more than a day or two discovering Balboa Park, you may want to purchase a "Passport to Balboa Park." The $21 passport is valid for a week and allows entrance to 12 museums (a $62 value). Passports can be purchased at the Visitors Center in the House of Hospitality building, (619) 231-1640, or at any participating museum.

This one-clown band attracts attention as he entertains on the walkways of Balboa Park.

Along with the visually impressive model trains is an in-depth exhibit that details the colorful history of railroads in the American Southwest.

The museum is open Tuesday through Friday, 11 AM to 4 PM; Saturday and Sunday, 11 AM to 5 PM. Admission is $3 for adults, $2.50 for students, military and seniors. Children younger than 15 are admitted free. The first Tuesday of the month is free admission day for the Model Railroad Museum.

Museum of Man
1350 El Prado (under the California Tower) • (619) 239-2001

San Diego's only anthropological museum is filled to the brim with treasures of the ages. In 1915 the Smithsonian Institution gathered a collection of artifacts, folklore and physical remains that were displayed as part of the Panama-California Exhibition. After the exhibition the collection became the Museum of Man, and today it holds more than 70,000 items, each one a symbol of cultures from ancient times to the present.

Ancient hunting spears, ceramic vessels, and delicately woven textiles are just a few of the objects on display. And each has a story to accompany it, taking you back to the days when the item was part of daily use.

The Museum of Man is open daily, except Thanksgiving, Christmas and New Year's Day, from 10 AM to 4:30 PM. Admission is $5 for adults, $3 for children 6 to 17, and free for kids 5 and younger. Everyone gets in for free on the third Tuesday of every month.

Museum of Photographic Arts
1649 El Prado, Casa de Balboa, Upper Level • (619) 238-7559

If you're like many Insiders, your photo treasures are limited to the occasional lucky snapshot. But we all appreciate those who have the talent to create spellbinding works of art with the camera. Some of the best are on display at the Museum of Photo Arts, one of the country's first and finest museums dedicated exclusively to photography.

Changing exhibits display critically acclaimed historical and contemporary work by some of the world's most celebrated photographers. In addition to its exhibits, the museum offers lectures, workshops and occasional film series. If during your visit you'd like more insight into exhibits, a guided tour is included with your admission on Sundays at 2 PM. The museum is open daily from 10 AM to 5 PM. Admission is $4 for adults; children younger than 12 are admitted free when accompanied by an adult. Admission is free to all on the second Tuesday of every month.

Insider's Note: The Museum of Photographic Arts is expanding, but while it increases its size by nearly fourfold, it will be closed through the spring of 2000. However, the exhibits will be moved to downtown's Museum of Contemporary Art in the interim, located at 1001 Kettner Blvd., San Diego, (619) 234-1001. Admission is $2 to the Museum of Contemporary Art and will include entry to the Museum of Photographic Arts during its stay there.

Museum of San Diego History
1649 El Prado, Casa de Balboa, Upper Level • (619) 232-6203

San Diego's history is rich with tales of townspeople determined to turn a town into a city. Despite numerous obstacles and bumps in the road, our dedicated founding fathers persevered. The Museum of San Diego History traces the city's development from 1850 to current times with displays of historical photos, costumes and artifacts.

The museum is operated by the San Diego Historical Society, which also makes its research archives available to the public. His-

---

INSIDERS' TIP

The San Diego Zoo provides special parking, restrooms, telephones and access to shows and exhibits for guest's with disabilities. Special ASL "signed" bus tours are available too. Call the Zoo's info line at (619) 234-3153 to arrange for an interpreter. Or call the TDD line at (619) 233-9639.

Photo: Robert Burroughs

Getting around Balboa Park is fun on this free trolley.

tory buffs spend hours in the archives, poring over photos and documents from the early days of San Diego.

Research archives are open Thursday through Saturday from 10 AM to 4 PM, and the fee for using the archives is $3; students research for free. The museum is open Tuesday through Sunday from 10 AM to 4:30 PM. Admission is $4 for adults; $3 for seniors, students and military; and $1.50 for children 5 to 12. Children younger than 5 are admitted free. Admission is free to all on the second Tuesday of each month.

Natural History Museum
Plaza de Balboa • (619) 232-3821

It's nearly impossible to get beyond the entrance foyer of the Natural History Museum, where the giant Foucault Pendulum swings back and forth hypnotically, slowly but surely measuring time by virtue of the Earth's rotation. The pendulum has been known to quiet unruly children and mesmerize adults for hours. Tear yourself away, though, because much more is in store.

Founded by the San Diego Society of Natural History, the museum traces it roots back to 1920, when it opened in Balboa Park. The facility encompasses 60,000 square feet and shares with visitors a fabulous collection of temporary and permanent exhibits. Don't miss the Scripps Hall of Mineralogy, or the diorama in the Hall of Desert Ecology. Kids will go nuts over the life-size Allosaurus skeleton in the paleontology exhibit and will gasp at the whale skeletons and oceanic specimens in the Ocean Ecology exhibit.

Hours at the Natural History Museum are 9:30 AM to 4:30 PM during winter months and 9:30 AM to 5:30 PM from mid-June through Labor Day. Admission is $6 for adults, $5 for seniors and military and $3 for children 6 to 17. Children younger that 6 are admitted free. The permanent exhibits in the museum are open free of charge on the first Tuesday of every month.

Photo: Ken Eckel

A jogger passes through the Spanish colonial arcades in Balboa Park.

Old Globe Theatre Complex
Located behind the Museum of Man
• (619) 239-2255

For more than 60 years the Old Globe Theatre has been presenting Shakespearean classics as well as contemporary plays and musicals. The Old Globe and its sister theaters in the Old Globe complex, the Cassius Carter Centre Stage and the Lowell Davies Festival Theatre, are nestled in a grassy enclave behind the Museum of Man. Visitors love strolling around the grounds and touring the Old Globe, which is a replica of the original Old Globe Theatre in London.

For more information about the Old Globe and its Tony Award-winning productions, please see the entry in our Arts chapter.

Pepper Grove

Pepper Grove is the perfect spot for a picnic. Lots of shady trees and wide, grassy areas give you the choice of eating in the shade at a picnic table or spreading out on the grass to bask in the sunshine.

Located behind the Reuben H. Fleet Space Theater (to the south of the theater), Pepper Grove is a great place for kids to burn off excess energy. It has three separate play areas with swings, climbing equipment and interactive structures. A parking lot is conveniently located right next to the area.

Reuben H. Fleet Space Theater and Science Center
Plaza de Balboa • (619) 238-1233

If you've never experienced an IMAX film, you're in for a treat. The space theater surrounds viewers with sound and with sights projected onto a giant domed screen. Here you can see IMAX films such as *Everest*, the story of the tallest Himalayan peak and one of the world's greatest climbing adventures.

The Exhibit Galleries in the Science Center contain more than 70 hands-on displays. Put your hands on the Lightning Globe and become a link in an electrical circuit. Find out how your heart works, or test your reaction time and coordination skills. All exhibits are science-related and highly entertaining for both kids and adults.

The Theater and Science Center are open from 9:30 AM to 6 PM Monday and Tuesday; 9:30 AM to 9 PM Wednesday, Thursday and Friday; 9 AM to 9 PM on Saturday; and 9 AM to 8 PM on Sunday. Show times vary, but there usually is a show every hour. Ticket prices for

Photo: Ron Garrison

The California Tower of the Museum of Man rises above the park and a tiled fountain.

Space Theater shows (which includes entrance to the Exhibit Galleries) are $8 for adults 13 and older, $6 for seniors 65 and older and $4 for children 3 to 12. Children younger than 3 are admitted free, but must sit on an adult's lap in the theater and will be directed to the lower left section. Admission to the Science Center Exhibit Galleries only is $2.50 for seniors and adults 13 and older, and $1.25 for children 3 to 12. Children younger than 3 are admitted free. Everyone is admitted free to the Science Center on the first Tuesday of each month.

San Diego Museum of Art
1450 El Prado (619) 232-7931

One of the country's leading art institutes, the San Diego Museum of Art has something for everyone: Italian Renaissance collections, Spanish and Dutch Old Masters, American art, nineteenth-century European paintings, and numerous other collections. Besides these permanent holdings, the museum holds year-round special exhibits too, such as the Jewels of the Romanov, Faberge Eggs and a special collection of Monet's works. We describe the museum in detail in our Arts chapter, but wanted to mention it briefly here, so you'll be sure not to miss it while you're in Balboa Park.

Hours are from 10 AM to 4:30 PM Tuesday through Sunday. Admission prices are $7 for adults; $5 for seniors 65 and older, young adults 18 to 24, and military; $2 for children 6 to 17 and free for children 5 and younger. On Fridays, Saturdays and Sundays, all admission prices are increased by $1. Admission to the permanent exhibits is free on the third Tuesday of every month.

San Diego Zoo
2920 Zoo Dr. • (619) 234-3153

The world-famous San Diego Zoo was founded in 1916, at the close of the Panama-California Exposition, by an enterprising local physician, Dr. Harry Wegeforth. He gathered a collection of about 50 animals, some which had been used during the exposition, and some that were part of various local menageries. Today the Zoo contains more than 4,000 rare and endangered birds, mammals and reptiles from 800 different species. More than just a place where animals hang out, the Zoo has long been dedicated to animal research with the goal of preserving endangered species. And you won't find any tigers or polar bears sitting listless and bored in cages. Enclosures and open spaces have been created to replicate the animals' natural habitats. Visit Tiger River, Sun Bear Forest, Scripps Aviary, Gorilla Tropics, Hippo Beach and Polar Bear Plunge, and you'll see what we mean.

The Children's Zoo, located inside the Zoo itself, is a favorite of the kids (and Mom and Dad too). Giant tortoises, goats and other gentle critters roam freely around the Children's Zoo, giving kids the opportunity for some hands-on interaction. Several animal shows are staged throughout the day in the main Zoo, including the Sea Lion Show and the Wild Ones, which showcases predators and prey from around the world.

Another must-see is the Giant Panda exhibit. Shi Shi and Bai Yun are here from China as part of a cooperative effort between the United States and China to study pandas and help raise funds for their protection. Shi Shi and Bai Yun are the only pair of giant pandas in the United States.

When you get hungry, choose from a wide range of snacks and all-American favorites at stands located throughout the Zoo. Or dine in style at one of several full-service restaurants, including the Treehouse Cafe and the Peacock & Raven Deli. Picnic areas are also located in convenient spots around the Zoo, and you're welcome to bring your own lunch with you. Lockers are available if you're not in the mood to tote your gear till lunchtime.

INSIDERS' TIP

Just in case you think you may miss out on shopping while you're discovering Balboa Park, guess again. Every museum has an expansive gift shop stocked with items related to the museum as well as gifts of general appeal.

The Zoo is open every day of the year from 9 AM until 4 PM, with extended hours during the summer, usually until 5 PM or 6 PM. Admission includes the Children's Zoo and all the animal shows. Prices are $16 for ages 12 and up, $7 for children 3 to 11, and free for children 2 and younger. Deluxe Admission includes a bus tour and Skyfari aerial tram ride, and is priced at $22 for adults, $19.80 for seniors 60 and older, and $12 for children 3 to 11.

Spanish Village Art Center
1770 Village Pl. • (619) 233-9050

Constructed in 1935 for the California Pacific International Exposition, the charming collection of buildings was meant to depict a picturesque village in Spain. At the conclusion of the exposition, a group of dedicated artists established the village as an arts center. Its only departure from that designation was during World War II, when the U.S. Navy used the village for temporary barracks. Today the center offers the creations of more than 100 artists, many of whom use the buildings as both studio and gallery.

Thirty-five individual galleries offer treasures in a variety of media: oil, watercolor, ceramics, sculpture, jewelry, wood carving, glass, photography and enamel. You can shop or just browse among the one-of-a-kind items every day except New Year's Day, Thanksgiving and Christmas from 11 AM to 4 PM. Admission is free.

Spreckels Organ Pavilion
Pan American Rd. E. • (619) 226-0819

John D. Spreckels, one of San Diego's founding fathers, presented the city with a gift on New Year's Eve in 1914, just before the beginning of the Panama-California Exposition: a beautiful pipe organ and a grand pavilion to house it. The organ has been in almost continuous use since that time. It contains 4,518 pipes ranging in size from more than 32 feet long to about the size of your little finger.

Year-round organ concerts are presented to the public on Sunday afternoons from 2 PM to 3 PM. Special summer performances are held on Monday nights during July and August from 8 PM to 9:30 PM. Even if there's no concert scheduled for the day you're in the park, be sure to inspect the pavilion and its stunning architecture; it's located at the south end of Plaza de Panama. Admission to all concerts is free.

Timken Museum of Art
1500 El Prado • (619) 239-5548

The Timken Museum of Art is devoted to the preservation of European and American paintings from the early Renaissance through the nineteenth century. Among its exhibits not to be missed is a collection of beautiful Russian Icons.

Like Balboa Park's other art museums, we cover the Timken in greater detail in our Arts chapter, but we want to make sure you add it to your itinerary while you're visiting the Park. Insiders refer to it as San Diego's "jewel box for the arts."

Hours are from 10 AM to 4:30 PM, Tuesday through Saturday, and 1:30 PM to 4:30 PM on Sundays. Admission is free.

Zoro Gardens
Between the Reuben H. Fleet Space Theater and the Casa de Balboa

Zoro Gardens were a favorite attraction during the California Pacific Exposition of 1935-1936. Why? Because the gardens were the site of a nudist colony. The chief of police, however, insisted that the women wear brassieres and G-strings, and that the men wear loincloths during daylight hours when visitors were likely to wander in.

Today there are no nudists, but the gardens are an inviting and usually cool spot for a break during your exploration of the park. The winding paths travel far back into the canyons and pass by beautiful plant and floral specimens. There is no admission charge.

San Diego is home to notable and eccentric events such as the Over-the-Line Tournament and the Mainly Mozart series.

Annual Events

Lots happens in San Diego, and on nearly every weekend you'll be faced with choices of what to attend, participate in or watch. Yeah, it's tough but somebody has to have fun.

Our goal with the list is to bring San Diego's special fun to you so we've included plenty of free events and festivals from the Bridal Bazaar and the Mother Goose Parade to the Rancho Santa Fe Rummage Sale (the primo sale of the year) to the Mainly Mozart Festival. We've also tried to blend the expected events with the unusual, notable, and eccentric ones, such as the Over-the-Line Tournament and the Mainly Mozart series. If there's an adult-only aspect, we've included that; where it's family fun, we've stressed that too.

Typically, the outdoor events include food booths, or you can pack a snack. We've listed the current fee or cost, if it's known. We also let you know when the event is free.

Remember when looking at the calendar of events that we've organized this chapter by months rather than region. Keep in mind that you'll want to call to double check locations and times, or to verify prices.

Many communities have mini-events and cultural activities that are big news for neighborhoods but are too small to be listed here. If you've just moved into the San Diego area and wonder what's happening, ask an Insider, or call the city's parks and recreation office, senior citizen centers or the public library. Events, athletic tournaments, community picnics and concerts are also often listed on bulletin boards.

We've tried to make it easy for you to use this list, by ordering events chronologically. So if an event happens in the beginning of any month, you'll find it among the first listings; if it's at the end of the month, you'll find it listed last.

January

Chinese New Year Celebration
Third Ave. and J St., San Diego
• (619) 234-4447

Go for the festival and stay for the fun with this celebration that presents the many cultures of China. There are traditional dancers, martial arts demonstrations by pros and students, cultural information, craft booths and food. The tea sets are especially worth a second look. The event is held for two days. Remember Chinese New Year doesn't always happen in January. Admission is $3 for adults, $2 for kids.

San Diego Marathon
The starting line is near Plaza Camino Real shopping center, 2500 El Camino Real, Carlsbad • (858) 792-2900

This 26.2-mile marathon draws runners, walkers and watchers from around the country. Last year the number of participants exceeded 8,000. This is a three-day weekend event with Friday activities featuring a golf tournament and Saturday activities including a Keebler Kids Marathon and a health expo, food, vendors and activities. The actual marathon is on Sunday and begins in Carlsbad near Plaza Camino Real shopping center. Call for entrance fees, which vary; Saturday activities and watching the marathon are free.

Bridal Bazaar
San Diego Concourse and Performing Arts Center, between A and C Sts. and First and C Aves., San Diego
• (858) 755-6601

Are you getting ready for the big day or dreaming of someday? The Bridal Bazaar, sponsored by Bridal Productions, provides everything a wedding planner could want. You'll find fashion shows, bridal helps, and hundreds of vendors with something new, something blue and something you just have to have. There are food booths to refresh you after all that bridal browsing. The event is free.

Local Authors Exhibit
San Diego City Public Library, 820 E St., San Diego • (619) 236-5818

This is an important event for Insiders and also for visitors who are interested in local authors. There are some best-selling writers among our literary crowd, including Victor Villaseñor. The month-long exhibit and author readings highlight the best the county has to offer. Call for library hours, information on readings, and, if you're a writer too, information on submitting your work. Admission to the readings is free.

Penguin Day Ski Fest
De Anza Cove at Information Center, Mission Bay • (619) 276-0830

During this ski fest, you won't see any of the penguins from Sea World; however, you will see brave (read that daring) water-skiers race around Mission Bay (no wetsuits allowed), and lots of people swimming and skiing in chilly ocean water. It's kind of crazy to be going in the water in winter, but that's where the fun comes in. The ski fest is from 9 AM to 1 PM. Call for details if you want to enter (watching is

free). There is always a party afterwards where you'll find food booths and places to picnic.

Rose Pruning Demonstration
The Inez Grant Parker Memorial Rose Garden/ Desert Garden, across Park Avenue from the Natural History Museum, Balboa Park, San Diego
• (619) 235-0004

Sponsored by the San Diego Rose Society, this demonstration at Balboa Park's rose garden will teach you the how-to's and what-for's of growing gorgeous blooms. The event is held from 9 AM to 1 PM. Rose Society members and volunteers trim, clip and coddle the more than 1,300 bushes found in the Park's knockout rose garden. Volunteers are encouraged to participate in the fun. Usually held toward the end of January, depending on the weather, the event is free. Call the society for the specific Saturday when the event is held.

Teddy Bear, Doll and Toy Festival
Scottish Rite Temple, 1895 Camino Del Rio South, San Diego • (760) 434-7444

You'll find everything imaginable at this weekend festival for professional collectors and those who appreciate the world populated by teddy bears, dolls and toys. With 200 or more vendors, this semi-annual event (it's in August too) is in its fortieth year. Admission is $5.

February

Anza-Borrego Desert Wildflowers Season
Anza-Borrego Desert State Park, Borrego Springs • (760) 767-4684 (for an events message), (760) 767-4205 (to speak with a park volunteer)

When spring comes to the desert the colors are breathtaking. It's a short blooming season and worth the drive. If you haven't visited Anza-Borrego "for the flowers," as Insiders say, then do not pass go until you've done so. Pack your camera, sunscreen and sense of wonder. Flowers do not bloom on a strict schedule so should rains come early, the blooms will too. A call to the park's visitors center can give you the status of the blooms. There are plenty of roadside opportunities for viewing the flowers, but if you love nature and flowers, you'll want to visit the information center at the park too. There's a $5 fee to enter the park, various charges for camping. See our Parks and Recreation chapter if you're a hiker or camper and want more information about outdoor opportunities at the park.

San Dieguito Half Marathon

Lomas Santa Fe and Highland Dr., San Dieguito County Park, Rancho Santa Fe • (619) 298-7400

This race is half the size of the San Diego Marathon and more do-able for less determined runners. The race, which begins at 8 AM, is held each February and goes through the San Dieguito County Park and surrounding community. There are hills so it can be a challenge. If you're not up to running, then do like plenty of other Insiders and walk it for a workout. Spectators can cheer for free. Call for entrance fees.

Annual Folk Fair

Balboa Park Club Building, Balboa Park, San Diego • (619) 479-8015

The fair is free; however, you'll want to bring some money since the ethnic clothes and pottery, especially the coffee mugs, are treats for any shopper. And there's plenty of food — from traditional American to exotic ethnic fare. The weekend event features more than 1,700 folk dances from all over the world. Some groups invite festival-goers to join in the dancing.

Jamboree by the Sea

Del Mar Fairgrounds, 2260 Jimmy Durante Blvd., Del Mar • (858) 489-5514

There's so much fun to squeeze in that this event lasts for three days. You'll marvel at the skill, the precision and the energy of the dancers. Come and watch them square, clog and round dance — it might encourage you to join the fun. This is an enjoyable family event and there's no charge for visitors.

Buick Invitational of California

Torrey Pines Municipal Golf Course, 11480 N. Torrey Pines Rd., San Diego • (619) 281-4653

San Diego's Torrey Pines Municipal Golf Course shines during this all-star golf competition. The best of the best play at this PGA event, which attracts more than 100,000 spectators. Weekday ticket prices range from $12 to $15. On the weekend prices are $15 for advance purchase and $20 at the gate. Call to verify ticket prices and availability, and plan to walk a ways from the parking locations. For more information about this event, check out the entries in our Spectator Sports and Golf chapters.

Cupid's Carnival

Spreckles Park, Seventh and C Sts., Coronado • (619) 522-7342

If it's romance you're looking for, head elsewhere. This is a high-intensity, giggling children's carnival that never goes out of style. It's Valentine fun for the family in this kidstuff event held annually on Coronado. There's a kissing booth, play area, games of chance (for a quarter a try) and an ice-cream sundae making event. The carnival is free.

San Diego International Auto Show

San Diego Convention Center, 111 West Harbor Dr., San Diego • (800) 345-1487

More than 32 domestic and foreign manufacturers roll out their newest and fastest and sleekest vehicles. You'll see auto design exhibits, cars of the future and past and exotic street machines too. Other attractions include the San Diego football team cheerleaders, the Charger Girls, and test-drives by NASCAR drivers. This is a weeklong event, with varying opening times and longer hours on Saturday. Admission is $8 for those 14 and older; children 13 and younger enter for $6, but on Sunday they get in free when they're with an adult; there are discounts for seniors and the military. Check newspapers, car dealers, chain supermarkets and local restaurants for discount coupons for adult admissions to this event.

Photo: Thom Vollenweider

With miles of immaculate beaches, San Diego's construction
isn't limited to bricks and mortar.

Four-Mile Couples Race
**San Diego Track Club, 6950 Genesee
Ave., San Diego • (800) 450-7382**

One of the many SDTC-sponsored events held in San Diego, this 4-mile run is fun for people of all fitness levels. You must have a partner. Since you'll be assigned a partner if you arrive solo, this may be a good place to let Cupid hit his mark. The run goes through Rose Canyon. Starting time is usually 8 AM. Call the SDTC for details on entry fees and starting times.

Mardi Gras in the Gaslamp
**Gaslamp Quarter, San Diego
• (619) 233-5227**

The Gaslamp Quarter hosts this parade and festival, which features music, food, and entertainment that might make you feel like you were in New Orleans. The parade, which starts at Fifth Avenue and K Street, begins in the late afternoon; however, the fun doesn't stop until the wee hours. The parade is free. Call the Gaslamp Quarter Association for details on the venues.

Daffodil Days Fine Art Shows
**Julian Town Hall, Main and Washington Sts.,
Julian • (760) 765-1857**

Although you may see some daffodils, this is an art show all the way. The show features the award-winning work of more than 50 fine artists whose paintings depict the beginning of this mountain community. Admission is free and if you think one of the paintings just must come home with you, you'll be in luck since much of the work is available for purchase. While you're here, be sure to

---

INSIDERS' TIP

Flower shows are held monthly at Balboa Park's Casa del Prado. Call (619) 583-9551 for information; there is no admission fee. One Insider's favorite show is the spectacular Mother's Day event featuring epiphyllums. (What's an epiphyllum? Look it up — it's worth knowing about).

eat some of Julian's famous apple pie. It will probably be for sale at the event, but if it's not (or it's all sold out), you can find it proudly offered at any local restaurant.

Silver Bay Kennel Club Dog Show
Del Mar Fairgrounds, 2260 Jimmy Durante Blvd., Del Mar • (858) 558-0507

This is a premier dog event that usually takes place the last weekend in February, although you'll want to call to confirm the dates. The Silver Bay show attracts more than 2,500 canine contenders vying for Best in Show (that's what the top dog is called). Judging begins about 8:30 AM on Saturday and continues through Sunday as dogs in various categories compete for titles and trophies. At any given time, there may be as many as 20 different competitions going on in the three huge indoor facilities. If you're a dog lover, this is the place to find everything you need for your pooch, from doggie hats to the latest in dog foods and canine treats. Be sure to catch the herding demos and dog obedience competitions as that's where training shines. The show is a family affair, and admission is free. So if you're wondering what's just the right breed for you and the kids, you can research your question nose-close to these beautiful dogs.

Vietnamese Tet Festival
2160 Ulric St., San Diego • (619) 277-6147

This festival will delight you with children's ethnic-costume contests, savory and satisfying foods, and dancing. There are traditional games, martial-arts demos, crafts and folk music. It's a multi-day festival. Call the number above for dates, admission and times.

March

Arbor Day at the San Diego Wild Animal Park
San Diego Wild Animal Park, 15500 San Pasqual Valley Rd., Escondido • (760) 738-4100

If you're younger than 11 and have an adult along, you get a free pass to the grounds on Arbor Day. Yes, there's a catch: You're invited to plant a tree. For all the fun you can expect at the Wild Animal Park, please take a look at the Attractions chapter. Adult admission is about $19.

Country Folk Art Show and Sale
Del Mar Fairgrounds, 2260 Jimmy Durante Blvd., Del Mar • (810) 634-4151

Do you love country folk art and crafts? Can't get enough of all things Americana? Then you'll go bonkers at this event that focuses on everything that's lovely about country. The admission fee varies for the three-day show and sale (check the local newspapers for discount coupons).

The operative word here is 'sale' because there will be something you'll just have to buy — a wrought-iron trivet, a book on Depression-era glass, or maybe (thinking ahead to Christmas) that dried-flower wreath that would look great in your Aunt Mabel's dining room.   Or buy a snack of homemade fudge or gourmet jerky and just browse. If you're an "I can make this" crafter, take a pencil and paper to gather ideas, because you'll see plenty of outstanding ones. Insiders recommend walking the entire nearly-2,000-booth exhibit hall before buying, unless you fall in love with a must-have work of country art. The event is held in the fairground's Bing Crosby Hall.

Marine Gear Swap Meet
The Marina at Chula Vista, 550 Marina Parkway, Chula Vista • (619) 691-1860

Calling the oars and crafts crowd: This is the boat and watersport-related swap meet of which dreams are made. What can you expect? A humongous parking lot heaped with good, used items. Here you'll find generators, compasses, scuba stuff, captain's hats and other stuff a boater can't live without. There are plenty of interesting objects for boating-gear collectors too. It's billed as a great day for the seafarer. Admission is free, but if you have stuff to sell, you'll need to call for pricing to rent a space.

Ocean Beach Kite Festival
4741 Santa Monica Ave., San Diego • (619) 224-0189

This is a build-it-yourself festival filled with the magic known as kites. There are prizes, a parade, food booths and demonstrations, and of course the kite-flying competition, held on the nearby beach. Come fly your own; walk it along in the parade. Or just come for the sight of them: triple-deckers, Japanese kites, fish-shaped kites and all manner of imaginative homemade flyers. This is great family fun and it's free for everyone.

Saint Patrick's Day Parade
Sixth Ave., San Diego • (619) 299-7812

If you've seen *Riverdance* and loved the high-stepping Celtic dancers, you'll have a treat here watching experts and novices kick up their heels. The parade also features marching bands (including ones carrying bagpipes) and civic volunteers from Rotary members to dogs for the blind (and the people who train them).

After the event there's an Irish festival. It's held in Balboa Park and you needn't be Irish to have a great time. There's plenty of food and that traditional St. Pat's day brew. Try one of the Irish varieties. Or if you're a hearty soul, you can sip a beer that's been "greened" just for the special day. There are drinks for the kids too. This is fun for the whole family. The parade and festival are free; food prices vary.

Borrego Valley Fly-In
Borrego Valley Airport, Borrego Springs • (760) 767-7415

Are you nuts for anything with a motor or wings? How about rare planes and antique autos? Then don't miss this two-day event held in Borrego Springs. Admission is free (there's a fee if you plan to enter a plane or vehicle). Parachuting exhibitions are outstanding (read that heart stopping) and airplane rides will get your adrenaline going. It's a great adventure for kids of all ages.

MS Walk
8840 Complex Dr., Ste. 130, San Diego • (619) 974-8640

The walks are held in various locations in Carlsbad and San Diego, and proceeds go to the Multiple Sclerosis Society. They're a great family activity for a worthy cause. Last year's participants included babies in strollers, folks

in wheelchairs, and well-mannered family dogs (with leash, collars, poop bags mandatory). The 5K and 10K give you a chance to meet people, do some good, and even get a T-shirt — provided your collected pledges total at least $95. (Should you or your group raise $5,000, there's a Nordstrom gift certificate for $500 that comes your way – Yes, you still get the T-shirt.) If you're new in town and want to get involved, the Society is always looking for volunteers. On the day of the walk alone, scores are needed for registration, to look after the rest stops, hand out T-shirts and clean up, too. Call the MS society for locations, pledge levels, dates, times and sponsorship information.

Recreational Vehicle Show
Qualcomm Stadium, 9449 Friars Rd. at Mission Village Dr., San Diego • (619) 296-1666

You'll want to hit the road after seeing the choices at the Recreational Vehicle Show. Last year there were over 1000 different motor homes, from the top-of-the-line to the more modest. All are available for your inspection. Need more reasons to go? How about great travel gear and accessories for the serious motor home owner and free admission?

April

Festival of Animation
La Jolla Museum of Contemporary Art, 700 Prospect St., La Jolla • (858) 459-8707

This film festival will tickle your funny bone and give you a new appreciation for the art of animated film production. The series, different each year, showcases prize-winning short films from around the world. Before the films were famous, we saw the now internationally acclaimed Wallace and Gromit films right here, and still feel like we "discovered" them. You might get to view a soon-to-be-classic too. Most of the festival's films have a PG rating; the R-rated ones screen late. Call ahead for the schedule, and if you're concerned about the ratings, ask about the content of the program. Tickets are $7; the program runs for 10 days. For more information on this event, see our Arts chapter.

Schooner Cup Regatta
Harbor Island and Shelter Island, San Diego Bay • (619) 233-3138

The largest schooner race on the West Coast and the largest charity regatta in America, it's the weekend of weekends for anyone who loves the spray of the sea. The race, held during the beginning of the month, raises funds for the Navy/Marine Corps Relief Society (providing help for military personnel and military dependents in time of personal need). After the race, there's a party that rocks the Voyager Room of the Kona Kai Continental Resort. The course begins at Reubens on Harbor Island, turns around at Point Loma and at the San Diego Bay. Watching the event is free, call for information if you want to participate in the event.

Surfing Contests
Varying locations, San Diego Beaches • (619) 223-7017

The South Coast Surf Shop, in San Diego, knows where and when you'll find these monthly competitions. You can also check with the local parks and recreation office or watch for notices in the newspapers. If "surf's up" is important news to you or you simply want to admire the skill and daring of surfers, then call for more info. Watching the event is free.

Flower Fields of Carlsbad
Palomar Airport Rd. and I-5, Carlsbad • (760) 431-0352

Insiders say that this event is not to be missed and with a six-week time slot (Mother Nature's in charge of the actual dates), you should be able to make this event and admire the awesome flower fields. The ranunculus, in shades too startling to describe, is the star in this explosion of colors. Months before the blooming season, growers stagger their plantings so that the flowering cycle stretches for a six- to eight-week period. And those flowers stretch for acres. You can catch a glimpse of the fields driving north on I-5 or by visiting the stores at the Carlsbad Company Stores (see our Shopping chapter). But we recommend, no, urge you to stop and pay the small entrance fee ($2 last year) to walk the fields. Camera buffs will want to pack extra film, and gardeners will want to visit the garden store for bulbs and bouquets. Picking flowers is strictly prohibited, as these are commercial fields. This is a perfect activity for the family.

Easter Egg Hunts
Carlsbad • (760) 434-2838
Coronado • (619) 522-7342
Fallbrook • (760) 728-5845
Oceanside • (760) 966-4530
Poway • (858) 679-4343
Santee • (619) 258-4100
Vista • (760) 758-7570

The hunts are scheduled in many communities throughout the county. There may be games and hat-making contests too. They are usually open and free for all egg and candy hunters younger than 10. Check with your local parks and recreations departments for details, times and dates.

Gaslamp Quarter Easter Hat Parade
Fifth Ave. and L Sts., Gaslamp Quarter, San Diego • (619) 233-5227

Come and stroll the Gaslamp in your Easter bonnet for this annual event that's

---

INSIDERS' TIP

Are you going to the Carlsbad Village Spring Faire? Parking is sometimes difficult. Why hassle when you can park at the city hall? It's at the corner of Carlsbad Village Drive and Pio Pico Avenue. (From I-5, take the Carlsbad Village Drive exit and go east. You'll see city hall and the parking lot at the first signal.) Parking is free. You can then walk the few blocks west (toward the ocean) to the fair.

family fun. There are hat-making activities for children from 9 AM to 10:30 AM. The parade starts at 11 AM and runs from Fifth Avenue and L Street and continues along Fifth to the Horton Grand Hotel. There's an Easter egg hunt and treats for children. The event is free.

Avocado Festival
Main St., Fallbrook • (760) 728-5845

Do you make a guacamole that has friends begging for the recipe? Would you like to taste avocado ice cream? Have you ever wondered if your child could be the next Little Miss or Mr. Avocado? Then don't miss this family-oriented outdoor street fair in downtown Fallbrook, which features recipe contests, booths selling arts and crafts, music, and lots of food — everything from ribs and potato salad (with chunks of avocado in it, of course) to burgers smothered in avocado and yes, even avocado ice cream. (Some say it's a tasty treat. We've never gotten up the gumption to try it.) Of course, there's plenty of guacamole too.

Are you aware that San Diegans eat more of it than any other county in the country? Be sure to check out the guacamole recipe in this chapter's Close-up. The event is usually held on a Sunday in mid-April, but call for dates. With no admission it's high time you attended this event.

Rose Society Annual Show
Balboa Park Club, Balboa Park • (619) 235-0004

Does a Double Delight or Queen Elizabeth rose that's blooming in your garden have what it takes to be Queen of the Day? Call for entry info, times, and rules. Spectators can watch as roses are judged by category, form and even fragrance. Before or after the show, be sure to walk around the rose garden, which

will be at peak bloom. Call for directions to the location at the park. Admission is free.

Lakeside Western Days and Rodeo
Calif. Hwy. 67 N. and Maple View, Lakeside • (858) 292-0092

Whoa baby, this much-anticipated event is locally known as the granddaddy of western fun. Visit it and you'll know why. The two-day celebration includes performances by nationally known western music groups and lesser-known ones too, and by school bands. There's a parade, booths, crafts, clothes, and food. According to Insiders who don boots and cowboy hats, this is the county western event of Southern California. General admission is $8; reserved seating is $11; kids younger than 12 are admitted free of charge.

Spring Garage Sales
Carlsbad • (760) 931-8400
Fallbrook • (760) 723-8838

If it's true that one person's trash is another's treasure, you could strike it rich with all the community-sponsored garage sales in San Diego County. Insider favorites include those in Carlsbad and Fallbrook. There is no admission fee for browsers; there is a charge for sellers who must reserve a spot. Come early for the best bargains.

Julian All-Photography Shows
Julian Town Hall, Main and Washington Sts., Julian • (619) 226-6964

This community-sponsored event showcases the work of Julian-area photographers. Here you'll find art photography, experimental photography (of the "what-is-that?" variety), and landscape photography. If you're a photo nut, this makes a nice outing. Many of the photographs are for sale, and the photographers are often on hand to discuss technique with you and perhaps be hired to take a photo. Call for details about admission and senior discounts. The weekend show, which is held late in April, runs from 1 PM to 6 PM. While you're there ask for a schedule of activities and events in Julian.

Wings over Gillespie
Gillespie Field, El Cajon
• **(888) 215-7000**

This aviation festival features more than 50 World War II planes and other vintage aircraft. You'll meet aviation celebrities, see aviation memorabilia and get close to antique cars, which are also featured at the event. It's family fun and educational too. Admission is $5.

May

Vista Garden Club Show/Plant Sale
1200 Vale Terrace Dr., Vista • (760) 724-3362

One Insider thinks this plant sale is the best-kept secret in North County — until now. Normally held near the beginning of May, the plant sale and flower show run from 1:30 PM to 5 PM on Saturday and from 10 AM to 5 PM on Sunday. Along with houseplants, you may be tempted with bonsai trees, cactus plants (which may be in bloom) and potted rose bushes. There are plants at prices for every gardener and the staff is helpful so bring your landscaping questions along. There's no charge for admission to the event.

Carlsbad Spring Faire
Grand and State Sts., Carlsbad
• **(760) 931-8400**

This event is billed as the biggest and best arts and crafts faire in Southern California (some say the world). The faire satisfies your expectations with arts, crafts, T-shirts, collectibles, antiques, books, tools, and gourmet foods. Then it takes you a step further with its size. Last year nearly 20,000 attended this first-Sunday-in-May event (there's another one on the first Sunday in November). The entire village area of Carlsbad is closed to traffic and crowds mingle through the displays. There is no admission fee. Parking can be tricky, so

be prepared to walk to the faire. There are free shuttles from Plaza Camino Real shopping center and the Carlsbad City Library.

Cinco de Mayo
Various locations throughout the county including:
Old Town State Historical Park, San Diego •
(619) 291-4903
Grape Day Park, Escondido
• **(760) 432-2893**
The Embarcadero, 849 West Harbor Dr., San Diego • (619) 235-4013
Christmas Circle, Borrego Springs
• **(760) 767-5555**

Our heritage shines during this May celebration and just about everyone turns out. Some cities celebrate on the closest weekend to May 5, so don't be thrown if the event doesn't coincide with your calendar. Look for Latin dancing for kids and adults, Mexican foods and activities for the family. Some festivals feature arts and crafts. Old Town's includes folkloric ballet and mariachi bands. Remember if you're coming from North County the commuter train called the Coaster doesn't run on Sunday. Admission is free.

International Gem and Jewelry Show
Del Mar Fairgrounds, 2260 Jimmy Durante Blvd., Del Mar
• **(858) 294-1640**

The local San Diego Gem and Jewelry Association sponsors this sparkling three-day event. Gems and jewelry are sold here at a variety of prices. So you can come just to look and learn or you might want to buy something too. Kids love the geodes, the lumps of golden-colored amber and the highly polished quartz that feels so smooth to the touch. They often come home with a handful of stones from the 10 cents-a-stone bins. Adults go for the uniquely designed bolos, necklaces, and rings studded with turquoise, jade, garnets and collectable stones.

Kids love the show, and since there's no admission cost, it's a fine family outing. Call for dates and times since they vary.

Annual Rummage Sale
Avenida de Acacias, Rancho Santa Fe
• (858) 756-4101

Sponsored by the Rancho Santa Fe Garden Club, this isn't your parent's idea of a rummage sale, but of course, you'd expect more from one of the county's premier communities. If you're a true bargain hunter you'll be in buyer's heaven. As with any rummage sale, early birds get the best selection. The two-day sale, held the first Friday and Saturday in May, begins at 9 AM and continues through the day. Proceeds are earmarked for charities, scholarships, and upkeep of the walking and hiking trails in Rancho Santa Fe. Admission is free.

Humphrey's Concerts by the Bay
2241 Shelter Island Dr., Shelter Island, San Diego • (619) 224-3411

Call or check local entertainment sections of the newspaper for a current list of concerts. Tickets sell out early so it pays to plan ahead. The concerts are outdoors, wonderful (read that romantic) on a balmy evening. They run through the summer. You'll see big name performers like the Beach Boys and lesser-known local celebrities too. The 1999 season includes performances by Dana Carvey ($33), the Righteous Brothers ($45), Eric Burdon and the New Animals ($34), and the Manhattan Transfer ($35). Ticket prices vary. Call for the times and prices of upcoming events. (See our Nightlife chapter for further information.)

Roar and Snore Camp Over
San Diego Wild Animal Park, 15500 San Pasqual Valley Rd., Escondido
• (760) 738-5049

Not only will you talk with the animals, but you'll get to sleep up close to them with this special series offered by the Wild Animal Park. Costs range from about $90 for adults to about $60 for kids 8 and older. There are hikes, instructional programs, campfires and al fresco dining (including a vegetarian choice). Bring a sleeping bag for the tent accommodations. This is a not-to-be-missed San Diego experience for all animal lovers. The camp happens on Friday, Saturday and Sunday summer evenings only; call for reservations and an equipment list.

June

Alpine Viejas Days
Alpine Town Center, Alpine
• (619) 445-2722

This annual event makes you feel like you've been transported back to the Old West. There are two days of action-packed activities from mock gunfights to Western dancing. Don't miss the barbecues. The Sunday parade down Main Street draws out the town. There is no admission fee.

Greek Festival
3655 Park Blvd., San Diego
• (619) 297-4165

Are you hungry for gyros and moussaka? Are you amazed by the skill and precision of traditional Greek dancers? This annual event, sponsored by Spyridon Greek Orthodox Church, gives you plenty to celebrate even if you can't claim Greek heritage. Be sure to check out the Greek imports and crafts. It's free to attend this event, which takes place at St. Spyridon Church.

San Diego County Fair
Del Mar Fairgrounds, 2200 Jimmy Durante Blvd., Del Mar • (858) 792-4252, (858) 793-5555 (24-hour event hotline)

This may be the biggest county fair you've ever attended, but don't let the scope and size put you off — there's old-fashioned fun to be had. The three-week event draws top country and rock 'n' roll musical performers, but hometown talent is also a big draw. There are baking contests, hobby displays (you've got to see the lint collection!), woodworking prizes, weirdest vegetable competitions, kids events and even wine and microbeer competitions.

What is the most popular event with the crowds? With the 10 and younger set it's the midway rides and the animal displays, which change every other day (4H is active in San Diego). Teens enjoy the vendors, the carny games and competitive events sponsored by schools and clubs.

Photo: CeCe Canton

The Carlsbad flower field "blooming" is an annual affair that attracts visitors.

The 20-and-older group appreciate all of the above along with displays, landscape exhibits, flower shows (you've got to see the roses), and food. The cinnamon buns are huge (and scrumptious) and the roasted corn on the cob is a bit of heaven. Food is pricey; pack a lunch or eat before you go and then buy treats. Free shuttles are available from various locations in the county. Single admission is $8. A "family pack," which consists of two adult admissions, two children's admissions, 20 ride coupons and four medium soft drink coupons, can be purchased for $24.95 at supermarkets and other retail outlets (but not at the fair). Here's an Insider tip: Watch the newspaper for a schedule of concerts and events.

The Jewish Community Center Festival of New Jewish Plays Lawrence Family Jewish Community Centers
Mantel Weirs Eastgate City Park, 4126 Executive Dr., La Jolla • (858) 457-3030

A distinguished series of staged readings of new plays that explore the Jewish experience, this program is now in its 12th year. The festival offers a dynamite array of drama, comedy and music with discussions following each performance so that participants can become part of the creative energies. Prices range from $100 for four performances to $12 for single performances, depending on the featured actors and on seating.

Mainly Mozart Festival
Various locations in San Diego and Mexico • (619) 233-4281

You've just gotta' love Wolfgang or forget going to this outstanding series of chamber music and piano concerts. The musical performances are sublime, to say the least, and are held in various locations throughout San Diego and Mexico. The concerts, which run for ten days, begin at 8 PM. Ticket prices vary so call for dates and availability as the festival books up fast. (To read more about Mainly Mozart, see the Arts chapter.)

Pala Mission Fiesta
Pala Mission Rd., U.S. Hwy. 76, Pala • (760) 742-1471

Help celebrate our Native American heritage with this little-known festival of Corpus Christi. The fiesta is held on the grounds of

Photo: Thom Vollenweider

Rodeo time means barrel racing and this rider is going for it!

Mission San Antonio de Pala and it includes dancing, food (a pit barbecue and Indian fry bread are not to be missed) and wonderful music. The fiesta is an outstanding, wholesome experience especially for the fourth grader in the family who studies California's rich heritage.

Portuguese Festa
2818 Addison St., San Diego
• **(619) 223-5880**

The reds and greens of the flag, the huge scarlet swirling skirts of the traditional dancers and the chords of the fado (a traditional Portuguese song) are what will stick in your memory. That and the aroma and taste of the foods you can try here. You'll not find hot dogs and burgers — and that'll suit you well. You might want to start with *caldo verde* (a green cabbage and spicy sausage soup) then move on to a hearty fish stew; be sure to save room for rice pudding with Port, *doces de ovos* (egg sweets) or *cauacos* (a hard, sweet biscuit). Billed as one of San Diego's longest running ethnic events, there's a parade, crown-

ing of the Festa Queen, dancing, music, and Portuguese foods that tempt any appetite. Admission is free; the event is usually held in the middle of June, but do call for the exact date.

Chili Cook-Off in San Marcos
2200 Sycamore Dr., San Marcos
• **(760) 744-1270**

This event is hot stuff and draws over 10,000 people to the Walnut Grove Community Park in the North County Inland community. It's a family event which includes entertainment — like those square dancers burning off calories before the chili is ready — and demonstrations, too. You might see folks making chili wreaths or designing ceramics with southwestern motifs. The food booths here sell everything from chili-flavored beef jerky to chili-flavored candy (a taste that has to be acquired, we believe). It's all hot fun, nonetheless. Bring your wallet, because you can buy one of those chili pepper wreaths, and chili pepper plants, and other chili pepper concoctions. Of course, you've got to be there for the chili competition, which is serious business. The cook-off runs from 10 AM to 6 PM. Admission is free.

Dr. Seuss Run/Walk for Literacy
Balboa Park and Seaport Village
• (858) 792-2900

With benefits going to the San Diego Council on Literacy even the Cat in the Hat would join this event. The 8K run is in Balboa Park; the 1-mile Fun Run is held at Seaport Village. There is a fee to run/walk the race. Spectators see it all for free.

July

Fourth of July Fireworks
Various locations
Marina View Park, Chula Vista
• (619) 691-5140
Old Town, San Diego
• (619) 220-5423
Coronado Beach, Coronado
• (619) 437-8788
Oceanside
• (760) 966-4530

Call for times and the best locations to see the spectacular displays. Some communities have 4th of July city picnics, others celebrate with water sport contests, such as surfing contests, along the beach. Check with your local parks and recreation department for what is happening on our nation's birthday.

Alpine Arts and Crafts Summer Fair
Tavern Rd. and Alpine Blvd., Alpine
• (858) 569-7615

There's always something going on in Alpine and this arts and crafts summer fair is worth a trip to the mountain community. There are wonderful homemade and handmade items from coffee mugs to cookies. You'll find food booths, craft demonstrations and music. It's all wrapped up in the

mountain village theme. Insiders say that the handcrafted tiles that can be used for trivets or coasters are worth the drive. Admission is free.

Del Mar Thoroughbred Horse Racing
Del Mar Fairgrounds, 2260 Jimmy Durante Blvd., Del Mar • (858) 755-1141

The mid-July through mid-September season is anticipated by locals and visitors alike, because these races bring the country's most illustrious horses and jockeys to San Diego. The venue is billed as the place where the "turf meets the surf", and from the grandstand you'll know why: The Pacific is the track's neighbor. The view is spectacular — it's often so clear you'll think you're seeing all the way to Hawaii. (Actually, what you're probably seeing is San Clemente Island.) Down on the track you'll be seeing the likes of the famous racehorse Cigar running his heart out.

This is the track Bob Hope, Bing Crosby and other celebrities used to flock to in the 40s. Today, you'll see the elite movers and fashionable shakers of San Diego. (Lots of Insiders go to the track to people watch as well as watch the ponies.) There's on-track wagering, and with a bet as low as $2 you can experience the thrill of the race. The events start at 2 PM. General admission is $3. See our Spectator Sports chapter for more information on the races.

Over-the-Line World Championships
Fiesta Island, Mission Bay, San Diego
• (619) 688-0817

The big networks wanted to put this annual event on television so that all of America could watch the fun. The hitch? The competitors would have to clean up one of their traditions: X-rated team names. "No way," said the Old Mission Beach Athletic Club which sponsors the beach soft-

Thoroughbred horse racing brings plenty of fast-paced excitement to the Del Mar Fairgrounds.

ball fest. Therefore, the adult-oriented event can only be seen in person. But you'll hear a lot about it at local nightspots, on radio and in the press. Admission is free. To read more about the Over-the-Line competition, see the entry in our Spectator Sports chapter.

Scottish Highland Games
Rancho Santa Fe Park at La Costa Meadows Dr., San Marcos
• **(619) 645-8080**

Do you love the music and energy of *Riverdance*? Do you adore the sound of bagpipe music? Do you think that shortbread should be one of the four food groups? Do you have a Scottish ancestor or two on your family tree? If you've answered "yes" to any of the questions above, then this event is for you. There are bagpipers and Celtic music, highland dancers and sporting competitions. There are imports and crafts from Scotland. And Scottish food too — don't miss the haggis (there's even vegetarian haggis for the non-meat eaters). An additional highlight is the sheep dog competition where the dogs follow a set of whistle commands as they herd flocks of sheep. Saturday features the Highland Dance Competition. Admission to this two-day event is $9 for one day, $15 for two days; children pay $7 for one day, $12 for two. The Games are usually the second weekend in July.

INSIDERS' TIP

Heading to the Del Mar Fairgrounds for the county fair? Traffic jams can be unpleasant, but there are alternatives. You can take the Coaster or one of the free shuttles. Watch the schedules, which can be found in the local newspapers. Some days kids and seniors need not pay admission fees.

U.S. Open Sand Castle Competition
911 Grove Ave., Imperial Beach (for info and full rules)
Imperial Beach Pier, Imperial Beach
• (619) 424-6663

This competition makes any sand architect marvel. The two-day event includes a parade at 10 AM on Saturday. The kids' competition starts at 2 PM with all children winning prizes (last year more than 300 kids joined the fun). Sunday is the day for serious competition; pre-entry for the competition is required. There are two classes: professional team (entry fee is $50) and amateur team (entry fee is $35). Sure it's sandy fun, yet consider that prize money is awarded for the sand structures, with $5,000 to the best in the professional competition. About 300,000 visit the free spectator event so parking can be at a premium. With fireworks beginning at dusk, it's a wonderful weekend at the beach that will truly spark your imagination.

August

Obon Summer Festival
Vista Buddhist Temple, 150 Cedar Rd., Vista • (760) 941-8800

This classical Japanese festival features the dances (odori) and displays of taiko (the incredible Japanese drums) along with ethnic foods and crafts. The festival is usually held in the middle of August and begins about noon on Saturday and Sunday and continues to 8 PM. The admission to this perfect cultural and family outing is free.

Toshiba Tennis Classic
Costa del Mar Rd. and El Camino Real, Carlsbad • (760) 438-5683

San Diego's premier women's professional tennis event comes to North County. Past lineups have included superstars Venus Williams, Martina Hingis, Monica Seles and Steffi

Graff. The nine-day event draws in excess of 70,000 spectators, including celebrities, movie stars and notable Insiders. Tickets range from $14 to $30 for individual days, with packages going for between $35 to $350. There is a charge for parking. See our Spectator Sports chapter for more information on this event.

Ringling Brothers and Barnum and Bailey Circus
San Diego Sports Arena, 3500 Sports Arena Blvd., San Diego
• (619) 224-4171

The Big Top doesn't get any better than this and draws kids of all ages. Be sure to see the Parade of the Animals, in which animals and performers walk down the city's streets from the Old Town Station (you can get there by taking the trolley or the Coaster) to the Sports Arena — a short walk but a thrilling spectacle. The parade is held the day before the circus begins. Seat prices at the circus are about $8.

Marine Corps Air Station Miramar Air Show
Miramar Marine Base, San Diego
• (858) 537-6365

This is an aviation expo that excites the entire family (parking and admission are free). There are displays and performances that will snatch away your breath, including flights by the Blue Angels. There's a twilight show on Saturday. Special seating in the grandstand and box seat area can be reserved by calling (619) 220-8497. The event takes place near the end of August.

Annual Julian Weed Show and Art Mart
Julian Town Hall, Main St., Julian
• (760) 765-1857

A weed is a weed is a weed when it's in your garden, but in this show a weed might be a work of art. Come see how the pesky plants can be arranged to delight the senses. Yes, arranged as one would a bouquet. The two-week event, held from 10 AM to 4 PM daily, includes a show of San Diego artists, so in addition to admiring weeds, you can also feast your eyes on paintings and sculpture, and ceramics and weaving and photography. Of course, you can always buy a slice of Julian's famous pie at this and all events that take place in Julian.

Admission is free.

A Taste of Summer Nights
Third Ave. between E and G Sts., Chula Vista • (619) 422-1982

Here's an opportunity to samples some of the excellent restaurants in Chula Vista, in one spot and on one evening. You might have barbecue from Love's or German food from House of Munich. Have a yen for Japanese food? In year pasts, that craving has been satisfied by Koto's. More than 15 restaurants participate in the outdoor event; music goes along with the $10 admission fee.

September

San Diego Bayfairs
Various locations
Chula Vista • (619) 426-2882
Oceanside • (760) 722-1534
Mission Bay • (858) 268-1250

The three-week celebration of the bay includes activities in the harbor areas from Oceanside to Chula Vista. There's fun for everyone with food booths, boats to drool over, classic car shows, displays, entertainment and demonstrations. The Mission Bay fair includes hydroplane races. Check local newspapers for other locations; events are usually free.

Street Scene
Gaslamp Quarter, between 4th and 6th Aves., Broadway and the waterfront, San Diego • (619) 557-8490

Downtown San Diego's Gaslamp Quarter turns into the biggest street fest imaginable with this three-day production that includes the most diverse collection of music, food and

performances contained in California. We're talking FUN for grownups (with some activities for the younger crowd scheduled early in the day). The music is loud and plentiful. It runs the gamut from rap to rock, from cool jazz to hot classical. Over 85,000 attended last year. Tickets are in the $25 range. Take the Coaster, the commuter train, or Trolley to make parking a non-issue. Be sure to check the schedules before you buy a ticket as the Coaster's timetable has been known to change.

Dia de la Independencia
Old Town State Historical Park, Old Town, San Diego • (619) 291-4903

Old Town celebrates Mexican Independence Day, September 16. (Mexican Independence Day actually begins at 11 PM on September 15 and continues through the next day.) You'll be treated to lots of music, dancers performing traditional steps and even a salsa-tasting contest. The mariachi bands are incredible, so wear your dancing shoes. Other cities and neighborhoods also celebrate this festival; check with your local parks and recreation department. Admission is free. Call to see exactly on what day the celebration will take place.

Thunderboat Races
Mission Bay, San Diego • (858) 268-1250

This event is technically called San Diego's Bayfair World Series of Powerboat Racing on Mission Bay. Insiders call them the Thunderboat Races. The excitement happens during a three-day weekend, usually in the middle of the month. The viewing is best at Crown Point, Fiesta Island and Vacation Island. And yes, the boats are loud and fast. The event includes the Thunderboats (the world's fastest boats), Formula 1 boats, unlimited lights, and drag boats. There are food booths and vendors. Buy tickets ahead and save $10. Tickets go for about $40 for all four days (kids get a discount). Check on the shuttles to get to the races from offsite locations and parking will be easier. (For more details, see the entry in our Spectator Sports chapter.)

Rosarito-Ensenada 50-Mile Fun Bicycle Ride
Call for official starting location
• (619) 583-3001

The annual Fall Baja cycling event attracts more than 8,000 riders of all skill and age levels. Starting at 10 AM from Rosarito Beach the route runs south along the two-lane free (libre) road to the finish line. The end point is in Ensenada, Baja California where there's a fiesta. Entry is $19; the T-shirt is an extra $10.

Art Festival in the Village of La Jolla
Prospect and Girard Sts., La Jolla •
(888) 298-3378

The festival features a quality, juried art show combined with live entertainment, kidstuff, gourmet food to sample and high-quality crafts to tempt your pocket book. Admission is free; call or watch the newspaper for info on free shuttles. Parking during the festival can be a challenge and parking regulations are enforced.

October

American Society of Interior Designers, Designers Showcase
Locations change each year
• (858) 571-7007

Do you want to see how the other half decorates? Check out ideas for your abode? Buy a ticket for this important design event which allows you to visit one of the grander homes in the area with interior designs by the best and brightest in San Diego. Nearly 20,000 walk through the selected home during the annual event and marvel at how the ASID designers unleash their creativity. Call for this year's site. Proceeds from the annual event go to St. Vincent de Paul Village, a San Diego facility for those in need of clothing, housing, food, care and shelter. Tickets cost about $20.

Oktoberfests
Various locations

Come celebrate fall with German-related festivals that happen in many of San Diego's cities. Some charge for entrance, but at others it's the food that carries a price tag. Insiders say the best Oktoberfest is at the German-American Club in El Cajon (located at 1017 S. Mollison Street), (619) 442-6637.

Tour de North County Bike Ride
Rancho Buena Vista High School, 1601
Longhorn Dr., Vista • (858) 450-6510

Choose your bike tour from 5- to 70-mile rides through North County Inland. The longer rides include some challenging hills. The focus here, at least for most cyclists, is fun and not speed. The big deal of the event, according to Insiders who have ridden it, is the French feast that follows the ride. The feast includes fruits, salads, sandwiches, yogurt and French bread, and the meal is included in the registration fee of about $20. Pre-registration is recommended. Helmets are required. There are sag wagons along the routes. And there's a free cycle safety check-up for all entrants.

Western Regional Finals Championship Rodeo
Lakeside Rodeo Grounds, U.S. Hwy. 67 and Mapleview Ave., Lakeside • (858) 292-0092

The championship full-scale, seven-event rodeo features top riders from 11 western states. The events include calf roping, barrel racing, saddle bronc riding, bull riding, team roping, bareback riding and steer wrestling. There's also mighty fine western grub, foot-tapping music, and wholesome, cowpoke fun for the whole family. Dust off your boots and get to Lakeside for the Championship Rodeo. General admission is $8, reserved seating $11; kids younger than 12 are admitted free.

INSIDERS' TIP

All during the month of October, kids 11 and younger can visit the zoo for free. On Zoo Founders Day, October 5, everyone is admitted free.

Mum Festival at the Wild Animal Park
San Diego Wild Animal Park, 15500 San Pasqual Valley Rd., Escondido
• (760) 738-4100

Shades of gold, red and burnt umber collide in bursts of color from the fall chrysanthemums that crowd the park during this annual botanical celebration. It's billed as the largest mum festival in the West and once you see it, you'll agree. Admission is about $20 for adults and includes the tram ride through the park.

Halloween Festivals and Haunted Houses
Various locations throughout San Diego County
Market Street, Gaslamp Quarter, San Diego • (619) 231-3611
Encinitas Halloween Festival, Encinitas
• (760) 943-1940

Almost every community in San Diego celebrates Halloween with fun houses, haunted houses, activities such as pumpkin-carving contests, and pin-the-tail-on-the-pumpkin games. Most of the activities are free. Adult Insiders like the Gaslamp Quarter's The Frightmare on Market Street. Tickets are about $20 and there's a costume contest, gourmet food booths (and fun food too), and plenty of partying in the clubs and restaurants in the Quarter. Families prefer the Encinitas Halloween Festival. This one is free and there are crafts and food for sale and costume contests along with trick and treating for the small set. The Encinitas festival is held between 5 PM and 10 PM on the last day of October, on First Street in Encinitas. Call your local parks and recreation departments for what's happening in your neighborhood.

November

Fall Village Faire
State St. and Grand Ave., Carlsbad
• (760) 434-8887

Similar to the Carlsbad Spring Faire (see May for details), this faire has a holiday flavor. It features Christmas crafts, decorations and oodles of holiday gift-giving ideas. There's a

certified organic farmers' market that sells perfect produce. The market is normally found near the intersection of Grand Avenue and Carlsbad Boulevard. Some Insiders go late in the afternoon when the vendors may be interested in doing some dealing. Others swear it's best to be there right at 8 AM when it starts. There's no cost for admission. Other communities, including the Gaslamp District and University Heights hold fall fairs.

Chrysler Classic Speed Festival
North Island Naval Air Station, San Diego
• (619) 283-5808

This is a day for speed demons and those who love the excitement of classic car competitions. The races feature top racing cars from the past. Here you might see restored Model T's, cool muscle cars from the 60s like the Mustangs, and immaculate old Corvettes. Cars race on a 1.5 mile course and the races take place from 9 AM to 4 PM. Best yet, you can get up close and look beneath some of the hoods. Adult tickets are about $20.

Score Baja 1000
Ensenada to La Paz, Baja California
• (818) 583-8068

This is an annual off-road race for cars, trucks and motorcycles, and it is much anticipated in the dirt-racing community. According to Insiders, this isn't the famous Dakar off-road race; hey, but it's treacherous nonetheless. The race covers the roughest terrain on the Baja California Peninsula and if you've ever driven in the area or flown over it, you know it's desolate. There's an entry fee for racing folks; viewing is free. The race starts early in the morning in Ensenada and attracts thousands. At the end in the city of La Paz, there's a fiesta and rowdy party that some parents might consider to be R-rated.

San Diego Jewish Book Fair
Lawrence Family Jewish Community Centers
Mantel Weirs Eastgate City Park
4126 Executive Dr., La Jolla
• (858) 457-3030

The entire family will enjoy this extravaganza of Jewish literature and culture, which

Photo: Thom Vollenweider

The dynamic Convention Center hosts events throughout the year.

includes appearances by guest authors who give readings and discuss their books. Here you can buy books on Jewish literature. Guests at past fairs have included Chaim Potok, Chaim Herzog, Amos Oz, and Elliot Adams. General admission for all readings and events is $20; individual events range from $10 to $14. Call for reservations and current prices.

Mother Goose Parade
W. Main and Chambers Sts., El Cajon • (619) 444-8712

El Cajon's chamber of commerce sponsors this parade, which is usually held the last weekend in November. It begins at 12:30 PM on W. Main and Chambers Streets and continues east on Main to Second Street then north on Second to Madison. This is an old-fashioned childrens' affair with lots of local turnout. You'll see floats, clowns, bands, equestrians, civic leaders and charitable organizations represented. There's no admission fee, so bring your lawn chairs or blankets for sidewalk sitting, and some cash for the food, peanuts, toys, banners and candy.

Annual Festival of Lights
Bazaar del Mundo, Old Town, San Diego • (619) 296-3161

The Bazaar del Mundo kicks off the holidays with this annual celebration that happens the weekend after Thanksgiving. It's a holiday tradition for many Insiders who especially enjoy the performance of dances from around the world. The Nativity scene is lighted and remains on display through New Year's Day. It's free and many families make the annual visit to get into the holiday spirit.

Palomar College Book Sale
1140 W. Mission Rd., San Marcos • (760) 744-7822

One of North County Inland's largest book sales with tons (and we're serious about that weight) of new, used and well-loved books. There are collections and specialty books such as autographed copies and rare collector items. Bibliophiles can find great buys here, as everything is priced to move from the campus to your home. Insiders recommend getting there early

Avocados: A Mainstay of San Diego-Style Eating

Do you know that San Diegans eat more avocados than any other regional group in the United States? If you love the shiny, sometimes bumpy green and glorious avocado, you know why. They're good in and on about everything that Insiders serve.

In case your school didn't teach Avocado 101 here's a primer so you can increase your avocado IQ:

Avocados are native to Mexico. Hernando Cortez, the Spanish explorer and

adventurer, discovered them in Mexico City in 1519. Montezuma II, the Aztec emperor, treated the avocado like a treasure, and according to legend it was offered as a gift to the Spanish conquerors. Much later in 1848, a year before gold was found at Sutter's Mill, Henry Dalton planted avocado trees in Southern California. In 1911 Carl

Schmidt traveled to Mexico and brought back other avocado varieties.

Schmidt, like others who first began farming the avocado, had some setbacks. His first grove was hit hard by the frost of 1913, and only one variety survived. Schmidt called it the Fuerte, the Spanish word for vigorous and strong, and it is still known by that name today. About the same time Rudolph Hass discovered the Hass (it rhymes with "pass") avocado. The Hass and Fuerte, along with the Zutano, Bacon, Pinkerton and Reed varieties, are the most popular with today's avocado growers and eaters.

Avocados are persnickety and need some pretty fine conditions to produce. Luckily, in San Diego, we have what it takes. Here avocados prefer living near the coastal strip (not more than 50 miles from the ocean) that stretches from San Luis Obispo to the Mexican border. Depending on the variety, trees have been known to grow from 20 to 60 feet tall. Most mature trees bear from 200 to 300 of the fruits a year. Some large Mexican trees have produced over 3,000 in a season.

The Hass variety has a thick, pebbly skin that turns purplish-black when ripe. You'll find this one in the store nearly year-round. The smoother varieties, such as the Fuerte, do not change color when ripe. The "greenskins" are ripe when they yield to a gentle pressure and

Photo: California Avocado Commission

More avocados are eaten in the San Diego region than in any other part of the country.

are available from November to April. And yes, each variety has a special flavor.

Even today in our high-tech society, avocados need to be harvested by hand using avocado shears called clippers. The fruits move from the picking stage to the packing stage and cold storage within hours. They'll hang out in cold storage either at the packinghouse or in trucks until they reach your supermarket.

Because avocados seem creamy, exotic, tempting and are often more expensive than other produce they're sometimes considered a luxury. Living in San Diego, however, we're treated to the best of the crop and often at incredibly low prices, especially when we get them at farmers' markets.

Along with the thought that avocados are just for special occasions, they've been given a bum rap in the nutritional department. Get it straight: They have no cholesterol; they're low in sodium and saturated fat and loaded with fiber and nutrients, such as vitamins B6, C, E, folate and potassium. It's the cheese, sour cream and other ingredients that many add to the fruit that make avocados dangerous for dieters. Avocado can be used as a healthy substitute for toppings such as butter, cream cheese and cheese, and in dips and spreads. Doing so you can get that creamy, green goodness taste with none of the cholesterol.

Photo: Califronia Avacado Commission

Okay, you're convinced—now you agree with Montezuma and most of the people who live in our county. Avocados are worth their weight in gold and are far more attainable. But what do you do when you bring avocados home and they're so hard you could break a window with them? It's simple. To ripen the fruit, place it in a fruit bowl at room temperature for a week. Or as Insiders suggest, place the fruit in a paper bag with an

Insiders eat avocados in soups, spreads, guacamole, on sandwiches, on bagels and straight from the shell.

apple to speed the process. Either way, check the ripening process every few days.

To prepare avocados, cut lengthwise around the large seed and rotate the halves to separate. Remove the seed by sliding the tip of a spoon gently beneath it and lifting it out. To peel, place the cut side down and remove the skin with a knife or your fingers.

Eat the fruit when ripe or store it in the refrigerator. After opening, sprinkle lemon juice on it to avoid browning and refrigerate it in an airtight container for 2 to 3 days.

Fallbrook's Avocado Days
First-Place Guacamole Dip

Competition was keen in a recent Fallbrook's Avocado Days Guacamole contest. Here's the first-place winning recipe entered by Bruce Taylor.

4 ripe Hass avocados
4 green onions, chopped
1 tablespoon finely chopped cilantro (Chinese parsley)
2 tablespoons lime juice
Salt to taste

Peel and blend avocado until it is as chunky or smooth as you prefer. Blend in other ingredients. Eat immediately or cover and refrigerate for up to four hours. It tastes best when made with San Diego-grown avocados.

Photo: Dale Frost/Port of San Diego

Sailing events are popular off the San Diego coastline.

and bringing a canvas tote bag to carry home your loot. The best books go first. The event is free and is typically scheduled for the last weekend of November. Call for the schedule or watch the event calendars in the local newspapers.

December

Old Town Holiday in the Park and Candlelight Tours
Old Town State Historical Park, San Diego • (619) 220-5422

Walk through the historic districts of San Diego, view the holiday period decorations, and listen to stories about the early days of Old Town. The candlelight tours, offered hourly from 6 PM to 9 PM during the holidays, begin at Old Town Historical Park. There's entertainment, caroling, and refreshments. Reservations are required. Donations are suggested. Old Town's shop owners decorate their stores and most are open late during the tours.

Parades of Lights
Various harbors

The parades feature boats of all shapes and sizes decorated for the holiday season. To get the best view of the Mission Bay Christmas Boat Parade, Insiders suggest watching it from Crown Point, on the east side of Vaca-

tion Island. For Oceanside's Boat Parade, anywhere in the harbor is perfect. For San Diego's, the best views are at Seaport Village. If you want to enter your boat, call or contact the local parks and recreation office or chamber of commerce. Remember to wear a jacket. It can be breezy and cool on December evenings. Most parades start about 7 PM; watching is free.

Holiday Parades and Celebrations
Various locations

Escondido's annual Christmas Parade begins at Escondido High School and runs along Broadway to Grape Day Park. Bring the family to see floats, cutest twin contests, local public servants riding the route and waving to the crowd, and plenty of horses and high school bands. This is an old-fashioned parade where families wave to the parade participants and neighbors meet and mingle. Ocean Beach has a parade and tree festival too. The parade there goes along Sunset Cliffs Boulevard to Newport Avenue and includes high school marching bands from around the county. At the end of Ocean Beach's parade, there is a holiday festival and community tree lighting. All are free events. For more information, contact the cities' chambers of commerce or park and recreation offices.

Great American Train Show

Del Mar Fairgrounds, 2260 Jimmy Durante Blvd., Del Mar • (630) 834-0652

This is a model railroad traveling show that comes to San Diego just once a year. It's a mandatory event for anyone who loves trains. You'll see train layouts on display, trains for sale, trains to operate, train gadgets and gizmos and train-related clothing. Adult admission is $5; kids 12 and younger are admitted free.

Wild Animal Park's Festival of Lights

San Diego Wild Animal Park, 15500 San Pasqual Valley Rd., Escondido • (760) 738-4100 x5140

Nairobi Village, the main shopping and eating area of the park, is even more appealing with sparkling holiday lights. The festival, which occurs the week before Christmas, features free children's activities from face painting to craft making to sliding and playing in Snow Hill. (The park has snow hauled in for the event.) There are carolers, programs and educational shows featuring live animals. Adult admission is about $19. Children 3 through 11 years of age pay $12.95; children younger than 2 are admitted free; Seniors (60 years and older) pay $17.95. There is a $3 parking fee.

Holiday Bowl

Qualcomm Stadium, 9449 Friars Rd., San Diego • (619) 283-5808

The Holiday Bowl, held in late December, features a football face-off between nationally ranked teams from the Big 12 and either the WAC or the Pac 10. Begun in 1978, the Holiday Bowl has earned a reputation for close games. This is a popular event in San Diego, so get your tickets early; they range in price from $29 to $50. (Read more about the Holiday Bowl in our Spectator Sports chapter.)

First Night Escondido

Downtown Escondido near the California Center for the Arts, Escondido • (760) 739-0101

This is an event that's G-rated for New Year's Eve so you can celebrate with the family. It's a no-alcohol event where you buy a button (that's your ticket) for $8 — less if you buy it before the event. The ticket allows you inside the roped-off performance areas and gives you access to all the fun. Last year Jeannie and Jimmy Cheatham (see the Close-up in the Nightlife chapter) and other top headliners were among the stars to perform. There's something for everyone from steel bands and chamber music to mariachi bands and acrobats. There's lots of food too — everything from pizza and hot dogs to foot-long sandwiches, ribs and chicken. Insiders always save room for the strawberry cheese cake and gourmet coffee. First Night begins at 6 PM and goes until the midnight fireworks. Proceeds from the admission support the arts community. Call your local parks and recreation department for other First Nights in the area.

Whale Watching

• (619) 557-5450, (619) 236-1212

The sand, the sun and the whales: What could be more San Diego? This event is free if you're on the beach or cliffs along the coast as the annual migration of California gray whales takes place. You may want to go out on a whale-watching boat (check the Attractions chapter). These gentle giants move through San Diego's waters to the warmer breeding grounds off the coast of Baja California. Insiders never tire of watching the event that continues through February. Some Insiders say that the best views are from the Cabrillo National Monument; others insist they're from the cliffs along Coast Highway from Carlsbad to Solana Beach.

With unlimited time and an unlimited budget, you could be out every evening attending a play, a concert, a musical or an art film.

The Arts

It's a common complaint among visitors to San Diego and even among some locals that San Diego is bereft of culture. Take it from us—that may have been true 25 years ago, but it simply isn't the case any longer and hasn't been for some time. Once an idea is established, however, it's hard to convince folks otherwise. So we'll just let San Diego's fine arts establishments and performers speak for themselves. You'll soon see that no matter what region of the county you're visiting, you'll find an abundance of galleries, museums, classical music performances, theaters and much, much more.

In North County Inland, Escondido, for example, has its own California Center for the Arts. East County's El Cajon has a fine Christian Community Theater. And small but distinguished theaters are easily found within the regions of North County Coastal and the South Bay. Within the city of San Diego, everything you could possibly look for in the arts is somewhere to be found.

During its season, the San Diego Opera features internationally renowned singers like Viveca Geneaux and Cecilia Bartoli. The Old Globe Theatre in Balboa Park, modeled after the original in London, not only continues with its cornerstone of Shakespearean plays, but has also presented everything from Molière to Mamet, from *Electra* to *Damn Yankees.* The La Jolla Playhouse has established itself by premiering several plays that have gone on to Broadway.

Around the county are more than 250 art galleries where you can find paintings, prints and sculptures by emerging as well as established artists. The East County is a treasure trove of galleries that feature Western art from the likes of Olaf Wieghorst and Remington. African art can be found in galleries all over the county, as can Aboriginal, Scandinavian, Indian, Chinese, Egyptian and just about any other type that piques your interest.

Traveling troupes have discovered that San Diego audiences enthusiastically embrace touring performances such as Broadway extravaganzas, ballet and ethnic dance shows like *Riverdance* and *Stomp.* These traveling groups are a welcome addition to the city's established performing organizations.

The film industry has started to emerge in San Diego, too, and several film festivals have sprung up in recent years. San Diegans have long enjoyed the Latino Film Festival and Spike & Mike's Classic Festival of Animation. In 1998 two new festivals were added to the mix, a Black Film Festival and the San Diego World Film Festival. All four draw filmmakers from all over the world, giving locals the chance to learn more about the history of filmmaking and to see some off-the-beaten-path movies.

San Diego has also begun to attract a growing enclave of writers. Victor Villaseñor, author of best-selling *Rain of Gold,* is a native of Oceanside, in North County Coastal. Joseph Waumbaugh, author of *The Onion Field* and numerous best-selling novels has adopted San Diego as his hometown, and scores of lesser-known but highly successful writers pen their works from somewhere around the county.

You can see that San Diego indeed is no slouch when it comes to the fine arts. With unlimited time and an unlimited budget, you could be out every evening attending a play, a concert, a musical or an art film. So when someone bemoans San Diego's lack of cultural accouterments, you can just smile knowingly and head to the opera while the uninformed spend another night in front of the tube.

In this chapter we'll give you a comprehensive description of all San Diego has to offer in the way of arts. We'll tell you where the best clusters of galleries are, where the best art-film houses are and how to get discount tickets occasionally. Like everywhere else in San Diego, dress tends to be on the casual side, even for nighttime performances of the symphony and the opera. You'll see everything from jeans to tuxedos, so whatever makes you comfortable is acceptable.

For current listings of performances, festivals and special gallery shows, check the "Night and Day" section of *The San Diego Union-Tribune* or the "Calendar" section of the free *San Diego Reader*, which can be picked up in convenience stores, libraries and bookstores all over the county. Both come out on Thursdays, and both provide in depth listings of everything going on in the arts in San Diego.

Classical Music

San Diego

La Jolla Chamber Music Society
Sherwood Auditorium
700 Prospect St., La Jolla
• (858) 459-3728

All year long the La Jolla Chamber Music Society presents classical music ensembles featuring national and international musicians. From October through April, the Sherwood Series is the big draw, presenting such notables as violinist Vadim Repin and the Takacs Quartet in the Sherwood Auditorium. The Celebrity Series, which is staged in May at downtown San Diego's Civic Theater, brings together a dazzling array of the world's most distinguished musicians and orchestras. Then, in August, the two-week Summerfest, also held at the Sherwood Auditorium, dazzles music lovers with a series of 14 concerts. Call for information on the individual series and their lineups as well as ticket price information.

Mainly Mozart Festival
121 Broadway, Ste 374, San Diego
• (619) 239-0100

The title of this festival spells it out: It's mainly a series of performances of the works of Mozart, but it also includes his 18th-century contemporaries, Baroque composers of the

late 17th-century and the romantic masters of the early 19th-century. Since 1988 the festival has successfully bridged the gap between the winter concert season of San Diego's primary performing arts groups and the major summer events. Many of North America's finest musicians are showcased every June in performances all over the county and across the border in Tijuana.

Even though the bulk of the performances are held in late spring, the festival has expanded in recent years to include special events year-round, such as the Spotlight Series held during the winter. For the most current performance schedule and to order tickets, call the number listed above. Ticket prices range from $30 for a single concert to $100 for a four-concert series.

San Diego Civic Youth Orchestra
4330 La Jolla Village Dr., Ste. 330, San Diego • (858) 484-9635

Gifted young musicians make up the San Diego Civic Youth Orchestra, a group dedicated to studying and performing the world's great orchestral works. Each year the organization embarks on an international tour to perform in music festivals around the world. Here at home, they delight and entertain audiences around the county with performances of such works as Tchaikovsky's *Nutcracker Suite,* Beethoven's Symphony No. 5 and John Williams's *Star Wars*.

Most performances are at Palomar Community College, at 1140 W. Mission Rd., San Marcos, but the group does travel around the county some. The season runs year-round. Call (619) 484-9635 for the current schedule.

San Diego Master Chorale
8813 Villa La Jolla Dr., Ste 2000B, La Jolla • (858) 453-6517

Originally founded as the choral arm of the San Diego Symphony in 1962, the Master Chorale split off into an independent organization in 1979. Consisting of 135 of San Diego's finest singers, the chorale produces its own concert season and joins other organizations occasionally for collaborative efforts.

Frequently the chorale will join the San Diego Opera and the San Diego Symphony for special performances.

The group performs all around San Diego County in a variety of settings from churches to outdoor stages. The repertoire includes a broad scope of music from master choral works to modern songs and show tunes. For information about the chorale's schedule, call (619) 453-6517.

San Diego Opera
1200 Third Ave., Ste. 1824, San Diego
• **(619) 232-7636**

There's little middle ground with opera: you either love it or hate it. But if you happen to be on the fence, we strongly suggest you take in a performance of the San Diego Opera; we suspect it'll make a convert of you. Since 1965 the San Diego Opera has been steadily maturing into a major community asset for San Diego. With General Director Ian Campbell at the helm since 1983, the character of the opera has evolved beautifully. Fiscally conservative and artistically daring, Campbell has led the opera to a point where its financial status is sound and its performances are a combination of the classics and the contemporary.

Campbell promises at least one contemporary opera each season, such as Gershwin's *Porgy and Bess* and Catán's *Rappaccini's Daughter*, the first Mexican opera ever to be performed in San Diego. Balancing out the new and unusual are the standard opera warhorses like Puccini's *Madam Butterfly* and Verdi's *Aida*.

Five operas are performed during the season, which runs from January through May. Information about subscriptions and tickets to individual performances are available by calling (619) 232-7636 or by stopping by the Civic Theatre box office. Ticket prices for individual operas range from $19 to $112. The opera performs in the Civic Theatre at Third Avenue and B Street in downtown San Diego.

San Diego Symphony
Copley Symphony Hall
1245 Seventh Ave., San Diego
• **(619) 220-6600**

Mired in bankruptcy, the San Diego Symphony ceased performing for a couple of years, but was revived in time for the 1998 Summer Pops season. Many of the symphony's original musicians returned, and under the leadership of Jung-Ho Pak, the symphony's new artistic director and principal conductor, the future looks bright.

The Summer Pops are always an Insiders' favorite, featuring such productions as *Beatlemania*, *Truly Tchaikovsky* and *Broadway, Just Off Broadway*. The venue for the Pops is at downtown's Navy Pier, at Harbor Drive south of Broadway. Ticket prices range from $10 for gallery seating to $40 for a champagne table and can be purchased through Ticketmaster at (619) 220-8497 or at the Symphony Hall box office.

The regular season performances include the Connoisseur Series, which runs from October through May. It features the traditional composers such as Beethoven, Tchaikovsky, Saint-Saens and Ravel. Ticket prices are from $15 to $50. For a different approach to symphony, you might try the Light Bulb Series, held occasionally from November through March. These interactive concerts combine music with guest speakers to put classical music in a whole new light.

The San Diego Symphony also has a Rush Hour Series, a Classic Film Series and a Family Series. All are designed to make classical music enjoyable to listeners of all ages and levels of appreciation. Ticket prices for the Light Bulb, Rush Hour, Classic Film and Family Series range from $10 to $35.

INSIDERS' TIP

The San Diego Opera has two free opportunities for opera fans: backstage tours conducted before every Friday night performance, and lunchtime concerts held at the San Diego Concourse (A and C Streets, First and Third Avenues) the Thursday after opening night. Call for further info at (619) 236-6510.

San Diego Youth Symphony
Casa del Prado
1800 El Prado, Balboa Park, San Diego
• **(619) 232-3232**

Founded in 1945 the San Diego Youth Symphony provides talented young musicians with the experience and discipline necessary for performing at a professional level. Most of the musicians are between the ages of 11 and 18, and the 300 or so members come from all over San Diego County and Baja California.

The Youth Symphony performs in various locations around San Diego, sometimes breaking the ensemble into just strings or just winds. Occasionally the group will join with the San Diego Master Chorale for a special concert. Whatever is on the agenda, these talented youngsters are always a delight to hear. Call (619) 232-3232 for updated schedule information.

Starlight Musical Theatre
2125 Park Blvd., San Diego
• **(619) 544-7827**

More commonly referred to as Starlight Opera, this organization has been delighting its patrons for decades with such easy to digest performances as *Hello Dolly*, *Camelot* and *Seven Brides for Seven Brothers*. All shows are held in the Starlight Bowl Amphitheater in Balboa Park, where you'll see lots of families picnicking on the grassy areas in the park before the show. Once the performance begins, be prepared for one of the quirks peculiar to Starlight Bowl. It's right under the flight path to San Diego International Airport, so every time a plane comes over, performers will freeze the action until the plane has passed and the actors can be heard once again. This happens 30 to 40 times during the performance, and kids especially get a kick out of watching for incoming planes and guessing when the action will freeze.

Ticket prices range from $15 to $46.50 (children 12 and younger are admitted free), and can be ordered by calling (619) 544-7827. Bring a cushion or a blanket to sit on — the hard seats may become uncomfortable . It tends to get somewhat cool in the evening, so be sure to bring a sweater or light jacket, too.

North County Coastal

San Diego Chamber Orchestra
2210 Encinitas Blvd., Ste. M, Encinitas
• **(760) 753-6402**

Established in 1984, the San Diego Chamber Orchestra's mission is to provide San Diego with a resident chamber orchestra of impeccable professional talent. The group performs music composed for smaller orchestras of 35 to 40 musicians, and it stages concerts in dozens of venues around the county, including the Museum of Contemporary Art, Fairbanks Ranch Country Club, and the California Center for the Arts, Escondido.

Single ticket prices range from $25 to $90, series tickets are from $50 to $165, and for an additional charge, VIP packages are available that include special seating and perks like champagne. Find out where the Chamber Orchestra is performing by calling (760) 753-6402.

Dance

San Diego

City Ballet School & Company
941 Garnet Ave., San Diego
• **(858) 274-6058**

San Diego's City Ballet is a nonprofit corporation that has been producing high quality ballet performances and outreach presentations since 1993. Each August the company offers free performances in the Organ Pavilion in Balboa Park, and, of course, the traditional *Nutcracker* is a must-see at Christmas time. City Ballet tends to stay with the familiar, staging such ballets as Shakespeare's *A Midsummer Night's Dream*. The venues vary as do ticket prices, but most tickets are in the $17 to $27 range.

City Ballet also has a strong educational program that provides training for professional and pre-professional dancers. It's "Discover a Dancer" program provides free ballet training for inner-city children in San Diego.

La Jolla Playhouse

This is a story of three Hollywood actors who were at the peak of fame and fortune in their film careers, but still longed for the purity of the stage. Gregory Peck, Dorothy McGuire and Mel Ferrer had dreams of opening a playhouse to bring live theater to California, where it was sadly lacking, and much to the good fortune of San Diego, they chose La Jolla.

Peck had grown up in San Diego and attended local schools. So it was only natural

that he should return to his roots. With the financial support of David Selznick and a solid core of local theater-lovers, the La Jolla Playhouse opened its first season in 1947 in the auditorium of La Jolla High School. The first production starred Dame May Whitty in *Night Must Fall*, a play in which she had been triumphant in both London and Hollywood. It was a great success and quelled all doubts about the threesome's venture. The future of the La Jolla Playhouse looked bright.

Peck himself performed in three plays at the La Jolla Playhouse during the next few years. Ferrer acted in three, as well, and McGuire in six, among them Tennessee Williams' *Summer and Smoke* and Noel Coward's *The Importance of Being Earnest*. In 1997 a new production of that same play opened the 50th anniversary season of the La Jolla Playhouse, and Peck and Ferrer were in the audience.

The early days of the Playhouse were filled with remarkable performances by notable actors including Jennifer Jones, Groucho Marx, Charlton Heston and David Niven. La Jolla quickly became a playground for the stars, and after each opening night the three founders could be found carousing with the likes of Desi Arnaz and Lucille Ball in the Whaling Bar at the La Valencia Hotel.

The Playhouse occupied La Jolla High School's auditorium for 18 seasons. Production ceased after the 1964 season for a number of reasons, the biggest being economic. It would take 19 years before the Playhouse presented another play; however, the dream of a La Jolla Playhouse never died. As early as 1954 local supporters were raising funds for the construction of a new theater, but that feat wasn't accomplished until 1982, when construction was completed on the current La Jolla Playhouse. Supporters were able to enlist the aid of UCSD's Dr. Roger Revelle, and as a

Photo: John Johnson

Neil Patrick Harris (left) and Christian Mena (right) sing in the West Coast premiere of *Rent* at the La Jolla Playhouse.

— continued on next page

result, the new Playhouse found a home in the Mandell Weiss Theatre on the campus of the university, where it remains today.

Under former artistic director Des McAnuff, the La Jolla Playhouse reopened in 1983 with Peter Sellars' production of *The Visions of Simone Machard*, which was later distinguished by the *Village Voice* as one of the 10 best regional theater productions of the 1980s. But it was the 1984 production of *Big River* that started the real buzz about the Playhouse. With its score by Roger Miller, *Big River* went on to Broadway and won seven Tony awards.

This was just the beginning of a tradition of Broadway-bound productions making their debut at San Diego's homegrown theater. *A Walk in the Woods* followed a few years later and quickly made its way to Broadway. So did Frank Galati's adaptation of *The Grapes of Wrath*.

But the real test of McAnuff's genius came in 1993, when playgoers gathered on a summer evening in July, anxiously awaiting the debut of The Who's groundbreaking rock opera *Tommy*. It was wildly successful among both the traditional playgoers and rock fans. Naturally it went on to Broadway, and the next year *Tommy* won five Tonys, including one for McAnuff. But those weren't the only Tonys San Diego felt pride in that year. During that same award ceremony the Playhouse received the Tony given annually to an outstanding regional theater.

That same year McAnuff stepped aside and passed the torch to Michael Greif, his former student and assistant. Continuing in McAnuff's tradition, Greif, who was nominated for a Tony Award for Best Director for *Rent*, brought that same production to the La Jolla Playhouse for its West Coast premiere. Greif also staged the world premiere of Barry Manilow and Bruce Sussman's musical *Harmony*. Greif's tenure extended into late 1999, when New York's Anne Hamburger took the reins as artistic director. Hamburger had established a reputation for bringing the theater to the people, staging productions in such unlikely locales as the Brooklyn pier, abandoned store-fronts and a Harlem street. She plans to continue such innovative techniques at the La Jolla Playhouse.

It has been 50 years since three actors with a germ of an idea started the La Jolla Playhouse. And each year, San Diegans take more and more pride in the quality of productions at the Playhouse. The combination of classics, popular musicals and plays, and groundbreaking productions has put the little theater on the national theatrical map.

Malashock Dance & Co.
1415 Old Globe Way, San Diego
• **(619) 235-2266**

A small company of seven dancers is led by its founder, John Malashock, a former principal dancer with Twyla Tharp in New York. The company maintains rehearsal and teaching studios in Balboa Park. Its mission is to advance the art and experience of dance through creative self-expression.

Malashock has an active year-round schedule, performing all over San Diego County, including the Old Globe Theatre. Call the number above for a current schedule of performances and for ticket information.

Film Festivals

San Diego

San Diego-Baja California Latino Film Festival
United Artists Theatre, Horton Plaza
475 Horton Plaza, San Diego
• **(619) 230-1938**

Presented annually in late February or early March by the Centro Cultural de la Raza, Latino filmmakers, writers and actors are showcased in a series of short and feature-length films.

The goal of the festival is to make the mass audience aware of talented Latinos who are making commercially successful films. Special guests have included noted filmmakers such as Moctezuma Esparza and actors Edward James Olmos and Joe Mantegna. Tickets for each screening are $7, and a festival pass can be purchased for $60. Tickets are available in advance through Ticketmaster at (619) 220-8497 or on the day of the screening at the theater box office.

San Diego World Film Festival
United Artists Theatre Horton Plaza
475 Horton Plaza, San Diego
• (619) 558-3456

New in 1998, this festival combines films screened solely for pleasure with those entered in a serious competition. Categories include Best American Independent Feature Film, Best Foreign Film, Best Major Studio Film and several awards for acting and screenwriting. Classic movies are shown, too, such as Woody Allen's *Manhattan* and *Waiting for Sunset* with Cliff Robertson and Robert Mitchum. The festival is spread out over 10 days, but as yet has not found a permanent spot on the calendar. Tickets are $7 at the door.

Spike & Mike's Classic Festival of Animation
Museum of Contemporary Art
700 Prospect St., La Jolla
• (858) 454-0267

Do you picture Porky Pig and Elmer Fudd when you think of animation? Do you associate animation with Saturday morning in front of the television with a bowl of Trix? Then you're in for a treat and an education at this festival. It's a combination of low-tech and high-tech. Some of the films, such as Don Hertzfeldt's *Lily and Jim*, take you back to the early days of animation, when cels were individually drawn by hand. Jan Pinkava's Oscar-winning *Geri's Game*, on the other hand, utilizes the latest in computer technology. The festival usually lasts about 10 days during the month of April, and screenings are held in the evenings. Tickets are $7 at the box office or $6.50 through Ticketmaster at (619) 220-8497.

South Bay

San Diego Black Film Festival
Cinema Star Theater
320 Third Ave., Chula Vista
• (619) 234-3456

Established in 1998, the Black Film Festival highlights vintage black films from the 1930s and 1940s, most of which are not available on video and are rarely screened. The festival, held in February to coincide with Black History Month, also includes a series of professional workshops on the film industry featuring actors, agents, directors and producers as panelists. Tickets for the first-night gala reception and screening are $30. Tickets for the other screenings are $7.50. Workshops are held at Mount Zion Missionary Baptist Church, 3045 Greely Avenue, San Diego. Admission is $5 in advance and $7 at the door. For information on advance ticket purchase, call the San Diego Film Commission at (619) 234-3456.

Galleries

San Diego

The Artists Gallery
7420 Girard Ave., Ste. 200, La Jolla
• (858) 551-5821

Many exceptionally talented artists call San Diego home, and the Artists Gallery is a favorite showcase. Owner Georgeanna Lipe, La Jolla's most noted watercolorist, offers the work of more than 30 artists in this cheerful

INSIDERS' TIP

Check our Annual Events chapter to see if there's a neighborhood festival going on while you're here. These are great places to find crafts and artwork created by local artists.

and colorful gallery. Original watercolors, oils, mixed media and sculpture are all available. The gallery is open Tuesday through Saturday from 10 AM until 5 PM.

Balton Art Glass
7863 Girard Ave., Ste. 101, La Jolla • (858) 456-8147

If you love the look and feel of beautiful glassware, stop in at Balton Art Glass. The collection features art glass created by artists from all over the United States and Europe, and most of these unique pieces are signed. Objects include hand-blown crystal vases and glassware, sculptures, paperweights and many decorative items. Most pieces are quite affordable, starting at around $5 for glass candy. Hours are from 11 AM to 6 PM daily.

Cosmopolitan Fine Arts
7932 Girard Ave., La Jolla • (858) 456-9506

La Jolla boasts many fine galleries, and Cosmopolitan is an Insiders' favorite. The gallery specializes in contemporary French impressionist and post-impressionist paintings by Cortes, Labrofont, Loir, Galien-LaLoue and M. Dyf. You'll also appreciate the American and European contemporary art on display by artists such as DyAns, Paco G., Uwe and Colomer. Hours are from 10 AM until 6 PM daily, and until 8 PM on Fridays.

Galeria Dos Damas
415 Market St., San Diego • (619) 235-0700

Should you wish to take home a true representation of artwork from the area, Galeria Dos Damas is the place to visit. It is well recognized as a showcase for emerging artists from Mexico and the Californias. Twelve shows are staged every year featuring both trained and self-taught artists, and the gallery is especially noted for finding and establishing new talent. Hours are from 12 PM to 5 PM Thursday through Saturday, and from 10 AM to 3 PM on Sunday.

International Gallery
643 G St., San Diego • (619) 235-8255

This is a huge gallery — more than 4,000 square feet of contemporary American crafts, including ceramics, glass, jewelry and wood. The rest of the world is well represented too, with African and Melanesian tribal art such as baskets, masks and sculpture. From Central Asia, North Africa and the Middle East are jewelry, kilims and textiles. The Gallery is open Tuesday through Saturday from 10 AM until 6 PM, and on Sunday from 11:30 AM until 4:30 PM.

IPGallery
641 B St., San Diego • (619) 702-5388

Nearly two dozen local artists present their unusual works here, displaying a variety of different styles and techniques. The IP Gallery specializes in exhibitions featuring artists such as Dodge Distad and Geoff Thomas. A recent exhibition showcased the works of some of San Diego's top female artists. Hours are from 11 AM to 6 PM, Monday through Saturday.

Soma Gallery
7661 Girard Ave., Suite 200, La Jolla • (858) 551-5821

The Soma Gallery offers contemporary painting, sculpture and photography by such internationally recognized artists as William Glen Crooks, Franco Nanartonis and James Renner. Special exhibitions are ongoing, with opening receptions the first night of each exhibition. Hours are from 10 AM to 6 PM Tuesday through Saturday, or by appointment.

INSIDERS' TIP

Art museums in Balboa Park offer free admission one day every month. The Museum of Photographic Arts offers free entry on the second Tuesday. Visitors to the San Diego Museum of Art and Mingei International Folk Art Museum are free on the third Tuesday. Admission is always free at the Timken Museum of Art.

Gospel singers at San Diego airport perform for special occasions and the arrival of special guests.

Spanish Village Art Center
1770 Village Pl., Balboa Park, San Diego
• (619) 233-9050

Spanish Village is a unique, concentrated collection of 35 studio/galleries that display the work of dozens of local artists. Many of the artists are on-site, creating their work as you watch.

You'll find artwork in a variety of media, including oil, watercolor, ceramics, sculpture, jewelry, woodcarving, glass, photography and enamel. There's no admission to Spanish Village, and it's open every day from 11 AM to 4 PM.

Stephen Clayton Galleries
1201 1st St., Ste. 111, Coronado
• (619) 435-6474

Lithographs by contemporary artists such as Red Skelton, Thomas Kinkade and Boulanger are the specialties at this gallery.

Even the artwork of children's author Dr. Seuss is represented. In addition to lithographs, you'll find a nice selection of modern sculpture. Hours are from 10 AM to 7 PM daily, but occasionally the gallery will stay open later on weekends.

Studio Gallery of Old Town
2501 San Diego Ave., San Diego
• (619) 294-9880

Animation is the cornerstone of this gallery, which features original work by such legendary artists as Chuck Jones, animator of Warner Brothers characters like Bugs Bunny and Daffy Duck. Fine art by internationally acclaimed photographers and artists such as Phil Broges, Karl P. Keonig, Carl Mydans and Robert Vavra is also displayed. The gallery is open Sunday through Wednesday from 10 AM to 6 PM, and Thursday through Saturday from 10 AM to 8 PM.

INSIDERS' TIP

At the foot of the San Diego-Coronado Bay Bridge, at the intersection of National Avenue and Crosby Street on the San Diego side, is Chicano Park. Within the park, Chicano artists have painted the abutments of the bridge with murals representing their history and social concerns. The result is an internationally acclaimed public art project.

North County Coastal

The gallery is open Monday through Saturday 10 to 7 PM and Sunday 12 noon to 5 PM.

Art & Accents
312 S. Cedros Ave., Solana Beach
• (858) 755-0062

To say that this gallery has wonderful pieces of art and the perfect accents for your abode is an understatement. You could be like us and find you really can't get a certain bronze sculpture or ceramic piece off your mind. You'll be tempted here by work from nationally recognized artists and local ones too. Choose from Venetian glass, paintings and fine Italian ceramics such as Vietre, Cottura, Mamma Ro, and Intrada. The store is open daily from 10 AM to 5 PM and is in the center of the Cedros Shopping District. (See our Shopping chapter for more on this area.)

Artist's Choice
1049 Camino Del Mar, Suite 4B, Del Mar
• (858) 259-4774

The gallery displays the art of the owner Angela J. Burkett who works in the classical tradition of early California plein-air painting. The gallery also features fine gift items and has a full line of custom frames. It also holds framing workshops for the do-it-yourself folks. Call for store hours.

Carlsbad Village Faire Gallery
300 Carlsbad Village Dr., Carlsbad
• (760) 434-9431

You may see a display of teddy bears at this gallery, or angels, or of mixed-media art that's on the cutting edge of "wow." This gallery's eclectic delights range from dollcraft to fine art and the collection varies from serious fine art paintings to whimsical music boxes. More than 50 San Diego artists are featured here. Daily hours are from 11 AM to 5 PM.

Enchanted Gallery
2650 Via De La Valle, #230, Del Mar
• (858) 792-6704

This truly is an enchanted gallery featuring the fine art of jewelry designers and acclaimed artists. You'll be treated to extraordinary sculptures and paintings. In addition, the store offers mineral and crystal specimens for sale.

Sana Gallery
115 N. Hwy. 101, Solana Beach
• (858) 755-5745

A few blocks from the Cedros Shopping District (see our chapter on Shopping), the gallery features changing exhibits, such as the recent show of minimalist and abstractionist art. Besides painting, you also might see jewelry, textiles, and sculpture. The gallery also features aboriginal art and artifacts from around the world. Gallery hours are Wednesdays through Sundays, 11 AM to 5 PM.

Susan Street Fine Art Gallery
444 S. Cedros Ave., Solana Beach
• (858)793-4442

This is one of the fine shops in the Cedros Shopping District. (See our listing in the Shopping Chapter about others stores in this area.) The store is open Mondays through Fridays 10 AM to 5 PM, and on Saturday the hours are noon until 4 PM. The selection is ever changing. If you love paper sculptures, you may be able to see them here; call to make sure that the gallery has some displayed. The work that's shown is by new talent as well as established artists.

Trios Gallery
130 S. Cedros Ave., Solana Beach
• (858) 793-6040

This unusual gallery features glass art, weaving and water features along with furniture that's art. Recently on display was work from California artists Albert Demattels, Jim Gibson, Rick Stava and James Hubbell. There's easy access from the Solana Beach commuter train station, the Coaster, to this store and the Cedros Shopping District. The gallery is open daily from 10 AM until 5:30 PM.

Zimbabwe Shona Sculpture
5600 Paseo Del Norte, Ste. 138, Carlsbad
• (760) 804-0600

The Spirits in Stone collection is a stunning exhibition of Zimbabwe's Shona stone sculpture. The store is located in the Carlsbad Company Stores (see our Shopping chapter) and exhibits are the stunning work of Africa's

Artistic inspiration comes easily with spectacular scenes like the Mission de Alcala.

newest generation of young men and women artists as well as masterpieces from Zimbabwe's best-known sculptors. Prices of the stone monuments range from $100 to thousands of dollars. The store is open daily 10 AM to 6 PM. During the December holidays, the store is open later.

North County Inland

Escondido Municipal Gallery
142 W. Grand Ave., Escondido
• (760) 480-4101

The shows at this gallery change focus often so it's worth stopping in to browse when you're in the neighborhood. At a recent exhibit there was an all-media exhibition of two- and three-dimensional art by local artists. The gallery is open Tuesdays through Saturdays, 11 PM to 4 PM.

Family Affair Gift Gallery
13330 Paseo del Verando Norte, San Diego • (858) 485-5850

The official North County Inland gallery to feature the works of Thomas Kinkade, the store is in Rancho Bernardo and also has an extensive selection of graphics, collector plates, figurines as well as fine art.

Store hours are Tuesday through Saturday 10 AM until 5 PM, Sunday 11 AM until 5 PM, and by appointment.

J & J Gallery and Framing
431 N. Escondido Blvd., Escondido
• (760) 747-8973

The gallery has paintings, prints, lithos, etchings, serigraphs, posters and sculpture. It's noted in the area for having contemporary and wildlife artwork, too. In addition, J&J offers home and business design services. The gallery is open Tuesday through Friday from 10 AM to 6 PM and Saturday 10 AM to 5 PM. It's closed Sundays and Mondays.

Poway Center for the Performing Arts
1598 Espola Rd., Poway • (858) 748-0505

The gallery at the Center exhibits the work of new and established artists. A recent exhibit included the inaugural show of the North County Printmakers of San Diego. The gallery is open Monday through Saturday 12 noon to 5 PM.

East County

Art World - Western Heritage Gallery
1266 Broadway St., El Cajon
• (619) 440-1041

According to Insiders who love Western or wildlife art, this is the primary gallery in Southern California. Many people travel from Los Angeles to visit it. More than 50 artists are represented here, including Bev Doolittle. You might also find the work of Harvey, Martensen, McCarthy, Tarpning, Wieghorst, Rodriguez, Cole, Larson, or Redlin. The store also carries numbered and fine-art prints and limited editions. The gallery is open Monday through Friday from 10 AM until 6 PM, and Saturday is open from 10 AM until 4 PM.

Julian Fine Art and Photography Shows
Julian Town Hall, Main and Washington Sts., Julian • (760) 765-1857

If you love art and want some fun, too, be sure to see the various fine art and photography shows you'll find in Julian. Call the number above for information on the usually-free shows held at Julian's Town Hall (and be sure to read our Annual Events and Shopping Chapter for more about Julian). Many artists, ceramists, weavers, and photographers live in the area. Some have shows from time to time but you can often see their work at various local shops and stores.

El Cajon Works of Art Gallery
764 Jamacha Rd., El Cajon
• (619) 588-8875

The gallery is open Wednesday through Saturday, 11 AM through 4 PM. There's a perfect blend of contemporary painting and sculpture by local and internationally known artists, such as Georgia Clemens.

South Bay

Frame Gallery
305 3rd Ave., Chula Vista
• **(619) 422-1700**

If you're a seeker of collectibles, this is the place for you. It would be hard to find a larger assortment of collectible figurines anywhere else in the county. If Snow Babies get you going, they're here in abundance. So are Disney figurines and tons of commemorative plates. The gallery also has a nice selection of Thomas Kinkade prints as well as several autographed prints of sports figures and Hollywood celebrities. A complete framing service is offered, too. Hours are from 10 AM to 5:30 PM, Monday through Friday, and from 10 AM to 5 PM on Saturday.

Museums

San Diego

Centro Cultural de la Raza
2004 Park Blvd., Balboa Park, San Diego
• **(619) 235-6135**

Indigenous, Mexican and Chicano arts and culture are exhibited in this internationally acclaimed museum/gallery. Even the outside of the museum is a work of art: Murals that cover its exterior walls depict the legacy of Chicano historical and mythological roots and traditions. Both traditional and experimental forms of visual and performing arts are presented in the museum, including film screenings, literary presentations and numerous workshops. Hours are from 10 AM to 4 PM Tuesday through Saturday, and 10 AM to 5 PM on Sunday. Admission is free, but donations are gratefully accepted.

Mingei International Museum of Folk Art
1439 El Prado, Balboa Park, San Diego
• **(619) 239-0003**

The word "Mingei" is used transculturally for "art of the people." Thus, traditional and contemporary folk art, craft and design representing the many cultures of the world are the focus at the Mingei Museum. You'll see exhibits such as "Dolls — Mirrors of Humanity," which showcases more than 200 objects, including an 18th-century dollhouse and a parade of dolls in vehicles of all kinds. Another recent exhibit was "The Art of Keisuke Serizawa — A National Treasure of Japan," a collection of Japanese textiles, book illustrations, paintings, folding screens and fans. All permanent and changing exhibits portray the essential arts that are satisfying to the human soul.

The museum is open Tuesday through Sunday from 10 AM to 4 PM. Admission is $5 for adults, and $2 for students and children 6 to 17. Admission is free for children younger than 6.

Museum of Contemporary Art
700 Prospect St., La Jolla
• **(858) 454-3541**
1001 Kettner Blvd., San Diego
• **(619) 234-1001**

Both locations of this museum have a long-established reputation for thought-provoking exhibitions as well as highly regarded permanent collections. For those who truly want to understand contemporary art, docent tours are available and are included in the price of admission. Recent exhibits have included *Double Trouble: The Patchett Collection*, a selection of works from Hollywood television producer, writer and publisher Tom Patchett. His collection includes work by Marcel Duchamp, Man Ray and many more important artists. Recently, San Diego artist Roman de Salvo,

---

INSIDERS' TIP

What's free on the first Wednesday of each month? Admission to the Visual Arts at the Center (the California Center for the Arts) in Escondido.

known for his ingenious transformations of everyday objects into imaginative and humorous sculptures, has been commissioned to create new works for the museum's indoor and outdoor spaces.

Lectures and commentaries are frequently scheduled, too. Both locations are open Tuesday through Saturday from 10 AM to 5 PM, and from 12 PM to 5 PM on Sundays. Evening hours at the La Jolla location are Wednesday until 8 PM, and at the Kettner Boulevard location on Friday until 8 PM.

Museum of Photographic Arts
1649 El Prado, Balboa Park, San Diego
• (619) 238-7559

Photography is one of the more intriguing art forms, and the Museum of Photographic Arts consistently displays stunning examples of the work of some of the finest international photographers. In addition to its permanent collection, changing exhibitions highlight the museum's dedication to displaying outstanding photography.

A 1998 exhibition, *Robert Capa: Photographs*, showcased a retrospective collection commemorating the work of the famed wartime photojournalist. Another recent exhibition presented the works of George Hurrell, whose celebrity images immortalized the faces of Hollywood. Exhibitions are usually combined with lectures and special programs that add to their appeal.

The museum is open daily from 10 AM to 5 PM. Admission is $4 for those twelve and older; children younger than 12 are free when accompanied by an adult.

Insider's Note: The Museum of Photographic Arts is expanding, and while it increases its size by nearly fourfold, it will be closed through the spring of 2000. However, in the interim, the exhibits will be moved to downtown's Museum of Contemporary Art, located at 1001 Kettner Blvd., San Diego, (619) 234-1001. Admission to the Museum of Contemporary Art is $2 and will include entry to

the Museum of Photographic Arts during its stay there.

San Diego Museum of Art
1450 El Prado, Balboa Park, San Diego
• (619) 232-7931

This venerable museum has a respectable permanent collection consisting of Italian Renaissance, Spanish Old Masters, American art, 19th-century European paintings and 20th-century paintings and sculpture. There's also a fine collection of American Indian paintings and a gallery dedicated to California Art.

It's the traveling exhibitions that draw the big crowds, though, and recent years have seen the Jewels of the Romanov visit the museum, as well as a huge collection of Faberge Eggs. The 1998 season featured *Monet: Late Paintings of Giverny from the Museé Marmatton*, an exhibit of 22 paintings by the famous French impressionist.

Hours are from 10 AM to 4:30 PM Tuesday through Sunday. Admission prices are $7 for adults; $5 for seniors, young adults 18 to 24, and military; and $2 for children 6 to 17. Children 5 and younger are admitted free. On Fridays, Saturdays and Sundays, all admission prices are increased by $1.

Timken Museum of Art
1500 El Prado, Balboa Park, San Diego
• (619) 239-5548

Known locally as San Diego's "jewel box for the arts," the Timken Museum is devoted to its select collection of European and American masterworks, which includes a small sampling of beautiful Russian icons. The Putnam Collection within the museum spans five centuries of art, from the early Renaissance through the 19th century. You'll see the works of artists such as Veronese, Bruegel, Cezanne, Clouet, Rembrandt and Reubens.

American artists are well represented, too, including Bierstadt, Copley, Heade and others. This is an outstanding small museum that's known nationwide for its critically acclaimed,

INSIDERS' TIP

Looking for the perfect gift to take back home to family or co-workers? The galleries often have less expensive collectibles and cards worth framing as well as pieces of art.

tasteful and well-lit setting for viewing its collection. The hours are from 10 AM to 4:30 PM Tuesdays through Saturday, and from 1:30 PM to 4:30 PM on Sunday. Admission is free.

North County Coastal

Carlsbad Children's Museum
399 Carlsbad Village Dr., Ste. 103, Carlsbad • (760) 720-0737

This museum has interactive exhibits and also exhibits art by children and children's artists. (Be sure to see our Kidstuff chapter for further details.) It's located near the beach and Carlsbad's State Street shopping district (see our Shopping chapter). This museum also has activities for kids ages 2 through 12.

During the traditional school year the hours of operation are limited, so call ahead. In the summer the museum is open between 10 AM and 5 PM. There's a $3.50 admission fee.

Oceanside Museum of Art
704 Pier View Way, Oceanside • (760) 721-2787

Located in the historic Gill Building, which was the old Oceanside city hall in the 1920s, the museum features local and international art. Its rotating exhibits include pottery, sculpture, paintings in watercolor and oil, and mixed media installations that sometimes include the work of local weavers. The museum is open Tuesdays through Saturdays, 10 AM through 3 PM. There is no charge for admission.

North County Inland

Heritage Walk Museum
Grape Day Park, 321 N. Broadway St., Escondido • (760) 743-8207

The gallery is open Thursdays, Fridays and Saturdays from 1 PM to 4 PM and there's no charge to view the photos and exhibits depicting the early days of Escondido. Take a picnic and make this a relaxing outing. There are plenty of shady areas and places for the kids to run around at the park.

The Visual Arts at the California Center for the Arts
340 N. Escondido Blvd., Escondido • (760) 738-4138

An always changing group of exhibits are on display here. Recently there was an exhibition of 20th-century still-life paintings from the Phillips Collection with work by artists Pablo Picasso, Georges Braque, Stuart Davis and Georgia O'Keeffe. In late 1998, the center hosted an exhibition of large-scale sculpture and installations by Los Angeles artist Ali Acerol and New York artists Andy Yoder, which included Acerol's brick furniture arrangements and a metal table set for thirty by Yoder, which provided an intriguing, contrasting view of domestic space.

With your ticket to a performance at the Center, you can visit the museum for free. Otherwise, ticket prices are $4 for adults, and $2 for children and students with identification.

Performance Venues

Art Film Houses

San Diego

Garden Cabaret
4040 Goldfinch St., San Diego • (619) 295-4221

From April through October, the Garden Cabaret "Cinema Under the Stars" presents its collection of classic films in a charming outdoor venue in Mission Hills. Films are

---

INSIDERS' TIP

For half-price, day-of-performance tickets to local shows, check out the Times Arts Tix Booth in Horton Plaza on Broadway Circle, next to Planet Hollywood. Or call (619) 497-5000 for a list of each day's half-price shows.

shown on Thursday, Friday and Saturday nights, and seating is at cabaret-style tables. Films shown include such classics as *It Happened One Night*, *From Here to Eternity*, *The Long Hot Summer* and *Harvey*.

Hillcrest Cinemas
3965 Fifth Ave., San Diego
• **(619) 299-2100**

This five-theater complex tucked away in the Village Hillcrest Shopping Center shows first-run foreign films and independent American films. The theaters are on the small side, lending a cozy atmosphere to the experience, but the amenities are modern and first-rate.

Ken Cinema
4061 Adams Ave., San Diego
• **(619) 283-5909**

Old-style theaters are rapidly falling by the wayside since the tidal wave of multiplex cinemas began taking their place. The Ken remains, however, and continually draws large crowds to its retrospectives and special showings. For instance, the theater has shown a retrospective of Kurosawa films, a series of Humphrey Bogart thrillers, Monty Python collections and all the *Godfather* movies. Classics are favored here, and there's always something interesting showing.

North County Coastal

La Paloma
471 S. Coast Hwy. 101, Encinitas
• **(760) 436-7469**

In all of the North County, this is the place for watching art films and viewing wild, weird or funny classics. Don't expect high brow stuff at this beach-town film house as most of the films are on the contemporary side of classic. For instance if you must see the 60s surf classic, *Endless Summer*, on the big screen once again, La Paloma is the place.

Cultural Centers

San Diego

San Diego Concourse Convention and Performing Arts Center
Third Ave. and B St., San Diego
• **(619) 570-1100**

This is a grand title for what actually is pretty much restricted to the Civic Theatre. Although the Concourse gets heavy use by conventions and trade shows, the performing arts are intelligently confined to the theater, which has the acoustics and the ambiance the Concourse does not. From January through May, the Civic Theatre is the exclusive home to the San Diego Opera. But once the opera season is over, watch out! Everything from *Cats* to *Miss Saigon* to *Riverdance* to *Stomp* makes an appearance at this gracious and graceful theater. If there's a popular Broadway production to be seen, chances are good that it will show up at the Civic Theatre.

As the holidays approach, you can take it to the bank that a traveling performance of *The Nutcracker* will turn up, and this is where you'll find the rare ballet that comes to town. The theater holds just under 3,000 people, but the seats in the upper regions virtually demand binoculars. So if you have your heart set on seeing a special concert or show, get your tickets early. Tickets can be purchased at the box office at the Concourse or by calling Ticketmaster at (619) 220-8497.

Simon Edison Centre for the Performing Arts
Old Globe Theatre, Cassius Carter Centre Stage, Lowell Davies Festival Theatre
Located behind the Museum of Man in Balboa Park • **(619) 239-2255**

Beautifully situated in Balboa Park, this complex consists of three theaters, including

Photo: San Diego Convention and Visitors Bureau

The Old Globe Theatre in Balboa Park, modeled after the original in London, not only continues with its cornerstone of Shakespearean plays, but has also presented everything from Molière to Mamet, from *Electra* to *Damn Yankees*.

the Tony Award-winning Old Globe Theatre. The other two are the 225-seat Cassius Carter Centre Stage, which is a theater-in-the-round, and the outdoor Lowell Davies Festival Theatre.

The three theaters stage year-round performances which range from the traditional Shakespearean classics (the 1998 season featured *As You Like It* and *Romeo and Juliet*) to world premieres such as *Getting and Spending* and *Paramour*. Christmas time always brings something to please the young ones, like *How the Grinch Stole Christmas*. Ticket prices range from $23 to $39 and can be purchased at the box office or by calling (619) 239-2255.

North County Coastal

Mission San Luis Rey
4070 Mission Ave., Oceanside
• (760) 757-3651

Is a mission just a mission? Not this one. At the Mission San Luis Rey in Oceanside you might be able to enjoy a Mozart concert, a

dance troop's performance or one by a choir of international fame. The events are sometimes held on the grounds of the historic mission and sometimes within the mission building. (See our Attractions chapter for more on this mission.)

At a recent concert the Vatican Choir performed. Call for upcoming events. Prices vary for every performance. Tickets for the recent Vatican Choir event ranged from $75 to $200. Sometimes there are receptions held before and after a performance.

Oceanside Museum of Art
704 Pier View Way, Oceanside
• (760) 721-2787

Located in the old Oceanside city hall, the museum sponsors theater, dance and musical performances, including chamber music concerts. Admission prices vary. At a recent performance of the Alouette Trio, an evening of works by women composers of the Romantic Era such as Clara Schumann and Rebecca Clarke, admission was $10 per person. Performances are usually held in the afternoon.

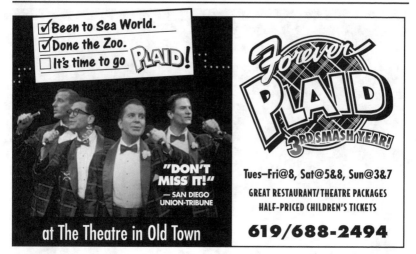

North County Inland

California Center for the Arts
340 N. Escondido Blvd., Escondido • (760) 738-4138

Will it be *Cats*, *The Music Man*, *Oklahoma*, *The Nutcracker* or Shirley Bassey, The Los Angeles Guitar Quartet or the *Pat Boone Show*? The performances at the California Center for the Arts run the gamut from serious to knee-tapping fun. Recently we attended a taping of National Public Radio's *What Do You Know?* with unflappable, wacky guy Michael Feldman, and the place was packed.

The center is located on a 12-acre campus. It's a world-class arts center that also includes fine educational programs. The Center was designed by the late renowned architect Charles Moore and includes a 1,538-seat concert hall and a 408-seat theater. It is a full-service conference center, too.

The theater brings troupes from around the globe to the inland community and brings Insiders and visitors from around Southern California to enjoy the varied programs. There are musical theater and Broadway shows, classical productions, dance and music from around the world, holiday programs, jazz and big band shows and family theater too. (See our Kidstuff chapter) Prices vary from about $16 to $60. Call for details and to get on the Center's mailing list.

Poway Center for the Performing Arts
1598 Espola Rd., Poway • (858) 748-0505

This cultural center provides live stage and musical performances for Insiders and visitors. Recent programs have included chamber music, a youth choir and a stunning performance of *Twilight of the Golds*, a contemporary social drama. This center seats 800 people but it's a popular venue, so make sure to make reservations early for popular programs. Call for a schedule of upcoming events. Ticket prices depend on the performance and seating location.

Theaters

San Diego

Horton Grand Theatre
444 Fourth Ave., San Diego • (619) 234-9583

Located in the heart of the Gaslamp Quarter, this small theater continuously presents crowd-pleasing plays that more often than not are held over. It's a fairly small theater but is comfortable and elegant. The 1998 season saw a long running of *Triple Espresso: A Highly Caffeinated Comedy*, which was brought back by popular demand. The theater is within a few blocks of all the Gaslamp's restaurants and clubs, so a performance can easily be combined with dinner and after-theater entertainment.

La Jolla Playhouse
2910 La Jolla Village Dr., La Jolla
• **(858) 550-1010**

This distinguished theater that was founded by actors Gregory Peck, Dorothy McGuire and Mel Ferrer is constantly on the cutting edge of world premiere plays and musicals that have a habit of finding their way to Broadway. Several Tony Award-winning plays have debuted here, including Roger Miller's *Big River* and The Who's rock opera *Tommy*. Classics are never ignored at the La Jolla Playhouse, however, and recent seasons have included such venerable plays as Ingmar Berman's *Nora* and Noel Coward's *The Importance of Being Earnest*. For the detailed history of the La Jolla Playhouse, be sure to read the close-up in this chapter.

Lamb's Players Theatre
1142 Orange Ave., Coronado
• **(619) 437-0600**

The history of the Lamb's Players Theatre is one of extremes. It started out in a Quonset hut in the East County, and now occupies a historic theater in Coronado, and along the way has grown into San Diego's third-largest theater organization, behind the Old Globe Theatre and the La Jolla Playhouse. Its resident acting company stages performances year-round, including plays like *The Secret Garden*, Arthur Giron's *Flight* and the nostalgia revue, *Boomers*. In addition, three holiday performances are presented every year at Christmas time.

Mystery Cafe
Imperial House Restaurant
505 Kalmia St., San Diego
• **(619) 544-1600**

Serious patrons of the arts might sniff haughtily at the idea of dinner theater, but sometimes ya just gotta do it. And the Mystery Cafe at the Imperial House is one of the best. Audience participation is not only encouraged it's expected, and plenty of laughs are guaranteed.

The long-running *Murder at the Café Noir*

has entertained guests with its hilarious blend of mystery and red herrings, and future performances are likely to be just as much fun. Along with the performance, a four-course meal is served.

San Diego Repertory Theatre
79 Horton Plaza, San Diego
• **(619) 235-8025**

Two subterranean theaters house the San Diego Repertory Theatre, the 550-seat Lyceum Stage and the 225-seat Lyceum Space. The season runs from autumn through spring, and the performances are eclectic: musicals, dramas and comedies. Most are fairly well known and familiar. At Christmas the Rep stages a two-week run of *A Christmas Carol*, presenting a different version each year. One year it was an African-American production; one year it was a musical version that featured dancing-food characters.

Sushi Performance Gallery
320 11th Ave., San Diego
• **(619) 235-8466**

Since 1980 Sushi has gained national acclaim as an adventurous alternative performance-art space. Whoopi Goldberg got her start here, and feminist performance artists Karen Finley and Holly Hughes have appeared too. Most evenings you can just show up and be assured of getting a ticket, and the dress is always casual. Sushi's performances require an open mind; most are edgy and thought provoking.

Theatre in Old Town
4040 Twiggs St., San Diego
• **(619) 688-2494**

An indoor, amphitheater-style house, the Theatre in Old Town presents familiar, favorite plays and musicals. *Forever Plaid* was booked for a short return engagement in early 1997, and by mid-1999 it was still showing, with no signs of decreasing in popularity. Perhaps by the time you make your way to Old Town, something else will be showing, but we doubt it.

Whether it's *Forever Plaid* or something else, this theater is worth a visit. The atmosphere is relaxed and casual, and all of Old Town is right outside the door.

North County Coastal

North Coast Repertory Theatre
987D Lomas Santa Fe Dr., Solana Beach
• (858) 481-1055

You might see a drama, comedy noir or, as often is the case, classics like *Auntie Mame*, *Fiddler on the Roof*, and *Our Town* in this 194-seat theater. The theater is intimate, elegant and comfortable, and unlike others in downtown San Diego, you can come as casually dressed or as gussied-up as you choose. Weekday performances start at 8 PM. On Saturday and Sundays there are two shows at 2 PM and 7 PM. Ticket prices are in the $17 range.

North County Inland

Avo Playhouse
303 E. Vista Way, Vista • (760) 726-1340 X1523 information; (760) 724-2110 for tickets.

The Avo Playhouse was recently renovated and now proudly supports the live-theater addicts of our communities. It is the winter-season home of the Moonlight Amphitheater, mentioned below. It's also an important North County venue for youth and community productions. You can get a schedule by calling the ticket number above.

Moonlight Amphitheater
1200 Vale Terrace Dr., Vista
• (760) 724-2110

An outdoor theater in North County Inland, the Moonlight Amphitheater produces musicals, comedies and dramas that you can watch under the stars.

For the kids and kids in all of us, *Cinderella* was performed. Other performances in the 1999 seasons include *Gypsy* and *Carousel*.

There is some seating, but if you plan to sit on the grass, bring low lawn chairs only or blankets and pillows. Lots of Insiders bring picnic suppers or, if they're coming from work, fast food. Call for an upcoming schedule and to get on the mailing list.

Patio Playhouse
1511 E. Valley Pkwy., Escondido
• (760) 746-6669

The Playhouse presents a range of live performances in comedy, drama, mystery and musicals. There are seven different shows presented each year and three youth theater shows. For the kids in the family, there was a recent performance of *Puss & Boots* and for adults the comedy *Breaking Legs*. Call for a schedule of events and the price of tickets.

Welk Resort Center
8860 Lawrence Welk Dr., Escondido
• (760) 749-3448, (888) 802-7469

In our Resorts and Spas chapter we covered the relaxing things you can do at the Welk Resort Center, but there's a whole lot more than spa-ing and golfing here. The Welk Resort's production team offers shows like the *Will Rogers Follies* and *Murder at Cafe Noir*, a mystery dinner theater. Prices range from $39 to $60 for most performances and shows usually start at 8 PM and at 7 PM on some Wednesdays. A before-the-show buffet is part of the plan.

East County

Christian Community Theater
1545 Pioneer Way, El Cajon
• (619) 588-0206, (800) 696-1929

The theater presents productions that the entire family will enjoy and often there are children's classics on the live theater "menu." The Christmas programs are especially popular and many Insiders make attending them a family tradition.

Rodeo Bar & Grill
10109 Maine Ave., Lakeside
• (619) 561-8673

Put on your cowboy duds, get your Stetson and take in the theater performances that are featured at this East County venue. Fun-loving live-theater fans from all over the county head for Rodeo Bar & Grill dinner theater. A recent program was *Showdown at the Rodeo Bar & Grill,* a rowdy, hilarious interactive play that's both comedy and mystery. The night we attended it was okay to openly root for the cowboy in the white hat. Dinner comes with the deal. The shows are scheduled for Saturdays at 7 PM, and the programs include a three-course meal for $29. Call for a listing of upcoming performances.

South Bay

Onstage Productions
Park Village Theatre
310 Third Ave., Ste. B-9, Chula Vista
• (619) 422-7787

If you like to get up close to the stage and see every little thing that's going on, try one of Onstage Productions' fine plays. The theater is intimate — only 50 seats — and sitting so close to the stage, you could almost believe you're part of the play. The quality of the plays is excellent. Onstage's 1998 season included A. R. Gurney's *The Dining Room* and Jack Sharkey's *The Murder Room*, a hilarious spoof of English murder mysteries. Call for the current schedule and for ticket reservations.

Something Different

Art Tours
1303 Cave St., La Jolla • (858) 459-5922, (888) 459-5922

Once you've visited all the galleries and museums and seen the performers make their magic, perhaps the muse will strike you, too. Consider signing up for an Art Tour, where you will be taken to a scenic location around San Diego — Coronado, La Jolla, Balboa Park, Torrey Pines or Mission Bay — and you can paint to your heart's content.

Professional art instructors will supply all the materials you'll need — paints, canvases, easels and brushes — and will help you explore your own creativity. You'll be greeted with a continental breakfast, and at lunchtime you'll enjoy a gourmet picnic of sandwiches, fruits and desserts.

Non-painters are always welcome; all locations offer much for the non-painter to see and do. The fee is $139 for painters and $45 for non-painters.

San Diego County has more than 100 parks where you can have lunch, fly kites, take a walk, discover a nature center or have a wonderful family outing.

Parks

When we first began talking about our favorite parks and how to steer you to the best ones, the conversation sounded like a trip down Memory Lane. We swapped stories of family reunions, Fourth of July picnics, playtime with dogs, and walks on shady trails. Then we realized that with more than 100 parks in San Diego County, we needed to narrow our focus and give you enough information so you could start gathering your own memories.

In this chapter you'll find parks where you can have lunch, fly kites, take a walk, discover a nature center or have a wonderful family outing. That was our specific focus. As in other chapters of the book, we've divided the material into regions and then listed those entries alphabetically. Of course our list isn't exhaustive; if you're looking for a neighborhood park, check the Yellow Pages of the phone book for a complete listing of parks in your region. If you want to visit a beach park, check out the sites listed in our Beaches and Watersports chapter.

Although we mention some wilderness areas in this chapter, you'll want to see our Recreation chapter if you want to know about other ones and the serious hiking, biking, climbing and other rugged activities that happen in them. Further camping possibilities are listed there too.

Besides the smaller parks listed here, where people can run after work or picnic at lunchtime, we've included some national forests and large regional parks and preserves too, and we've sometimes narrowed in on certain areas within them. Cleveland National Forest, for instance, takes up a major section of the East County, and offers some superb places to picnic, camp, walk and hang out. Since Cleveland National Forest is huge, we haven't just said, "Head east, friends." Instead we've done some of the scouting for you and selected some parks within the area that are special, such as Palomar Mountain State Park and Cuyamaca Rancho State Park.

But large or small, all the parks here offer outdoor fun for adults and are just right for families too. If you're visiting with children, though, remember safety precautions. It makes sense to watch small fry when they're playing at the tot lots and running through campgrounds and picnic areas. When you're hiking alone or with another person, it's wise not to roam into unfamiliar and isolated areas after dark. Pets, on 6-foot leashes and with a responsible owner, are normally welcome in county parks, but not in all city parks. They must be attended at all times, and it might be smart to call to find out if Fido is welcome. Or you can check the signs you'll see posted at most park entrances.

We've included special information to make your park visits more enjoyable. For example at Blue Sky Ecological Reserve you might see vultures and foxes, but you won't find drinking fountains. You'll need to bring your own water. At Laguna Mountain Recreation Area, you can reserve a place for some thrilling nightlife — if you're into stargazing. Star parties are held during the summer months. Further when there are specific hours of operation or if the park has unusual restrictions we've noted that.

Laws against picking wild flowers, removing plants, tampering with the archaeological resources or the animal and natural features from state, county and city parks are strictly enforced. If one is found doing so, a stiff fine becomes part of your park experience.

Some parks let you reserve picnic areas for parties and reunions. For some camping areas, the reserved list is long. It's always sound advice (in our popular county) to make park reservations well in advance of the date you plan to visit. See the gray box for phone numbers of major camping locations and the individual parks for more details.

Wait no more. Pack a lunch and grab the sunscreen or hat. Now let's head out and explore San Diego parks.

Phone Numbers for Major Camping Locations

San Diego County Parks: (858) 694-3049; (858) 565-3600 reservations

California State Parks: (858) 642-4200 information; (800) 444-7275 for reservations

National Park Service: (619) 557-5450 information; (800) 365-2267 for reservations

U.S.D.A. Forest Service: Cleveland National Park (858) 673-6180; National Forest Recreation Reservations (800) 280-2267

San Diego

Kate Sessions Memorial Park
Soledad Rd. and Loring St. in Pacific Beach, San Diego • (858) 581-9927

Named for famed horticulturist Kate Sessions, this 79-acre park is a tranquil spot overlooking Mission Bay. During summer months it's an ideal location for picnicking, especially for those who want to avoid the traffic and congestion of the beach areas but still want to take advantage of those ocean breezes (which, by the way, make this a favorite spot for kite-flying).

For those who crave a hike, a two-mile hiking trail, lined with coastal sage scrub and other native plants and trees, winds its way through the park and up and down a canyon. If you prefer something less challenging, there's also a paved walking path — perfect for walking off that big picnic lunch. This is a well-equipped park with plenty of picnic tables,

barbecues, playgrounds for the kids and restrooms.

Lake Miramar
Scripps Lake Dr. off Scripps Ranch Blvd., San Diego • (619) 668-2050

Do you like to just get out and walk? So do many Insiders, and Lake Miramar is one of the most popular places for walkers, joggers and skaters. The distance around the perimeter is just under 5 miles, which makes for a perfect workout, whether you're strolling, running or on wheels. Plus, the hiking trails around the lake provide the opportunity to feast your eyes on lots of native vegetation and waterfowl.

The lake is a good spot for game fishing, too, and you're likely to reel in rainbow trout, bass, sunfish and channel catfish. Take a few minutes to linger on the dam. On a clear day you'll be able to see Mt. Soledad and the Pacific Ocean to the west.

Plenty of picnic areas are available, as are concession stands and restrooms. The lake closes for 30 to 60 days each fall.

Marian Bear Memorial Park
Accessible from either Regents Rd. or Genesee Ave., south off Calif. Hwy. 52, • (858) 581-9952

One of the nicest things about San Diego is that it has maintained so much open space within its urban areas. Marian Bear Park is a 466-acre expanse of woodland and trails that runs the length of San Clemente Canyon. You'll feel like you've left the city far behind as you make your way through the dense live oak trees, sycamores, willows and tons of native grasses and shrubs.

Hikers will enjoy the 7 miles of trails, and mountain bikers are welcome to use the park's maintenance roads. You'll often see mountain bikers practicing their moves here. This is a peaceful spot for a picnic, and there are lots of picnic tables to accommodate you.

INSIDERS' TIP

The staff at camping and outdoor-equipment stores can give you the current conditions at many wilderness park areas – so ask if you're wondering about needing tire chains or if you're worried about closures due to dry weather and high fire danger.

Mission Bay Park
2688 E. Mission Bay Dr. (Visitors Center), San Diego • (619) 221-8901

As this is technically classified an aquatic park, we'll cover Mission Bay Park more thoroughly in our Beaches and Watersports chapter. But we also mention it here because it offers more than just watersports.

What was once a stretch of mud and marshlands began its transformation into Mission Bay Park in 1960. At 4,600 acres, it's the largest facility of its kind the world created by dredging, filling and landscaping. The park and picnic areas are used for volleyball, softball, kite flying and horseshoes. The 27 miles of bayfront and 17 miles of oceanfront beaches are probably the county's most popular place for bicycling, skating, jogging or just strolling along and people watching.

Facilities are excellent — boat rentals, docks and launches, beaches, picnic tables, fire rings, restrooms and playgrounds for the kids all make the park perfect for whatever recreation you have in mind. Even if you plan no more than a snooze on the grass while listening to the seagulls and the water lapping on the shore, you can't go wrong with Mission Bay Park.

Mission Trails Regional Park
1 Father Junipero Serra Trail, San Diego • (619) 668-3275

Imagine this: 5,820 acres of open space with nearly 50 miles of hiking and biking trails. Add to it the highest point within the city of San Diego, Cowles Mountain (read about what a great hike this is in our Recreation chapter), and stone outcroppings for rock climbers. Let's keep going. Mission Trails Regional Park even has its own lake — Lake Murray — and it's open year-round for fishing.

We're not through yet. An impressive Visitor and Interpretive Center provides all the sights and sounds to be found within the park with videos, photography and interactive exhibits that describe the geology, history, plants and animals found in the park. The best spot for picnicking within the park is around Lake

INSIDERS' TIP

It's never wise to ignore Nature. Even on days when it's just sprinkling along the coast, the rains can be heavy inland, often causing flash (read that dangerous) floods. Take the advice of park rangers and use common sense when exploring off the beaten track.

Murray, and the paved trail around the lake is ideal for jogging and walking.

Presidio Park
Taylor St. and Presidio Dr., San Diego
• (619) 692-4918

This is the site of Father Junipero Serra's first mission in California, and it's where San Diego was born. Although the mission was moved to a new location a few years after it was built, a museum now stands on top of the hill where it once stood. Surrounding the museum is a beautiful, tree-filled park with gently sloping grassy hills.

The museum itself is worthy of a visit; it's a visual history lesson of the beginnings of San Diego. But if you're just looking for recreation and a picnic, this is a fantastic spot that's easy to get to and close to everything. Plenty of picnic areas are available, and so are basketball courts, ball fields and volleyball courts. A pitch-and-putt golf course is within the park for those looking to work on their short game. Restrooms are conveniently scattered throughout the park.

Tecolote Canyon Natural Park
Tecolote Rd. off I-5, San Diego
• (858) 581-9952

For the explorer, this is one of the best parks in town to while away the hours, absorbing the quietness and observing native plant and animal life. Hiking trails meander back and forth across Tecolote Creek in this 970-acre park, and you'll wander through wooded glades of willows, live oaks and sycamores.

Tecolote has a nature center featuring exhibits on canyon ecology, natural history and Native Americans. The nature center also offers lectures and guided walks through the park. Restrooms are available at the nature center. This park isn't set up for picnicking,

but if you bring your lunch along with a blanket to spread out, the rustic atmosphere can't be beat.

North County Coastal

Guajome County Park
• Guajome Lakes Rd, near Mission Ave., Vista • (760) 565-3600

To find this 599-acre park, exit Interstate 5 on Mission Avenue in Oceanside and drive about 7 miles east. Nature trails ramble for miles through the lush wilderness here. There are equestrian trails too. The marsh area is popular with serious bird watchers and the lakeshore is a well-liked fishing spot. You'll find camping available in 35 developed sites (with showers for campers). There are plenty of picnic and barbecue areas along with a play area and convenient restrooms. Near the parking lot is an information kiosk that has brochures about the area. Nature tours and walks are held periodically; call for times and dates.

San Elijo Lagoon Ecological Reserve
Manchester Ave. exit off Interstate 5 in Encinitas
• (858) 565-3600, (760) 436-3944

There are nearly 300 different species of birds that can be seen at this North County Coastal reserve. One Insider recently spotted egrets, blue herons, coots and an array of ducks. This is one of the county's best-preserved wetlands. The 1,000-acre reserve has more than 7 miles of walking trails that wind through chaparral and marshes. Depending on the season, you'll see ferns and wildflowers.

Docent-led nature walks are held every second Saturday of the month at no cost. The

---

INSIDERS' TIP

If you're a bird watcher, don't miss the Kendall-Frost Marsh Reserve in Mission Bay Park. More than 100 species of waterfowl can be seen. The Reserve is at the north end of Crown Point Drive, between Lamont and Olney Streets.

Photo: San Diego Convention and Visitors Bureau

Parks provide beach access for this young family fishing off the rocky shoreline.

walks begin at 9 AM. Call for starting points and routes.

Torrey Pines State Reserve
N. Torrey Pines Rd., one mile south of Carmel Valley Rd., Del Mar
· (858) 755-2063

This is the sanctuary for the noted and rare Torrey pine. On the 1,750-acre reserve you could count more than 4,000 of these once-endangered trees, but it's far more fun to visit the indigenous plant garden where you can see, touch and smell the plants native to this coastline park. In the spring and early summer, you'll find native wild flowers mixed among the sage and chaparral-loving plants. Nature walks are held on weekends at 11:30 AM and 1:30 PM.

The reserve is open daily from 9 AM to sunset. Dogs are not allowed and picnicking and trail bike riding are prohibited.

North County Inland

Blue Sky Ecological Reserve
Espola Rd., north of Lake Poway Rd., Poway · (858) 679-5469

A wonderful addition to the "outback" parks in the county, Blue Sky Ecological Reserve has 700-acres of wilderness. There's a mixture of chaparral, riparian woodland and coastal sage scrub that gives off a wonderful aroma when blended with San Diego sunshine. The area is home to coyote, deer, foxes, and snakes of many varieties. For the bird watcher, of special note might be gnatcatchers, vultures and hawks.

In this reserve and other parks be sure to walk on the trails and sit on benches rather than rocks and fallen logs. This is snake country and our reptile friends don't like to be surprised.

Drinking water isn't available at the park and walkers are instructed to bring enough to drink. The park is open during daytime hours. Bikes, horses and vehicles are prohibited in the reserve. Near the parking lot is an information kiosk with a display of plants and animals that are native to the area. Guided nature walks are offered on weekends at 9 AM and 4 PM; call for information and reservations.

Lake Hodges
Lake Dr. off Via Rancho Pkwy., Escondido · (760) 668-2050

The 1,234-acre shoreline park on Lake Hodges is a popular place for walking, boating, bike riding and picnicking. While not for

Photo: Dale Frsot/Port of San Diego

Families picnic in beautiful, beachside Chula Vista Bay Park.

the small-sized people in your family, Insiders recommend the 15-mile trail for the long-distance walking family. The trail passes through open grassland to marshlands, making it a wonderful place to see birds and other wildlife. According to those Insiders who love to fish, the lake is teaming with bluegill and catfish (permits are required). Motorboat and rowboat rentals are available and there's a sailboat launch if you bring your own. Swimming isn't allowed in the lake. The park has restrooms.

The area is open March through November on Wednesdays, Saturdays and Sundays from sunrise to sunset.

Lake Poway Recreation Area
Lake Poway Rd, off Espola Rd., Poway
- **(858) 679-5466 information**
- **(619) 679-4342 reservations**

Lake Poway is a 35-acre recreational area that's popular in this youthful community. There is a 60-acre reservoir for boating and fishing, and it's stocked with trout in the fall and winter and catfish in the summer. Nonmotorized boats are available for rental Wednesday through Sundays year-round.

There are two playgrounds for the younger set. There are picnic areas, a nature trail and a concession stand that's open year-round. The eight campsites have running water and restrooms.

Los Penasquitos Canyon Preserve
Black Mountain Rd., west from Interstate 15, Rancho Penasquitos
- **(858) 538-2480**

The reserve is about 3,700 acres and you'll find woodlands, scrub oak and chaparral. There are walking trails, but bikes are allowed only on the service roads. Depending on the season, some of the trails may be closed; the Preserve is open from 8 AM to sunset daily. There are two historic adobe structures on the site, built in 1825 and 1910. Guided tours of the adobes are held every Saturday at 11 AM.

Palomar Mountain State Park
19552 State Park Rd., Palomar Mountain
- **(760) 742-3463, (760) 788-0250, (800) 444-7275 for camping reservations**

As you reach the fork in S-7, one way leads to Palomar Mountain State Park and the other takes you to the national forest and the observatory. The sign is clear but the choice may be hard. This is a popular year-round picnic, walking and camping area for Southern California because it stays green for most of the year. (Be prepared to bring along chains during the winter if you head toward Palomar Mountain for some fun in the snow. You may not be allowed to drive up to the top without them.)

At the park you'll find some rambling walking trails. The Doane Valley Nature trail is about a 3-easy-mile walk; most of it is on flat ground. The hike to the observatory, according to the self-guided trail markers, is about 4 miles with some climbing. Therefore, this isn't the right trail for tiny people in your family, but kids older than 10 will probably love the challenge. Request a trail brochure from the ranger station staff as you drive into the park.

For those who love to picnic, you'll find eating areas and camping spots with barbecues. Many Insiders picnic on Thanksgiving and Christmas, and the outings have become family traditions. There are also developed campsites. Speaking of picnics and camping, become "bee" wary. The bees and yellow jackets (a hungry, hazardous wasp) can be a serious fun-deterrent during the late summer and fall when they swarm around campgrounds and picnic areas. They can be frightening and dangerous for small children and the family pooch. Steer clear of swarms and bring along insect repellent.

The observatory and museum, at the end of County Road S-6, are open from 9 AM to 4 PM daily throughout the year. (Find out more about them in our chapter on Attractions.) There's a small gift shop that's open daily between July 1 and August 31 and weekends only the rest of the year.

East County

Anza-Borrego Desert State Park
Borrego Springs • (760) 767-4684 (for an events message), (760) 767-4205 (to speak with a park volunteer)

There are more than 600,000 acres of desert within this State Park for camping, picnicking, walking, biking and hiking. Here you'll see plants from the silver cholla and jumping cholla (a prickly cactus that will earn your respect if you happen to mess with it) to the agave (or century plant) and indigo bush (with its cobalt blue flowers). There's wild life too, from big jackrabbits to bigger coyotes.

It's a flora and fauna paradise for naturalists of all ages. See our Attractions chapter for details about the wild flowers which bloom here in early spring and turn the desert into a breathtaking burst of exotica. If you're bringing kids with you, get each one a "disposable" camera and let them snap their favorite flowers. When the photos are developed, see if they can identify the flowers and plants in their snapshots.

At the park, you'll find 500 primitive trails (remember to take water — this is the desert). Borrego Palm Canyon has 117 developed campsites, five group sites and a hiking trail that leads to an oasis of palms and shaded pools that's always unexpected even if you've hiked the park 20 times. Tamarisk Grove has 25 developed campsites. Call the park and ask to have the latest newsletter sent or scout out books on the park at bookstores and libraries. The more you read about the region, the more you'll understand why it's important to respect the delicate ecosystem of our deserts.

If you're adventurous, there are primitive campsites dotted here and there throughout the park and are given out on a first-come, first-served basis. The rangers will make suggestions on equipment you'll need. Remember, you'll need to pack in your water and pack out the trash. The equestrian camp has 10 sites and a corral. The visitor center, located 1 mile west of Borrego Springs on West Palm Canyon Drive is open from 9 AM to 5 PM daily. There's a $5 charge to enter the park; camping fees range from $16 to $22, depending on the month and the day of the week. Weekend rates are $22 a day.

Cuyamaca Rancho State Park
Calif. Hwy. 79 between Hwy. 78 and I-8, eastern San Diego County • (760) 765-0755

This is a state park that's worth visiting again and again,, whether you come for a short walk or plan to disappear for a while in the wilderness. There are more than 120 miles of

San Diegans enjoy a great day in the sun at Mission Bay Park.

walking and equestrian trails. The wilderness area covers 25,000 acres in East County including heavenly wildflower meadows, Green Valley Falls and the ruins of a gold mine, the Stonewall mine. There are two developed campgrounds with 166 units, group campsites and cabins. There is even an equestrian campsite.

Lake Cuyamaca is popular for fishing, boating and bird watching. Playing on the shore is allowed, but swimming isn't. Motorboats and rowboats are rented throughout the year. During the summer, paddleboats are available. Call (760) 765-0515 for rental information and reservation. The park has a museum too, displaying Native American artifacts; it's open weekdays 8 AM to 4:30 PM and weekends 10 AM to 4 PM. Call for park hours.

Laguna Mountain Recreation Area
County Rte. S-1, six miles northeast of Pine Valley • (619) 445-6235 (for information), (619) 473-8547 (for the information center)

Located within the Cleveland National Park, you'll find 8,600 acres of recreation area with more than 20 miles of trails. The Pacific Crest Trail is a 6-mile path where every turn presents Kodak opportunities.

The visitors center has information on safety, hiking and campfire programs along with the summertime star-gazing parties. The center is open Friday 1 PM to 5 PM and weekends from 10 AM until 5 PM. There are several hundred developed camping sites, some open year-round, others only during the summer months.

Lake Morena County Park
Lake Morena Rd., off Calif. Hwy. 94, or Buckman Springs Rd., off Interstate 8, near Campo • (858) 694-3049 (information), (858) 565-3600 (reservations)

Part of the Cleveland National Forest, which stretches through San Diego County and into Orange County, Lake Morena is a lakefront park that covers about 3,250 acres. The terrain is rocky foothills with scrub oak and chaparral. Here you'll find the Pacific Crest Trail

INSIDERS' TIP

Love the outdoors? Want to make new friends? The County of San Diego Department of Parks and Recreation is eager for reliable volunteers to run programs and become docents. Call (619) 694-3049 for more information.

that excites hikers of skill. You'll also find easy walking trails for young kids.

If you're into camping, this is a choice park. There are 86 developed campsites, 58 with RV hookups, and 2 campsites for disabled campers. There are scores of picnic areas. You'll also find primitive campsites at the northern end of the park.

If you're into fishing, call the "fish report hotline" at (619) 478-5473 for the latest report. Fishing is popular here, and bass, bluegill, catfish, crappie and stocked trout crowd the lake — at least that's what we've heard from those who love the sport. There's a rowboat launch and motor and rowboats are available for rent.

To blend a bit of history into the outing, stop at the nature center and museum. There's antique farm equipment (yes, you can tell the children, people really did use these tools). There's a nice-to-see collection of barbed wire, birds' nests and a listing of record-setting bass. The park and museum are open weekdays from 9:30 AM to 5 PM, weekends from 9:30 AM to sunset.

Santee Lakes Regional Park
9040 Carlton Oaks Dr., Santee
• (619) 448-2482

Popular Santee Lakes Regional Park offers a profusion of picnicking, jogging, lounging, boating and fishing opportunities. There's a developed campground with 152 sites with RV hookups, a general store, a swimming pool and rec center along with a laundry room. To add to the fun there are horseshoe pits, volleyball courts and a large playground. Kids will immediately take to the places to fly kites, throw a softball and enjoy the San Diego weather.

South Bay

Sweetwater County Park
Summit Meadow Rd. off San Miguel Rd.,
Bonita • (858) 694-3049

If your idea of the perfect day at the park includes hiking or horseback riding, Sweetwater may be the place for you. Its 580 acres of open space and trails include more than 8 miles of hiking and equestrian trails that run along the Sweetwater River and the southern shore of the Sweetwater Reservoir. If that's not enough, a 4-mile paved bicycle and equestrian trail runs from the western end of the park to San Diego Bay.

Sixty developed campsites are in the park (see our chapter on Recreation for more camping information), and picnic sites are available. Sweetwater is a wilderness park that is dedicated to preserving the area's riparian habitat.

Tijuana River National Estuary Research Reserve
Caspian Way and 3rd St., Imperial Beach
• (619) 575-3614

A bird watcher's delight, this 2,500-acre salt marsh reserve boasts more than 300 species of migratory birds. See them for yourself as you wander along 6 miles of trails that cross the reserve. There's a visitor center that has exhibits on local ecology and the species of birds you're likely to see. The center also offers guided nature walks on weekends.

Winter is the best time to see migratory waterfowl; in springtime acres and acres of chaparral-covered hillsides are blanketed with colorful wildflowers, putting on a display that only Mother Nature could create. The visitor center is open Wednesday through Sunday.

The perception that locals and visitors spend much of their time in pursuit of recreation is no myth.

Recreation

Looking for something to do? You won't have to look far — San Diego is famous for its abundance of recreational activities, both indoor and outdoor. The perception that locals and visitors spend much of their time in pursuit of recreation is no myth. From bicycling to bowling to hang gliding to inline skating, the opportunities are endless. So endless, in fact, that we've devoted entire chapters to watersports and golf. In this chapter we'll cover everything else and give you enough information to get you started on your favorite sport.

We'll tell you where the nicest bike paths are, and where to find the county's best hiking and walking trails. If being airborne appeals to you, we'll direct you to places where you can hook up with a hot-air balloon or a hang glider. For the earthbound enthusiasts, we'll keep you busy but safely anchored.

Part of the appeal of San Diego is that you can combine relaxation with fresh air, exercise and a ton of fun. We encourage you to try something new while you're in town. Rent a pair of inline skates and glide up and down the boardwalk at Mission Beach. Once you have the hang of it and can direct your attention elsewhere, you'll discover that this is one of the best sports in the world for people watching. Or join an impromptu game of volleyball at the beach or in any of the county's many parks.

A couple of good sources for organized (and usually free) hikes, walks, bicycle tours and many other current activities are Thursday's "Night and Day" section of *The San Diego Union-Tribune* and *The San Diego Reader*. The *Reader* also comes out on Thursdays and is distributed free at record stores, bookstores, drug stores and many other businesses throughout the county. They both have comprehensive listings of things to do around town. Whatever you decide to do, keep in mind that safety precautions aren't just for kids. Use common sense and heed the advice of professionals. We don't want to have to visit you in the hospital. And even though the temperature is usually mild, don't forget your sunscreen.

Ballooning

Ever since the movie *Around the World in 80 Days* focused attention on ballooning as a mode of transportation, the fascination for those brightly colored, soaring globes has held steady. If you'd like to quietly glide through the sky above San Diego, several balloon companies are eager to make your dream come true.

California Dreamin' Balloon Adventures
162 S. Rancho Santa Fe Rd., #F35, Encinitas • (800) 373-3359

Soar high above the earth on a sunrise ride over the wine country in Temecula or a sunset ride over Del Mar. Riders receive a photo and certificate at the conclusion of the ride. The sunrise ride is $128 per person and includes a continental breakfast; the sunset ride is $148 per person Monday through Friday, $158 per person Saturday and Sunday, and includes champagne and hors d'oeuvres.

Skysurfer Balloon Co.
1221 Camino del Mar, Del Mar • (858) 481-6800

Sunrise balloon rides in Temecula's wine

country include a picnic breakfast upon landing. Sunset coastal excursions in Del Mar offer on-board champagne. Rates are $135 per person Monday through Friday, and $145 per person on Saturdays and Sundays.

Bicycling/Mountain Biking

Whatever your pleasure — gentle, flat surfaces or more challenging hills and terrain, — you'll find it somewhere around town. Designated bike paths are clearly marked on many San Diego streets, and great off-road trails are located throughout the county. One of the best street rides is along the coast, from Mission Beach north to La Jolla. It hugs the shoreline for most of the way, but when it does veer inland for a block or two, you'll be treated to a peek at some magnificent homes. For mountain bikers, the Iron Mountain trail in East County is a moderately difficult favorite. Trailheads are located on California Highway 67 at Poway Road and Calif. 67 at Ellie Lane.

Bicycles can be rented at several locations; we've listed a few below, along with Gravity Activated Sports, a company that guides thrilling organized tours. Rental rates vary, but you usually can rent a cruiser for $5 per hour. Full-day rates range from $10 to $25. Mountain-bike rentals are usually a few dollars more. Most bike shops provide maps that highlight street bike paths and off-road trails all over the county, or you can pick up a map at the Caltrans office at 4040 Taylor St., San Diego, (619) 231-2453. Remember, bicycle helmets are recommended for all and required by law for children younger than 18.

Bike 101
211 N. Highway 101, Solana Beach
• (858) 793-5431

Bike 101 specializes in mountain bikes that can be ridden either off-road or on the street. Rentals are available by the hour or by the day.

Bikes and Beyond
1201 First St., Coronado
• (619) 435-7180

Beach cruisers and mountain bikes can be rented by the hour, half-day or full day. The shop is located in the Ferry Landing Marketplace. A wide variety of cycles is available for adults and kids.

Bike Tours San Diego
509 Fifth Ave., San Diego
• (619) 238-2444

This shop specializes in hybrid bikes (a cross between a road bike and a mountain bike) and mountain bikes. Also available for rent are hard-to-find mountain bikes with front suspension. Free pick-up and delivery are offered, and all bike rentals come with locks, helmets and maps.

Carlsbad Cycle World
325 Carlsbad Village Dr., Carlsbad
• (760) 434-5698

Hybrid and mountain bikes can be rented here, and for a $10 fee, bikes will be delivered and picked up. Bikes are rented by the hour, day and week.

Gravity Activated Sports
16220 Calif. Hwy. 76, Pauma Valley
• (760) 742-2294, (800) 985-4427

GAS is famous for the "Palomar Plunge" a 16-mile, 5,000-foot guided bicycle descent that includes a tour of the Palomar Observatory, bike and equipment rental, lunch, T-shirt, photo and certificate of achievement. The cost is $80 per person. Also ask about their cycling wine country tours, the desert descent and off-road tours.

Hamel's Action Sports Center
704 Ventura Pl., San Diego
• (858) 488-5050

A fixture in Mission Beach for decades, Hamel's rents a full range of bicycles and mountain bikes for the whole family. Its turreted, castle-like building is located right next to Belmont Amusement Park in Mission Beach.

Photo: Dale Frost/Port of San Diego

This smiling fisherman's catch has the attention of a group of children.

Bicycle Clubs

For organized cycling adventures, we suggest you contact one of the following clubs:

San Diego Bicycle Club
P.O. Box 80562, San Diego, CA 92138
• (858) 495-2454

This is the oldest bicycle club in San Diego and has members of all ages. Its focus is on racing, and members are trained by experienced cyclists that have both racing and coaching backgrounds. The club organizes several races throughout the year.

San Diego Bicycle Touring Club
P.O. Box 1941, Chula Vista, CA 91912
• (619) 426-8192

Geared mostly for the bicyclist who likes to cruise, this club nevertheless offers some challenging rides. Members schedule a weekly Sunday ride that takes place in locations all over the county.

North County Cycle Club
P.O. Box 127, San Marcos, CA 92079
• (760) 471-2239

Three groups make up the membership of NCCC: The Cruisers, who are laid back and like to enjoy the scenery while they ride; The Roadies, who are fast, intermediate to advanced riders who like to pick up the pace a little; and The Spokey Dokes, who are the mountain bikers of the group. All three sections schedule regular rides.

Billiards

The game of billiards has been enjoying a resurgence in recent years, a fact borne out by the increasing number of billiards parlors in San Diego. Plus, you can usually find a table or two in many bars around the county.

INSIDERS' TIP

Thinking of trying hang gliding? Wind conditions at Torrey Pines are consistently the best from February through April, even though you'll be able to fly whenever a good wind comes up.

Photo: Dale Frost/Port of San Diego

Imperial Beach Pier is a great place for fishing, strolling and ocean-viewing.

But for pure, uninterrupted billiards, we recommend you visit one of the facilities devoted primarily to the game.

Billiard Gallery Sports Grill
717 N. Escondido Blvd., Escondido
• (760) 743-7665

With a full sports bar, grill and 26 pool tables, you can't go wrong here. Rates range from $5 per hour for daytime hours during the week to $8.50 per hour for weekend nights.

Fiesta Billiards
1770 Palm Ave., San Diego (South Bay)
• (619) 429-1800

For $5 per hour you can play pool to your heart's content on one of 28 tables. Or relax with a cocktail and a snack when you need a break from the action.

Pacific Q Billiards Club
1454 Encinitas Blvd., Encinitas
• (760) 943-9929

Play pool on 13 gorgeous tables for $3 per player, per hour, up until 7 PM, Sunday through Thursday. After 7 PM, the price is $4 per player, per hour, and $5 on Friday and Saturday. Pizza, salads, sandwiches and buffalo wings are the standard fare, and Pacific Q serves more than 70 brands of beer.

Society Billiard Cafe
1051 Garnet Ave., San Diego
• (858) 272-7665

In addition to 15 regulation pool tables, Society Billiard Cafe has a bar that serves cocktails, beer and wine from around the world. Pizza, salads and sandwiches can be enjoyed at the on-site restaurant, which also has patio dining. Rates range from $3 per hour, per person, during the day to $10 per hour on weekend nights.

Bowling

One sport that never goes out of style is bowling. San Diego has several bowling alleys where you can enjoy a leisurely game or two, or if league play is more to your taste, all alleys provide that, too. Prices vary considerably from facility to facility and depend on the day of the week and the time of day. You can bowl a lane for as little as $2 or as much as $8 per person, per hour. All facilities have spe-

San Diego Marathon

Imagine this: It's a perfect early morning winter's day in San Diego. That means the sun is out and it's in the mid-60s and sure to jump 10 degrees by lunch. The scene could be tranquil; however, with over 8,000 people warming up, stretching, and psyching up to compete in this event, all is far from serene.

The annual San Diego Marathon is the second-oldest marathon on the West Coast. Begun in the late 50s by the San Diego Track Club, it was originally run from Oceanside to Mission Bay. It moved to North County in December of 1990.

Change is constant in San Diego, and usually brings improvements. This new race was no exception. When the current organizing company, In Motion Inc., was hired to orchestrate the event, it turned into a not-to-be-missed happening that continues to score high marks with runners, watchers and supporters.

When In Motion moved the race to North County Coastal in 1990, it increased its national exposure and changed the race into more than a recreational activity. It's a community event now. (FYI: In Motion, Inc. is a company owned and run by Insiders: Lynn Flanagan and her daughters, Ellen Flanagan and Christine Flanagan Adams.)

The marathon is held in the middle of January. If you'd like details for the next run, call In Motion at (858) 792-2900 or watch the local press. The company also coordinates a fitness-training program for those interested in running but who might not be in shape. The 25-week regimen is designed to help everyone, regardless of age or fitness level, to participate in the race — and have some fun too.

Even if you don't run, there are still exciting things to do at the three-day All About Fitness Expo, which is held in conjunction with the race. The expo is free. It's a big deal and thousands come to see the latest in exercise equipment, tasty healthy foods — including energy bars and smoothies —, and meet some local celebrities, from the mayor to the winners of the previous years' races. Keep in mind that this isn't just a San Diego marathon or a three-day program — it's a West Coast event.

All the races (there are choices) start and end at Carlsbad's Plaza Camino Real shopping center at El Camino Real and Marron Road, about 40 minutes north of downtown San Diego. You can find it by driving

Photo: In Motion, Inc.

There's a marathon run for everyone. Most exciting? The one in which you are entered.

— continued on next page

north on Interstate 5, then following Highway 78 east about 1 mile.

The featured event is the marathon (26.2 miles) where runners run northern San Diego's coastline. Lynn Flanagan, founder of In Motion, Inc. explains: "The marathon, and half marathon, are run on a gently rolling out-and-back course along the ocean. All marathon events are run on a closed course with safety provided by the Carlsbad Police Department." Mother Nature supplies perfect days.

The half marathon is recognized as one of the fastest races of that distance in the United States, and Lynn says that it draws the very best field of American runners. The Marathon Relay, which offers 25 different divisions, including law enforcement, military, non-profit, financial, and medical, is open to five-member teams. Southern California's businesses and civic clubs always participate in this event, which draws lots of cheering supporters of the various teams.. Children 12 and younger are winners no matter how they place in the Keebler Kids Marathon Mile. Wheelchair competitors compete in the marathon too, and the purse is sizable (last year it was $2,000). Many of the events are covered by national television, including ESPN, and magazines such as *Outdoor Life*. The local press and TV crews are always on the spot.

The San Diego Marathon is good for San Diego. The organization helps local non-profit associations find ways to use the marathon for fund-raising, and programs like the Special Olympics, Blind Recreation Center, the Autism Association and Volunteers on Probation have done so. The sponsor list last year included Southwest Airlines, Vons, Sparkletts Water, BMW, Gatorade, ESQ Watch, Cloud 9 Shuttle and the Carlsbad Convention and Visitors Bureau.

Schedule of Events

Friday
San Diego Marathon Golf Tournament
All About Fitness Expo   3:00 to 7:00 PM

Saturday
Cliff Bar 5K Run/Walk   8:00 AM
All About Fitness Expo   8:00 AM to 5:00 PM
Keebler Kids Marathon Mile   9:30 AM
Vons Carbo Dinner   5:00 to 8:00 PM

Sunday
Walk start, marathon   5:30 AM
Early marathon start   6:30 AM
Half marathon start   7:00 AM
Wheelchair start   7:25 AM
Marathon start   7:30 AM
Marathon Relay   7:30 AM

INSIDERS' TIP

Are you an amateur photographer? Capture some of San Diego's most beautiful images at Mission Trails Regional Park. The dramatic stone outcroppings are captivating subjects for shutterbugs.

cials, like $1 days, and discounts for seniors and kids, so be sure to call in advance to find out prices and lane availability.

AMF Eagle Bowl
945 W. San Marcos Blvd., San Marcos
• (760) 744-7000

Forty lanes with automatic scoring make AMF Eagle Bowl a modern, up-to-date facility. If you're looking for something a little different, try moonlight casino bowling on Friday nights and extreme bowling on Saturday nights. You'll find a snack bar, lounge and pro shop on the premises.

Brunswick Premier Lanes
845 Lazo Ct., Chula Vista
• (619) 421-4801

Brunswick Premier has 48 lanes, a pro shop, a snack bar and a full-service lounge. This is a busy facility, so reservations are highly recommended. A variety of bowling opportunities are offered for kids and seniors, too.

Kearny Mesa Bowl
7585 Clairemont Mesa Blvd., San Diego
• (858) 279-1501

Forty lanes provide ample opportunity for bowling on even the most crowded days. A sports bar with satellite television is a popular hangout, as is the snack bar and video arcade. The fully stocked pro shop has everything you'll need in the way of equipment.

Mira Mesa Lanes
8210 Mira Mesa Blvd., San Diego
• (858) 578-0500

Mira Mesa Lanes is a relatively new bowling facility with 44 modern lanes and an automatic color scoring system. On the premises is everything you'll need to make your bowling day a complete experience: a sports bar, snack bar, well-stocked pro shop and video arcade.

Parkway Bowl
1280 Fletcher Pkwy., El Cajon
• (619) 448-4111

Parkway Bowl has long been a family entertainment center in East County. Its 60 lanes include eight that are equipped with bumpers just for kids — which means no gutter balls.

All lanes have automatic scoring, and the facility has a pro shop, bar and snack bar.

Surf Bowl
1401 S. Coast Hwy., Oceanside
• (760) 722-1371

If bowling by the sea appeals to you, the Surf Bowl is the place. With 32 lanes, a snack bar and lounge, you'll find everything you need for an enjoyable afternoon or evening at the lanes. The on-site pro shop is fully stocked for all your equipment needs, too.

Camping

Is your idea of camping truly roughing it with just a tent and few essentials? Or do you prefer a more upscale form of camping, say, in an RV or a park that has all the luxuries of home? Whatever your heart's desire, San Diego has the perfect campsite for you.

We have private camps, county camps, state camps and national forests, all with as many or as few amenities as necessary to satisfy the adventurer in you. Here we give you a sampling of some of the area's best and most popular campgrounds. You may want to check some of the camping sites described in our Parks chapter too. But if you want an in-depth listing of the dozens of sites throughout the county, try calling the county's park and recreation department at (858) 694-3049 or the state's park and recreation department at (619) 220-5422. Or look for camping guides and books at your local library or bookstore. Most camps accept advance reservations; be sure to call ahead to find out. Rates change frequently, so be sure to check for current prices.

Agua Caliente County Park
1 mile southwest of Agua Caliente Springs, off County Rd. S2
• (858) 565-3600

Heaven in the desert is the best way to describe Agua Caliente. Two naturally fed mineral pools are the main attractions here. One is a large outdoor pool kept at its natural 96 degrees; the other is indoors, heated and boasting Jacuzzi jets. The 140 campsites accommodate tents or RVs with full or partial hook-ups. Hiking trails, horseshoe pits, shuffleboard courts and a children's play area provide plenty of entertainment for campers. Campsites rent for $15 per night, and reservations can be made 12 weeks in advance.

Campland on the Bay
2211 Pacific Beach Dr., San Diego • (858) 581-4260, (800) 422-9386

Every campsite at Campland comes with a beach, a bay and a rollicking good time. Right on the shores of Mission Bay, this private camp has 568 spaces, most of which can accommodate either tents or RVs. All sites have electricity and water, and 420 of them come equipped with sewer hook-ups. Campers can enjoy the two pools on the premises along with showers, picnic tables, playground, recreation room and tons of water activities. Summer rates range from $23 per night for a tent site to $100 for Campland's Supersite, which is a private site overlooking the bay with a Jacuzzi, washer and dryer, gas grill and cable TV. Reservations are accepted up to two years in advance.

Laguna (Cleveland National Forest)
3 miles northwest of Mount Laguna, off County Rd. S1 • (858) 673-6180

Camping in the Laguna Mountains is back-to-nature with just the basics, but a more beautiful and peaceful spot would be hard to find. The state-owned Laguna campsite has 103 tent sites and 20 RV sites. You will find running water, primitive toilets, barbecues, fire rings and picnic tables. Swimming (in a stream) is a one-mile hike from the campground. Rates are $10 per night, and all campsites are available on a first-come, first-served basis.

South Carlsbad State Beach
5 miles south of Carlsbad, via County Rd. S21 • (760) 438-3143 (information), (800) 444-7275 (reservations)

This is a rare campsite set on the beaches of Carlsbad and perfect for those who wish to combine camping with water sports. Surfing, fishing or simply swimming are all right at your feet here.

The site includes showers, restrooms, fire

These horses will be taking visitors for rides in the Cuyamaca Mountains.

Photo: Thom Vollenweider

Photo: Dale Frost/Port of San Diego

Good friends get together for a day of sailing.

rings and picnic tables. The campground has 220 tent or RV sites, and prices range from $17 to $23 per night. Reservations can be made up to seven months in advance.

Sweetwater Summit
Off Summit Meadow Rd., Bonita
- **(858) 565-3600**

Sixty campsites accommodate tents, RVs and horse trailers. Several sites have horse corrals, and all have water and electricity. Horse trails galore are the main attraction here. Other amenities include restrooms, showers, barbecues, picnic tables and a large group area.

As with all county parks, reservations are accepted up to 12 weeks in advance. Rates range from $12 to $16 per night. Horses add an extra dollar to the fee. To get to the campground take Bonita Road east until it becomes San Miguel Rd. Turn left on Summit Meadow.

Climbing

Indoors or outdoors, rock climbing is quickly becoming the sport of choice for many locals and visitors alike. Indoor facilities are available for climbing, lessons and equipment purchase or rental. For outdoor climbing, we highly recommend you take advantage of an organized climb, especially if you're a newcomer to the sport or unfamiliar with the area. Outdoor climbing areas are abundant throughout San Diego County, but you can't go wrong with the recommendations and guidance of professionals.

Adventure 16 Outdoor and Travel Outfitters
4620 Alvarado Canyon Rd., San Diego
- **(619) 283-2374**

312 Horton Plaza, San Diego
- **(619) 234-1751**

INSIDERS' TIP

Two small books are gems of information on some of the best hiking trails in San Diego County. Check out Sean O'Brien's *12 Short Hikes*. He has written one each for mountain hikes and coastal hikes in San Diego County, and they're available at most local bookstores.

The travel experts at Adventure 16 specialize in group climbs all over the county. This is also a great place to get top-notch instruction in the art of rock climbing. Outdoor clothing, gear and boots are available for purchase or for rent.

Solid Rock
2074 Hancock St., San Diego
• **(619) 299-1124**
13026 Stowe Dr., Poway
• **(858) 748-9011**

This indoor climbing facility offers 30-foot seamless, textured climbing walls and a multitude of apparatuses for practicing techniques such as bouldering, top-roping and lead climbing.

Hours are from 11 AM to 10 PM Monday through Friday, 9 AM to 9 PM Saturday and 11 AM to 7 PM Sunday. Day passes can be purchased for $10, Monday through Friday before 5 PM. After 5 PM and on weekends, a day pass is $12. Children 16 and younger are always charged $10. Lessons are available and may be required of inexperienced climbers.

REI Recreational Equipment
5556 Copley Dr., San Diego
• **(858) 279-4400**

In addition to offering clothing, gear and boots for purchase or rental, REI has a small indoor climbing wall for enthusiasts to get a quick (and free) taste of what rock climbing is like.

Vertical Hold Climbing Center
9580 Distribution Ave., San Diego
• **(858) 586-7572**

This center has an indoor 10,000-square-foot climbing wall and welcomes beginners to advanced climbers. Beginning climbers are required to take instruction. Hours are from 11:30 AM to 10 PM Monday through Friday, 10 AM to 10 PM Saturday and 10 AM to 8 PM Sunday. Day passes are $12.

Hang Gliding

Hang gliding, or paragliding as it is frequently called, is as close as you can get to flying without actually having wings. For the thrill of a lifetime, soar above the beautiful Torrey Pines coastline and enjoy unparalleled stillness and serenity while navigating either a hang glider or paraglider. All fliers must have an advanced license to soar on their own, but you can experience the thrill right away by taking a tandem flight with a licensed pilot.

UP San Diego
2800 Torrey Pines Scenic Dr., La Jolla
• **(858) 452-9858**

Located at the historic landmark Torrey Pines Glider Port, UP San Diego offers training courses ranging from beginner to advanced. The three- to four-day beginner course teaches the basic skills necessary to fly under direct instructor supervision. The cost is $495. For a one-time thrill, try a tandem flight. No instruction is necessary — you glide with an experienced pilot. The cost is $125.

Hiking

We proudly declare that there is no better place in the world than San Diego for hiking over a variety of terrain, from mountain to desert to coastal trails. While we may be overstating the case just slightly, if you're a dedicated hiker, you will not be disappointed here. If you'd like to meet new friends and prefer to hike with a group, check Thursday's "Night and Day" section of the *San Diego Union-Tribune*. It usually has a long list of organized hikes from which you can choose.

If you prefer the solitude of hiking on your own or selecting your own location, we'll highlight a few of the best hikes here. For comprehensive maps and lists of hiking trails, check with any sporting goods store or bookstore.

INSIDERS' TIP

If you plan to test your skills at one of San Diego's indoor climbing facilities, morning hours are the least crowded time. By early afternoon, there may be more climbers around you than you want to contend with.

Photo: Dale Frost/Port of San Diego

The steady ocean breezes make the bay a great place to learn to windsurf.

Be sure to pack lots of water and sunscreen, and if you're planning to make a day of it, include a picnic lunch and some basic first-aid supplies. San Diego does have its share of dangerous critters too, so be alert for rattlesnakes (even on the coast) and mountain lions.

Cuyamaca Rancho State Park
10 miles northeast of Alpine

If diversity in hiking is what you're after, this hike is the ticket. This is a somewhat strenuous hike that will take you along streambeds, through pine and oak forests, meadows and sagebrush. The trailhead is right at the parking lot. Head north on the East Side Trail, and you'll wander alongside the Sweetwater River for a bit before you start to climb. Some long climbs await you, but the reward is an unequaled scenic vista. This trail is not marked well in some places, so we advise you to have either a map or clear directions before you set out. The trail length is 4.7

miles, and it should take you about 2½ hours. As always, be sure to take more water than you think you'll need. To get to the trailhead, take Interstate 8 east to Calif. 79, turn left (north) and drive five miles to a large parking lot on the right side.

Mission Trails Regional Park
1 Father Junipero Serra Trail, San Diego
• (619) 668-3275

Mission Trails contains almost 6,000 acres of hiking, mountain biking and equestrian trails that meander through mountains, valleys and lakes. Staff members from the Visitors' Center offer guided hikes daily. One of the best hikes in the park (no guide is necessary) is to the top of Cowles Mountain. At 1,591 feet, it's the highest point in the city of San Diego. To reach the trailhead from the coast, drive east on I-8 to Mission Gorge Road, then turn left (north). Drive 5 miles to Golfcrest Road and turn right (south). Head up the hill for 1 mile to the parking lot on the left. You'll hike up a series of

Photo: San Diego Convention and Visitors Bureau

Glider enthusiasts like to hang glide off the Torrey Pines cliffs.

switchbacks to the top of the mountain, a 3-mile hike. The views are spectacular.

Rancho Peñasquitos Canyon Preserve
10 miles north of downtown San Diego

Hike through oak trees and lush meadows on this 6½-mile trail before descending to the canyon floor where you'll be surrounded by giant boulders. During winter and spring, a stream forms small waterfalls between the boulders, making this a perfect spot for a picnic. You'll hike up a canyon for a while before returning to the grove of oaks and the main trail back to the parking lot. The hike takes about 2½ hours. To get to the trailhead, take 1-15 north to Mira Mesa Blvd. Turn left (west) and travel one-half mile to Black Canyon Rd. Turn right and drive to the parking lot, which is one mile ahead on the left.

San Elijo Lagoon Ecological Preserve
Encinitas, North County Coastal

This is an easy 4-mile hike that you can stretch into a two-hour stroll. Once you leave

the parking lot, you'll make a series of right turns until you pass underneath the freeway. Turn left (south) and follow the trail that travels alongside the lagoon. Signs along the way will point out some of the endangered species that inhabit the preserve. At the end of the trail is a lovely view of the Pacific Ocean. To get to the trailhead, take I-5 north (from the city of San Diego) to Manchester Ave. Turn left (east) and drive a quarter mile to a small dirt parking lot just across from the entrance to the preserve.

Horseback Riding

Grab your cowboy hat, pull on those boots and climb on a horse for a different view of San Diego. Whether you prefer riding on the beach or in the wilderness, both are available for short rides of one hour or longer rides up to a full day.

Canyon Side Trail Rides
12115 Black Mountain Rd., San Diego
• **(858) 271-8777**

See nature at its most pristine from atop a

horse as you ride into the Los Peñasquitos Preserve. Owner John Barker offers professional trail horses and guides seven days a week. Rates start at $20 per hour with discounts for multiple-hour rentals. Full-day rides include a barbecue. Call for reservations.

Holidays on Horseback
24928 Viejas Blvd., Descanso
• **(619) 445-3997**

Located in the Cuyamaca Mountains in San Diego's East County, Holidays on Horseback offers wilderness rides from one and a half hours up to nine hours. The rate for a one-and-a-half-hour ride is $25; a two-hour ride is $35 and a three-hour ride is $50 and includes chips and dips. If you ride for four hours the fee is $60 and includes a picnic lunch. Call for reservations.

Sandi's Rental Stable
2060 Hollister St., San Diego (in the South Bay) • **(619) 424-3124**

At Sandi's you'll be fitted with a saddle and introduced to your horse as soon as you arrive. Absolute beginners to experienced riders are welcome. Several riding tours are offered, but the most popular are the three-hour beach ride for $40 per person and the one-hour river trail ride for $20 per person. No reservations are necessary.

Ice Skating

Hard to imagine ice skating in San Diego? Believe it or not, it not only exists, it thrives. Several local skating rinks have public hours for amateur skaters to test their skills gliding across the ice. Remember, even if it's summertime it can get chilly inside the rinks, so dress appropriately.

Ice Chalet
4545 La Jolla Village Dr., San Diego
• **(858) 452-9110**

Located in the University Towne Center mall, Ice Chalet offers public ice skating seven days a week. If you need lessons, teachers are on hand to help get you upright and moving forward. The rink is available for private parties too, in case you're looking for someplace unique for your next gathering. Because the rink is located in the UTC shopping mall (See our Shopping chapter), there's the added benefit of a food court surrounding the rink, and parents can shop while kids skate. Rates are $9 per person and include skate rental. Public hours vary from day to day, so be sure to call ahead.

Iceoplex
555 N. Tulip St., Escondido
• **(760) 489-5550**

This modern facility in North County Inland has a fixed public skating schedule. Monday through Friday you can skate from 8:30 AM to 11:30 AM and from 1:30 PM to 5:15 PM. Wednesday evenings from 7:30 PM to 9:30 PM are for public skating, too. Friday and Saturday evening hours are from 7:30 PM to 10:15 PM. Saturday and Sunday afternoon times are from 1 PM to 4:30 PM. Admission is $6.50 for adults and $5.50 for children 12 and younger. On Sundays families can buy a $17 pass that admits two adults and two children. Skate rentals are $2.25 for figure skates and $2.50 for hockey skates.

San Diego Ice Arena
11048 Ice Skate Pl., San Diego
• **(858) 530-1825**

This skating rink offers public skating every day. Hours change from day to day, so

---

Speedwalkers get their workout along one of many harbor walkways.

call ahead for current hours. A complete sport shop is on the premises, and both individual and group lessons in figure skating and hockey are offered. Skating rates are $5.50 per person; skate rental is $2.50. This is the best spot in the county to learn to play hockey.

Laser Tag

Advanced technology has created new and innovative ways to play, and nowhere is that more true than in a laser-tag venue. Laser tag is an interactive adventure that combines computer technology with action-oriented team play. Players don a special pack and take a laser-pulse phaser into intricately designed play areas where they score points for their team by "tagging" opposing team members.

All ages are welcome, but players should be at least 7 years old to get maximum enjoyment from the game.

Laser Storm
9365 Mission Gorge Rd., Santee • (619) 562-3791

Players receive a brief introduction to the game, put on lightweight vests and headsets, then enter a futuristic arena with phasers in hand. The object here is to seek, find and deactivate opposing team members and their base station. The arena is full of barriers, strobe lights, police beacons, sentries, roboscanners and many more obstacles to add to the fun and the challenge. Games last for approximately 10 minutes, and the cost is $3.50 for the first game and $2.50 for subsequent games.

Laser Storm is open from 1:30 PM to 4:30 PM Monday through Friday, and from 6 PM to 10 PM on Tuesday and Thursday, 6PM to 9 PM on Wednesday, and 6 PM to midnight on Friday. Saturday's hours are from 10:30 AM to midnight, and Sunday's are from 1:30 PM to 7 PM.

Ultrazone
3146 Sports Arena Blvd., Ste. 21, San Diego • (619) 221-0100

Laser tag at Ultrazone starts in the Briefing Room, where players get specific game and equipment instruction, learn safety rules and are divided into teams. Once inside the 4,000 square-foot arena, players are confronted with a fog-filled, UV-blacklit environment crammed full of mazes, passageways, ramps and obstacles on several levels.

The game typically lasts for about 15 minutes, and the cost is $6.50 per game. Hours are from 4 PM until 11 PM Monday through Thursday and from 2 PM until 2 AM on Friday. Saturday hours are from 10 AM until 2 AM, and Ultrazone is open from 10 AM until 11 PM on Sundays. During summer months, starting time is at noon during the week.

Martial Arts

If mastering one of the many martial arts piques your interest, you'll find no shortage of schools or disciplines tailored to your unique desires. From judo and karate to tae-kwan-do and Thai kickboxing, you'll find a huge variety of studios and classes. We've listed a few studios here that cater to the whole family, mainly to get you started. If a particular discipline interests you but isn't mentioned here, never fear. It's bound to be taught somewhere in San Diego. If you call any of the numbers listed below, you're likely to get a good referral. Class rates vary widely depending on the level of instruction and number of classes.

Academy of the Martial Arts
9850 Hibert St., San Diego
- **(858) 566-9500**
3333 Midway Dr., Ste. 100, San Diego
- **(619) 223-9869**

Kenpo karate, Daito Ryu ju jutsu and taichi chuan are the specialties here. The instructors promise you can learn to paralyze an attacker with a single finger. Special family rates are offered where one member pays, and the rest study at no additional charge. Classes are available for men, women, children and groups, and private classes and workshops are offered, too.

International Self Defense Center
12657 Poway Rd., Poway
- **(858) 748-5829**

This 4,000 square-foot facility was established in 1967 and offers classes in Shaolin kung fu, kempo, karate, jiu jitsu, aikido, kickboxing, tai chi and meditation. Students develop confidence, peace of mind, strength and flexibility. The arts of concentration, courage and patience are all taught with a sense of humor. The facility includes a bag room and a weight room.

Twin Dragons Kenpo
6924 La Jolla Blvd., La Jolla
- **(858) 454-5413**

All styles and all ranks are welcome at Twin Dragons for classes in karate, boxing, grappling and Thai kickboxing. Since 1969 this state-of-the-art studio has given classes for adults and children. In addition to boxing-ring and bag training, video training is provided in each of the offered disciplines. Martial arts supplies are also available on-site.

White Dragon Schools
191 El Camino Real, Ste. 212, Encinitas
- **(760) 451-3116**
225 N. Magnolia Ave., Santee
- **(619) 441-1144**
7127 University Ave., La Mesa
- **(619) 461-2760**
5953 Balboa Ave., San Diego
- **(858) 277-7557**

Since 1985 the instructors at White Dragon Schools have been teaching men, women and children the arts of Yang tai chi, Chinese kickboxing and choy li fut for health, self-defense and discipline. The classes are designed to be fun and to improve self-confidence and mental attitude. The four facilities are large and fully equipped, and private lessons are included at no extra cost.

Paintball

Here's a treat for those looking for something a little different. Paintball has taken firm root as a game filled with fun, thrills and strategy. Players seek out opponents with the intent of eliminating them with a brightly colored blob of paint. Come alone, bring a friend or organize a group, and get ready for a unique experience.

Borderland Paintball Park
13531 Otay Lakes Rd., Jamul
- **(858) 536-4257**

Borderland's paintball competition consists of two teams playing the classic "capture the flag" game in an outdoor park. The staff is always on hand to assist you with equipment needs, explanation of the rules and general tips to enhance your paintball day. The park is open Saturdays and Sundays from 9 AM to 4:30 PM and is also available on weekdays for prearranged private parties. Guests must be 10 years or older, and those younger than 18 must have signed parental consent to play. Admission is $15 for adults and $8 for children 10 through 15. Equipment rental packages are $20.

Hidden Valley Paintball Park
25320 Lake Wohlford Rd., Escondido
• **(769) 737-8870**
Owner Mr. Paintball (otherwise known as Stan Burgis) likens the sport to the cops-and-robbers games we played as kids. Like the competitions at Borderland, Hidden Valley's games are of the capture-the-flag variety. Mr. Paintball emphasizes safety while ensuring that participants have a good time. Folks can play on either outdoor fields or in indoor venues.

Paintball can be played on weekends from 8 AM to 4PM. Full-day admission is $15.00; half-day is $10.00. Hidden Valley also offers camping, mountain biking and a team-building rope and obstacle course.

Parachute Jumping

Come on, admit it — haven't you secretly dreamed of experiencing the rush of free falling through the sky and watching the ground come closer and closer? If you've got a bit of the daredevil in you, here's your chance to indulge the fantasy.

Parachutes Over San Diego
13531 Otay Lakes Rd., Jamul
• **(619) 421-0968, (800) 707-5867**
Located in East County, about 20 minutes from downtown San Diego, you can train, jump and land at a private airfield — all in the same day. The company offers USPA Certified tandem, accelerated free fall and static line instruction. Instruction and jumps range from $155 to $295.

Racquetball

Although racquetball isn't the rage that it once was, there still are dedicated players who hit the courts with regularity. Some fitness centers and clubs have racquetball courts and will allow the public to play without purchasing a membership. But your best bet is to try one of the public courts listed below. They charge a per-person rate for one hour's play, but if the courts aren't busy, you can keep playing for no additional charge.

Courthouse Fitness & Jazzercise
1010 S. Santa Fe Ave., Vista
• **(760) 724-6941**
Three racquetball courts are available for public play at this facility, and reservations are accepted up to a week in advance. Rates are $6 per person before 3 PM and $10 per person after 3 PM. The $6 rate applies all day on Saturdays and Sundays. Hours are from 5 AM to 9:30 PM Monday through Thursday, 5 AM to 8 PM on Fridays, 6 AM to 6 PM on Saturdays and 7:30 AM to 6 PM on Sundays.

American Athletic Club
2539 Hoover Ave., National City
• **(619) 477-2123**
Rates range from $6 to $7 per person depending on the time of day. The club has six courts and is open Monday through Friday from 6 AM to 10 PM, Saturday from 7 AM to 6 PM and Sunday from 8 AM to 6 PM.

La Mesa Racquetball
4330 Palm Ave., La Mesa
• **(619) 460-3500**
Racquetball can be played on nine courts here, 365 days per year. The courts are open from 9 AM to 11 PM Monday through Friday, and 7 AM to 10 PM Saturday and Sunday. Rates range from $5 to $7 per person. An added bonus in case you push yourself too hard is the on-staff chiropractor.

Skating/Skateboarding

As in most cities, the popularity of skating and skateboarding seems to be in direct proportion to the intolerance for the sports. The city of Del Mar, for example, discourages skating and skateboarding wherever it can within the city limits. Both are also prohibited in Balboa Park, but for good reason. There's always such a large group of people milling about that combining wheels with slow-moving feet would be a recipe for disaster.

Never fear, however. We'll get you rolling safely and legally in some of the best spots in the county. Do it on your own, or join an organized skate to meet new friends and discover new skating places.

Mission Bay Park

Miles and miles of paved (and wide) walkways are shared equally by walkers, joggers, skateboarders and skaters. Choose from the beach or bayfront boardwalk or the pathway that meanders from the beach all the way around the various bays and inlets that make up Mission Bay Park. There are no restrictions here, except for an 8-mile-per-hour speed limit on the boardwalk.

San Diego Skate Club
• **(619) 544-4553**

This organization meets on Fridays at 7:30 PM at various locations throughout the city of San Diego for a group skate. Helmets are required, wrist guards and other padding are recommended.

Temecula Skate Park
42569 Margarita Rd., Temecula
• **(909) 694-6480**

Temecula Skate Park may be a bit off the beaten path, but skaters and skateboarders flock to this park designed and built especially for them. Plentiful bowls, lifts and jumps will test your skills and challenge even the most talented daredevils on wheels. For the complete lowdown on this one-of-kind park, see the Close-up in our Daytrips chapter. Hours are Monday through Friday from 1 PM until 9:30 PM, Saturday from 10 AM to 9:30 PM and Sunday from 1 PM until 6:30 PM. The entrance fee is $5.

Tennis

Looking for a game of tennis? You're in luck. Many hotels have their own courts, but if yours doesn't, you'll find quite a few public courts throughout the county. Here we list the most centrally located within our five regions.

George E. Barnes Tennis Center
4490 W. Pt. Loma Blvd., San Diego
• **(619) 221-9000**

Twenty hard courts and four clay courts are available for public play daily. Walk-on prices are $5 for the day for adults; children 18 and younger play for free. Courts are open daily from 8 AM to 9 PM.

Chula Vista Tennis Center
900 Otay Lakes Rd., Chula Vista
• **(619) 421-6622**

This is a small tennis center with only four courts located on the campus of Southwestern College, but the good news is that there's no charge for play.

The courts are staffed by a tennis pro, and lessons are available. If you are interested in taking lessons you can sign up with the tennis pro. Hours are from 8 AM to 7 PM, and play is on a first-come, first served basis.

Coronado Tennis Association
1501 Glorietta Blvd., Coronado
• **(619) 435-1616**

Eight courts, three of them lighted, are available on a first-come, first-served basis. Play is free, and courts are open from dawn until 10 PM.

La Jolla Tennis Club
7632 Draper Ave., La Jolla
• **(858) 454-4434**

The courts never close here, so if you can see, you can play. The lights, however, do go off at 9 PM. No reservations are accepted for the nine courts; play is strictly on a first-come, first-served basis and is always free.

Lake Murray Tennis Club
7003 Murray Park Dr., San Diego
• **(619) 469-3232**

Ten newly resurfaced courts are waiting for players. A fee of $4 allows you all-day play. Hours are from 8 AM to 10 PM Monday through Thursday, 8 AM to 8 PM Friday and 7 AM to 8 PM Saturday and Sunday.

Morley Field
2221 Morley Field Dr., San Diego
• **(619) 295-9278**

This tennis center has 25 courts and is open from 8 AM to 8 PM weekdays and from 8 AM to 6 PM on weekends. An all-day individual permit is $4. Courts are assigned on a first-come, first-served basis. The best time to get a course is between 11 AM and 5 PM.

Photo: James Blank/San Diego Convention and Visitors Bureau

Sailing the harbor at sunset can be a memorable experience.

Pala Mesa Resort
2001 Old Hwy. 395, Fallbrook
• **(760) 728-5881**

Four lighted courts are available for public play at this North County Inland resort. Rates are $8 per hour per court. Hours are from 7 AM to 10 PM.

Volleyball

Volleyball in San Diego is a big deal, especially beach volleyball. Newcomers and visitors will notice, however, that it's not a particularly well-organized sport. Most games consist of groups of friends who set up a net and start playing when the mood strikes them. If you happen to be at the beach or at one of the county's parks and see a game in progress, chances are you can join in. But the best way to assure a game is to organize it yourself.

One way to meet others who share an interest in the sport is to sign up for lessons. Or if you're really serious about your volleyball, there's a coed league in Poway that plays indoor volleyball once a week (see the information that follows).

Beach Volleyball Classes
• **(888) 742-4763**

Classes are held at Ocean Beach every week from 6 PM to 7:30 PM. Beginners meet on Thursdays, and intermediates meet on Tuesdays. Call for information and registration. The 10-week class is $125, and classes fill up, so make your reservation early.

Four-on-Four Coed Volleyball League
Meadowbrook Recreation Center
12320 Meadowbrook Lane, Poway
• **(858) 679-4343**

Games are held every Monday at 7 PM at the Meadowbrook Recreation Center. Teams consist of six players and must have at least two women. The registration fee is $30.

Walking

Sometimes there's a fine line between walking and hiking, but for those who truly love to stroll around city streets or even take an easy nature walk, hundreds of spots exist for both.

The beauty of walking is that, other than a good pair of shoes, no special equipment is needed, no reservations are required, and you can do it just about anywhere. If you like to confine your walks to paved sidewalks, no prettier place can be found than the walkway around Mission Bay, or the coastal streets and walkways in La Jolla. But any neighborhood in the county will provide the requisite fresh air and exercise.

Some prefer walking as a solitary pursuit, others like to walk with a friend or a group. If an organized walk sounds like it might be of interest to you, check out one of the many walking organizations listed below. You'll have your pick of organized nature walks, neighborhood walks, backcountry walks or any other kind of walk you can possibly imagine. And you'll have the added pleasure of making new friends.

Encinitas Walkers
• (760) 753-3212, (760) 634-3165

Every Monday, Wednesday and Friday this group meets at Starbucks Coffee in the Lumberyard Shopping Center, 947 South Coast Highway 101, Encinitas, at 7:30 AM. Different walks are scheduled for every meeting.

Gaslamp Quarter Walking Tours
410 Island Ave., San Diego
• (619) 233-4692

Combine exercise with a little bit of history as you take a guided walking tour through San Diego's historic Gaslamp Quarter. Prices are $5 for adults and $3 for seniors and students. Tours depart at 11 AM every Saturday.

Joy of Walking
4170 Balboa Ave., San Diego
• (858) 483-1831, (760) 945-7830

A free class that offers a one- to two-mile walk followed by exercises is offered Tuesday and Thursday from 8 AM to 9:30 AM.

La Jolla Walking Tours
Meet at the Colonial Inn, 910 Prospect St., La Jolla • (858) 453-8219

At 10 AM every Friday, Saturday and Sunday, La Jolla Walking Tours offers a two-hour guided tour that combines exercise with stories of La Jolla's history and famous residents, past and present. The cost is $9. Call for reservations.

Sierra Club
11220 Clairemont Mesa Blvd., San Diego
• (619) 299-8733

The Sierra Club offers a number of hikes in different locations throughout the county. Interested individuals are invited to the club orientation at 7 PM on the second Wednesday of each month.

Walkabout International
835 Fifth Ave., San Diego
• (619) 231-7463

Walks are scheduled every day of the year by this well-known group. Call for the current schedule of events.

Picture yourself sailing across the smooth waters of Mission Bay in a kayak or a sailboat. You can even rent powerboats and take the whole family water skiing.

Beaches and Watersports

What's the first thing everyone, including locals, thinks of when they think San Diego? Why, beaches, of course. Long stretches of white sand, sparkling blue ocean, sunny days basking in the warm California sunshine with your toes buried in the sand — all these images float through the minds of those hankering for sun and surf. Guess what? It's no myth. Those magical beaches do exist, and we're about to give you the skinny on each and every one of them. Even better, there's never a fee to use any of San Diego's beaches, just an occasional parking charge.

For those of you who want to interact with the blue Pacific, but prefer a little more activity than just dreaming away the day with maybe a splash in the water to break things up, we also have a whole bunch of watersports you can indulge in. We'll show you where to rent jet skis, surfboards, scuba equipment and more. If fishing is what sends you to nirvana, we'll point you to the best piers and sportfishing expeditions. We'll give you the scoop on licensing requirements and where to get your equipment. We'll even tell you what fish you can expect to reel in.

Picture yourself sailing across the smooth waters of Mission Bay in a kayak or a sailboat. You can even rent powerboats and take the whole family water-skiing. Or try something new and rent a wind surfer. With just a short lesson, you can be sailing across the water

with nothing but a sail and a surfboard to move you along. And don't think you need to bring a lot of stuff with you. Virtually everything you need, from basic equipment like a boat to wetsuits and life jackets, is either easily rented or comes as part of a package.

Now we have a few words of caution for you. The Pacific Ocean can be deceptive. It looks calm and beautiful, but it can pack a wallop. Even the most serene lake or swimming pool has its dangers too, so we urge you to bring your common sense along and take the advice of a couple of longtime beach rats: If you plan to go in the water, know how to swim. If you're not a swimmer, don't you dare go in the pool or ocean past your ankles. Rip currents in the ocean are hard to spot and can get a hold of you before you know what's happened. A rip current is sort of like a narrow but very powerful river that's heading back out to sea. They tend to form in the deepest points along the ocean floor, pulling everything with them as they flow seaward. Even the strongest swimmers have a healthy respect for rip currents.

If you're in a boat, always wear a life jacket and make sure all children wear them, too. Should a mishap occur, you won't have time to put one on, so you're well advised to just keep it on at all times.

If you heed some simple guidelines about rip currents and other potential dangers, though, you should have no problem. First and foremost, whether you're swimming in the ocean or a pool, be sure it's protected by a lifeguard, and pay attention to all warning signs, especially those regarding rip currents. Lifeguards can spot them and will post red flags where they have formed. That's a clear signal to avoid swimming in that area. Should you get caught in a rip, swim parallel to the shore in either direction until the pull of the current subsides. Then you can swim in to shore.

www.insiders.com
See this and many other **Insiders' Guide®** destinations online.
Visit us today!

Lifeguards advise you to swim with fins. They use them; you should, too. Also, never swim when you've been drinking. Alcohol impairs your judgment and your physical capabilities. Avoid using things like Boogie Boards or rafts as swimming aids if you're a weak swimmer. You shouldn't venture any farther with a raft than your swimming ability would normally take you. Finally, if you get into trouble, simply wave your arms. Lifeguards recognize this as a distress signal whether you're in the water or on the shore. You'll get immediate attention.

In addition to heeding safety tips, you'll need to follow the few rules and regulations that exist to make going to the beach a pleasure for everyone. The permissibility of alcoholic beverages varies from beach to beach. Most don't permit alcohol at all, but some will allow it between certain hours. Signs are posted at all beaches advising you of current regulations. Bottles are never permitted on beaches, so bring your beverages in cans or in plastic. Fires can be built in provided fire rings only, and many beaches have them. And never bury coals in the sand — they don't go out for hours, and some unsuspecting beachcomber may stumble upon them and end up with a bad burn.

You might expect that San Diego overflows with marinas since we spend so much time in and on the water. And although there are quite a few, they're mostly private. You can rent a temporary slip at a hotel marina if you're a guest, but arrangements should always be made in advance. Vacant slips are hard to find, so we don't advise that you sail into town

unexpectedly and expect to find a marina to accommodate you.

Now that we've given you the heads up on how to stay out of trouble, let us urge you to throw caution to the wind and explore all the possibilities that coastal life has to offer. And remember, you don't have to have any special knowledge or skill to take advantage of most watersports. Experienced captains are always on hand to pilot a boat for you, or to take you on a tandem windsurfer, or teach you to water-ski. But if that sounds like just too much activity, then do as we do. Grab a beach towel, some no-brainer summer reading, lots of sunscreen, and hit the sand. You'll feel remarkably mellow at the end of the day.

We've listed the beaches in geographical order, from north to south, and have tried to point out the characteristics and quirks that distinguish each. We've included a few that don't have lifeguard service or facilities such as restrooms, but do have something special that tends to attract locals. Just be advised that these aren't places to take the kids. Watersports are listed by activity, with a description of the sport along with where to go to get the necessary equipment.

So put the sightseeing aside for a day and head to the water. Find out firsthand what it is about San Diego's beaches, lakes and pools that make this town such an enviable place to hang out.

Beaches

San Onofre Surf Beach
I-5 and Basilone Rd., San Onofre

This is one of the most popular surfing beaches along the coastline in San Diego County. Insiders call it "Trestles" and it's known around the world for truly cool surfing. Many people say it's the best surfing spot in the entire state.

Once you exit the freeway (at the Basilone Road exit), follow the blue signs for beach access and parking. There's a $3 entrance fee to park your car. The north end of the beach has a wide, sandy shoreline that's good for walking, swimming and sunset watching. The south end is more narrow and covered with large beach stones — here's where the surfers hang out. The beach is walkable for about four miles in either direction. The beach has lots of restrooms, cold showers, running water, some picnic tables and fire rings. Shade is limited. There are public phones near all the restrooms. There is no lifeguard on duty; for emergencies, you'll have to call 911.

Oceanside Beaches
Oceanside

You can locate the Oceanside beaches by simply driving west on most of the Oceanside city streets. Oceanside beaches all have wide sandy shores, which are great for lounging, picnicking, sunbathing and yes, even swimming. Surfing is especially good between Tyson Street Park and the Oceanside Pier, just south of Mission Avenue. There's a tot lot and restrooms at Tyson Street Park.

Pacific Street runs all along the ocean in Oceanside and there's beach access between Wisconsin Avenue and Morse Way. There is free and metered parking, with handicapped spaces provided. Parking is at a premium, however, so be prepared for a walk to the water during the summer months and especially on the Fourth of July when beaches are busy.

Buccaneer Beach, 1506 South Pacific Street, is popular with families because of its wide sandy shore. The YMCA brings the summer surf-day campers here for lessons (see our Kidstuff chapter for other activities at this beach). The beach is patrolled 24 hours a day by police, and there are lifeguards at Buccaneer too. The beach has picnic tables, barbecues, some shade, and a public telephone.

Just south of Buccaneer Beach is a popular surfing place with a width that varies with the seasons and the tides. Parking is scarce

and illegal parking will nearly guarantee you a ticket. There's no lifeguard on duty here.

Eaton Street, at the south end of Pacific Street, fronts the gated community of St. Malo. Security guards at the St. Malo gated community watch the private beach; however, all beach below the high-tide line is public, so you can still walk through without fear of trespassing.

Carlsbad Beaches
Carlsbad

The beaches begin south of Buena Vista Lagoon. Carlsbad City Beach, the first of the string we present here, has some sand at high tide; at low tide, it's a wide and popular spot for surfers rather than walkers and swimmers. There are no facilities at the north end of this beach, which is open from 6 AM to 11 PM daily.

To access the beaches where there are facilities and lifeguards, you can walk the beach steps down from Ocean Street, Christiansen Way, Grand Avenue or Carlsbad Village Drive straight to the sea. After Carlsbad Village Drive stops at the ocean, turn left to Ocean Street and then merge into Carlsbad Boulevard. Here you'll find street parking (although it's at a premium) and flights of stairs to reach the sand. Beach access signs, indicating how to get to the water, are everywhere. The Carlsbad beaches, by the way, are only about three blocks west of the Coaster station. So if you'd like to visit this community's water and sand and would rather not drive north, check the Coaster's schedule.

Whatever you decide, be sure you're wearing comfortable shoes, either to walk from the station or from that parking place wherever you may find it (at least most parking is free).

There are cold-water, open public showers at Christiansen Way and Tamarack Avenue and restrooms, telephones and lifeguard stations all along the shore. You'll see fire rings

Photo: CeCe Canton

Several California grey seals come ashore during heavy surf at La Jolla.

along the beaches as well. Where Tamarack Avenue ends at the Pacific Ocean there is a public parking lot. You can't, however, expect to find a spot on beautiful sunny days.

Directly above the beach is the well-maintained Carlsbad Seawall, a 4-foot-high barrier between the cliffs and the sea. It was built to help maintain the integrity of the cliffs since erosion and generations of ground squirrels, who also love beach life, have weakened the earth. You can stroll on the walk that follows the seawall.

Or, at street level, there's the popular beach-view sidewalk for strolling, skating, jogging or briskly walking from Carlsbad Village Drive all the way to Cannon Drive — a good 5-mile trek. Lots of folks who work in Carlsbad take brown bag lunches, or buy fast food, and eat at the tables along the beach. Lots of folks walk here in the evenings — including many Insiders with leashed canine companions.

(Dogs are not allowed on the lower level of the seawall walkway and you will be ticketed if you don't scoop up after a pet's potty stop.) At the street level, there are picnic tables and benches, and there's some shade too.

South Carlsbad State Beach
Poinsettia Dr. and Carlsbad Blvd., Carlsbad

To reach this state beach, exit Interstate 5 at Poinsettia and drive west. There's a day fee of $3 to enter the limited-area parking lot; there is no charge to enter if you walk in. It's a popular beach campground and those who want to camp here make reservations months in advance. Even in winter it's nearly always full. From the campground, there are eight exits to the narrow pebbled beach. There are lifeguard towers. Beach walking isn't easy with all the stones, but surfing is supposed to be outstanding.

At the campground there are restrooms, tables, fire rings, shade and a food store.

Beacon's Beach
Encinitas

Exit I-5 at Leucadia Boulevard and head west, then follow the "Beach Access" signs toward Diana Street. Beacon's Beach has a small parking lot that's open from 6 AM until 10 PM. There is a public telephone and steps down to the heavily pebbled beach. There are no lifeguards. This is a surfers' beach and parking is often a problem since it's so limited. Insiders park legally where they can find a place and walk a number of blocks to the beach.

Moonlight State Beach
Encinitas

Exit I-5 at Encinitas Boulevard and drive west. There is parking on C Street and Third Street. This is one of the nicest beaches in North County: a place where kids can run and parents can play. There are restrooms, public phones, a snack bar, running water, showers, fire rings and picnic tables. Moonlight State Beach is a popular swimming beach with lots of wide sandy areas that make walking fun. This beach is about a five-block walk from the commuter train station.

Swami's
Encinitas

Just below Sea Cliff County Park, where First Street and Highway 101 merge, is Swami's. There are restrooms, tables, barbecues and public telephones at the park on the bluff. Above the beach is a romantic sunset-watching spot and an excellent place to whale watch during the winter months. To get to the surfing beach — no sand, just pebbles — there are stairs. Swami's is known worldwide for surfing so whether you do it or just watch it, you may want to add this Insider's favorite place on your list of places to visit. There's a lifeguard tower.

San Elijo State Beach
Cardiff

Just south of Swami's is San Elijo State Beach. There's a campground here and facilities from showers to snack foods; there's a $3

Photo: San Diego Convention and Visitors Bureau

A crowd gathers to watch the beach artists perform their magic during the annual Sand Castle event in Imperial Beach. The Imperial Beach pier reaches out to the ocean in the background.

charge if you want to park in the campground. There is limited street parking along Highway 101. You'll find the stairs to the beach at the campground, too. It's another San Diego pebble beach so you'll need to wear sneakers unless your feet are tough. San Elijo State Beach is locally known as "Cardiff Pipes." There are lifeguard stations.

Cardiff Seaside Park
Cardiff

Exit I-5 at Lomas Santa Fe Drive, drive west to First Street (which may be marked Highway 101) to find this pebbled beach. At low tide you might even be able to find some sand. There are restrooms, showers, lifeguard stations and nearby you'll find restaurants.

Tide Beach
Solana Beach

You can reach this swimmer's beach, i.e., there's sand, by exiting I-5 at Lomas Santa Fe Drive. Drive west past First Street (which in places may be marked Highway 101) to Acacia Avenue. Turn right to Solana Vista Drive and you'll see the sign for Tide Beach. Parking is limited and most Insiders realize that they just have to park a distance away and hike to the ocean. There is a lifeguard tower and a wide shoreline that's good for walkers.

Fletcher Cove
Solana Beach

Just south of Tide Beach, you'll notice this one has sand; there's a parking lot at Plaza Street and South Sierra Avenue. Fletcher Cove, also locally known as Pill Box Beach, is popular with fitness walkers and families. The beach is open between 6 AM and 10 PM. There are restrooms, showers, telephones and fire rings.

Dog Beach
Del Mar

Insiders started calling it Dog Beach because you can let Fido off the leash here, and the name stuck. Exit I-5 at Via de La Valle and

turn right on Hwy. 101. There's roadside parking; handicap access is difficult since you'll be crossing dirt paths and must hike up and down some cliffs. Look for the beach access signs. Dog Beach is found between Via de La Valle and the San Dieguito River. The area is also called "Rivermouth."

Insiders sometimes forget to explain a few things about Dog Beach. As much fun as it sounds, not all dog owners bring friendly, kid-loving pets to the beach. If you're planning a family outing and Fido is already panting, talk to the kids about dog safety before you hit the sand. Make sure your canine companion is current with all vaccinations, isn't aggressive and doesn't infringe on others. Then you can hope that others do the same.

Del Mar Beaches
Del Mar

The beaches in Del Mar are wide, and wonderful for family times, beach walking, and swimming. The Del Mar beaches are typical of postcard photos friends and family have sent you when they've visited San Diego. The beaches are open 24 hours a day. The central lifeguard tower is staffed between 9 AM and 8 PM; additional towers add staff as beach use demands. There are no fire rings or tables here, but portable barbecues are permitted. Parking is always at a premium.

Above Del Mar Beach is Seagrove Park with a tot lot, picnic tables, benches, grassy picnic areas and places to spread a blanket, but no other facilities. This is a popular, brown-bag lunchtime area for those who work in Del Mar. There's metered parking and controls are enforced.

Torrey Pines State Beach
Del Mar

Exit I-5 at Carmel Valley Road and turn left at Torrey Pines State Beach. There is some roadside parking, but the beach access isn't easy since you'll have to scramble down the cliffs to the water. There is a parking lot with a

---

INSIDERS' TIP

For an up-to-the-minute surf report for the entire coastline, call Encinitas Surfboards at (760) 753-0506.

It's a great day for families in the sun on Mission Bay Beach.

$3 entry fee where you'll have access to restrooms and public telephones. There's beach access from the parking lot.

Here's where you'll find the entrance to Torrey Pines State Beach, a 1,750-acre park with picnic tables, walking trails, sandy and pebbled beaches, and restrooms. Along the beach are lifeguard towers. Picnics are permitted on the beach, but not in the wildlife preserve area.

Unique along the coastline is the Torrey Pines State Beach underwater park. It is protected and maintained for marine research and enjoyment by scuba and snorkel divers.

Black's Beach(es)
Del Mar/Torrey Pines

Even many Insiders don't know that there are two Black's Beaches. The beaches divide at the bottom of the curving trail that leads from the beach access path at Torrey Pines State Beach. The path to the right is Black's Nude Beach. Here swimsuits are optional. To

the left at the waterfront, nude sunbathing and nude swimming aren't permitted. There are no facilities or lifeguards on either beach.

La Jolla Shores Beach
La Jolla

La Jolla Shores is a favorite hangout for teenagers and families. It's a wide, sandy beach nearly a mile long, with a gently sloping ocean floor. Waves are usually fairly gentle — just the right size for those who want a taste of wave action without being bowled over every time a set rolls in. Separate water areas are reserved for swimming and surfing. Restrooms and showers are located 100 yards north and south of the main lifeguard tower, which is staffed daily. Kellogg Park, a nice grassy area for those who don't like sand in their peanut butter and jelly, is located behind the tower.

To get to La Jolla Shores, take La Jolla Village Drive west from I-5 south, or Ardath Road from I-5 north. Follow the signs to Torrey

Pines Road and head south. Turn right on La Jolla Shores Boulevard and left on Camino del Oro to the beach. A free parking lot runs the length of La Jolla Shores, but it fills up quickly during summer months. Then you're on your own. You can park on adjacent streets, but you will probably end up with a big hike ahead of you. It's a good idea to drop your companions and all your gear at the beach if the lot is full, then only one of you has to make the trek from car to beach.

La Jolla Cove
La Jolla

To reach La Jolla Cove, follow the directions for La Jolla Shores, but continue on Torrey Pines Road to Prospect Street. Turn right and follow the road to Coast Boulevard. The cove is in the 1100 block. Swimming, snorkeling and scuba diving are the activities permitted at the cove. It's a north-facing cove and has unusually coarse sand, but water visibility is usually excellent, sometimes as much as 30 feet, which is why so many divers and snorkelers frequent the waters here. Grassy Scripps Park is immediately adjacent to the cove and is a fine place for a picnic. Lifeguards are on duty year-round, and a public restroom with showers is located in Scripps Park. This is a great place to bring the family, especially the little ones who might be overwhelmed by big waves. Come early, though, parking is limited to what's available on the street.

Marine Street Beach
La Jolla

This is a local's hangout for those who like to toss Frisbees, sunbathe and scuba dive. From La Jolla Boulevard, the main street that runs north/south through La Jolla, turn west on Marine Street and drive to the foot of the street. Parking is limited to what's available on adjacent streets. The drawback to Marine Street Beach is that there are no facilities and no lifeguard service. Perhaps it's the isolation that draws people here, but Insiders know there's something else, too: a wicked shore break that challenges even the most experienced body surfers. If rough and tumble in the waves sounds like a day in heaven, this may well be the ideal spot for you. Otherwise,

you might prefer to stick to one of the more conventional beaches.

Windansea Beach
La Jolla

Windansea is both a swimming and surfing beach distinguished by its sandstone rocks that take the place of sand. It offers a secluded and scenic atmosphere for sunbathing; swimming and surfing are a bit more of a challenge, and this is not a recommended place for diving. To reach Windansea, turn west off La Jolla Boulevard to Neptune Place, and park wherever you can find a spot on the street.

Like Marine Street Beach, Windansea has a shorebreak, a condition on steep beaches that produces hard-breaking surf right at the shoreline. Experienced swimmers and surfers know to take care while entering and exiting the water to avoid injury. Lifeguards are present only during the summer months.

Bird Rock
La Jolla

Take Bird Rock Avenue west off La Jolla Boulevard and drive to the end of the street to find this unusual beach. Bird Rock is not a beach for swimmers or sunbathers, but surfers, divers and bird watchers love it. Conditions for both surfing and diving are usually top notch, but the big draw is the beach's namesake: Bird Rock. It's a huge boulder that sits right off the coast and plays host to scores of visiting sea birds. Bring your binoculars. No facilities or lifeguard staffing is available at Bird Rock. Parking is limited to what's available on the surrounding streets.

Tourmaline Surfing Park
La Jolla

No swimming is allowed at this designated surfing park, but surfers, sailboarders and scuba divers flock to Tourmaline in droves. Turn west off La Jolla Boulevard onto Tourmaline Street and head for the large parking lot. Surfers love the year-round reef break, and divers enjoy the underwater scenery. There's a nice picnic area for those who'll be staying shoreside, and restrooms and showers are conveniently situated in the park. Lifeguard service is provided year-round.

Photo: San Diego Convention and Visitors Bureau

Long sunny days often find surfers and beach-goers on the shoreline even as the sun is setting. This surfer leaves the water at the end of the day.

North Pacific Beach
San Diego

This mile-long beach stretches south from Tourmaline Surfing Park to Crystal Pier, which is located at the foot of Garnet Avenue, the main drag through Pacific Beach. To reach the beach, take the Grand Avenue/Garnet Avenue exit from I-5 and drive west to the beach. It's a beach that's protected by high cliffs, and it has separate water areas for swimming and surfing. Lifeguards staff the beach from spring break through the end of October. Scuba diving is not recommended here because of the heavy use by surfers and sailboarders, and also because there just isn't too much undersea life in this area. Restrooms and showers are located at the foot of Diamond Street and Law Street on the south end and at Tourmaline on the north end. You can park either in the Tourmaline lot or on nearby residential streets.

Pacific Beach/Mission Beach/ South Mission Beach
San Diego

A continuous 2 miles of sand bordered by a cement boardwalk stretches south from Crystal Pier, at the foot of Garnet Avenue, to the channel entrance to Mission Bay. It's the busiest and most popular beach in the county during the summertime. People watching is a preferred activity, and the boardwalk provides plenty of it. Joggers, walkers, inline skaters, skateboarders and bicyclists combine to form a never-ending parade of entertainment. The beach itself has separate water areas for swimming and surfing. Lifeguards staff the main lifeguard towers at the foot of Grand Avenue in Pacific Beach, West Mission Bay Drive in Mission Beach and Avalon Court in South Mission Beach. During the summer months, additional lifeguards staff seasonal towers that are sprinkled along the beach. Public restrooms and showers are located on all three beach areas.

This is one of the few beaches in the county where alcohol is permitted — but not on the boardwalk and between the hours of 8 AM and 8 PM only. Those hours are subject to change, as the city is trying to reduce them, so be sure to read the signs posted along the beach. Scuba diving is not recommended here

because there's not much underwater sea life, and the water is usually crowded with swimmers and surfers. To reach any of these beaches, take any of the streets or courts west from Mission Boulevard. Parking is on nearby residential streets, and is extremely tight, except for South Mission Beach, which has a large parking lot.

Mission Bay Park Beaches
San Diego

More than 4,600 acres make up Mission Bay Park — half water and half land. The park has 27 miles of shoreline, 19 of which are sandy beaches. To find Mission Bay, take the West Mission Bay Drive exit from I-8 west and follow the signs — they're plentiful and easy to follow. You'll see just about everything here: power boaters, sail boaters, rowers, water skiers, picnickers, joggers and even swimmers. The many coves and inlets provide scenic spots for a day at the beach, and the gentle bay is often preferred by families with small children. Lifeguard staffing usually begins around spring-break time, and continues on the weekends until summer, when it becomes daily. After summer, weekend staffing continues until the end of October. Between November and spring break, there's no lifeguard staffing on any of Mission Bay's beaches. Restrooms and showers are liberally sprinkled throughout Mission Bay. A bonus is that most of the swimming beaches have large parking lots.

Ocean Beach
San Diego

A wide, sandy beach, O.B. is populated mostly by locals and visitors who are staying in the area. Drive west on I-8 until the freeway ends at Sunset Cliffs Boulevard. Follow Sunset Cliffs Boulevard to Newport Avenue. Turn right, and park in the large lot at the Ocean Beach Municipal Pier or in one of the auxiliary lots along Abbott Street. Surfing is especially popular just north of the pier, and there are separate water areas for swimming. The main lifeguard station is staffed year-round, and additional stations are set up during the summer. At the north end of O.B. is Dog Beach, a place where owners can take their dogs and let them run free. Keep in mind that even

Photo: Dale Frost/Port of San Diego

Sailboats gliding by on the sparkling water of Mission Bay always capture the notice of onlookers.

though disposal facilities are provided, some dog owners aren't too scrupulous about cleaning up after their pooches. So this is not a great place for an afternoon stroll. Restrooms and showers are located at the foot of Abbott Street and at the foot of Brighton Avenue.

Sunset Cliffs Park
San Diego

Take I-8 west to Sunset Cliffs Boulevard, and follow it until you see an impressive sight: towering cliffs with surf pounding at the base. This is one of the best spots in San Diego to watch a sunset or go tidepooling. Staircases at the foot of Bermuda Avenue, Santa Cruz Avenue and Ladera Street will lead you down to small, secluded beaches from which you can surf, scuba dive and swim. It's important to note that the cliffs are soft and continuously eroding, so mind the warning signs and use only specified approaches to the beaches. A few parking lots are sprinkled along the cliffs; otherwise, street parking is usually easy to find. There are no lifeguards or other facilities.

Coronado City Beach
Coronado

Aside from being one of the prettiest beaches in San Diego, long, wide and sandy, there's some romance attached to Coronado Beach, too. It's the Hotel del Coronado that lends the romance, and rightfully so. It's hard to feel less than royal when you're sunbathing with the grand hotel as a backdrop. This is a great family beach with lots of room to spread out. Crowds are well behaved and the beach is always spotlessly clean. Fishing, swimming and surfing are all given separate water areas, and nearby Sunset Park is a large grassy area for picnickers and Frisbee throwers. Once you're on the island of Coronado, take Orange Avenue west to the beach, and park wherever you can find a spot on residential streets. Plenty of lifeguards and restrooms are provided.

Silver Strand State Beach
Between Coronado and Imperial Beach

From Coronado, take California Highway 75 south to the signs that point the way to the beach. From Imperial Beach, take the Palm Avenue exit from I-5 and drive west until it veers north to Silver Strand Boulevard. Silver Strand State Beach has something unique in San Diego: clamming. It's typically an East-Coast activity, but you should be able to dig up some of the tasty mollusks at Silver Strand. Also look for the tiny silver shells for which the beach was named. They cover the 2 miles of shoreline on the narrow spit of land between the ocean and San Diego Bay. The north end of the beach is a little more isolated than the south end and is a popular nude-sunbathing area. There are facilities galore here: picnic areas, restrooms, lifeguard stations and RV camping.

Imperial Beach

Of all the county beaches, Imperial Beach has probably the largest concentration of locals, but visitors are always welcome, too. It's a vast, sandy beach that's popular with swimmers, surfers and boogie-boarders. It's also home to the annual sand-castle competition (see our Annual Events chapter for more details on this ultra-fun event), which draws a ton of people every August. The Imperial Beach Pier, at the south end of the beach, is a favorite with folks who like to fish. Grassy picnic areas are available, as are restrooms and year-round lifeguard service. Drive west on Palm Avenue from I-5 until you reach the ocean. Parking is tight, as it is at most beaches, but you should be able to find something either in one of the lots or on nearby residential streets.

Watersports
Freshwater Fishing

Freshwater fishing is a popular hobby with lots of Insiders and visitors too, and our lakes and piers support this pastime. For instance at **Lake Miramar**, Lake Miramar Scripps Lake Drive off Scripps Ranch Boulevard, San Diego (619-668-2050), you can fish for rainbow trout, bass, sunfish and channel catfish.

Mission Trails Regional Park, with its **Lake Murray**,1 Father Junipero Serra Trail, San Diego (619- 668-3275) is open year-round for fishing. **Lake Poway Recreation Area**,

People enjoy the sun and the surf on Imperial Beach.

Photo: Dale Frost/Port of San Diego

Lake Poway Rd, off Espola Road., (Poway 858-679-5466), has a 60-acre reservoir for boating and fishing. The lake is stocked with trout in the fall and winter and catfish in the summer months.

Lake Morena County Park, Lake Morena Road, off California Highway 94, or Buckman Springs Road, off I-8, near Campo (858-694-3049) has a "fish report hotline" at (619) 478-5473. Fishing is popular here, and bass, bluegill, catfish, crappie and stocked trout crowd the lake — at least that's we've heard from those who love the sport. There's a rowboat launch, too.

Guajome County Park, Guajome Lakes Road, near Mission Avenue, Vista, (760-565-3600), gives you the chance to fish and picnic or bird watch all in the same developed park and wildness area. The park is nearly 600 acres, with trails. The lake has shore fishing and is popular with kids from the area.

Lake Poway Recreation Area, Lake Poway Road, off Espola Road, Poway, (858-679-5466) is a 35-acre recreational area. The 60-acre reservoir is stocked with trout in the fall and winter and catfish in the summer months. Only nonmotorized boats are allowed on the lake.

At **Cuyamaca Rancho State Park**, Calif. Highway 79 between Highway 78 and I-8 in eastern San Diego County (760-765-0755), you can fish, boat and paddle boat around the lake. No swimming is allowed. You can rent a motorboat for $6 that will seat five, and if you want to spend the day on the water, the price is only $25. Paddleboats run from $6 (for a two-person boat) to $7 (for a four-person boat) for an hour (there's no fishing off the paddleboats). At Cuyamaca, the rental shop doesn't take reservations, but opens up at 6 AM each day. Call (760) 765-0515 for more information about the boats and regulations.

Be sure to read our Parks chapter for information on all the lakes that have fishing, boating and watersporting possibilities. If you prefer to cast your line in the ocean, see this chapter's section on Sport Fishing. Wherever you go, be sure you have your fishing license with you. You're required to have one, unless you're fishing off a pier or unless you are 16 years old or younger. A freshwater fishing permit is $27.05; a saltwater permit is $18.65, and for both it's $29.70. They're good between January and December. Most bait and tackle shops and sport fishing outfitters sell licenses. Just fishing for a weekend? For $10 you can buy a two-day freshwater license.

Kayaking/Canoeing/ Wave Riding

Be your own skipper and get up close and personal with water and wildlife by using or renting a kayak or canoe. Check with local regulations if the posted signs are unclear as to whether boating is allowed. This varies. For instance, at Lake Hodges in Escondido, Lake Drive off Via Rancho Parkway, (619-668-2050), you can take these small boats around the lake, but in other wildlife preserve areas, including Buena Vista Lagoon, found between Carlsbad and Oceanside in North County Coastal, boats are prohibited.

Aqua Adventures Kayak School
4901 Morena Blvd., San Diego
• (858) 272-0800

If you're pricing kayak rentals, be sure to call this store. At $18 a day, the price is hard to beat. You can also arrange for kayak instruction and take advantage of the ocean and river kayaking trips and tours. Call the store to get a brochure and to be placed on their mailing list.

California Water Sports Rentals
4215 Harrison St., Carlsbad
• (760) 4334-3089

Located at Snug Harbor Marina in North County Coastal, this store provides everything you need for a watersporting good time, including instruction on use and safety.

You can rent kayaks and canoes for $12 to $18 an hour. You can rent Wave Riders for $40 to $60 for an hour, and the equipment can be shared with up to three people. When you rent motorized equipment, you'll also be shown a seven-minute safety and instructional video. They like having first-timers come to Snug Harbor Marina and make sure there are plenty of instructors on the beach for additional help. You can also take classes on these sports at the marina. Snug Harbor also has a pro shop, snack bar and picnic tables.

Carlsbad Paddle Sports
2780 Carlsbad Blvd., Carlsbad
• (760) 434-8686

For paddle sports and kayak fun, Insiders use this store, which is more than a place to rent equipment. Knowledgeable staff here provide instruction, lead adventure trips and can tell you about local paddling possibilities. They sponsor paddles at the La Jolla sea caves and in Oceanside harbor. If you need equipment, it's $40 for an eight-hour kayak rental. Ask about their "two-fer" specials (so you and a friend can kayak for the price of one).

The adventure trips to Catalina and Baja aren't just for the adventurous; the staff is well qualified to instruct even novice kayakers. The trip to Catalina Island includes everything from wetsuit to kayak, food to tent; you just bring a sleeping bag. No, you don't kayak across the rough Pacific to Catalina, but take the ferry out of San Pedro, near Los Angeles. The actual paddling is about 6 miles of kayaking. The cost is $315 per person.

The trip to Baja is less expensive, although you must bring everything you'll need (except the kayaks, which are provided). The paddling trip is about 8-miles long and costs $150 per

---

INSIDERS' TIP

If you decide to visit Del Mar's Dog Beach or Ocean Beach, where dogs are permitted, keep in mind that dogs are dogs. Some dogs are friendly and some dogs are not. And there are irresponsible beach-goers who "forget" to clean up after Fido. You may have to watch where you step, sit down or play in the sand. If you are not a dog lover, head to another of our area's fine beaches.

person. Participants meet at a designated spot on Baja's western coastline. For Baja or any of the treks, you'll want to follow the checklist the store gives you when you pre-register.

REI-Recreational Equipment Inc.
5556 Copley Dr., San Diego
• (858) 279-4400

If you don't want to transport your kayak to San Diego or if you want to try the sport without buying one, REI is your ticket. It's $40 to rent an ocean kayak for one day, and $15 for each subsequent day. For those who are not members of the REI association, there's a security deposit of $150. The store's savvy staff reminds you to reserve a kayak if you want it for a holiday weekend. The store also has a full line of outdoor accessories for sports from camping to biking, and rents lots of other equipment. See our Recreation chapter for more about REI's climbing wall.

Resort Watersports
Catamaran Hotel, 3999 Mission Blvd.,
Pacific Beach • (858) 539-8696
Bahia Hotel, 998 W. Mission Bay Dr.,
Mission Beach • (858) 539-7696

For rentals of watersporting equipment and lessons, Resort Watersports is a one-stop shopping and outfitting emporium. Single and double kayaks range from $13 to $16 for an hour's rental. There is a discount if you want to rent them for a day. The staff shows you how to use the equipment and then lets you get out on the bay or ocean. Call first to reserve equipment since this is a popular shop.

Southwest Kayaks
2590 Ingraham St., San Diego
• (619) 222-3616

On Dana Landing, near Sea World (see our Attractions chapter), Southwest Kayaks rents, sells and instructs kayakers. There are free demonstrations on Mission Bay almost every weekend. Call the store for details if you want to see what this sport is all about.

Rental prices for kayaks are $10 for an hour, $25 for a half-day, and $35 for a full day. Insiders recommend taking the three-hour lessons for beginners that cost $45 and are scheduled for weekends.

The store also has a free newsletter. The newsletter provides kayaking tips and tricks and talks about the trips, including those to the Channel Islands (off the coast of Santa Barbara), Baja and around Catalina.

Photo: CeCe Canton

Heavy surf crashes over the sea wall at Children's Pool in LaJolla.

Windsport
844 W. Mission Bay Dr., San Diego
• **(858) 488-4642**

This is a full-service kayaking and windsurfing shop where you can buy and rent kayaks. They also have kayaking accessories from lifejackets to designer sunscreen. The price for a sit-on kayak is $13 for an hour, $36 for four hours and $45 for a full eight-hour day. You'll get some basic instructions from the craft-smart staff before they set you free to paddle the bay. If you'd like further instruction on other kayaks, a two-hour private lesson is just $60. Be sure to call ahead to rent or arrange lessons.

Sailing and Power Boating

San Diego is a sailor's dream come true. You can sail on the bay or just around a marina. You can sail up and down the coastline and never lose sight of land. You can head for Catalina, the Channel Islands or even Hawaii (as long as you know what you're doing).

You can also sail on some of our local lakes. **Lake Hodges**, at Lake Drive off I-15 and Via Rancho Parkway, Escondido (858-668-2050), has a small boat launch. There's a shady picnic area, parking and tiny grocery stories in the area should you forget to bring lunch. (See our Parks chapter for more places to boat and sail on our lakes.)

Many marinas have sailboats to rent and depending on the size and length of time you'll be on it, they are priced accordingly. If you want to sail around San Diego Bay you can get a 14-foot Capri for as little as $18 an hour. Visitors and Insiders rent the boats for a few hours to see the city from a different vista, right on the water.

With the small, two-person sailboats, you may be restricted to the bay and marina and will be asked to show that you're competent with the boats before you leave the dock. There's usually a security deposit that's required when you rent a small boat. For larger sailing crafts, you may have to take a test cruise with an instructor (for a fee) and only then will you be able to set sail. Many of the sailboat rental companies have sailing clubs and lessons. Local parks and recreation offices in coastal communities like Oceanside will have sailing and other watersport classes, too.

Harbor Sailboats
2040 Harbor Island Dr., San Diego
• **(619) 291-9568**

You don't have to take lessons here to get into a sailboat. You will have to show you know what you're doing though when a staff member checks you out before untying the mooring ropes. Prices range from $80 for four hours on a 22-foot Capri to $475 for a full day aboard a Beneteau. If you're headed to San Diego and have made up your mind to sail, just call and reserve a craft. Remember that over holiday weekends (and we're talking Thanksgiving and Christmas, too) and the summer months, boat availability may be limited. By renting boats here, you get yacht club discounts, instruction for all levels and can enjoy other club and cruising experiences. There's a pool, deli and restaurant on-site.

Resort Watersports
Catamaran Hotel, 3999 Mission Blvd., Pacific Beach • (858) 539-8696
Bahia Hotel, 998 W. Mission Bay Dr., Mission Beach • (858) 539-7696

As mentioned above, Resort Watersports is the place to rent everything from kayaks to wave runners. They also rent powerboats (a 16-foot powerboat will cost you $65 for an hour, $195 for four hours). They rent sail boats too. The Capri sailboats, 14-, 18- and 22-foot lengths, range from $18 to $30 for an hour and there's a saving if you want to rent in four-

INSIDERS' TIP

Be aware that some beaches are "surfing only" beaches during specific hours of the day. Check the signs as you enter the beach area.

Photo: San Diego Convention and Visitors Bureau

With the luxury of some palm trees for shade and the Coronado Bridge in the background, this group is enjoying one of the many "perfect" beach days that San Diego is famous for.

hour periods. Call to reserve boats and for more information.

San Diego Sailing Club and School
1880 Harbor Island Dr., San Diego
• (619) 298-6623,
• (800) 606-9224

Here's a club and school that has different levels for novice, experienced and extremely experienced sailors. The initial cost of $275 gives you unlimited access to the 19-foot Rhodes sailboat, club facilities (such as a pool area and restrooms) and basic sailing lessons. The club's location is right on the harbor. Many Insiders visit the club for drinks after a day's sail. It's a beautiful location to lounge and watch the sun set.

Scuba Diving

The good news is that San Diego has some excellent locations for scuba diving. The bad news is that you must be a certified diver in order to get your tanks filled and legally dive. If you're in town for a week or so, you can get certified in as little as four days and then be able to discover and explore the fascinating underwater world. However, even though the intrepid diver can find lots of interest in local waters, most scuba divers head elsewhere. The reason is that the water tends to be cold most of the year, and a consistent surge can keep things murky underwater. Sometimes visibility is limited to a foot or less. So many head for Catalina Island or Mexico, where the water is warmer and clearer. For those who insist on testing the waters locally, here's where to point your snorkel.

Once you're a certified diver, the best spots for diving are La Jolla Underwater Ecological Reserve and the kelp beds off Point Loma. You're likely to see California's state fish, the

tiny but brilliantly colored orange Garibaldi, as well as huge Manta Rays and countless varieties of large fish. Keep in mind that if you're diving in the ecological reserve, it's prohibited to remove anything — even a shell. And since the Garibaldi is a state fish, harming one little scale on its tiny body can get you a night in jail and a hefty fine. Look, but don't touch.

Boat diving is also popular here; you can choose from half- and full-day trips to the Coronado Islands in Mexico or trips around local waters. Safety is a big issue with scuba diving, so always remember what you've been taught: Dive with a buddy and observe all the safety rules your instructor has pounded into your head.

The Diving Locker
1020 Grand Ave., San Diego
• (858) 272-1120
405 N. Highway 101, Solana Beach
• (858) 755-6822

Since 1959 the instructors at the Diving Locker have been teaching the skills of scuba to thousands of would-be divers. Lessons start at around $150 and include four pool sessions, four classroom sessions and five ocean dives. Students are required to provide their own mask, snorkel, gloves and booties. The Diving Locker also offers certified divers full equipment rentals for $35.

San Diego Divers Supply
4004 Sports Arena Blvd., San Diego
• (619) 224-3439

For $99 plus the cost of materials (which brings the price up to about $160), San Diego Divers Supply offers a four-week certification class for new divers. You'll learn the basics in pool classes and on an ocean dive. Once certified, the store can fill all your equipment needs at a deep discount. Rental equipment is available, too.

INSIDERS' TIP

Dangerous sea critters aren't too much of a problem at San Diego's beaches. But watch out for the occasional floating jellyfish that can inflict a painful sting. Also, when you first enter the ocean, it's a good idea to shuffle your feet along the sandy floor to shoo away the rare stingray that might be napping in the sand.

Photo: San Diego Convention and Visitors Bureau

La Jolla Cove is beautiful and has become a popular beach for swimming and sunning.

Water Education Training
2525 Morena Blvd., San Diego
• (619) 275-3483

For $99 W.E.T. will give you a one-hour lesson, then accompany you on a dive off La Jolla. This isn't full instruction, but you'll get a good taste of what scuba is like. Full certification classes are offered too, ranging from about $150 for group lessons to $550 for private lessons. Boat dives are also offered by W.E.T.: For $49.95 you can dive for a half-day off Point Loma or La Jolla; $79.95 will buy a half-day's dive in Mexico.

Snorkeling

If the time and expense involved in full scuba certification put you off, try snorkeling. With just a mask, snorkel and fins, you can explore the underwater world for as long as you can hold your breath. Or you can float serenely on the surface, eyes downward and breathing easily through your snorkel. There's much to be seen that's close to the surface and the shore of the beach, and equipment is easily rented or purchased. All sporting goods stores sell snorkeling equipment, and getting it there might be the best way to go if you want equipment that fits.

Ocean Enterprises
7710 Balboa Ave., San Diego
• (858) 565-6054

Both sales and rentals of snorkeling equipment are available here. Rates for a 24-hour rental are $5 for mask and snorkel and $5 for fins.

OE Express
2158 Avenida de la Playa, La Jolla
• (858) 454-6195

You can either purchase or rent snorkeling equipment here. Daily rental rates are $5 for mask and snorkel and $5 for fins. OE Express also offers full scuba training and equipment.

Play It Again Sports
1401 Garnet Ave., San Diego
• (858) 490-0222
8366 Parkway Dr., La Mesa
• (619) 667-9499

9969 Mira Mesa Blvd., San Diego
• (858) 695-3030

If you're in the market to purchase snorkeling equipment (or any watersport equipment, for that matter) this is a great place to check out. The store specializes in new and used equipment, and you can find everything from a mask to a wetsuit here, all at a big discount.

Sport Fishing

Most sport fishing boats operate year-round in our perfect San Diego weather. On the off chance there's another El Niño year headed our way, call to confirm your fishing plans before you head to any of our harbors.

With those sport fishing-boat companies we've included, you can expect to sail out along the coast. Many varieties of fish can be caught, depending on the season. The Japanese current that travels along the entire coast of California is home to albacore, tuna, marlin, shark, yellowtail, barracuda, bonito, calico bass, sand bass, halibut and rock cod.

Before deciding on an expedition, consider what's included in the price, such as gear and food. Other factors are important too, like how the boats are equipped the number of passengers, facilities on board, the size of the boats and the experience of the crew.

For other charter boats not listed here, check the Yellow Pages under "Fishing." We've listed prices, but always remember to ask about discounts; if you're going with a group you may be able to get one. Remember, too, you'll need a fishing license. Yearly saltwater permits are $18.65, but you can purchase a one-day license for only $6.85; your captain (or crewmember) should be able to sell you one (see the Freshwater Fishing section for further information on fishing licenses).

Captain Ward Lindsay
2803 Emerson St., San Diego
• (619) 523-0520

The captain runs *My Fair Lady*, a 50-foot sport-fishing trawler that's definitely on the high-end of luxury, and it's priced accordingly (in the $1,000-a-day bracket). The boat takes on six fishing fans. The company offers part-day, full-day and two-day trips. Food (full meals that are well prepared), gear and bunks are included. Because of the record highs in catches for the last few years, reservations are required and it's recommended that you call days ahead to secure your plans. What can fishing folks expect to catch? Depending on the season it could be yellowtail, calico bass, rock cod, or albacore tuna.

Fisherman's Landing
2838 Garrison St., San Diego
• **(619) 221-8500**

Charter boats are available with Fisherman's Landing for fishing for tuna and yellowtail. The company specializes in long-range trips from two to 23 days. The cost of an overnight trip on a 65- to 95-foot trawler is from $108 to $185, depending on the charter or limited load options. Sales of equipment and bait are available.

H&M Sportfishing Landing
2803 Emerson St., San Diego
• **(619) 222-1144**

H&M specializes in deep-sea fishing along the coastline and further from shore. They offer half-day and longer trips. Tackle sales and rental of equipment are available. To rent a rod it's $12 for a rod that extends to 500 feet, and $15 for a trawling rod. Cost, including the fishing permit for a 24-hour trip is $108 to $158 depending on the number in the party or if you want to reserve the entire boat. Boat sizes range from 65- to 85-foot crafts. Reservations are recommended.

Photo: Dale Frost/Port of San Diego

The Ferry Landing Marketplace on Coronado Island is a great picnic spot.

Seaforth Sportsfishing
1717 Quivira Rd., San Diego
• **(619) 224-3383(information and reservations),**
•**(619) 224-6695 (fish report)**

Seaforth has half-day, full-day and twilight trips and is conveniently located in Mission Bay. The company has tackle and bait for sale and equipment rentals are available. Specialty trips include shark and rock cod in season and this company fishes the waters off the Coronado Islands. For the partial day trip, 7 AM until 4 PM, the cost is $33 for adults and $27 for children 15 years old and younger. For the two-day sports fishing trip, 10 PM until 10 PM the following day, the cost is $108 per person and includes sleeping accommodation but not food.

Surfing

San Diego County has world-renowned surfing beaches including "Trestles," "Pipes" and "Swami's." These are supposed to be the premiere spots to catch any wave. If you're visiting and have to see the sport San Diego-style or are into the surfing scene, you'll be in good company year-round. See this chapter's "Beaches" section for information on these and other surfing spots.

If you want to enjoy or participate in surfing contests, check out our Annual Events chapter for more information. The contests are often televised by ESPN and the local television channels.

We also have some pretty cool surf shops. Here are a few Insiders' favorites.

The Beach Company
1129 S. Coast Hwy., Oceanside
• **(760) 722-2578**

The surf shop prides itself on its large selection of merchandise, lots of it at unexpected and wonderfully affordable prices. They want to make the sport affordable for everyone. The store carries surfboards, body boards, and wetsuits. They also sell swimwear, sportswear, and footwear, including those surfer-style soft leather boots imported from Australia. In addition, should you have ding problems, they have a technician right at the store who can help.

Just bring in your board, and they'll offer you a quote for repairs.

California Surf-n-Sport
617-619 Pearl St., La Jolla
• **(858) 454-4580**

Smack dab in the middle of La Jolla's upscale shopping district (see our Shopping chapter), this wonderful store is for you if you're California dreamin' of surf paraphernalia. They have surfboards (and buy used ones), wetsuits, clothing (with all the right labels) and body boards. If you're already going shopping or dining in La Jolla, step inside, and you'll be certain to find the right outfit to make your San Diego stay truly cool.

Emerald City Surf Shop
3126 Mission Blvd., Ste. G, San Diego
• **(858) 488-9224**
1118 Orange Ave., Coronado
• **(619) 435-6677**

Insiders swear that Emerald City Surf Shops have the best prices on brand-name surf gear, so some trek from the North County and East County to come to the stores. The Mission Boulevard store is in Mission Beach and is located near the roller coaster in Belmont Park (see our Attractions chapter). The Coronado store is just one block north of the famous Hotel del Coronado (see our Hotels chapter). Emerald City is also a store for buying wave boards, jet skis, water skiing and other surf and watersport supplies.

Hansen's
1105 1st St., Encinitas • (760) 753-6595 (for the "board" room — surf boards only, that is),
(760) 753-1869 (all other merchandise)

Hansen's is the place to come for all the fashion-conscious surf lines of clothing and watersport accessories. That said, many Insiders think of Hansen's as "too touristy." They still come here, though, during sales and if they need something the other stores just don't have. The store carries body boards, water skis, wetsuits, new and used surfboards and in-line skates too. The store is about 2 blocks north from Swami's (see our Beaches in this chapter) so after you have the right gear, you can hit the waves or watch those who know

Palm trees and soft breezes grace this evening paradise.

what they're doing. If you want the surf report in Encinitas, you can call (760) 753-6221.

Longboard Grotto Surf Shop
978 N. Hwy. 101, Encinitas
• (760) 634-1920

Want to browse and buy at a store that real surfing Insiders come to? Then Longboard Grotto is it. Granted, it's a bit of a hodge-podge of merchandise from longboard to eggs (yes, the kind you eat for breakfast) to books, videos and memorabilia on surfing and the sport. It's fun and funky and an experience whether you've moved here or are cruisin' the coast.

If you're driving along the coast highway (Calif. Hwy. 101), stop in for a look-see. As for the eggs: Although it once sold other products than surf gear, the store has been selling eggs for more than 20 years. Some folks call it "that egg store." Insiders come here to buy eggs, so okay, it's an Insider thing. Does everything Insiders do have make sense?

Ocean Snow Surf Shop
1272 Auto Park Way, Escondido
• (760) 747-7873

This store in North County Inland is the place to find everything from tips on the best surfing spots and the newest suggestions on

sunscreen to wetsuit wearing recommendations and yes, even surfboards, too. Ocean Snow Surf Shop has been a mainstay of the area since 1980 and can supply your clothing and sports needs with quality logo brands.

Offshore Surf Shop
3179 Carlsbad Blvd., Carlsbad
• (760) 729-4934

Offshore Surf Shop can outfit you in everything from a perfect-fit wetsuit to reef sandals and shoes. Yes, they sell new and used surf boards. If you're looking for something special, say an antique long board, put in your request here. The store has a full line of men's and women's beachwear from shorts to logo T-shirts and bathing suits. They can also tell you about the surf along Carlsbad State Beaches. Call for the surf report before you head to the coast.

South Coast Surf Shop
5023 Newport Ave., San Diego
• (619) 223-7017

This is your place to find out about upcoming surfing contests and buy surfing and water gear and other equipment. The store also has surf and sports clothing and sometimes has used equipment for sale. It's an Insiders' place to hang out and talk about surfing too.

Sun Diego

Fashion Valley Mall, 7007 Friars Rd., San Diego • (619) 299-3244
North County Fair Mall, 272 E. Via Rancho Pkwy., Escondido
• (760) 489-2332

These surf shops in malls are a stretch for Insiders who are devoted to serious surfing. Many shun them as gauche, others as too commercial. But these same folks also admit that the stores have a place in the county.

So if you find yourself far from the beach and at the mall and say you need some surf wax, a T-shirt or want the latest copy of a surfing magazine, stop in. The stores, and more are springing up in malls in the county, have equipment that goes beyond surfing, namely snowboarding and skateboarding merchandise. They have an extensive line of apparel for kids, men and women too, and if you're looking for truly cool sunglasses, Sun Diego can help you out.

Surf Rider

1909 S. Coast Hwy., Oceanside
• (760) 433-4020

If you're looking for surf gear, shoes, and accessories, Surf Rider, formerly the Hobie Oceanside, always offers a big selection of top-quality merchandise, including the designer labels you may be looking for. They have a fine selection of long boards and also rent them for $12 for a half day, $18 for a full day. There's a $250 security deposit on the boards and they do take major credit cards for merchandise and the deposit.

Witt's Carlsbad Pipelines

2975 Carlsbad Blvd., Carlsbad
• (760) 729-4423

If you were to create a surf shop for a movie set or television show, you'd build it just like Witt's (as Insiders refer to the store). It's a bit crowded, loaded with surf stuff and all of the staff has that truly-San Diego surf look down pat, including the warm friendly smiles. If you're from a part of the country or world that doesn't have surf shops and you want to see the ultimate example, head to Witt's and take some

snaps shots of the store to show the folks back home. This could be one of your favorite memory-making experiences.

Located on the corner of Carlsbad Village Drive and Carlsbad Blvd., near Fidel's restaurant and the antique stores of Carlsbad (see our Restaurants and Shopping chapters), the shop has been a mainstay of the Carlsbad community since the early 1980s. It's also located about four blocks south of the Coaster station if you decide to take the commuter train.

At Witt's you'll find Insiders shopping and talking about surfing. It's a welcoming, low-key place with a dedication to service. No surfing question is too basic and no one will laugh if you can't figure out how to get into a skin-tight wetsuit. They want you to succeed at the sport and while the more upscale stores might sell you unnecessary stuff, at Witt's you can depend on solid advice.

Two Insider tips: Witt's has great sales every spring and fall. And Witt's offers trade-ins on surfing stuff. If you've outgrown your board or wetsuit or want to trade up, Witt's can make you a tidy deal on new gear. Just ask.

Swimming

Swimming isn't limited to just beaches; you can get a pool fix at any number of public and municipal pools around the county. Or you might enjoy spending a day at one of the two water parks in the county, Whitewater Canyon in Chula Vista or The Wave Waterpark in Vista (check our Attractions chapter for all the details). Many health and fitness clubs have pools that are open to the public for a small fee. And if you're staying at a hotel, you probably need venture no farther than a few steps outside your room. Just in case you want to swim with the locals, though, we'll give you some options.

Municipal pools offer swimming lessons for all ages, from toddlers up to adults, in groups or individually. Lessons start at around $28 per child for ten group lessons and go up from there, depending on age and type of lesson. Recreational swimming hours vary from pool to pool, so be sure to call before you go. At San Diego pools, admission is $2 for adults and $1.50 for children younger than 16. Admission prices for pools in other cities around the county are indicated separately. The San Diego municipal pools listed here are the ones that are open year-round. For a complete listing of San Diego pools, call the Swim Hotline at (858) 685-1322.

San Diego Municipal Pools

Allied Gardens
6707 Glenroy St., San Diego
• (619) 235-1143

Bud Kearns Memorial Municipal Pool
2229 Morley Field Dr., San Diego
• (619) 692-4920

Clairemont
3600 Clairemont Dr., San Diego
• (858) 581-9923

Swanson
3585 Governor Dr., San Diego
• (858) 552-1653

Tierrasanta
11238 Clairemont Mesa Blvd., San Diego
• (858) 636-4837

Vista Terrace
301 Athey Ave., San Ysidro
• (619) 424-0469

North County Coastal
Carlsbad Community Swim Complex
3401 Monroe St., Carlsbad
• (760) 434-2860
Designated hours for lap swimming and recreational swimming are offered here; call for the schedule, which tends to vary because of special events. Admission is $2 for adults who are Carlsbad residents, $3 for adult non-residents and $1 for children 17 and younger.

North County Inland
Woodland Park Aquatic Complex
671 Woodland Pkwy., San Marcos
• (760) 746-2028
Operated by the city of San Marcos, this pool has a 50-foot water slide as well as a water basketball hoop. Admission is $2. Call for public swimming hours.

East County
Fletcher Hills Pool
2345 Center Pl., El Cajon
• (619) 441-1672
Public swimming hours are available every day, but tend to vary and are scheduled around lessons. Admission is $1.50 for adults and $1 for children ages 3 to 17.

South Bay
Parkway Pool
385 Park Way, Chula Vista
• (619) 691-5088
You can get your laps in here or merely splash around if the spirit moves you. Admission is $1.50 for adults, $1 for seniors and children ages 6 to 17.

Water-Skiing/Jet-Skiing / Windsurfing

One reason that San Diego is a watersport paradise is that you have choices. You can jet ski, water ski and windsurf in the ocean, on our bays or in many of the local lakes. Check with the rangers, however, if you're entering state or community parks and before you put the boat in a lake. Some lakes may allow sailing, but not jet skiing, so ask first.

California Water Sports Rentals
4215 Harrison St., Carlsbad
• (760) 4334-3089
Whether you're a seasoned windsurfer, water-skier or jet skier, or a novice and barely

INSIDERS' TIP

Sunscreen is a must. Parents must be vigilant with their kids to make sure it's reapplied every couple of hours and after swimming.

Photo: Dale Frost/Port of San Diego

Spending time on or near the water is a San Diego pastime.

have your toes wet in the sport, the staff at California Water Sports Rentals can tell you how to do it and stay safe. You can also have fun at this marina because it's a complete watersport haven.

Located at Snug Harbor marina, even some Insiders don't know about this place, although you'll see it as you drive north on I-5 between Cannon Road and Tamarack Avenue. If you want to make sure you'll get to rent the equipment you crave, call ahead to reserve it. Your choices are wide: They even offer a motor boat with driver for skiing. The cost for water skiing is $45 for a half-hour and $85 for an hour; up to three people can ski at this price. The rental shop can outfit you with a boom to teach kids to water ski and can also provide instruction on barefoot and regulation skiing. Along with jet skis ($40 for an hour),

California Water Sports Rentals has wake boarding too.

The store gives classes on watersports too and welcome enthusiasts of all levels. There are picnic areas, a snack bar, and a small beach, and the harbor is just minutes from a grocery store and all the fast-food restaurants in Carlsbad. To get there, exit I-5 at Tamarack Avenue, turn right at Adams Avenue and follow the signs to Harrison Street.

Monkey Sea Monkey Doo Rentals
1551 Shelter Island Dr., San Diego
• **(619) 222-9625**

Monkey Sea Monkey Doo Rentals is the exclusive Sea Doo jet boat rental company in San Diego. If you want to rent a jet ski for two for eight hours the price is as low as $27.50 per hour. For one hour, it's $55, and they do have other rates depending on how long you want to ski.

Resort Watersports
Catamaran Hotel, 3999 Mission Blvd., Pacific Beach • (858) 539-8696
Bahia Hotel, 998 W. Mission Bay Dr., Mission Beach • (858) 539-7696

For rentals of watersporting equipment and lessons, Resort Watersports is one-stop shopping and outfitting. Single kayaks range from $13 to $16 an hour. Wave riders for two people are $70 an hour. You don't have to be a pro here, either, since the staff will instruct you, and make sure you've mastered the skills needed before they let you take your craft to the water. You can also get pedal boats, windsurfers, SunKats and larger sailboats here. It's best to call and make reservations for the equipment you need.

It's five-star golf here;
that's why golfers
throughout the country
drag along their clubs
when they're headed to
our fair city.

Golf

"It's five-star golf," say avid players about the courses in San Diego. That's why championship golf tournaments are held here and why golfers throughout the country drag along their clubs when they're headed to our fair city.

For duffers, like "your" Insiders, there are plenty of courses where we can have fun, enjoy the sport and keep some self-respect intact.

In this chapter, we'll given you the goods on the good places to play. As you look over the listings, be aware that these aren't the only places in the county. The Yellow Pages of your phone book will give you a full listing.

What you have here are the ones we like and recommend to friends and family. And we've included all the extraordinary ones, like Oaks North Golf Course, the ultimate executive course located in Rancho Bernardo. In each case we've tried to sketch out what makes them especially worthy of inclusion — what makes them winners.

If there's an extra cost for the cart, or something special you need to know, like a dress code, we've added that. Most of the courses here have driving ranges and putting greens. However, we haven't repeated those under the driving range category. The driving range entries are strictly that, except for Surf & Turf in Del Mar, in North County Coastal, with its miniature golf area. Here you can play a really short game and it's also fun for the shorter crowd (the kids in our families).

Like restaurants and shopping districts, golf courses sometimes change with time. For instance, one course in North County Coastal had a reputation for well-maintained fairways and manicured greens and for years before developments spread up the coast, it was the only place to play north of Del Mar. Then the owners sold it. Now, rumor has it, when it rains more than a teaspoon, the dry fairways become mudville. So it's smart to call to make sure you'll get what you expect and to verify the greens fees, too.

We've divided our chapter into public golf courses, executive courses and driving ranges, with entries under each category following our usual geographic order. At all of the courses and ranges, you can rent clubs and at most you have to look clean and casual. At the Four Seasons Resort Aviara, for instance, you'll want to spiff up a bit more, since this is an upscale course.

We've omitted those country club and resort courses where you need to be a member or guest to play. Keep in mind, however, that at courses connected to hotels, like the one at the La Costa Resort and Spa in Carlsbad, you can get great golf-package deals. So you can play where Player plays

If you're determined to golf when visiting San Diego, if you want to play at a popular time or if you're traveling a distance, call ahead. Some courses, like Torrey Pines, which hosts the PGA tour, hold tournaments. We provide phone numbers so you can get the scoop and be sure you'll get a tee time.

Golf Courses

San Diego

Balboa Park Municipal Golf Course
2600 Golf Course Dr., San Diego
- **(619) 570-1234 (reservations)**
- **(619) 239-1660 (pro shop)**

First opened in 1915, Balboa recently underwent a comprehensive, two-year renovation. Located in the heart of Balboa Park, it has spectacular views of the San Diego skyline and the Blue Pacific from many of the holes. Seemingly short at 5801 yards from the white tees, the par 72 course can reach out and bite you when you least expect it. The bulk of the first nine climb in and out of a canyon while the back nine has some new holes that require pinpoint accuracy.

The signature sixth hole is a par 3 that requires you to sail your tee shot over a ravine filled with ball-eating brush. If you hedge your bets and blast one over the green, 193 yards away, you'll have to chip back up from a swale beneath the green. This is a good course for straight hitters with lots of patience. A driving range with mat tees will get you warmed up, as will a putting green and chipping area. The venerable clubhouse overlooks the 1st and 18th holes. Greens fees during the week are $30; on weekends the fee is $35. A special twilight fee of $18 takes effect at 3 PM from November through March and 4 PM from April through October. City residents pay a discounted fee if they carry a resident card, which can be purchased for $12 at the course. The resident greens fee is $17 during the week, $19 on weekends and $9 for twilight play. Golf cart rental is extra: $20 during the week and $22 on weekends. There are no restrictions on walking.

Coronado Municipal Golf Course
2000 Visalia Row, Coronado
• (619) 435-3121 (reservations),
(619) 435-9485 (pro shop)

This is one of the most underrated courses in the county, mainly because it can be tricky getting a tee time, so lots of golfers don't even try. But if you're persistent, you'll be pleasantly rewarded. A beautiful new clubhouse opened in 1997, and the 9th and 18th holes have been recently rebuilt, too. But the course's greatest claim to fame is that on June 10, 1996, President Bill Clinton shot a 79 here, breaking 80 for the first time in his golfing career.

The par 72, 6317-yard course is flat and open, and it stays in the shadow of the San Diego-Coronado Bay Bridge for most of the front nine. Still, you'll face two par 5s within the first four holes, so keep your driver polished. A couple of ponds guard the 8th and have been known to swallow many an errant ball. The approach to the 8th is long and requires accurate shooting to avoid the ponds. Fortunately, the back of the green slopes down to hold those shots from far back in the fairway.

Greens fees are $20 for everyone, everyday. Cart rental is $12 per person. The twilight rate is $10, with cart rental going down to $7.

Mission Trails Golf Course
7380 Golfcrest Pl., San Diego
• (619) 460-5400

Nestled in a canyon at the foot of stately Cowles Mountain, Mission Trails has undergone considerable renovations in recent years, bringing much-needed improvements to this popular course. Most of the greens have been resodded, resulting in a putting surface that's a bit more predictable than in years past. It's a par 71, 5603-yard course that has lots of ups and downs in the fairly rugged terrain.

The signature hole is the 16th, the longest par 4 on the course. It's noted not so much for its difficulty — it's a not-too-daunting dogleg right — but for the beautiful view of Lake Murray as you approach the green. If you're walking, keep in mind that the climb to the 18th green is a steep one. Greens fees are $22 Monday through Thursday, $25 Fridays and $31 on weekends. Cart rental is $11 per person. The course also has a 28-station driving range and putting, chipping and sand practice areas.

Riverwalk Golf Club
1150 Fashion Valley Rd., San Diego
• (619) 698-4653

San Diego's newest public golf course opened in the spring of 1998 in the heart of Mission Valley. Three nine-hole courses combine to produce the par 72, 6156-yard Mission/Presidio course, the par 72, 6033-yard Mission/Friars Course and the par 72, 6277-

---

INSIDERS' TIP

Twilight golf is sometimes your best bet for getting in a round at your preferred course. A bonus is that the rates are cheaper.

yard Presidio/Friars Course. Presidio is longer and straighter than Mission and is favored by brute-force hitters. Mission has several doglegs and lots of water, so accurate golfers tend to fare well here. Friars has long, undulating fairways that tend to produce unexpected bounces. Thirteen of the 27 holes are protected by four lakes and the San Diego River. If you can distract yourself from your game for a few moments, you'll appreciate the beauty of the waterfalls, wildlife and wetlands flora that are all over the course.

The second hole on Mission is a short par 4 with a dogleg left and a narrow landing area. It calls for precision shots. Slice it, and you're in the water. Hook it, and your ball will be bouncing among the cars driving by on Fashion Valley Road. Greens fees include a cart and are $75 Monday through Thursday, $85 on Friday and $95 on weekends. You can walk, but the greens fee will be the same as with a cart. There's a two-sided, lighted driving range with practice greens adjacent to the course.

Torrey Pines Golf Course
11480 N. Torrey Pines Rd., La Jolla
• (619) 570-1234 (reservations),
(858) 452-3226 (pro shop)

When the PGA makes its tour stop at Torrey Pines in February of each year for the Buick Invitational, millions of television viewers across the country are awed by the splendor of the course with its emerald green fairways and stunning views of the towering cliffs and the ocean beyond. As a result, when visiting golfers find their way to San Diego, playing Torrey is a must. We won't lie to you — it's hard to get on, but not impossible. For those who manage to get a tee time, it's an experience of a lifetime.

Divided into two courses, the North and the South, it's a day of golf that can bring even seasoned golfers to their knees. Most prefer to play the tougher South Course, mainly because that's where the pros play the last two rounds of their tournament. But the par 72, 6326-yard North Course has the most picturesque (and tricky) hole you've ever seen. It's a par 3, and from the tee you look out over the Pacific, south to downtown La Jolla. Once you recover from the splendor of the view, the hole itself is waiting to humble you. The green slopes from back to front and is guarded by bunkers on both sides and in front, too. Shoot over the green and kiss your ball bye-bye. It'll be gone forever in a sharp, brush-covered dropoff.

On the par 72, 6705-yard South Course, the 18th hole presents the most difficulty. It's the only hole with a water hazard on the South Course, and was made famous by pro golfer Bruce Devlin, who sank several shots into the pond that fronts the green, ending his hopes of winning the tournament in the early 1970s.

Today it's known as Devlin's Billabong. The big decision for amateur golfers is whether to lay up in front of the pond or go for broke and shoot for the green on the second shot. Either way, the results have been known to break a grown golfer's heart.

Greens fees are $47 during the week and $52 on weekends, not including cart rental, which is $28 per cart. Twilight golf, which begins at 3 PM from November through March and 4 PM April through October, is $26. City residents with a $12 resident card (which can be purchased at the starter's window at either Torrey or Balboa) pay $20 during the week, $22 on weekends and $11 for twilight golf. The driving range and practice facilities are top-notch.

North County Coastal

Four Seasons Resort Aviara Golf Club
7447 Batiquitos Dr., Carlsbad
• **(760) 603-6900**

Here's the only Arnold Palmer-designed course in San Diego County and it's also considered one of the longest and toughest. Golfing Insiders say it's one of the best, too. But with this much beauty to surround you it really doesn't matter if you're playing the finest game ever. Every hole has a panoramic view of the mountains, the lagoon and the azure Pacific.

The 18-hole course has been featured in *Golf Digest* and *Golf* magazines as one of the top courses in the United States. There are four sets of tees measuring 5007 yards to 7007 yards. This allows golfers of various abilities to enjoy the play. The course is open to all, but the driving range and practice facility is available for guests only. Greens fees range from $85 to $140 and include a cart. You can reserve a tee time up to six days in advance.

The signature hole is the 18th, a par 4.

When asked about the hole, Arnold Palmer said, "A picturesque finishing hole with a wide fairway." Then he added this Insider's tip: "Direct the tee shot towards the fairway bunkers away from the lake. The shot to the fairway is visually exciting with the rock and waterscape highlighting the approach." For a complete look at all that happens at this resort (beyond playing where Palmer plays), check out our Spas and Resorts and Restaurants chapters.

Remember this is a lavish resort. If you stroll into the pro shop in cutoffs and flip-flop sandals, you'll be reminded that upscale golf attire is required.

Call the resort for information on golf and spa package deals.

Morgan Run Resort and Club
5690 Cancha de Golf, Rancho Santa Fe
• **(858) 756-3255**

A semi-private resort and club that's open to the public (after 11 AM each day), Morgan Run is a superbly groomed, 27-hole championship course designed by golf course architect Jay Morrish. This is Rancho Santa Fe and you will be playing the course that has challenged the rich and famous golfing set.

The course is constantly upgraded, with memorable water features and a series of challenging and notable holes — so many great ones even the course pros can't agree on which is the signature hole. Most Insiders and the majority of club pros say that it's the 8th north. It's challenging, but the best part is that it looks out over scenic views of the backcountry. During horse racing season at the Del Mar Fairgrounds (see our Annual Events chapter), there are golf packages that include seating and shuttle service to the Del Mar Thoroughbred Club.

Greens fees are about $80, slightly less at twilight, which in golf language here happens at 2 PM, golf carts are not required. but you pay the same whether you use one or not.

INSIDERS' TIP

Would you love to play golf in Mexico? Look over our South of the Border chapter for some suggestions on challenging courses.

Photo: San Diego Convention and Visitors Bureau

Golfers enjoy a game played next to the waters edge.

North County Inland

Castle Creek Country Club
8797 Circle R Dr., Escondido
• **(760) 749-2877, (760) 749-2422**

If your idea of a good game of golf is to play on a course that has big trees, beautiful fairways and flawless greens, then Castle Creek Country Club is your course. Castle Creek's golfers come here to play golf and have fun.

It's a par 72, 6396-yard, 18-hole course and the signature hole is number 14. To make this one, without losing balls or adding a lot to your score, you'll be expected to drive over a creek, hit to the right and then make it over a small lake. Oh yes, don't forget that there's a huge oak tree guarding the hole.

Challenging and fun, Castle Creek's greens fees are about $30 for the 18-hole course, $15 for just nine holes and weekends and holidays slightly more. Carts cost extra (total greens fee with cart is $35). You can reserve a tee time up to seven days in advance of your game time. There's a driving range, putting green, pro shop and snack bar near the first hole.

Doubletree Carmel Highland Resort
14455 Penasquitos Dr., San Diego
• **(858) 672-9100, (858) 672-2200**

You can see the course from Interstate 15 in the Rancho Bernardo, Carmel Mountain area of San Diego. There's a short-game practice area, nicely maintained and always very green, and the 18-hole par 72, 6428-yard championship course. The signature hole is number 5; it's a long par 5 that twists slightly.

If you're an early bird, greens fees before 9 AM are only $33, after that it's in the $50 range for weekdays. Saturday, Sunday and holidays it's $60 and all greens fees include the cart. The convenience of this course makes it popular for the seniors, so it may be busy during the workweek. Just call ahead if you have weekday flexibility because you'll most likely need a reservation.

San Luis Rey Downs
31474 Golf Club Dr., Bonsall
• **(760) 758-3762, (800) 783-6967**

This par 72 course measures 6750 yards and while the overall length isn't that long, the course is a challenge for players. For us duffers, the better word might be difficult. It's not that the course isn't beautiful — it is. You see, there are #?$! mature trees, deep greenside bunkers, tight fairways and water hazards galore. There are also wonderful ocean breezes...wonderful when your opponent is at the tee and you've already placed your ball on the green.

Monday through Friday, fees are about $30; the shared cart is $10 for each player. Saturday, Sunday and holiday fees are about $60, including the cart.

The signature hole is the 15th. It's long and narrow and deceptive. Just when you think everything is perfect, a caboose gets in your way. Yes, a train caboose is on the golf course with a resort sign attached. With the wonderful breeze (see the paragraph above), your ball could be swept straight at that obstacle. Trust us on this one.

Pala Mesa Resort
2001 Old Hwy. 395, Fallbrook
• (706) 728-5881, (800) 722-4700,
(877) 725-2637

Tucked away in Fallbrook, just off Interstate 15 in North County Inland, Pala Mesa is considered one of the best truly traditional courses in the county because of the stately trees and manicured greens and extensive fairways. Lots of seniors and those with weekday flexibility come here Mondays through Fridays.

The course is lush and especially delicious, we think, in the fall when the trees hugging the fairways change colors. Pala Mesa has rolling fairways, edged with pines and sycamores and a challenge at every turn. The mountain views are spectacular on the 6502-yard course. It's a par 72 with a 131 slope. It's also home to Golf Digest School so if you need a few tips or some advice on that swing, you can reserve time with an instructor.

The signature hole is the 11th because of the view. You get a 360-degree panorama portrait of the area. Don't be shy about admiring it. If you have room for a camera in your golf bag, it's worth taking one along to take this shot back home.

Greens fees after 1:30 PM during the week are about $30; on the weekend, carts are required, and the greens fee (including the cart) is $80.

East County

Carlton Oaks Country Club
9200 Inwood Dr., Santee
• (619) 448-4242

Carlton Oaks Country Club has a challenging 7088-yard, Pete Dye-designed course. This is the course where Curtis Strange hit a 1-iron to the 18th and made eagle to win the NCAA individual title and assure Wake Forest of the team title.

There are meandering creeks, clusters of mature trees, and a strategically undulated peninsula fairway. Carlton Oaks greens fees Monday through Thursday are $65; Friday through Sunday the fee is $75, cart included. There are package deals that include lodging, breakfast and dinner with prices that could entice you; call for information.

The signature hole here is the 12th, a par 3 that's on an island. (Take extra balls if you play like we do!) There's also a driving range, full-service pro shop and cafe to make your day complete.

Singing Hills Resort
3007 Dehesa Rd., El Cajon
• (619) 442-3425

Spread over gently rounded fairways and hugged by rugged mountains, Singing Hills offers golfers of all abilities challenging and fun play. There's a choice of three 18-hole courses, two 18-hole championship courses and an executive course.

You may have already seen Singing Hills

INSIDERS' TIP

In an informal poll conducted recently by *The San Diego Union-Tribune*, Torrey Pines was rated number one with Insiders. Steele Canyon was another highly rated favorite.

on ESPN. It has been the site of numerous PGA, LPGA, USGA and SCGA championships, in addition to hosting the School of Golf (for women, juniors and seniors). The courses were designed by Ted Robinson.

During the week, greens fees are in the $30 range; on weekends, you can expect to pay about $50. Carts are available for $10 per person. Golf packages are available. The course is busy on weekends so call ahead to reserve a tee time.

This is a sunny course so you may want to wear a hat and use sunscreen. East County can be warm in the summertime so pack a bottle of water in your golf bag.

(Be sure to see our Restaurants chapter about the restaurant and grand brunch served here at Singing Hills.)

Steele Canyon Golf and Country Club
3199 Stonefield Dr., Jamul
• (619) 441-6900

The 27-hole championship golf course in this golf community was personally designed by Gary Player. When you play it you'll feel Gary's respect for the game and his appreciation for nature.

The Canyon Ranch course requires strong shot-making abilities over breathtaking elevations; the signature 5th hole is elevated — and we're talking high up. The Ranch Course winds through the fields of a working ranch and it's the 3rd hole, called Parachute, that's the challenge. Again, here you'll be challenged with the elevation. The Meadow Course meanders along the valley floor with woodlands and streams surrounding you. You might spy rabbits and lots of birds. For the Meadow course, it's the 6th hole that most remember. Here you must hit the ball over a deep ravine to make it to the green. The Canyon Ranch course is 6700 yards, the Canyon Meadow course is 6666 yards and the Meadow course is 7003 yards.

There's a practice facility including a target-oriented driving range and two large putting greens. Monday through Thursday the greens fee is about $50. Friday it is $60 and on the weekends and holidays in the $70 range. Late weekday is a bargain for this course at about $45. There's no extra charge

for carts. You can reserve starting times up to six days in advance.

What? You didn't pack your clubs? Fear not. At Steele Canyon you can rent Titleist clubs just like the set you own back home. Heck, you might just want to leave your clubs at home to see what it feels like to play with Titleists.

South Bay

Bonita Golf Club
5540 Sweetwater Rd., Bonita
• (619) 267-1103

Most of the fairways are lined with trees at this South Bay course, which is scenic if you hit straight, but trouble if you hook or slice. It's a fairly short par 71 course at 5832 yards, so concentrate on accuracy rather than long drives. Watch out for water, too. The Sweetwater River meanders through six holes, and a large pond comes into play on another two. Bunkers are sparse, thankfully.

The signature 13th presents a couple of choices, both of them doubtful. It's a par 5 dogleg left that has both the river and a big pond to contend with. If your tee shot is too short, you just might have to lay up short of the river on your second shot. Conversely, if you blast your drive into the stratosphere, you're likely to plunk it into the pond.

Warm up on the driving range, putting green and chipping/sand practice area that are all set around a large clubhouse with a nice sports bar and restaurant. Greens fees are $18 on weekdays and $26 on weekends. Carts are an additional $12 per person. Twilight golf is $12 during the week and $16 on weekends.

Chula Vista Golf Course
4475 Bonita Rd., Bonita • (619) 479-4141

Former PGA star Billy Casper helped design this municipal course in the early 1960s. It's short on trees and pretty flat, but don't let the lack of scenery fool you. It's a par 73 course that plays longer than its 6186 yards. Only a few holes don't have water to bedevil you, and the last three holes on the back nine are straight into the wind, which is usually strong in the afternoon.

The par 4 6th is the toughest hole on the course. The wind comes in from the west and has a habit of knocking your drives down to a conveniently located bunker. Second shots demand a long iron or fairway wood to reach a skinny little green that has bunkers on both sides.

A nice grass-tee driving range is on the grounds, as is a putting green and chipping/sand practice area. Greens fees are $20 on weekdays and $26 on weekends. Carts are $11 per person extra. Twilight fees are $12 during the week and $15 on weekends.

Eastlake Country Club
2375 Clubhouse Dr., Chula Vista
• (619) 482-5757

At first look, you might think the computer-equipped carts at Eastlake are little more than a gimmick. But once you get used to the information you can get at the push of a button, you may well be hooked. Screens on every cart provide exact distances to the pin, along with helpful hints about the idiosyncrasies of each hole. They can't help your swing, though, so that part is up to you.

The par 72, 5834-yard course has fairways that are lined with nearly 2,000 young trees, six lakes, three waterfalls and dozens of sand traps. Most holes have bunkers placed right about where your drive should land. Approaches are narrow but clear, with bunkers guarding either one side or the rear of the green. It's usually the par 3s that are the sticklers, and the 12th at Eastlake is one of them. A head wind can play havoc with your tee shot, and water laps right at the putting surface. It's also protected by a couple of bunkers to the right and directly behind.

Greens fees are $50 Monday through Friday, $65 on weekends, and include the computerized cart. Twilight golf (after 2 PM) is $26 on weekdays and $39 on weekends. A luxurious three-building clubhouse complex offers all the after-golf amenities, and there's a grass driving range, two chipping/sand practice areas and two putting greens.

Executive and 9-Hole Courses

San Diego

Balboa Park 9-Hole Course
2600 Golf Course Dr., San Diego
• (619) 570-1234

If you're too short on time or talent to tackle the main course at Balboa, the nine-hole is more than adequate as a second choice. It underwent a renovation at the same time the main course did, and the effort actually improved a course that was already too much fun. It's a par 32, 2175-yard course that has some of the same hazards as the big course — big trees and bunkers.

Most fairways are lined with trees, and errant shots can easily end up in the next fairway over on the several holes that are adjacent, going up and back. Players tend to be accepting of this, and it's probably one of the few places where you look ahead and behind before you hit the ball. This is a good course for walk-ons in the late afternoon. Greens fees are $15 every day; $6 with a $12 resident card.

Mission Bay Golf Course
2702 N. Mission Bay Dr., San Diego
• (619) 490-3370

This is the only course in San Diego that has lights for nighttime play. It's a fun course with 18 holes that stretch into a par 58 of 2719 yards. Each nine has seven par 3s and two par 4s. The best is saved for last, with the 18th

---

INSIDERS' TIP

Try walking on at some of the more popular courses like Torrey Pines and Balboa. Singles and even twosomes can usually get a game with a minimum wait because of cancellations and no-shows.

being the longest hole on the course at 291 yards.

If you play at night, our best advice is to hit it straight. The lights are bright, but should you wander too far from the fairway, you'll probably have some trouble finding your ball because the lights are aimed at the tee boxes and the greens. Greens fees are $15 on weekdays and $17 on weekends. Most everyone walks on this course, but a few carts are available for those with disabilities. You can also play nine holes for a discounted rate of $10 during the week and $12 on weekends after 2 PM.

Presidio Hills Golf Course
4136 Wallace St., San Diego
• **(619) 295-9476**

A nine iron and a putter are all you'll need to navigate this charming pitch-and-putt course in historic Old Town. You'll see veteran golfers out here working on their short games, and the course is designed to test even the best. It opened in 1932 and has all par 3 holes ranging from 45 to 100 yards. Just in case you don't think you'll be challenged, wait until you get to the 17th hole, which requires a tee shot over an extremely tall and wide tree to reach the green.

This is a good place for kids (and grownups) who are just learning the game, too. Greens fees are $7 every day. No reservations are necessary, and it's fairly easy to walk on and tee off within a few minutes. There's a nice snack bar on the course that's housed in one of the oldest adobe structures in Southern California.

Tecolote Canyon Golf Course
2755 Snead Ave., San Diego
• **(858) 279-1600**

Designed by Robert Trent Jones Sr. and Sam Snead, this course is widely known as one of the toughest par 3s in California. You might not pull every club in your bag, but we guarantee you'll be challenged. The course is in a narrow canyon with swirling winds that make club selection a creative sport. Four par 4 holes range from 299 to 339 yards, and the total yardage is 3161 on the par 58 course.

The fun starts at the 1st hole, where you tee off from the top of a cliff to the green below. It's a feel-good hole that's easy and gives you false confidence for the rest. By the time

Photo: San Diego Convention and Visitors Bureau

Golfers from around the world enjoy Torrey Pines Golf Course for its challenge and scenery.

you get to the killer 11th, you'll have figured out that this is no walk in the park. The 299-yard, par 4 11th begins at the farthest point of the course, and lots of trees and the edge of the canyon provide trouble on the right. Most lay up short of the creek that runs through the fairway, then play a 9-iron up to the green, which is guarded by a trap.

Greens fees during the week are $16 to walk and $25 to ride. On weekends it's $20 to walk and $29 to ride. There's a lighted driving range with half grass and half mat stations, a practice putting green and a small chipping area.

North County Coastal

Emerald Isle
660 El Camino Real, Oceanside
• (760) 721-4700

Emerald Isle is billed as North County's "most challenging executive course," and it's the hills that get your attention if you're walking the course with its full 18 holes. Emerald Isle is a comfortable, unpretentious place to play and where you can have family fun. If you've never been into mingling with the Rolex watch crowd or you're a beginner, Emerald Isle could become your favorite.

Prices are right here. On weekdays, it's $16 before 1 PM and weekends $20 before 1 PM, after which the price drops a few dollars. There's a putting green, spacious driving range, and snack bar. Emerald Isle's staff offers instruction, whether you need a few tips or a series of lessons with the pro.

Rancho Carlsbad
5200 El Camino Real, Carlsbad
• (760) 438-1772

This executive golf course, "Rancho" as it's known by Insiders, is right off El Camino Real, near LEGOLAND California (see our Kidstuff chapter), the Carlsbad Flower Fields

(see our Annual Events chapter) and shopping (see our Shopping chapter). It is an Insiders' favorite. Not that many people frequent it so you'll rarely have to wait long, even if you don't call ahead to reserve a tee time.

While executive courses usually don't have signature holes, we like the 9th. There's a long narrow fairway and the green is elevated. Should you hit the ball way out in the rough on this hole, remember you're playing in the backcountry and watch where you step. Snakes have been known to think that the brush adjacent to the 9th is their home.

There's a shady putting green and a driving range (buy your tokens for the ball machine at the pro shop). You can browse through the pro shop and visit the snack bar. You can eat inside or on the patio. The entire package here is wrapped in mature trees with plenty of shade even on warm days. If it's been raining or looks like a storm's on the way, call to make sure Rancho is open. On wet days management closes the course to avoid destroying the fairways. It's $11.50 during the week and $14.50 on weekends to play a round on the full 18-hole, par 56 course. This course is tucked out of traffic and it's quiet.

North County Inland

Lake San Marcos Executive Golf Course
1556 Camino Del Arroyo Dr., San Marcos
• (760) 744-9092

Lake San Marcos has flat, inviting fairways that make play, especially for the less experienced, a whole lot of fun. It's popular with seniors who enjoy the perfect weather and gentle breezes in San Marcos.

A par 58 course, Lake San Marcos can be busy as there are always tournaments going on. The price is right, too. It's only $11 after 2 PM every day of the week. Golf carts are available every day for $16.

INSIDERS' TIP

If you need help getting a tee time at your preferred course, try calling Stand-by Golf at (888) 825-4653 for guaranteed same-day and next-day discounted times.

Welk Resort Center
8860 Lawrence Welk Dr., Escondido
• **(760) 749-3225, (800) 932-9355**

Hidden away in the lushness of the foot-hills and about an hour's drive from down-town San Diego, the courses here delight avid players and novices too. Surprisingly, the cost of playing at the resort can be reasonable. For instance, at the Fountains and Oaks executive courses, the fees are less than $14 to walk and play after 2 PM on weekdays and include the cart. Of course the fees are significantly higher on weekends and during prime play times.

Every hole is beautiful and with the warm, sunny days of summer that last well into the evening, you might be wise to play late in the afternoon. Some of the fairways are steep, but they make for a good bit of exercise if you're walking the course.

The yardage, designed by David Rainville, is 1837 at the Oaks and 4002 at the Fountains. If you want a golf getaway, call about golf packages. Some include lodging at the resort (see our Spas and Restaurants chapters) and unlimited golf with a cart to play either course.

Oaks North Golf Course
12602 North Oaks Dr., Rancho Bernardo
• **(858) 487-3021**

This is it: our Insiders' favorite executive course. Actually there are three 9-hole courses that easily add up to a pleasurable day out.

Oaks North is stunning with long and short fairways that make it fun for experienced golfers (you see lots of them) and duffers, too. There is a dress code here — you'll need to wear nice shorts or khakis and golf shirts (or shirts with collars). The prices range from about $30 during prime play time to about $12 for 18 holes in the late afternoon. A cart will cost you $8 extra per person, and unless you always get a cart when you golf, forego it here. The walk is worth the price of admission.

Call ahead to reserve a tee time. There's a snack bar and shaded patio for an after-golf ice tea or soda or beer.

East County

Singing Hills Resort
3007 Dehesa Rd., El Cajon
• **(619) 442-3425**

See the listing above for information about this beautiful course. The executive course has narrow fairways and well-tended greens. The challenge of the course happens to be focused on those sneaky, big, beautiful trees clustered here and there. If we didn't know better, we'd vow that they can jump in front of a perfectly placed ball and force it into the rough.

At the executive course, it's $14 for 18 holes, $10 to play the same holes late in the day. Golf carts are available every day for $10 per person. Call to reserve a tee time.

South Bay

National City Golf Course
1439 Sweetwater Rd., National City
• **(619) 474-1400**

This is a quick-play par 34 nine, and many golfers play around twice, completing a full round in about four hours. It's a narrow canyon course that can be lots of fun for straight hitters. Those who lean left or right are in for some creative second shots. The fairways are very narrow, especially on the only par 5, the 525-yard second. Water comes into play on three holes.

Greens fees are $8.50 for nine holes and

INSIDERS' TIP

Most golf courses have already switched to soft spikes only. If your golf shoes still have metal spikes, consider changing before you show up at the golf course ready to play. Otherwise, you can get them changed easily in the pro shop before you tee off.

Photo: James Blank/San Diego Convention and Visitors Bureau

An aerial view of Torrey Pines Golf Course shows where famous golfers have challenged the game.

$13.50 for 18 on weekdays. Weekend fees are $11 for nine and $17 for 18 holes. Carts are $8 per person.

Driving Ranges

San Diego

Family Golf Center, Harborside
801 W. Ash St., San Diego
• (619) 239-4653

Located on the west end of downtown San Diego, this range is a favorite of downtown workers who will often spend lunch hours working on their swing. It's a double-deck facility with 80 mat tees, 16 grass tees, a putting green and a chipping/sand practice area. What

makes this range unusual is that you can hit from two directions, the north end or the south end, and it's completely encased in netting to prevent wild shots from landing on the busy adjacent streets.

Buckets of balls range from $3 to $6. Seniors can hit for half price on weekday mornings. The range is open weekdays from 7 AM to 10 PM, Saturday from 8 AM to 10 PM and Sunday from 9 AM to 9 PM.

The Links at Carroll Canyon
5605 Carroll Canyon Rd., San Diego
• (858) 642-0181

This is the newest of all the golf ranges in the city of San Diego, and it's got a lot of perks, like 74 stations on two levels. All stations have both a mat and a little plot of grass that's replaced every few days. In addition to the tee stations, there's an 18-hole, par 58 grass putting course with distances ranging from 35 feet to 114 feet. It's $10 to play the putting course, or $5 if you rent a bucket of balls for the range.

Buckets are from $4 to $12 if you use the mats, and from $5 to $16 if you hit off the grass. You can also work on your short game at a 75-yard chipping-practice area. Facilities include a golf shop, lockers, deli and a club-repair shop. The lighted range is open from 7 AM to 10 PM daily.

Stadium Golf Center
2990 Murphy Canyon Rd., San Diego
• (858) 277-6667

When this range first opened, passersby thought aliens had landed because the lights were so bright and visible from such a distance. What evoked images of E.T. in some is a benefit to those who use the range because you can see just where your shots land, even in the dead of night.

With 48 mat tees and 24 grass tees, there's rarely a problem finding an open tee here. The landing area is long and grassy and has seven target greens. One of the nicest features is the 10,000 square-foot bent-grass putting green that's available for play (along with the chipping and sand practice areas) for $3 for the first half-hour and $1 for each additional half-hour. Bucket prices range from $4.50 for 45 balls to $13 for 225 balls.

North County Coastal

Family Golf Center
2711 Haymar Dr., Carlsbad
• (760) 720-4653

The Family Golf Center in Carlsbad is tucked behind a hill and a strip shopping center right off Calif. Highway 78. Exit at El Camino Real. You might not know it's there until you're

past the exit. Call for directions if you don't have a good map because the location is extra nice; it's worth going out of your way to find this driving range.

The center is big, with more than 100 stations where you hit the ball off imitation grass. It's rarely crowded — we know because we've been here a lot. (Hey, we were doing research for the book and someone had to see if we could recommend it to you.) At this center (there are other Family Golf Centers in the county) there's a well-stocked pro shop. The range also has tournaments. You can arrange for lessons here too.

The putting green is of the plastic-turf style. It's well maintained but might disappoint someone who seriously wants to practice his or her short game. We find it fun nonetheless. Six dollars will get you a big bucket of balls. Get the tokens in the pro shop.

Olympic Resort Hotel & Spa
6111 El Camino Real, Carlsbad
• (760) 438-8330

Here's a driving range for the serious golfer and anyone who wants a challenge. At Olympic Resort Hotel & Spa there are 48 deluxe stations. There's a practice bunker and four — count 'em — four putting greens. You can also arranged for PGA instructions and take advantage of video lessons on state-of-the-art equipment. Down side? The range is situated so that in the late afternoon or early evening (depending on the time of year) you're hitting straight into the sun. So for about an hour you'll need sunglasses or simply schedule your practice session for another time.

Surf & Turf Driving Range
1555 Jimmy Durante Blvd., Del Mar
• (858) 481-0363

Surf & Turf is easy to get to. Just exit Interstate 5 at Via De La Valle in Del Mar and head toward the ocean. Make the first left turn onto Jimmy Durante Boulevard. You can't miss it. The range is across from the Del Mar Fair-

INSIDERS' TIP

The Four Seasons Aviara Golf Club has one of the longest and toughest courses in the county.

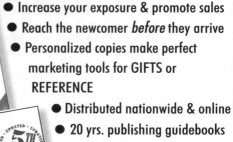

grounds. The staff here offers individual and group lessons. The range is lighted and open daily from 7 AM until 9 PM.

If you're from a part of the country that has lush, green driving ranges and you come here in the summer, you might be surprised. While the stations have astro-turf, from about June through October, you'll be hitting balls into dirt.

Keep in mind that when the horses are running (during racing season) and during the four weeks the Del Mar Fair is being held, traffic can be unpleasant. If you're uncertain of what's happening at the fairgrounds or the track, call the driving range about traffic conditions before you set your sights on hitting golf balls here. If you want to play some strictly-for-laughs golf after hitting a bucket of balls, Surf & Turf has a place to play miniature golf, too.

North County Inland

Thunderbird Driving Range & Training Center
26351 N. Centre City Pkwy., Escondido
• **(760) 746-0245**

Conveniently located right off I-15 (take the Deer Springs Road exit), the Thunderbird is well lighted and popular. The down side is that the highway traffic can be noisy.

There's a pro shop and snack bar. A large bucket of balls will cost you $6.

Vista Golf Practice Center
1850 Thilbodo Rd., Vista
• **(760) 727-0008**

This driving range is smack-dab in suburbia, so if you're visiting or living in Vista, San Marcos or the surrounding communities, you're in luck. Be aware, however, that others have also discovered its convenience and it can be busy.

There's a putting green and pro shop where you can arrange for lessons or get a few tips from the pro. Call ahead if you're interested in lessons.

East County

Fletcher Hills Golf Range
1756 Weld Blvd., El Cajon
• **(619) 449-6311**

Fletcher Hills is popular with golfers who live in East County and can get there during the daylight hours. You see, there are no lights so they sell the last bucket at 7 PM in the summer. In the winter, it closes earlier. A large bucket of balls will cost you $5.East County

South Bay

Bonita Golf Center
3631 Bonita Rd., Bonita
• **(619) 426-2069**

Rent a bucket of balls and swing away on this lighted range that has 30 grass tees and 18 mat stations. The first 175 yards of the range have small target areas that are marked by flags for those accuracy shots. If you just want to swing away and see how far you can drive, distance markers are placed beyond the target areas.

Next to the pro shop is a putting green and a large sand/chipping practice area. If you bring your own balls, it's $4.50 per hour to use the practice facilities, but if you rent a bucket, it's free. Balls rent for $2.50 for a small bucket of 25, $4.50 for 60 and $5.50 for 100. Hours are 8 AM to 8 PM daily.

Family Golf Center, The Palms
540 Hollister St., San Diego
• **(619) 424-3213**

Located just off I-5 in the South Bay, the 42 hitting stations here are half grass and half mat. The landing area is grassy, and target flags and yardage markers are sprinkled throughout. A bonus is a nice chipping course with nine holes ranging from 30 to 70 yards. Buckets of balls are $4 and $6. The range is lighted and is open from 8 AM until 9 PM daily.

In addition to the standards — football, baseball, hockey, golf, tennis and auto racing — San Diegans are blessed with a couple of oddball (but highly entertaining) sports spectacles.

Spectator Sports

San Diegans have a reputation for being fair-weather fans — literally and figuratively. Whether or not that reputation is deserved is up for debate, but the fact is that professional sports teams struggle at times to generate sustained interest among local fans — unless, of course, the team is in the hunt for a championship. If the Padres or the Chargers are having a dismal season, chances are that more than a few Insiders will look elsewhere for entertainment, mainly because there's so darn much to do here. Why waste an afternoon or evening watching the hometown boys turn in yet another lackluster performance when you could bask on the beach or sip champagne at an outdoor concert by the bay?

That said, don't think for a moment that we don't love our sports teams. Scores of rabid fans attend every home game (and many away games, too) simply out of sheer devotion and loyalty, regardless of the standings. And when the team is winning or an out-of-town superstar is making an appearance, tickets can be hard to come by.

In addition to the standards — football, baseball, hockey, golf, tennis and auto racing — San Diegans are blessed with a couple of oddball (but highly entertaining) sports spectacles. Among them is Over-the-Line, a three-person-per-team softball game invented by some local beach guys who believed that running the bases interfered too much with their beer drinking. From that inauspicious philosophy was born a game that now is celebrated every summer in a two-week tournament that draws players and spectators from all over the world and somewhere along the line has earned some actual credibility.

The X Games have been to San Diego twice, bringing along such extreme sports as sky surfing, bicycle stunt riding and the downhill luge. Everyone hopes they'll be back for future meets. Another repeat performer is the Super Bowl. In 1998 both the event itself, and its weeklong festivities were so successful that it looks as though the NFL will be adding San Diego to its regular rotation for future Super Bowls.

Although San Diego does not have a professional basketball team at the moment, there is no lack of exciting sporting events to fill the gap. Thunderboats — high-speed racing boats — roar across Mission Bay in an annual competition, thrilling onlookers with their death-defying speeds. A short trip south of the border is all you need to see the ancient and historic sport of bullfighting. And the beautifully renovated Del Mar Thoroughbred Club plays host to the Sport of Kings every summer.

We'll fill you in on them all in this chapter. Some sports are annual events; some are held during a regular season. We'll give you dates, ticket prices and venues, all you have to do is make up your mind what appeals to you most. You're likely to find a sporting event to watch on any day of the year. And if it's a nice day, which it usually is, ignore the lure of the beach. The sun will be out at the stadium, too, and we guarantee you'll have a great time.

Qualcomm Stadium
9449 Friars Rd., San Diego
• **(619) 641-3131**

Home games for Padres baseball, Chargers football and San Diego State University

Baseball action gets intense when the San Diego Padres take the bat.

Aztec football are all held at Qualcomm Stadium. Located in Mission Valley, the stadium is just north of Interstate 8, between Calif. Highway 163 and Interstate 15. Parking is a hefty $6 per car for Padres and Chargers games, $5 for Aztec football games and $7 for all other special events, so we strongly urge you to carpool. Bus service to home games is provided by North County Transit, (760) 722-6283, and San Diego's Metropolitan Transit, (619) 233-3004. If you taxi your way in, rest assured that you'll find one waiting for you following the game in the stadium parking lot. One of

the best ways to get to Qualcomm is by way of the San Diego Trolley. The trolley departs from locations all over town and takes you right to its station in the stadium parking lot, just a short walk from the gate.

Bottles, cans and liquid containers are not allowed inside the stadium. The exception is baby bottles and containers with formula. Food may be brought into the stadium, but coolers, backpacks and packages must fit underneath your seat, and bags and purses are subject to inspection at the gate. Smoking is not allowed in any of the seating areas or in the field-level

INSIDERS' TIP

If you plan to attend OMBAC's Over-the-Line Tournament, remember the organizers' safety motto: No bowsers (dogs), bottles or babies.

Tony Gwynn, San Diego Padres

You're sitting in the stands at Qualcomm Stadium, barely into your bag of roasted peanuts. It's the bottom of the first inning, and the number-three batter is about to move into position. The buzz of the crowd suddenly quiets. A familiar figure moves toward the batting box, and you can almost feel the excitement building. Then the announcer says, "Number nineteen, TONY...GWYNN!" The crowd goes wild, exploding in cheers and applause, as Mr. Padre takes his stance. Chances are Tony will get a hit; he usually does. He's flirted with batting .400 a couple of times, the only player in modern baseball to approach the milestone passed by Ted Williams so many years ago. One thing is certain, though, Tony Gwynn is one of the most beloved Padres in the history of the team.

Tony has been with the San Diego Padres since 1982, and along the way has accomplished some pretty impressive feats. He's the all-time club leader in batting average, hits, runs, doubles, triples, stolen bases, RBI and games played. On top of those achievements, he holds eight batting titles, five Gold Glove Awards and has been voted to the All-Star Game 10 times. And he has no plans to retire in the near future.

What really distinguishes Tony Gwynn from the average baseball superstar goes beyond statistics. Tony is a hometown son, having graduated from San Diego State University, and his ties to San Diego are strong. Throughout his major league career he has been committed to working within the community, particularly with disadvantaged children. Talk to the Padres' front office, and they'll rattle off no less than a dozen charitable organizations to which Tony dedicates his time and energy. Tony and his wife, Alicia, have also established the Tony and Alicia Gwynn Foundation, which funds many organizations supporting needy children. Each year he hosts the Tony Gwynn Celebrity Golf Classic to raise money for the foundation, and during the off-season, he spends a good chunk of time instructing kids from all over the country who come to learn the fine points of the game at the San Diego School of Baseball.

On the field and in the clubhouse, Tony is a leader, one who leads by example. He's invariably the first to arrive at Qualcomm Stadium on game day, and you won't often find him fooling around — he's too busy taking extra batting practice. When spring training

Photo: San Diego Padres

San Diego Padres right fielder, Tony Gwynn.

begins, Tony is there long before the other players roll in. The records he breaks and the numbers he amasses are all testament to Tony's dedication to the team and his impeccable work ethic.

Needless to say, as much as he loves San Diego, he is even more adored by the

— continued on next page

community. There's no posturing with Tony. He's open and cheerful whether confronted with reporters grilling him for details or youngsters seeking an autograph. When his Poway neighborhood held a parade, organizers would have no other grand marshal than Tony. The only problem was, the Padres made the playoffs, and a game was scheduled for the exact time as the parade. So the city of Poway asked Alicia and their two children, Anthony and Anisha, to step in for him, which they gladly did. And no one doubted that Tony was there in spirit.

In 1997 San Diego State University honored Tony by naming its new, state-of-the-art baseball stadium for him. Tony Gwynn Stadium was recently named one of the top stadiums in college baseball by *Baseball America*, and Tony makes frequent appearances to cheer on the Aztecs.

Not content with breaking new ground in San Diego, in 1998 the Padres' right fielder joined Rod Carew for a youth batting clinic in Culiacan, Sinaloa, Mexico. This landmark event for Culiacan Little Leaguers raised funds for their program, the Tony and Alicia Gwynn Foundation and pediatric cancer research here in the United States.

Tony will finish his major league career in San Diego. Padres owner John Moores has seen to that already, extending his contract beyond the millennium to when Tony thinks his aging body will have had enough. His talents seem only to improve with age, however. In each of the past five seasons, he has bettered his batting average. Who knows? He may yet break .400. Whether he does or not, one truth is immutable: Tony Gwynn is a class act, through and through.

concourse. Smoking is permitted in the plaza, loge and view concourses.

Tailgating is a popular way to kick off a game. Gather your friends, some food and drink, and have an impromptu party in the parking lot. Just remember that tailgaters must confine themselves to their own parking space.

Baseball

San Diego Padres
Qualcomm Stadium, 9449 Friars Rd., San Diego • (619) 280-4636

May 27, 1968, was an exciting day for baseball fans — San Diego was awarded a National League franchise, the San Diego Padres. Now approaching the end of its third decade as a major league team, the club has amassed some statistics that have little to do with hits and runs: The Padres have seen four owners and fourteen managers over the years. And it was 1975, seven years after the team's inception, before the club climbed out of the cellar.

It took another eight years of fluctuating between fourth place and last before every-

thing clicked. In one memorable season, in 1984, the Padres soared. Not only did they beat San Francisco to win their division, they came back from an early deficit in the National League Championship Series to snatch the pennant away from the Chicago Cubs. The beleaguered Padres were going to the World Series!

No matter that the Series proved to be anticlimactic — the Pads dropped four of five to the Detroit Tigers — they had made it to the big show. Never was a city more proud of its team. Winning seemed almost irrelevant. It's a good thing, too, because subsequent years brought more of what fans were used to. The team dropped to third place in their division the following year, then fourth, then last, a position they seemed most comfortable with.

Days of glory finally returned, though. In 1994 John Moores and Larry Lucchino bought the team, and a new and better era began. The quality of the team improved dramatically with the acquisition of players such as Ken Caminiti, Steve Finley, Wally Joyner, Greg Vaughn and Kevin Brown, who joined veteran slugger Tony Gwynn. And by the dog days of summer 1998, the Padres returned to the

Photo: Thom Vollenweider

The San Diego Qualcomm Stadium hosts events that draw sports fans from across the nation.

World Series, only to suffer an even more ignoble fate than before — being swept by the New York Yankees. After that season, all the aforementioned players (with the exception of Joyner and Gwynn) moved to other teams. So the Padres are once again rebuilding.

But a new baseball-only ballpark is in the works. A joint venture by the Padres and the city of San Diego will produce a place for the Padres to call home just east of downtown's Gaslamp Quarter. The new ballpark should be completed in time for the 2002 season. And as ever, each new season inspires a new round of hopes and dreams for baseball fans.

To fulfill their commitment to community involvement, the Padres ownership founded the Padres Scholars program, in which players donate funds that ownership matches dollar-for-dollar. Each year, twenty-five $5,000

scholarships are awarded to financially disadvantaged middle schoolers. Also, the club is refurbishing or building 60 Little Padres youth baseball fields in San Diego and south of the border. The Padres' history includes such notable players as Randy Jones, Rollie Fingers, Gaylord Perry, Ozzie Smith, Steve Garvey, Gary Sheffield and Fred McGriff. More than a dozen Gold Glove Awards belong to Padres' players (five to Tony Gwynn alone), and the team boasts three Cy Young Awards for pitching. But history doesn't win today's pennants. Fortunately the future looks bright. With quality ownership, young but talented players and loyal, exuberant fans, it's easy to believe that division championships, league championships and that elusive World Series championship will soon grace the Padres' record books. So grab the kids and head for

INSIDERS' TIP

Try one of Rubio's famous fish tacos while you're attending a game at Qualcomm Stadium. Available on the concourse of the Plaza, these delicacies are pure Southern California.

Qualcomm Stadium. Padres fever is contagious.

Ticket prices range from $5 to $22 for individual games. Season tickets range from $195 to $1,760 and are available in ½-season and full-season packages. Tickets may be purchased at Gate F in the stadium, from Ticketmaster by phone, (619) 220-8497, or by Ticketmaster Online. Call (619) 881-6500 for information on season ticket packages.

Football

San Diego Chargers
**Qualcomm Stadium, 9449 Friars Rd.,
San Diego • (619) 280-2121**

The histories of the San Diego Chargers and the Padres have followed an eerily parallel course. Just as the Padres are not frequent contenders in the World Series, the Chargers have made it to the Super Bowl but one time, in 1995. And like both the Padres' contests, the Charges faced a powerhouse opponent in the Super Bowl — the San Francisco 49ers — and were soundly trounced.

The loss didn't put a dent in the enthusiasm of fans, though. Game day always finds a sea of blue- and gold-clad aficionados who are ever loyal to their beloved "Bolts." (The Bolt refers to the streak of lightning on the Chargers' uniforms.) Owner Alex Spanos is committed to putting together a winning team, as evidenced by General Manager Bobby Beathard's maneuvering for a high draft pick in 1998, so the team could acquire Washington State's Ryan Leaf. Leaf is the team's new hope — a quarterback they hope will lead them to years of winning seasons and, with any luck, back to the Super Bowl. Time will tell.

Team members have shown a devotion to San Diego by diving headfirst into charitable ventures. Foundations, charity golf tournaments and Junior Chargers organizations are just a few of the ways in which players give back to the community. Earlier Chargers players such as Lance Alworth, Rolfe Benirschke and Dan Fouts set the example, and modern-day players like Junior Seau and Natrone Means follow it well. More than just sports heroes, players are truly community leaders.

Whether the Chargers are having a winning season or not, you can always count on sellout crowds whenever their perennial nemesis, the Oakland Raiders, are in town. One step below the Raiders in terms of rivalry are the Denver Broncos. But whoever the team is playing, the excitement is unparalleled. Whether you're visiting or a newcomer to San Diego, be sure to take in a Chargers game. You won't be sorry.

Individual home-game tickets are available at the Chargers' ticket office, Gate F at the stadium, or by calling Ticketmaster at (619) 220-8497. Prices range from $20 to $58. For information on season tickets, call (619) 280-2121. Prices range from $200 to $550 for regular seating, and from $890 to $2,000 for Gold Club seating.

San Diego State University Aztecs
**Qualcomm Stadium, 9449 Friars Rd.,
San Diego • (619) 283-7378**

Most Insiders are just as proud and loyal of the Aztecs as they are of the Chargers. Home games commonly draw more than 40,000 fans to the Q (as Qualcomm Stadium is often called) to cheer on the team led by head coach Ted Tollner. Prior to the opening of Qualcomm Stadium in 1967, San Diego State played its games in Aztec Bowl, located on campus, or in Balboa Stadium downtown. Neither facility was large enough to hold the masses clamoring for tickets, so the move to Qualcomm was a welcome one.

The Aztecs will compete in the Western Athletic Conference until the end of the 1999 season against teams such as UNLV, BYU, Air

---

INSIDERS' TIP

At the Del Mar Thoroughbred Club, everyone has a unique wagering technique. One Insider says she always bets on gray horses. Another places wagers solely on the basis of the color of the jockeys' silks.

When the San Diego Chargers are in action on the field, San Diego is cheering.

Force and Wyoming. After that, the Aztecs will split off with several other members of the WAC to form a new conference called the Mountain West Conference. Typically, the NFL draft eyes SDSU closely, and many players have gone on to greater glory in professional football, Fred Dryer, Willie Buchanon and Marshall Faulk among them. Tickets to home games range in price from $7 to $27; SDSU students with ID are admitted free, but tickets must be picked up in advance. Tickets are available at Gate F in the stadium, at the SDSU ticket office on campus or by phoning (619) 283-7378.

Holiday Bowl
Qualcomm Stadium, 9449 Friars Rd., San Diego • (619) 283-5808

For more than 20 years the Holiday Bowl has featured a football face-off between na-tionally ranked teams from the Big 12 and either the WAC or the Pac 10. Since its inauguration in 1978, the majority of games have been won by a margin of one touchdown or less, and most have been decided in the final two minutes. It's no wonder the Holiday Bowl has earned a reputation as America's most exciting bowl game.

The hometown San Diego State Aztecs made an appearance in the Holiday Bowl in 1986 and put on one of the best shows ever. The Aztecs held off the Iowa Hawkeyes until the final four seconds, when an Iowa field goal gave the team a one-point edge over the Aztecs and a final score of 39 to 38.

Holiday Bowl tickets are available in advance by calling the Bowl ticket office at (619) 283-5808. Ticket prices range from $29 to $50. The game is held in late December.

INSIDERS' TIP

Even though days are warm during the summer, nights can be chilly clear through July. If you go to a nighttime Padres baseball game during the early summer months, be sure to bring a warm jacket or even a blanket.

Photo: Bob Yarbrough/San Diego Convention and Visitors Bureau

Hard-hitting excitement reigns in this Del Mar polo game.

Photo: Bob Yarbrough/San Diego Convention and Visitors Bureau

Auto Racing

El Cajon Speedway
1875 Joe Crosson Dr., El Cajon
• (619) 448-8900

Choose from a heap of racing events: NASCAR, Spec Trucks, Grand American Modifieds, Stock Cars and Destruction Derbies, to name a few. The Cajon Speedway is a 3/8-mile track on 40 acres adjacent to Gillespie Field Airport in El Cajon. The track has turns banked to 18 degrees for great racing. Regular race events include a Trophy Dash, Heat Races, Semis and four Main Events.

Mid-March through mid-October is the racing season. Ticket prices for adults are $8 for the east side, $7 for the west side. Children 6 to 12 get in for $3; kids younger than 6 are admitted free when accompanied by an adult. Parking is $1. The parking lot opens at 5 PM. Qualifying begins at 5:05 PM, and the first race is at 7 PM.

Bullfighting

El Toreo de Tijuana
Blvd. Agua Caliente at Blvd.
Cuauhtémoc, Tijuana
Plaza Monumental
Playas de Tijuana, Tijuana
• (619) 232-5049

If you have an appreciation for the ancient sport of bullfighting, head south of the border to one of two bullrings in Tijuana. Dating back to 2000 B.C., bullfighting is a combination of ritual and mortal combat, pitting man against beast in a graceful but deadly battle. El Toreo de Tijuana and Plaza Monumental present some of the world's leading matadors.

Bullfights are held from May through September. The sport is extremely popular in Mexico, so you're encouraged to purchase your tickets in advance. Tickets are available in San Diego at the Five Star Tours depot, 1050 Kettner Boulevard, and in Tijuana at a

---

INSIDERS' TIP

Kids love the interactive games in the plaza concourse of Qualcomm Stadium. During baseball season they can try their luck at the batting contest or have the speed of their pitching gauged by radar.

This young sports fan knows how to add enjoyment to his game-day activities.

booth on Avenida Revolución between Calle 2a and Calle 3a. Tickets are $11 for general admission, and from $23 to $39 for reserved seats. The most expensive tickets are those located in the shade, closest to the floor of the ring.

Golf

Buick Invitational
Golf Tournament
Torrey Pines Golf Course, 11480 N.
Torrey Pines Rd., La Jolla
• (619) 281-4653

The annual PGA Tour men's tournament makes its way to Torrey Pines every February for a week of special events topped off with the 4-day professional competition. Sponsored by the local Century Club, this is the only PGA Tour event held on a municipal course — and a more beautiful one would be hard to find. Beautifully manicured fairways and greens are located on the bluffs above La Jolla, and the views are spectacular.

Crowd favorite Tiger Woods took the championship in 1999, which means he'll be back to defend his title.

Practice rounds are held Monday and Tuesday, a Pro-Am featuring local and national professionals is Wednesday, and the competition runs from Thursday through Sunday. For exact dates of the tournament and to order tickets, call the Century Club at (619) 281-4653, or Ticketmaster at (619) 220-8497. Advance season badges can be purchased for $50. Single-day tickets during the week are $12 in advance, $15 at the gate. Weekend single-day tickets are $15 in advance, $20 at the gate.

Hockey

San Diego Gulls Hockey
San Diego Sports Arena, 3500 Sports
Arena Blvd., San Diego • (619) 225-9813

If you enjoy watching one of the fastest games in professional sports, then Gulls ice hockey is for you. The San Diego Gulls play in the South Division of the West Coast Hockey League, and have consistently made the finals in the Taylor Cup Championship series.

The season runs from October through March; the playoffs run into April. Ticket prices range from $11 to $16, and are available at the Sports Arena Box Office or by calling Ticketmaster at (619) 220-8497.

Horse Racing

Del Mar Thoroughbred Club
2260 Jimmy Durante Blvd., Del Mar
• (858) 792-4242

Bing Crosby and his Hollywood buddies envisioned a horse palace by the sea where they could play all day and party all night, and thus was born the Del Mar Thoroughbred Racing Club. Bing was there to greet the first fan through the gate on July 3, 1937, and even now, each racing day begins with a recording of Bing singing, "Where the surf meets the turf in old Del Mar." The racing runs from late July through mid-September, and the track is still a favorite of Tinsel Town celebrities.

Some of racing's top California-bred horses have set records at Del Mar, including Bertrando and Best Pal, and one of the sport's all-time favorite jockeys, Willie Shoemaker, holds the records for most wins all-time and in one season. The track's most exciting day ever was in 1996, when the mighty Cigar attempted to break Citation's 16 consecutive wins record, only to be upset by an unheralded horse.

Races are held daily, except Tuesdays. First post is at 2 PM, except on Fridays when first post is at 4 PM. General admission is $3; reserved grandstand seating is $4. Clubhouse admission is $6; reserved clubhouse seating is $4. Reserved seats for any day may be purchased at the ticket office at the racetrack.

Hydroplane and Power Boat Racing

Thunderboats Unlimited
Mission Bay Park, San Diego
• (619) 268-1250

Since 1964 Unlimited Hydroplanes and other classes of powerboat racing have been held on Mission Bay. The stars of the spectacle, 3-ton monster Unlimited Hydroplanes, bring thrills and chills to spectators with their rooster-tail-spewing power. East Mission Bay's Bill Muncey Course is named for the sport's all-time greatest star, who was instrumental in bringing Unlimited Hydroplane racing to San Diego.

Loyal Chargers fans in their team colors make sure their cheers are heard.

Photo: Thom Vollenweider

Here is an aggressive sport for beach lovers — women's professional volleyball.

Nighttime fireworks, demonstrations by Navy SEAL teams and performances by the Sea World Beach Band entertain spectators between and after races. Kids will love the in-line skating, skateboard demonstrations and interactive games and rides.

Held in September, three racing venues are available for spectators: East Vacation Isle, Fiesta Island and Crown Point Shores. Your ticket is good for all three locations, and shuttles run continuously between the venues. Tickets for a 3-day pass are $30 for adults, $10 for children 7 to 12 and free for children 6 and younger. Single-day tickets, sold only to adults, are $20 for Friday, and $25 for Saturday or Sunday(no single-day tickets are sold to children). Three-day pit passes are $25; single-day pit passes are $20 for Friday and $25 for Saturday and Sunday. Children younger than 4 get in free. Preferred three-day parking is $30; single-day is $10 for Friday, and $15 for Saturday or Sunday. Three-day general parking is $20. To order tickets, call (858) 268-1250.

Motocross Racing

Carlsbad Raceway
6600 Palomar Airport Rd., Carlsbad
• (760) 727-1171

The county's only motocross track is home to a series of bike races for all classes: beginner, novice, intermediate and expert. Races are scheduled at various times throughout the year, usually in a series of eight races spread over three or four months. Call to find out exact dates.

Admission is $10 at the door. Gates open at 8 AM; racing starts at 11 AM. A catering truck is located at the racetrack, or you can bring a lunch with you.

Polo

San Diego Polo Club
14555 El Camino Real, Rancho Santa Fe
• (619) 481-9217

For pure primal excitement, nothing compares to the thrill of eight mounted riders thundering downfield in pursuit or defense of a goal. The object of polo is to move a ball through the goal in six periods of play called "chukkers." Each chukker is seven minutes long, and there are no time-outs except for injuries or penalties.

The San Diego Polo Club holds its matches on Sundays from June through September. Pre-match festivities include picnics, tailgating, polo demonstrations, kids' activities and complete food and beverage service. Spectators have one responsibility — during the intermission between the third and fourth chukkers, fans are asked to make their way to the field and stomp down the divots unearthed by the ponies. It's a great tradition and a chance to meet other polo aficionados, too.

Matches begin at 1:30 PM and 3 PM. Admission is $5.

Sand Softball

Over-the-Line World Championship Tournament
Fiesta Island, Mission Bay, San Diego
• (619) 688-0817

The Old Mission Beach Athletic Club (OMBAC) consists of a group of friends who organized in 1954, mainly to sponsor beach volleyball. From the beginning OMBAC has been most famous for Over-the-Line, a game invented by its members. Three players per team compete on a rectangular field with a triangle at its tip, pointing toward the batter. The spot where the base of the triangle abuts the rectangle is "the line." The object is for the batter to hit the ball over the line without being fielded by the opposite team. In keeping with OMBAC's philosophy of maximum pleasure with minimum effort, no base running is involved.

Now evolved into a major tournament, this annual ritual occurs every second and third weekend in July, and thousands of fans flock to Fiesta Island to watch it. One of the signature characteristics of the tournament is the team names. Entrants are encouraged to be as creative as possible, and the result is a collection of names that are bawdy at best and downright crude at worst. This is not an ideal event for kids. But for people watching, lots of sunshine and an interesting game, it can't be beat.

Hot dogs and soft drinks are sold at the

This crowd keeps a close eye on the action at the Over-the-Line Tournament.

tournament, but you're welcome to bring your own food and drink. Bottles are not permitted. The tournament runs from 7 AM to 7 PM, and admission is free. As parking is limited on the island, you are encouraged to catch one of the many shuttles that run continuously from the beach area and other locations around town (these are publicized in the days before the tournament). Be sure to bring a beach chair or towel so you can spread out and get comfortable

North County Coastal region. The tournament attracts top stars and the excitement is non-stop. Held on the grounds of the posh La Costa Resort and Spa, this is professional tennis at its best.

The first week in August is the usual time for the tournament, but call the box office at (760) 438-9220 to get the exact dates. Tickets range in price from $7 for practice rounds to $30 for the finals. We strongly advise you to purchase your tickets as far in advance as possible, as they usually sell out early. Tickets are available at the box office at La Costa Resort or through Ticketmaster at (619) 220-8497.

Soccer

San Diego Flash
San Diego Mesa College
• **7250 Mesa College Dr., San Diego**
• **(858) 581-2120**

The San Diego Flash is an A-League soccer team, which is one level below Major League Soccer. Playing its inaugural season in 1998, the Flash competes in the Western Conference's Pacific Division with Seattle; Vancouver, WA; California; San Francisco; Orange County and U.S. Pro-40 Select. Coach Ralf Wilhelms was a player for the former San Diego Sockers, a team from a defunct indoor soccer league. He has put together a multinational team of young players complemented by seasoned veterans.

The season runs from April through September, and all home games are held on the San Diego Mesa College campus. Tickets are $10 for adults and $6 for children 16 and younger, seniors 65 and older and members of the military.

Tennis

Toshiba Tennis Classic
La Costa Resort and Spa,
Costa Del Mar Rd., Carlsbad
• **(760) 438-9220**

Every August the women's professional tennis tour stops in La Costa, in San Diego's

College and High School Sports

San Diego State University's athletic teams are the college powerhouses in town; they get national recognition in nearly every sport. But plenty of other college teams are not only noteworthy, but also provide a ton of entertainment for spectators. Insiders know that USD's Toreros consistently shine in football, basketball, baseball, volleyball and soccer. The Tritons of UCSD compete on a national level in a number of sports, and Point Loma Nazarene has strong athletic teams too.

Let's not forget our community colleges. Their intercollegiate sports are every bit as competitive as their four-year counterparts. And for the ultimate sports experience, go to a high school game. With more than 60 county high schools, all of which have sports programs, you're sure to find a game of some kind on just about any day of the week.

This is sports at its purest form, and the rivalries between teams are intense. Remember, these youngsters are the superstars of tomorrow. Join the parents, faculty and boosters at any high school game. You won't be disappointed.

San Diegans like to visit the desert communities, Disneyland, San Juan Capistrano Mission, and Temecula's wine country.

Daytrips

Why leave the San Diego area even for a daytrip? That's a good question.

We have nearly a never-ending supply of places to see and things to do right here in our amazing county. But folks here do want to get out and about; they like to visit the desert communities, Disneyland, San Juan Capistrano mission, and Temecula's wine country. It's fun to explore.

We selected the trips for our Daytrips chapter using two simple principles: 1) They had to be special and ones we'd recommend to friends and family, and 2) They had to be do-able in one day.

With places like the El Pueblo de Los Angeles Historic Monument, you will have to travel to Los Angeles, about three hours north by car. But you don't have to drive the freeway to reach the area. You can take Amtrak and get there in about 2 hours without once thinking "gridlock." You'll exit at Los Angeles Union Station, just a block from your destination. But you won't want to rush right over. Stop for a moment to enjoy the renovation and art deco design.

You'll need to drive, though, to the desert communities of Palm Springs, Rancho Mirage and Indio, but it's a relatively short trip of about 2 hours, so many people go there for the day. Traffic is normally light, compared to that of Orange County and Los Angeles. The desert scenery is gorgeous. And you'll be treated to the sight of snow-covered mountains most of the year, Mt. San Jacinto, and an electricity-generating windmill farm as you take the Palm Springs exit from Interstate 10. So get a map, gas up the car (or get your train ticket) and let's see where these daytrips will take you.

The Deserts

Whether you go for the hot display of spring flowers or the hotspots of shopping, eating, golfing and celebrity watching in Palm Springs, the desert communities are perfect daytrips. Many Insiders go to the desert cities when it's cool and damp along the coast, and our usually constant sunshine is covered over with cloud. Some prefer to visit during the summers when there are great deals on tennis, golf and food packages.

Anza-Borrego Desert State Park
200 Palm Canyon Dr., Borrego Springs
• (760) 767-5311 (the park),
(760) 767-4205 (visitor's center)

Every year about 600,000 visitors travel to the park to camp, enjoy desert hikes and walks, and see the spring flowers. (Please see our chapter on Annual Attractions and Parks for more tips.) At the park's visitor center — the best place to start — you'll find information and brochures about the area. The center holds naturalist's talks, fossil programs, garden walks, nature hikes, campfire programs, and activities for "junior" rangers. The visitor center is open from October through May, 9 AM to 5 PM. During the summer, the center is open weekends and holidays only. There's overnight camping and other options at the park too. Be sure to see our entry in the Parks chapter for more information on Anza-Borrego.

The Desert Cities
Palm Springs Desert Resorts Convention and Visitors Bureau
69-930 Hwy. 111, Suite 201,
Rancho Mirage • (760) 770-9000
City of Palm Springs Visitor and Information Center
2781 N. Palm Canyon Dr., Palm Springs
• (800) 347-7746

A fashionable resort city, Palm Springs is known worldwide for celebrities, perfect winter temperatures and football field-sized swimming pools. Once considered the playground for the rich and famous, today Palm Springs and the desert communities such as Palm Desert, Indio and Rancho Mirage have transformed themselves into family areas. And yes, there are still plenty of celebrities who make their homes here. Golf, tennis and spa packages abound at the hotels and resorts, and during the winter "snow birds" flock to the areas from colder climes.

From San Diego, you reach the desert towns by traveling north on Interstate 15 and connecting with Calif. Hwy. 60 or Interstate 10. The 60, as Insiders call it, is a winding mountain road in some places, but a safe drive nonetheless. Whatever choice you make, just head east and you'll be heading in the right direction. The trip from San Diego is about 2 hours and traffic is hardly ever heavy.

For shopping fun while you're in the area, don't miss a stop on I-10 about 17 miles west of Palm Springs at the **Cabazon Outlet Stores**. Here you'll find a rest stop (restrooms and food) blended with outlet shopping that Insiders say is the best in the area. Stores include outlets for Nike, Eddie Bauer, Maidenform and Esprit.

For the mildly adventurous types, photo enthusiasts and the outdoor guy or gal, the **Palm Springs Aerial Tramway** is a must-do when you're in the desert. Kids love it. Call for hours of operation as they change depending on the season (760) 325-1391. To take the tram, exit I-10 at California Highway 111 and head toward Palm Springs. Exit again at Tramway Road and follow the signs. The entrance is about 3 miles up the road toward the mountain. Once the admission fee is paid (about $18 for those twelve and up; about $12 for kids over 5), you'll board the tram, which transports passengers 2.5 miles from Valley Station in Chino Canyon (at an altitude of 2,643 feet.) to and from Mountain Station (at 8,516 feet) at the east edge of Long Valley. The trip

www.insiders.com

See this and many other **Insiders' Guide®** destinations online.

Visit us today!

in an enclosed, hanging gondola isn't the jaunt for those who avoid heights or are uncomfortable in enclosed areas. If you love scenery from a bird's eye view, this is a spectacular way to see the mountains and the entire Coachella Valley below. On any blistering summer's day, you can leave Palm Springs in 100-degree-plus weather and feel a chill (maybe play in snow) on top of the mountain. At the summit you'll find a cafeteria, observation area, picnic spots, museum, gift shop and snack bar along with walking and hiking trails.

Once you're back down in the desert, you can take a celebrity-spotters bus tour (760) 770-2700 with **Palm Springs Celebrity Tours**. The 2½-hour tours cost $17 for adults, $15 for those 60 and older, and $8 for students. (You can call ahead for reservations and they're recommended during the popular winter season and during the film festivals.)

You can shop along **Tahquitz Way**, with stores such as Gucci and Saks beckoning you inside. And from ice cream parlors to chic dining establishments, you can choose a place to satisfy your daytripping appetite. You can take in a museum, too. **The Palm Springs Desert Museum** (101 Museum Dr. (760- 325-0189) has exhibits on Western and contemporary art and the human and natural history of the Coachella Valley. Call for dates and performance information; the museum holds events from drama to dance. General admission is $6.

Los Angeles Area

Traveling the freeways to Los Angeles requires patience, yet if you go, you'll wonder why you don't make the trip more often.

Good Golly Miss Molly — They're Grinding

And they're thrashing and getting some air. Yep, you guessed it. These folks are on skateboards and happily involved in a sport that's growing by the second.

Once you tell your kids about this daytrip to Temecula, just over 80 miles from downtown San Diego, be prepared to be pestered until you actually make the trek north on Interstate 15. It's worth the drive to see this model skateboard park and perhaps even try your own luck at the sport. You can rent safety equipment when you arrive, so the excuse, "Gee, honey, I don't have a helmet," won't cut it here.

Temecula's skateboard park is located at Rancho California Sports Park and shares space here with ball fields, places for inline skating, and a roller hockey rink. It's open to kids of all ages, seven days a week. Weekday hours are 1 PM until 9:30 PM. Saturday hours are 10 AM to 9:30 PM, and on Sunday it's open from 1 PM until 6:30 PM.

The park features challenging areas for beginners and special times for anyone who has yet to put on skates. Those who are really good at the sport will just have to try it to believe the air they get flying off a ramp.

There are bowls, lifts and jumps to sample, a fun box and one area that looks like a pyramid with a flat top. A favorite is the Embarcadero steps, a series of cement stairs that resemble those that might lead down from a building. Each obstacle holds a thrill for skaters who live and breathe the tricks and maneuvers that sometime make a parent's heart stop.

— continued on next page

Photo: City of Temecula

Flying off a ramp, negotiating stairs, and catching "air" from a side-wall are part of the fun at the spectacular Temecula Skate Park.

Kevin Thatcher, skateboard guru and an editor for the skateboarding magazine *Thrasher* was one of the park's designers. His patience paid off during the process and he was impressed when he finally skated the park on its opening day — June 27, 1996. "It's bad, rad, gnarly and groovy...It should provide a lot of thrills, definitely. It's far and away better than any facility in America."

Why the excitement about an acre that's covered with cement shaped into hills and valleys and vaguely resembling a swimming pool that's been drained? That answer requires more questions, starting with: Is skateboarding illegal in your hometown and on your city's sidewalks? If you've said yes or have seen warning signs prohibiting skaters, you're not alone. But imagine for a minute outlawing baseball? Or soccer? Imagine telling fitness walkers to get off the hiking trails or face a fine?

The concept is hard to envision, yet that's what has happened to skateboarders in many cities, including ones here in San Diego County. Thatcher and other advocates of skateboarding continue to remind us that in most areas, skateboarders are treated like lowlife hoods. Many communities have forbidden the sport, yet provide no alternatives. Temecula is one of a small handful of communities that had the foresight to find a solution.

In the spring of 1993, the City of Temecula heard pleas from skaters and skateboarders who wanted to practice their sport. While some store and business owners screamed that they wanted skating enthusiasts run out of Dodge, other citizens in this progressive area knew the truth: What skateboarders lacked was a safe, well-run venue. It took time and lots of planning, but public opinion and soil were turned. What emerged was the Rancho California Sports Park.

It cost about $300,000 to build the 1-acre skating utopia. It costs another $62,000 for annual upkeep; these costs are easily offset by fees.

The park has been enormously successful, judging by the skate park's mountainous pile of waivers (each skater must sign one), and by the park's growing reputation. City officials from around the country have toured the facility. Herman D. Parker, deputy director of Temecula's Community Services Department, says, with a good measure of pride, that "there's even been interest in the park from planners in London, England."

Julie Pelletier, Temecula's recreation superintendent, points out one of the unique factors in the park's success: "Many cities have opened parks, but they are not manned. We have a staff of seven." Pelletier also mentions other reasons the skate park is so popular: "A lot of professional skaters live in Southern California." She adds that the park draws not only kids but lots of adults too. "It really caters to all ages," she says. Whatever explains it, the park has become a mecca for beginners and pro skaters alike.

And the rules don't drive them away either. Of course there are some —that's to be expected. You must sign a waiver form. Temecula residents with proof of residency must pay an annual $1 fee and a $2 entrance fee for each session. (A session lasts about two hours.) Non-residents must pay a $5 entrance fee. All skaters younger than 18 must have a parent or guardian sign an information form or waiver to use the facility. Parents of skaters who live in Temecula must visit the park in person to fill out the form. Children younger than 7 must be accompanied by an adult.

While spectators can't enter the park while skating is occurring, there are plenty of grassy areas. It's fun just to watch and marvel at the skill and balance of those who put on skates or ride skateboards. There's a snack bar outside of the rink, restrooms, an equipment rental service, a tot lot and plenty of parking. On holiday weekends be prepared to wait for a turn.

No bicycles, food or drink are allowed in the park and any skirmishes between skaters are dealt with promptly. But these disputes rarely happen. And for broken bones? There have been a few, but the bad injuries are kept down since all patrons must wear appropriate safety gear (wrist guards, elbow pads, kneepads and helmet) that is in good condition. Skateboards and skates must be in good condition, too.

The park fulfills the dreams of skaters of all ages. The roller hockey rink accommodates state-of-the-art league play for in excess of 2,000 youths per year. That's quite an accomplishment since only a short time ago these youngsters had nowhere to play but parking lots and public streets. Now rather than practice their sport on the blacktops of malls and public roads, the skaters can enjoy a safe, well-supervised and challenging place to participate in their sport.

For more information on the Temecula Skate Park, contact the City of Temecula at (909) 694-6480 or (909) 694-6410.

There's so much here: from chi-chi Beverly Hills, with its shoppers' heaven, Rodeo Drive; cultural centers and museums; incredible ethnic events and lesser-known historical districts.

To really get around LA you'll need a car and a good city and freeway map. If you'd prefer to leave the driving to others, local parks and recreation offices in your region often sponsor daytrips to events happening in Los Angeles, such as taping of television shows and the theater. So you can figure out ways to see the city without battling traffic.

Here we've included a daytrip to L.A.'s historic district that can be reached without a car. It's directly across the street (a busy one, but with cross walks) from Amtrak's Union Station. While you're passing through Union Station, be sure to admire all the renovation that's taken place in the last few years. Looking at the section done in art deco may remind you of the days when Clark Gable and Dorothy Lamour and Bob Hope and all the celebrities of the 30s, 40s and 50s traveled by train.

El Pueblo de Los Angeles Historic Monument
Alameda, Arcadia, Spring and Macy sts., Los Angeles • (213) 628-1274

This is a wonderful historic district and the site of the 1781 pueblo. The original colony in the area, El Pueblo reflects the ethnic background and heritage of the diverse groups who settled here. Some of the landmarks have been restored.

You can visit the Avila Adobe (10 E. Olvera St.), Olvera Street (the oldest shopping area in the city and filled with stalls that sell Mexican handicrafts and foods) and Pico House (home to the last Mexican governor of California, Pio Pico). Its rich variety of architectural styles and convenient location makes this momument an especially nice daytrip.

If you drive, expect the trip to take about two hours (more in heavy traffic). Call for docent tours and a listing of special events, such as the Cinco de Mayo celebration.

Universal Studios Hollywood
100 Universal City Plaza, Universal City • (818) 622-3801, (800) 3777-5072

Since the early 1960s Universal Studios has been the world's number one motion picture and television theme-park attraction. For those who want an Insiders' look behind the scenes of the entertainment industry, this is the place to visit.

The attraction is about 2 hours from downtown San Diego, often longer during peak driving times. Take Interstate 5 north through Orange County and Los Angeles to where Cali-

INSIDERS' TIP

When visiting amusement parks with children, remember that for safety reasons some rides prohibit youngsters who are less than 40 inches tall. Call ahead for restrictions if you're traveling with small ones.

Photo: San Diego Convention and Visitors Bureau

Driving through the Anza-Borrego Desert during the springtime, you may be thrilled to see the desert in bloom.

fornia Highway 101 and Interstate 5 intersect. You cannot miss it.

Since the attraction opened, more than 90 millions guests have been on the Universal lot where history-making films and television shows have been filmed. Today, guests still thrill to attractions such as Jurassic Park — The Ride, WaterWorld — A Live Sea War Spectacular, and Back to the Future — The Ride.

During the summer, the park is open from 7 AM until 11 PM, and in the winter it is open from 9 AM until 7 PM. Admission for adults is $34 and for children ages 3 to 11 is $26; there's a 2 percent tax added to all tickets.

Orange County

Orange County — all of it — is filled with daytrips for anyone who wants to explore. In this section, we're giving you a taste of what you'll find in Orange County.

Remember when driving in Orange County, it's well worth avoiding the freeways during peak commuter times and to find alternative routes if possible. Carry a map, should there be a snag in traffic. Listen to the radio channels that give traffic updates, too. Doing so will make your daytrip a snap.

Crystal Cathedral
12141 Lewis St., Garden Grove
• **(714) 750-3836**

For the sheer joy of seeing this masterful piece of architecture, you'll want to visit the Crystal Cathedral. It was designed by famed architect Philip Johnson.

The Cathedral resembles a four-pointed star with 10,000 panes of glass covering the web-like translucent walls and ceiling. The tickets for the pageants of "The Glory of Christmas" and "The Glory of Easter" (the two internationally known events) sell out long before the seasonal performances. Call well ahead

for reservations if you have your heart set on seeing these.

If you attend the performances, you'll be treated to music that seems to echo from heaven. Some of the "actors" are live animals that, well, play animal parts in the programs.

Visitors are welcome at the cathedral Monday through Saturday 9 AM to 3 PM. Sunday hours for the Christian, nondenominational worship are 9:30 AM and 11 AM. There is a Spanish service at 12:45 PM.

Disneyland
1313 Harbor Blvd., Anaheim
• **(714) 781-4565**

Space Mountain, Frontierland and the whole new Tomorrowland are just a sample of the fun that's in store at Disneyland. The theme park is as much Southern California as oranges, surfers and blue-sky days. The park is about 90 miles north of San Diego and there are signs to get you to Disneyland displayed on I-5 at Katella Avenue in Anaheim.

A wonderful family tradition, Insiders and visitors from around the country make the theme park part of their vacation plans. It's open every day with more than 60 major attractions, 50 shops and 30 restaurants from sit-down places to snack-food walk-up counters.

Adult admission is $38; children's admission is $28; and senior (60 and older) admission is $36. The park is open Monday through Friday from 10 AM to 6 PM, Saturday and Sunday from 10 AM to midnight; during the summer the closing hours are extended. So honestly, isn't it time you hummed a few bars of "It's A Small World" and returned to Disneyland?

Knott's Berry Farm
8039 Beach Blvd., Buena Park
• **(714) 220-5200**

Knott's Berry Farm is a fun, family theme

INSIDERS' TIP

For special values on accommodations, attractions and events in the desert communities, call year round for a *Hot Summer Values* brochure, from the Palm Springs Visitor and Information Center at (800) 347-7746.

park that celebrates California and the West. There are six areas: Old West Ghost Town, Indian Trails, Wild Water Wilderness, Fiesta Village, The Boardwalk and the world-famous Camp Snoopy (home of the Peanuts gang).

Within the park are 30 shops and restaurants. Here you can buy that fabulous Knott's boysenberry jam and lots of other Knott's jams too. Gift baskets — nice to take back home with you — are available too. At the not-to-be-missed Mrs. Knott's Chicken Dinner Restaurant you can sample some of that famous delicious fried chicken. The park is open every day but Christmas from 9 AM until midnight between late June and Labor Day. The rest of the year the hours are Monday through Friday 10 AM until 6 PM, Saturday 10 AM until 10 PM, and Sunday 10 AM until 7 PM. To get to the park, which is about 90 minutes from San Diego, drive north on Interstate 5, then take Calif. Hwy. 91 west to the Beach Boulevard exit, then head south. Unlimited-use tickets are $29.95 for adults and $19.95 for seniors 60 and older and for children ages 3 to 11.

Mission San Juan Capistrano
31522 Camino Capistrano, San Juan Capistrano • (949) 248-2048

Padre Junipero Serra founded this mission in 1776 and every year the swallows migrate to the grounds on Saint Joseph's day, March 19. The swallows are not aware that humans try to clock their arrival and flock to see the birds coming back. Depending on weather conditions throughout the world, the birds may arrive early or late, but visitors come nonetheless.

Padre Serra's Chapel at the mission is the oldest building, still in use, in the state. For youngsters in the fourth grade who study California history, the trip to the mission is sometimes the most impressive field trip of the year.

On the grounds you'll see examples of 200-year-old adobe homes, the rustic Western train station and antique stores. There are often crafts demonstrations and docent tours.

The mission is within walking distance of the Amtrak train station depot in San Juan Capistrano and many Insiders take the train

Photo: San Diego Convention and Visitors Bureau

Cattle graze near Julian in a quiet pasture setting.

Graceful palms stand watch along coastal highways and through surrounding areas.

and a picnic lunch for a day at the mission. If you're driving, exit Interstate 5 at the Calif. Hwy. 74 exit and drive west, following the signs to the mission. There is no admission fee. Within a few blocks of the mission, there are boutiques, cafes, antique shops and bookstores.

Movieland Wax Museum
7711 Beach Blvd., Buena Park
• (714) 522-1154

The Movieland Wax Museum, about 90 miles from downtown San Diego, lets you get up close and personal with the stars from movie-making history. Since the early 1960s, the museum has been documenting the world of film by adding celebrities to their wax collection. Currently, there are more than 275 figures including replicas of Julie Andrews, John Wayne, Bette Davis, Tom Selleck, Michael Jackson and Gloria Estefan. At the museum, you'll see sets from *Star Trek*, *Bonanza*, *The Wizard of Oz,* and *The African Queen*. The museum is open daily 9 AM to 7 PM. Admission is $12.95 for adults, $10.55 for seniors 55 and older, and $6.95 for children ages 4 to 11. To get to the museum, drive north on Interstate 5 to Buena Park, taking Calif. Hwy 91 west. Exit on Beach Boulevard.

Temecula

Temecula is a favorite daytrip. Head north on I-15 past Escondido. You may want to stop along the way as you take this daytrip — perhaps at Lawrence Welk Village to visit the

---

INSIDERS' TIP

On the major highways leading out of San Diego, there are checkpoints administered by the U.S. Border Patrol. Because the checks can slow traffic and especially if you're heading north into Orange County on I-5 during commuting hours, it pays to add an extra half-hour on any trip time when using these routes.

winery and Deer Park or at one Fallbrook's many farmers' stands filled to the brim with fresh vegetables and fruits. You'll see these as you exit Interstate 15 at California 76, going either east or west. Just 6 miles farther along the interstate, you'll find the valley of Temecula in Riverside County.

Temecula and Rancho California are fast-growing, family communities. For the daytripper, the area is a treasure trove of possibilities. Be sure to read this chapter's Close-up about the famous skateboard park that's located in this sprawling community.

Antique Shopping District
Old Town Temecula Historical Preservation District
Front St., Temecula • (909) 699-8138

Front Street in Temecula may be as close to heaven as any antique hunter could imagine without going through the pearly gates — at least that's what some Insider antique lovers say. In a multi-block area, you'll find more than 20 stores. Call the number above for a brochure of the stores or ask for a brochure when you arrive in Temecula's shopping district. The area also has family-style restaurants and specialty food spots.

Temecula Skate Park
42569 Margarita Rd., Temecula • (909) 694-6410 or (909) 694-6480

This model skate park is a favorite among serious and fun-loving skateboarders and in-line skating enthusiasts of all ages and abilities. The park consists of a competition 64-foot diameter bowl with ramp entry and a 10-foot-wide apron that connects the upper bowl with a street plaza skate area. In the street area are the pyramid, fun box, curbs, ramps, stairs and a 20-foot handrail.

Don't fret if you've forgotten your safety equipment. The park had thought about you and you can rent everything you need. See the Close Up in this chapter for more details.

Temecula Wine Country

Temecula Valley Vintners Association
• (909) 699-3626, (800) 801-9463

When in Temecula, do like other visitors do and take the wine country tours. Call the Vintners Association at the phone number above for a map or call one of the wineries mentioned below for directions.

This is southern California's largest wine-producing area, and within the valley of Temecula you can visit more than 12 wineries, each offering samples of their distinct products.

According to the vintners, this is perfect wine country because of the combination of geography, micro-climate and well-drained soil. The 1,500-foot elevation and cool summer nights add to the grape-growing and wine-making magic.

The wineries range in size from one that produces about 1,000 cases a year to large-scale wineries with production exceeding 100,000 cases each year.

The following are just a sampling of the wineries you'll discover in Temecula.

Baily Vineyard & Winery
3833 Rancho California Rd., Temecula • (909) 676-9463

The vineyard and winery produces award-winning wines available only at the tasting room. Open daily 10 AM to 5 PM, there's a picnic area, a gift shop and special events. Baily Vineyard and Winery is known for it's Chardonnay, Muscot Canelli and Riesling.

INSIDERS' TIP

Heading to the desert region in February? Add the National Date Festival in Indio, in Imperial County, to your "to do" list. The festival features camel and ostrich races and Arabian Nights musical pageants. Call the Indio Chamber of Commerce at (800) 444-6646 for more information and the specific dates.

Hart Winery
41300 Avenida Biona, Temecula • (909) 676-6300

This winery specializes in handcrafted, barrel-aged red wines and dry, full-bodied white varieties. Tasting is available daily from 9 AM until 4:30 PM. There's a cost $2 per person and it includes a winery logo glass you can take home. Hart Winery, according to in-the-know Insiders, does an excellent Fene Blanc, and the Barbera and Merlot are outstanding.

Van Roekel Vineyards & Winery
34567 Rancho California Rd., Temecula • (909) 699-6961

This vineyard and winery is the newest in the area, and has already developed premium wines. Tasting is daily from 10 AM to 5 PM. There's a picnic area and a shop that sells gourmet cheeses, deli items and a wide selection of wine-related gifts. You'll want to taste and of course bring home Van Roekel's Chardonnay, Chenin Blanc and Syrah Rose.

Shopping is the sport of choice for most visitors who cross the border.

South of
the Border

¡*Bienvenidos a Mexico!* Most visitors to San Diego (and most locals, too) sooner or later end up South of the Border. The lure of Mexico is irresistible. Added to that lure is the fact that the U.S.-Mexico Border is only a 20-minute drive from Downtown San Diego, which makes for an easy daytrip or even an after-dark excursion. Many Insiders make regular forays to Tijuana for an evening on the town. Fine dining is abundant, and Tijuana has several nightclubs that are popular among revelers of all generations, be they Xers, Nexters or Boomers.

Beyond the border city of Tijuana lie the resort towns of Rosarito Beach and Ensenada. Both are within easy daytrip or weekending distance. The pace is a little slower in these beach towns, but you'll still get a good sampling of the flavor of Mexico. Rosarito has beautiful beaches and was popular during the 1930s and 1940s as a getaway for Hollywood stars. Ensenada has an active nightlife and is known for its excellent sport fishing.

Along the way, between Tijuana and Ensenada, are some favorite stops. One is Puerto Nuevo, which once was a sleepy fishing village, but in recent years has evolved into an enclave of restaurants that specialize in the local catch — namely, lobster. No trip South of the Border is complete without a taste of lobster Mexican-style, cooked to crispy perfection and served with rice, beans and plenty of butter for dipping.

Golfers head for Bajamar, the posh resort about halfway between Tijuana and Ensenada, or Real Del Mar, just a few miles south of the border. The golfing is excellent at both courses and the facilities are first-rate. Folks who are serious about their fishing go south to Ensenada or southeast, to San Felipe on the eastern coast of the Baja California Peninsula. Boats depart regularly from San Felipe in search of record-breaking marlin, swordfish, yellowtail and sailfish in the Sea of Cortez.

Tijuana is the city that draws the most visitors, though, and there's no shortage of attractions. Shopping, dining, bullfights and cultural performances and exhibits all await the intrepid explorer. We'll introduce you to the highlights in this chapter and give you lots of tips for planning your trip and finding things to do once you get there. Most places South of the Border accept American dollars and major credit cards in addition to the Mexican peso. If credit cards are not accepted at an establishment, we've made a note of it.

Getting There and Getting Back

The border crossing at San Ysidro (at the southern end of Interstate 5) is open 24 hours; the Otay Mesa crossing at the eastern end of Interstate 905 is open daily from 6 AM to 10 PM. Travelers crossing the border into Mexico are usually waved through with few, if any, formalities. When you return to the United States, you must stop for inspection by U.S. Customs officials. Usually you will be asked a few questions, like your place of birth, where you've traveled and what you're bringing back with you, but occasionally returning travelers will be asked to stop for a secondary inspection. It's a fairly rare occurrence and only happens if customs inspectors suspect you might have exceeded your permissible duty-free articles or are attempting to smuggle contraband.

Driving

If your idea of a trip into Mexico is a leisurely expedition, stopping here and there, without a set agenda or time schedule, then you should drive. A word of caution, however. Driving in Tijuana is not for the weak of heart. Traffic is usually heavy, street signs and directions are often in short supply and are all in Spanish, and the driving habits of both locals and tourists are, shall we say, exuberant. Plus, Tijuana is chock-full of traffic circles. Getting stuck in one can be frustrating and disorienting. Just remember to bear right and follow the counter-clockwise flow of traffic. Also, watch for one-way street signs, which are numerous. If you're used to driving in large foreign cities such as Rome or Paris, then Tijuana will be a piece of cake. If the prospect sounds a little intimidating, you might be better off taking taxis or signing on with a tour group.

Should you decide to drive, take I-5 south to the San Ysidro border crossing. From Interstate 805, drive south to I-905, and go east to the Otay Mesa border crossing. The San Ysidro crossing is recommended for easiest access to downtown Tijuana; Otay Mesa is generally used for access to Tijuana's international airport. Once across the border and into the downtown Tijuana area, you'll find plenty of on-street parking and pay lots. Most shopping centers offer free parking. You can also drive all the way to the border, park in one of several security-guarded lots, and walk across. The fee ranges from $2 to $3 for half an hour, but tops out between $6 and $10 for 24 hours.

If you're driving a rental car, be sure to check with the rental agency to see if they allow their cars to be driven across the border. Of the larger rental agencies, Avis, Budget and Enterprise do allow travel into Mexico. But policies change, so be sure to check ahead of time.

Insurance

This is important. Be sure to purchase Mexican auto insurance before you cross the border or immediately after crossing. Mexican authorities recognize insurance policies issued only by companies licensed to transact insurance sales in Mexico. Your American policy is not valid. If you're involved in a traffic accident while in Mexico, a Mexican insurance policy will pave the road to an easy resolution. The laws are different in Mexico; you're presumed guilty until proven innocent, even in something as minor as a fender-bender. If it's determined that you are at fault, and you don't have a Mexican policy, you will be expected to pay for the damages on the spot. If you can't, you'll be taken to jail.

Mexican insurance policies are available through the Auto Club and from a number of companies that have set up shop on both sides of the border. You can't miss them — their signs are easily visible from the freeway and from streets on the other side. They all are licensed and reputable, and any one of them can write a policy to cover the time you spend in Mexico.

Alternative Transportation

Public transportation is a highly recommended method for a trip across the border. The San Diego Trolley Blue Line goes all the way to the San Ysidro border crossing for a fare of $1.75, then you can walk across the border and catch a taxi for the short drive into town. Or you can join the crowd of people who enjoy walking into town, an easy stroll of less than a mile. A typical taxi fare from the

---

INSIDERS' TIP

The U.S. Consulate is located on Calle Tapachula near the Agua Caliente Racetrack. The telephone number is 011-52 (66) 81-74-00.

border or for a drive within town runs about $6 to $7. You might be able to negotiate a lower fare, but be sure to establish what the fare will be before you take off.

Greyhound Bus Line also has a quick trip from its downtown station, which can be reached from any of the other stations throughout San Diego County, to the San Ysidro border crossing. See our chapter on Getting Here, Getting Around for more information on Greyhound and its terminals in the different regions.

One of the easiest ways to navigate Tijuana and regions beyond is by joining a tour group. You can sign up for half-day, full-day or even overnight tours to Tijuana and beyond, and leave the worries of driving to the tour company. Here are two companies that offer South-of-the-Border tour packages.

Gray Line Tours San Diego
1775 Hancock St., Ste. 130, San Diego
• (619) 491-0011

Gray Line's half-day Tijuana tour takes visitors to the heart of Tijuana's shopping district. The fee for adults is $28, and for children 3 to 11 is $15. Or try a full-day trip to Ensenada.

You'll journey south along the Baja coastline, stopping at the Rosarito Beach Hotel, then traveling on to Ensenada for shopping, lunch and a complimentary margarita. The fee is $54 for adults and $37 for children ages 3 to 11.

San Diego Scenic Tours
2255 Garnet Ave., Ste. 3, San Diego
• (858) 273-8687

Tour guides entertain you with the history and culture of Tijuana as you take in the sights before alighting on Avenida Revolución, the city's main shopping street. You'll have plenty of time to shop, have lunch at one of many fine restaurants in the area or simply sit and enjoy mariachi music while sipping a frosty margarita. Both full and half-day tours are available, with prices starting at $26 for adults and $13 for children ages 3 to 11.

More travel tips

Citizens of the United States and Canada do not need tourist cards if you are traveling only as far south as Tijuana or the rest of the border zone, which includes Ensenada on the

INSIDERS' TIP
If you see a traffic sign that has a big "E" with a slash through it, that means "no parking."

west coast of the Baja California peninsula and San Felipe on the east coast. However, if the length of your stay exceeds 72 hours or you plan to journey beyond Ensenada or San Felipe, a tourist card for each traveler is required. Tourist cards can be obtained in the United States from Mexican consulates or Mexican tourism offices. The Auto Club of Southern California and the California State Automobile Association also have supplies of tourist cards, or check with your travel agent. Travelers must fill in the necessary information and have either a valid passport or a birth certificate. It's always a good idea to keep identification and proof of citizenship with you while traveling in Mexico (drivers license, military ID, voter registration card, passport, birth certificate).

English is spoken most everywhere in Tijuana, but knowing a few Spanish words can be helpful, especially *por favor* (please) and *gracias* (thank you). Don't be afraid to try a few words from your Spanish-English dictionary. You'll endear yourself to the locals. And remember that a smile is always the universal language.

Tijuana and the border area are duty-free zones, and you can pay for your goodies with U.S. dollars, Mexican pesos, traveler's checks or credit cards. Returning U.S. citizens are allowed up to $400 worth of merchandise for personal use once in every 30-day period. You also are allowed one liter of alcoholic beverages. Keep in mind that most fruit and vegetables are not allowed to cross into the United States.

Now let's clear up some common misconceptions. Yes, Tijuana is a great place to buy fireworks. No, you may not bring them back into the United States. If you try, they will be confiscated and you'll be subject to a hefty fine. You've probably also heard about the great deals you can get on prescription medications in Tijuana. You *must* have a valid prescription in order to bring medications back across the border. And in some cases, a prescription from your doctor is not enough; one from a Mexican doctor might be required. You can most assuredly save money on some expensive medications by buying them in Tijuana, but be absolutely certain you know ahead of time what the regulations are. Do not

rely on the pharmacist. Check with U.S. Customs or the Mexican Consulate before you go.

Ready, Set, Go

Now that we've gotten all the caveats out of the way, get ready for a one-of-a-kind experience. Granted, Mexico is not for everyone. It's a different way of life, different customs, different culture, different food and a different language. But take our word for it: a trip South of the Border is a must. You'll have the time of your life and will create memories that'll stay with you forever.

We urge you to be prepared, though. Plan ahead, follow the guidelines we've given you, and you'll have smooth sailing. And have a margarita for us. Lift your glass and say, *"¡Salud!"*

Accommodations

Should you decide to stay for a spell, several nice hotels and resorts are available where you'll be quite comfortable. Keep in mind that the level of service may not be what you're accustomed to back home, but in most cases, you'll find most of the amenities and special touches you're accustomed to. Plus, you'll get much more for your dollar than you can in the United States.

Price Code

The price code indicates the cost of accommodations for two for one night. Tijuana hotels typically do not have price hikes during the summer season, so the fees quoted are reliable any time during the year.

$	$50 to $100
$$	$101 to $150

Tijuana

Grand Hotel Tijuana
$ • 4500 Blvd. Agua Caliente, Tijuana
• (800) 472-6385, 011-52 (66) 81-70-00
Twenty-four stories of plush rooms offer a

beautiful view of the golf course at the Tijuana Country Club. Be sure to specify a golf-course view; the view from the other side of the hotel is less than cheerful. Rooms are posh, with sitting areas, light-oak furnishings and queen or king-sized beds. An elegant French dining room is a favorite among guests as is the busy cafe in the sky-lighted atrium. In addition to its 422 rooms, the hotel has a pool, sauna, tennis courts, a health club and a lively nightclub.

Hotel Lucerna
$-$$ • 10902 Paseo de los Heroes, Tijuana
• (800) 582-3762, 011-52 (66) 34-20-00

Authentic Mexican atmosphere combines with modern amenities to make the Hotel Lucerna an Insiders' choice. It has 168 rooms and nine suites, and features a sunken lobby, an open-air cafe, and a courtyard garden. The hotel's swimming pool is in the midst of the garden and is surrounded by palm trees. In addition to the cafe, there's a French restaurant, a cocktail lounge and a nightclub. Rooms have double, queen or king-sized beds, cable television and fully appointed baths. The more expensive rooms have a courtyard view. Rooms overlooking the street tend to be noisy,

although their price will be on the low end of the scale.

Rosarito

Rosarito Beach Hotel & Spa
$-$$ • Blvd. Benito Juarez, Rosarito
• (800) 343-8582, 011-52 (661) 211-06

This is *the* place to stay in Rosarito Beach. Made famous in the 1930s and 1940s by legions of Hollywood stars who originally came south to escape the constraints of prohibition, the resort hasn't lost any of its luster over the years. The grand lobby and ballroom still retain the magic of years gone by. The resort's 280 rooms and suites have all been renovated over the years and are modern and efficient, if somewhat small. Rooms are available in beachfront low rises or in the tower. The upper floor ocean view rooms are the most expensive.

In addition to the beach, two pools with slides and wading areas cater to families. Singles bar hop among the three watering holes or relax in one of the three Jacuzzis or the sauna. Basketball, tennis and racquetball are all available, too. In a 1930s mansion next

Photo: San Diego Convention and Visitors Bureau

Going south of the border? Some visitors take in a bullfight when they are in Mexico.

door is the Casa de Playa Spa. It's a full-service European-style spa that offers massages, herbal wraps, saunas and hot tubs. Chaberts restaurant, specializing in both steaks and French cuisine, is also on the grounds of the resort.

Ensenada

Estero Beach Resort Hotel
$ • On Highway 1, 6 miles south of Ensenada • (800) 762-2494, 011-52 (617) 669-25

This is truly an Insiders' favorite. Tennis, horseback riding and boating are just some of the activities to occupy your time while at Estero Beach. Located right on the beach, it's also an excellent spot for bird watching. A winding road lined with flowers leads up to the main entrance, and several gardens on the property invite long, quiet strolls.

The resort has 108 rooms and suites, which are modern and well maintained. Rooms in the Palenque wing are more expensive than those in the Tikal wing, but are a better choice. Suites are in a two-story building that fronts the ocean. Also available are cottages with kitchenettes and patios that are popular among honeymooners. Both double and queen-sized beds are available. A restaurant is also on the premises.

San Felipe
San Felipe Marina Resort
$-$$ Carretera San Felipe Aeropuerto, San Felipe • (858) 558-0295, 011-52 (657) 715-68

Just a little south of town is this ever-expanding complex of hotel rooms, timeshares and condos. Sixty hotel rooms are available, and all are decorated in a Mexican-Mediterranean style with white-tiled floors and woven rugs. Lots of folk-art accents adorn the rooms,

and they all have balconies or patios, most with views of the Sea of Cortez.

Visitors have their choice of the beach or two pools, one of which is indoors and is a popular hangout on cool days. Next door is an RV campground, and plans are in the works for a 100-slip marina.

Attractions

People often forget that Tijuana is a major city, and as such has developed a number of worthy attractions over the years. When you've had your fill of shopping and dining, check out some of the attractions that are unique to Mexico or at least uncommon elsewhere.

Sporting Events

El Toreo de Tijuana
Blvd. Agua Caliente at Blvd. Cuauhtémoc, Tijuana
Plaza Monumental
Playas de Tijuana, Tijuana
• (619) 232-5049

If the ancient sport of bullfighting intrigues you, two bullrings in Tijuana present some of the world's top matadors. Dating back to 2000 BC, bullfighting is a combination of ritual and mortal combat, pitting man against beast in a graceful but deadly battle.

Bullfights are held from May through September. The sport is extremely popular in Mexico, so we encourage you to purchase tickets in advance. Tickets are available in San Diego at the Five Star Tours depot, 1050 Kettner Boulevard, and in Tijuana at a booth on Avenida Revolución between Calle 2a and Calle 3a. Tickets are $11 for general admission, and from $23 to $39 for reserved seats. The most expensive tickets are those located in the shade, closest to the floor of the ring.

INSIDERS' TIP

If you drive south of Tijuana, you'll soon encounter toll roads. The fares are usually around $1 (they fluctuate with the peso), and you can pay in U.S. currency or Mexican pesos.

Caliente Race Track
**Blvd. Agua Caliente and Tapachula,
Tijuana • (619) 231-1910**

Try something new and spend an afternoon or evening watching greyhounds race. Greyhound racing is held year-round, and Agua Caliente has full wagering facilities. In addition to the dog races, there's a full race and sports book. Satellite wagering is available on football, baseball, hockey, soccer and all major North American thoroughbred horse racetracks. Greyhounds run nightly at 7:45 PM and on Saturday and Sunday at 2 PM. General admission is free. Turf Club seating is $5, which includes a $5 betting voucher.

Museums

Mexitlan
**Ave. Ocampo and Calle 2a, Tijuana
• 011-52 (66) 38-41-01**

In this outdoor museum visitors can see more than 200 scale models of the most important monuments, buildings and archeological sites of Mexico. You'll be enthralled by the miniature pyramids, temples, Gothic cathedrals and modern stadiums. Samples of traditional music and arts can also be enjoyed. Mexitlan is open Tuesday through Sunday from 9 AM to 5 PM. Admission is $3.35 for adults; children younger than 12 are free.

Tijuana Cultural Center
**Paseo de los Héroes and Avenida
Independencia, Tijuana
• 011-52 (66) 84-11-32**

For a little bit of Mexican history and culture, stop in at this modern complex. The museum features archaeological, historical and craft displays, and the art gallery shows changing exhibits. The center also has an OMNIMAX space theater that has daily films in both Spanish and English. The 1000-seat performing arts theater offers a variety of musical and dramatic performances. The Cultural Center is open daily from 11 AM to 9 PM. Admission to the museum is around $1.25 for adults and $.75 for children (prices fluctuate).

Wax Museum
**Calle 1 near Avenida Revolución, Tijuana
• 011-52 (66) 88-24-78**

Some travelers cannot visit a new city without seeking out the local wax museum, and the one in Tijuana is worth a look-see. Mixed in with the standard representatives of Hollywood are figures from Mexican history, such as Emiliano Zapata and Pedro Infante. International historical standouts are featured, too. You can get nose to nose with the likes of Mahatma Gandhi and Mikhail Gorbachev. Hours are from 10 AM to 10 PM daily. Admission is $3 for adults, $2 for children 6 through 12 and free for children younger than 6.

Fishing

Fishing South of the Border has traditionally had a mystique attached to it that's hard to explain. Maybe it's the whole idea of "going fishing in Mexico" that sounds so appealing to the diehard fisherman. Truth is, the fish bite no better down south than they do off the coast of San Diego, but that doesn't stop hordes of fishermen from packing their tackle and catching a boat in the quest for a record-breaking yellowtail.

In the border zone, Ensenada and San Felipe are the two hot spots. San Felipe is about 120 miles south of San Diego on the eastern Baja California peninsula. You can sign up for a variety of fishing expeditions including single-day trips, extended-trip charters or just to go out for a few hours and back again. Fishing trips that last only for a day or less are best arranged on-site. Prices are up to the individual captain and are usually negotiable.

For longer trips, here are two agencies on the U.S. side of the border (although they're in

---

INSIDERS' TIP

Fishing in Baja California is always good, but the best months are from August through October.

Orange County, north of San Diego) that will help you make your arrangements in advance.

Ensenada

Ensenada Clipper
8194 Havasu Cir., Buena Park
• **(714) 994-1872**

San Felipe

Tony Reyes Fishing Tours
c/o The Long Fin
4010 E. Chapman Ave., Ste. D, Orange
• **(714) 538-8010**

The longer trips are up to six days on vessels large enough to provide a good level of comfort for die-hard seekers of that trophy fish. Most everything you might need is built into the cost of the trip, including fishing gear, meals and a Mexican fishing license. Cost of such trips vary widely, ranging from $150 for a two-day adventure and up to $500 or more for six days at sea. The cost will also be affected by the number of people joining you and whether or not you need gear.

Many varieties of fish inhabit the waters on both sides of the Baja peninsula. You're likely to hook tortuava, croker, corvina and, of course, the much-sought-after marlin. The beauty of a charter trip arranged through one of the companies listed is that you can combine the captain's extensive knowledge of Baja fishing with whatever you have in mind to create an ideal trip.

Golf

San Diegans are serious about their golf. From the occasional hacker to the smooth swinger with a low handicap, golfers jump at any chance to play, and that includes forays South of the Border to take advantage of some excellent courses.

Bajamar Ocean Front Golf Resort
K-77, Ensenada Toll Rd.
• **(800) 225-2418, 011-52 (615) 501-61**

Past Rosarito Beach and on the way to Ensenada is this Insider's golf-resort favorite.

It's about a 50-minute drive from the border, and golfers often stay for a day or two to fully take advantage of the links-style courses. Three nine-hole courses combine to provide different challenges. The par 71 Lagos to Vista Course is 6968 yards with a 74.9 rating and a 143 slope.

The rugged Baja California coastline provides an incomparable setting, and you'll undoubtedly see a few road runners sprinting through the fragrant desert lavender. It's a tough course, and the brutal rough tends to swallow balls. Bring lots of them — one Insider lost 20 in one round. Hole number 11, a par 4, 500-yarder, has a waterfall and a large lake sheltering a green that doesn't seem to have any flat spots. Most golfers feel that a par on this hole is as big an achievement as a hole in one.

Bajamar has a putting green but no driving range. Both men's and women's locker rooms are huge and nicely outfitted. The clubhouse has a pro shop, a restaurant and a bar in an observation tower with a 360-degree view. A luxury hotel and condos make up the balance of the resort, and special golf/accommodations packages are available. Greens fees include a mandatory cart and are $60 Sunday through Thursday and $70 Friday, Saturday and holidays. Reduced rates are offered for late afternoon play, and a $20 replay fee is available at any time.

Real Del Mar Golf Resort
K-19.5, Ensenada Toll Rd.
• **(800) 803-6038, (619) 475-4666,**
011-52-(663) 134-01

Just 12 miles beyond the border crossing, Real Del Mar is another outstanding course down south. Like Bajamar, Real Del Mar overlooks the coastline and is a challenging course with seven lakes and 50 bunkers. Its looks are deceptive, seemingly benign, and yet the course will reach out and bite you when you least expect it. Its fairways are narrow, and some of the greens are elevated on pedestals. If you miss one, you've got your work cut out for you. The par 3 18th consists of an immaculately appointed tee box and a beautiful green — and nothin' but *agua* in between. Making par on this one is cause for a post-round celebration.

Shopping is the sport of choice for many who come to Mexico. Here, a shopper admires some embroidery on Avenida Revolución in Tijuana.

Club pro Fred De Cain welcomes all levels of players, and facilities include a putting green and driving range, luxury clubhouse with men's and ladies' locker rooms, sauna and gym. Should you decide to stay for a few days, the luxurious Marriott Residence Inn at the golf course offers a complete European-style spa, tennis courts, swimming pool and Jacuzzi. The par 72 course is 6,403 yards of manicured fairways and greens, with a rating of 70.5/131 slope. Greens fees are $55 Monday through Thursday and $65 Friday, Saturday, Sunday and holidays. Tee times are available seven days in advance.

Nightlife

Locals South of the Border love their nightlife. So do the hordes of Americans who regularly cross the border just for a taste of something different. You'll find everything from rock bands to traditional Mexican mariachi music. The drinking age in the border zone is 18. Remember that it's against the law to drink alcoholic beverages on public streets. Sometimes a cover charge will be required, but it depends on how heavy the crowd is at the time, and the amount will vary accordingly.

Tijuana

Baby Rock Disco
Paseo de los Héroes and Ave. Diego Rivera, Tijuana • 011-52 (66) 34-24-04

From the outside, Baby Rock appears to be a gigantic rock. Once inside, you'll find a modern dance floor and loud, loud, loud rock music. This obviously is a favorite among the younger set, but don't be surprised to see a fair amount of older party-lovers dancing the night away. Lots of Americans habituate Baby Rock.

Bar San Marcos
Calle 5 and Avenida Revolución, Tijuana • 011-52 (66) 88-27-94

The best way to find this tucked-away spot is to look for a building called "Le Drugstore Tijuana," next to the Hotel Caesar. The Bar San Marcos is inside. Once through the door you'll mix with an equal number of visitors and locals, all enjoying the sounds of a 10-piece mariachi band. Be sure to check out the shining 1940s bar.

Ensenada

Hussong's Cantina
113 Avenida Ruiz, Ensenada • 011-52 (617) 832-10

You cannot go to Ensenada without stopping in at the legendary Hussong's. It has been an institution in the seaside town since 1892, and even though its hype is bigger than its reality, it's still a great party bar. If you want a table, be sure to arrive by early afternoon, and be prepared to dodge a raucous crowd. Both mariachi and ranchera music are played nonstop. Hussong's serves beer only.

Restaurants

Dining South of the Border offers many pleasant surprises. Of course, it's easy to find many eateries that offer the familiar combo plates of enchiladas, tacos and burritos. But that's mostly to satisfy American palates; it's not true Mexican cuisine. Try one of the gems listed below for traditional delicacies from all regions of Mexico. You won't be sorry. You'll also be happy to find that a full gourmet meal can be enjoyed for a price that might bring you an appetizer and a cocktail in the states. Toss caution to the wind, and try something new and unusual.

INSIDERS' TIP

Tipping South of the Border is the same as it is in the United States. Fifteen percent is customary. The exception is taxis. You need only tip if the driver has given you a special tour or service.

Photo: Bob Yarbrough/San Diego Convention and Visitors Bureau

Terrific items and great bargains in Tijuana make shoppers return again and again.

Price Code

Prices given indicate the cost of dinner entrees for two, excluding beverages and tip)

$	Under $15
$$	$16 to $30
$$$	$31 to $40

Tijuana

El Zaguan
$$ • Paseo de los Heroes, Zona Río (at the Abraham Lincoln statue), Tijuana • 011-52 (66) 34-67-81

You *will* find tacos and quesadillas here. They *will not* be what you're used to. Quesadillas with mysterious but delicious fillings are a delightful way to start, then you can proceed to savory *tacos de barbacoa*, lamb wrapped in cactus leaves and spices and slow-cooked in a pit. Beef and seafood dishes are offered, too. The house favorite is *calamares rellenos*, squid stuffed with crab meat and served with a divine sauce.

El Zaguan serves lunch and dinner daily.

La Fonda de Roberto
$$ • Blvd. Cuauhtemoc No. 2800, Tijuana • 011-52 (66) 86-57-17

A mainstay in Tijuana for many years, La Fonda offers an array of appetizers and entrees with regional flair. Try the house specialty, *chiles en nogada*. Large chiles are stuffed with beef and pork along with a mixture of nuts, raisins, fruits and spices. The chiles are then fried and served with a walnut sauce.

La Fonda's appetizers are hard to resist. Tiny corn tortillas are served with a spicy cactus salad or stuffed with a variety of meats and chiles. The restaurant serves lunch and dinner Tuesday through Sunday.

La Mansión de Quetzal
$ • Esteban Cantú No. 2630, Tijuana
• 011-52 (66) 86-33-51

This unique restaurant offers traditional regional dishes from the nine different Mexican states. You can create an entire meal that might come directly from a kitchen in Veracruz, or you might sample courses from a combination of cuisines from, say, Yucatán, Campeche and Michoacán.

The star of the menu is a fork-tender, double-layered beef filet, stuffed with Oaxacan cheese and mushrooms and surrounded by an avocado sauce that could make you swoon. From Campeche you might try the coastal coconut-fried shrimp served in a cantaloupe bowl. Another standout is a spicy lamb dish served with nopal cactus from Tlaxcala.

Salads and desserts are equally intriguing, like the flaky *buñuelos* from Tlaxcala that are covered with cinnamon and sugar and served with a plum sauce. The restaurant serves breakfast, lunch and dinner daily.

Rosarito Beach

Mariscos de Rarito Vince's
$-$$ • 77 Blvd. Benito Juarez,
Rosarito Beach • 011-52 (661) 212-53

Lobster fresh from coastal waters is what draws hungry diners to this popular restaurant, especially lobster served Mexican style, grilled and presented in the shell. Other seafood specialties are offered, too, including a freshly grilled fish of the day.

The restaurant also has a deli for those looking for a meal on the go. Lunch and dinner are served daily. Credit cards are not accepted.

Ensenada

El Rey Sol
$$$ • 1000 Avenida Lopez Mateos,
Ensenada • 011-52- (617) 817-33

Imagine a combination of French and Mexican cuisine. Hard to picture? Let us assure you that the result is worth a trip to Ensenada. This is a family-run restaurant that opened in 1947. The building is quaint, and the dining room is decorated with stained glass windows and heavy oak furniture.

Seafood, poultry and beef dishes with a French flair are all served with appetizers, and the traditional Mexican dishes are outstanding — like the *machaca*, a mixture of dried beef, onions, pepper and eggs. Breakfast, lunch and dinner are served daily. Reservations are recommended, as it's a popular place.

Shopping

Shopping is the sport of choice for most visitors who cross the border, for a couple of reasons. First, the area's duty-free status provides substantial savings on imported merchandise such as perfumes, jewelry, cosmetics, leather goods, watches and apparel. Second, shopping for Mexican arts and crafts, curios and souvenirs in downtown Tijuana, Rosarito Beach and Ensenada is an unparalleled experience. You'll find many unique objects plus lots of designer knockoffs. Shopkeepers expect you to bargain, so sharpen up your negotiating skills and wrangle yourself a good deal.

Tijuana also has several excellent shopping malls that rival those across the border. Here, one does not negotiate the retail price, but you'll still find that prices are much lower than they are in the United States. Before you go overboard, though, remember your $400 per-person duty-free maximum. Most stores, both in the shopping centers and downtown areas, are open from 10 AM to 9 PM daily.

Tijuana

Avenida Revolución, Downtown Tijuana

This is the oldest tourist shopping street in Tijuana and is usually a first stop for visitors. Both sides of the street are lined with arcades, curio shops and apparel stores. Nearly everything you would look for elsewhere in the city is available here, with the bonus of a high-voltage ambiance. The street is crowded with bars and eateries in addition to the shops, and revelers of all ages flock to Avenida Revolución simply because it's so much fun.

Photo: Bob Yarbrough/San Diego Convention and Visitors Bureau

Aztec Indian Dancers perform in traditional costumes.

Don't neglect the streets surrounding Avenida Revolución. They all are popular shopping areas, and if you expand your shopping trip by just a block or two, you'll find lots of shops selling Mexican arts and crafts, as well as clothing.

Avenida Revolución can be reached on foot from the border by following the pedestrian walkway that starts just beyond the border crossing and leads straight to the downtown shopping area, of which Avenida Revolución is the main street. It's a short, mile-long walk, and it's very common to see folks walking from the border rather than driving or taking public transportation.

Plaza Rió Tijuana
Paseo de los Héroes, 96 and 98 Rió Zone, Tijuana • 011-52 (66) 84-04-02

This is a shopping center located within the fairly new Rio Tijuana development. It's the largest shopping center in northern Mexico with more than 100 shops. Several major Mexican department stores anchor the center, and you'll find lots of specialty stores, bakeries, restaurants and a movie theater.

Plaza Fiesta
Paseo de los Héroes 9415 Rió Zone, Tijuana • 011-52 (66) 84-27-14

Located across the street from Plaza Río Tijuana are the traditional Colonial-style buildings of the Plaza Fiesta, a collection of small shops and eating places. Next door to Plaza Fiesta is Plaza del Zapato, which offers thousands of shoes of all styles and colors.

Rosarito

Shopping in Rosarito is more relaxed than in Tijuana, but you'll find the same bargains, only in a more concentrated location. The majority of Rosarito's shopping is found along one street — Benito Juarez — which is the main street through town. At the south end of town is the Rosarito Beach Hotel, which has its own shopping arcade. Here you'll find duty-free imports, designer goods, arts and crafts, clothing and many items from Guatemala.

For more shopping, follow the main street south, out of town, and you'll wander into a huge marketplace that features curio shops, pottery and cement statuary and fountains. As you stroll along the street, you'll see many furniture shops that display locally crafted pieces made from wrought iron, willow and specialty woods.

Ensenada

Seventy-five miles south of the border you'll encounter yet another kind of shopping experience. Ensenada has long been a cruise-ship stop, and as a result, the merchandise for sale is extensive. As in Rosarito, all of Ensenada's shopping is along the main street — Boulevard López Mateos — and it's just a block from the waterfront.

The history of the real estate market in San Diego is one of excess. Either the market is booming and prices are excessively high, or housing prices have gone bust. Rarely is moderation the name of the game.

Neighborhoods and Real Estate

After a few days in San Diego, visitors and newcomers inevitably reach the same conclusion — San Diego is nothing but a very big small town. Insiders just nod their heads and smile. That's what pleasantly distinguishes San Diego from other big cities. Even with a population of 2.8 million countywide, San Diego has somehow managed to hold on to its small-town flavor while enjoying the advantages of a major metropolitan city. Most everything you would look for in New York or San Francisco is here: theater, opera, museums, first-class restaurants and vibrant nightlife. But the sense of community that you find in smaller cities is here too. And nowhere is that sense of community stronger than in the neighborhoods.

San Diegans appreciate and enjoy all the cultural and entertainment opportunities available to them, but they place even more value on life within their neighborhoods. Community pride is fierce. Almost without exception, neighborhoods within both the city and county limits have planning groups to monitor growth and plan activities. Residents care very much about what happens down the street and around the block.

Over the decades, each neighborhood within San Diego County has developed its own unique characteristics. Take Poway and Rancho Bernardo, for example. Both are located in North County Inland; in fact, they're very close to one another. But they could hardly be more different. Rancho Bernardo is an interesting combination of high-tech industry, golf courses and retirement communities. Poway, on the other hand, has a strong working-class population that focuses its energy on local festivals, politics and public school issues.

Farther south, in San Diego, is the neighborhood of Mission Hills. With its stately mansions and high-ticket real estate values, it makes a strangely genteel neighbor for adjacent Hillcrest, a buzzing, active neighborhood with a highly concentrated gay population. Somehow it all works, though.

Then there are the neighborhoods that have cute quirks. Burlingame, for example, a tiny area in North Park, is distinguished by its red concrete sidewalks — the only community in the entire county to sport such a feature. Birdland has a quirk of a different sort. Tucked away between Linda Vista and Serra Mesa, all its streets are named after birds: Hummingbird Lane, Peacock Drive and Nightingale Way, to name a few.

We'll take you through the individual neighborhoods, region by region, so you can get an idea of the variety of lifestyles, architectural styles and just plain old standout features — and there are many. You'll surely find something that appeals to you. Just keep in mind that in the city of San Diego alone there are more than 100 separate, identifiable neighborhoods. So we'll group many of them together and give you an idea of the characteristics of the general area.

One of the best ways to get a good idea of what an individual neighborhood is like is to attend one of its annual festivals or celebrations. Check out the listings in our Annual Events chapter or pick up a community newspaper in a neighborhood library, coffeehouse or convenience store. You'll undoubtedly find a parade, block party or arts festival that will give you the feel for what the area is like. Chat with the locals. You're sure to get an earful.

www.insiders.com

See this and many other
Insiders' Guide®
destinations online.

Visit us today!

Real Estate — A Tale of Boom and Bust

The history of the real estate market in San Diego is one of excess. Either the market is booming and prices are excessively high, or housing prices have gone bust and buyers can snatch up a property for well below market value. Rarely is moderation the name of the game.

We seem to be on the leading edge of another boom period, where prices go through the ceiling, bidding wars break out whenever a property hits the market and buyers are forced to put together some creative financing to purchase even the most modest property. Right now housing prices are seeing double-digit increases, seemingly overnight. But interest rates are at a historic low, which is a strong motivator for many buyers to find some way to wiggle into their dream house.

Here's the scary part: The median price for a single-family resale home in San Diego County is about $250,000. That's a daunting figure, we know. And it's the main reason San Diego habitually makes the least-livable city lists that come out periodically. The cost of living otherwise is quite affordable. It's that darned real estate that makes you swallow so hard.

The good news is that bargains can still be found if you're willing to be a little flexible in terms of neighborhoods and amenities. Many young families are buying homes in some of the older neighborhoods in the county and restoring the homes to pristine condition. As more and more people catch on to the idea, revitalized neighborhoods are emerging from older, more rundown ones, and whole communities are being reborn.

Outlying areas are growing rapidly too, as folks move farther away from central San Diego in search of more affordable housing. Traditionally, housing costs in North County Inland, East County and the South Bay have been somewhat easier on the wallet than those in North County Coastal and some of the prime areas in San Diego. This adds a bit of a commute to the mix, but city planners are committed to making that commute as easy as possible. Currently their main focus has been on North County routes into the city. Freeways are being widened and ways to increase usage of special commuter lanes are being tested.

The rental market seems to rise and fall with real estate values, and right now rental units are at a premium. They also are on the expensive side. The average monthly rent for a one-bedroom apartment in the county is more than $800. Ouch! But again, do your homework, and you should be able to find a nice place in the neighborhood of your choice. Some of the best units for the best value are listed in the classifieds by their owners. Just be prepared to make an immediate decision and have cash in hand for first and last month's rent, plus a security deposit.

As we introduce you to the various neighborhoods throughout the county, we'll also try to give you an idea of housing prices. Aside from a few communities like Rancho Santa Fe and La Jolla, where home prices always have more digits than you want to know about, most neighborhoods have a wide range of prices. Modest cottages can usually be found right around the corner from some pretty impressive houses in most neighborhoods.

We'll steer you toward some good resources too that will help you find a house, condo, apartment or whatever your heart de-

Photo: Thom Vollenweider

Craftsman-style homes are abundant in San Diego's older neighborhoods.

sires. Real estate brokers are abundant, and we'll give you the heads-up on some of the best. We'll also list home buyers' and apartment guides to help make your search easier.

San Diego

Beaches: Pacific Beach, Mission Beach, Ocean Beach

Beach life is different. It's special. It requires forbearance — forbearance for the tourists in the summer, the inflated housing prices year-round and the damp air that sometimes settles in, threatening to never leave. But as soon as the sun pokes its head through the clouds, all the challenges of beach life are forgotten, and the benefits are abundantly clear.

The three beach areas in San Diego are so different they may as well be on three different planets. Those who live in **Pacific Beach** are generally twenty-something career people in search of fast times and the club scene, and they have minimal housing requirements. Apartment complexes are seemingly everywhere and are the residences of choice for

this crowd. Sprinkled amongst the younger set, however, are residents who have called P.B. home for years. They have the same pride of ownership and community spirit that you would find elsewhere, but they also have an affinity and tolerance for the exuberance of their youthful neighbors. Together they add up to more than 41,000 residents, making Pacific Beach by far the most densely populated beach community.

A half mile or so inland in Pacific Beach is where many homeowners have found housing prices that are within reach, and an lifestyle that still qualifies as beach living. Single-family homes range from about $195,000 on the far east end of P.B to $1.5 million for beachfront houses or for some of the stately homes in the hills. Condos range from $75,000 for a one-bedroom unit to $300,000 for something with a few more bells and whistles.

Mission Beach is a tiny isthmus only two blocks wide between bay and beach, and it stretches south from P.B. to the jetty at the mouth of the San Diego River. The vast majority of cottages, apartments and condos in Mission Beach are rentals. This is where the college crowd settles in during the winter and vacationers rent during the summer months.

A few hardy souls have made Mission Beach their permanent home, but you'll find few families here. As in P.B., housing prices range from $195,000 for a small, run-down fixer-upper cottage to well over $1 million for beachfront property.

Ocean Beach is another story. Its northern edge is the southern jetty across the channel from Mission Beach, and it continues south to Sunset Cliffs and Point Loma. Sometimes called the Haight-Ashbury of San Diego, O.B. was an enclave for hippies and flower children during the late '60s and early '70s. Many of the erstwhile hippies stayed on, bought houses and raised their children here. Other beach-lovers have discovered modern-day O.B., found it to their liking and have settled in, resulting in a population of more than 13,000. Still, much of the flavor of the community is reminiscent of that interesting generation of 30 years ago, only these days in a much more refined sense. The public beach in O.B. is one of the best in the county, and the downtown village in the community boasts dozens of excellent antique stores, casual restaurants and one-of-a-kind boutiques.

Housing prices in O.B. are among the best bargains for home buyers, ranging from $130,000 to $190,000 for condos, and $150,000 to $550,000 for single-family homes. A lot of quality lies in between, so those who crave the beach existence can usually find something that matches their expectations and their budget. Rental prices in all beach areas tend to be a bit higher than in other parts of San Diego, averaging about $900 for a small apartment. You can find them cheaper, but bear in mind that the lower the rent, the lower the quality of the rental. College students don't seem to have a problem with a dearth of amenities, but the older crowd might find rental life too much like roughing it.

Downtown and Golden Hill

Fifteen years ago, no one lived Downtown except for down-on-their-luck transients and drug dealers who inhabited the streets and seedy flophouse hotels that populated the area. A lot has changed in 15 years, and now downtown boasts a number of ultra-modern high-rise condominiums, townhouses and artists' lofts. Buyers are flocking to the downtown area because massive redevelopment projects have resulted in a hip and trendy neighborhood, combined with fine restaurants, shopping, theaters and clubs. Plus, many appreciate the convenience of being able to walk to work or take a quick trolley ride to offices outside the downtown area.

The area's appeal continues to increase, and so do housing prices. Single-family housing is nearly nonexistent, and condominiums range from $175,000 to $1 million-plus for a unit in the posh Harbor Club high rise. Lofts are somewhere in between and have become quite popular; more and more seem to be springing up every day. Even though loft prices are somewhat less than the pricey condos, they're pretty much bare bones. You usually get walls and plumbing, the rest is up to you.

Just to the east of Downtown is **Golden Hill**, a community of mostly single-family homes developed in the early days of San Diego. Many of the homes are stately Victorian gems from the turn of the century, and some have been beautifully refurbished. Like Downtown, Golden Hill has seen a period of blight, but is rapidly recovering. Much of it borders Balboa Park and the park's golf course, so it features some outstanding scenic properties.

Housing prices are still very affordable in Golden Hill. Houses start at less than $100,000 and top out at around $300,000. Condos are mostly in the $60,000 to $100,000 range. Many of the houses are in need of some TLC, but smart buyers are snapping them up, recognizing that Golden Hill is one of the up-and-coming communities in San Diego.

Kearny Mesa, Serra Mesa, Birdland

Although designated as three separate neighborhoods, **Kearny Mesa**, **Serra Mesa** and **Birdland** are so similar that they often are thought of as one. They do have their distinctions, though. There's no mistaking when you're in Birdland, for all the streets have an ornithological designation. Serra Mesa overlooks Qualcomm Stadium and has a couple of brain-teasing street names: Unida Place and Haveteur Way (sound them out — you'll get it). And **Kearny Mesa** is the location of the first major business district in San Diego outside of Downtown. So they do have their distinguishing features, but the housing remains much the same from area to area: mostly modest tract houses that have nevertheless been well maintained and upgraded over the years to accommodate growing families. Houses cost between $150,000 and $230,000; condos range from $75,000 to $150,000.

Eastern: Tierra Santa, Allied Gardens, Grantville, Del Cerro, San Carlos

Tierrasanta's development began in the late '60s, and it is a glowing success story. Located across Interstate 15 from Kearny Mesa, it has matured into an eye-pleasing community that focuses on families. The schools are great, housing prices have stayed within reach and an amazing number of first-time buyers have stayed in the area rather than moving to bigger houses elsewhere. Houses are priced from around $185,000 to $335,000, and condos range from $100,000 to $180,000.

Southeast of Tierrasanta are **Allied Gardens**, **Grantville**, **Del Cerro** and **San Carlos**, another group of communities that share common characteristics. Del Cerro is slightly more upscale than the others, featuring more custom homes with more floor space. But the solidly built tract homes in Allied Gardens, Grantville and San Carlos have held their value over the years. Grantville was one of the first neighborhoods in San Diego because of its proximity to Mission San Diego de Alcalá. It once consisted of dairy farms, but along with Allied Gardens and San Carlos was fully developed in the mid-'50s and '60s. Now the

neighborhoods are welcoming back children of the original homebuyers. This generation is either buying their parents' homes or ones nearby, a testament to the appeal of the community and its affordability. Houses range from $150,000 to $300,000, and condos go from $80,000 to about $130,000.

Many Del Cerro homes are distinguished by their glorious views of Mission Valley and beyond. On clear days the ocean, ten miles to the west, is easily visible. As a result, housing prices are quite a bit higher than in neighboring communities, starting at about $175,000 and going as high as $750,000. Del Cerro has a much-sought-after condo complex, called Del Cerro Heights, perched on the side of a hill overlooking the valley. The units are huge and hard to come by. They also extract a steep price. In today's market, it's not unusual for one to go for upwards of $300,000.

La Jolla and Torrey Pines

It seems as though everyone has heard of **La Jolla**. From Omaha to Orlando, folks have heard tales about the beauty and opulence of the seaside village that some say is like Beverly Hills — only with a view. Some, however, are surprised to learn it's part of San Diego, and many La Jollans wish its location were an even better-kept secret. Residents are close-knit and protective, and they fiercely guard the natural beauty and mystique of their neighborhood.

Although Jolla is not a word found in the Spanish dictionary, the word "joya" means jewel, and the two words are pronounced the same. That's close enough for the 30,000 or so residents who inhabit the palm tree-lined hills and shores of La Jolla. The jewel by the sea it is, and a more appropriate description would be hard to find. La Jolla sits squarely on top of some of the most valuable real estate in the United States. Million-dollar homes

Housing near the naval base can fill up quickly when the fleet is in.

are the rule rather than the exception. And if a view of the Blue Pacific comes with the house, the price tag goes way up. To lucky residents, no amount of money is too great to have the opportunity to settle in what inarguably is one of the most glorious spots on earth.

For visitors (and many residents, too) it's the downtown village that draws them to La Jolla. Prospect Street and Girard Avenue, the two main streets in the village, are crammed with art galleries, chi-chi boutiques and trendy (but fabulous) restaurants. Insiders know souvenirs can be found in La Jolla, but you'll have to search if you're looking for the ubiquitous snow globe with a surfer and a starfish in it. Trinkets to remind you of your trip to La Jolla are more likely to require currency with Ben Franklin's face rather than Abe Lincoln's.

The beaches are the stuff dreams are made of and offer a little something for everyone. There's Tourmaline, exclusively a surfers' beach, and the Children's Pool, a manmade cove with tiny, gentle waves to delight youngsters. Then there's La Jolla Cove, a treasure trove for snorkelers and scuba divers, and the white sands of La Jolla Shores, a favorite of families.

Monetary considerations aside, just look at faces of residents as they sip their coffee and mimosas and nibble their croissants on a restaurant deck overlooking La Jolla Cove on any Sunday morning, and you'll understand that they believe they're living in heaven. And if heaven is a place where the most controversial political issue of the day is whether the townspeople should install parking meters or not, then La Jollans are right to guard their secret well.

Just to the north of La Jolla, is **Torrey Pines**. The campus of the University of California at San Diego is in Torrey Pines; so are many of the high-tech and biotech companies that are becoming such a significant force in the local economy. Many professors and scientists spend their daylight hours in Torrey Pines, and then take a short drive down the coast to their homes in La Jolla.

The two communities are inextricably linked. The "town and gown" atmosphere is an integral contributor to La Jolla's social scene, and the educational and scientific community in Torrey Pines is heavily dependent on the generosity of its La Jolla benefactors. Drive south along Torrey Pines Road and you can almost feel the waves of brain power exuding from UCSD. Then as soon as Torrey Pines Road turns into La Jolla Boulevard, you can sense the luxury and see the beauty of this stunning oceanfront community.

Housing prices in both neighborhoods will make most people wince. A simple, tiny condominium can go for $175,000. Start adding such amenities as bedrooms, and you'll be pushing $500,000. Houses range from $350,000 to the sky's the limit.

Mid-City East: Kensington, Talmadge, Normal Heights, North Park, College Area

Atop a long mesa overlooking Mission Valley lie the neighborhoods that make up the mid-city area of San Diego. Rich in history and even richer in modern-day personality, these communities are home to San Diegans who enjoy a sense of neighborhood, but savor the proximity to urban amenities, too.

Kensington is one such neighborhood. Developed in 1910 by a Canadian expatriate, it was named for the famous London borough. A stroll down the sidewalks of today's Kensington reveals the developer's original intent: Stately English Tudor houses are plentiful. The twist is that they are intermixed with houses sporting San Diego's traditional Spanish architecture, white walls, red tile roofs and all. Strangely enough, the result is an appeal-

ing combination of the two styles, and the well-manicured landscaping attests to current owners' neighborhood pride.

Across the canyon from Kensington is its sister community of **Talmadge**. Silent film stars and sisters Norma, Constance and Natalie Talmadge lent their name to the subdivision and were further rewarded for their generosity by having individual streets named for them too. Norma, Constance and Natalie Drives are the main streets that take you through this well-kept, quiet area. Real estate agents know that people who live in Kensington and Talmadge are rigorous defenders of their neighborhoods and are vocally active in local politics. Kensington's housing prices are slightly higher than those in Talmadge, ranging from $175,000 for a small fixer-upper to $1 million. One factor that may tend to inflate that range is that several bona fide mansions dot the northern rim of Kensington's mesa. Condos are much more reasonable, starting at around $75,000 and topping out at about $200,000. In Talmadge the range is from $150,000 to $350,000 for houses, and condos are about the same as in Kensington.

West of Kensington and Talmadge are the neighborhoods of **Normal Heights** and **North Park**. Housing tends to be more affordable in both areas, ranging from $75,000 to $350,000 for houses and $65,000 to $200,000 for condos. Both neighborhoods have suffered periods of neglect. The neighborhoods are rebounding, though, and many of the houses are remarkable. Along with the standard array of Spanish styles are some of the best examples of Craftsman cottages in San Diego. Many have been refurbished, many more are awaiting a dedicated owner to restore them to their original glory.

North Park and Normal Heights are in the early stages of redevelopment, but there is no doubt that the two neighborhoods have huge potential. That's why savvy homebuyers are

INSIDERS' TIP

Every neighborhood has its little secrets. One of the nicest in Hillcrest is the Spruce Street Pedestrian Bridge. A suspension bridge linking Front and Brant Streets, it was built in 1912, is 375 feet long and rises 70 feet above the canyon floor.

taking advantage of the real estate bargains now, before prices start to climb.

Finally, there is the **College Area**, called so because it's home to San Diego State University. This area too is an older San Diego neighborhood, but like its communities to the west is seeing an influx of younger families seeking good quality, affordable housing. The presence of the university helps maintain the value of the surrounding neighborhoods and is seen by most as a community asset. The cost of a home in the College Area ranges from $110,000 to $390,000, while condos sell between $75,000 and $175,000.

All the mid-city neighborhoods are good places for families. And community pride has generated a new wave of restaurants, local watering holes, coffeehouses and retail shops.

Mid-City West: Mission Valley, University Heights, Hillcrest, Mission Hills, Middletown

Mission Valley, named for San Diego Mission de Alcalá, is a valley that runs east-west between two overlooking mesas. Bisecting the valley is the San Diego River. The Valley, as its called, has the distinction of having no single-family homes. It has plenty of apartments and condominiums, though, that mostly attract a younger crowd that appreciates the central location. The San Diego Trolley runs through the Valley, and Mission Valley and Fashion Valley shopping centers are a stone's throw from one another and right on the trolley line. Condo prices range from $65,000 to $300,000, and apartment rental rates average $800 for a one-bedroom unit.

Hillcrest and **University Heights** are right next door to each other and are similar in housing styles. The difference is that University Heights is strictly residential, while Hillcrest is anything but. The village area of Hillcrest is almost a miniature Gaslamp Quarter with fabulous restaurants, way-cool shops and trendy clubs. Hillcrest also has a large gay population that has been instrumental in revitalizing the area. Pride of ownership is clear as you drive down the streets of both Hillcrest and University Heights. Immaculately maintained

houses and yards show off their owners' efforts. Many Craftsman-style houses dot the streets of the two neighborhoods and can still be purchased without having to win the lottery. Houses range from $150,000 to $700,000, and condos range from $125,000 to $400,000.

Mission Hills is a rare, old neighborhood that has never endured a downturn. The beautiful houses, many of which were built at the turn of the century, maintain their original elegance. Second- and third-generation families keep returning to Mission Hills, and they do so for a number of reasons. First is its beautiful location, of course, overlooking Mission Bay and Presidio Park, the site of the original mission founded by Father Serra. Second is its central location. Tucked in at the intersection of Interstate 5 and Interstate 8, it's close to everywhere. Third is its proximity to Hillcrest. It may seem an odd juxtaposition to have a predominantly gay neighborhood right next to a stately, old-money community, but the two intermingle beautifully. Housing prices are high in Mission Hills. Single-family homes range from $200,000 to upwards of $1 million. Condos range from $150,000 to $400,000.

Rounding out Mid-City West is **Middletown**. Originally called Little Italy, this is where the Italian community laid its roots. Even today you'll find an abundance of old-style Italian restaurants lining the streets of Middletown. You'll also find Italian Community Centers and an occasional bocce ball tournament. It's a close-knit community, even though many of its members have left the area. Those who remain cling to their heritage, and an unmistakable aura of pride and satisfaction permeates the area. Houses range from $100,000 to $250,000; condos from $75,000 to $165,000.

Northeastern: Mira Mesa and Scripps Ranch

Mira Mesa is a bedroom community of mainly tract houses that began in the late '60s. It provided a much-needed source of affordable housing for young families, especially military families in search of off-base living quarters. The neighborhood has stood the test of time and is still a haven for families. Schools,

La Jolla is an upscale area with a diversity of homes and condominiums.

shopping centers and restaurants have all made their way into Mira Mesa. So much so, that it is nearly a self-contained community. Housing prices remain affordable, ranging from $125,000 to $250,000 and most of the houses are built with families in mind: lots of bedrooms, baths and family rooms. Condos range from $75,000 to $150,000.

Just to the southeast of Mira Mesa lies the newer and slightly more upscale neighborhood of **Scripps Ranch**. Housing prices are substantially higher than in Mira Mesa, from $200,000 to $485,000 for houses, and from $120,000 to $300,000 for condos. But you're purchasing more square footage and more atmosphere. Nestled among eucalyptus trees, the community has a kind of country flavor, and yet it's a commuter close to downtown San Diego. The houses are tract homes, as they are in Mira Mesa, but are bigger and have many more amenities. Plus, the entire community is within walking distance of Lake Miramar, which has jogging and bike trials around the perimeter. Many Scripps Ranch homes have a view of the lake too. It's a serene setting, and you can't help feeling you're someplace much farther away from the bustle of the city.

Northern: Linda Vista, Clairemont, University City, Sorrento Valley

To the east of I-5 are the long-established communities of **Linda Vista** and **Clairemont**. So long-entrenched is Linda Vista that it has the distinction of being the home of the first shopping mall in the United States. Small in comparison to the mega-malls we're familiar with today, it nevertheless put the tiny community on the map. Today Linda Vista is known for its most prominent neighbor: the University of San Diego.

Surrounding much of Linda Vista is Clairemont, which comprises the neighborhoods of Bay Ho and Bay Park too. Large in area and population (Clairemont is home to some 80,000 residents), the area has a melting pot of inhabitants, from young families in to retired folks who have been living in the same house for more than 50 years.

Linda Vista and Clairemont can't be considered suburbs, because they're right in the heart of the city. But quiet streets and neighborhood block parties blend right in with the shopping centers, strip malls and other businesses that all coexist in a wonderful mix of everything that's good about San Diego. Plus, the beach is ten minutes away. Clairemont and Linda Vista both border Tecolote Canyon Park, a nature reserve with oodles of hiking trails and one of the top-rated executive golf courses in California. Housing prices are reasonable in both communities, unless you happen upon one of the lucky Clairemont homes that has a panoramic view of Mission Bay and the ocean. Then you're likely to pay upward of $400,000 for a three-bedroom house. But the range for the rest is from $140,000 to $280,000 for houses, and $120,000 to $220,000 for condos.

University City, a slightly more upscale version of Clairemont, is located just to the north. The community is a little newer, and the houses are a little bigger. Other than that, it has the same neighborhood feel that Clairemont boasts. The north end of University City has been taken over by apartment buildings because of its proximity to UCSD. Rental rates are quite high, $1,000-plus for apartments. Housing prices range from $175,000 to $450,000; condos from $75,000 to $250,000.

North of University City is the new community of **Sorrento Valley**. Sorrento Valley itself isn't new — it has long been a center for San Diego's high-tech businesses and industries. But it's only recently that housing developments have begun to spring up. Like any new community, it'll take time to develop a personality of its own, but the folks who have already settled in are working hard to do just that. Houses range from $300,000 to $450,000, and condos start at $175,000 and top out at $250,000.

Point Loma and Coronado

At the tip of the Point Loma peninsula sits the Cabrillo Lighthouse, a monument to the explorer who claimed San Diego for Spain. From the base of the peninsula to its tip are located some of San Diego's prettiest houses and longest-established neighborhoods. One of the most prolific industries in days gone by was tuna fishing, an enterprise started by San Diego's Portuguese community. Most of that community remains ensconced in **Point Loma**, where Portuguese festivals, food and culture are abundant.

Somewhere along the way others discovered Point Loma too, and took advantage of the hillside property on either side of the peninsula to build houses that command magnificent, unobstructed ocean or bay views. The biggest drawback to life in Point Loma is the nearby airport. Lindbergh Field's runway is aimed right at the Loma Portal area of the peninsula, and residents endure airplane noise all day long, from 6:30 AM until nearly midnight. With a little extra soundproofing insulation and the advent of newer, quieter planes, it has become more bearable of late, and most feel it's a small price to pay for the beautiful houses and views they get in exchange.

Across the bay is the neighboring island of **Coronado**, with its 29,000 residents. Technically it's not really an island — it's the tip of a narrow spit of land that reaches north from Imperial Beach, near the U.S.-Mexico border. But Coronado residents like the idea of it being an island, and few outsiders are ungenerous enough to disagree, so an island it is.

Coronado has the distinction of having more retired navy admirals than any other location in the country. But it's not just military brass who have discovered the charm of the island. It's an ideal place to raise a family — good schools, low crime and beautiful beaches

---

INSIDERS' TIP

One of the best sources for trivia about San Diego County neighborhoods is Evelyn Kooperman's *San Diego Trivia*. Kooperman is a native San Diegan and a reference librarian at the San Diego Public Library.

Photo: Dale Frost/Port of San Diego

Many neighborhoods are adjacent to wonderful parks and beach areas.

are among its attributes. And the downtown village of Coronado is so picturesque it looks like something out of a movie. Quaint shops, theaters and restaurants line Orange Avenue, the main drag through town.

Coronado and Point Loma have one thing in common: exorbitant real estate. In Point Loma you can still find the occasional fixer-upper to fit your budget, say for $175,000. Houses can easily top $1 million, especially if they have one of those coveted views. Condos are a little more affordable, from $110,000 to $350,000. Bargains are not to be found in Coronado, however. A rock-bottom fixer-upper on the island can easily go for $300,000, and the mansions don't seem to have an upper limit. One that was on the market for quite a while (and had the distinction of a presidential visit during the mid-1990s) had a ticket of more than $7 million. Even condos make you catch your breath, ranging from $200,000 to $1.3 million for a luxury dockside unit in the Coronado Cays complex.

North County Coastal

Carlsbad and La Costa

Carlsbad and its La Costa district are like fraternal twins, forever joined with similar backgrounds. Yet there's a world of difference in the twins' approach to San Diego living.

Starting with **Carlsbad**, which stretches from the city of Oceanside way down the coast to Encinitas, and inland to Vista, you'll find a family community, blended with small stores and shops. There's a real downtown area in this town. In it you'll find city hall, the main branch of the library, great restaurants (and some beach hangouts and clubs), supermarkets, antique shops, beauty salons and all you'd expect in a small town. (If you love to shop for antiques, be sure to read about Carlsbad's antique district in our Shopping chapter.) There are also the usual downtown office buildings — but they're never more than three stories high — and hotels and motels, from posh resorts to more thrifty establishments.

In addition, Carlsbad offers some tourist attractions. Be sure to read about Carlsbad's newest one, LEGOLAND California, in our Kidstuff Chapter.

The neighborhoods are a mix of ethnic backgrounds and their population is young: The median age of residents is 36 years. With about 70,000 residents (including those in the La Costa section), Carlsbad is a thriving area.

The beach property of Carlsbad includes million-dollar oceanfront homes. New homes in Carlsbad not along the shore are in the $300,000 to $600,000 range.

Resale homes to the west of I-5 are sometimes less expensive, but don't count on it. Apartments on that side cost an average of $850 a month for a one-bedroom.

On the east side of I-5, most resale home prices are between $250,000 to well over $400,000. These are not custom homes, mind you. They are remodeled or well-maintained sixties track houses that once sold for $6,000. Now add an ocean view to this equation, and even if you can only see it by standing on your tiptoes and craning your neck through a second-story window, you can easily add to that figure.

Carlsbad has a nice range of condos. Those found in neighborhoods with apartments sell for about $130,000. But expect to pay way more than that for those with ocean views.

Now let's look at **La Costa**, the area south of Carlsbad and adjacent to the La Costa Resort and Spa. In this upscale area there are condos, some apartments and lots of family homes.

There are multi-million dollar homes, too. As in Carlsbad, it's not unusual in today's booming real estate market for a house to be sold even before a broker can decide what to put in an advertisement. Because the moment the rumor begins to circulate that a house is up for sale, bids immediately appear. As one Insider recently found out, if you fall in love with a neighborhood, you need to drive around it often, and be prepared to jump in with an offer (with lender info all in place), since Carlsbad and La Costa homes aren't on the market long.

Schools are good in the Carlsbad-La Costa neighborhood, the city government listens to the voters, and crime is lower than in other cities. Air quality (except for a few days in autumn when LA's smog invades the coast) is excellent, and the quality of life makes Carlsbad's neighborhoods desirable. The down side? Those who commute south or east face miles of slow-and-go — and that's on a good day. We're talking gridlock. Carlsbad residents are a resourceful lot, and many take the Coaster, work flex hours, and get jobs closer to home to avoid the grind that can start as early as six in the morning.

Del Mar

Del Mar has a laid-back beach-tourist feel that visitors expect to find when visiting San Diego. Regardless of the time of day, there are people outdoors. Some are walking, jogging or playing beach sports. Others come out to mingle at the cafes and coffeehouses that are sprinkled through town. When that first group goes back to work or school, the next wave takes its place and the cycle continues until late in the evening. Del Mar is an outdoor town and home to outdoor institutions like a polo club, racetrack and the Del Mar Fairgrounds where there's something happening outdoors nearly every weekend. (Be sure to read our Annual Events chapter for

INSIDERS' TIP

Call Local Talk for tips on San Diego County real estate: (858) 569-1010 in San Diego, East County and South Bay; and (760) 631-6001 in North County Coastal and Inland. Punch in the following codes for info: 2110 for the role of a real estate agent, 2115 for selling tips, 2120 for buying tips, 2125 for leasing tips.

some of the great things that happen at the fairground.)

Del Mar is only 1.8 square miles and the residents (a number that hovers at about 6,000) like it that way. While some of the county's communities have less desirable areas, Del Mar is Del Mar and that means charming. In the section of Del Mar that's found west of I-5, the custom homes are in older neighborhoods with established landscaping and shady twisting streets. East of I-5, past the multistory business offices seen from the freeway, are a sprawl of planned neighborhoods whose homes have red Spanish tile roofs and perfectly green lawns.

Housing prices have soared in this coastal community and as we go to press, it looks like this trend will continue. The average house in Del Mar, probably a three- or four-bedroom resale home, can be bought for between $580,000 to more than $1 million. A good number of homes have ocean views, which can tack on a cool hundred grand or more to that price tag. Those homes on the beach may be smaller, but alas, still go for the big bucks. The typical Del Mar home is a spacious, custom dwelling with a nice-sized family lot. The community is close enough to the city of San Diego to make the commute tolerable.

There's some apartment living in Del Mar, but you're more likely to find a condo for rent. Rents are in the $1,200-a-month range for apartments. The price of renting a house could easily soar to $5,000 a month, depending on location. The price of condos ranges from $475,000 to $115,000; the median is $300,000.

Encinitas

Encinitas, with its official boundaries incorporating the towns of Cardiff and Leucadia, is half the size of Carlsbad, and enjoys a youthful community spirit. At one time, Encinitas, Leucadia and Cardiff-by-the-Sea (Insiders just call it Cardiff) were three distinct locales. But in 1986 they grouped together to form the city of Encinitas. Yet even after more than ten years, each area strives to keeps its individuality.

Driving north along I-5 from San Diego, you'll first see Cardiff, with its older, established family homes set on rolling hills. Most homes in Cardiff have an ocean view (or at the very least relish in those Pacific breezes). There are schools, supermarkets, sidewalk cafes and sandy beaches in this town. The overwhelming flavor of Cardiff is casual.

Encinitas, the hub of the community, is filled with the energy of its growing families. It's going somewhere — and just where that is concerns residents. This pristine city strives for a clean and wholesome image that sets it apart from many other beach cities. As with other coastal communities, Encinitas has a downtown with shops, cafes, restaurants, businesses and specialty stores lining Pacific Coast Highway and along the few blocks on either side of it. Inland, that is on the east side of I-5, are most of the city's homes, typically in planned communities with shopping centers and strip malls.

If Insiders think that Cardiff is quiet, Leucadia could be accused of taking a full-time siesta. It has sleepy neighborhoods with architectural jewels mixed in with simpler homes. There's more elbowroom here too: There are still a good number of undeveloped lots available should you want to build.

Leucadians are reluctant to promote growth, and take an active part in the decisions that affect their part of Encinitas. Years ago when the city wanted to put in sidewalks on some of the peaceful roads, the voters quickly nixed that. "No change needed," they said firmly. Today Leucadia continues to be a serenely sweet town.

Resale homes in Encinitas, in all three areas of the city, are in the $260,000 neighborhood; new homes in planned communities can be substantially more. One upscale abode just sold for over $750,000. Condos are close to the resale homes figure, with the average condo selling for about $200,000. Apartments close to the ocean can rent from $750 to more than $3,000; those without an ocean view are usually in the $1,000 category. Houses and condos in family neighborhoods rent for more.

Oceanside

Oceanside, incorporated on July 3, 1888, was one of the first cities in North County Coastal. It's the largest of the cities, too, with more than 40 square miles within its boundaries. Housing prices vary in this ethnically diverse, working-class community.

You may be able to find a tiny, older house, a real *Home Improvement* fan's fixer-upper, for $80,000. A resale home in a family part of town will run about $200,000 and up. Newly built homes in planned developments can exceed $250,000. But don't be mislead by these figures. Oceanside's best properties sell for more than $500,000, depending on location, view and neighborhood. Condos range from $120,000 to the higher figures just cited. There are more rental units in Oceanside than in other parts of North County Coastal due to the military presence in Camp Pendleton. Rent prices vary with location and are somewhat lower than those of Oceanside's neighboring cities.

Oceanside rightfully bursts with pride at all it has to offer. There are well-established parks, big sandy beaches, a respected community college and a recreation system that brings programs to kids, adults and seniors. And currently it's trying to shake off that "Oceanside is just another military town" stigma. Whatever it's doing, it's doing it right. More new businesses, enterprises and manufacturing groups are coming to town and that means more jobs and more families. As we go to press, there's a major beach-area resort in the discussion stage. Clearly, the city of Oceanside is moving comfortably into its new image.

Rancho Santa Fe

The community that Insiders refer to as "the Ranch" doesn't come with a visible price tag. As the cliché goes: If you must ask the price of property in Rancho Santa Fe, you may not be able to afford it.

Having said that, we want to add that some of our favorite Insiders live in this community where multi-million dollar homes are the norm, yet we still pal around with them like they are regular folks. That's the nice part of the community; everything is understated. The Ranch has the feel of just another upscale San Diego town. The median price for a home here (we're talking spacious home with plenty of prime property, perhaps a pool and a tennis court — the kind you see in better decorating magazines) is about $2 million. Condos, if you can find them, are selling for about $500,000. Rentals here are traditionally handled by agents and can be anything from a condo near the tiny downtown to oversized mansions on oversized lots with matching monthly rental fees.

Streets are tree lined and inviting. As you drive through the Ranch, you can glimpse mansions tucked behind the lush landscaping. Traffic is regulated and slower than in other cities. Parking can be a challenge, especially during the lunch hours. People know each other and those who work in the Ranch often walk to work and walk at lunch. People meet at the post office often since there is no home mail delivery in the Ranch.

Rancho Santa Fe feels safe and is rather old-fashioned. The downtown is small, with exclusive jewelry shops, clothing boutiques, the usual doctors' and dentists' offices, and a supermarket. You'll find the busy post office there too. The cafes and restaurants are fun to try; menu choices are no more expensive than you'd expect in other parts of the region.

Solana Beach

Solana Beach is hugged by Del Mar and Encinitas. The city seems to have the best of its neighbors' best qualities, plus an added shot of adrenaline. There's energy everywhere. Check out the downtown area along the Pacific coast highway: You'll see early-morning, lunchtime and evening walkers and runners, parents pushing kids in strollers, business people on break and out for a browse and shoppers claiming prizes in those famous Cedros Street antique stores. (Be sure to read our Shopping chapter for information on the stores in the Cedros Design District.)

This is a family town too, with good parks and schools and recreational activities. Residents in Solana Beach think about the environment — the ocean is their best neighbor — and recycling programs abound. Many residents also opt for a cleaner form of transportation. After one Insider rode the commuter train, the Coaster, during a rainy winter, she reported that more business people seem to get on and off in Solana Beach than at any other station.

The town has an excellent blend of family homes, condos and some apartment living. The high end for resale real estate is about $650,000 while the low end hovers above $250,000. New homes in planned communities average about $500,000. Condos have a wider range since some are built overlooking the ocean and garner bigger price tags. Recently a condo sold for $800,000, yet the average condo now goes for about $250,000, if you can find one. Again, it's all in the location. Rentals, if you can find them, average about $1,000 for an apartment or very small home.

North County Inland

Escondido

Escondido seems to have been transplanted from another time. It's a hometown, with a downtown, downtown merchants, and a civic pride rivaling that of any Midwestern community. People live and work in this town that's situated in North County Inland, about an hour's drive (in traffic) from downtown San Diego. That's not saying there aren't those who brave the rush and commute out of Escondido using I-15.

The drive can become a gridlock similar to that found along I-5 along the coastal communities, and yet a lot of people who work in San Diego and East County drive in from Escondido daily. While there are express buses that take commuters into San Diego and diamond lanes for car-poolers, there's no commuter train yet.

With the recently built California Center for the Arts, a multi-purpose facility with a multi-story theater, culture has come to Escondido. (Be sure to read more about the center in our Arts chapter.) The center draws big time performers from around the world and if you want tickets you need to plan ahead.

Obviously, highbrow opportunities are not lacking, but people like the community fun produced by this town too. There are parades, arts and crafts fairs, and picnics and historical tours of houses built in the late 1880s, which is about the time the city was incorporated. Back then it was a hub of agricultural activity.

Less than ten years ago you could still visit avocado and citrus packinghouses and working orchards within the city limits.

Escondido has a blend of older and newer neighborhoods. You may find smaller houses, family homes, at the low end of the real estate price tag in the $200,000 range and more posh family abodes netting close to $600,000. The range reflects the location. Condos are in the $150,000 range and apartments and rental homes, depending on the location, can be found for between $700 and $2,000.

Fallbrook and Valley Center

There's lots of fresh air in these communities that are situated about an hour and a half northeast of downtown San Diego. You'll also find working avocado and citrus orchards, people who love horses and dogs, and lots of families who've chosen these communities for the elbowroom. You'll also find some retired folks since golf courses are abundant and close at hand. See our chapter on Golf.

The cities provide a nice combination of stores, services, and eateries. In both towns, there's a main street and neighbors who still stop and chat. The schools encourage civic pride and there are lots of family activities from Fallbrook's Avocado Days to Valley Center's local art fairs.

Homes in this area are usually custom-built, and situated on hillsides — both communities are known for the views of tree-studded mountains and miles of open backcountry. Most have at least an acre of ground, some quite a lot more. People who want to have horses and other farm critters often move to these communities for the land and friendship of other animal lovers.

The average home, as we go to press, is re-selling for about $380,000. New homes are easily $100,000 more. Condo and apartment living is limited. With the real estate boom beginning, it's unclear if prices will rise as they have in other cities in the area. If you're reading this book a year or two after publication, don't be shocked if prices have gone up. There's a general feeling that the real estate market in Fallbrook and Valley Center is about to explode.

If it's country hillsides you're longing for, the outlying areas like Julian may be the focus of your home hunting.

Rancho Peñasquitos and Poway

The communities of Poway and Rancho Peñasquitos (or just Peñasquitos as Insiders call it) are grouped because they are lively, family towns with a younger than average population. If you move to Peñasquitos or Poway your neighbor might be a doctor who works at Scripps Hospital, a local landscaper with a thriving business, a computer genius who interfaces with colleagues over the Internet or someone in public service or the military. People and professions blend well in these cities which offer planned communities with tree-lined streets.

Homes in Poway and Peñasquitos are slightly more expensive than those in neighboring communities. Resale homes average about $300,000; Peñasquitos house price tags are about $340,000. New homes in both cities, in well-planned developments, are about $450,000. Condos average about $150,000 and some rental houses and condos go for $800 to $2,000 a month.

There are a few apartments, but most people look for condos and homes in this family-oriented, newly developed area.

Rancho Bernardo

Rancho Bernardo is many things to many people. Seniors think of it as the perfect retirement community, because of its lovely weather, great services, easy freeway access and super golf courses. Families think of it as a family town. And large corporate entities such as Hewlett Packard see it as the perfect business site. Whatever you name this inland city that's actually part of San Diego proper, you'll find a bucketful of reasons why people live here.

Just off I-15, about 40 minutes north of San Diego, the community stretches out on both sides of the freeway. There are shopping centers, parks and golf courses, excellent medical facilities and a number of colleges. The University of California, San Diego, has a satellite center in the area.

The range of housing prices is extreme

and again depends on location. It tops at $1 million yet can go as low as $150,000 for a small, fixer-upper (if you can find one that someone is selling).

Condos average about $160,000, although there are not that many that go up for sale. You can figure that rental homes and apartments will begin at about $1,000 and skyrocket straight up if you're in the market for a six-bedroom, six-bath home on the 9th green with a back view of a private country club.

San Marcos, Vista and Bonsall

These "sisters" are happily connected by proximity. To the newcomer they seem to be very much alike, with planned developments, acres of roofs topping lowland and hillside alike and clustered areas of shops and malls. They are all family towns, where younger people are beginning their lives. Each is unique, however, and that's where your choices enter the picture.

San Marcos is home to the brand new California State University, San Marcos. The campus graces one of the hills just off California Highway 78. Having CSUSM in San Marcos will eventually provide the city with that college feeling and cultural activities. Right now everyone in the community is still getting used to saying all those initials — and also to the new civic center, increased traffic, and the change from a rural to a suburban environment.

Home prices in San Marcos average about $190,000 and in planned communities they can top out at about $500,000. Condos run at a little less (about $150,000). You'll have to look for houses and condos if you want to rent in this community; apartments are scarce.

Vista is more established than San Marcos. It has older neighborhoods, and if you're a handy person, you might just find a fixer-upper here. Recently a house in Vista, in an older part of town, sold for about $85,000. It needed a lot of work, but the asking price was right. The mid-range for resale homes is $185,000; new ones can be in the $350,000 bracket. Condos come with a price tag as low as $130,000. This is still a deal for North County, which is within twenty minutes of the coast.

Bonsall, connected to Vista on the south and Oceanside on the east, is spread out amongst winding roads meandering through groups of custom and owner-built homes. It has the feel of a backcountry town. People stable horse and farm animals, meet friends at the feed store, and then dash to work in their expensive 4X4 or foreign car. Home prices have actually dropped slightly in the area (no one can figure out why) and this year resale prices are in the $220,000 bracket. With that said, the newspaper recently featured an open house at a Bonsall resale. The asking price was $400,000 and included an ocean view (on a very clear day), three acres of land and a swimming pool. You won't find rental apartments or condos here; most dwellings in Bonsall are homes.

East County

Alpine

Unlike the other communities in East County, Alpine was a planned community (we're talking the planner of the late 1800s). It started in life as Viejas Stage Stop. The town originated when drivers hauled supplies to the mines in the Cuyamacas and returned with gold destined for San Diego. Further along, the Butterfield Stage line allowed passengers to get out at the stop and shake off some of the dust. As more people began passing through, more services came to the area.

Today Alpine remains where it started, but now there's an interstate highway, not a dusty trail, connecting it to the cities of San Diego. There's a cozy downtown with cafes and stores and friendly smiles on peoples' faces. And if you're searching for the perfect glamorous outfit or a fine wine or want to do some serious shopping (as in a huge mall), then you'll have to go down the hill and into San Diego or to one of the other communities in East County. That's what folks do in Alpine and don't think twice about the trip.

Resale homes range in price from $150,000 to $500,000 and as with other San Diego ranges, the wide spread occurs because of the amenities and locations. You may find a rental home in Alpine, but don't expect to find condos or apartments.

Julian and Ramona

Julian and Ramona are known for their quiet country, feel-good environments. While some folks live in Ramona and work in San Diego, few if any people commute "down the mountain" from Julian into the urban areas. In these towns you'll find sprawling ranches, quaint custom homes, and plenty of wide-open spaces. That makes the area especially attractive to people who like to spread their wings, and add some horses, hiking trails, and natural habitats to their estates. Houses are normally custom-built. The few condos you can find go for about $150,000.

Julian, of course, is known for the western-town atmosphere and not-to-be-missed apple pie. The town is tucked within Cleveland National Forest. It's a favorite community for artists, writers, crafts people and those who own the local establishments from bed and breakfast inns (there are more than 20 in town) to the pie shops and antique stores. Folks are friendly in Julian and enjoy knowing they live in a desirable area. When houses come up for resale, they carry a $250,000 to $300,000-plus price tag. New custom homes can easily exceed $1 million.

Think of a town in Wyoming, without the really big mountains and all that snow, and you have an idea of **Ramona**. With its annual dusting of snow and warm, dry summers, it's an ideal location for those who want to get just far enough away from it all. Within town are enough stores, services and shops for more than the basics of life. Yet if you need something special Escondido or San Diego are where you need to head. The city is over an hour from San Diego, and about 30 minutes from Escondido. Resale homes range from rambling ranch styles that might go for about $250,000 to new custom abodes that cost more than $500,000.

El Cajon, Lakeside and Santee

The cites of El Cajon, Lakeside and Santee are neighbors and have been linked since the founders of Mission San Diego de Alcala chose this valley area to graze cattle.

In more recent times they were thought of as bedroom communities to San Diego, but that's changed. Now they are thriving as younger families select these cities to put down roots. There's a feeling of renewed vigor, excitement and youthful energy. There are plenty of activities for kids and parents coordinated by local parks and recreation centers. There are parades and rodeos (see our Annual Events chapter about the Lakeside Rodeo), Easter egg hunts and outdoor music, arts and crafts festivals.

The housing ranges from modest to elaborate; prices follow along that range. You may find a home in a working-class neighborhood for about $130,000 and another that's been renovated right across the street for $300,000. Some Insiders believe that as more people come to San Diego, the reasonable homes will be snapped up before agents even put a sign on the lawn.

You will find condos and rentals in these areas, and these are especially attractive to those needing a place (with an okay commute) close to SDSU. Condos average about $100,000, and apartments, depending on the size, can be found for about $700 a month.

Jamul, Borrego Springs and the desert communities

Like Palm Desert did twenty years ago, the desert communities — including those of Jamul and Borrego Springs — could very well boom at any second. However, as some skeptics point out, that feeling has been around for a long time.

Tourists and snowbirds flock to the desert during the mild falls, wonderful winters, and delightful springs. Town people stay year-round and love that hot, dry desert air.

Home prices, when you can find one that's available for resale, are in the $220,000-plus bracket. Those who want to enjoy desert living normally purchase land and build their dream house. As for condos, as one Insider who wanted to find a winter home recently said, "Good luck!" Rumor had it that there was a condo for sale in Borrego Springs — just rumor mind you — and three people made offers and five more were trying to get their financial packets in order so they could do so, too.

La Mesa and Spring Valley

La Mesa and Spring Valley were once considered backcountry by those cosmopolitan settlers of San Diego and people who made homes along the coast. Nowadays, young families, retired people, students and professionals continue to go east to find their perfect homes.

It's a little-known bit of trivia that **La Mesa** was originally known as Allison Springs. Early settler and rancher Robert Allison purchased a part of the area to graze sheep. Then it was renamed La Mesa Springs, and finally in 1912, when it was incorporated as a city, the name officially changed to what we call it today.

The Native American name for **Spring Valley** was Meti. For a while the mission padres called it the Spanish equivalent to "The Springs of St. George." Finally, early farmer August Ensworth settled in the area. The story goes that he asked his young daughter for the perfect name and Spring Valley was born.

People continue to discover quality of life in East County and there's a good mix of housing here. With luck, one can still find an older home for about $150,000. Recently a three-bedroom, one-bath home in the business area sold for $125,000. Another newspaper ad featured a "Doll House," one-bedroom, one-bath home with an asking price of $90,000. Condos go for about the same.

Homes in family neighborhoods, near services, parks and schools, begin at $250,000. New development homes can easily be seen in the $300,000 to $500,000 range.

South Bay

Chula Vista and Bonita

Chula Vista is the second-largest city in San Diego County, with a population of around 153,000. It was originally part of El Rancho de la Nación, a huge area of land in the South Bay that was once part of Mexico but ended up as part of California when it was granted statehood. From the 1890s through the early 1900s it was known as the lemon capital of the world because the world's largest lemon orchard existed there. Nowadays it is a vital, bustling city.

Newcomers and longtime residents of San Diego are gravitating in increasing numbers to the developments in Chula Vista. Prices are usually more affordable, and the master-planned communities offer grand amenities for families. The EastLake development, for example, has a manmade lake, complete with sandy beaches, and a first-rate public golf course. Another master-planned community Otay Ranch, is in the early stages of development and promises to rival the appeal of EastLake. Housing prices vary widely. In the urban area of Chula Vista, prices are as low as $60,000 for a condo and $100,000 for a single-family home. In the outlying subdivisions like EastLake, Rancho del Rey and Otay Ranch, prices rise to as much as $200,000 for condos and $500,000 for houses.

City leaders lobby hard to entice new industry to Chula Vista, and recent years have seen the opening of a giant water park and an official Olympic Training Center. Both are bringing greater recognition to Chula Vista, as well as an increase in tourism.

Neighboring **Bonita**, an unincorporated area, has a gentrified rural atmosphere complete with horses, stables and an occasional farm animal. Residents of Bonita prize their detachment from city life and local politics, preferring the peace and quiet of country living. However, the benefits of the city are easily within reach. Chula Vista is just a short drive away. Houses are typically sprawling ranch style with larger than average lots that range from $190,000 to $575,000. Condominiums are generally in the neighborhood of $175,000.

Imperial Beach

Imperial Beach is the most southwesterly city in the continental United States. Its motto in the 1940s was "Where the sun and the surf spend their continuous honeymoon." A little outdated today, the motto is still not too far off the mark. Imperial Beach was first settled in the 1880s by a developer who intended it to be a beach resort for residents of the Imperial Valley, a desert community east of San Diego. Though it achieved that status, other people soon discovered its charm, and it now draws visitors from all over.

Today Imperial Beach is home to the world's biggest sandcastle contest (see our Annual Events chapter for details), which attracts amateur and professional sandcastle artists from all over the world to compete in the annual event. Beachfront condos sprinkle the shores, and folks from landlocked cities like to make Imperial Beach their home during the summer months. Its proximity to Mexico is a big attraction too. A self-contained, incorporated city, Imperial Beach has its own city council that attends to hot issues of the day. For the most part, though, the community tends to be laid back and casual, a mecca for surfers.

Condos range from $60,000 to $350,000 for beachfront properties. Houses range from $100,000 to $175,000.

National City

National City was the second established city in the county after the city of San Diego. It was founded and developed by the Kimball brothers, Frank, Warren, Levi and George. The brothers were the purchasers of El Rancho de la Nación, a 26,000-acre plot of land (of which Chula Vista was also a part). They laid out the town, founded a number of businesses and helped establish the olive and citrus industries. The houses the Kimball brothers built for their families were the first genuine houses in the county — the so-called houses in Old Town, in San Diego, weren't much more than four adobe walls with a crude roof. Some of the lovely mansions later built by the Kimballs still stand today.

Modern-day National City is a working-class town, with many of its residents employed by nearby National Steel and Shipbuilding Company. The city is also noted for its Mile of Cars, the largest concentration of auto dealers in the county.

Houses are modestly priced, ranging from $95,000 to $175,000. Condominiums are from $60,000 to $80,000.

San Ysidro, Otay Mesa and Nestor

San Ysidro and **Otay Mesa** are two southern communities that abut the U.S.-Mexico border. Thus their combined population of 59,000 includes a high proportion of Hispanic-Americans and many businesses that cater to shoppers who cross the border from Tijuana. The history of San Ysidro is unconventional. Most cities have a beginning that leads to a period of development, then a modern incarnation. San Ysidro started and stopped.

It began as a utopian colony founded by William Smythe in the early 1900s. Smythe named the colony Little Landers to reflect his philosophy of life. He believed that his group of land owners needed only enough land to raise food for their families and have a little extra to sell. Their motto was "A little land and a living." The colony was fairly successful until a flood in 1916 wiped out the farms. All that remains of Little Landers today is Smythe Avenue.

Recent years have seen lots of development in San Ysidro and Otay Mesa, both of which boast relatively new housing projects. Houses range from $135,000 to $160,000, and condos are in the $75,000 to $90,000 range.

Nestor is a community of just under 17,000. It, too, began as a farming community, only its residents were mostly Japanese. The Japanese farmers pretty much disappeared, though, during World War II when most were placed in internment camps. Today Nestor focuses on its schools. Its middle school and high school are invariably among the first to come up with new programs to stimulate young minds and encourage a love of learning. And community service is as deeply ingrained in residents of Nestor as is getting out of bed in the morning.

Housing prices start at $120,000 and go up to $200,000, while condos range from $75,000 to $100,000.

Shopping for a Home

By now you've probably figured out that real estate is of prime value in San Diego. So it should come as no surprise to learn that there are more than 8,000 Realtors, agents and brokers doing business around town. The commonly held theory is that every single resident of San Diego is either in the business himself or has a brother-in-law, a cousin or a buddy who is. Many companies are long established with excellent reputations. Others have a tendency to come and go.

If you're relocating to San Diego, we can suggest several ways to select a Realtor to best serve your needs. Probably the safest and most reliable route is to work with one of the national chains. They all have offices in every neighborhood, community, nook and cranny in the county, and if you call one of the relocation numbers listed below, you'll be hooked up with a Realtor who is intimately familiar with the areas you might be considering.

Otherwise, a referral from a friend is usually reliable. Or if you have your heart set on a particular neighborhood, we've included a list of a few long-standing independent agencies for each region. With so many from which to choose, it's obviously a buyer's market. So we strongly suggest you interview potential agents. Ask questions, find out about their standard policies and what they can do for you. It doesn't hurt to ask if their commissions are negotiable, too.

National Real Estate Offices

Century 21 National Referral Service
• (800) 4-HOUSES

Since the early 1970s Century 21 has saturated the country with its local offices with the intent of making home buying a happy and satisfying experience for its clients. With 26 offices and nearly 500 agents in San Diego County, Century 21 has become a major force in the real estate industry here.

Century 21 is the world's largest franchiser of residential real estate brokerage offices, thus their agents and brokers receive the very best in training, management, administrative and marketing support. If you call the number listed above, a friendly representative will provide a referral to a San Diego Century 21 office. The only hitch is that you need to know the zip code of your desired area. Alternatively, you can call any Century 21 office nationwide, and agents will be happy to help you find just the right office to suit your needs.

Coldwell Banker Residential Brokerage
• (800) 488-6683

Colbert Coldwell founded his company in 1906 after the San Francisco earthquake, mainly as a result of his disapproval of agents who were taking advantage of vulnerable homeowners. His philosophy was to place the customer's interest above all, and that philosophy remains the driving force behind Coldwell Banker today.

With 18 offices in San Diego County, the company is committed to making the real estate process easier and more accessible for everyone. If you call the number above, you will receive a home price comparison index as well as information about the area of your choice and a referral to a nearby agent.

Coldwell Banker has a long history of integrity, exceptional service and customer satisfaction.

Prudential California Realty
• (888) 888-7356, (619) 792-3885

With corporate offices in the North County Coastal community of Del Mar, Prudential California Realty is one of the main real estate players in San Diego. The company has nearly 30 offices countywide with more on the drawing board.

By calling the relocation information number above you can find the right agent to fit your special needs and one who speaks your personal language. You will also receive a free relocation packet that includes details about our region and average home prices. It also provides a good sketch of our neighborhoods.

As one of the perky and helpful information specialists says, "We like to provide counseling as well as home buying data. Our goal is to assist buyers to homes where they feel comfortable." With information like that, Prudential California Realty takes the mystery out of finding the right home for you.

RE/MAX Realtors
• (800) 227-3629, (619) 549-2700

With nearly 25 offices throughout the county, RE/MAX has more than 350 agents in our region. Each agent is determined to serve your needs and support San Diego. RE/MAX people are strong on community involvement and support volunteerism in the communities they serve. The type of involvement for a RE/MAX associate is as varied as the neighborhood he or she lives and serves. One might spend time with a scouting program and another help provide expertise with Habitat for Humanity.

Says Fred Christiansen, president of the RE/MAX Brokers/Owners Association of San Diego County, "Elbow grease is what it takes in today's world. It means rolling up your sleeves and plenty of shoe leather. RE/MAX agents believe that investing in our communities makes our neighborhoods better places to live, work and grow." Founded in 1973, the RE/MAX organization sells more property than any other firm with offices worldwide.

Local Real Estate Offices

San Diego

Willis M. Allen Co.
2904 Canon St., San Diego
• (619) 226-7800
1131 Wall St., La Jolla
• (858) 459-4033
1424 Camino del Mar, Del Mar
• (858) 755-6761
6024 Paseo Delicias, Rancho Santa Fe
• (858) 756-2444

Since 1914 Willis Allen Co. has been serving San Diego's real estate needs, specializing in the coastal areas of Point Loma, Pacific Beach, La Jolla, Del Mar and Rancho Santa Fe. More than 100 agents combine to make Willis Allen San Diego's most prestigious firm

specializing in luxury properties. The company is also the exclusive affiliate of Sotheby's International Realty.

Carol Carol Real Estate
4108 Adams Ave., San Diego
• (619) 281-2000

A veteran of the real estate industry since 1985, Carol Carol opened her own office in 1991 in the Kensington area. Carol specializes in Kensington, Talmadge, Normal Heights, University Heights and North Park, but also covers other San Diego areas. You can rest assured that she will represent you well. "I will only work in an area if I feel I know enough about it to be helpful to my client," Carol says. In addition to helping folks with their real estate needs, she has made a lasting impression in Kensington and the surrounding neighborhoods. Whenever a community problem arises, Carol serves as the liaison between residents and the city council.

Thomas Realtors
3941 Utah St., San Diego
• (619) 296-6343

Hal Thomas and his energetic agents have been placing happy buyers in their dream homes since the late 1960s. His office is located in North Park, and although he started out specializing in that neighborhood and its surrounding communities, Hal has since branched out to cover most of San Diego, even some South Bay neighborhoods. "We're here to serve," says Hal. And serve he does, as is evidenced by the fact that much of his business consists of referrals from satisfied customers.

United Realtors, Inc.
9330 Mira Mesa Blvd., San Diego
• (858) 578-8181

"We are #2; our clients are #1." So says United Realtors owner Richard Higgins who, along with his 10 agents, specializes in the neighborhoods of Mira Mesa, Rancho Peñasquitos, Poway, Scripps Ranch and much of the greater San Diego area. Matching clients with the perfect house for their needs has always taken precedence over simply making a sale, and the staff at United Realtors make the search for a home a pleasant one.

Ursula K. Younie Co.
7817 Herschel Ave., La Jolla
• (858) 454-3023

Since the early 1950s the Younie Company has been assisting homebuyers and sellers in San Diego County. Owners Larry and Barbara Anderson have been at the helm since 1978 and are committed to matching the perfect house with the perfect buyer. The Andersons and their 22 agents specialize in properties in La Jolla, Bird Rock and Point Loma, but occasionally branch out into other neighborhoods such as Del Mar, and Rancho Santa Fe.

North County Coastal

Dyson and Dyson Real Estate Associates
437 S. Hwy. 101, Solana Beach
• (858) 755-0500

This locally owned agency specializes in properties of all shapes, sizes and prices in Carlsbad, La Costa, Solana Beach, Del Mar, Fairbanks Ranch, Rancho Santa Fe, Carmel Valley, and La Jolla. Dyson and Dyson has a long-time reputation within the county as one of the leading independent agencies. With a strong team commitment to those who are buying another home or are relocating to our area, the agency's goal is to match a client with the perfect home. Sometimes it's a home for retirement or leisure and sometimes it's for a young, energetic family that needs plenty of room and a big back yard.

Back to the Basics Real Estate
609 W. Vista Way, Oceanside
• (760) 721-8700
245 E. Vista Way, Vista
• (760) 726-4841

Bill Aldredge and Doreen Northway, partners in Back to Basics, are in the real estate business for the long run. Bill and Doreen deal with a plethora of listings, and treat every client like an ESP (Extra Special Person). "We work to find out what people want and need in a home," explains Bill. The partners ask plenty of questions, from what the client considers an okay commute to their particular need for special schools and services. Bill says, "We're here for clients 110 percent, and our clients always come first. We strive for a great match between a home and our clients."

Barksdale Properties, Inc.
1116 S. Coast Hwy., Oceanside
• (760) 722-6161, (800) 722-6161

As a broker for more than 22 years, owner Paula Barksdale and her ultra-conscientious staff are committed to customer service. They know that part of the job includes educating buyers regarding the current market. The office handles properties throughout San Diego, and they know North County Coastal extremely well, with listings that run from new track-development homes to mobile homes.

Barbara McLain Properties
2715 Carlsbad Blvd., Carlsbad
• (760) 434-6161

A true Insider, Barbara McLain has been in the area more than 28 years and her knowledgeable staff includes those specializing in beachfront and vacation property. The company feels especially gratified when clients return because of relocation or the acquisition of rental properties.

Ranch and Sea Realty
6965 El Camino Real, Carlsbad
• (760) 929-8585

Eric Waite, owner and broker, and his staff of 60 hold down the four offices of this Insider's real estate agency. People turn to Ranch and Sea because of the strong one-on-one commitment to clients. Specializing in North County Coastal property, you'll see Ranch and Sea's signs on homes up and down the coast. Locally owned, and with Eric's strong Insider's ability to do business in San Diego, the agency supplies quality services time and again.

North County Inland

Selitsch Properties
1215 E. Vista Wy., Vista
• (760) 758-9420, (800) 828-3528

"With this climate people who are relocating to San Diego County are sold before they come," says Kathy Selitsch, who is a partner with husband, John, at Selitsch Properties. The company has been in Vista for more than 20 years. The professionals at Selitsch have seen lots of changes with home buying and home building at the top of the list. The 11 agents know North County Coastal and North County Inland and handle listings from ranch property to homes in our retirement communities.

Hidden Meadows Realty
10320 Meadow Glen Way E., Escondido
• **(760) 749-4640**

Allen and Jean Hemphill are cheerleaders when it comes to this tiny, upscale community of 1,100 custom homes. Allen says, "We're a mom and pop operation, with old-fashioned determination to please clients." Hidden Meadows, as Allen points out, is located directly above Lawrence Welk Village, technically in the county of San Diego, but with an Escondido address.

When people find this area, with its exclusive golf course, they say, "Whoa, how do I get a house here?" and Allen, Jean and the four agents of Hidden Meadows Realty help them do just that.

Real Estate Market
1660 E. Mission Rd., Fallbrook
• **(760) 728-5878**

Judy and Arnold Hogarth are partners in the first real estate office you'll see as you drive into this North County Inland community. These Insiders have been in the business 13 years. Judy explains, "We get a lot of walk-in clients. These are people who love Fallbrook and just want to see if it's possible to move here." The good news is that Judy, Arnold and their staff of six can make it happen. "Affordable housing and lots, some 4-acre parcels well within reach, are still available."

High Point Realty
1875 E. Valley Pkwy., Escondido
• **(760) 743-5755**

Gary M. Weiler and his staff of seven have been with High Point Realty since 1977. Insiders all, the team specializes in North County Inland properties with knowledge about all areas of San Diego. "We really enjoy working with first-time buyers and with the services here in house, we can help young families and those who are relocating to get into that perfect home."

Panda Realty
13715 Poway Rd., Poway
• **(858) 748-8850**

Linda and Arthur Bell are partners in Panda Realty and in marriage. Along with their staff of five agents, they focus on properties in the Poway and the North County Inland area. Linda says, "While fewer houses are available in Poway — because so many people want to live in this Insiders' neighborhood — there is property for sale. We can help connect people to their perfect house or dream lot and work with them toward achieving that dream house." Linda further explains that "Most clients who come into Panda are already pre-qualified for loans or ask that the red tape be taken care of immediately." In today's market, as most agents agree, it pays to be ready.

East County

Sprague Realty
2110 Main St., Julian • (760) 765-0035

In business for over 30 years, Sprague Realty has five agents who are actively interested in their own community. People turn to Sprague. The company handles listings in and around Julian. The agents at Sprague want to know what you want. Then they can work with you to make a dream come true.

Western Realty
2226 Alpine Blvd., Alpine
• **(619) 445-6201**

Broker and owner Skip Harned has owned Western Realty since 1972. People settle in East County after visiting or seeing the mountains, ranches, and extra space. Some also decide on the spot to buy or exchange their current home for one in the area. "That's what I enjoy most — the exchanges," says Skip, and says that sometimes it can be as complicated and fulfilling as playing a big board game. Others on the Western Realty team of six specialize in ranches, mountain retreats,

Photo: James Blank/San Diego Convention and Visitors Bureau

Folks who settle in Coronado commute to downtown San Diego across the graceful San Diego-Coronado Bay Bridge.

residential property and custom homes. All members specialize in customer satisfaction.

South Bay

All City Realty
660 Telegraph Canyon Rd., Chula Vista
• (619) 421-1300

"All City says it all," according to owner Michael Joseph. "Even though we specialize in the South Bay, we send people up north too." When he says "up north" he means to North County. Michael is proud of the fact that All City staffers are relocation specialists as well as local real estate experts. Since 1978 All City's staff has been covering ever larger areas; they now sell homes in Chula Vista, Otay Mesa, Imperial Beach and National City.

Colwell Realty
134 Palm Ave., Imperial Beach
• (619) 423-2444

Since the late 1970s Kenneth Colwell has been using his real estate expertise to match homebuyers with their dream homes. When people get a glimpse of Imperial Beach and like what they see, they usually gravitate to Ken's office. Ken and his staff concentrate their efforts in Coronado, Imperial Beach, parts of Chula Vista and South San Diego. The company motto is "Helping you make your move," and you can count on Ken to make it as easy on you as possible.

Homes International
4045 Bonita Rd., Ste. #11, Bonita
• (619) 421-9000

Owner Carlos Lopez has been assisting home buyers all over the South Bay since the mid-1980s, especially in Chula Vista and Bonita. Integrated into his business is a strong philosophy of community first, a sentiment incorporated into the company logo. Carlos and his staff are dedicated to helping students. For every house sold by Homes International, $250 is donated to a scholarship fund. Additionally, you'll often find Carlos planting trees around the South Bay to help beautify the community. Homes International is a full-service agency that will fulfill your real estate needs, and a plus is that you'll feel good about doing business with a company that does so much good for the community.

San Diego Real Estate Group
4308 Vista Coronado Dr., Chula Vista
• (619) 427-9000

"The client is the top priority," says San Diego Real Estate Group owner Larry Williams. Larry, his wife, Sue, and their seven agents have been serving the South Bay since 1987. They've built their reputation and their business the long, hard, slow way. According to Larry, sometimes that's meant passing up the big money, because for him it's been more important to have a satisfied client. They're perfectionists when it comes to finding just the right home for their buyers.

Apartment Hunting

Just as you can find magazines to help you buy a home, so can you find guides to help you rent an apartment. Located in the same places as home buyers guides — racks in supermarkets, drugstores and convenience stores — these free guides will give you an idea of how the rental market stacks up in San Diego County.

Apartments For Rent
9682 Via Excelencia, Ste. 100, San Diego
• (858) 530-2295

Serving all of San Diego County, *Apartments for Rent* is published every two weeks. It is broken down by region and features full-color photos of apartment complexes around the county. The guide also has a comprehensive list of amenities and restrictions of each complex (it will tell you for instance, about pet policies). It also includes contact phone numbers and maps. When it comes to driving time, this guide can be a big time-saver.

San Diego ApartmentNet
2425 Camino del Rio So., Ste. 230,
San Diego • (619) 682-5470

Within the first few pages of this monthly guide is an all-inclusive map that clearly details the regions of San Diego. The apartment listings that follow are broken down by these specified regions and include amenities, rental rates and contact phones. The guide also has a section on short-term rentals and furniture rentals.

Homebuying Magazines

Even if after digesting all our neighborhood descriptions you still feel in the dark about San Diego real estate, a good way to get a feel for what's out there is to pick up one of several free magazines or guides. They all have photos, descriptions, prices and referrals to real estate agents. Look for the following magazines in racks at the front of most supermarkets and drugstores, and some convenience stores too.

Harmon Homes
9682 Via Excelencia, Ste. 100, San Diego
• (858) 689-7381

Broken down into several editions by region, this twice-monthly magazine features resale properties with thumbnail descriptions and photos. Each property also has a referral to the listing agent.

Homebuyers Guide
17780 Fitch, Ste. 195, Irvine, CA
• (949) 476-3055

A monthly publication that covers all of Southern California, the *Homebuyers Guide* is restricted to new developments. A color photo of a model accompanies each description, along with an area map, contact phone number and price range.

San Diego has more than 600 public schools, some 300-plus private schools, and scores of community colleges, colleges and universities.

Education and Child Care

Education is as essential to residents of San Diego County as a healthy dose of outdoor activity. While that might oversimplify our need for it and commitment to it, we're sincerely proud of the opportunities that exist for those in search of knowledge.

Sure, the rare curmudgeon will say the entire system is headed you-know-where and in a you-know-what. But rather than focus on what's wrong with education in San Diego County, parents, teachers, and students find that there's lots that's right.

To give you a quick sketch of our educational system, consider this: There are more than 600 public schools, some 300-plus private schools, and scores of community colleges, colleges and universities (which we describe in our Higher Education chapter). Now factor in the educational programs that range from Platt College's architectural drafting and computer graphic-design classes to the College of Food-San Diego's cooking, baking and fine-dining classes, and it won't take any "book learning" to see the diversity of instruction, education and training San Diego offers.

Child care is also an issue close to the hearts of San Diego residents and we wish we could tell you we have answers to working-parents' quandaries. Like our co-workers in every part of the nation, we're faced with the fact that sometimes there are no perfect choices for the care of our kids. We've tried to provide resources to get you started, however, in your hunt for safe, happy day care and after-school programs, which we assure you can be found in San Diego. We've included a couple of special camps for kids too.

Education

Public Schools

Under the authority of the San Diego County Office of Education, 6401 Linda Vista Road, San Diego (858- 292-3500), there are about 600 public schools, kindergarten through 12th grade. That number grows each year as more people are drawn to our perfect climate and excellent school system.

The breakdown of schools is impressive, too. There are independent study schools, special education schools (a selection that addresses special needs from learning challenges to hearing impairments). And there are alternative schools and continuation schools for students who learn best outside the traditional high school environment

Each year more than two-thirds of all graduating seniors go on to higher education. The number is never exact, since some seniors take classes and work part-time or return to college after working for a year. For a complete look at the opportunities for higher education in San Diego County, be sure to read our Higher Education chapter. Many high school seniors attend our community colleges. Others focus on our excellent colleges and universities, often referred to as "alphabet soup," with school acronyms from CSUSM and USD to SDSU and UCSD.

Quite a number of San Diego's learners seek out other educational arenas such as the no-cost programs offered by the Office of Education. Non-traditional students seem to be everywhere these days as they learn new skills or retrain in another career. Classes offered by the Regional Occupation Program (ROP) help these students pursue myriad educational choices. (Call 858-292-3611, or stop by one of the campuses listed in the gray box.)

ROP courses are diverse. Sure, they include the expected computer skills and welding. But you can also learn about media production, auto engine performance, cabinetmaking, the travel industry, grocery operations, dog and cat grooming, international trade and fashion design. ROP may be one of the best educational bargains in San Diego. The classes are free. Some courses require a small materials fee. Some classes are held during the day; quite a number are evening classes. Lots of San Diego adults and high school students take ROP classes for the joy of learning new things.

Regarding the basics of education, the good news is that San Diego students are doing well. Our students' Stanford Achievement Test scores may not be as high as some districts', but that's by no means an indication that our schools aren't working. Many of San

www.insiders.com

See this and many other **Insiders' Guide®** destinations online.

Visit us today!

Diego's students are just beginning to learn English, so that's reflected in the tests. And some students are disadvantaged too, which always presents challenges for any school district. In spite of this, the county's 11th graders outperformed the national average in history. And San Diego County's students fluent in English generally outperformed their counterparts elsewhere in the state and country. Second through eighth-grade students, however, were lower than the national average in spelling, a result which, once again, probably reflects socioeconomic and language factors. Looking at results reflecting individual districts, based on the test, the districts of Rancho Santa Fe, Del Mar and Carmel Valley were in the top 10 percentile. Printed copies of test scores per district are available by contacting the San Diego County Office of Education and individual school districts.

The results from this statewide, systematic testing were put under a microscope, correlated and compared. The end results went beyond, "Gee what do we do with these numbers?" Administrators and teachers instead said, "Let's set goals and achieve them." Many school districts, including San Diego Unified, the state's second-largest school district with 167 campuses, have done just that. Their objective is to eventually judge students, teachers and principals, not by test scores, but by overall change and improvement. They hope to raise scores in 2000 and 2006, but they know that they can't just focus on scores.

Test scores and rating of districts are only numbers. As Solana Beach Superintendent Ellie Topolovac, recently said, "It's one indicator, but it's not the total picture. Some children can be brilliant, but they just don't test well."

Photo: Scripps Institution of Oceanography, UCSD

Educational opportunities abound for these San Diego youngsters learning about sea life firsthand at the Stephen Birch Aquarium-Museum.

The consensus with the "report card" on our schools is that social variables not only complicate the test results but the actual testing as well. This conspires against making true district-to-district or school-to-school comparisons.

If you'd like to know more about the public schools in the area in which you're thinking of living, make an appointment with the school's principal or the district's superintendent. And for a listing of public schools in your area, look under "Schools" in the Yellow Pages. You can find a specific school by name in the White Pages of the phone directory.

Private Schools

In San Diego there are more than 300 private educational opportunities. The choices range from the tiny type, with two or three students, to those with worldwide prestige.

As in many other larger cities and regions, the vast majority of San Diego's private schools focus on specific religious beliefs. For example, nearly every Catholic parish in San Diego has an elementary school, which in turn is affiliated with a Catholic high school. If you're interested in religious schooling for your kids, contact your pastor or the advisor for your church or synagogue. Tuition varies a great deal, according to the size of the facility, its location, courses and staff.

In addition to those schools with a religious affiliation, there are about 10 other well-respected private schools here in San Diego. These private kindergarten-through-12th-grade schools are all college preparatory. These private schools can only be described as on the high side of expensive. The price tag sometimes exceeds $6000 for a child to attend a private elementary school for one year.

Most parents in San Diego County are comfortable sending their children off each day to one of our public schools. For one thing, San Diego is not one of those cities where many parents feel that private schools are a necessity. Besides, most of the private schools are out of financial reach for San Diego parents. So here we give you just a sampling. Check the Yellow Pages under Schools for other private schools.

Army-Navy Academy
2605 Carlsbad Blvd., Carlsbad
• **(760) 729-2385, (800) 762-2338**
The Army-Navy Academy is a distinguished North County Coastal military school. The

Academy is right on the beach and about 4 blocks north and east of the Coaster commuter train station in downtown Carlsbad. A year-round boarding school, the Academy's students number about 250 boys in the seventh through 12th grade program. Students come from every corner of our globe and right from Carlsbad, too. Instruction is diverse and intense, and yes, students wear military-style uniforms. Included in the curriculum is an award-winning ROTC program, honors programs, English as a second language program, full athletics and a 14:1 student to teacher ratio. Ninety-five percent of the Army-Navy Academy graduates go on to college; many attend one of the military academies like West Point.

La Jolla County Day School
9490 Genesee Avenue, La Jolla
• (858) 453-3440

A co-ed school, the respected La Jolla County Day, as it's known to Insiders, has an enrollment of about 1,000 students, kindergarten through 12th grade. This is a college prep school. After graduation, it's likely that its students will go on to notable universities like Harvard, MIT and Stanford.

Montessori East County Preschool and Kindergarten
10017 Maine Ave., Lakeside
• (619) 561-0902
Montessori American
3604 Bonita Rd., Chula Vista
• (619) 422-1220
Mission Bay Montessori Academy
2640 Soderblom Ave., San Diego
• (619) 295-7591

For the younger crowd, Montessori schools are sprinkled throughout the county. All the schools are privately owned, so curriculum varies. The Montessori East County Preschool and Kindergarten has 12 students; Montessori American, a kindergarten only, has 27 students, and the Mission Bay Montessori Academy is a K through 6th grade private school with nearly 300 students.

Vocational and Technical Schools

We'd be lax if we didn't point out some of the outstanding private vocational and technical schools in San Diego. Here are a few to give you a taste of what you can find if you're looking for specialized education. For a complete list of technical and vocational schools, consult the Yellow Pages under Schools. Remember, if you're looking for technical and vocational programs, review the cost-free possibilities with ROP, mentioned above; ask plenty of questions; and talk to graduates before spending your money.

The Advertising Arts College
10025 Mesa Rim Rd., San Diego
• (858) 546-0602

Devoted exclusively to advertising, graphic design and computer arts, TAAC offers traditional four-year bachelor's degrees, three-year associate degrees and professional certificates. Among the more than 60 courses in the curriculum are broadcast copywriting, multimedia design, graphic design visualization and general education classes in sociology, psychology and ethics.

Many students already have jobs in advertising and want to improve their skills, while others attend to develop a career in the field. Students develop ad campaigns in class, and their work is critiqued by other students and professors. Facilities include fully equipped classrooms, video cameras and monitors, still cameras, audio recording equipment, visualization systems, duplication machines, scanners, printers computers and transfer stations.

California College for Health Sciences

222 W. 24th St., National City
• (619) 477-4800, (800) 221-7374

Although based in San Diego County, this college has been a leader in distance education since 1978. It offers certificate programs specifically designed to meet the needs of working adults in the healthcare field, including certificates in healthcare ethics, polysomnography, business essentials, community health education, gerontology and health psychology. Associate of science degrees are offered in respiratory technology, respiratory therapy, electroencephalography and allied health.

In addition, bachelor of science degrees can be pursued in either the School of Health Sciences or the School of Business, and a master of science degree is available in community health administration and wellness promotion. More than 7,000 students are enrolled nationwide, and independent study schedules are personalized for each student. Faculty members and student advisers are readily available to assist students. California College for Health Sciences is accredited by the Accrediting Commission of the Distance Education and Training Council.

California Culinary Academy College of Food — San Diego

5504 Hardy Ave., San Diego
• (619) 229-6480, (800) 229-2433

At San Diego's branch of the California Culinary Academy, students are trained in the basic knowledge of kitchen skills. The curriculum is designed to cover all the skills the food industry requires, including safety and sanitation, tasting, chopping, carving, baking and complete navigation of the kitchen.

Courses include such comprehensive subjects as flavor recognition, knife skills, stocks and soups, sauces, breakfast cookery and many more.

The San Diego campus offers a certificate of basic professional culinary skills, which can be completed in 24 weeks on a full-time basis, or in 44 weeks on a part-time basis. The certificate is fully transferable into an 18-month associate of occupational studies degree program at the San Francisco campus. Faculty members at the San Diego campus are all distinguished industry professionals with years of experience and outstanding credentials and awards.

California Institute for Human Science

701 Garden View Ct., Encinitas
• (760) 634-1771

The California Institute for Human Science, an accredited postgraduate university, is committed to scholarly excellence in the training of holistic practitioners/scientists in the disciplines of general psychology, human science and clinical counseling psychology. It provides graduate level education and training services.

Founded by the distinguished Dr. Hiroshi Motoyama, the institute's unique offering of diverse graduate programs is designed to prepare the mature graduate student to contribute meaningfully as a professional and a scholar in the emerging global society.

The California Institute for Human Science has daytime, weekend and evening courses and workshops, many of which are accredited for Continuing Education Units (CEU's) for healthcare professionals.

Coleman College

7380 Parkway Dr., La Mesa
• (619) 465-3990
1284 W. San Marcos Blvd., San Marcos
• (760) 747-3990

Founded in 1963 to support the then just budding computer industry, Coleman College has established itself as a resource and cornerstone of private technical education in San Diego. Classes are small, typically about one instructor to 10 to 15 students, often less. The

San Diego Regional Occupation Programs

The programs offered at these locations range from computer skills training to landscape management. Not all locations run the same programs, so call for a catalogue. You may also be able to find catalogues at a public library.

East County ROP Center
181 Fletcher Pkwy., El Cajon • (619) 579-8323

Escondido High School
3750 Mary Ln., Escondido • (760) 739-7309

Metro ROP Service Center
6735 Gifford Wy., San Diego • (858) 627-7208

Oceanside Instructions Center
2080 Mission Ave., Oceanside • (760) 439-5534 X 767

Palomar Community College
1140 W. Mission Ave., San Marcos • (760) 744-1150

Poway Unified District
13626 Twin Peaks Rd., Poway • (858) 679-2560

Ramona High School
1401 Hanson Ln., Ramona • (760) 788-5015

South County ROP Service Center
1355 2nd Ave., Chula Vista • (619) 691-5611

Southwestern College
900 Otay Lakes Rd., Chula Vista • (619) 482-6377

Vista Adult School
305 E. Bobier Ave., Vista • (760) 758-7122

coursework is intensive. Classes are held in the day and evening and start-up cycles occur often. Coleman's innovative curriculum gives career training first so students can become qualified for a computer-related position in a matter of months. Longer programs include those for associate's, bachelor's and master's degrees.

Programs include computer information science, computer engineering technology and computer applications and networks. The college also has a placement service for graduates and those seeking part-time employment while studying at Coleman.

Contractors Licensing Service
340 Vernon Way, Ste. C, El Cajon
• (619) 440-2122

Contractors Licensing Service, established in 1965, provides exam preparation programs. There are on-campus classes, home-study programs and even crash-course curriculum. In addition to the educational segment, their services include, but are not limited to, send-

A young San Diego student prepares to board the school bus.

ing in student forms to the state and weekly progress checks with the state to ensure a timely issuance of licenses.

Design Institute of San Diego
8555 Commerce Ave., San Diego
· (858) 566-1200, (800) 619-4337

This college is devoted exclusively to education in interior design and is accredited by the Foundation for Interior Design Education

Research as well as the Accrediting Council for Independent Colleges and Schools. Founded in 1977, the institute provides students with a broad understanding of the profession, developing creative, technical and analytical skills while at the same time providing an understanding of the historical and social foundations of design. Students also learn the practical aspects of business.

The faculty consists of practicing interior

designers, architects, artists, historians, environmental psychologists, lighting designers and a multitude of other professionals who augment the design industry. The four-year program offered leads to bachelor of fine arts in interior design. Facilities include high-tech, spacious classrooms, drafting studios, exhibition spaces, computer lab, lighting lab, sample room and media center.

Fashion Careers of California College
1923 Morena Blvd., San Diego
• (619) 275-4700

Students interested in a career in the fashion industry can obtain a certificate or a specialized associate of arts degree in either fashion merchandising or fashion design here. The curriculum includes internships and study tours to New York and Los Angeles, and as part of the program, students work on fashion shows and other outside activities in the fashion industry in San Diego.

Certificates in either merchandising or design can be obtained in one academic year; associate of arts degrees take two years. Students receive hands-on training from top professionals and are out in the fashion world making contacts while they're students. Credits earned at the college are fully accepted at major colleges for the applied arts throughout the country.

Kelsey-Jenney College
201 A St., San Diego
• (619) 233-7418, (800) 734-4625

Since 1887 Kelsey-Jenney has been preparing students with the knowledge and skills that enable them to qualify for entry-level careers in business, industry, and the medical and legal fields. The instruction is job-oriented, designed to develop the highest level of language, business and technical skills. Accredited by the Western Association of Schools and Colleges, the college offers degree programs in accounting, administrative assistance, business management, legal secretarial work, paralegal studies, medical assistance, court reporting and computer networking technology.

Courses may be taken during the day or in the evening at either the downtown campus or the northern campus at 7310 Miramar Road, San Diego. Students are required to complete course work in general studies in addition to their chosen field.

Pacific College of Oriental Medicine
7445 Mission Valley Rd., Suite 105, San Diego
• (619) 574-6909, (800) 729-0941

As interest in holistic medicine and practices becomes more widespread, folks are pursuing academic knowledge to become practitioners themselves. Accredited by the National Accreditation Commission of Schools and Colleges of Acupuncture and Oriental Medicine, this college offers a wide variety of degree and diploma programs at its San Diego campus. Students can study to become a master of traditional oriental medicine, holistic health practitioner, massage therapist, massage technician, Oriental body therapist, Chinese health exercise specialist and many more.

The college offers flexible scheduling for working adults, and students can take courses at either the San Diego campus or at the sister institute in New York. The New York campus offers a diploma of acupuncture in addition to the same course offerings in San Diego. Tours and consultations are always welcomed.

Palomar Institute of Cosmetology
355 Via Vera Cruz, San Marcos
• (760) 744-7900

A cosmetology and manicurist school, stu-

INSIDERS' TIP

In the recently conducted Stanford Achievement Test, called the Stanford 9, San Diego County public school students came out within 10 percentile points of the national average in virtually all subjects and grades.

dents here study and prepare to pass the State Board Examination. The goal of the school is to provide all students with the knowledge they'll need to be highly employable. Potential occupations that are available after completing the courses include hair stylist, facialist, manicurist, make-up artist, and cosmetic and beauty product representative.

In addition, Palomar Institute of Cosmetology provides a teacher trainee program. The program is suited for those who are already licensed cosmetologists and want to train to teach in a school of cosmetology.

Platt College
6250 El Cajon Blvd., San Diego
• (619) 265-0107

Platt College provides comprehensive, professional education programs and associate of applied science degrees in computer graphic design, multimedia, drafting technology and architectural drafting. One of the college's primary goals is to help students find careers related to their field of study, so they maintain an active Placement Assistance Program for their graduates.

In the graphic design program students learn form, color, typography and the development of design skills. Multimedia is an extension of the graphic design program, in which students apply the technical knowledge and creative skills they've acquired in the integration of text, illustrations, photos, sound, voice, animation, music and video on computer. The drafting technology and architectural drafting programs combine knowledge of manual drafting and computer-assisted drafting training.

Rawhide Vocational College
W. Lilac Rd., Bonsall
• (760) 758-0083

Here's a California, state-approved, two-year college for anyone who has the horse-sense to be crazy about horses. Rawhide Vocational College has classes in horsemanship, practical veterinary medicine, farm and ranch management, horse science, breeding, teacher training, animal science, practical animal management, farm shop and Christian education. About 50 students are in the study program during the traditional school term.

The campus, which looks like a real cowboy-style western town, is located about 45 miles from downtown San Diego. You'll find a library and dormitories and all the college trimmings here as well as more than 130 head of high-quality quarter horses. The goal of the college is to prepare men and women, in a Christian atmosphere, for leadership and the responsibilities of ranch and camp management. Further, the goal is to help students attain high-level skills in horsemanship, horse training, horse science, stockmanship and camp recreation. The successful graduate will be employable as a riding instructor, professional horse trainer, livestock director or manager of an equestrian center.

Travel Experts Training School
3505 Camino del Rio S., #220, San Diego
• (619) 281-4333

Travel and tourism is one of San Diego's largest industries, offering an abundance of career opportunities. At Travel Experts Training School students can study to become travel agents, tour operators, flight attendants, airline representatives, and reservationists for the hotel, cruise, rail and car rental industries. Since 1976 the school has provided the facilities and resources necessary to train students in theoretical knowledge and practical skills in their chosen field.

All faculty members are trained professionals in the field in which they teach. Among the classes offered are world geography, worldwide rail transportation, cruises, airline computer training and worldwide tours and land arrangements. The school is accredited by the California Council for Private Postsecondary and Vocational Education.

University of Humanistic Studies
380 Stevens Ave., 210, Solana Beach
• (858) 259-9733

University of Humanistic Studies (UHS) students and graduates often call the university "the school for second lives." The administration is proud of that title.

Having achieved success in other careers, students come to the accredited UHS for new or renewed direction and a second life. Most desire a way to evolve into a new person and a bigger person. At UHS, one can work to-

This youngster is admiring the elephant lights at the entrance to
the San Diego Wild Animal Park.

ward a bachelor of arts in Humanistic studies. Students can enroll in a master's program for marriage, family and child counseling; sports counseling; and leadership development. Some are working toward doctorates in psychology, philosophy and sports psychology. The university also offers degrees or certificates in areas such as Expressive Art Therapy and Tibetan Buddhist psychology.

UHS was started in 1989 as a low-cost counseling resource for the community and an internship/practicum site for university students. Today students come from all over the country for the unique, focused coursework. There are day, evening and weekend classes to accommodate the working schedules of adults. UHS provides a humanistic education emphasizing personal development, maturity and wisdom equally blended with technical and professional skills. The university teaches the concepts of humanistic philosophy and acknowledges the individual's capacity for choice, self-healing and spirituality.

Child Care

To make child care concerns and questions a bit less overwhelming, we've done part of the legwork for you. Securing appropriate child care for the kids of working parents is a personal issue. You know your child better than anyone, so we haven't composed a list of what we think would be good choice for child care, daycare or home care. Instead we provide some resources for making choices and mention just a few almost universally accepted facilities you may want to contact.

As you review the choices for child care, whether from the phone book or one of the giveaway magazines found at the grocery store, it's crucial to check references, make impromptu visits, and ask plenty of questions. Of course, you'll want to do all this before you leave that little one in anyone else's care.

If your child requires individualized attention or special medical care, you may want to talk with your pediatrician, healthcare provider or school district. They may be able to make referrals.

The San Diego County Family Child Care Association is another source of information. You can contact them at (760) 736-2598 to get information on providers. To find out about licensed day care in your area, you can call the help info line of California State Community Care Licensing Board (858) 467-4388.

Religious and academic private schools often have extended day-care programs. A number of YMCA's in San Diego (see our chapter on Kidstuff) provide after-school activities for kids for a fee. You can reach the YMCA Childcare Resources Service at (800) 481-2151 or (619) 521-3055. Some school district elementary schools also provide this service.

Here on vacation or a business trip and need help caring for kids?

If you're wondering how to keep the kids happy and safe while you're doing business and enjoying San Diego, the first step to the care issue may be a talk with the concierge or reservations desk staff member. Often hotels, resorts and spas have contacts with licensed and bonded babysitters and nannies (see our Spas and Resorts chapter). Some resorts have "camps" with special kid-style activities.

For instance, the Four Season's Resort Aviara, 7100 Four Seasons Point in Carlsbad, (760) 603-6800, has a Kids for All Seasons program, offered during the weekends, summer months, traditional school breaks and holidays. About $30 pays for a day of fun with supervised activities and nature hikes, a kids' pool, indoor playroom and a teepee for storytelling time. All of the staff members are CPR certified.

The Commodore Kids Club, at Loew's Coronado Bay, 4000 Coronado Bay Road, Coronado, (619) 424-4416, has supervised programs for kids ages 4 to 12. Activities include arts and crafts, Ping-Pong, board games and movies. The cost is $40 for each child. Evening care facilities are available for $25 per child.

All of San Diego's universities are deeply involved in the surrounding community, and they never hesitate to exchange ideas and resources among themselves.

Higher Education

Almost without realizing it was happening, San Diegans took a look around one day and discovered that the area had quietly turned into a remarkable enclave for higher education. Anchored by three major universities — San Diego State University (SDSU); the University of California, San Diego (UCSD); and the University of San Diego (USD) — the educational scene comprises more than 50 institutions for higher learning. Rapidly gaining in stature are Point Loma Nazarene University and California State University, San Marcos, both of which will soon be considered major universities themselves. Also multiplying in number are several well-respected business colleges. And finally, dozens of trade, technical and vocational schools (which we cover in our Education and Child Care chapter) round out the higher education scene. It's really no wonder that so many fine institutions have sprung up in San Diego. After all, it's a piece of cake to draw students. The combination of excellent academics and the San Diego lifestyle is irresistible.

San Diego State University is the granddaddy of them all, established as the Normal School in 1897 by the California Legislature. It moved to its current site on Montezuma Mesa in 1931, where it evolved into the dominant liberal arts university it remains today. It's younger brothers and sisters do not suffer by comparison, though; they enhance its presence with their different focus and programs.

The university community is a crucial component of San Diego's industry. The majority of students stay put after they graduate, and they are the future of the county's business and industry. Working hand-in-hand with the local scientific community, UCSD produces the next generation of high-tech, biotech and engineering talent so desperately needed. With its first-rate law school, USD keeps the legal community filled with talented lawyers. All the universities are deeply involved in the surrounding community, and they never hesitate to exchange ideas and resources among themselves. For example, The three majors established a library consortium to trade books among their students. When a student at one university requests a book from another, it is usually delivered the same day. This spirit of cooperation makes for a better educational experience for all.

In this chapter we'll give you an Insider's look at the major universities, the up-and-coming institutions, the colleges geared toward working adults and the excellent community colleges. We'll also talk about extended studies programs affiliated with the universities, where adult students with or without degrees can enhance their knowledge and skills or par-

INSIDERS' TIP

If you're planning to attend a San Diego State University football game at Qualcomm Stadium, make sure you're wearing the traditional Aztec colors: red and black.

ticipate in certificate programs. Unless otherwise specified, all colleges are accredited by the Western Association of Schools and Colleges.

Keep in mind that we're giving you the best-known and most well-established colleges here. Plenty more await you, and if the ones described here don't fill your bill, there almost surely is an institution around town that will be perfectly tailored to your needs.

Four-year Universities and Colleges

California State University, San Marcos
Barham Dr., San Marcos,
• **(760) 750-4000**

The new kid on the block in San Diego County, CSUSM opened its doors to students in the fall of 1990 as the 20th campus in the 23-campus California State University system. Nestled in the foothills of North County Inland, the 304-acre campus is home to some 4,700 students who attend one of three colleges: Arts and Sciences, Business Administration and Education. The university is growing rapidly — by design. Projected student enrollment by the year 2020 is more than 18,000.

The three schools at CSUSM offer 19 majors, 14 teacher-credential programs and 7 master's degree programs. The average age of the students is about 25. Of the 170 faculty members, 91.8 percent have a doctoral or terminal degree. The university is just starting to field some athletic teams, beginning with track and field, and within the next few years should be competing in many of the major sports.

Chapman University
7460 Mission Valley Rd., San Diego
• **(619) 296-8660**

Chapman University is the seventh oldest university in California. An independent liberal arts college, it is composed of the Wilkinson College of Letters and Sciences and six schools: the School of Business and Economics, the School of Communication Arts, the School of Education, the School of Film and Television, the School of Music and the School of Law.

The university offers more than 40 fields of undergraduate study, graduate study programs and teacher-credential programs in a unique 10-week term format. Geared toward working adults, many classes are offered during lunchtime, evening hours and Saturdays at its Mission Valley headquarters and five other locations around San Diego. Chapman makes a point of catering to the military population in San Diego and gives credit for military training and experience. About 1,000 students are enrolled in Chapman's San Diego locations.

Christian Heritage College
2100 Greenfield Dr., El Cajon
• **(619) 588-7747, (800) 676-2242**

Tucked away at the base of Shadow Mountain in East County's El Cajon, Christian Heritage College has a liberal arts curriculum. Founded in 1970 with a Christian-oriented mission, learning in all CHC's academic programs is biblically focused.

In addition to its halls of learning, the 34-acre campus has playing fields and a swimming pool for intercollegiate and intramural sports for men and women students. Christian Heritage has more than 20 undergraduate academic programs, including Aviation Technology, Sports Medicine and Biblical Studies to augment the more traditional disciplines. Because of its small student population of approximately 560, individualized attention is the norm. The student-teacher ratio is 15 to 1.

National University
4121 Camino del Rio S., San Diego
• **(619) 563-7100, (800) 628-8648**

Based in San Diego, National University has 20 campuses throughout California, nine in San Diego County alone. Its enrollment of 11,300 full-time equivalent students makes it the third largest private university in California. National offers a one-course-per-month format for both undergraduate and graduate programs, with most classes held in the evenings and on Saturdays. The average age of students is 34. Sixty-eight percent are gradu-

University of San Diego

For decades the University of San Diego has been known around town as "that little Catholic college up on the hill." For a long while that was a relatively accurate assessment. It isn't any longer. That little Catholic college has grown up into a major university, and each year, USD gains in stature nationwide, consistently ranking in the top 100 on *U.S. News & World Report*'s annual ranking of institutions of higher learning.

Close-up

Officially chartered by the State of California in 1949, USD began as the vision of Bishop Charles Francis Buddy. Newly consecrated as Bishop of the Diocese of San Diego in 1937, the bishop visited his friend and colleague, Mother Rosalie Hill, superior vicar of the San Francisco College for Women. He shared with her his dream of inaugurating a Catholic college in his new diocese and hoped that she and the Religious of the Sacred Heart would join him in his quest.

Mother Hill eagerly accepted the challenge. By 1944 they were surveying sites, finally settling on a stunning piece of property in Linda Vista. The property, situated on a long mesa at the west entrance to Mission Valley, consisted of more than 100 acres overlooking Mission Bay, Old Town and historic Presidio Hill, where Father Junipero Serra established his first mission in California. Bishop Buddy and Mother Hill named the site Alcalá Park, in honor of San Diego de Alcalá; the university had come one step closer to reality.

The two were committed to building two separate colleges, the College for Men (which included the School of Law as well as a seminary) and the College for Women, but agreed that, to provide social interaction, the two colleges should remain close to one another. When Mother Hill began looking at designs, she decided that the architecture should be an adaptation of Spanish Renaissance because of its lasting appeal, its softness of detail and its widespread use throughout California. From the beginning to the present, all campus buildings have remained true to the Spanish Renaissance architectural style, a tradition that has resulted in unparalleled beauty and a proud heritage for the college.

Ground was broken in 1948, and the first classes in the College for Women were held in 1950. The two colleges remained separate for two decades, but began allowing reciprocal course registration in the late 1960s. Finally, encouraged by Vatican II, the College for Women and the College for Men merged in 1972 to become the University of San Diego.

In the nearly three decades that have passed since the merger, the university has grown with lightning speed, gaining in reputation and recognition throughout the United States. Today USD draws students from around the world

Spanish Renaissance architecture is faithfully adhered to in University of San Diego buildings.

— continued on next page

who are in search of an education that combines superior academics with a strong philosophy of values and ethics. Complementing the academic side of life at USD are strong intercollegiate and intramural athletic programs, campus ministry, fraternities and sororities, clubs and organizations and a committed and wide ranging community-outreach program.

During the 1996 U.S. presidential campaign, USD received national exposure when it played host to one of the candidate debates. Those who watched the debate, which was televised live internationally, saw a beautiful campus and a flawless production. The preparations, however, were far from matter-of-fact. Shiley Theater, the venue for the debate had to be gutted. New seats were added, air conditioning had to be installed, and at the last minute, the stage had to be extended to accommodate the debate's town hall format. Most interesting were the special alterations made in the theater and around campus to allow the Secret Service to effectively protect the candidates. University President Alice Hayes admitted she was a little nonplused by the prospect of snipers on the roof, but she dealt with the all the anomalies of the debate with style, grace and practicality. And in the end, all the preparations paid off. The debate went off like clockwork, and USD got a gold star and national acclaim for its role as the perfect host.

Today, as visitors walk down Marian Way through the center of campus, the beauty of the buildings, the plaza and fountain, and the lush landscaping are almost more than the senses can absorb, particularly against a backdrop of the crystal blue waters of Mission Bay and the Pacific Ocean beyond. But a few moments spent talking with USD's students will reveal that the university means much more to them than beautiful surroundings and a panoramic view. For them, USD means an opportunity for a values-based educational experience, one that enriches their personal growth as well as their minds. In this achievement, USD has been wildly successful. And the little college on the hill has now become a jewel in the crown of higher education in San Diego.

ate students and 32 percent are undergraduate students.

Founded in 1971, the university is committed to adult learning in a convenient and practical way. New courses begin each month, so students can enroll at any time during the year. Its headquarters are in Mission Valley, but learning centers and campuses are spread throughout the area, with three located on military bases. Three schools — the School of Management and Technology, the School of Education and Human Services and the School of Arts and Sciences — offer more than 40 undergraduate and graduate degree programs, and 11 teaching credentials.

Point Loma Nazarene University
3900 Lomaland Dr., San Diego
• (619) 221-2273

Founded in 1902 as Pasadena College, Point Loma Nazarene University moved from Pasadena in 1973 to its current location atop the bluffs of Sunset Cliffs on the Point Loma peninsula. After the move, the college changed its name to Point Loma Nazarene to reflect its new location. The campus spreads over 90 acres, all with a breathtaking view of the Pacific Ocean. Founded in 1902, PLNU now has an enrollment of more than 2,500 undergraduate and graduate students from all across the United States and 25 foreign countries.

The University, an institution of the Church of the Nazarene, offers liberal arts curriculum in an environment of Christianity in the evangelical and Wesleyan tradition. Undergraduate degrees in 60 major fields of study are available, plus several pre-professional programs and graduate degrees. Of its faculty, 72 percent have doctoral degrees. Point Loma Nazarene has a variety of extracurricular activities including clubs and organizations, fraternities and sororities, campus ministries and intercollegiate athletics for men and women students. The student-faculty ratio is 15 to 1.

San Diego State University

College Ave, north of Montezuma Rd.,
San Diego • (619) 594-5200

Part of the California State University system, SDSU celebrated its centennial in 1997. Belying its reputation as one of the top party colleges in the country, SDSU's academic excellence is nationally recognized.

It is the largest institution of higher learning in San Diego, with a student population of more than 30,000 and an average student age of 25. Located atop Montezuma Mesa on the eastern border of the city limits, the campus occupies more than 4.5 million square feet in 44 academic buildings, including the new 320,000-square-foot Malcolm A. Love Library. Although SDSU is considered a teaching university, it has strong research programs too: Faculty members receive $60 million yearly to conduct research programs.

Seventy-four undergraduate-degrees are offered; there are also 54 master's and nine doctoral programs. Further emphasizing the university's pursuit of academic recognition is the presence of five multi-disciplinary honor societies on campus: Golden Key, Mortar Board, Phi Beta Kappa, Phi Eta Sigma and Phi Kappa Phi.

Complementing the academic side of education are the outstanding varsity athletic programs. Ten of the 17 intercollegiate sports have been ranked in the nation's top 20 since 1980. Aztec teams have won national championships in volleyball, track and field, basketball and football. The new Tony Gwynn Stadium, funded by San Diego Padres' owner John Moores, opened for Aztec baseball in 1997, and Aztec basketball has a new home, too, in the Cox Arena, a facility that seats 12,000.

Most Insiders feel pride of ownership in San Diego State University, whether they're alumni or not. Locals flock to the campus for concerts, lectures or to use the library. And on game day, everyone is an Aztec.

University of California, San Diego

Gilman Dr. and La Jolla Village Dr.,
La Jolla • (858) 534-2230

San Diego State University may be the most well known college in town, but there's little doubt that UCSD is the most prestigious. The scenic campus overlooking the Pacific Ocean consistently ranks in the top 10 in the nation among public colleges and universities according to *U.S. News & World Report*. The university boasts a faculty that includes five Nobel laureates and a former astronaut, and has state-of-the-art research facilities. It attracts the highest caliber students too. Approximately 95 percent graduated in the top 10 percent of their high school class, with an average GPA of 3.9 and average SAT scores of more than 1,200.

The university consists of five colleges: Eleanor Roosevelt College, Earl Warren College, Thurgood Marshall College, John Muir College and Revelle College. Each college has its own philosophy, general education requirements and staff, but students may pursue any major at each of the colleges. Eighty-four undergraduate majors are available along with more than 30 graduate programs. Additionally, six joint doctoral programs are offered in conjunction with San Diego Statue University.

The student population is about 15,000 in the undergraduate colleges and approximately 2,500 in graduate programs. Students at UCSD average just over four years to degree, a rarity these days, and the student-teacher ratio is 19 to 1.

Because of UCSD's close ties to San Diego's high technology, wireless communication and biomedical industries, its students have an advantage in securing internships, summer jobs, graduate school and careers. Triton intercollegiate teams have won several national championships, and more than 60 percent of students participate in intramural sports. Social, athletic and leadership oppor-

INSIDERS' TIP

Make a point of visiting the Founders Gallery at the University of San Diego to see exhibitions by community, student and alumni artists. Open to the public, the gallery is located in Founders Hall on the USD campus.

tunities include 200 student clubs and organizations.

University of San Diego
5998 Alcalá Park, San Diego
• **(619) 260-4600**

A private Catholic institution, USD sits on a 180-acre hilltop campus overlooking Mission Bay. The university offers a liberal arts curriculum and is known for its commitment to teaching, values-oriented programs and community involvement. More than 50 undergraduate and graduate degree programs are available to USD's 6,600 students, including doctoral programs in education and nursing. Five schools comprise the university: the College of Arts and Sciences, the School of Business Administration, the School of Education, the Philip Y. Hahn School of Nursing and the School of Law (see School of Law entry that follows).

International study programs in England, France, Germany, Italy, Spain, Mexico and Japan are increasingly popular among USD's students, as are on-campus ROTC, Freshman Preceptoral and Paralegal programs. Ninety-seven percent of faculty members have a doctoral or terminal degree, and the student-faculty ration is 18 to 1. Sixteen intercollegiate sports are available along with dozens of club sports and intramurals.

Law Schools

California Western School of Law
225 Cedar St., San Diego
• **(619) 239-0391**

California Western began as a small law college called Balboa Law College in 1924. Located in downtown San Diego. It was accredited by the American Bar Association in 1962 and admitted to the Association of American Law Schools in 1967.

The student population totals more than 700, the student-faculty ratio is 16 to 1. An average of 80 percent of California Western's students pass the bar exam on the first attempt. Special programs include a Center for Child Advocacy, a Center for Study of Telecommunications Law, a Clinical Internship Program, an International Legal Studies Program,

an Institute for Criminal Defense Advocacy and a Sports and Entertainment Law Program.

Thomas Jefferson School of Law
2121 San Diego Ave., San Diego
• **(619) 297-9700**

Founded in 1969, Thomas Jefferson School of Law is a private, independent law school whose mission is to provide legal education to a diverse array of students. The campus is located in Old Town and consists of two Spanish-style buildings that overlook San Diego Harbor. In 1996 the law school received provisional accreditation from the American Bar Association, which affords its students all the benefits of an ABA-approved law school.

Dedicated to individualized instruction, class sizes at Thomas Jefferson average fewer than 30 students. Faculty and administration recognize that law school is a stressful experience, thus they provide maximum accessibility and many support services to help provide students with the necessary skills to successfully complete their course of study.

Special programs include a Judicial Internship Program that permits students to clerk for federal and state judges, and Field Placement Programs that provide opportunities for working with attorneys in public agencies. Thomas Jefferson offers a three-year, full-time or a four-year, part-time program.

University of San Diego School of Law
5998 Alcalá Park, San Diego
• **(619) 260-4528**

Founded in 1954, USD School of Law is accredited by the American Bar Association and is a member of the Association of American Law Schools and The Order of the Coif, the most distinguished rank of American law schools. The law school offers degrees of juris doctor and master of laws. Additionally, joint degree programs are available in conjunction with USD's graduate schools: a master of business administration, a master of international business and a master of arts in international relations.

The student population is approximately 1,100, and both full-time and part-time programs are offered. The full-time program requires 3 years for completion; part-time stu-

Photo: Thom Vollenweider

This futuristic structure is the library at the University of California at San Diego.

dents usually need four years of evening study plus one summer to complete the degree.

The Center for Public Interest Law at USD is an academic center for research, learning and advocacy for the disadvantaged or underrepresented in state administrative proceedings. Likewise, the Children's Advocacy Institute is a legal advocacy and research center that promotes the health and well-being of California's children. Yet another special program at the law school is the Patient Advocacy Program, which works to ensure the rights of the mentally disabled.

Community Colleges

San Diego's community colleges often serve as an intermediate step between high school and university. They usually offer two-year associate degree programs along with specialized certificate courses and vocational studies.

Grossmont-Cuyamaca Community College District
8800 Grossmont College Dr., El Cajon
• (619) 644-7010

The district includes both Cuyamaca College and Grossmont College, which offer custom contract courses for foreign nationals in addition to its traditional programs. The district works with overseas groups to design courses that fulfill their specific educational goals, including English language courses and introduction to American culture.

Cuyamaca Community College
900 Rancho San Diego Parkway,
El Cajon • (619) 660-4000

Opened in 1978, Cuyamaca offers a comprehensive curriculum of lower division courses and academic preparation for transfer to any of the California State University or University of California campuses. It also has a variety of technical-vocational, engineering and other professional programs and general education courses.

Cuyamaca College's 165-acre campus is located on a scenic hillside east of San Diego. The college serves about 4,500 students in daytime, evening and Saturday classes. Additionally, Cuyamaca offers Telecourses, which are delivered via cable television.

Grossmont Community College
8800 Grossmont College Dr., El Cajon
• (619) 465-1700

Officially opened in 1961 with classes held at a local high school, Grossmont College moved into its permanent quarters in 1964.

The 135-acre campus in El Cajon is characterized by its open landscape and abundance of trees, which create an environmentally pleasing setting for its 16,000 students.

Like Cuyamaca, Grossmont offers dozens of associate-degree, certificate and transfer programs. Students here benefit from additional programs: student services, which provides academic and vocational support; and learning resources, which supports and supplements instructional programs. Grossmont also has a community continuing education program.

MiraCosta Community College
1 Barnard Dr., Oceanside
• (760) 757-2121 (Oceanside Campus)
3333 Manchester Ave., Encinitas
• (760) 944-4449 (San Elijo Campus)

Opened in 1964 to serve the educational needs of North County Coastal students, MiraCosta's Oceanside campus is located on a 168-acre hilltop site with panoramic views of the Pacific Ocean to the west and the mountains to the east. Seventeen miles south is the San Elijo campus, 48 acres nestled below the bluffs and overlooking the San Elijo Lagoon reserve. The Oceanside campus has a student population of 6,000, and about 3,000 attend classes at the San Elijo Campus. Approximately 1,000 students alternate between the two.

MiraCosta offers freshman- and sophomore-level courses in preparation for transfer to a four-year university. Transfer agreements are established with most California public universities, including UCSD, SDSU and CSUSM. Also offered are dozens of certificate job-training courses as well as associate of arts degrees.

Both campuses offer diverse organizations, clubs and activities along with intramural and some intercollegiate sports.

Palomar Community College
1140 W. Mission Rd., San Marcos
• (760) 744-1150

Serving North County Inland, Palomar's 200-acre San Marcos campus houses up-to-date classroom and laboratory facilities, the largest research library in North County, a planetarium, athletic playing fields, the Boehm Art Gallery, the 400-seat Brubeck Theatre, a Wellness/Fitness Center and a 47-acre arboretum. In addition to its phenomenal facilities, Palomar was named by the Community College Journal as one of three flagship community colleges in the United States for its emphasis on learning.

More than 25,000 students take classes at the main campus, over the Educational Television channel and at several Education Centers throughout North County. Students may choose from more than 130 associate degree and certificate programs as prelude to transfer or for vocational preparation. Palomar also offers foreign language immersion programs in Cuernavaca, Mexico; Costa Rica and Paris.

San Diego Community College District
3375 Camino del Rio S., San Diego
• (619) 584-6960

All three of the colleges in the San Diego Community College District, City College, Mesa College and Miramar College, have transfer agreements with the University of California, the California State Universities and other universities and colleges as well.

San Diego City College
1313 12th St., San Diego
• (619) 230-2400

Occupying four square blocks on the outskirts of downtown San Diego and next door to its namesake, San Diego High School, City College is the oldest community college in the San Diego District. Serving some 12,000 students, the urban campus offers an array of two-year associate degrees and certificate programs. Emphasis is on vocational studies.

The City Knights compete in intercollegiate baseball, basketball, cross country, soccer, volleyball and tennis. City College is distinguished by its on-campus radio station, KSDS-FM, San Diego's only 24-hour jazz radio station. The station won the Marconi Award for Excellence in Radio in 1993.

San Diego Mesa College
7250 Mesa College Dr., San Diego
• (858) 627-2600

Among the largest community colleges in the nation, the 24,000-student campus of Mesa

San Diego State University's Aztec football games draw fans from
all over San Diego County.

College is situated in the geographic heart of San Diego, in Kearny Mesa. Sprawled over 104 acres, the college offers more than 70 degree and certificate programs, and has one of the highest student-transfer rates among the 106 community colleges in California.

Special programs include a comprehensive array of allied health programs in dental assisting, medical assisting, physical therapist assisting, radiological technology and animal health technology. New curricula in biotechnology and biochemistry have been recently introduced, and a new Learning Resource Center, complete with the latest computer technologies, opened in 1998.

San Diego Miramar College
10440 Black Mountain Rd., San Diego
• (858) 536-7800

Opened in 1969 on 120 acres of undeveloped land north of what was then the Miramar Naval Air Station, Miramar College initially concentrated on law enforcement and fire science training. It has since broadened its curriculum to include the same general education requirements as its sister colleges, City and Mesa, to better serve its student enrollment of more than 10,000.

Miramar is approved by the office of Private Post-secondary Education for the training of veterans, as well as by the U.S. Department of State and the U.S. Immigration Service for international student education.

Southwestern Community College
900 Otay Lakes Rd., Chula Vista
• (619) 421-6700

The jewel of South Bay, Southwestern College was established in 1961, and construction was completed in 1964 on its 156-acre campus in eastern Chula Vista. Over the years the college has evolved into a facility that serves a diverse range of educational needs for its 17,000 students, including preparation for transfer, pursuit of two-year associate of arts degrees, courses for personal development and job enhancement, and acquisition of new occupational skills.

Specialized programs include hazardous material handling, emergency medical services training and new electronic and manufacturing technologies. Because of its closeness to the U.S.-Mexico border, Southwestern provides special focus on the maquiladora industry (bi-national manufacturing enterprises), importing/exporting regulations, international law and foreign trade zones.

Extended Studies Programs

All three public universities in San Diego County offer outstanding extended studies programs for individuals pursuing professional certificates, university course credits, professional development or just general knowledge and information. The mission of extended studies programs is to fulfill the lifelong knowledge and skill-development needs of individual citizens, businesses and the community at large. Classes are usually geared toward working adults and are held at flexible times during the day, evenings and weekends.

California State University, San Marcos, Extended Studies
Foundation Classroom Building,
CSUSM Campus, San Marcos
• (760) 750-4020

Among the highlights of CSUSM's extended studies program are community education courses, workshops and seminars. The American Language and Culture Institute here

---

INSIDERS' TIP

Campus tours of UCSD are available from Monday through Saturday at 11 AM. Stroll through the peaceful environment surrounded by eucalyptus trees, and be sure to see the extraordinary artwork, such as the mosaic snake pathway that leads to the library, an architectural wonder in itself. Call (858) 534-1935 for tour reservations.

holds intensive classes for international students wishing to pursue an education at American colleges and universities. At the Open University, students can take regular university classes without going through the formal admission process. Online courses are available, too.

San Diego State University College of Extended Studies
Gateway Center, SDSU Campus, San Diego • (619) 594-5152

San Diego State's extended studies program specializes in professional and executive development and training for some of San Diego's leading organizations. It also offers certificate programs in which participants become recognized specialists in a variety of fields. Unique among extended studies programs is SDSU's program for retired adults. The American Language Institute offers intensive English language courses. Telecourses and Internet courses are also widely used.

University of California, San Diego, Extended Studies and Public Programs
Extension Complex, UCSD Campus, La Jolla • (858) 534-3400

In addition to the main extension complex on the UCSD campus, the extended studies program offers classes at three other locations in La Jolla and one in Rancho Bernardo to serve North County residents. Programs at UCSD Extension focus heavily on the telecommunications industry, information technologies, teacher education, applied healthcare, business management and international languages. In addition to those specialized fields, a wide variety of general courses are available. Online courses are increasing in popularity too.

San Diego is one of the nation's leaders when it comes to trauma care.

Health and Wellness

Emergencies happen. Even the best-planned vacation or business trip can be interrupted by a visit to a doctor or hospital emergency room.

When relocating, it's always a challenge to find the right medical assistance for ourselves and our families. In this chapter we'll provide some help in locating the services you may sometime need. Keep in mind that this chapter is not comprehensive. There are nearly as many healthcare centers in San Diego as there are parks, beaches, and shopping centers. The ones we present are representative of what's out there.

A great feature of San Diego is its diversity of healthcare and wellness facilities. According to a study conducted by the Northwestern National Life Insurance Company, San Diego receives high marks on access to healthcare. We have more than 75 healthcare facilities and hospitals in the county, and all our major hospitals have intensive-care and critical-care units. We also have six specifically designated trauma centers. That means when serious trouble hits, according to trauma specialists, you can be at a trauma center in minutes. In fact, San Diego is one of the nation's leaders when it comes to trauma care.

San Diego is unique in that its trauma centers work together with the County Division of Emergency Medical Services to create a true system. That system, which coordinates the efforts of physicians, hospital staff and county health officials, was put together in 1984, and was immediately successful: The county trauma death rate dropped by 55 percent in the first year. And according to Mike Casinelli, executive director of the Trauma Research and Education Foundation, (headquartered in San Diego) it "reduced preventable deaths from a 1982 high of 21 percent to less than 1 percent today." Mike points out that our system is often referred to as "the finest in the nation."

The San Diego Trauma Care System consists of the County Department of Health Services, the Division of Emergency Medical Services, other pre-hospital providers and those six trauma centers: Children's Hospital and Health Center, Palomar Medical Center, two Scripps Hospitals, Sharp Memorial Hospital and UCSD Medical Center.

So to say you're in good hands in San Diego is a truism. And our expert care isn't limited to emergencies. Insiders take health seriously and as the county has grown, so has the variety of treatments available. These are offered not only by our small but sophisticated facilities, but also by state-of-the-art hospitals. Scripps Hospitals are major research centers and provide the best, most innovative care available in the United States. The Scripps HealthCare System is a benchmark for care in the area.

At Fallbrook Hospital, a smaller facility in North County Inland's community of Fallbrook, not only will you get high-tech treatment, but you may be paid a special visit during your stay. Fallbrook Hospital is one of the county's facilities that encourages visits from therapy pets (with a human volunteer). Whether your special visitor is a golden retriever or a calico cat, there's nothing like a visit from a pet to speed healing.

Our county also offers excellent mental health facilities, alternative medical care, walk-in facilities and drug- and substance-abuse treatment centers. You'll want to check the Yellow Pages in the telephone directory under your specific need. The sections on home healthcare, mental health, physical therapists, nurses and nursing registries as well as clinics and care for the disabled will help you find services. In this chapter we've included the major healthcare facilities, including information on mental healthcare, hospice programs, and alternative care. The hospitals are listed alphabetically by region. The sections on mental health, hospice and alternative care are a countywide overview.

Hospitals

San Diego

Children's Hospital and Health Center
3020 Children's Way, San Diego
• (858) 576-1700, (800) 788-9029

Opened in 1954, Children's Hospital's mission continues: to "restore, sustain and enhance the health and development potential of children." It is now the region's only designated pediatric trauma center and the only area hospital dedicated exclusively to caring for kids, birth through adolescence.

Out of the 292 licensed beds, 24 are designated as Pediatric Intensive Care and 33 as Neonatal Intensive Care. The staff of 700 physicians serves about 10,000 inpatients and 200,000 out-patients each year. The facility includes Pediatric Intensive Care and Neonatal Intensive Care.

From its 12 outpatient clinics to the hospital in Kearny Mesa, Children's Hospital serves all the communities in the area. It is also active in numerous outreach programs including health education, early intervention and counseling for drug and alcohol abuse, childhood immunizations, child-abuse prevention and child safety issues. In partnership with other community-based organizations, like the Greater San Diego Chamber of Commerce and the Safe Kids Coalition, the hospital sponsors the Children's Center for Healthier Communities for Children, which links San Diego families with the educational tools and community services they need to raise healthy kids. Children's Hospital also works with local schools, businesses, government and law enforcement agencies.

A recent addition to the hospital is the Leichtag Family Healing Garden. The elements of hope and beauty and life are represented in this garden, which is designed to provide a blend of integrative wonder and peaceful respite. The garden is available to patients, children, parents and staff.

Kaiser Permanente Medical Care Center
4647 Zion Ave., San Diego
• (619) 528-5000, (619) 528-3290 (directions to county facilities)

Centrally located in San Diego, this medical center serves those who belong to the Kaiser Permanente group. Here and at various other Kaiser facilities in the county, members can access treatments for anything from addictions to women's health problems. Although there is a Kaiser Hospital in El Cajon, patients go to the Zion Avenue facility for any care that

---

INSIDERS' TIP

The AIDS Foundation maintains a toll-free number for questions and assistance. They can be reached at (800) 600-AIDS.

requires a stay in the hospital. There are about 400 beds in this large hospital.

Other Kaiser facilities have pharmacies on campus; check the white pages of the phonebook. The one at the Zion Avenue hospital, however, is open seven days a week. This hospital also features a well-staffed emergency facility where patients are treated for life-threatening and non-life-threatening needs. As we go to press, there's rumor that a fully staffed Kaiser Hospital may be built in the North County.

Scripps Hospital, La Jolla
9888 Genesse Ave., La Jolla
• (858)457-4123

Scripps Hospital has been in its present location since 1964 and now includes a huge array of high-tech medical options and services. Many believe that the Scripps Hospital healthcare system is the finest in the country. It's by far the most extensive health provider in the county. For instance, Kaiser Permanente subcontracts with Scripps Hospitals for various services, such as cardiac treatments and surgical procedures, rather than performing the procedures at their facility. Scripps is also part of the Trauma System. Recently, all medical professionals at Scripps facility were linked to a new Lifesaver Nurse Call that keeps track of the personnel and makes them available to patients within an instant. The facility has more than 1,500 employees, including 719 physicians and 614 nurses. Six hundred volunteers also help Scripps provide the best of care. The 600-plus bed facility is located on a 43-acre campus in the heart of the Golden Triangle area of San Diego

Sharp Cabrillo Hospital
3475 Kenyon St., San Diego
• (619) 221-3400

Sharp Cabrillo serves the beach communities of San Diego with a full range of services. Opened in 1958, the 300-bed facility has more than 540 affiliated physicians providing 24-hour emergency services. In 1996 the hospital linked its clinical serves with Sharp Memorial.

At the Chest Pain Center one can drop in just to check if those pains are indigestion or a more serious concern. That's an important function for visitors who might not know where to turn, especially if they have heart-related concerns. There's home health and hospice care along with services for seniors, from wellness checks to fitness classes.

Sharp Mary Birch Hospital for Women
3003 Healthcare Dr., San Diego
• (858) 541-3400

Opened in 1992, this hospital provides services for women in all stages of life. In a single location and with more than 300 beds, the hospital, which has its own pharmacy, focuses on complete care, including normal and high-risk obstetrics, laboratory and diagnostic testing for women and infants, and in- and outpatient gynecological care. It is known for its Sharp Fertility Center and the services of the Sharp Perinatal Center, an ambulatory center for women experiencing high-risk pregnancy. The hospital continues to be recognized nationally as one of five similar facilities dedicated to women's care.

Sharp Memorial Hospital
7901 Frost St., San Diego
• (858) 541-3400

With more than 500 beds, Sharp Memorial on Frost Street is Sharp HealthCare's largest hospital. As one of San Diego's trauma centers, it handles more than 1000 trauma cases annually. Also a provider of cardiac care, each year it performs 2,000 cardiac cauterizations, 800 angioplasties and 480 cardiac surgeries.

Opened in 1955 and staffed by more than

INSIDERS' TIP

Local Talk, with directions for use found in the front of the Pacific Bell Yellow Pages phonebook, includes short recorded messages about medical and health issues. When calling within the local area, the phone call is free.

1,100 physicians, it is especially known for outstanding programs in cardiac care, trauma care, cancer treatment, pulmonary-care services, rehabilitation and multi-organ transplantation.

Memorial also offers extensive outpatient care and prevention programs. Its Sharp Senior Health Center offers health groups and services for seniors.

Sharp Coronado Hospital
250 Prospect Pl., Coronado
• **(619) 522-3600**

This 204-bed acute care hospital was established in 1942 and continues to serve the Coronado community. The hospital has four operating rooms, an intensive care unit and a 24-hour emergency room. It provides obstetrical services, sub-acute and long-term care, and rehabilitation therapies.

The Motion Center, a state-of-the-art fitness facility, provides therapy and fitness programs for patients, outpatients and the community. In addition to operating the Villa Coronado skilled nursing facility, the hospital also offers senior services such as skin cancer screening, mature drivers' courses and health-education classes.

North County Coastal

Scripps Hospital, Encinitas
354 Santa Fe Dr., Encinitas
• **(760) 753-6501**

This state-of-the-healing-arts hospital joined the Scripps Health system in 1978 with nearly 200 beds available. The hospital's staff includes over 600 trained professionals. You'll also find a caring team of more than 300 volunteers. Within the campus are licensed acute-care beds and sub-acute (skilled nursing) beds to provide extensive care for in- and outpatients.

Tri-City Medical Center
4002 Vista Way, Oceanside
• **(760) 724-8411**

Three years in a row, Tri-City Medical Center, in North County Coastal was ranked among the nation's top 100 hospitals. This 300-bed facility at the Oceanside center includes an around-the-clock emergency room to provide on-the-spot care and dispense life-saving procedures. The hospital's location makes it especially convenient to freeway travelers.

North County Inland

Fallbrook Hospital District
624 E. Elder St., Fallbrook
• **(760) 728-1191, (800) 647-6464**

The Fallbrook Hospital District, a 146-bed healthcare organization, has served the people of Fallbrook, Bonsall, Rainbow, Deluz and Temecula Valley since 1950. It provides both high-tech care and loving high-quality caring, to North County Inland residents.

The staff calls it "a hospital without walls," since it offers home-health nursing, a hospice program, private home services, and a nurse-monitored walking regimen (part of their Cardiac Rehabilitation program). At the hospital proper, you'll find a women's center and services, a skilled nursing facility, and radiology, oncology and emergency programs. You'll also find active volunteers who bring a pet-therapy program to patients.

Palomar Medical Center
555 E. Valley Pkwy., Escondido
• **(760) 739-3000**

Located in the heart of Escondido this 299-bed acute-care hospital boasts North County's only trauma center. In addition, it has a 24-hour emergency department and the area's first state-of-the-art cardiac, oncology and gen-

---

INSIDERS' TIP

If you or a family member must go to the emergency room, call ahead to let them know you're coming and the reason for the visit. To find the one nearest you, check the Yellow Pages under "Hospitals."

eral medical/surgical center. The Birth Center offers mothers high-tech medical care in private suites.

This facility is part of the Palomar/Pomerado Health System and shares certain services with Pomerado Hospital. Among them are radiology services, a hospice, and an industrial medicine program. Palomar Medical Center is also a designated Kaiser Permanente emergency center.

Pomerado Hospital
15615 Pomerado Rd., Poway
• **(858) 485-6511**

A 109-bed acute care hospital located in the rapidly growing Poway area, this hospital has a round-the-clock emergency center. Along with the fine medical and surgical care, the hospital provides the kind of caring atmosphere not found in some mechanized hospital settings. Pomerado shares a healthcare board with Palomar Hospital; the two facilities share radiology and hospice services, healthcare boards and an industrial medicine program. This facility is part of the Palomar/Pomerado Health System.

Some medical staff at the University of California at San Diego are involved in ongoing research programs.

East County

Grossmont Hospital
5555 Grossmont Center Dr., La Mesa
• **(858) 465-0711**

Affiliated with Sharp HealthCare, this is the largest and most comprehensive hospital in East County. Grossmont has been serving the community more than 40 years and currently has more than 300 beds. In addition to acute-care services, it offers cardiac care, women's services, rehabilitation, orthopedics, cancer treatment, pediatric care, mental health services, a hospice program and hyperbaric medicine. Also, the hospital has a comprehensive sleep-disorder program unique in the area.

The hospital operates the David and Donna Long Center for Cancer Treatment and Cardiovascular Diagnosis, which was the first cancer center in San Diego County. In addition, there's a Senior Resource Center and Women's Health Center on-site.

Scripps Hospital, El Cajon
1688 E. Main St., El Cajon
• **(619) 440-1122**

Joining the Scripps Health group in 1993, this East County hospital provides the same excellent health services offered by others in the system's network (See the Scripps hospital entry in the San Diego section).

The facility has nearly 200 beds and 397 employees, with close to 300 medical staff members. It is located on a 16-acre campus. The hospital's auxiliary volunteer members take extra care to give patients and visitors special care.

South Bay

Paradise Valley Hospital
2400 E. 4th St., National City
• **(619) 470-4321**

Along with fine general medical care, Paradise Valley offers outstanding service in the areas of cardiology and oncology. Here you'll also find 24-hour emergency and walk-in services and the New Life Family Center. Prospective parents come here for childbirth classes and then to have their babies in a comfortable homelike atmosphere. There is also a nursery. The 243-bed campus also includes a Center for Health Promotion, which sponsors programs to quit smoking, and a walking club. The hospital also offers pediatric services and a transitional-care skilled nursing service.

Scripps Hospital, Chula Vista
Fourth and H Sts., Chula Vista
• **(619) 691-7000**

Serving people throughout the South Bay, this is another in the string of Scripps Hospitals. Centrally located in Chula Vista on a 13.5-acre campus, it has more than 300 beds and a staff of more than 500 nurses and physicians. It offers a plethora of healthcare and life-affirming services (For more information on Scripps hospitals, see the entry in the San Diego section). The facility joined the Scripps Health system in 1986.

Sharp Chula Vista Medical Center
751 Medical Center Ct., Chula Vista
• **(619) 482-5800**

Sharp Chula Vista Medical Center is a comprehensive medical center in South Bay. The hospital offers a variety of services including outpatient surgery, cardiac-care programs and facilities, a certified cancer treatment program and a full scope of programs for women in all stages of life.

The hospital opened in 1944 and recently underwent an extensive renovation in order to offer high-tech services that should serve area patients well into the next century. The 306-bed center provides 24-hour emergency care, and is equipped with a heliport. A women's and infant's pavilion provides obstetric and gynecological services.

Mental Health Services

Mental health facilities are often included in many of our county's hospitals. In this listing you'll find some that provide comprehensive care. Note that the entries are in a general countywide group rather than listed by geographical area as we've done previously.

One facility, Sharp Mesa Vista in San Diego, is an involuntary detention center for the care of acutely-ill patients who are judged to be a danger to themselves, a danger to others or are gravely disabled as a result of a psychiatric illness. Others facilities listed specialize in substance-abuse problems. Note, too, that you'll find emergency numbers and crisis hot lines in the Gray Box found in this chapter.

In the phone book's Yellow Pages, you'll find a listing for Mental Health. When calling, you'll want to ask about the specific services offered and whether your healthcare coverage provides for those services.

Charter Behavioral Health System of San Diego-North
11878 Ave. of Industry, San Diego
• **(858) 487-3200**

All calls to this mental health hospital are answered confidentially by a highly trained staff who can offer options. The system, established 25 years ago, offers treatments for emotional, behavioral, alcohol and drug problems. It provides assistance with depression, anxiety, sexual abuse and stress disorders. Serving the needs of children, adolescents, adults and seniors, the hospital is also a CHAMPUS approved provider.

San Luis Rey Hospital
335 Saxony Rd., Encinitas
• (760) 753-1245

With a 24-hour-a-day help line, this hospital specializes in drug and alcohol treatment. It accepts most insurance programs and will provide assistance and treatment for depression, anxiety, and sexual and physical abuse. Programs are geared for individuals and families.

Sharp Mesa Vista Hospital
7850 Vista Hill Ave., San Diego
• (858) 694-8300

Sharp Mesa Vista is the largest freestanding psychiatric hospital in San Diego County. The 150-bed facility was opened in 1963 and became affiliated with Sharp HealthCare in 1998. It offers premier psychiatric services with a medical staff of nearly 300.

Treatment programs are designed for specific patient populations including adults, children and chemical dependents. It shares services with the Navy's adult psychiatric inpatient program, its child and adolescent psychiatry program and the department of obstetrics.

Immediate-Care Facilities

While walk-in clinics are found throughout the county, we'd recommend that you consider visiting a hospital's emergency room if you're in need of immediate care. That's what most Insiders do, and when our visiting friends and family need to see a doctor quickly, it's where we take them. Our hospital emergency rooms provide excellent, state-of-the-art medical services on a round-the-clock basis. And most are within 20 minutes of any place you might be in San Diego. No matter what your immediate need, you'll be directed to the level of care you need, often within minutes of your arrival.

That said, walk-in clinics are available for those who prefer them. Usually found in strip malls, these centers can treat non-life threatening injuries and illnesses. They will treat anyone, but if you think you may want to use their services, you might want to check with your insurance carrier. If you have a life-threatening illness, some HMOs will pay for treatment at a hospital emergency room but not pick up the tab for walk-in clinic treatment.

Keep in mind that if you do not have insurance or your carrier cannot be billed for the services you require, you'll be required to pay when services are rendered, regardless of whether you go to a hospital emergency room or to a walk-in clinic. You'll find listings for walk-in clinics and immediate-care facilities listed under "Clinics" in the phone book's Yellow Pages.

Alternative Care

Alternative healthcare isn't everyone's cup of java, yet for those who choose to seek health and wellness in some of the ancient traditions, the choices in San Diego are excellent.

Your best bet when seeking alternative medical care is to ask for referrals from people you know and trust. Remember, you can also call and ask questions about the practitioner's methods, background and certification.

When making an appointment, discuss the expected treatment and costs in detail, along with possible side effects. It's fair, too, to ask for references.

Most alternative healthcare facilities offer a full "menu" of services. These might include acupuncture, shiatsu and acupressure techniques. The services may help you quit smoking or provide drug-free solutions to pain or

INSIDERS' TIP

Before traveling anywhere, including South of the Border, write down the prescription medications you're currently taking. Keep the list in your wallet. Should you need medical help, the list could be a lifesaver.

alternative therapies for women's health problems. The Yellow Pages give a complete listing of practioners in the areas of chiropractic, acupuncture, herbology, holistic medicine, Chinese herbal therapies, therapeutic massage and other treatments. Swedish/circulatory massage, sports massage and foot reflexology are additional health-wise options you may wish to explore.

Hospice Care in San Diego

Hospice care has long been a part of San Diego's healthcare picture. Most hospice organizations have in-home services and several are available for residential stays for terminal illness.

San Diego Hospice, 4311 3rd Ave., San Diego (619) 688-1600, is a county leader in hospice care and the oldest hospice in the area for persons facing a life-limiting illness.

In North County Coastal, you can contact **Hospice of the North Coast Community Outreach**, 5421 Avenida Encinitas, Carlsbad, (760) 431-4100. This program reaches those who prefer care within their homes; however, the staff can coordinate licensed residential care, too.

In North County Inland, Hospice care can be coordinated by **Fallbrook Hospital District,** 624 E. Elder St., Fallbrook (760) 728-1191), for both in-facility care and at-home hospice assistance.

Also in North County Inland is **Elizabeth Hospice**, 150 W. Crest St., Escondido (760) 737-2050, or (800) 797-2050. The program is open to those whose disease prognosis is measured in months, not years, and who are seeking comfort not cure. Patients may elect to stay at home or at a licensed facility. The Elizabeth Hospice team, working as part of the Palomar/Pomerado Health System, includes medical directors, registered nurses, social workers, the clergy, home health aids and volunteers. It is a model program: one that never forgets that patients are people.

Some of the county's hospitals also offer hospice programs and, in addition, there are private hospice plans. The hospitals that provide hospice care include Sharp Cabrillo Hospital, Grossmont Hospital, Fallbrook Hospital and the Palomar Pomerado Healthcare System in Escondido and Poway.

Wellness and Healthcare

Good Numbers to Keep Handy

For emergency or health-related questions and concerns, these phone numbers could help. Crisis lines are operated around the clock.

Throughout San Diego a call to 911 will bring police, ambulance and paramedic services, most within five minutes.

Alcohol AA Abuse Hot Line	(800) 333-4313
Airport Travelers Aid	(619) 231-7361
Border Patrol	(619) 662-7251
Crime Victim's Crisis Line	(760) 688-9200
Customs, U.S.	(619) 557-5360
Doctor Referral	(800) 628-2880, (800) 727-4777
Domestic Violence Services - YMCA	(619) 234-3164, (619) 270-4504
Dentist Referral	(619) 275-0244
Harbor Patrol	(619) 221-8985
Highway Patrol (State Police)	(619) 296-6661
Mental Health Counseling	(760) 753-1245
Poison Center	(619) 543-6000, (800) 876-4766
Teens Helping Other Teens	(800) 400-6780
Womens' Resource Center, 24-hour help line	(760) 757-3500

INSIDERS' TIP

Before calling your doctor or one in the area, jot down symptoms and/or concerns. That way you can leave a clear message. If you're staying in a hotel or motel, make sure your message includes your room number.

Folks who call San Diego home typically stay here when retirement beckons.

Retirement

With the perfect weather, relaxed lifestyle and great outdoor opportunities, most Insiders take leisure time as seriously as those who choose not to continue with a career. We believe that regardless of one's age, San Diego is easy on the body and soul.

Most who retire in San Diego immediately feel right at home here; after all, our seniors are a valued part of every neighborhood. Folks who call San Diego home typically stay here when retirement beckons. Others move from those places where the white stuff accumulates each winter — and we're not talking beach sand. The up side, of course, is the weather and numerous outdoor activities. This is a watersport and golf paradise (just check out our chapters on these topics). The down side of retirement in San Diego is the cost of living. The county is one of the more expensive areas in the United States; yet our senior population continues to increase.

In a recent report it was determined that about 15 percent of San Diego's population is 55 or older. In some neighborhoods, such as Rancho Bernardo, San Marcos and Rancho Santa Fe, that percentage is considerably higher. In Poway however, all those young families probably make it lower. Yet in every community in our county there's a comfortable mix. See our chapter on Neighborhoods and Real Estate to get a feel for the area's communities.

Regardless of age, Insiders love to sit at the marinas and watch the sailboats, picnic at Balboa Park on lazy summer days, and hike or bike in the wilderness areas, with cameras slung around our necks. The only real difference is that some of us have to get back to work on Monday and the other group goes out to find more fun.

In this chapter we've identified some opportunities for the 55-plus group. We've included information on senior centers and senior programs. These organizations have senior advocacy staff members. We've pointed out some senior publications and given information on how seniors can get special help if they should need it. We have included a smattering of residential options that include multi-level care. These facilities abound in San Diego County, so we've tried to point out some ways you can compare the many choices before you sign on the dotted line.

Senior Living – Housing Options

Choosing the right retirement place can be tricky unless you do your homework. Location is, of course, a chief issue. If you prefer sea breezes to the inland area's dry summertime air, then a coastal home is best. However, as you've noted in the Neighborhoods and Real Estate chapter, it's somewhat more expensive to live near the ocean. If family, friends, church or synagogue and community services are important, take these into consideration. For instance, let's say you're a member of Kaiser Permanente and know you'll need to visit a medical facility often. If you choose to

---

INSIDERS' TIP

Think 10 years into your future when buying a retirement home. A one-story house will probably work best. Before you buy, consider ways the house might be modified for wheelchair access.

live in East County's Borrego Springs for the glorious winter months, you'll be faced with an hour's drive to visit your doctor.

If you're interested in retirement living in San Diego County check the telephone book Yellow Pages under Retirement and personally visit the facilities or communities that strike your fancy. You'll want to make a scheduled visit and pick up a brochure or talk with someone on the sales staff. You may even want to stop by at another, unannounced, time.

Depending on the facility, you'll want to discuss with the staff the options for care, chat with the activities director as to what really goes in at the facility — including discounts on theater tickets and trips. You'll want to have lunch on-site to taste the cuisine and mingle with the other residents. And you'll want to socialize with the residents to see how you might fit in. Be sure to find about medical care and to ask for references. You may want to speak with the family members of residents to get their opinions of the facility, care level etc.

Some privately owned rental units throughout the county prefer seniors; some can help apartment dwellers arrange for rent reduction through HUD. To find a senior rental housing and those complexes specifically geared to seniors, we recommend contacting the senior center in the community where you want to live.

As your selection of a retirement home or apartment narrows, think of security. Are you most comfortable in a gated community? Are you interested in having a security officer on-site at night? Is a medical staffer essential? Will you want a multi-level facility (one that provides multiple levels of care) so that should the time arrive, skilled nursing care is avail-

able? Do you want to live in a community that only caters to those interested in independent living? And what about shopping? Is it convenient or is there a van to take residents to the stores they like? Does the facility schedule trips to the library or make sure that residents have access to community programs including church or synagogue services?

As you tour various senior communities, think about ease of access for today and later. While it might be fun now to dash up a flight of stairs to your two-story condo with a view, five years from now those stairs may become tedious. When buying a townhouse consider how it might be outfitted for any special equipment needed later in life. Can a ramp be built for the front steps? Will the bath be big enough should a wheelchair be required?

Finally, you might consider how much of your current furniture will reasonably fit into your new home. Those communities listed below have furniture rentals available should you want to see what it's like to live in the area before having all your furnishing shipped.

If you've decided to simply buy a private home in a neighborhood or in a planned community, see our Neighborhoods and Real Estate chapter for descriptions of neighborhoods and a listing of real estate agencies. This is another source of great information on San Diego housing. An agent can help you find the best location, assist with red tape to get your financial approvals in order, and then help you zero in on a house, condo or apartment that's priced right and fits your personal needs.

So look over some the entries we provide to get a feel for what's out there. Once you know what to ask and what you want, you should be able to find your perfect retirement

www.insiders.com

See this and many other **Insiders' Guide®** destinations online.

Visit us today!

home. Below we give you a taste of the types of retirement living options found in San Diego County. Special note: Most have a waiting list. (Remember that this is just a sample; San Diego has lots more options, so be sure to use the Yellow Pages too.)

Atria Courtyard at San Marcos
1590 W. San Marcos Blvd., San Marcos
• (760) 471-9904, (800) 864-0600

Beautifully landscaped grounds and the convenient North County Inland location draw seniors to this community. While most who live at Atria Courtyard are independent, the facility also offers assisted-living options (meals, housekeeping, and transportation, as well as staff checks for medication and medical conditions. There is a heated swimming pool, spa, walking paths, rose gardens and a putting green. Beach walks, shopping, cultural events and movies are favorite outings for the active crowd who live here. The complex, with studio, one-bedroom and two-bedroom apartments (some facing the courtyard and rose garden) is close to grocery stores and other everyday shopping. Small pets are always welcome. Rents start at about $2,000 a month; this includes housekeeping, activities, and two meals a day.

Chateau La Jolla Inn
233 Prospect St., La Jolla
• (858) 459-4451, (800) 452-5652

Chateau La Jolla Inn is carefree living with an elegant touch that's not grandiose, just comfortable and designed with ordinary people in mind. Choose from studios, one- and two-bedroom apartments and enjoy three meals daily.

This is an independent living complex; however, medical care can be provided on an as-needed basis for long-term residents. There's complimentary limo service, cultural activities, socials, classes, fitness programs

and loads of events. Shops, boutiques, and cafes are within blocks. About a half-mile north of Chateau La Jolla Inn are all the temptations of La Jolla. (You can read more about this city on the Pacific in our Real Estate and Neighborhoods chapter.) Monthly rents begin at about $2,000.

Fredericka Manor
183 3rd Ave., Chula Vista
• (619) 422-9271, ext. 22

There's no entrance fee or deposit for this senior complex that really is one of the nicest you'll find. To say that the individual cottages are cozy doesn't do them justice — they are down right darling and inviting. The grounds are pristine and the people who choose to live at Fredericka Manor are typically active folks. In addition to the cottages, you'll find apartment-style living in an eight-story tower, assisted-care and skilled nursing. There's also an adult daycare center on-site.

The facility is located on 24 garden-like acres with paths and ponds and walkways and gardens. Living options range from a utility studio to a penthouse suite; prices go from about $1,200 a month and up. All of the units are maintenance free (including the cottages) and come with housekeeping services.

There are various meal options. You'll find 24-hour-a-day security and medical response, transportation, programs and cultural events. And a friendly staff.

North Park Towers Apartments
4602 Kansas St., San Diego
• (619) 284-0104

Secure living for adults and seniors is available at North Park Towers Apartments. There's full security, senior activities, pool, and exercise and game rooms. There's an elevator for residents who aren't comfortable climbing stairs. The garden apartments are comfortable and clean. They begin at about $500 and the two-bedroom units are slightly higher. Those who come to live here have typically downsized their homes and bring along their favorite pieces of furniture to give the apartment a homey touch.

The Patrician
4025 Pulitzer Pl., San Diego
• **(858) 455-9188**

Located in La Jolla's Golden Triangle area, the facility is newly renovated and a luxury senior community. There are elegantly furnished common areas, spacious one- and two-bedroom apartments, fully equipped kitchens and walk-in closets.

You'll find easy access to shopping, hospitals, and services. Activities and transportation, a gated underground parking structure and the private park-like entrance all pull seniors into this independent living community. There are balconies or patios for all apartments; some units have fireplaces. Annual leasing is available; a security deposit of $400 is required. Monthly rents range from $795 for a one-bedroom apartment to about $1000 for a two-bedroom apartment.

The White Sands of La Jolla
7450 Olivetas Ave., La Jolla
• **(858) 454-4201, (800) 892-7817**

A Southern California Presbyterian Home, this exceptional community offers three levels of care, should you ever need the options. We're talking ocean close. It's the only retirement community in the country that boasts immediate access to those waves. This is understated luxury in the finest sense, with lovely rooms, some more pricey and spacious than others. Amenities include housekeeping, delicious meals, and transportation. At the end of Pearl Street in La Jolla, it is also blocks from the shops and restaurants that have made this city famous throughout the world. It's an interesting bit of trivia that more than 55 percent of the residents at White Sands have at least a master's degree. That's a high number for people who are in the 75-to-80-year age group.

Although the complex isn't new, it is constantly renovated and is extremely well maintained. There is a $1000 fee to have your name placed on the waiting list. The entrance fee ranges from $37,000 to $1.5 million, depending on the apartment and whether you must have an ocean view. Monthly fees vary from $1,200 to $2,500 for a spacious apartment.

Senior Organizations

You'll find weekly listing of clubs, hobby groups, volunteer needs and special activities in the *North County Times* and *The San Diego Union-Tribune*. Most organizations that help seniors always need dependable volunteers to deliver meals, stop and visit shut-ins and provide helping hands at activities. Volunteering is a great way to make new friends and learn new skills.

Alzheimer's Association
8514 Commerce Ave., San Diego
• **(858) 537-5040**

This organization provides and coordinates a countywide effort to give information and referrals. They also offer respite programs, support groups, and education programs. The organization coordinates "Safe Return" system, a wanderers alert program.

City of San Diego, Senior Citizen Services
202 C St., San Diego • (619) 236-6905

Services include referrals for medical and psychological services, and housing. This office also issues senior identification cards. Seniors who don't drive can use these cards to

---

INSIDERS' TIP

If you're looking for skilled nursing, assisted living, and multi-stage housing (where one can arrange for full care), pick up an issue of *San Diego Eldercare Directory*, (619) 281-6400. The book lists everything from day care and respite care for adults to in-home solutions and transportation for the disabled.

Senior citizens enjoy a day in Balboa Park playing a rousing game of lawn bowling.

get discounts on bus fares, at restaurants, for accommodations and for other services. This office also offers discounts for special events and tours, helping seniors get out to enjoy a play, for example, or a performance of the opera.

Jewish Family Service Senior Services
2930 Copley Ave., San Diego
• (619) 563-5232

This office is open to all seniors, and services are available on a sliding scale. Licensed clinical social workers here give free consultations to provide information and recommendations on physical and mental-health issues. You'll find people willing to take time and help on issues of housing, managed care, adult day care and counseling. There is even a hot meal delivery service available.

Lifeline Community Services
200 Jefferson St., Vista
• (760) 726-4900

Lifeline provides information and referrals for senior services. This office can provide information on adult day care, advocate for seniors concerned about medical bills or treatment, and provide transportation to seniors who are unable to drive. Lifeline also offers shared-housing match services

Meals-On-Wheels
2437 Morena Blvd., 2nd fl., San Diego
• (619) 275-7800, (800) 573-6467
Central San Diego • (619) 275-7810
North County Coastal • (760) 753-1036
North County Inland • (858) 451-8611
East County • (619) 447-8782
South Bay • (619) 420-2782

This agency provides two home-delivered meals per day to seniors who are ill or disabled for a suggested fee based on a sliding scale. The association accommodates special and restricted diet choices, too. Dependable volunteers are always needed.

National Association of Hispanic Elderly
22 W. 35th St., Ste. 127, National City
• (619) 425-3734

This organization helps Hispanic seniors with social and economic concerns and provides programs to help with housing and employment.

Senior Centers

Most communities throughout the county have senior centers. The easiest way to find them is by calling each city's main phone number or its parks and recreation office. The phone numbers are listed in the telephone book for each region. Senior centers and activities geared to our senior community are also available at our county's religious centers. Many churches provide meal service, counseling, support groups and housing referrals. Our hospitals take an active part in helping seniors with a variety of programs, from those addressing substance and elder abuse to those offering respite and hospice assistance. Be sure to look at the Healthcare and Wellness chapter for some tips to finding medical and wellness programs.

It's always best to call and find out what your neighborhood's center has available as things do change. Most serve a well-balanced hot lunch every weekday for a suggested donation of about $2. A number of the centers can arrange for delivery of hot mid-day meals to the homebound. Many of the centers have bilingual staff members, who serve as translators for elderly Spanish-speakers needing assistance with medical care or housing .

Senior citizens can stay physically fit and young at heart playing tennis.

The programs at the centers may include exercise and stretch classes, painting and craft activities, language arts and writing, bridge and poker, dance classes and performances and discussions of current events. Most of the centers offer tax and financial information, senior advocacy programs and medical check-ups. Some centers have social workers on staff and weekly support groups that deal with many issues, from grief management to dealing with stress. Most of the services are free; however, it's always wise to ask.

A growing number of centers have classes coordinated with our YMCA program and lo-

---

INSIDERS' TIP

To stretch your dollars, don't forget to ask about senior discounts, whether you're visiting the San Diego Zoo or attending the opera. For instance, Palm Springs Aerial Tramway, (760) 325-1391, gives a $3 discount for seniors who want to ride the tram. See our Daytrips chapter for more tips on discounts

cal colleges. For instance, Palomar Family YMCA, 1050 N. Broadway St. Escondido, (760) 745-7490, holds senior fitness classes including low-impact aerobics, senior water aerobics, strength training and line-dancing workouts. Fallbrook Senior Citizen Centers, 399 Heald Lane, Fallbrook, (760) 723-9282, offers writing and colleges classes through Palomar College. Other centers provide transportation from your home to the center and then get you back after lunch, a dental or medical appointment, grocery shopping or a daytrip.

If you have a talent you can share, whether it's tax accounting or tuba playing, let the coordinator at the senior center you visit know about your skill. Centers are constantly on the watch for interesting classes, helpful volunteers and those with special skills who want to share them.

Have you just moved to a new retirement community? What better way to make new friends than at a senior center? Or how about taking a class? You'll find brochures and class schedules at local city offices, the library, parks and recreation departments, and at senior centers too. Be sure to also pick up a copy of *New Wave: Get Up & Go* magazine for a monthly listing of senior activities; the full address is listed below.

For a complete listing of senior centers, refer to *San Diego Eldercare Directory*. The publication is free and is updated yearly. Copies are available at San Diego Gas and Electric offices (addresses are in the phone book) throughout the county and at Sharp HealthCare hospitals (see our chapter on Healthcare and Wellness).

Senior Publications

Get Up & Go! (formerly Senior Highlights and Senior World Newsmagazine)
500 Fesler, Ste. 101, El Cajon
• **(619) 593-2900**

This is a free monthly newsmagazine for maturing adults and has a fine blend of articles and useful advertising. A recent issue included an interview with John Glenn and a feature on substance abuse among seniors. You can find copies at most grocery stores, video stores and senior centers.

San Diego Eldercare Directory
ReVisions Resources
P. O. Box 600751, San Diego, 92160
• **(619) 281-6400, (619) 525-7777.**

A free, annual publication listing senior services from healthcare to legal advice along with living options such as assisted care and skilled nursing services. It's available at San Diego Gas and Electric offices throughout the county, Sharp HealthCare System, and various other locations.

More Senior Resources

Adult Protective Services .... (619) 283-5731

Area Agencies on Aging (known as AAAs
or Triple As) or Councils on Aging .... (858) 560-2500 or (800) 339-4661

American Association of Retired People (AARP) .... (202) 434-3525

American Red Cross, Wheels Service .... (800) 921-9664

Community Care Licensing, San Diego County .... (858) 467-2367

RSVP, Retired Senior Volunteer Program .... (858) 505-6399

Sharp Senior Source (part of Sharp HealthCare) .... (800) 827-4277 ext. 65

Even though the city has only one major newspaper that covers the entire county, there's plenty of competition from community newspapers.

Media

Once San Diego was established as a full-fledged city, it wasn't long before journalists began surfacing, eager to report the daily news. Even though the city has only one major newspaper that covers the entire county, there's plenty of competition from community newspapers. More than 50 community and neighborhood newspapers are published, and although some come and go, many have become old-timers in their respective neighborhoods.

Radio runs the gamut from adult contemporary to news/talk, and, of course, all three television networks are represented, as well as Fox and the WB. The city has a fledgling film industry and the San Diego Film Commission has recently been formed to coordinate the various production companies wanting to take advantage of San Diego as a filming site. Among the feature-length movies shot in San Diego are *Top Gun*, *The Lost World*, and *Mr. Wrong*. A couple of television series have been filmed here too, including the popular series *Silk Stalkings*. Even today you're likely to run into a film crew somewhere around the county filming *Pensacola: Wings of Gold*.

The following listings should give you a good idea of what's available to read, watch and listen to locally.

Newspapers

Newspapers listed here are the major dailies and weeklies, and those that cover a broad area of the county. For news and information specific to a neighborhood or community, look for weekly or bi-weekly publications that are easily found in neighborhood newsstands, coffeehouses, convenience stores and restaurants.

Daily

North County Times
207 E. Pennsylvania Ave., Escondido
• **(760) 745-6611**
   North County's only full-sized daily newspaper has nine zoned editions covering Escondido, San Marcos, Valley Center, Ramona, Fallbrook, Bonsall, Poway, Rancho Bernardo, Oceanside, Carlsbad, Vista, Encinitas, Cardiff and Solana Beach. It features international, national and local news and sports. Comparable to *The San Diego Union-Tribune*, the paper focuses on local news and editorials that pertain to North County. Its expanded Sunday edition features special sections on lifestyle, entertainment and real estate. The paper has a circulation of 95,000.

The San Diego Union-Tribune
350 Camino de la Reina, San Diego
• **(619) 291-3131, (800) 244-6397**
   Founded in 1868 by William Jeff Gatewood, *The San Diego Union-Tribune* is the oldest business in San Diego County and the second-oldest newspaper in Southern California. It began as a weekly and has been a daily since 1871. *The San Diego Union-Tribune* is the end product of a 1992 merger of *The San Diego Union* and *The Evening Tribune*, which was founded as an afternoon newspaper in 1895.
   John D. Spreckels, a San Diego founding

father, took over as publisher of *The San Diego Union* in 1890 and subsequently founded *The Evening Tribune*. He remained publisher until 1926, and after his death the two newspapers were purchased by Colonel Ira C. Copley. The Copley family has remained at the helm since 1947, with Helen Copley as the newspaper's current publisher.

The original building occupied by the newspaper still stands in Old Town State Historic Park. Today the *Union-Tribune* is published from an editorial and administrative building and printing plant in Mission Valley, not far from its original location in Old Town.

Five separate editions are published daily: San Diego City, North County Coastal, North County Inland, East County and South County. On Tuesdays a tabloid insert called "Computer Link" is featured that gives the latest news and information on computer-related topics.

Thursday editions have the tabloid "Night and Day" section, which has a wealth of information about night life, concerts, special events, performing arts, movies, restaurants and leisure activities throughout San Diego County.

Sunday's edition features special sections on travel, the arts, and homes, and has many feature-length articles to help pass the time on a lazy Sunday morning. Circulation on weekdays is 380,500; Sunday's is 455,660.

Almost Daily

Daily Californian
1000 Pioneer Way, El Cajon
• (619) 442-4404

Published five days a week, the *Daily Californian* reports news affecting the East County cities of El Cajon, La Mesa, Spring Valley, Lemon Grove, Santee, Lakeside, Rancho San Diego, Jamul, Alpine and the surrounding communities. It publishes an expanded Wednesday edition with a circulation of 40,000. The *Daily Californian* also covers issues dealt with by the various East County city councils and has a comprehensive editorial and commentary section.

San Diego Daily Transcript
2131 3rd Ave., San Diego
• (619) 232-4381

A broadsheet newspaper, the *Transcript* is published Monday through Friday and covers business, financial, legal, construction, real estate, and government news and includes legal notices, as well. The *Transcript* created the San Diego Stock Exchange and is the only publication to provide listings of every publicly traded corporation based in San Diego. Its circulation is 10,000.

Weekly and Semiweekly

Beach and Bay Press
4645 Cass St., San Diego
• (858) 270-3103

This community news group publishes four weekly newspapers that cover issues of interest to residents of coastal San Diego from Ocean Beach north to La Jolla. The *Beach and Bay Press*, the *Peninsula Beacon*, the *La Jolla Village News* and the *Golden Triangle News* together reach some 62,000 readers. Each paper has occasional features on local personalities and brings readers up to date on political issues affecting their neighborhood. Opinion polls are a common feature, too, giving readers the chance to make their voice heard.

INSIDERS' TIP

Looking for a job? How about an apartment, or even a used surfboard? Your best bet is the Sunday edition of *The San Diego Union-Tribune* with its expanded classifieds section.

Photo: CeCe Canton

A scene from an upcoming movie is being filmed on location in downtown San Diego.

Forum Publications
3434 Grove St., Lemon Grove
• (619) 469-0101

Every Tuesday and Thursday six separate community newspapers are published by Forum Publications: *La Mesa Forum*, *El Cajon Eagle*, *Spring Valley Bulletin*, *Lemon Grove Review*, *Lakeside Leader*, and *Santee Star*. Each newspaper covers items of interest to readers in their respective communities. All six have a combined circulation of 18,600. Although most of the content is folksy, community news, the papers do include government issues that have a direct effect on residents.

La Jolla Light
450 Pearl St., La Jolla • (858) 459-4201

The *La Jolla Light* and its sister newspapers, the *University City Light* and the *Clairemont Light*, are published weekly. Together these community newspapers cover the areas of La Jolla, Torrey Pines, the Golden Triangle and Clairemont, and reach 54,000 readers. The *La Jolla Light* and the *University City Light* focus on "town and gown" news about the interaction between UCSD and the residents of La Jolla. With less of an educational slant and more of a community focus,

the *Clairemont Light* has stories about residents and neighborhood activities in Clairemont.

Pomerado Newspapers
13247 Poway Rd., Poway
• (858) 748-2311

Published weekly, the Pomerado Newspapers include the *Poway News Chieftan*, the *Corridor News* and the *Rancho Bernardo News Journal*. In addition to the communities of Poway and Rancho Bernardo, coverage includes Rancho Peñasquitos, Carmel Mountain Ranch, Sabre Springs and Scripps Ranch. Besides neighborhood news, the papers feature profiles of community leaders and in-depth features on issues affecting these North County cities, such as local politics and real estate development. Each week 44,800 readers are reached.

San Diego Business Journal
4909 Murphy Canyon Rd., Ste. 200,
San Diego • (858) 277-6359

The *Business Journal* provides weekly news and commentary on San Diego County businesses and industries to 18,500 readers. Each issue has news, features and columns

A film crew sets up for a screet scene in the Gaslamp Quarter.

about San Diego's business environment. Its national award-winning weekly lists of businesses, agencies and services and its annual *Book of Lists* keep readers in touch with San Diego's growing industries. It is part of a national chain of business journals in major cities. The *Business Journal* can be purchased at newsstands throughout the city of San Diego and is also available by subscription.

Sun Newspapers
2841 Loker Ave. E., Carlsbad
• **(760) 431-4850**

The *Sun* group of newspapers publish individual newspapers that cover items of local interest to readers in the North County Coastal communities of Carmel Valley, Del Mar, Solana Beach, Rancho Santa Fe, Carlsbad, Encinitas and Oceanside. Published on Thursdays, the newspapers have a combined circulation of 65,500. Articles include updates on community activities, opinion pieces and local politics. Beach issues are always a hot topic, and the *Sun* pays close attention to what politicians are doing on behalf of residents.

Magazines

San Diego Home/Garden Lifestyles
4577 Viewridge Ave., San Diego
• **(858) 571-1818**

Local architecture, interior design and gardening are the features of this monthly magazine. It also includes articles on remodeling, art, local personalities and San Diego issues.

INSIDERS' TIP

The best lowdown on the club scene is found in *The San Diego Reader*. This ultra-cool weekly will help you decide which of San Diego's numerous clubs is the most happening.

The monthly guide to arts, culture and entertainment is an excellent source for information about what's happening in San Diego. The magazine's circulation is 45,000.

Special-Interest Publications

San Diego Magazine
401 West A St., San Diego
• **(619) 230-9292**

The first city magazine in the country, *San Diego Magazine* celebrated its 50th anniversary in 1998. This glossy monthly contains a selection of articles about San Diego, past and present, and its notable political, social and business leaders. The magazine also has an extensive thumbnail-review section on arts, entertainment and restaurants. It has a circulation of over 53,000 and can be purchased at newsstands, supermarkets, and bookstores or by subscription.

San Diego Metropolitan Magazine
656 6th Ave., Ste. M, San Diego
• **(619) 233-4060**

San Diego Metropolitan is a monthly newsprint magazine that focuses on the downtown community. Its emphasis is on downtown businesses, arts, retail and human-interest items. Downtown redevelopment, urban real estate and political happenings are subjects that are frequently covered, and at least one local business leader is profiled in depth each month. Monthly columns cover legal issues, money matters and the business of sports. It's distributed free to 50,000 readers.

Uptown Newsmagazine
3911 Normal St., San Diego
• **(619) 299-6397**

San Diego's largest free monthly community newspaper, the *Uptown* is distributed to over 25,000 readers in Downtown, Middletown, Old Town, Mission Hills, Hillcrest, University Heights, Mission Valley, North Park, Normal Heights, Kensington Mission Beach, Pacific Beach, the Gaslamp Quarter, Coronado and Golden Hill. Each issue typically has in-depth features on local issues and personalities, as well as commentary and editorial pieces. Unlike most other local newspapers *Uptown* publishes articles and stories submitted by local writers.

ComputorEdge
3655 Ruffin Rd., San Diego
• **(858) 573-0315**

San Diego's free computer magazine is published weekly, and 85,000 copies are distributed to newsstands, computer stores and libraries. It contains feature articles and columns with information on software and hardware for the computer buff. For true aficionados, *ComputorEdge* has a calendar of events to keep computer-heads entertained and up to date, as well as a listing of local websites and user group lists. The magazine also has a classifieds section advertising computers and accessories for sale.

Entertainer
12760 High Bluff Dr., Ste. 310, San Diego
• **(858) 259-1822**

This entertainment and lifestyle magazine has articles featuring the most up-to-date news in movies, theater, dining, music, travel, sports and nightlife in San Diego's North County Coastal and Inland communities. 40,000 copies are distributed free every other Thursday and can be found at libraries, convenience stores and bookstores. The *Entertainer* is a comprehensive source for information and reviews on everything from the newest Greek restaurant to the hottest local band to the latest movies.

Gay & Lesbian Times
3911 Normal St., San Diego
• **(619) 299-6397**

With a circulation of 15,750, the *Gay & Lesbian Times* is San Diego's largest publication specifically for the gay community. Heavy on guest commentaries, the newspaper also has news and articles of interest to gays and lesbians. The *Gay & Lesbian Times* extensive arts and entertainment section covers nightlife that often is neglected in mainstream publications. It's most easily found in libraries, bookstores and coffeehouses in the Hillcrest and downtown areas.

Get Up & Go!
500 Fesler St., Ste. 101, El Cajon
• (619) 593-2900

Get Up & Go! is a monthly tabloid published for readers 50 and older. It covers issues of interest to seniors such as travel, recreation, health, finance and lifestyle. Each issue has feature articles about HMOs and exercise, for example, as well as the continuing columns "Moneywise," "Health," "Entertainment," "Lifestyles" and "Travel." Available free throughout the county at libraries, and drug and convenience stores, 90,000 copies are published monthly.

La Prensa San Diego
1950 5th Ave., San Diego
• (619) 231-9180

Bilingual *La Prensa* is published weekly and distributed throughout San Diego County, from San Ysidro in the South Bay to Oceanside in North County and east to El Cajon. It's available free of charge at libraries, government buildings, coffeehouses and convenience stores throughout San Diego County. In publication since 1976, *La Prensa* views the news and events through a Hispanic/Chicano perspective. A continuing feature is its "Noticias de Mexico" column, which is a collection wire-service news items from Mexico. The newspaper reaches 30,000 readers.

Mabuhay Times
9580 Black Mountain Rd., Ste. C,
San Diego • (858) 693-6043

This twice-monthly newspaper is published primarily for the Filipino and Asian-American community. Articles are mostly in English, with two or three in Tagalog. The publication covers international, national and local news, and gives special attention to local events and cultural festivals for the Asian-American community. Its calendar of events, advertising and classifieds are geared toward Filipino and Asian residents. Its circulation is 38,000, and it can be obtained by subscription or at newsstands throughout the county.

San Diego Family Magazine
1475 6th Ave., San Diego
• (619) 685-6970

Published monthly, this free magazine is full of articles, columns, advice and helpful hints to benefit families. Pick up a copy at libraries, drug stores and convenience stores all over the county. Monthly features include columns titled "Family Science," "Health Tips," "Classes" and "Resources," as well as in-depth articles on parenting, camps, teen issues and safety. It includes a comprehensive directory of private schools as well as a listing of classes for youngsters. The magazine is distributed to 120,000 readers.

San Diego Parent
3160 Camino del Rio S., Ste. 313,
San Diego • (619) 624-2770

San Diego Parent is a monthly magazine distributed free to 80,000 readers. It features monthly columns on parenting classes, health notes and family fun, as well as feature-length articles on topics such as vacation options, summer camps and exercising. Each issue also includes a calendar of events for parents and kids. It's usually located right next to *San Diego Family Magazine* in libraries, drug stores and convenience stores.

The San Diego Reader
1703 India St., San Diego
• (619) 235-3000

This free weekly tabloid is noted for its comprehensive pullout entertainment section. The pullout gives detailed information and reviews on the arts, dining, sports and things to do around San Diego. Each issue also contains feature articles and columns about San Diego life and politics. The *Reader* is distributed to locations throughout San Diego County and reaches 156,000 readers.

San Diego Voice and Viewpoint
1729 N. Euclid Ave., San Diego
• (619) 266-2233

Distributed weekly throughout San Diego County, the *Voice and Viewpoint* is a publication geared toward the local African-American community. The newspaper prints local and national news, editorial and commentary, and it recognizes African-Americans of distinction in special features. It includes a weekly calendar of events, and its circulation is 18,900. The newspaper can be purchased at newsstands throughout the county.

SLAMM (San Diego Lifestyle and Music Magazine)

4241 Jutland Dr., Suite 211, San Diego
• (858) 581-3879

A bi-weekly tabloid, *SLAMM* features articles and reviews on the local film, theater, album, radio, TV and concert scene. Repeating columns are "Sordid Tales," real-life experiences from the nightlife scene, and "Reel News," clever and hip movie reviews. Each issue also has a local band directory and a listing of who's playing in which club. It has a circulation of 76,000. Pick up a copy at libraries, coffeehouses, music stores and many restaurants throughout the county.

Television

Like most other cities, local television stations have beloved anchor people and quirky personalities whose goal is to inform and entertain. With a good antenna the major network stations as well as Fox and the WB can be pulled in without cable. But reception is iffy, and most San Diegans subscribe to cable. The three network affiliates, Channels 8, 10 and 39, and local Channel 51 all have news broadcasts throughout the day.

Local TV Stations and Their Network Affiliates

KFMB Channel 8 (CBS)
News at 5:30 AM, 4 PM, 5 PM, 6:30 PM, 11 PM
KGTV Channel 10 (ABC)
News at 5:30 AM, 5 PM, 6:30 PM, 11 PM
KNSD Channel 39 (NBC)
News at 5:30 AM, 4 PM, 5 PM, 6 PM, 11 PM
KPBS Channel 15 (Public TV)
KSWB Channel 69 (WB)
KUSI Channel 51 (Independent)
News at 5:30 AM, 10 PM
XETV Channel 6 (Fox)
XEWT Channel 12 (TVA-Tijuana)

Cable Providers

Three main cable companies cover the majority of San Diego County. For the most part, each has exclusive rights to its area, and the area is divided roughly as follows: south of Interstate 8 and part of North County is Cox Communication's territory, north of Interstate 8 and Coronado belong to Time Warner Cable TV, and the part of North County that Cox doesn't have is covered by Daniels Cablevision. Confused? Obviously there's quite a bit of overlap, so if you have any doubt about which cable company controls your area, call any one of them. They'll be able to help you figure it out. Basic cable service can be purchased for around $15 per month, which will tune you in to the network stations as well as a few local independents. But if you wish to take advantage of the more than 75 premium and special-interest channels available in San Diego, expanded packages can be added.

Cox Communications (San Diego)

1535 Euclid Ave., San Diego
• (619) 262-1122

Area Covered: Alpine, Santee, Lemon Grove, Jamul, Rancho San Diego, National City, Imperial Beach, Chula Vista, Poway, and portions of San Diego, La Mesa, Del Cerro, El Cajon and Pine Valley.

Cox Communications (North County)

520 W. Valley Pky., Escondido
• (760) 599-6060

Area Covered: Escondido, San Marcos, Ramona, Leucadia, some of Cardiff, Vista, Oceanside, Camp Pendleton, Solana Beach, Encinitas, Olivenhain, Fairbanks Ranch and Rancho Santa Fe.

Time Warner Cable

8949 Ware Ct., San Diego
• (858) 695-3220

Area Covered: Del Mar, La Jolla, Poway, Rancho Santa Fe, Mission Valley, Mission Beach, Pacific Beach, Bay Park, Linda Vista, Clairemont, University City, Serra Mesa, Tierrasanta, Mira Mesa, Rancho Bernardo, Rancho Peñasquitos, Carmel Valley and Scripps Ranch.

Daniels Cablevision

5720 El Camino Real, Carlsbad
• (760) 931-7000

Area Covered: Lake San Marcos, Carlsbad,

Fallbrook, Del Mar, parts of San Marcos, Vista, Encinitas and Solana Beach.

Radio

Whatever your favorite format, you're likely to find it somewhere on the dial. Some stations come in clear in some parts of the county and not so clear in others. If a station's signal originates in North County, for example, it'll be clear and strong in the northern regions, somewhat weaker in San Diego and probably nonexistent in the South Bay. Don't give up, though. The old boom box has plenty of entertainment to please every taste.

Adult Contemporary
1450 AM KSPA
94.1 FM KJQY
95.7 FM KMSX
96.5 FM KYXY
100.7 FM KFMB
102.1 FM KXST

Alternative
550 AM KCR
1320 AM KKSM
98.9 FM XHMR

Children
1240 AM KSON (Radio Disney)

Christian
910 AM KECR
1210 AM KPRZ
100.1 FM KBNN
107.9 FM KWVE

Classic Rock
94.9 FM KBZT
101.5 FM KGB

Classical
540 AM XTIM
92.1 FM KFSD

Country
97.3 FM KSON

Jazz
88.3 FM KSDS
98.1 FM KIFM

Oldies
1360 AM KPOP
94.9 FM KBZR
101.5 FM KGB
103.7 FM KPLN

R&B/Soul
92.5 FM XHRM

Rock & Roll
91.1 FM XTRA
105.3 FM KIOZ
107.1 FM KLYY

Spanish
800 AM XEMM(Spanish Variety)
860 AM XEMO(Banda Music)
1040 AM KURS(Music/Information)
1420 AM XEXX(Spanish News/Sports)
1470 AM XERCN(Ranchera/Norteña)
1550 AM XEBG(Sports in Spanish)
88.7 AM XHITT(Tijuana Public Radio)
91.7 FM XTIM(Banda/Norteña)
97.7 FM XTIJ(Radio Amor)
99.3 FM XHKY(Fiesta Mexicana)
102.5 FM XHUAN (Ranchera)
102.9 FM KLQV(Mexican Ballads)
104.5 FM XLTN(Radio Latina)
106.5 FM KEBN(Ranchera/Banda)
107.3 FM XHFG(Romantic Spanish)

Talk
600 AM KOGO(Talk/News/Rush Limbaugh)
690 AM XTRA(All Sports)
760 AM KFMB(Talk/News/Padres Baseball)
1000 AM KCEO(Talk/News)
1130 AM KSDO(Talk/News/Sports)
1170 AM KCBQ(Talk/Entertainment)
89.5 FM KPBS(National Public Radio)

Top 40/Dance
90.3 FM XHTS
93.3 FM KHTS

Many visitors, regardless of their faith, attend mass at one of our missions.

Worship

While driving around our easygoing communities from Pacific Beach and Alpine to Bonita and Fallbrook it might seem that Insiders are too laid back to care about spiritual beliefs and values. If you've already read the Attractions, Shopping and Balboa Park chapters you might be asking yourself: "How do they have time when there's so much to do?"

The answers are simple: Yes, we care and yes, we make time.

People who live in San Diego are concerned about spiritual health. To find out for yourself, attend any religious service on any day of the week. You'll see that the notion that we're too lazy to make the service or meeting just isn't true.

San Diegans are diverse, and run the gamut from conservative and orthodox to outrageous and unconventional. But you already know that if you've read any of the book. So you won't be surprised to learn that our places of worship also reflect a variety of spiritual preferences.

Whether we attend a nontraditional service or one that's steeped in ancient customs, religious beliefs are alive and active throughout the county.

But while our beliefs are both strong and diverse, we all still live that San Diego lifestyle, and so we hope you won't be shocked to learn that when we attend our churches, centers, temples and synagogues, we may show up in shorts and sandals. Even at the most conservative services, the faithful walk in with bare knees and toes. If you're here from a conventional part of the country that could surprise you, but look around. People in San Diego are comfortable in their breezy wardrobes as they mix with congregation members who might prefer to be dressed to the nines. Hey, this is San Diego, so dress-wise, nearly anything goes.

Services

The choices of religious services available throughout the county are extensive. If you're here on a vacation, finding a worship center that's right for you might be as easy as looking in the Yellow Pages of your hotel's phone book. Someone on the staff at the front desk should be able to tell you which of the listings are closest. Many visitors, regardless of their faith, attend mass at one of our missions. The services are a way to touch San Diego's rich history and feel the past of our diverse community. (Be sure to read over our History chapter for more about religion's role in our past.)

Unlike other cities around the United States, San Diego County's religious centers are not on every corner; most will require a drive to get there. The good news is that if you're attending a Sunday morning service, the freeway traffic will usually be light. But as always, allow extra time for unplanned gridlock.

INSIDERS' TIP

The Church of Jesus Christ of Latter Day Saints, California Temple, is that huge white building you'll see when driving north on Interstate 5 in La Jolla. Although only open to visitors who are members of the church, the building's architectural grandeur can be appreciated by all. For church members, tours are scheduled every 30 minutes; call for a schedule. The temple is located at 7474 Charmant Drive, San Diego, (858) 622-0991.

The Friday edition of *The San Diego Union-Tribune* has a directory of religious services which includes church addresses, phone numbers and times of services. However, not every San Diego house of worship is included. So think of this resource as a starting point. For instance if you're visiting Bonsall and you want to find a Roman Catholic service close to this North County Inland city, you could call one of the Roman Catholic churches listed in the telephone directory and ask for the name of the Catholic church nearest you.

If you're moving to San Diego, you may decide on specific neighborhoods or parts of our county that will be close to the house of worship of your choice. Some congregations have groups for teens and seniors; others are geared to the needs of single people. Some churches offer services for the hearing-impaired and extensive child-care and preschool programs. Some centers have senior day-care programs and cultural events. Some are focused around the young family unit with everything from after-school programs to family campouts and church camps. As most churches do, a number of churches in our region specifically support our gay and lesbian community.

We have so many types of worshiping communities, in fact, that it will be hard to choose. You could visit a new church or spiritual center nearly every weekend for a year and still find more to explore. And that's one more wonderful thing about San Diego.

As you visit and consider where you'll put down your spiritual roots, remember it's okay

to call and ask about the philosophies being shared or the programs in which the religious group is involved. If singles groups or senior day care are important, see if your needs are met as you connect with the congregation.

When you do decide on your new spiritual "home," you'll probably feel like you belong right away. People are friendly here in our county and you won't feel like a stranger for long.

www.insiders.com

See this and many other **Insiders' Guide®** destinations online.

Visit us today!

History of Worship in San Diego

The Mission Basilica San Diego de Alcala, the first in the chain of 21 missions established in California, still holds services and celebrates christenings and weddings. It's been doing so since July 16, 1769 when Father Junipero Serra celebrated the first mass there. In North County Coastal, Mission San Luis Rey in Oceanside continues to hold services in Spanish as well as English. Tours of both missions are available and the gardens and museums alone make them popular tourist attractions. (Be sure to read about the missions in our Attractions chapter.)

While the first European settlers who founded San Diego were Catholic, many other religions came to San Diego with the farmers, cattle owners, and tradespeople that began to call our county home. (See our History chapter for more information on early settlers.)

As they cleared the land, established homesteads and tried to figure out how to get

---

INSIDERS' TIP

On Good Friday and the Sunday before Easter, *The San Diego Union-Tribune* has a countywide listing of sunrise and traditional Easter services. Some services, while not held at the crack of dawn, are still held quite early. Those at the Las Flores Church of the Nazarene, 1400 Las Flores Drive in Carlsbad, (760) 729-0231, begin at 7 AM and are held again at 8:30 AM and 10 AM. Many of these services, including those at the Las Flores Church, are held outdoors. It can be coolish on Easter, so if you're determined to wear a new spring outfit, bring a jacket.

Photo: Courtesy of St. Vincent de Paul Village

Saint Vincent de Paul's Village is one of America's most highly respected, creative, and responsible providers of opportunity and services to those in need.

water to make everything grow, these independent folks were determined to feed their souls, too. Just as it happens today, not everyone could decide on that spiritual "meal" or how it should be served, so diverse churches and houses of worship sprang up around the county.

If you stepped back in history, 50 or 100 years, you'd find a spiritual scene much like today's. On any Sunday you could choose to attend a spiritualist church or a Baptist church or a Catholic one. The only difference between then and now is that today you'd have even more choices. San Diegans are proud of this diversity.

Humanitarian Activities

Our scores of religious institutions also happen to be a vital part of humanitarian activity in San Diego. At any one of them you may find a way to express your own faith by helping with these efforts. At Saint Vincent De Paul's Mission in San Diego (see the Close-up in this chapter) volunteers assist those who need a helping hand emotionally, physically and spiritually. If you volunteer here you might be asked to read a book at the day-care center, help with distribution at the food bank, serve lunch, or work at a fundraiser. The main center is

INSIDERS' TIP

Christmas worship and midnight services are offered at many of San Diego's churches and at our historic missions. Insiders enjoy the history and the pageantry of attending mass at the missions. Check the Yellow Pages of your phone book for numbers and call for service times.

Father Joe: God's Hustler

He's been called a "genius," a "saint," and a "hustler." He's been referred to as a "con artist," and "that guy you wanta' watch." Perhaps what best describes Father Joe Carroll is "anomaly." Here's a Bronx-born priest who successfully fought the system to institute one of the nation's most effective programs for alleviating homelessness and its causes. And while Fr. Joe started out in South Bronx, the miracle happened here in San Diego.

Born in New York City's South Bronx in 1941, Joe Carroll was raised in a fiercely close-knit neighborhood where people valued roots. One of eight Carroll kids, he was part of a family that never forgot to pray for "the less fortunate," although all of them at the time were living in a two-room apartment. Fr. Joe says, "Given those circumstances, we'd be homeless today."

When he relocated to Southern California at age 22 with $50 in his pocket, Joe Carroll had one desire: to be a millionaire. What he got was something entirely different.

Joe's easy and gregarious personality, coupled with the compassion for the poor he'd learned as a child, eventually led him to the priesthood. Following his ordination in 1974, Fr. Joe immersed himself in parish work, where he also found outlets for his businessman's instincts. Parish life enabled Fr. Joe to apply fund-raising skills, which he used among his growing cadre of friends and supporters. Those skills would become for Fr. Joe a magnetic extension of his vision. This vision, which originally had a more personal nature, turned into one of universal proportions.

Visions like Fr. Joe's are contagious and this one eventually caught the interest of Bishop Leo T. Maher. The Bishop was appalled by the numbers of San Diegans sleeping nightly in cars, in the parks and on the public beaches. He dreamed of a comprehensive center to address their immediate needs. Believing Fr. Joe to be the only man capable of spearheading such a project, he assigned Father Joe the task.

"I'm not exactly what you'd call a saint who wanted to work with the homeless," Fr. Joe admitted in a recent interview for *San Diego Magazine*. In that robust laughter that fills any room,

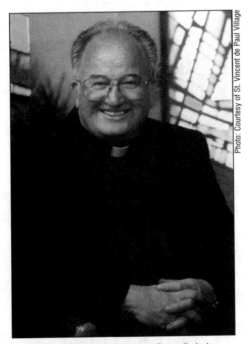

Photo: Courtesy of St. Vincent de Paul Village

We know him as Father Joe. Formally he's called Rev. Msgr. Joseph Carroll, president of Saint Vincent de Paul Village.

regardless of size, he added, "Basically, I'm just a New York hustler—a con man who can make things happen."

He accepted Bishop Maher's task with his usual gusto. Daunted but determined, Fr. Joe leased a hotel and set about understanding the causes of homelessness. He also devised a plan for an urban oasis that would provide not only emergency care, but a free clinic, a public school, a children's library and play area, rooms for 350 residents, and a kitchen serving 2,000 meals daily. The center would also offer resources where "street" people could search for work, brush up on professional skills and prepare for job interviews. The cost of this plan? Try $11 million and change.

Like dynamos with less lofty persuasions, Fr. Joe scrounged for money. It came. The big break happened when a local television station aired his public-service spot. Viewers were captivated. "I'm a hustler," said the man in the clerical garb. Then he grinned and added, "And I want your money." Then as images of San Diego's homeless families were shown in the same commercial, Fr. Joe explained the need for a residence where people could galvanize themselves and work toward another try.

Fr. Joe's plan worked, and worked well. He became an instant celebrity and offers of help poured in from every corner of the county. The con man became famous and his work celebrated. One Insider likes to tell about the times Fr. Joe was honored at various social functions: "He even made appeals for the center during grace." With God's help and through the hands of compassionate Insiders, the millions were raised. The dream turned into reality.

Opened in September 1987, the Joan Kroc Center is situated in what was once one of San Diego's seediest neighborhoods. Rising from its modest surroundings, the structure is a beacon of hope to the nearly 2,000 residents and non-resident homeless who partake of its services every day. It's been called the "Taj Mahal of homeless shelters," and building it took five years of selling, begging, wheeling, dealing, arm-twisting, hand-shaking and Fr. Joe's brand of friendly persuasion. That center is all business and Fr. Joe is at the helm.

An outspoken conservative, the good Father doesn't believe in handouts. "Handouts are not the answer to today's volatile economy. People have to learn how to take care of themselves; that means learning how to spend, how to save and how to maintain security for themselves and their families. We don't want to see our residents come back. If they do, then its time to re-evaluate our methods. Part of our job is to instill personal responsibility, tenacity and the will to succeed. Of course the onus of this process lies squarely on the shoulders of our residents. But we have to help them to recognize that they can do it."

Since its opening day, the "Miracle of 15th Street," as the Joan Kroc Center is lovingly called, has become just one in a series of six structures comprising the Village and bursting out of that original dream. Actually located at 3350 E Street, San Diego, the center and its satellite sites provide a plethora of services including residential programs for neglected teens, low-income graduates of the Village, persons living with AIDS and many more state-of-the-heart programs to teach and help.

In the Village family are medical programs, counseling and chemical dependency help, computer training programs, the meal plans and the Village's Harbor Summit School. The school provides more than 120 resident children with education, techniques to bolster self-worth, social skills and a sense of security. There's also a child development program for parents who are seeking employment and education. Additional programs coordinated with the school include tutoring, family literacy, children's therapy, medical services, a foster grandparent program, parenting classes and teen and pre-teen clubs. "Yet, there's still work to be done," says Fr. Joe, and smiles

— continued on next page

with pride when discussing another Village. Because there are other villages now. The one in Las Vegas helps that city's growing homeless population and has become the largest facility of its kind in the state of Nevada.

Today, Fr. Joe's Villages continue to lead the country in non-government solutions to homelessness. Each case manager, counselor, administrator, volunteer and donor seeks greater opportunities for people who come to the center. And Fr. Joe Carroll remains at the center of the activity. He is a clear-headed, determined businessman meeting the demands of severe federal cutbacks. After getting to know Fr. Joe, or about him, you won't be surprised that he's always looking for good volunteers — to serve meals, conduct medical exams or teach someone how to read. To volunteer and be part of Fr. Joe's plan, call (619) 233-8500 X 1122.

"Genius," "saint," "hustler," whatever the title, when it comes to Fr. Joe Carroll, the message is simple and just: hope for the world.

located at 3350 E Street, San Diego, (619) 233-8500.

The Salvation Army's centers at 4170 Balboa Avenue, San Diego (858-483-1831) and 825 Seventh Street, San Diego (619-239-6221 X19), have Sunday and midweek services and provide shelter, clothing and food for some of our less fortunate citizens. The Salvation Army always needs volunteers too.

Talk with the pastor, rabbi, or head of your spiritual center to find out about volunteer opportunities sponsored by your group. While many religious groups cry out for financial support, it's often the priceless gift of willing hands that is the greatest contribution you can make.

Cultural Activities

Our religious centers are more than sites where we join one another to worship. They're often places to enjoy the arts and cultural activities, or centers where people can help themselves to a better life here on earth.

For instance, the First United Methodist Church of San Diego, 2111 Camino Del Rio South, San Diego (619-297-4366), recently sponsored a performance by soprano Patricia Minton and pianist Stephen Sivcochi. The program was filled with music, comedy and a joyful sing-along.

Our houses of worship often become places to work on relationships and family issues. They serve as resource centers accessible to all. Turning Point Church, 12269 Oak Knolls Road, Poway (858-748-7478) recently offered Gary Smalley's "Hidden Keys to Loving Relationships," a seminar on forming strong bonds for couples. The cost was only $2.50 for the evening seminar and child care was available.

The Taoist Sanctuary of San Diego, 4229 Park Boulevard, San Diego (619-692-1155), extends a summer open house every Tuesday evening during June, July and August. At the open house, you can hear an introduction to the Taoist philosophy and enjoy demonstrations of Tai Chi Chuan, a healing exercise system, and the martial arts.

Lawrence Family Jewish Community Centers, Mandell Weirs Eastgate City Park, 4126 Executive Drive, La Jolla (858-457-3030), provides the community with a Jewish Film Festival and Jewish Book Fair.

INSIDERS' TIP

Most religious services welcome visitors dressed in California casual; i.e., it's not necessary to wear suits or dresses and high heels. If you're in doubt, call first. On any first visit, slacks and a blazer are always appropriate.

This eclectic "menu" of services continues far beyond the traditional scope of church activities. St. Paul's Cathedral, Fifth Avenue and Nutmeg Street, San Diego (619- 298-7261), holds a variety of concerts, but they also have dinner theater performances.

The First United Methodist Church of Chula Vista, 915 Paseo Ranchero, Chula Vista (619-656-2525), recently sponsored a concert of George and Ira Gershwin music, which charged very small admission fees.

Churches and synagogues often sponsor garage sales too. Safe Harbor Ministries, a non-denominational center at 5150 Jackson Drive, La Mesa (619- 583-9736) sponsors an important one every June. The sale begins at sunrise and ends in midafternoon. Such activities form a strong sense of social community within church groups, and often are used as fundraisers which help promote humanitarian missions.

So if you're looking for a place to worship, to put your faith to work in social service, and to enjoy the companionship of others, our community has much to offer. As with all of San Diego, just ask some Insiders and you'll receive a cornucopia of choices.

Index of Advertisers

Index

Going Somewhere?

Insiders' Publishing presents these current and upcoming titles to popular destinations all over the country — and we're planning on adding many more. To order a title, go to your local bookstore or call (800) 582-2665 and we'll direct you to one.

Insiders' Publishing • P.O. Box 1718 • Helena, MT 59624
Phone (406) 443-3021 • Fax (406) 443-3191 • *www.insiders.com*